PROVERBS 1–9

VOLUME 18A

THE ANCHOR BIBLE is a fresh approach to the world's greatest classic. Its object is to make the Bible accessible to the modern reader; its method is to arrive at the meaning of biblical literature through exact translation and extended exposition, and to reconstruct the ancient setting of the biblical story, as well as the circumstances of its transcription and the characteristics of its transcribers.

THE ANCHOR BIBLE is a project of international and interfaith scope: Protestant, Catholic, and Jewish scholars from many countries contribute individual volumes. The project is not sponsored by any ecclesiastical organization and is not intended to reflect any particular theological doctrine. Prepared under our joint supervision, THE ANCHOR BIBLE is an effort to make available all the significant historical and linguistic knowledge which bears on the interpretation of the biblical record.

THE ANCHOR BIBLE is aimed at the general reader with no special formal training in biblical studies; yet it is written with the most exacting standards of scholarship, reflecting the highest technical accomplishment.

This project marks the beginning of a new era of cooperation among scholars in biblical research, thus forming a common body of knowledge to be shared by all.

William Foxwell Albright
David Noel Freedman
GENERAL EDITORS

THE ANCHOR BIBLE

PROVERBS 1–9

A New Translation
with Introduction and Commentary

BY
MICHAEL V. FOX

THE ANCHOR BIBLE
Doubleday
New York London Toronto Sydney Auckland

The Anchor Bible
PUBLISHED BY DOUBLEDAY
a division of Random House, Inc.
1540 Broadway, New York, New York 10036

Library of Congress Cataloging-in-Publication Data
Bible. O.T. Proverbs I–IX. English. Fox. 2000.
Proverbs 1–9: a new translation with introduction and commentary /
by Michael V. Fox. — 1st ed.
p. cm. — (The Anchor Bible; v. 18A)
Includes bibliographical references.
1. Bible. O.T. Proverbs I–IX—Commentaries. I. Fox, Michael V., 1940–
. II. Title. III. Series: Bible. English. Anchor Bible. 1964; v. 18A.
BS192.2.A1 1964.G3 vol. 18A
[BS1465.3]
220.7′7 s—dc21
[223′.7077] 99-30321
CIP

ISBN 0-385-26437-2

Printed in the United States of America
September 2000

First Edition

10 9 8 7 6 5 4 3 2 1

ACKNOWLEDGMENTS

◆

The National Endowment for the Humanities helped make this work possible by granting a fellowship that allowed me time to work on the book. The University of Wisconsin Graduate School also provided research funding, as did the Weinstein-Bascom Professorship endowment and the Halls-Bascom Professorship endowment. I also thank the Wisconsin Society for Jewish Learning for ongoing support, which greatly facilitated my efforts. My student assistant Rick Painter provided valuable corrections and comments.

Above all, David Noel Freedman's famous editorial work enhanced the precision and quality of this book. Some of his insights are cited in the Commentary as DNF.

This commentary includes material in modified form from my following articles or portions thereof:

"Words for Wisdom," *ZAH* 6 (1993) 149–69.

"The Pedagogy of Proverbs 2," *JBL* 113 (1994) 233–43.

"*ʾAmon* Again," *JBL* 115 (1996) 699–702.

"The Strange Woman in Septuagint Proverbs," *JNSL* 22 (1996) 31–44.

"The Social Location of the Book of Proverbs," pp. 227–39 in *Texts, Temples, and Traditions: Essays in Honor of Menahem Haran* (Winona Lake, Ind.: Eisenbrauns, 1996).

"Words for Folly," *ZAH* 10 (1997) 4–17.

"Ideas of Wisdom in Proverbs 1–9," *JBL* 116 (1997) 613–33.

"Who Can Learn? A Dispute in Ancient Pedagogy," pp. 62–77 in *Wisdom, You Are My Sister* (FS R. E. Murphy), ed. by M. L. Barré (Washington: Catholic Biblical Association, 1997).

"What the Book of Proverbs Is About," VTSup 48 (1997) 153–67.

CONTENTS

◆

PREFACE

◆

RECENT BOOKS

The manuscript of this volume was submitted in August 1996. Though it has undergone considerable revision since then, publications that reached me subsequently could be treated only sporadically, if at all. Three commentaries unavailable during the preparation of this volume will be used in volume II: Richard Clifford, *Proverbs* (OT Library); Roland E. Murphy, *Proverbs* (Word Bible Commentary); and R. Van Leeuwen, *Proverbs* (New Interpreter's Bible).

TRANSLATIONS

Translations from Sumerian and Akkadian are usually quoted from B. Foster's *Before the Muses* (BTM) or B. Alster's *The Instructions of Suruppak* (1974). Translations from other languages, unless otherwise noted, are my own. To help the reader find the context of the quotation, a reference to an easily accessible translation is added in brackets (usually M. Lichtheim's *Ancient Egyptian Literature* [AEL], though her translations may differ from the ones provided here). See further the Bibliography.

USING THIS COMMENTARY

This commentary is intended as a resource for different kinds of reading and study. Its modular organization is intended to help readers select the discussions relevant to their own purposes.

Commentary. The exegesis proper requires no knowledge of Hebrew and can be read without reference to the more technical investigations.

Excursuses. Issues that emerge from the exegesis and are of importance to Proverbs as a whole are explored in excursuses within or following the comments on each unit.

Philological and technical notes (small type). Matters of more specialized interest, in particular, analyses of philological problems and discussions of scholarly theories and interpretations, are discussed in embedded notes.

Textual Notes (at the end of the volume): A textual commentary identifies variants in the major textual witnesses and describes the underlying interpretations implied in the ancient translations, particularly the Greek. The purpose of this appendix is to establish possible Hebrew variants. The *choice* of variants is a literary-critical task and undertaken in the commentary proper.

Subject to the caveat in Prov 27:1b, the second volume will complete the commentary and conclude with essays on the broader interpretive, literary-critical, ideological, and historical issues.

TRANSLITERATION

In the body of the commentary I use a broad romanization, which is simply intended to recall the Hebrew word to the reader. The vowel letters in final position, such as final *heh* and *yod*, are represented by *h* and *y*, since they recall the written form (and are not pronounced in English either), e.g., *malkah, dibrey*. *Mapiq-heh* is written *-hh*.

A narrow romanization is used in the indented philological comments and, when needed, the textual notes.

In romanizing the Hebrew texts underlying the LXX and Syriac translations, I transcribe the consonantal text only, which is what those translators had before them. Occasionally, vocalization is indicated to suggest the translator's interpretation.

A PRACTICAL PRONUNCIATION GUIDE

The sounds represented by the different transliteration letters were distinct in biblical Hebrew, though some of these distinctions are not preserved in Western pronunciation. For practical purposes, the letters can be pronounced as follows:

Consonants: ʾ, ʿ silent; *ḥ* = rough "h," as in "Loch"; *ṭ* = "t"; *ṣ* = "ts"; *q* = "k"; *š* = "sh"; *ś* = "s."

Vowels: *a, ă* = "ah," as in "father"; *ay* as in "my"; *e* = "eh" as in "bet" or "ay" as in "way"; *ĕ* = "eh"; *ey* = "ay" as in "way"; *i* = "i" as in "bit," at end of a word = "ee" as in "bee"; *o, ŏ* = "o" as in "go"; *u* = "u" as in "you."

Principal Abbreviations, Terms, and Sigla

For abbreviations not listed below, see the List of Abbreviations in *The Anchor Bible Dictionary* (Vol. 1, pp. lii–lxxviii).

ABBREVIATIONS

ABD — Anchor Bible Dictionary
abs. — absolute
AEL — *Ancient Egyptian Literature*, Lichtheim 1973–80
ÄHG — *Ägyptische Hymnen und Gebete*, Assmann 1975
Ant — Antinoe Papyrus (prophetologion; 8th c.), Zuntz 1956
Aq — Aquila
AS — *Ägyptologische Studien*, Firchow 1955
AW — *Altägyptische Weisheit*, Brunner 1988a
b. — Babylonian Talmud
Baum. — Baumgartner 1890: *Etude Critique*,
BDB — Brown, Driver, and Briggs, *Hebrew and English Lexicon of the Old Testament*
BH — Biblical Hebrew, *including Ben Sira*
BHS — Biblia Hebraica Stuttgartensia
BTM — *Before the Muses*, B. Foster 1993
BWL — *Babylonian Wisdom Literature*, Lambert 1960
CATSS — Computer Assisted Tools for Septuagint Studies: Hebrew-Greek Parallel Aligned Database
CG — Cairo Geniza Biblical MSS (cited from the BHS apparatus)
cl. — clause
CLEM — *Late-Egyptian Miscellanies*, Caminos 1954 (translation and commentary of LEM)
CML — *Canaanite Myths and Legends*, Gibson, 1978
COHL — *Catalogue des ostraca hiératiques littéraires de Deir el Médineh*. See Posener in Bibliography
coll. — collective
const. — construct
CSP — Cook 1997: *The Septuagint of Proverbs*
CTA — *Corpus des tablettes en cunéiformes alphabétiques*, Herdner, 1963
D — D-stem, Piel (Aram Pael)
DCH — *Dictionary of Classical Hebrew*, Clines 1993ff.
Di Lella — *The Wisdom of Ben Sira*, AB 39, Patrick W.

Skehan and Alexander A. Di Lella, 1987

DNF — David Noel Freedman, editorial communication

Dp — D passive, Pual

Dr — D reduplicated stem, Polel

DSS — Dead Sea Scrolls

DSST — *The Dead Sea Scrolls*, García Martínez 1994

Dt — Dt-stem, Hitpael (Aram ʾetpaal)

EM — Encyclopedia Miqraʾit 1965ff.

ET — English translation

FAL — *Fragen an die altägyptische Literatur* (E. Otto Gedenkschrift), Assmann et al. 1977

fem. — feminine

FIFAO — *Fouilles de l'Institut français d'archéologie orientale*

FS — Festschrift

G — G-stem, Qal

GBH — *A Grammar of Biblical Hebrew*, Joüon and Muraoka 1991

GELS — *A Greek-English Lexicon of the Septuagint*, Lust et al. 1996

Gk — Greek

GKC — Gesenius, Kautsch, and Cowley, *Gesenius' Hebrew Grammar*, 1910

Gp — G passive

Gt — ʾEthpael (Aram)

H — H-stem, Hiphil

HAHL — *Handbook of Ancient Hebrew Letters*, Pardee 1982

HALAT — *Hebräisches und Aramäisches Lexikon*, Baumgartner and Stamm 1967–90

HB — Hebrew Bible (including Aramaic portions)

HO — *Hieratic Ostraca*, Černý and Gardiner 1957

Hp — H passive, Hophal

IBHS — *Introduction to Biblical Hebrew Syntax*, Waltke and O'Connor 1990

impf. — imperfect

impv. — imperative

inf. — infinitive

IW — *Israelite Wisdom*, Gammie et al. 1978

JPSV — Jewish Publication Society Version, 1965–82

juss. — jussive

K — Ketiv

KAI — *Kanaanäische und Aramäische Inschriften*, Donner and Röllig 1962

KÄT — Kleine ägyptische Texte

Kenn. — Kennicott 1776–80: *Vetus Testamentum hebraicum cum variis lectionibus*

KJV — King James Version

KTU — *Die keilalphabetischen Texte aus Ugarit*, Dietrich et al. 1976

l. — line

LÄ — *Lexikon der Ägyptologie*, Helck and Eberhard 1972ff.

LAE — *Letters from Ancient Egypt*, Wente 1990

Lag. — De Lagarde 1863: *Anmerkungen zur griechischen Übersetzung der Proverbien*

LEM — *Late-Egyptian Miscellanies*, Gardiner, 1937

LEWL — *Late Egyptian Wisdom Literature*, Lichtheim 1983

LRL — *Late Ramesside Letters*, Wente 1967

LSF — *Die Lese- und Schreib-*

	fehler im AT, Friedrich Delitzsch, 1920
LXX	Septuagint (ed. Rahlfs) LXX^A = Septuagint, Codex Alexandrinus LXX^B = Septuagint, Codex Vaticanus LXX^S = Septuagint, Codex Sinaiticus Other MSS according to the Göttingen Septuagint numeration
masc.	masculine
Mezz.	Mezzacasa 1913: *Il Libro dei Proverbi di Salomone*
Mid.	Midrash
MH	Mishnaic Hebrew
MK	Middle Kingdom (Egypt)
MS, MSS	manuscript(s)
MT	Masoretic text (edition used: BHS)
N	N-stem, Niphal
NK	New Kingdom (Egypt)
O.	ostracon
ODeM	Ostracon from Deir el-Medineh (see Posener, FIFAO series)
OG	Old Greek, the (reconstructed) original Septuagintal text
OHDM	*Catalogue des ostraca hiératiques littéraires de Deir el Médineh*, see Posener 1938
OK	Old Kingdom (Egypt)
OL	Old Latin (Vetus Latina) translation
om.	omit(s)
Pap.	papyrus
pass.	passive
per.	person
pf.	perfect
pl.	plural
$^{pl.}$	*syamē*, the plural marker in Syriac words
PN	personal name
poss.	possessive

ptcp.	participle
Q	qeré
RA	*Reallexikon der Assyriologie*
rco.	recto
RH	Rabbinic (Mishnaic) Hebrew[1]
SAIW	*Studies in Ancient Israelite Wisdom*, Crenshaw 1976
SAL	*Studien zu altägyptischen Lebenslehren*, Hornung and Keel 1979
sfx.	suffix
sg.	singular
SIANE	*The Sage in Israel and the Ancient Near East*, Gammie and Perdue 1990
sim.	similarly
Sir	Ben Sira (Ecclesiasticus)[2]
SPOA	*Sagesses du Proche-orient ancien*, 1963; see "Sagesses" in Bibliography
Sym	Symmachus
Syr	Syriac: the Peshitta translation (Leyden edition)
SyrH	Syro-Hexapla
TDOT	*Theological Dictionary of the Old Testament*, Botterweck and Ringgren 1974ff.
Tg	Targum, the Aramaic translation (for other MSS, see Healey 1991: 3–4)

[1]For statements about RH vocabulary with no further reference, see the relevant entry in Marcus Jastrow, *A Dictionary of the Targumim, etc.* (New York: Pardes, 1950).

[2]References indicate MS or version only when there are differences significant to the matter under discussion. For abbreviations of MSS and discussion of textual witnesses see Di Lella 1987 (pp. 52–59).

	Tg^L = de Lagarde, *Hagiographa Chaldaice*, 1873
	Tg^Z = Zamora text (= San Bernardo 116-Z-40), dated 1517 C.E.; in Díez Marino 1984
Theod	Theodotion
TS	*The Tale of Sinuhe and Other Ancient Egyptian Poems*, trans. Parkinson 1997
TWAT	*Theologisches Wörterbuch zum Alten Testament*, Botterweck and Ringgren 1970ff.
var(s).	variant(s)
vso.	verso
Vul	The Vulgate (Jerome's Latin translation)

TERMS

Dittography	The accidental double copying of a letter or group of letters.
Haplography	The accidental omission of a letter or group of letters because of its similarity to the letters next to it.
Homeoteleuton	The accidental omission of text due to the copyist skipping from one word to a later word with the same or similar ending.
Ketiv	"Written," the consonantal form of a Hebrew word in the body of the text.
Parablepsis	The accidental skipping of material in the process of copying or translating.
Peshiṭta	The ancient Syria translation of the Bible; see the introduction to the Textual Notes.
Qeré	"Read"—the way a Hebrew word is written in a Masoretic note, when this differs from the Ketiv. The Qeré is best understood as an alternative reading, not an emendation or correction of the Ketiv.
Septuagint	The ancient Greek translation of the Bible, abbreviated as LXX; see the introduction to the Textual Notes.
Targum	The ancient Aramaic translation of the Bible; see the introduction to the Textual Notes.
Vorlage	(German, used as an English word): The Hebrew text that an ancient translator had before him.

SIGLA

*	hypothetical or reconstructed form. (In Bibliography, indicates a work referenced by name of author only.)
=	equals; i.e., the same as or *virtually* the same as
≠	not equal to, substantively different from
≈	similar to, congruent with
//	parallel to
⟨ ⟩	judged to be a later addition
{ }	not in MT; supplied
$^α, ^β, ^γ ^δ$	Superscripted Greek letters mark line (stich) divisions

within the LXX (e.g., 22:8$^{\alpha}$ = the first line within verse 8, not an additional verse. For the latter, roman letters are used (e.g., 22:8a), to agree with Rahlfs. See the explanation in "Verse Numbering within the Septuagint" in the introduction to the Textual Notes.

INTRODUCTION

INTRODUCTION TO THE BOOK OF PROVERBS

◆

I. ON READING PROVERBS

When we look at life honestly, as the sages of ancient Israel surely did, we see goodness, beauty, and justice, but we also see evil, ugliness, and injustice. And we see that God, who demands just action and rational behavior, often acts in ways that are apparently unjust and bewildering. The books of Qohelet (Ecclesiastes) and Job confronted these inequities and sought ways to make the best of the hand we are dealt in a game whose rules are often murky.

Proverbs too responds to life's vicissitudes, and it does so no less honestly than the two more adventurous Wisdom books. By no means oblivious to life's uncertainties and ambiguities, the authors of Proverbs—countless generations of unknown sages—seek to provide firm principles to guide us through life: not a set of dogmas or a book of laws, but precepts, norms, and guidelines for securing a life of well-being, decency, and dignity. The same is true of foreign Wisdom literature, in which tradition Proverbs is deeply rooted.

But Proverbs introduces a novel principle: wisdom.[3] Wisdom, as conceived in Proverbs as a whole, is not just a set of prepackaged traditional truths or wise teachings. It is the power of the human mind, both in its intellectual faculties and in the knowledge it can gain, hold, and transmit. Wisdom both transcends the individual mind and resides within it. God possesses it and, we are taught, it can be ours as well.

Proverbs' guiding belief is that the human intellect—wisdom—founded on fear of God and tutored in traditional teachings, is the prime virtue of character, and as such is the necessary (and almost sufficient) means for creating a life of success—materially, physically, socially, and morally. Where this principle comes from and how it is thought to work are questions that will be explored in the course of the commentary. But for now consider this: The diverse anonymous sages whose words are embedded and reworked in the book of Proverbs are making a bold, by no means self-evident statement. They are declaring faith in the ability of the human mind, for all its frailties, to illuminate the darkness and guide us aright, "For the precept is a lamp and the teaching a light" (6:23a).

---

[3] I capitalize "Wisdom" when referring either to the literary genre or to personified Lady Wisdom. When referring to the faculty of wisdom or the content of wise teaching, I use the lower case. The distinctions cannot always be maintained. At the beginning of sentences, I remove ambiguities as necessary.

II. Place in the Canon

Proverbs belongs to the Writings or Hagiographa, the third division of the Hebrew canon. There are varying traditions on the order of the books in the Writings (as well as in the Prophets). In the section that concerns us, two orders are given: (1) Psalms–Job–Proverbs (thus in the view of the Tiberian Masoretes and in the Leningrad and Aleppo codices and the major Spanish MSS; likewise in the Talmud [*b. Baba Batra* 14b], which differs with regard to other books) and (2) Psalms–Proverbs–Job (Ashkenazi manuscripts and early printed editions). The first arrangement has greater antiquity. In spite of the variations, the three books are consistently grouped together as the three "poetical books" by virtue of sharing a peculiar accentual system. In the Septuagint, however, the Solomonic books are grouped together and follow David's book. The usual order is thus Psalms + Odes–Proverbs–Ecclesiastes–Song of Songs–Job.

A rabbinic tradition tells that the ancient sages, prior to Hezekiah, sought to withdraw Proverbs from general circulation. In the course of interpreting Prov 25:1, Abba Shaul says:

> At first the [ancient sages] said, "Proverbs and the Song of Songs and Qohelet should be withdrawn [read *yᵉgānnᵉzû*], because they said, "These are proverbs and not part of the sacred writings." And they did withdraw them, until the men of Hezekiah [thus read] came and explained them. (Avot deRabbi Nathan A 1:4)[4]

The issue is not the canonicity of these books but their suitability for general reading.[5] The ostensive issue in the case of Proverbs (at least as Avot deRabbi Nathan interprets Abba Shaul's tale) was the erotic language of Prov 7:7–20, which was open to misinterpretation. The story is a fiction that seeks to explain the mention of Hezekiah in Prov 25:1 and to assert that the problems in Proverbs and the other two books were recognized and somehow resolved exegetically.

On the title of the book and its names, see the Commentary on 1:1.

III. The Divisions of Proverbs

The book of Proverbs is composed of six distinct parts, commonly called "collections." This term is appropriate to the central parts but not to chapters 1–9 or the appendices in chapters 30–31, which are not compilations of proverbs. I will

[4]See the discussion in Haran 1996: 293–94 (q.v. on the variants) and chapter 5, *passim*.

[5]The entire discussion of the "withdrawal" of biblical books is a fiction meant to show awareness of the difficulty of these books and to claim that the difficulties were exegetically resolved. See M. Haran 1996: 301f. and chapter 5.

designate the major divisions "Parts," a neutral label that accommodates different histories of composition. Some parts can be subdivided on the grounds of different emphases and preferred proverb types. Additional likely subdivisions are IIa (10–15) and IIb (16:1–22:16) and Va (25–27) and Vb (28–29), though there is no indication that these subdivisions ever existed independently. For the subdivisions of Part I, see pp. 44f.

	Verses	Heading or Contents
I	1:1–9:18	"The proverbs of Solomon the son of David, king of Israel" (1:1)
II	10:1–22:16	"Proverbs of Solomon" (10:1)
III	22:17–24:22	"Words of the Wise" (22:17, emended)
IV	24:23–34	"These too are of the wise" (24:23)
V	25:1–29:27	"These too are proverbs of Solomon, which the men of Hezekiah king of Judah transmitted" (or "redacted") (25:1)
VI	30:1–31:31	Appendices
	VIa 30:1–14	"Words of Agur son of Yaqeh the Massa[ite]" (30:1)
	VIb 30:15–33	(Numerical epigrams)
	VIc 31:1–9	"The words of Lemuel, king of Massa, which his mother taught him" (31:1)
	VId 31:10–31	(The Excellent Woman)

IV. Text

The basis for this commentary is the Masoretic Text (MT). This is the only Hebrew form of Proverbs extant in its entirety, but it is not the only form there ever was. Variant readings can be recovered with varying degrees of certainty, mainly from the ancient translations. Ancient variants are not necessarily better than the MT, but sometimes they are earlier and are to be preferred to the MT. Often, however, we can accept both variants, the Masoretic and the recovered forms, as valid alternatives, for proverbs are, by their nature, highly mutable. Proverbial sayings undergo constant change, in both oral and written transmission, and some of the changes are *developments* rather than mere errors. Copying errors do occur, however, and when the MT is obscure and violates the well-established rules of Hebrew grammar, we do less violence to the sages' teachings by emending the text than by squeezing meaning from it by tortuous decryptions.

In the reconstruction of variant texts, the ancient Greek (LXX) and Syriac (Syr) translations are the oldest and most valuable. For a fuller discussion of the textual evidence, see the introduction to the Textual Notes.

V. Dating

The notion of "dating" a text, a traditional concern in Bible studies, is not quite germane to the book of Proverbs. The book by its own testimony is a collection of sayings from an indefinite number of sages (see 24:23) over a number of generations, at a minimum from Solomon's time (mid-tenth century) to Hezekiah's (eighth to seventh centuries; see 25:1). In fact, the Solomonic ascription is untenable (see comment on 1:1), and Hezekiah is not the end point.

Some sayings speak about kingship as a present reality, and so probably belong to the First Commonwealth, which came to an end in 587 B.C.E. The first part of the book, Prov 1–9, is later than the others because it serves as the introduction to the proverb collections. A Persian or early Hellenistic dating is likely for the latest strata of the book. A few proverbs show Aramaisms or late usages. Some parts of Prov 1–9, especially chapter 8, seem to me to be a response to Greek philosophy, though this is an uncertain basis for dating. The end point of the process was well before Ben Sira, who was writing in the early second century B.C.E., for he was strongly influenced by Proverbs.

No further precision seems possible in the dating of the individual proverbs or the collections. We know that some proverbs and literary units have precursors in ancient Egyptian Wisdom, but that does not help date the proverbs we have, in their present form, for they have undergone much development since their Egyptian forerunners.

The literary form of the material provides little help in dating, even relatively. Individual proverbs, whether "folk" or "artistic," written or oral, were produced long before and long after the time of ancient Israel. (This is contrary to Westermann's assumption that since oral wisdom "flourished" before literary wisdom, the short, presumably oral, sayings in Proverbs are older than its longer, presumably literary discourses [1990: 10–13; ET 2–5]. The age of the genres says nothing about when individual proverbs and poems were composed.)

Prov 1–9 introduces and tells us how to read the rest of the book and so must be later. See "The Dating of Proverbs 1–9" in the introduction to Part I.

VI. The Authors and Their Social Setting[6]

The authorship of Proverbs was traditionally ascribed to Solomon (10:1; 25:1). On the reason for—and inaccuracy of—this ascription, see "Solomon and the Title of Proverbs" in the Commentary on 1:1. The collection headers themselves recognize that the work is a sampling of the collective wisdom of ancient Israel.

---

[6]This section is based on my essay "The Social Location of the Book of Proverbs" (1993b), which should be consulted for a more detailed argument, in particular, with regard to the social ideal projected by the book.

Anonymous and unnumbered "sages" are mentioned in 22:17 (emended) and 24:23. Two of the sages, Agur (30:1) and Lemuel's mother (31:1), are apparently foreigners.

The social setting of the book of Proverbs is open to dispute, but it is clearly a secular work. It makes no pretense to an origin in divine revelation or inspiration. God is never quoted or addressed. It never had a role in the ritual life of Israel, in neither temple nor synagogue. In fact, it never was, and still is not, a subject of deliberate study in the rabbinic academies. With the exception of a few passages, it treats everyday life, not the grand affairs of state, history, cult, or law. It gives guidance in challenges we all face: how to get along with people, how to be a good and decent person, how to make the right choices in personal and business affairs, how to win God's favor and avoid disaster—all issues of great importance, but still modest and prosaic ones.

Scholars are divided as to whether the social setting of the proverbs collected in this book was the scribal school or village life. The argument focuses particularly on the earlier proverb collections in chapters 10–29.

Some scholars, notably H.-J. Hermisson (1968), locate the setting of Wisdom Literature in schools connected with the royal court. Though (he grants) the proverb collections may not have been written for the schools, they were certainly used in schools that trained children of the upper class for the royal bureaucracy. While Hermisson grants that the book probably does incorporate some oral folk sayings, he regards the collections we have as literary texts. B. Lang too sees the origin of the book of Proverbs (though not all its material) in the schools (1986: 7–11).

Though a presumptive case can be made for the existence of schools in ancient Israel, there is no *positive* evidence for them until well into the Hellenistic period, when Ben Sira refers to a *beyt midraš*, "house of study."[7]

The arguments for the existence of schools in Israel are exhaustively presented by Hermisson (1968: 97–136) and A. Lemaire (1981 and 1984) and cautiously affirmed by G. Davies (1995). F. Golka (1983, 1993, chapters 1–2) disputes their existence and proposes that education took place in a "famulus" or apprentice system. But there is no evidence for this besides a vague parallel to the presumed practice on Old Kingdom Egypt, which Golka assumes was at a "similar stage of development" to the United Monarchy (1993: 10). (If that were so, we could just as well parallel the Middle and New Kingdoms, which definitely had schools, to later periods in the Israelite monarchy, when Proverbs was composed.) Jamieson-Drake (1991) analyzes archaeological data and concludes that there is no evidence for schools in pre-exilic Judah, but he grants that a school in Jerusalem in the eighth to seventh centuries would be consistent with the evidence of increased regional economic activity (p. 155). (He does not consider the needs of *temples* for more than informal tutelage.) R. N. Whybray (1974, *passim*) argues that nothing in the Bible points to a professional class

---

[7]Thus lack of evidence does not prove nonexistence, since no one claims that Ben Sira invented the school.

Ben Sira's *beyt midrash*, lit. "house of study," mentioned in the much misunderstood 51:23, is a metaphor for his book. The passage concludes the book and recommends it to the reader. Through this "school," one may gain wisdom "without money" (v 25). The metaphoric use, however, presumes a known reality.

(better: "caste") of wise men called *ḥăkamim* and that there was no "Wisdom School" in the sense of an ideological-political faction.

Though the Hebrew writing system was vastly simpler than those used in Egypt and Mesopotamia, future priests and administrators had to learn much more than just reading and writing. It is likely that there were schools attached to the temple and possibly the court, as in Egypt and Mesopotamia, because there is little reason for *anyone* to write if only a scattered few can read. The massive and intricate priestly lore in particular would require temples. Like the temples had libraries in Egypt and Mesopotamia, the Second Temple in Jerusalem had a library, and these would form a locus for advanced learning, like the "House of Life" associated with Egyptian temples. It is unlikely that the First Temple alone lacked such a center of learning. See further Lemaire 1990: 176–80.

But the existence of schools is really a separate issue from the origins and setting of Wisdom Literature. There certainly were schools in Egypt, and Wisdom Literature was one of many genres used and copied in them, but that does not mean that these books were written *for* the schools or that we are to imagine them as a transcription of the words of teachers to pupils.

The Egyptian wisdom instructions (our best non-Israelite analogues to Proverbs) do not present themselves as written for schools. The books are ascribed to men from a variety of professions and classes,[8] ranging from king and vizier to ordinary scribes of different rank. Some ascriptions may be fictitious, but some certainly are not, for their authors are too individual and unillustrious to be likely typological fictions. Duachety, Amenemope, and Anii[9] are examples of this. The "scribe of the tomb" Amennakhte is a known historical personage.[10] Even when fictive, ascriptions show what an Egyptian reader could be expected to envision as the setting of wisdom instruction. The ostensive, and often actual, authors are men from various walks of life who are speaking to their actual sons.

In the "Letter of Menena," a father writes to his "son and apprentice" Payiri and refers to the advice and teachings he gave him formerly (and which the son is now ignoring). It is unquestionably his actual son he is addressing.

An interesting variation is the case of the friends Amennakhte and Hori, the fathers of Horisheri and Horimin, respectively, who apparently wrote "instructions" to *each other's* sons. Hori wrote an instruction to Horisheri after Amennakhte's death, urging him to emulate his father. These are real men writing to real individuals. We know about the careers of the two fathers, and neither was a schoolteacher. Amennakhte was (among other things) a scribe in the House

[8]The scribes in Egypt, and probably in Israel, belonged to a variety of social classes. They ranged from ordinary village scriveners (who would write personal letters or petitions for a fee) to members of the highest echelons of palace service.

[9]Foreign Wisdom texts are cited by name of author (putative or real). For information on them, see later "Wisdom Literature: A Survey" and the Bibliography.

[10]At least five of Amennakhte's works are extant: a poem of nostalgia for Thebes, a satirical poem, two hymns to Ramses IV, and a hymn to a god (Bickel and Mathiew 1993: 38; translations pp. 35–48). This example shows that Wisdom literature was not the product of a certain "school" of scribes but that the same men could author different types of works, both religious and secular. By the same token, there is no reason to suppose that the authors of Israelite Wisdom belonged to a certain "school" and subscribed to a distinctive ideology.

of Life (a scribal center in the temple that included a library and probably a school), but he does not call himself a schoolteacher (*sbꜣw n pr ꜥnḫ*). (See Bickel and Mathieu 1993.) This variation presupposes that the father-to-son setting of wisdom instructions was the norm.

The father-to-son setting is maintained in Proverbs, at least as a fiction, consistently in chapters 1–9 and occasionally elsewhere (19:27; 23:15, 19, 26; 24:13, 21; 27:11; cf. 31:1–2). The father's reminiscence in Prov 4:3 of the education he received from his own father envisions education in the family, not the school. This impression is reinforced by mention of the mother's teaching in Prov 1:8 and 6:20, since "mother" can hardly mean schoolmistress. Education, which is the goal of Wisdom Literature, is not identical with schooling.

On the other side, C. Westermann (1990; ET 1995) holds that the older collections of Proverbs (chapters 10–29) comprise mainly oral folk sayings which originated in the daily life of agrarian villages, among the smallholding farmers, craftsmen, laborers, slaves, and housewives in pre-exilic times (1990: 27; ET 17, and *passim*). Prov 1–9 and numerous additions to the older collections are from the postexilic schools. F. Golka (1983; 1986; 1993: 4–53) supports this theory. R. N. Whybray (1990, *passim*) locates the proverbs among the smallholding farmers, neither rich nor poor. Related to this trend is C. R. Fontaine's emphasis on the oral origins of wisdom and on the family as the setting of instruction, which was shared by mother and father (1993). Fontaine does not deny the subsequent formulation of this wisdom within schools.

Westermann locates the bulk of the proverbs among the "simple people" ("einfachen Menschen"; p. 75; ET 60) in small agrarian villages at a preliterate stage of culture (1990: 10, 45, 75; ET 2, 33, 60). Extrapolating from proverbs (or proverb parts) that he considers folk sayings, he paints an idyllic picture of village society—a "modest, staid, bourgeois world."[11] The communitarian, egalitarian ethic of the proverbs is their way of life.

While most scholars recognize that many, perhaps most, of the sayings in Proverbs are in origin oral folk sayings, some of which may well have originated in small villages, this setting does not dominate the book. The folk-literature approach tends to slight the diversity of sources by overlooking clues to an urban setting, such as references to goldsmithery (17:3; 27:21), fine jewelry (e.g., 25:11, 12), and messengers (e.g., 10:26; 22:21; 25:13), which have no role in the small village. Many of these adages address well-to-do landowners rather than smallholders; for example: "As for him who withholds grain—the nation (*lᵉʾom*) will curse him; but blessings come upon him who distributes food" (*mašbir*) (11:26). A *mašbir* is a major distributor—a central grain distributor—and small farmers could not afford to withhold grain. Similarly, when slaves are mentioned, it is from the perspective of their owners, people who are concerned with efficient discipline of slaves (29:21), whom only the better-off could afford to buy and keep.

[11]"Es ist eine nüchterne, solide, bürgerliche Welt" (p. 27).

A fair number of proverbs indicate a setting in the royal court, describing kings and governors and giving advice to their servants and ministers. Some proverbs speak from the perspective of people who have to deal with kings; for example, "Do not put on airs before the king, and do not stand in the place of the mighty. It is better that he say to you, 'Come up here'" (25:6–7), and "The king's anger is angels of death, but a wise man can assuage it" (16:14). F. Golka (1986 and 1993: 16–35) contends that these proverbs are not evidence of origins in the court because they are critical of the king and have parallels in African folk sayings. Such proverbs, however, are not deeply critical of kingship itself but only recognize kings' power and the damage that they can do, and in any case people close to kings can see them with critical eyes.[12] Royalty is a prominent theme throughout chapters 10–29. Chapters 28–29, in particular, seem to form a sort of manual for a monarch. Together with the reference to the editorial work by the men of Hezekiah in 25:1 (which I find credible), they show that the court was the decisive locus of Wisdom creativity. Since we cannot imagine courtly proverbs seeping down to be collected by the "folk," we must presume an upward movement. Everything we have was channeled to the court and through it. The flow cannot be supposed to move in the other direction.

The royal servants (whom we may call the "king's men," following a usage implicit in Prov 25:1[13]) should not be imagined only as rich courtiers. It would have included literate clerks and officials of high and low degree, much like the men whom Ben Sira addresses and to whose caste he belonged. When Ben Sira says, "Among the great, do not act their equal" (32:9), he is speaking to men who may come into contact with the grandees but are not *of* them.

The king's men had their hand in the formation of Proverbs, and they reached deep. What did they do? Surely they did not undertake paroemiological fieldwork in the villages, gathering and publishing folk sayings. Ben Sira gives us a glimpse into the way that folk proverbs could migrate into literary collections.

> If you are willing, [you will receive knowledge]. Incline your ear that you may gain discipline. [Stand in the company of the elders, and attach yourself to whosoever is wise.] Desire to hear every discourse [*śîḥah*], and let no perceptive proverb [*m^{e}šal binah*] escape you." (6:33–35[14])

This advice (written by a scholar to a reading audience) shows an appreciation of oral discourse as a source of wisdom.[15] A scholar should be attentive to intelligent conversation and perceptive proverbs. It is a small step from here to re-

---

[12] I debate the validity of Golka's arguments in "The Social Location of the Book of Proverbs" (1993b: 234–35).

[13] "The men of Hezekiah"; compare 1 Kgs 10:8 (MT), *ʾănašeyka* "your men" // *ʿăbadeyka* "your servants."

[14] From Hebrew MS A, supplemented (in brackets) from the Greek.

[15] As does Ptahhotep's observation that "Fine discourse is more precious [lit. "hidden"] than emeralds, but it is to be found with the maids at the grinding stones" (§1; ll. 58–59).

calling such sayings, along with written proverbs one has read, and embedding them in one's own creations. In such a process, the very notions of "author" and "redactor," "original" and "later," intertwine inextricably.

Such a process accounts for the great diversity and the even greater unity in Proverbs. The diversity comes from the varied sources, the unity from the redactors' individual creative activity. The redactors' intervention was radical and determinative, going far beyond just attaching "later additions" to existing proverbs. They did collect sayings and add some of their own, but, most important, they *selected*. They chose what to include and what to ignore, and what they included, they reshaped. Observe that Ben Sira does not simply advise the reader to retain the proverbs he hears. He advises the remembering of *wise* proverbs. The proverbs preserved must meet the redactor's, not the "folk's," notion of wisdom.[16]

While the sayings in Proverbs are drawn from different social groups, including the "folk" and the literati, it was a series of editors who ultimately determined what was included and what was excluded. Learned clerks—at least some of them the king's men, others perhaps serving post-exilic provincial administrations—were the membrane through which principles, sayings, and coinages, folk and otherwise, were filtered. The central collections of Proverbs are their filtrate, a largely homogeneous one. In the end, it is *their* work and *their* idea of wisdom that we are reading, and it is, not surprisingly, ideologically quite coherent.

To the proverb collections, later authors affixed longer poems, particularly in chapters 1–9 and 30–31. We will also have to take into account the possibility of miscellaneous insertions throughout the book, though these are very hard to determine. What emerges, even if we cannot know the details of the process, is a book that is representative of many domains of ancient Israelite society through numerous generations.

Proverbs is a slice of a tradition that preceded ancient Israel and continued beyond it. This tradition comprised the creation, reshaping, and transmission of wise sayings and teachings about how to live a righteous, productive, and happy life. The Israelite tradition had predecessors in the ancient Near East and successors in Jewish Wisdom texts. These are surveyed here in "Wisdom Literature: A Survey."

The tradition was in constant evolution, and it is arbitrary at what point of development we cease to apply the genre label "Wisdom Literature." But the enterprise does not disappear, and the descendants of Wisdom Literature may be traced beyond the Bible and Apocrypha into Jesus' sayings,[17] rabbinic midrashim, apothegms and sayings (see here "Later Works Affiliated with Wisdom

[16]A fair portion of the folk proverbs found elsewhere in the Bible would not have qualified as wisdom by the standards of Proverbs. "The fathers have eaten sour grapes, and the children's teeth stand on edge" (Ezek 18:2), for example, is a self-serving gripe that shifts the blame to the father, and "One who puts on his armor should not boast like one who takes it off" (1 Kgs 20:11) is a bellicose taunt.

[17]On these, see J. G. Williams 1981: chapter 3.

Literature"), medieval Jewish ethical wills or testaments (Abrahams 1948), and even modern Hebrew proverb collections.[18] When a Jewish scholar in the Middle Ages read the book of Proverbs and reused its language, teachings, and forms in his testament to his sons, he was doing essentially the same thing as the Hebrew scribe who read the book of Amenemope (or a descendant thereof) and reshaped it into Prov 22:17–23:11.

VII. COMMENTARIES USED[19]

Biblical commentary is a collective enterprise. All commentaries, including the present one, absorb and integrate earlier interpretation. Coming to grips with past exegesis is not only preparatory to commentary but also integral to it, because genuine discovery and progress in humanistic studies come through the unending dialectic within the community of readers, not through sudden solitary insights.

I try to identify the authors of distinctive interpretations and to refer the reader to commentaries and studies that provide fuller arguments for important ideas, even ones I do not accept. Often, however, my commentary assimilates and reworks the earlier insights in a way that makes it impossible to assign credit for the various components of the results.

Rather than attempting to wade through the massive numbers of commentaries on Proverbs, I have selected several (listed here) to follow consistently. I chose them not because I agree with them more often than with the others but because they take distinctive approaches to exegesis and provide different kinds of assistance. I call on a range of other commentaries as the need arises. Most often, the commentaries cited constitute only a sampling of those holding a particular interpretation.

I give special attention to the medieval Jewish *peshaṭ* ("plain sense" or "literal") commentators. Medieval Jewish commentary has largely been neglected in academic Bible scholarship, though a great many of the ideas of modern commentators arose first among the medievals, and many of their brightest insights are absent from later exegesis. I emphasize that I do provide a representative survey of medieval Jewish exegesis to Proverbs. Much of this exegesis, even in the literalistic commentaries, consists of ethical-religious moralizing and homilies, or seeks to fit the ideas and terminology of Proverbs into the concepts of medieval philosophies. These matters require a separate study. I use the medieval commentaries as I do the modern ones, mining them for insights and suggestions in the course of forming my own interpretation.

---

[18]Collections that draw from the entire range of Jewish literature are A. Hayman's *ʾOṣar Divrey Ḥăkamim Upitgᵉmeyhem* (Tel Aviv, 1935), M. Waxman's *Mišley Yisraʾel* (1933), and I. Davidson's *ʾOṣar Hamᵉšalim vᵉhapitgamim* (Jerusalem 1957).

[19]Commentaries (and a few other works marked by an asterisk in the bibliography) are referenced by the name of the author only, ad loc. unless otherwise indicated.

I give less attention to midrashic interpretations of Proverbs, since those are distant from my own essentially *peshaṭ* exegetical approach. For a translation and discussion of Midrash Proverbs, see Visotzky 1990 and 1992. I am not versed in patristic and medieval Christian exegesis and largely leave it aside. Some citations may be found in the commentaries of Delitzsch and Toy. With regard to medieval Christian interpretations, see B. Smalley's *Medieval Exegesis of Wisdom Literature* (1986).

TRADITIONAL JEWISH COMMENTARIES REGULARLY USED, IN APPROXIMATE CHRONOLOGICAL ORDER (for Further Information, See the Bibliography)

Saʿadia Gaon (882–942)
Rashi = R. Shlomo ben Isaac (1040–1105)
Riyqam = R. Yosef Qimḥi (ca. 1105–70)
Radaq = R. David Qimḥi (1160–1235?)
Ramaq = R. Moshe Qimḥi (12th c.)
Hameʾiri = Menahem ben Shelomo Hameʾiri (1249–1316?)
Ralbag = R. Levi ben Gershom, or Gersonides (1288–1344)
Kaspi = Yosef ibn Kaspi, Commentary II (1279–1340)
Naḥmias = Yosef ben Yosef ibn Naḥmias (14th c.)
Ibn Yaḥyah = Yosef b. David ibn Yaḥyah (1494–1534)
Malbim = Meir Loeb b. Yechiel Michael (1809–79)[20]

MODERN COMMENTARIES REGULARLY FOLLOWED

Franz Delitzsch 1873
C. H. Toy (ICC) 1899
Arnold Ehrlich 1913
N. H. Tur-Sinai 1947
William McKane (OTL) 1970
Otto Plöger (BKAT) 1984
Arndt Meinhold (ZBK) 1991

[20]In spite of Malbim's date, in his methods and assumptions he belongs to the older tradition of Jewish commentary.

The present commentary cannot fairly summarize the rich and varied contributions of modern scholarship to the study of Proverbs and Wisdom Literature. For such a survey, the reader should consult R. N. Whybray's clear and wide-ranging topical history of recent research, *The Book of Proverbs: A Survey of Modern Study* (1995).

VIII. Terms and Definitions

POETIC UNITS

1:15	a	My son, don't go in the way with them,
	b	don't step upon their path,
1:16	a	for their feet rush to harm,
	b	make haste to shed blood.

Verse:	A verse (e.g., 1:16) is determined strictly by the Masoretic accents and the numbering in Hebrew editions and is not necessarily a poetic unit.
Line:	In the example, there are four lines. A verse usually has two lines, occasionally three. "Lines" are assigned letters corresponding to the lines in the translation.
Couplet:	Two lines, usually in parallelism, forming a thought-unit, are a couplet. In the example, v 15 is one couplet, v 16 another. Most proverbs consist of a single couplet of two parallel lines.
Tristich:	A unit of three parallel lines, relatively rare in Proverbs.
Quatrain:	Two closely associated couplets (e.g., 1:15 + 16).

Hierarchy of subdivisions, small to large: Strophes–Stanzas–Sections–Units–Parts

FREQUENTLY USED TERMS FOR TYPES OF SAYINGS (These designate not discrete categories but rather emphasize different aspects of proverbial sayings.)

Adage	A traditional saying used and transmitted in oral performance. An adage gains its credibility by long and general acceptance.
Admonition	A warning against improper behavior, usually given in vetitive (negative imperative) form.
Aphorism	A statement of an insight.[21]
Apothegm	A pithy saying or observation.

[21] J. G. Williams (1980: 37–39) says that an aphorism has the following features: It is an assertion, apparently self-explanatory, which states something as if it were a priori. It offers insight as process and can provoke another series of reflections. It is typically paradoxical, offering a different way of looking at things. It is concise and unites sound and sense.

Epigram	A brief poem making a single point.
Precept	A rule of behavior, whether formulated as advice or as an evaluative statement that is easily translated into a rule. I use this term to translate *miṣwah*, usually rendered "commandment."
Proverb	Used for all types of short sayings in the book of Proverbs and in other works of the genre.

IX. Translation

Different purposes call for different types of translations. In a commentary such as this, whose purpose is to aid in study and scholarship, the first goal of the translation must be to produce a clear and readable sentence that represents at least the surface meaning of the text. Many literary features, such as deliberate ambiguities, sound patterns, and wordplays, are often lost in translation and will sometimes be remarked on in the Commentary as appropriate.[22] Above all, the extraordinary concision of the Hebrew is invariably lost in the English.

Proverbs are "wisdom in a nutshell" (M. Salisbury 1994: 438). Most sayings in the book of Proverbs consist of two sentences juxtaposed in such a way that the words and images play off against each other and suggest a web of meanings. J. G. Williams describes the effect thus: "Within each sentence there is a juxtaposition of images which are projected stroboscopically: they are seen quickly side by side, then they are shut off" (1980: 41). Williams uses a mimetic translation[23] to suggest this effect, alongside a paraphrastic rendering to convey the meaning (hyphenated words represent single words in the Hebrew):

toḥelet mᵉmuššakah	*maḥalat leb*
wᵉʿeṣ ḥayyim	*taʾăbah baʾah*
hope drawn-out	sickens mind
and-tree-of life	desire come (13:12)

Hope drawn out drains the heart,
but a desire fulfilled is paradise.

---

[22] Consistency of number was apparently not a rule of Hebrew style, and singulars often stand parallel to plurals. Such fluctuations occur throughout Proverbs and will not usually be discussed in the Commentary. Since a literal translation would jar in a way the imbalance in Hebrew does not, the translation will often smooth out singular-plural inconsistencies without implying emendation of the original.

[23] The concept of "mimetic translation," which I prefer to "literal," is not Williams's but James S. Holmes's (*Translated!* 1988: 25–28). Mimetic translation attempts to imitate the linguistic features of the original and aims at consistency in correspondences between the vocabulary of the source and the target. Mimetic translation "tends to have the effect of re-emphasizing, by its strangeness, the strangeness which for the target-language readers is inherent in the semantic message of the original poem" (ibid., pp. 27–28). Nevertheless, I will use the more standard "lit." when rephrasing my own translation in mimetic form.

ḥośek šibṭo	*śone᾽ b^e^no*
w^e^᾽ohăbo	*šiḥăro musar*
sparer-of rod	hater of his son
and-who-loves-him	applies-to-him discipline

Save your strap and spoil your son;
if you love him let him learn discipline. (13:24)
(Williams 1980: 43)

Even the stripped-down "stroboscopic" rendering is less compact than the Hebrew, while the natural feel and lucidity (as well as the alliteration) of the Hebrew diction are completely lost. The book of Proverbs still awaits a translation that conveys the concision, rhythm, and memorability of the Hebrew, a task that probably requires sharp paraphrase (for an attempt to work out a method of doing so, see Salisbury 1994). An example of how such a paraphrase could work is the snappy rephrasing of 13:24a that arose in English oral tradition: "Spare the rod and spoil the child."

Most sayings in Proverbs are couplets, with the two lines carefully counterpoised in equivalent or (more often) antithetical parallelism. R. Alter (in an enlightening essay on the literary mechanisms of proverbs) nicely describes the effect of this regularity as "a didactic and mnemonic neatness of smoothly balanced statements clicking dutifully into place" (1985: 164). This smoothness is functional, since "the wisdom itself derives from a sense of balanced order, confident distinction, assured consequence for specific acts and moral stances" (164). But the simplicity is often deceptive, because "meaning emerges from some complicating interaction between the two halves of the line," an interaction enhanced by the way that words, syntactic patterns, and cadences "have a strong tendency to press closely against one another, generating complications of meaning by virtue of the sheer tightness of the frame in which they are held" (164f.). As Alter observes, this effect is often (and perhaps inevitably) blunted in translation, but we can still keep our eyes open for such complications and watch for surprises, for these allow us to grasp the particular and unforeseen message of the proverb.

For the most part, chapters 10–29 are made up of independent proverbs or apothegms: compact pieces of knowledge that jingle around in the memory like coins in one's pocket, waiting to be "spent" in a social transaction, sometimes, but not necessarily, in combination with other such coins. Reading such sayings will require special strategies, especially since many were coined to be heard, not read. But first, in chapters 1–9 (and occasionally elsewhere), we read wisdom of a very different sort: longer, sometimes expansive, magisterial poems, carefully crafted as the products of reflection and interaction with other texts.

With regard to "gender sensitivity," a matter currently of some concern, neither the present translation nor the discussion of it attempts to impose an alien gender neutrality on an undoubtedly male-oriented text. Proverbs speaks to males and their concerns. Sometimes it is explicit, as when the son is addressed.

When women are spoken of, whether in warning or complaint or commendation, it is from the standpoint of their value, danger, or irritation to men. Often the social or religious role assumed in the text is not specific to one sex, but when it is, it is always the male's. We may be sure that daughters too received moral instruction at home,[24] but that is not the setting that Wisdom literature chooses as its backdrop. Nevertheless, in terms of current applicability, the teachings of Proverbs are for the most part relevant, with only modest transposition, to both sexes.

X. WISDOM LITERATURE: A SURVEY

A. THE GENRES OF WISDOM

The book of Proverbs belongs to an international Wisdom tradition that began some two thousand years earlier in Egypt. This tradition was productive in Egypt, Palestine, Syria, and Mesopotamia.

No definition of Wisdom literature will identify precisely which works belong and which do not.[25] But we should not think of Wisdom literature as a field that can be marked out and fenced in. Wisdom literature is a *family* of texts. There are clusters of features that characterize it. The more of them a work has, the more clearly it belongs to the family. In fact, in the case of Wisdom literature, the family resemblances are quite distinctive, especially among the didactic texts. For practical purposes, the more a work resembles Proverbs, the more useful it is for comparison. But even works on the margins of Wisdom, such as the Egyptian school letters or the "Eloquent Peasant," can be used in comparisons insofar as there are resemblances relevant to the issue under discussion.

There are two main genres of Wisdom books: didactic Wisdom and critical (or speculative) Wisdom. The second class is amorphous. Works belonging to it are not necessarily skeptical. Their common feature is that they reflect and comment *on* doctrines and values found in didactic Wisdom literature rather than directly inculcating them. Job and Psalms 49, 73, and 88 belong in this category. Qohelet contains much critical or reflective material, but as a whole it presents itself as a teaching about how to live one's life and is to be classed as

---

[24]See n. 83.

[25]Whybray (1978) and Lichtheim (1997: 1–8), among others, have emphasized, or perhaps overemphasized, the difficulties in defining Wisdom literature. Lichtheim says that no Egyptian words in the semantic field of knowledge/understanding are identical to "wisdom," and that is true, but it is true of the Hebrew equivalents as well. Most translation-glosses are approximations, and we have to use them while observing the differences between the glosses and the original. I do this here in "Words for Wisdom and Folly in Proverbs." There is no reason to hesitate about applying the term "Wisdom literature" to Egyptian and Mesopotamian instructions just because it is a modern coinage or one based on Israelite literature (thus, e.g., Lambert, BWL 1–2; Buccellati 1981; Lichtheim, ibid.). If the word is used too loosely (as it sometimes is, for example, when applied to Esther or the Joseph story), it is an appropriate label for a fairly cohesive genre.

didactic—which is how the epilogue describes the work of Qohelet and other sages (Qoh 12:9–14).

Didactic Wisdom, the genre to which Proverbs belongs, is almost always cast as the words of a father to his son. The didactic books formulate some teachings as observations in the third person and others as admonitions in the second person, but both types aim at inculcating right attitudes and behavior. The teachings are not revelation and are never spoken by a god (except when the teacher is Pharaoh). With a few exceptions in Ben Sira, gods are never quoted or addressed in the body of the works. In content, the advice is both religious and worldly, but the focus is on successful and worthy behavior in mundane affairs. The advice is always directed to individuals, not a national grouping. It shows little interest in affairs of state, except when the pupil happens to be the king, in which case the national concerns belong to his personal realm of activity. Didactic writings are composed of short proverbs and of somewhat longer maxims on a single theme. (Insofar as a book diverges from this, as in the "Loyalist Teaching" or the Wisdom of Solomon 11–19, it diverges from the "core" of the family.)

A fair number of Wisdom books have reached us from Egypt and Mesopotamia. (They are listed at the beginning of the Bibliography.) These present many parallels to Proverbs, some of them strong enough to suggest direct influence.

In one case in particular, there is strong evidence for direct (though not immediate) foreign influence. In 1924, Adolf Erman argued that Prov 22:17–23:11 is a translation of selected passages from the Instruction of Amenemope.[26] This thesis has held up well to scholarly scrutiny. In fact, there is evidence for Amenemope's influence elsewhere in Proverbs. The existence of a secure case of transmission from Egypt to Israel strengthens the probability that it happened with other Wisdom books, formulas, and sayings as well. However, even in the case of Amenemope, the contact was probably mediated. We need only posit that sometime in the centuries following its composition in the twelfth to eleventh centuries B.C.E., Amenemope was translated into Hebrew or its Canaanite predecessor, and that this book, or a reworking thereof, was copied and read in Palestine until its sayings and forms became part of Israelite wisdom. The relation between Amenemope and Proverbs will be discussed in comments on Prov 22:17–23:11, as well as at Prov 1:1–7 and a few other verses that may be derived from Amenemope at some remove.[27]

Other Wisdom books, too, help us understand the literary and intellectual context of Proverbs. I will mention some of these parallels in the course of the

[26]The collection extends through 24:22, but the parallels with Amenemope end at 23:11. The entire collection (Part III) includes parallels to other Wisdom books too; see Washington 1994b: 139–45. As the title "Words of the Wise" suggests, the collection is a miscellany of older Wisdom maxims.

[27]Washington (1994b: 136) lists the following cases of likely dependence outside Prov 22:17–24:22:

Proverbs	Amenemope	Proverbs	Amenemope
15:16, 17:1	9.7–8; 16.11–14	20:9	19.18
16:11	18.2, 23	20:19	22.11
17:5	24.9	27:1	19.11, 22.5–6, 23.8–9

commentary, without implying that every parallel is an "influence" or a *homology*, that is to say, a similarity due to genetic influence or borrowing. It may be an *analogy*, a case of similar ideas arising independently in similar literatures. Analogies, too, give insight into how a certain theme, form, or idea was treated in ancient Wisdom literature. Both sorts of parallels can support a certain interpretation of the Proverbs passage, though their weight is not decisive, for an idea can change radically in the course of transmission.

Even the earliest texts can be used for comparison, because the Egyptian school tradition was a continuous one. The oldest texts were copied and reworked and quoted by later authors down to Ptolemaic times, with quotations of ancient texts sometimes appearing as late as in Coptic literature.

There were many opportunities for Egyptian texts to be translated into Canaanite dialects, including Hebrew. During the Egyptian empire in Palestine (late sixteenth to late twelfth centuries B.C.E.), there were scribes literate in Canaanite, Akkadian, and Egyptian, who were in frequent contact with the Egyptian court and royal administration. Mayors of towns in Palestine sent their sons to Egypt as hostages to loyalty, and the sons received an Egyptian education. The mayors themselves had to appear in the Egyptian capitals for certain festivals. Egyptian officials, which is to say, scribes, were often sent to Canaan on official duties (see Redford 1992: 198–203). Texts translated by such people could have been transmitted as part of the Canaanite literary heritage, which Israel inherited and reshaped.

Israel was never out of contact with Egypt, and the translation and transmission of Egyptian literature may have taken place in the period of the monarchies as well. Egyptian interaction with Asia increased in the Saite period (665–525 B.C.E.). After that, Egyptian Wisdom was not being cultivated in hieratic but in demotic, and the transmission of the classical books to Hebrew becomes very unlikely.

B. WISDOM BEFORE PROVERBS

1. Egypt

The following Wisdom instructions have been preserved well enough to be usable. (There are also numerous fragments of unidentified, largely lost Wisdom books.) For sources, see the Bibliography.

Old Kingdom (Dynasties 3–8; ca. 2650–2135 B.C.E.)

Djedefhar (or Ḥordjedef): Ascribed to a Fifth Dynasty prince, but extant texts much later. A sentence is even quoted in a first-century C.E. text. The extant portions recommend mortuary preparations.

Kagemeni: This instruction is actually *to* Kagemeni, spoken by his father the vizier, whose name is lost. The extant portion of the text advocates a quiet demeanor and moderation in eating. An epilogue reports that the vizier gave the instruction in written form to his children, including Kagemeni, who later became vizier.

First Intermediate (Dynasties 9–11 [first half]; ca. 2135–2040 B.C.E.)
Merikare: Spoken to King Merikare by his father, a monarch apparently named Cheti. Much of the advice is relevant only to the royal office and concerns topics such as repression of political incitement and rebellion, mustering troops, and performance of religious duties. The king speaks of his own accomplishments but also, extraordinarily, confesses his guilt in failing to prevent the desecration of mortuary monuments. He describes the judgment of the dead and advocates truth and justice. He concludes with a meditation on divine retribution and a hymn to the creator.

Middle Kingdom (Dynasties 11 [second half]–14; ca. 2040–1650 B.C.E.)
Amenemhet: A political apologia in the guise of a Wisdom instruction delivered by King Amenemhet I to his son, Sesostris I. Amenemhet describes in vivid terms a successful palace coup that apparently left him dead. Hence Amenemhet is speaking from the realm of the dead, as in a tomb autobiography, and he uses formulas from that genre. The gist of his "teaching" is: *Trust nobody.*

In the NK Pap. Chester Beatty IV (6.13–14), the actual author of this text is identified as the scribe Chety, who is the same as the Duachety mentioned later.

Ptahhotep: The book is set in the reign of Isesi in the Fifth Dynasty (2388–56 B.C.E.), but the language and the extant manuscripts belong to the early MK and the book was probably composed then. (The earliest MSS are from the mid-Twelfth Dynasty.) This long book is preserved intact on the earliest papyrus (Prisse) and extensively on two others from the NK.

In the prologue, the vizier Ptahhotep, approaching death, describes the miseries of old age and asks of Pharaoh permission to appoint his son as his successor, called a "staff of old age." He receives permission to do so and to instruct him in "the words of the ancestors." There follow thirty-seven maxims (varying from four to eighteen lines in length), each on its own topic. Ptahhotep prescribes proper behavior for various levels of officialdom and good relations with other people, including superiors, inferiors, wife, friends, and friends' wives. He cultivates the virtues of moderation, generosity, honesty, and modesty. In an epilogue, he compares two kinds of sons, those who can "listen" and those who refuse to do so.

Duachety son of Duauf: This is one of the most popular Wisdom books, with more than 250 copies of the whole or sections remaining. It offers instruction to a boy beginning scribal school, in two parts: (1) Encouragement to love book learning, with a "satire on the trades," which depicts the hardships of all occupations other than the scribal. Such "satires" became a commonplace of educational texts. (2) Miscellaneous advice, especially about social behavior: avoid quarrels, be modest and reserved, relay messages accurately, treat your mother well, and the like.

"Loyalist Teaching": The main witness to this is the stele of Sehetibre. The middle section is an "instruction" preaching loyalty to the king.

"A Man to His Son" (actual title, "The Instruction Which a Man Made for His Son"): This anonymous teaching promotes the virtues of quietness and obedience and praises skills in rhetoric and interpretation. It praises the king's power and the virtue of loyalty to him. It describes the king's power to aid the unfortunate and to make "the last be first." The conclusion again warns against "hot" talk and urges quiet, reserved speech. Many difficulties remain in the reconstruction of this text.

Ramesseum Papyri I and II: Fragmentary papyri containing various observations and sayings. Ramesseum I has a frame narrative about a scribe, Sisobek, who was imprisoned and placed in danger. After his release, he declaims on the unpredictability of human fortunes and the futility of indulgence in passion and loquacity. He offers various counsels, particularly on proper demeanor in speech. (A very similar device introduces the later books of Anchsheshonq and Ahiqar.) The ideal of the silent man is prominent.

New Kingdom (Dynasties 18–20; ca. 1550–1080 B.C.E.)

Amenemope:[28] An "educational instruction" (*sb'yt mtrt*[29]). In thirty numbered chapters, each with its own message, the scribe Amenemope teaches his son "the way of life" and advocates the ideal of the "truly silent man," who accepts God's will in serenity and trusts in his justice.

Amenemope's ideal is not (as sometimes thought) fatalism and resignation to human impotence and divine caprice. Amenemope is, after all, claiming to show the way to success in all regards (see his prologue, discussed later, pp. 72f.). Rather, he urges a confident reliance on God's wisdom.[30] To be sure, material success cannot be secured, for God's will is ultimately inscrutable. It can, however, be fostered, above all by moral and personal virtues. These virtues include composure and reserve, honesty, and kindness. One must show respect for the manifold varieties of God's creation, including the defenseless and weak, who are under God's special protection. The great vices are dishonesty, lack of self-control, and greed, which is evidenced in straining too hard for success.

Amenemhet Priest of Amon: A tomb autobiography that includes a brief moral instruction.

Amennakhte: The extant counsels (addressed to Amennakhte's apprentice Horimin, the son of his friend Hori; see later). It urges dedication to study, emphasizing personal cultivation.

---

[28]Washington 1994b: 11–24 reviews the evidence carefully and argues for a date in the later Twentieth Dynasty, about 1186–1069 B.C.E. For Washington (chapter III), the economic difficulties and social corruptions of that time are the social background to Amenemope's teachings.

[29]A title in Ramesside instructions. It is the most precise equivalent to what we call a Wisdom instruction.

[30]The Egyptian Wisdom texts often speak of "god" or "the god" in the singular. This is not indicative of monotheism but of henotheism—that is to say, the practice of speaking of the god relevant to a particular situation as if he were the sole deity (Hornung 1982: 15–32, 230–37). It is like referring to "the president" in the Constitution or a civics text.

Anii: An "educational instruction" by a scribe of the (mortuary) temple of Queen Nefertari. Anii addresses behavior in the personal sphere: good speech, proper demeanor toward superiors, and conformity to rank and custom. He tells how to treat one's wife, family, friends, and family spirits. He insists on proper deportment in the temple and at festivals. Throughout, he underscores the importance of remaining calm and composed. He also urges his son to study the ancient writings.

In an extraordinary epilogue, Anii and his son debate the ways and limits of education; see the excursus "Can Everyone Learn?" in the Commentary to 9:6–10.

Ḥori: An "educational instruction" addressed to the son of his deceased friend Amennakhte (see previously), telling him to become a scribe like his father.

O. Petrie 11 ("Instruction According to Old Writings"[31]): A brief list of "don'ts." Two other ostraca of this sort are extant, both fragmentary.

Pap. Chester Beatty IV: A miscellany of Wisdom texts: §1 ethical advice; §2 praise of ancient scribes and the immortality of writers; §3 the advantages of the scribal occupation; §4 religious counsels; §5 the miseries of a soldier's life; §6 character education; §7 praise of the scribe Cheti.

These seem to have been originally independent texts, but there are signs of deliberate selection and organization. They are all directed to young scribes. They speak of the responsibilities of the powerful toward the weak and the rules of etiquette for keeping in favor with the gods and men. They encourage the pupil in his studies by praising the scribal art for bestowing enduring fame on writers and for freeing its practitioners from hard labor.

Related Works

Some other works are relevant to understanding Egyptian pedagogical and ethical principles, in particular:

The *Kemit* ("The Compilation") (Eleventh Dynasty): A much-copied miscellany of model texts for school use. There are three main parts: (1) Epistolary greeting formulas. (2) A short narrative, including a letter. (3) Sentences in the style of ideal biographies and Wisdom instructions. Its maxims emphasize the need for a quiet, reserved demeanor and dedication to the study of the ancient writings.

"The Eloquent Peasant" (MK): A peasant who has been cheated lambastes the local official for shirking his obligation to give him justice. In high rhetoric, he praises justice and condemns its violation.

Model letters (MK, NK; examples in CLEM, *passim*): Numerous model letters were copied in the scribal schools. Of particular interest are those that depict student life. Written by a father or teacher to the neophyte scribe, they chastise him for laziness in his studies and moral dissipation.

---

[31]The title is found on a different ostracon (HO 88, vso.). Its connection with O. Petrie 11 is uncertain. But since one "do not" admonition is preserved after the title, the title probably headed a series of "do not" instructions, though perhaps not this particular one.

Menena (NK: Rameses III–IV): A literary letter chastising a son/apprentice for wandering about and living a dissipated life.

"Satirical Letter" (NK): A long missive, perhaps fictional, in which one scribe berates a colleague for his professional incompetence and challenges him to answer some hard questions and explain how to perform certain tasks that might be demanded of an educated scribe.

2. Mesopotamia and Syria

Shuruppak (or Suruppak): There are three Sumerian versions, dating from ca. 2500 B.C.E. to ca. 1800 B.C.E. and a fragment of an Akkadian translation, ca. 1100 B.C.E. The author—a legendary wise man—is praised for his wisdom and eloquence. He offers his eldest son a string of miscellaneous counsels, both practical and ethical, mostly in the form of one-line vetitives ("do not" . . .), sometimes with brief motivations appended.

Shube'awilum: Delivered by a father to a son who is about to leave home. He offers advice on a variety of topics, such as voyages, taverns and companions, the bad child, quarrels, and the choice of a wife and an ox. He concludes with a statement on man's ephemerality. In a version found at Emar, the son enters into debate with his father and says that death renders wealth useless.

Ahiqar (6th c.; in Aramaic, then widely translated and revised): The introduction tells how the vizier Ahiqar was sentenced to death in a frame-up but later delivered. He then delivered a long series of practical counsels and religious moralizings with strong similarities to Proverbs. (There are different versions of this story.) Topics include discipline of sons, avoidance of bad slaves, generosity with wine, care in speech, avoidance of the king's anger, resignation to the will of the gods, and the importance of calm and controlled behavior. An innovation is the introduction of illustrative animal fables. An important unit (ll. 94a–95) praises heavenly wisdom; this is discussed here in "The Origins of Personified Wisdom." In spite of its references to foreign gods, the Aramaic version was transmitted by Jewish communities. A few sayings in Proverbs have strong parallels in Ahiqar and may derive directly from it.[32]

Other Texts: There are many tablets holding numerous short proverbs, some of them of popular origin. See BWL 213–80 and Alster 1975b.

---

[32]Examples of parallels:

Proverbs	Ahiqar
4:23	98
Chapter 8	94b–95
23:13–14	81–82
25:15	105–6
27:3	111

On the personification of wisdom in Ahiqar, see "Literary Personifications: A Foreign Personification" in Essay 2.

C. WISDOM AFTER PROVERBS

1. *Egypt*

The Brooklyn Wisdom Papyrus; Anchsheshonq; Phibis ("The Demotic Wisdom Book"); **Louvre Demotic Papyrus 2414**: Starting in the sixth or fifth century B.C.E., a new form of Wisdom book developed, mostly in demotic, a late form of Egyptian writing. The hieratic Brooklyn Wisdom Papyrus, the earliest of this genre, is more discursive and prosaic than the others, which are probably of Hellenistic, perhaps late Hellenistic, origin.

These teachings are composed of long strings of self-contained sentences, usually in the form of one-line sayings arranged in topical groupings. They give practical advice but also emphasize the paradoxical nature of life and man's inability to understand it or to secure success. In form and content, these differ radically from the older Egyptian Wisdom books and should not be used in describing the background of Proverbs, especially since Proverbs is probably the earlier. They show West Semitic as well as Greek influence.

2. *Hellenistic Judea*[33]

Qohelet or **Ecclesiastes** (from the fourth or third century B.C.E.): This is in large part a speculative, critical work, which undermines, intentionally or not, many of the axioms of more conventional Wisdom literature. Nevertheless, the epilogue recalls Qohelet as a wise teacher (12:9), and the book holds many sayings and counsels that would be entirely at home in the book of Proverbs.

Ben Sira (ca. 180 B.C.E.):[34] This was written in Hebrew, and several Hebrew manuscripts are extant, but they are all incomplete, and much of the book remains only in Greek and Syriac. The Greek translation was undertaken by his grandson.

Ben Sira (or Ecclesiasticus) is a lengthy Wisdom book dealing with a broad range of personal and public behavior, along with religious and ethical principles. The counsels are frequently organized by topic or fashioned into longer poems. Ben Sira places emphasis on the fear of God. Important innovations are his identification of wisdom with Torah and his emphasis on obedience to Torah and dedication to the study of Israel's sacred texts. The book ends with a hymn praising God's work in creation (42:15–43:33) and a long paean to Israel's

---

[33]For a comprehensive and authoritative study of post-biblical Hellenistic Jewish Wisdom literature, including Sira, Wisdom of Solomon, Pseudo-Phocylides, and the Qumran texts, see Collins 1997.

[34]There is great confusion in the chapter-verse numbering of Ben Sira, particularly in 30:25–33:13a and 33:13b–36:16a, which are in reverse order in all extant Greek MSS (the original order is preserved in the Old Latin; see Di Lella, p. 56). I have followed Di Lella's practice in his AB commentary (p. x). He uses the parenthetical numbering in Ziegler's Göttingen edition, for this represents the original order of these two blocks, which are reversed in the extant Greek MSS. I sometimes give the alternative (Greek) numbering in brackets. When there are minor disruptions in verse numbering, I follow Di Lella's practice, without giving the alternative numbers.

ancestors, which culminates in an encomium on the priest Simon son of Yohanan (44:1–50:24). Appendices include an autobiographical poem on Ben Sira's attainment of wisdom and his life's work (51:13–20).

Ben Sira's main inspiration is the book of Proverbs. He borrows its forms, phrases, and ideas, quotes it, and reshapes its material. He can often be read as the earliest interpreter of Proverbs.

Commentary and bibliography: Skehan and Di Lella 1987 (AB; referenced as "Di Lella"). Translation: NRSV Apocrypha (1991) and other translations of the Apocrypha. Greek text: Göttingen Septuagint (J. Ziegler 1980). Hebrew text and commentary: M. Z. Segal, 1958.

Qumran Wisdom Texts: Recently, a number of wisdom texts from the Dead Sea have become available. While some of the works that have been labeled "sapiential" or "wisdom" are only vaguely connected to the ancient Wisdom literature, others have strong affinities of genre and theme, notably "Sapiential Works" A and C; "Beatitudes" (4Q525); "Wiles of the Wicked Woman" (4Q184), which describes a seductress-prostitute, based on Prov 7; a collection of prudential maxims, mostly in "do not" form (4Q424); and parts of the "Ways of Righteousness" (4Q420–21). These are mainly instructions in matters of attitude and faith, in part imitating Proverbs' gnomic forms. The Qumran wisdom texts are translated by García Martínez in DSST 379–94 and by Harrington 1996, *passim*, with commentary and discussion.

Wisdom of Solomon (37–41 C.E. according to Winston 1979 [AB, pp. 20–25]; sometimes dated in early first century B.C.E.): The book was written by a Hellenized Jew of Alexandria to encourage pride and faith in the Jewish religion. It is rooted in the tradition of Jewish Wisdom Literature, which includes exhortatory discourse like the Wisdom of Solomon. It belongs to the genre of *logos protreptikos*, the exhortatory discourse, a union of philosophy and rhetoric, which attempts to urge people to adopt some line of action (Winston, pp. 18–20). The book's main themes are theodicy and immortality, Solomon's pursuit of wisdom and wisdom's glory, and wisdom's power in history. Particularly the exhortation to wisdom in 6:1–21 and Solomon's praise of wisdom in chapters 7–9 draw upon Jewish Wisdom traditions.

Commentary and bibliography: Winston 1979 (AB). Translation: NRSV Apocrypha (1991); and other translations of the Apocrypha.

3. *Later Works Affiliated with Wisdom Literature*

Tobit (3rd–2nd c. B.C.E.): A moralizing tale that includes a father's testament to his son (4:4–19) reminiscent of the admonitions in Prov 1–9.

Pseudo-Phocylides (1st–2nd c. C.E.): A Hellenistic Jewish gnomic work inspired by Jewish law but propounding a universal ethic, thus showing the compatibility of Jewish law and Greek thought.

Pirqey Avot ("Sayings of the Fathers"): A compilation of gnomes or aphorisms of Mishnaic sages through the first century C.E. Many sayings derive directly from the Bible or cite it for prooftexts.

The New Testament holds material that belongs in the Wisdom tradition. In particular, the Sermon on the Mount (Matt 5–7), where Jesus is instructing his disciples using sapiential forms of assertion and argumentation, can be classified as Jewish Wisdom literature. The Sermon on the Plain (Luke 6:17–49), too, is indebted to the Wisdom tradition. In this case, the audience is a broader public. Public teaching—"teaching the people knowledge"—is among the wise man's activities (Qoh 12:9; cf. Sir 15:5).

Rabbinic sources quote and collect adages. These can be found in many places. Concentrations are found in the Talmud (*b. Baba Qama* 92a–b and *b. Bikkurim* 17a), parts of *Avot d'Rabbi Natan, Derekh Erez Rabbah, Derekh Erez Zuṭa*, and elsewhere. The last mentioned work is especially close to the earlier apothegmatic tradition.

The Geniza Wisdom Book:[35] This medieval book, possibly Karaite in origin, is composed of couplets in praise of wisdom (meaning Torah) and piety. It imitates Proverbs' language and forms (Rüger 1991).

Jewish Ethical Wills (Abrahams 1948): These wills or (better) testaments are medieval descendants of Wisdom literature. They are instructions written by men in their maturity for the religious-ethical guidance of their sons and, sometimes, daughters. The testaments are family wisdom but nonetheless literary.[36] The father addresses his son or sons and, through them, speaks to a larger reading audience. The form became popular and was sometimes used as a fictional literary setting, but other testaments were written for an author's actual children.[37]

Medieval Ethical Poems: A number of medieval Hebrew poets continued the Wisdom tradition by citing old proverbs in new (often rhyming) form and adding counsels of their own. Examples are the ethical tracts *Musar Haśkel* by Hai Gaon and *Ben Mishley* ("The Son of Proverbs") by Shmuel Hannagid, both writing in the early eleventh century. Both offer worldly wisdom in rhymed couplets and often cite and reformulate the sayings of Proverbs.

None of the later works is quite like Proverbs, but Proverbs was not quite like *its* predecessors. The Hellenistic, rabbinic, and medieval books are continuations of Wisdom literature and belong to the life and history of the genre, not to something beyond it, a *Nachleben* or *Nachgeschichte*, to which Wester-

---

[35]Thus, correctly, Rüger (1991: 15), who prefers a twelfth-century C.E. dating, contrary to Berger's improbable first-century C.E. dating (1989: 77). There are a number of medieval Hebrew texts that emulate biblical models.

[36]J. Bergman (1979: 74–103) has aptly compared Egyptian Wisdom Instructions to the Ethical Testament genre. E. von Nordheim (1985, vol. 2, *passim*), on the basis of a careful form-critical study, concludes that the Hellenistic Jewish testaments have their social setting in Israelite Wisdom, which, in turn, was an extension of ancient Egyptian and Mesopotamian Wisdom literature, to which the genre of testament belongs (2.94–107). The approaching death of the author is not, however, an essential assumption of the testament.

[37]G. Couturier (1962: 293–309, esp. 308–9) describes Babylonian and Israelite wisdom as "the sum of the life-experiences of a father transmitted to his son as a spiritual testament." This is an apt formulation of the form of Prov 1–9, though not of the book as a whole.

mann (1990: 121–23; ET 106–7) assigns all Wisdom literature after the book of Proverbs. Wisdom literature continued long after the Bible Wisdom. Indeed, the production of Wisdom literature, in the sense of instructions in living a successful and righteous life, formulated as the product of human intellect rather than as revelation or textual interpretation, never ceased.

WORDS FOR WISDOM AND FOLLY IN PROVERBS

◆

Biblical Wisdom literature has recourse to a large group of words to designate the wisdom it describes and inculcates and the types of persons who possess these attributes. There is a correspondingly rich vocabulary for folly and its possessors. The distinctions among these terms are often not essential for understanding a verse, since Proverbs includes several intellectual powers in its concept of wisdom and praises them all together, nor is it much concerned with drawing fine distinctions among the types it condemns. Nevertheless, these words for wisdom and folly and their possessors are used repeatedly in expressing the most important of Proverbs' teachings and concepts, and we should try to ascertain their lexical meanings, the basic concepts they bring to the text.

It is important to distinguish between lexical and contextual meaning, which is to say, between the nuclear meaning a word contributes to the new context and the enriched and complex meanings it receives by interaction with its new environment.

It is impossible to find a single English equivalent for each Hebrew term, and the glosses listed here are not used consistently throughout the translation in this commentary.

For convenience, the following survey lists the words in English alphabetical order (ignoring the *ʾaleph* and the *ʿayin* signs). Certain clusters of near-synonyms that tend to appear in collocation or parallelism will be noted. Biblical references are given as examples of the usages listed and do not account for all occurrences and nuances. For full argumentation, see my articles in *ZAH* (Fox 1993d, 1997d).[38]

I. Wisdom

1. *bînāh, mēbîn, nābôn*	4. *ḥokmāh, ḥākām*
2. *daʿat, yôdēaʿ*	5. *mᵉzimmāh*
3. *ʿēṣāh, yôʿēṣ*	6. *mûsār*

[38] All these terms, positive and negative, have equivalents in Egyptian Wisdom, though generally they do not correspond exactly. In the following glossary, I set aside comparisons (except for some footnotes) and attempt to determine the meaning of the words from inner-biblical analysis only. (I include Ben Sira as essentially "biblical" Hebrew.) For a full comparative study, see N. Shupak, *Where Can Wisdom Be Found?* (1993). Shupak has a useful discussion of the uses of the Hebrew words for wisdom and folly (pp. 232–56). I differ from Shupak in my attempt to distinguish the lexical content of the words from what is said about the persons and powers designated by them.

7. *ʿormāh, ʿārôm*
8. *śēkel*
9. *taḥbûlôt*
10. t^{e}*bûnāh, mēbîn, nābôn*
11. *tûšiyyāh*

II. Folly

1. *baʿar*
2. *ḥăsar lēb, ḥăsar lēb*
3. *ʾiwwelet, ʾĕwîl*
4. k^{e}*sîlût*, k^{e}*sîl*
5. *lāṣôn, lēṣ*
6. p^{e}*tayyût, petî*[39]

I. Words for Wisdom

Hebrew words do not always mean exactly the same thing as the English words used to translate them. Usually the overlap is considerable, but sometimes there are significant differences. This is so in the case of the word "wisdom" itself. There are two ways in which "wisdom" is commonly used in English.

The weak sense of "wisdom" is prudence, good judgment. It is often reflected in the adjective "wise," as in "It was wise to buy that car." No deep understanding of life is implied. *Ḥokmah* and t^{e}*bunah* are often used this way, especially outside Proverbs. The strong sense, which entails an array of powers and qualities, refers to an unusual trait of character and intellect. Wisdom is always prudential, conducive to the individual's well-being, but it weighs the effect of an action on others as well. It is an ethical quality, never merely instrumental. It is also a quality of character, for it entails not only the knowledge of the right ends but also the will to pursue them.[40]

Proverbs' treatment of wisdom as an inherently ethical virtue is a novel idea, not a lexical shift in the words for wisdom. Proverbs does not suddenly give the wisdom words an idiosyncratic or technical meaning. The wisdom words mean what they always meant. If they did not, Proverbs would fail to communicate with the readers, for they would not realize that something new was being said. What has changed is what Proverbs says *about* the intellectual powers they represent. The *concept* of wisdom has changed. This concept was not and never has been static. As Eugene Rice says of the idea of wisdom in Western philosophy:

> Wisdom was an ideal of twenty-two centuries. It described the highest knowledge men were capable of and the most desirable patterns of human behavior. It mirrored man's conception of himself, of the world, and of God. . . .

---

[39]*Nabal* ("scoundrel") is not included because this term does not primarily signify a cognitive failing.

[40]This description of wisdom from a philosophical perspective draws, in particular, on Bien 1988, Blanshard 1967, and, above all, Godlovitch 1981.

> Word and definition remain static; the idea itself is transformed by the changing needs and aspirations of successive epochs, centuries, and even generations. (1958: 2)

1. *BÎNĀH* "UNDERSTANDING"; *MĒBÎN* "DISCERNING MAN"; *NĀBÔN* "ASTUTE MAN," "SENSIBLE MAN"

Binah designates the faculty of intellectual discernment and interpretation, the exercise of that faculty, and the product thereof, in words or deeds. Unlike *t^{e}bunah*, *binah* is not necessarily practical, though it may be brought to bear in pragmatic decisions. See the later section on *t^{e}bunah*. For the differences between *binah* and *ḥokmah*, see the discussion of the latter.

Binah includes reason, the intellectual faculty used in solving problems and deducing truths, as well as intellect, the ability to comprehend meanings and perceive relations and causes. The raw faculty of *binah*, insofar as it is possessed by an individual apart from application, is similar to the modern concept of intelligence, except for the modern assumption that intelligence is innate. *Binah* is a mental power or activity, not an inherently moral virtue.

Knowledge produced by *binah*, whether one's own or another's, is itself *binah*. *Binah* in this sense is sometimes the object of *yadaʿ* "know" and *lamad* "learn" (Isa 29:24; Job 38:4; 1 Chr 12:33). In Daniel, *binah* refers to a special kind of knowledge, namely, the interpretation of esoteric messages (1:20). *Binah* can also refer to a particular interpretation, as in Dan 8:15, where Daniel prays for *binah* of a vision and receives the explication from Gabriel.

A *mebin* ("understanding, intelligent person") is one who has (or can impart) *binah*. The *mebin* is perceptive and can interpret signs. Daniel says, "I was puzzled about the vision and *ʾeyn mebin* there was no one who could understand [or "explain"] it" (8:27). Lady Wisdom says that the *mebin* sees that her words are all honest" (8:9a). The faculty in question is not the competence to succeed in life or get things done but the ability to discern the true nature of a message. The *mebin* can interpret men's spirits (Prov 28:11) and quickly gets the point of a rebuke (Prov 17:10).

A *nabon* is the possessor of either *binah* or *t^{e}bunah*. *Binah* is ascribed to the *nabon* in Isa 29:14 and Deut 4:6, and a *nabon* is able to analyze puzzling situations (e.g., Gen 41:39; Hos 14:10; cf. Prov 15:14; 19:25; Sir 31[34]:26 Heb). Thus the *nabon* is astute. He may also have practical good sense, that is to say, *t^{e}bunah*; see, for example, the use of *nabon* in Gen 41:33 and Deut 1:13.

A slight difference between *nabon* and *ḥakam* is suggested by Prov 16:21a: "The wise of heart (*ḥăkam leb*) is called *nabon*." The *ḥăkam leb* has the faculty of gaining expertise, even before he has particular knowledge; such a one is called *nabon*. Thus *nabon* can refer to one who has the capability of gaining *binah*. This is supported by Prov 14:6b, "but knowledge comes easily to the *nabon*"; compare 15:14.

2. *DA^cAT* "KNOWLEDGE"; *YÔDĒA^c* "KNOWLEDGEABLE MAN"

Daʿat is the broadest of the wisdom words. It appears that everything designated by any of those words could also be called *daʿat*. It is broader even than English "knowledge," insofar as it includes minimal acts of awareness and innate intellectual capacities apart from learned information and skills. *Daʿat* is cognition itself—*any* cognition, from minimal awareness to elevated sagacity.

Daʿat can be knowledge of specific facts, propositions, or entities, such as good and evil (Gen 2:9); God (Hos 4:1; 6:6; Prov 2:5); or God's ways (Isa 58:2; Job 21:14). *Daʿat ʾĕlohim* "knowledge of God" means "knowing" him to the extent of understanding his manifest behavior and demands.

As the broadest of the wisdom words, *daʿat* encompasses the entire range of knowledge. Because of its scope, *daʿat* can refer to cognition too elementary to be called *ḥokmāh*, even minimal acts of cognition and awareness of the obvious. Derivatives of *y-d-ʿ* can signify awareness. For example: one who kills another *bibli-daʿat* "unawares," "unintentionally" (Deut 4:42; cf. Deut 19:4; Josh 20:3; Job 9:5; Jer 50:24; Ps 35:8; Prov 5:6), or sins unintentionally (Lev 5:18). *Daʿat* includes ordinary, easily accessible knowledge that all can have, if they do not deliberately refuse it. The psalmist of Ps 119 does not claim to have *ḥokmah* or even ask for it. He seeks *daʿat* and "good discernment" (*ṭub taʿam*) as a reward for faithfulness and study of the commandments (v 66). Job's assertion, *ʿal daʿtᵉka ki loʾ ʾeršaʿ*, "you know that I am not wicked" (Job 10:7), means that Bildad is aware of a fact, one that requires no learning to know that of which he is cognizant, even against his will. One cannot have *ḥokmah* involuntarily.

"Knowledge of God" is not erudition in theological esoterica or divination. (The exception is *daʿat ʿelyon*, Num 24:16, as noted later.) It is awareness of how God behaves in human affairs, and it is available to all and required of all. *Daʿat ʾĕlohim* is equivalent to *daʿat dᵉrakay*, "knowledge of my [God's] ways" (Isa 58:2). Having knowledge of God is required of all, which is not true of *ḥokmah*. See the excursus "Knowledge of God," at 2:5.

Daʿat can be knowledge on the high end of the spectrum and overlap *ḥokmah*, both as erudition and as sagacity in living. This usage is specially frequent in Wisdom literature; for example, "For the Lord gives wisdom (*ḥokmah*), from his mouth is knowledge and good sense [*daʿat utᵉbunah*]" (2:6). Compare 1:7 with 9:10. They are indistinguishable in Qohelet (see, e.g., 1:16 and 12:9). Though we are accustomed to consider *ḥokmah* as the word epitomizing the wisdom taught in Proverbs, *daʿat* occurs almost as frequently as *ḥokmah* in Proverbs (41 times to 43 times) and means "wisdom" no less than *ḥokmah* does.

Daʿat can be knowledge beyond one's scope: "Knowledge is too wondrous for me, so lofty I cannot attain it" (Ps 139:6); Agur says the same of *ḥokmah* (Prov 30:3a). *Daʿat* can refer to esoteric wisdom such as the diviner's (Isa 44:25) or Enoch's (Sir 44:16; cf. 1 Enoch 68:1; 82:1; Jub 4:17).[41] *Daʿat ʿelyon*,

---

[41] *Daʿat* is esoteric knowledge, "hidden from man," in 1QS 11.6; cf. 10.24.

"knowledge of [i.e., "from"] the High One," is accessible only to the seer (Num 24:16). It is erudition in Dan 1:4 and 12:4. *Daʿat* can refer to the artisan's skill (e.g., Exod 31:3; 35:31) and be indistinguishable from *ḥokmah* in that sense. But the word itself does not imply an unusual degree of erudition.

Though *daʿat* can almost always be translated "knowledge" and refers to the process of cognizance or the objects of knowledge, it can occasionally refer to an innate faculty, a capacity one may have prior to gaining knowledge. Deutero-Isaiah says, "And [the idol maker] lacks the intelligence [*daʿat*] and good sense [*tᵉbunah*] to say, 'Half of it I burnt . . .'" (44:19; cf. Jer 10:14). "Wisdom" would not be required to deduce something so obvious. Sir 3:25 says that *daʿat* is a precondition for *ḥokmah*.

3. *ʿĒṢĀH* "PLANNING," "DESIGN"; *YÔʿĒṢ* "ADVISER," "PLANNER"

ʿeṣah is essentially *deliberation*: careful thinking and planning, the resolution arrived at by such thinking, and the capacity for such thought.

A plan spoken to others (e.g., Job 29:21; Prov 12:15) is advice or counsel, as *ʿeṣah* is usually glossed. Deliberation with others is consultation (Judg 20:7; 2 Kgs 18:20; Isa 8:10; 29:15). But an *ʿeṣah* is not necessarily spoken to others (see, most clearly, Ps 13:3; Prov 20:5; Isa 46:10). Though "plan" or "advice" is usually a good gloss for *ʿeṣah*, these notions are not inherent in the word's lexical meaning. The noun *yoʿeṣ*, however, as a professional designation, seems always to refer to an adviser.

4. *ḤOKMĀH* "EXPERTISE," "WISDOM"; *ḤĀKĀM* "EXPERT," "WISE MAN"

It should be remembered that *ḥokmah*, though translated "wisdom," does not have exactly the same meaning as the English word, which was previously defined. But it is the word that Wisdom literature most often uses in designating the intellectual and moral quality it sets as its goal. The following observations define the meaning that *ḥokmah* has in the language as a whole.

Ḥokmah is essentially a high degree of knowledge and skill in any domain. It combines a broad faculty (including the powers of reason, discernment, cleverness) and knowledge (communicable information, that which is known and can be learned). Both facets are always implied by the word *ḥokmah*; one cannot have *ḥokmah* purely as a potential or as mere inert information. This duality makes it difficult to find a single English gloss for *ḥokmah* because English (as well as a set of modern assumptions about the nature of intelligence) tends to distinguish, perhaps too sharply, between knowledge and intelligence. In the Bible, there is an assumption that gaining the former enhances the latter.

The nearest English equivalent that encompasses its semantic range is "expertise." The *ḥakam* is the possessor of *ḥokmah*, an expert. "Expertise" has different connotations from *ḥokmah*, insofar as the former tends to be confined to a narrow range of functions, whereas *ḥokmah* can extend to knowledge in a broad domain. However, with the proviso that one may be an "expert" in right living and good character, the two terms are comparable. For stylistic reasons, a translator might prefer to vary the rendering in accordance with context, and "wisdom" is often best because it allows the richer range of connotation that *ḥokmah* often possesses.

The domains of knowledge in which *ḥokmah* may manifest itself include (a) Craftsmanship ("skill") (e.g., Exod 35:31; 36:4; Isa 40:20, and often elsewhere in the HB). This includes professional proficiencies, such as in lamenting (Jer 9:16) and business (Ezek 28:5). (b) Knowledge gained through the study of books and lore ("learning"; "erudition" if extensive) (e.g., Jer 8:8; 9:22; Qoh 1:16; Dan 1:4; Sir 14:20; 51:15). This includes the magical and mantic arts (e.g., Exod 7:11; Isa 47:10; Esth 1:13). (c) The ability to understand the implications of situations and interpret signs and text ("perceptiveness," "astuteness," "reasoning ability") (e.g., 2 Sam 14:20; Jer 9:11; Hos 14:10; Ps 107:43; Job 34:34; Qoh 8:1; Sir 3:29). (d) Skill in devising stratagems and plans ("cleverness") (e.g., 2 Sam 14:2; 20:16; Jer 18:18; Job 5:13; Qoh 4:13). (e) Good judgment in practical and interpersonal matters ("good sense," "prudence"; equivalent to *t^ebunah*) (e.g., 1 Kgs 5:9; Job 39:17; Qoh 2:3; 7:10; Sir 11:1). This usage is closely related to the next category but does not necessarily entail moral virtue. (f) Wisdom, knowledge of right living—"right" in both the ethical and pragmatic senses. This aspect of wisdom is close to English "sagacity." These domains overlap, and more than one may pertain in a single occurrence of the word.

Ḥokmah is not inert knowledge. You could memorize the book of Proverbs and not have *ḥokmah*. *Ḥokmah* always implies ability to carry out what one knows. But it is never an innate talent devoid of knowledge. Inborn talent apart from acquired knowledge can be called *ḥokmat leb* (e.g., Exod 31:6; 35:25; 36:8; Prov 10:8; cf. Exod 35:25).

Proverbs consistently applies the word *ḥokmah* to wisdom as manifest in the skill and knowledge of right living in the enriched sense (see category f). This is because the sages are making strong claims for the powers of human expertise.

Wisdom of this sort may be manifest in numerous aspects of behavior, such as practical and interpersonal matters (e.g., Prov 10:14; 11:30; 12:18; 16:14; 31:26); cleverness (14:8; 21:30); the reasoning (e.g., 4:7, first occurrence;[42] 24:3; 29:15); learning (e.g., 1:5, 6 [*ḥakam* = learned man]; 4:7, second occurrence; 14:6; 16:16); the words that convey knowledge (e.g., 1:7; 3:13; 5:1; 10:31; 30:3); ethical-religious attitudes (9:10; 15:33 and often). But these distinctions are matters of emphasis, and usually *ḥokmah* refers to these qualities all together. Proverbs teaches that there is a global intellectual power—wisdom—that can be called upon in all endeavors and that is inherently righteous and almost always effective.

---

[42] "The first step to wisdom is: get wisdom!" I take this to mean that to attain the universally desired faculty of *ḥokmah* (including reasoning, cleverness, intelligence, and so on) one must first absorb the teachings. This sentence plays on the word *ḥokmah*; compare Sir 38:24.

The sages of Proverbs are aware that the word *ḥokmah* can refer to an expertise that is not wise, but it denies its actuality: "There is no *ḥokmah* or know-how [*t*^{e}*bunah*] or planning [*ʿeṣah*] against the Lord" (21:30), none, that is, that can defy God's will.

5. *M*^{e}*ZIMMĀH* "SHREWDNESS," "CIRCUMSPECTION," "DISCRETION"

The notion common to derivatives of *z-m-m* is hidden, private thinking; the notions of planning and scheming (the meaning given in the lexicons) are extensions of the primary sense. Sometimes *m*^{e}*zimmot* are not actually schemes, that is, secret plans for achieving something, but just hidden thoughts (e.g., Ps 10:4; Job 21:27–28). Since scheming requires keeping one's thoughts secret, the faculty of *m*^{e}*zimmah* is often employed for immoral and harmful ends (e.g., Ps 10:2; 21:12; 37:7; Sir 44:4). But *m*^{e}*zimmot* are not intrinsically evil. God's own plans are called *m*^{e}*zimmot* (Jer 23:20; 51:11; Job 42:2).

In Proverbs, too, the connotations of *m*^{e}*zimmah* can be both negative (12:2; 14:17; 24:8) and positive (2:11; 5:2; 8:12). In the latter usage, *m*^{e}*zimmah* is circumspection or discretion. The verb *zamam* has a corresponding semantic range.

6. *MÛSĀR* "DISCIPLINE," "CORRECTION," "EDUCATION"

The core notion conveyed by *musar* is the teaching of the avoidance of faults. In line with its root-meaning, *y-s-r* "punish," "inflict," *musar* is originally, and usually, a lesson intended to correct a moral fault. The goal of *musar* is always (except for the ironic use in Prov 16:22b) a moral insight or a quality of moral character. (Sira extends this realm into what we would probably consider decorum or good manners rather than morality.)

As Malbim (commenting on 1:2) observes, *musar* is always given by a superior to an inferior, who is morally obligated but not forcibly compelled to listen and learn. *Musar* is used only of authoritative correction and discipline, never of counsel such as one might offer a superior (that would be *ʿeṣah*).

Musar is basically correction, whether by verbal rebuke or by physical punishment. This is clear, for example, in Job 5:17: "Happy is the man whom God chastises [*yokiḥennu*]; do not despise the *musar* of Shadday." Outside Proverbs and Ben Sira, there is always a prior failing that calls for correction. *Musar* requires repentance: "And [God] opens their ear for *musar*, and he says that they should repent [*y*^{e}*šubun*] of iniquity" (Job 36:10). This is usually the case in Proverbs too, where *musar* is frequently parallel to or conjoined with *tokaḥat* "chastisement" and synonyms (3:11; 5:12; 6:23; and often). *Musar* means "punishment" in, for example, Prov 22:15 and 23:13. The phrase *tok*^{e}*ḥot musar* "the chastisement of *musar*" in Prov 6:23 shows that *musar* is a verbal lesson that gives chastisement. Prov 8:33 probably refers to correction; compare 13:18.

As a means to knowledge, *musar* may take the form of punishment, ranging from a beating (Prov 13:24; 22:15; 23:13), to personal affliction, perhaps in the form of illness (Prov 3:11; Job 5:17), to national calamity (Ps 50:17). Or it may be a verbal reprimand and warning (e.g., Jer 7:28; 17:23; Prov 12:1; 13:18). Prov 23:12 also speaks of punishment, as the next verse shows. The frequency with which *musar* parallels *tokaḥat* "reproof" and *gaʿarah* "rebuke" indicates that it never entirely loses the connotation of chastisement or its connection with the root-meaning of *y-s-r*, "punish."

The corrective lesson may come from one's own experience of punishment (e.g., Jer 2:30; Job 5:17), from observing it (Ezek 5:15; Prov 24:32), or, less frequently, from hearing words of correction (e.g., Jer 7:28; Zeph 3:2).

The word occasionally has an extended sense in Proverbs and Ben Sira, where it may mean admonition or *preemptive* correction, a warning given prior to the failure. The man who observes the sluggard's field in disrepair takes *musar* (Prov 24:32) so as to avoid the defect himself. Ben Sira's "lesson [*musar*] about both wine and bread" (34:12) does not chastise the reader but admonishes him to avoid failings such as greed; similarly 41:14. Since the "correction" can precede the violation, the word can become nearly synonymous with *ḥokmah*, as in Prov 1:2, 3, 8. In Sir 6:22 ("For *musar* is like its name"[43]), *musar* designates the entire process of attaining wisdom, which Sira describes as arduous (6:23–31).

Musar can refer to the substance of the teaching conveyed by correction. In Prov 4:13 ("Take hold of *musar*, don't let go. Guard it, for it [*hiʾ*] is your life"), *musar* is identified with *ḥokmah* (and treated as feminine); see v 11. Sira says that Solomon "overflowed" with *musar* (47:14), meaning the teaching he imparted. Other examples: Prov 8:10; Sir 41:14; 42:8; 50:27. This usage belongs to later texts and show an extension of the earlier meaning.

A further extension of the term occurs when the lesson to which *musar* refers does not even contain admonitions. This is the case in Prov 4:1 and 13. The term then means simply "moral teaching" or the like; thus too in 8:10; 19:20 (// *ʿeṣah*); and Sir 47:14.

7. ʿ*ORMĀH* "CUNNING"; ʿ*ĀRÛM* "CUNNING PERSON"

ʿormah is the talent to devise and use adroit and wily tactics in attaining one's goals, whatever these may be.

ʿormah (noun) and *ʿarum* (adj.) are commonly used of guile (Gen 3:1) and scheming (Exod 21:14; Josh 9:4). Even the devices of the "wise" can be called *ʿormah* (Job 5:13, with the variant *ʿorem*).

In Proverbs, *ʿormah* and the cognate verbs refer to cunning used legitimately (1:4; 8:5). Lady Wisdom attests to the respectability of *ʿormah* by declaring her

---

[43]The parallel line suggests that Sira parses *musar* as "set apart," from *s-w-r*: "and it is not present [*nekoḥah*] to many people."

proximity to it (8:12) and offering to teach it (8:5). Outside Proverbs, *ʿormah* and its cognate verb and adjective are applied to morally valid intelligence only in Sir 6:32, in the Manual of Discipline (1QS X 24; XI 6), and in the Damascus Covenant (X 3–4, where the *ʿormah* is divine).

In Proverbs, *ʿormah* is not native cunning but rather the shrewdness that a *peti* (uneducated, naif) lacks and must acquire (1:4; 8:5). If a *peti* sees a scoffer beaten, he will *yaʿrim*, "wise up," from *ʿ-r-m* (19:25).

8. *ŚĒKEL* "DISCRETION," "GOOD SENSE"; *MAŚKÎL* "DISCREET MAN," "MAN OF GOOD SENSE"

A distinct meaning of *śekel* is "regard," that is to say, the way others see one (Ps 111:10;[44] Prov 3:4; Sir 35:2; possibly 1 Sam 25:3); this is discussed at 3:4. When *śekel* refers to a kind of wisdom, its core meaning is "insight," the ability to grasp the meanings or implications of a situation or message. *Śekel* is consequently discernment or prudence, the ability to understand practical matters and interpersonal relations and make beneficial decisions. It later comes to include intellectual understanding and unusual expertise.

This intellectual power is not an inherently ethical virtue. It may be used for deceit (Dan 8:25, if correct). The addition of *ṭob* "good" (Prov 13:15; 2 Chr 30:22) suggests that *śekel* is not inevitably used for the best. Usually, however, it is. A man's *śekel* gives him patience (Prov 19:11) and avoids much social conflict. Job accuses his interlocutors of lacking *good sense* (Job 17:4). A fool despises the *śekel* of another's words. This is probably their prudence rather than a deep intellectual penetration. When possessed by officials, *śekel* can save a city (Sir 10:3b). Being the antithesis of "unrestrained" (*paruaʿ*; 10:3a), *śekel* involves prudence and self-control.

In line with this usage, the *maśkil* is a prudent person, such as a son who stores up provisions during the summer (Prov 10:5), a man reserved in speech (Prov 10:19), and a good wife (Prov 19:14; Sir 26:13; cf. 14:35; 17:2). These are not deep intellectual qualities or learning, but the common sense accessible to all. In Amos 5:13, the *maśkil* is the cautious man concerned for his personal well-being, not the insightful or gifted one.

In later texts, the insight of *śekel* extends to the intellectual understanding or "decoding" of messages, including more rarefied intellectual expertise. It refers to interpretation in Neh 8:8, where the insight (*śekel*) imparted to the people is not the method or ability to interpret, but the purport or message communicated by the text. In Daniel, the *maśkil* is the man who can interpret events (12:10) and teach others (11:33, using the same verb).

Śekel in later usage refers also to sagacious words, such as Ben Sira advises the banquet master to conceal at a banquet rather than interfering with the music

---

[44] Ps 111:10 is disputable, but *śekel* there probably refers to the good regard of others, as in Prov 3:4, where it is a synonym of *ḥen* "favor."

(Sir 35:3f.). Expressing one's *śekel* in v 3 is rephrased as *tithakkam*, "show yourself wise," in v 4. This is not simple discernment or prudence, which Sira would not counsel to conceal in any circumstance. It is, rather, one's erudition or profound thought, which one might be tempted to put on display during a banquet. When Sira says that "no *śekel*" (// *kol dabar*) is hidden from God (42:20), he is definitely referring to the more recondite realms of knowledge.

9. *TAḤBÛLÔT* "STRATEGY," "GUIDANCE"

The LXX glosses the word by *kybernēsis* ("steering" or "navigation") in Prov 1:5; 11:14; and 24:6, and uses the verb *kybernan* in Prov 12:5.[45] The LXX (followed by most scholars) is implicitly deriving the word from *ḥebel* "rope" (of a ship) or *ḥobel* "sailor," hence "navigational skills," hence skill in making one's way through life, or "knowing the ropes" (McKane 1970: 266). *Taḥbulot* is translated by *desmoi* in Sir 35:16a, so that whether or not the etymology is correct, an association between this word and "rope" could be made (and see n. 46). Nevertheless, the etymology and the noun pattern are uncertain. The Peshitta (= Targum) renders the term abstractly, *mdabranuta'* "leadership," "guidance."[46]

A derivation from *ḥebel*, "rope," would allow equally well the gloss "designs" (thus Dhorme 1967: 566). The notion of "design," "plan" fits the various contexts better than "steering," "guidance." *Taḥbulot* are stratagems or designs that can be put to any purpose, such as in waging war (11:14 = 24:6 // *ʿeṣah*). They are something that an intelligent man can learn from reading the book of Proverbs (1:5). As the parallel line (*yišmaʿ ḥakam w^e yosep leqaḥ*) indicates, *taḥbulot* is a more sophisticated level of knowledge than the guidance that the callow youth will gain (1:4).

Taḥbulot are in themselves ethically neutral. They may even be used in cheating (12:5b [// *maḥš^e bot-* "plans"]). This is one of the few instances where Proverbs concedes the existence of mental powers that might be put to bad uses. Sir 37:17 recognizes that the effects of *taḥbulot* can be for good or evil.

10. *T^e BÛNĀH* "GOOD SENSE," "COMPETENCE"; *MĒBÎN* "INTELLIGENT, SENSIBLE (MAN)"; *NĀBÔN* "SENSIBLE MAN"

Binah and *t^e bunah* often occur together (in that order) in reference to the same teachings. But an examination of the contexts where each is used alone indicates a distinction: *T^e bunah* is the pragmatic, applied aspect of thought, operating in the realm of *action*; it aims at efficacy and accomplishment, whereas *binah* is the conceptual, interpretive activity of thought (and the outcome of

[45]LXX lacks Prov 20:18; *kybernēsis* is supplied from Theod in Job 37:12a. In Sir 37:17, the Greek (*alloiōseōs*) does not correspond well to the MT.

[46]Shupak (1993: 313–14) considers the term equivalent to Egyptian *ṯs*, "knot," hence "utterance," "wise saying." But *ṯs* does not mean "rope," and *taḥbulot* does not mean "saying."

such thought). It operates in the realm of meaning and aims at insight and comprehension.

T^e^bunah is the competence to deal with the exigencies of life, and it generally implies a follow-up in action, or at least the expectation of one. *Tᵉbunah* does not require an understanding of causes, significances, and implications, though one may certainly have both. In short, *tᵉbunah* is know-how, whether in the execution of a particular task or in social relations generally. English "competence" may be the closest equivalent of *tᵉbunah*. In the realm of everyday activities, "good sense" is an appropriate gloss.

The "man of *tᵉbunah*" in Proverbs is competent in human relations; he is patient (14:29; 17:27), quiet (11:12), and reserved (18:2). He draws out other people's thoughts (20:5). He walks the straight path (15:21) and enjoys behaving wisely (10:23). These virtues are in the realm of attitudes and social skills rather than intellectual penetration and comprehension.

11. *TÛŠIYYĀH* "RESOURCEFULNESS," "COMPETENCE," "WITS"

Tušiyyah (which appears almost exclusively in Wisdom literature) denotes clear, efficient thinking in the exercise of power and practical operations. It is used in determining a course of action and dealing with difficulties rather than in comprehending intricacies or deducing conclusions. It is thus aligned with *tᵉbunah* rather than *binah*. *Tušiyyah* also refers to decisions and strategies produced by such thinking. *Tušiyyah* spoken to others is a form of counsel (Job 26:3). In this regard, it is a close synonym of *ʿeṣah*.

Tušiyyah confers power, personal and political. These powers are deployed particularly in dealing with conflict or crisis, or at least a tension. It is usually associated with words for help, strength, aggression, and defense (Job 5:12; 6:13; 12:16; 26:3; Prov 2:7; 3:21 [cf. 22]; Prov 18:1; several of these are in a context of strife). It is also used of God's providential control of history (Isa 28:29). Crafty, tricky men may possess this faculty. The sages esteemed *tušiyyah* for the protection it provides the wise (Prov 2:7; 3:21).

II. WORDS FOR FOLLY

The essence of folly is lack of good judgment, with consequent distortions in moral and practical choices. One who persistently fails in this respect fits Kant's definition of the fool as "one who sacrifices things of value to ends that have no value" (*Anthropology* 1.49). Folly may arise from a variety of causes, such as moral debasement and distorted ethical values (in the case of the *ʾĕwil*); smug mental sloth (the *kᵉsil*); arrogance and disdain (the *leṣ*); flightiness (the *ḥăsar leb*); ignorance (the *baʿar*); and mindless naiveté (the *peti*). We can arrange the types of fools on a continuum from ingrained moral defect and unchangeability to relative innocence and improvability: *ʾewîl–lēṣ–kᵉsîl–ḥăsar leb–baʿar–petî.*

All of the folly words imply moral culpability, not lack of native intelligence. An exception is *peti,* who can be a *peti* in BH (Ps 116:6; Hos 7:11 calls a dove *potah ʾeyn leb*). Elsewhere, the word implies a voluntary situation. *Baʿar* can mean ignoramus without necessary connotations of moral culpability (see Prov 30:2), but the *baʿar* is a fool when his ignorance results in distorted judgment. In most cases, even the *peti* and the *baʿar* are assumed to have the potential to learn and are thus responsible for their condition if they remain mired in it. The other folly words connote willful and blameworthy defects of character.

We cannot define the folly words simply by redescribing the things said about fools. The behaviors imputed to different types of fools are not enough to distinguish them from one another. We must also consider what contexts the words are *not* used in. Many foolish actions, after all, can be ascribed to various sorts of fools, though not to all of them. A brilliant scientist, for example, who was nasty to people might for that reason be called a "jerk" or "fool" or *ʾĕwil.* He would not be called a "dullard," "simpleton," or *baʿar,* and probably not a *kᵉsil.*

1. *BAʿAR* "IGNORAMUS"[47]

The *baʿar* is an ignoramus. Animal-like brutishness is his earmark. Etymological associations with "beast" (*bᵉʿir*) are often activated: "But I am a *baʿar,* lacking knowledge. I am a beast with you" (Ps 73:22). "The man who is a *baʿar* does not know (this)" (Ps 92:7). "I am more a *baʿar* than a man, and have not in me human perception" (*binat ʾadam*) (Prov 30:2).

The term *baʿar* does not necessarily denote a pernicious defect. When Agur (Prov 30:2) and the Psalmist (73:22–23) use this word in declaring their ignorance, they are not confessing sin but asserting the power of their untutored faith. Nevertheless, ignorance is one step away from moral debasement because it makes one less open to correction (Prov 12:1). Compare Jer 10:14, 21.

2. *ḤĂSAR LĒB* "MINDLESSNESS";[48] *ḤĂSAR LĒB* "MINDLESS, EMPTY-HEADED PERSON"

The expression *ḥăsar leb* is unique to Proverbs and Sira; *ʾeyn leb* "lacking a mind" (Jer 5:21; Hos 7:11) is a synonym, and *libbo ḥaser* "his mind is lacking" in Qoh 10:3 conveys the same idea. In this phrase, *leb* always refers to faculties we would consider specifically cognitive, namely, the ability (or willingness) to make a prudent, sensible decision. Hence, *leb* is better translated "mind" in this phrase—or even "head," since the expression means the same as the English

[47] *Baʿar* 5x (2x Prov). The participle *bōʿărîm* means "ignorant" in Ps 94:8, while in Ezek 21:36 it refers to brutish men, barbarians.

[48] The abstract occurs in Prov 10:21.

"empty-headed." It has a precise equivalent in Egyptian *iwty-ib.f* "one who lacks a heart," which refers to the senseless, imprudent person rather than the arrogant or wicked fool (Shupak 1993: 187). It can even refer to the humble believer. Since the Hebrew expression is found only in Wisdom literature, it is likely an Egyptianism.

The imprudence of the *ḥăsar leb* may involve an immoral and vile act, as in Prov 6:32, but it may also reveal itself in lesser types of indiscretion and mindlessness, such as pursuing vain things (Prov 12:11), guaranteeing a loan (Prov 17:18), and being lazy (Prov 24:30). Since the term *ḥăsar leb* does not necessarily imply deeper corruption, it is nearly identical to *peti* (Prov 7:7; 9:4; 9:16); compare Hos 7:11 and Sir 16:23. In Sir 6:20, *ḥăsar leb* parallels *ʾĕwil*, but the words probably refer to different types of person.

3. ʾ*IWWELET* "FOLLY," "PERVERSE FOLLY"; ʾ*ĔWÎL* "FOOL," "KNAVE"

Commenting on Prov 1:7b, Alsheikh observes that *ĕwilim* are not idiots or madmen, for these would not bother either to esteem or to despise discipline. Rather, "one is called an *ʾĕwil* who vacates (*yeḥasser*) his mind from choosing good and rejecting evil." This is correct. *ʾiwwelet* is the willful refusal to make moral choices. *ʾiwwelet is moral corruption from the standpoint of its impact on judgment and reason.* Though the *ʾĕwil* may be shrewd and expert in some ways, he is rendered stupid in important regards by his warped values and distorted vision.

The words *ʾĕwil* and *ʾiwwelet* are associated as synonyms and antonyms not only of wisdom words but also of words for moral or immoral actions and traits: *yiššer leket* "walk straight"; *ʾăšāmôt* "guilty deeds"; *ṭāmēʾ* "(morally) impure"; *ʾeyn musar* "lacking moral discipline." *ʾiwwelet* is essentially a moral pathology. In fact, a rendering such as "knavishness" is often to the point.

However clever he may be superficially, the *ʾĕwil* is morally obtuse. The princes of Zoan are called both *ḥăkamim* and *ʾĕwilim* (Isa 19:11) because they are blind to God's plans (12–15). Likewise, Israel is an *ʾĕwil* "stupid sons" (*banim sekalim*) who do not know God their father. Yet they do have *ḥokmah* of one sort: they are *ḥăkamim . . . leharaʿ* "experts in doing evil" (Jer 4:22; cf. 5:4). The promise that *ĕwilim* will not wander in the holy way (Isa 35:8) has in view their moral failings. The psalmist confesses his *ʾiwwelet* parallel to his sin and iniquity (Ps 69:6; cf. Ps 38:6). The actions of the adulterer in Prov 5 are labeled *ʾiwwelet* and *ʾeyn musar* "lack of moral discipline" (5:23; see also Ps 107:17).

ʾiwwelet is persistent and irremediable in the *ʾĕwil* (Prov 27:22), but it may appear episodically in others. Prov 22:15 asserts that "*ʾiwwelet* is attached to a lad's heart, but a 'disciplinary beating' can remove it from him." This is not ingrained moral perversion, but an immature waywardness and recalcitrance. The psalmist confesses to *ʾiwwelet* (Ps 69:6), but this is humble hyperbole. A true *ʾĕwil* would not feel the need for moral cleansing.

4. *K*ᵉ*SÎLÛT* (*KESEL*) "STUPIDITY," "DOLTISHNESS"; *K*ᵉ*SÎL* "DOLT," "OAF"[49]

Kᵉsilut is smug mental sloth with respect to its impact on judgment and reason. It is stupidity that comes from obtuseness and complacency, not merely from inadequate intelligence. If the *ʾĕwil* is obtuse by virtue of his moral perversion, the *kᵉsil* is, or probably will become, morally perverse by reason of his obtuseness.

Several times *kᵉsil* (never *ʾĕwil*) appears in association with *baʿar* (and cognates) meaning "ignoramus" (Ps 49:11; 92:7; 94:8). The verbs *kasal* and *baʿar* are used in describing wooden idols in Jer 10:8, which are, we might say, "blockheads," the epitome of stupid, dense things.

Kᵉsil "stupid man" and *kesel* "stupidity" are cognate to *kesel* (var. *kislah*) "hope," "confidence." *Kesel* refers to hope and confidence of all kinds, whether pious and praiseworthy (Ps 78:7; Prov 3:26; Job 4:6) or foolhardy and shortsighted (Job 8:14; 31:24; Ps 85:9). There is an easy semantic move from confidence to overconfidence, and from there to smug obtuseness. Various verses assume the connection between (over)confidence and stupidity. Prov 1:32b says that "the complacency [*šalwah*] of *kᵉsilim* will destroy them." The *kᵉsil* "trusts in his own heart" (Prov 28:26).

The *kᵉsil* lacks clarity of vision. Outside Proverbs, at least, this deficiency is not inherently evil. The old king in Qoh 4:13 who is a *kᵉsil* and no longer able to take precautions suffers from senile witlessness, not ethical debasement.

The *kᵉsil*'s oafishness erupts into all he does. He blunders into others' quarrels (14:16). He quickly consumes the goods that happen to be in his house (21:20). The *ʾĕwil*, by contrast, does not lack wit or narrow prudence, at least in short-term considerations.

Self-satisfaction is conducive to silly self-indulgence, so when a fool is shown as mirthful, he usually is called a *kᵉsil*, as in Prov 19:10. He is inclined to mindless amusements rather than facing reality—a trait that Qohelet seems to envy (Qoh 7:4, 5, 6). Only Qoh 7:9 says that *kᵉsilim* suffer from anger; that is Qohelet's way of saying that anger is self-destructive and stupid.

The *kᵉsil*'s stupidity renders him incompetent in speech, a frequent theme in Proverbs (26:6, 7, 9). He is inanely voluble (Prov 29:11; Qoh 5:2; see also Prov 15:14; 18:7; Qoh 10:12). In contrast, verbal incompetence is not ascribed to the *ʾĕwil*.

A *kᵉsil* is not necessarily an *ʾĕwil*, but lacking intellectual keenness, he is inclined to speak *ʾiwwelet* (Prov 12:23; 15:2, 14), to possess it (14:8; 17:12, etc.), and to repeat it (Prov 26:11). His stupidity twists his values so that he easily slides into wickedness and stays there (10:23; 13:19).

The *kᵉsil* is ignorant, clumsy, and unhelpful (Qoh 2:14; 10:2, 15), as well as smug and self-destructive (Qoh 4:5).

---

[49] A virtual synonym, *siklut, sakal*, appears often in Qohelet and once in Sira but is not used in Proverbs.

There is little hope of educating the *k^e^sil* (Prov 17:10), but it is not inconceivable (see Prov 8:5b), whereas there seems to be no thought of improving the *ʾĕwil*.

K^e^sil is associated with *peti* in Prov 1:22, 32; and 8:5, whereas *peti* and *ʾĕwil* are kept distinct. (*Poteh*, however, is parallel to *ʾĕwil* in Sir 31[34]:7 and Job 5:2.) The manifestations of *p^e^tayyut* and *k^e^silut* are much the same, but in the *peti* they are caused by inexperience, in the *k^e^sil* by smugness.

5. *LĀṢÔN* "SCORN," "INSOLENCE"; *LĒṢ* "SCORNFUL, INSOLENT MAN"

The *leṣ* (commonly translated "mocker") is both arrogant and scornful. These are two sides of one coin, for, as Kaspi says, "The *leṣ* is the haughty man; he is wise in his own eyes, and therefore mocks whomever rebukes him" (comment on Prov 1:4). Still, the contexts that employ *leṣ* (rather than, say, *geʾeh* or *yahir*, which also mean "proud") are primarily concerned not so much with the culprit's feelings of pride as with his insolent and disdainful treatment of others. The *leṣ* may be apt to deride and mock others, but nowhere is he clearly shown doing so.

Prov 21:24 defines the character of the *leṣ*: "The arrogant insolent man [*zed yahir*]—'*leṣ*' is his name; he acts in the rage of insolence [*b^eʿ^ebrat zadon*]." The essence of *laṣon* is *hybris*, a quality that naturally issues in contempt for others. The connection with *zed* "the arrogant man," also appears in Ps 119:51a: "Arrogant men [*zedim*] mocked (?) me [*hĕliṣuni*] severely." Compare Sir 38:18, where *zd wlṣ* is treated grammatically as a singular. The antithesis between *leṣim* and the humble in Prov 3:34 highlights the characteristic arrogance of the former. In Isa 29:19–21, the three types who afflict the humble and poor are the "brutal man" [*ʿariṣ*], the "impudent" [*leṣ*], and "those who diligently pursue iniquity" [*šoqdey ʾawen*]. In Isa 28:14, *ʾanšey laṣon* "men of insolence" is explicated by parallelism with *moš^e^ley haʿam hazzeh* "rulers of this people." These are the men who boast that they have made a covenant with death and are protected by deceit (28:15). Their words do not express mockery so much as cynicism and insolence. In their audacity, they imagine themselves immune from punishment.

Proverbs points out the *leṣ*'s resistance to chastisement (9:7–8; 13:1; 15:12; cf. Isa 29:20–21; Sir 3:28). His character prevents him from attaining learning, even if he should seek it (Prov 14:6; cf. Sir 15:8; 38:18), for the ability to learn from others requires a certain suppression of ego. He must be punished, not so much to change him as to warn others (19:25, 29; 21:11).

6. *P^e^TAYYÛT* (VAR., *PETI*, PL. *P^e^TĀYÎM*) "CALLOWNESS," "NAIVETÉ," "GULLIBILITY"; *PETÎ* "CALLOW, NAIVE, GULLIBLE (PERSON)"

P^e^tayyut is inexperience and gullibility. The root-meaning "be gullible" (cf. *pittah* = "seduce," "tempt") is maintained in the noun (Prov 14:15).

The *peti* is not inherently culpable. Indeed, outside Proverbs he never is. God himself watches over the *p^eta'im* (Ps 116:6), and his teachings make them wise (Pss 19:8; 119:130). In Ezek 45:20, the *peti* is just a simpleton, and the synonymous participle *poteh* is used of an innocent dove in Hos 7:11.

Proverbs, however, tends to interpret any intellectual flaw as tantamount to a moral one. With their absolute faith in education, the sages of Proverbs consider being a *peti* a matter of choice. The callow are thought to *love* their callowness (1:22). They have a proclivity for backsliding (1:32) and even for the deep corruption of *'iwwelet* (14:18; "inherit" folly means that they will get this at a later stage). At the same time, their malleability leaves them open to learning and improvement (8:5; 9:4, 6; 19:25; 21:11). Indeed, according to the Prologue, the *peti* is the primary audience of Proverbs' instructions (1:4). But as long as the *peti* remains stuck in his naiveté and callowness, he belongs to the class of fools and can be placed parallel to *leṣim* and *k^esilim* (1:22; 8:5).

INTRODUCTION TO PART I, PROVERBS 1–9

◆

I. THE COMPONENTS OF PROVERBS 1–9

The structure of Part I differs fundamentally from the rest of the book of Proverbs. The components of Part I are long, cohesive units, as described here. These units form two series, each with its own origins, concepts, and messages. In the rest of Proverbs, there are a few longer poems, particularly in chapters 30–31, but for the most part the significant units are short sayings, usually in the form of self-standing couplets. These are proverbs as the term is usually understood in English. The proverbs sometimes have ties to their contexts and can form thematic clusters, but the basic interpretive units are usually the individual sayings. They require a special approach to exegesis, one appropriate to the atomistic character of the collections and sensitive to the proverb's autonomy, which enables it to function in a limitless variety of life situations. In Part I, in contrast, interpretation must focus on and be governed by the longer literary units rather than the shorter sayings and statements within them. (I discuss the internal literary history of Part I in Essay 1, "The Formation of Proverbs 1–9.")

The literary units of Part I are of two types: "lectures" and, interlaced among them, "interludes." The lectures are father-to-son discourses, the interludes are, for the most part, reflections on wisdom.

Lectures (I–X) and Interludes (A–E)

Prologue: 1:1–7

I.	1:8–19	Avoid Gangs
A.	*1:20–33*	*Wisdom's Warning*
II.	2:1–22	The Path to Wisdom
III.	3:1–12	The Wisdom of Piety
B.	*3:13–20*	*In Praise of Wisdom*
IV.	3:21–35	The Wisdom of Honesty
V.	4:1–9	Loving Wisdom, Hating Evil
VI.	4:10–19	The Right Path
VII.	4:20–27	The Straight Path
VIII.	5:1–23	Another Man's Wife and One's Own

C.	*6:1–19*	*Four Epigrams on Folly and Evil*
IX.	6:20–35	Adultery Kills
X.	7:1–27	Beware the Seductress
D.	*8:1–36*	*Wisdom's Self-Praise*
E.	*9:1–18*	*Two Banquets*

A. THE TEN LECTURES

The ten major units in Prov 1–9 are sometimes called "instructions" (Whybray) or "discourses" (McKane). I designate them "lectures" to give a more precise notion of their nature: a father lecturing his son or sons in moral behavior. ("Instruction" will refer to the wider genre attested throughout Wisdom literature.) There is considerable agreement on the boundaries of the lectures. Their general outline was first identified by R. N. Whybray (1965b: 33–52), though he excluded much of the material as secondary.

Each lecture has three major constituents: exordium, lesson, and conclusion. These have parallels in classical Greek rhetoric, in which the components of an oration are called the *exordium*, *propositio*, and *peroratio* (Plöger, pp. 23–24).

(1) *Exordium*. The introduction to the lesson, comprising
(a) an *address* to the son or sons ("my son . . .");
(b) an *exhortation* to hear and remember the teachings (e.g., "Listen . . . to your father's instruction; neglect not your mother's teaching" [1:8]);
(c) a *motivation* that supports the exhortation by extolling the teachings' excellence and value to their possessor (e.g., "for these are a graceful garland for your head, and a necklace for your throat" [1:9]).

These elements can be repeated within the exordium and recur later in the lesson.

(2) *Lesson*. The body of the teaching, imparting the message peculiar to the lecture (e.g., "My son, if criminals lure you, don't give in . . . for their feet rush to harm, make haste to shed blood" [1:10–16]).

(3) *Conclusion*. A summary statement generalizing the teaching of the lesson (e.g., "'No bird is caught in a net which is set out in plain view of him.' Yet *these* lie in wait—for their very own blood, set an ambush—for their very own lives" [1:17–18]). The conclusion sometimes ends with a capstone:
(a) *Capstone*. An apothegm that reinforces the teaching and provides a memorable climax (e.g., "This is what happens to everyone who grasps ill-gotten gain: it robs him who holds it of life" [1:19]).

1. *Instructions Elsewhere in Proverbs*

A few units outside Part I belong to the genre of instruction,[50] though they show significant differences from the lectures, which should also be classified as instructions. The components of instructions appear in Prov 22:17–24:22 (Part III) and 31:1–9 (Part Vc).[51] Part III includes subunits, but the boundaries are uncertain, since the topics are varied and the units brief. There are no units organized exactly like the lectures of Part I, but there are still strong resemblances.

In Part III, the components of the exordia are interlaced among diverse proverbs, mostly couplets and quatrains on a variety of subjects. Longer thematic units are 23:1–8; 23:29–35; and possibly 24:3–9, though these lack exordia and conclusions.

Prov 22:17–24:21 is best described as a single, loosely structured instruction. It is a miscellany of proverbs and epigrams drawn largely from foreign sources. Prov 22:17–22 is the exordium to the entirety.

In Prov 31:1–9, the speaker addresses "my son" (*b^eri*, in Aramaic; v 2) and expounds on a single theme (royal comportment), but there is no exhortation or motivation. In spite of structural differences, there are significant similarities between the exordia of Part I and comparable elements in Parts III and Vc. Parts III and Vc include addresses to "my son" (23:15, 19, 26; 24:13; 31:2), exhortations to hear and remember (22:17; 23:12, 19, 22–23, 26; 24:13–14a), and motivations of exhortations (22:18, 20; 23:15b–16, 24, 25; 24:14b).[52]

The formal components of the instruction, then, were available to the author of Part I, but he organized them in a more consistent design.

2. *Instructions in Foreign Wisdom Literature*

In foreign Wisdom, too, the three elements appear but in a different distribution. Typically (in Amenemope, for example), the definitive features belong to the work as a whole, not to its constituent discourses. These discourses (e.g., Amenemope's "stanzas") do not each display the complete structure.

The Egyptian instruction genre was studied by Kayatz (1966: 15–75), who described its basic form as comprising (1) a prologue, whose purpose is expressed by one or more infinitives (the infinitival construction is, however, rare; see "Prologues to Wisdom Books," after 1:1–7); (2) a series of self-contained units, some introduced casuistically ("If . . ."), others by imperatives; (2a) a motivation or substantiation (*Begründung*) in each unit. Prov 1–9 is structured quite differently. The Prologue is

---

[50]The "instruction" genre is described by McKane (pp. 6–10), with an extensive survey of Egyptian and Mesopotamian instructions (pp. 51–182). My formal description differs somewhat from Whybray's and McKane's, but the basic identifications coincide.

[51]Thus McKane, pp. 7, 369–70, 407.

[52]The exhortations of Part III use a number of verbal phrases in commanding obedience. Some appear in Part I as well: *hiṭṭah* (*n-ṭ-h*) *leb/ʾozen* "incline the heart/ear" (22:17; cf. 2:2); *nṣr* (G) "guard"—but with "my ways" as object (23:26 qere), not words for wisdom; *šamaʿ* "listen" (22:17; 23:19, 22; as in 1:8; 4:1, 10; 5:7; 7:24; cf. 8:6, 32, 33; also 19:20); the conditional formulation with *ʾim* (23:15; as in 2:1, 3, 4); *qanah* (*ḥokmah/ʾemet/musar/binah*) "acquire (wisdom/truth/instruction, understanding"; 23:23; as in 4:5, 7). Others are not paralleled in Part I's exhortations: *ʾaššer badderek* ("go straight in the way"; but cf. Wisdom's invitation in 9:6); *yadaʿ ḥokmah* "know wisdom" (24:14a); *habiʾah lammusar libbeka, w^eʾozn^eka* "bring your heart, your ear" (namely, to instruction) (23:12); *ḥakam* (G impv.), "become wise"; *natan leb* lit. "give the heart" (23:26; cf. 27:11); *šyt* (G) *leb* "set the heart" (22:17); introduction of exhortation by an analogy (24:13–14a).

similar. Then each unit has its own introduction, the exordium, with its own motivating sentences. The "lessons" likewise have various types of motivations. These differences suggest considerable development between the Egyptian instruction form and the lectures of Prov 1–9, which means that the formal parallel is not evidence for an early dating of Prov 1–9. We should also observe that some of the formal features Kayatz describes also appear in the Mesopotamian instructions of Shuruppak and Shube'awilum.

B. THE INTERLUDES

There are five interludes outside the framework of the lectures. The relation of the interludes to the lectures and to one another will be discussed in "The Formation of Proverbs 1–9," Essay 1. I regard the interludes as later additions by different authors. Interlude C is rather extraneous, but the other four are thoughtful reflections on a theme found in the lectures, the excellence of wisdom. The interludes are probably by different authors, but each one seems to know the contributions of his predecessors and to be responding to them. Their ideas are discussed in "Ideas of Wisdom in Proverbs 1–9," Essays 3–4.

II. MASORETIC DIVISIONS (*PISQAʾOT*)

The earliest preserved unit divisions are Masoretic *pisqaʾot* "sections." The existence of *pisqaʾot* is mentioned as early as *Sifra* (Lev 1:1), ca. third century C.E. A *pisqaʾ* is indicated by beginning a verse on a new line or, if the preceding line is complete, leaving one line blank. (The letter *peh*, for *pᵉtuḥah* "open" is used as well, but inconsistently.) The *pisqaʾot* are maintained in formal manuscripts, such as the Aleppo and the Leningradensis. The *pisqaʾot* of Prov 1–9 are as follows:

> *1:1–7*; *1:8–19*; *1:20–33*; *2:1–22*; 3:1–10; **3:11–18**; **3:19–35**; 4:1–19; **4:20–5:6**; [5:7–23]; [*6:1–5*; *6:6–11*; *6:12–15*; *6:16–19*]; [*6:20–26*; *6:27–35*]; [*7:1–23*; 7:24–27]; [*8:1–21*; *8:22–31*; 8:32–36]; **9:1–9**; **9:10–18**

These divisions are based on content, and almost all agree with the units demarcated previously (as lectures or interludes) or with sections of them, which will be defined in the Commentary. I have italicized cases when we agree on the boundaries (of units or sections) and bracketed *pisqaʾot* that constitute sections of my units. Disagreements are marked by boldface. Even in cases where we disagree on the compass of a unit or section, the starting or ending points usually coincide (3:11; 3:18; 4:20; 5:6).

It is interesting that the Masoretes begin a *pisqaʾ* at exhortations beginning *wᵉʿattah* "and now" (5:7; 7:24; 8:32), which always introduces a new exhortation. They did not, however, always recognize the addresses to "my son" in the exordia as starting a new unit (3:21; 4:10; 5:1).

This comparison shows that the boundaries of the divisions of Prov 1–9 proposed here (which are widely recognized by modern commentators) are natural and were recognized in ancient times.

III. THE DATING OF PROVERBS 1–9

With the possible exception of the appendices in chapters 30–31, Prov 1–9 is the latest stratum of the book, since it serves as an introduction to the later chapters. It is, however, very difficult to determine its date.

The instruction form, to which genre the major units (lectures) of Prov 1–9 belong, is attested in Egyptian and Mesopotamian Wisdom from earliest times. Kayatz believes that this consideration eliminates the grounds for a late dating of Prov 1–9, and she dates the unit to the monarchic period (p. 135). But the formal features she observes do not show that the lectures are *early*, but only that they belong to an ancient genre. The lectures are, as noted previously, a developed stage of the genre.

The current tendency is to place Prov 1–9 in the later Achaemenid period, more specifically after the middle of the fifth century B.C.E. Maier (1995) has argued this most extensively. She bases her conclusions on a lengthy description of the social-historical conditions of the Achaemenid period (pp. 25–68), which she believes are reflected in these chapters (pp. 262–69). It is, however, difficult to see anything that ties Prov 1–9 specifically in that period, even assuming the accuracy of her (largely theory-driven) description (see especially the features she summarizes on pp. 66–68). Later periods are certainly not excluded.

Maier argues that the characterization of "opponents" as self-aggrandizing criminals (1:10–19 and 2:12–15) indicates the viewpoint of the "solidarity group" of the Achaemenid-Judean upper class ("solidarischen Gruppe der Oberschicht," p. 265). But nothing here is peculiar to the Persian period. There were always upper classes, and they didn't like being robbed and killed. Nor did the other classes. (It's not as if we knew that the men portrayed as criminals were actually just ambitious entrepreneurs from outside the traditional upper class who were then "characterized" tendentiously as being cutthroats. They were created for the text and exist in it, and there they *are* cutthroats.)

Maier (like H. Washington [1994a]) also believes that the warnings against the "Strange Woman" (in particular, the *nokriyyah*) grew out of the struggle against exogamy in the mid-fifth century (Ezra 10:6–44; Neh 13:23–27). But the Strange Woman is not foreign (see the arguments in "Who Is the 'Strange Woman'?" after Lecture II), and she is certainly not trying to marry the foolish youth (after her divorce?). In any case, marriage with foreigners hardly disappeared after the fifth century. As for the notion that the warning is also directed against sexual contact with Jewish women outside the family or clan (p. 265), that simply does not come into Proverbs' purview (or Ezra-Nehemiah's). And although Tobit prefers (anachronistically) to have his son to marry within his tribe, Naphtali (4:12, in MSS BA), at no period was such a marriage considered an evil. In Proverbs, nothing suggests that the strangeness of the Strange Woman, who is in any case a resident of the same city, consists simply in belonging to another tribe.

A. Meinhold (p. 76) says that the exhortation to tithe from *all* one's produce in Prov 3:9 suggests that people were stinting on donations, and this reminds him of the problem raised in Persian-period texts (Mal 3:6–12; Neh 10:36–39; 13:10–13). But Prov 3:9 does not have a particularly polemical tinge, and in any case it is hard to believe that people always paid their temple donations in full in earlier or later times.

There has not yet been a thorough historical-linguistic study of the Hebrew of Prov 1–9. The language is neither clearly late nor early. The Phoenicianisms and features with Ugaritic parallels (adduced, and probably exaggerated, by

Albright [1955]) may have resided in the language from an earlier period.[53] The absence of distinctively late (or proto-Mishnaic) features may be due to the modeling of the language of Part I on the style of the earlier proverbial collections, Parts II–V.

Just how late Part I should be dated is more difficult to ascertain. There are likely allusions to Jeremiah in Part I (see "Interlude A and Jeremiah" after chapter 1), which would indicate a postexilic dating, though not securely.

Certain features of Part I and some verses elsewhere suggest an early Hellenistic setting. The social background implied (with the *qahal-ekklēsia* as a judicial forum) resembles the setting of Ben Sira more than Ezra-Nehemiah (see the comment on 5:14). Proverbs nowhere shows a concern with separating Jews from foreigners, which was the great challenge in the fifth century. In fact, the social and intellectual concerns of Prov 1–9 evinced in favor of an Achaemenid dating are equally present in Ben Sira, which was written about 190–180 B.C.E.

The universalistic outlook of Prov 8 reflects a more intellectually cosmopolitan period than the Persian. The message fits a time when Jewish traditions were in competition with foreign currents of thought. (See "Wisdom as a Universal" in Essay 4.) The subtext of Part I, especially chapter 8, is that Jews need not look outside their own intellectual traditions (*ḥokmah*) to find the kind of thought so esteemed among the gentiles. Moreover, the concept of wisdom in the story of Wisdom's origins seems to show a certain awareness of Greek styles of thought (see "Wisdom as a Universal, in Essay 4). These features would not be impossible prior to the Macedonian conquest but are more likely after it.[54] These considerations, however, are far from decisive. While the characteristics of Part I allow for a Hellenistic dating, they do not prove it.

---

[53] *Yapiaḥ* "witness" (6:19), is attested in Ugaritic, but the vocable could have been learned from Prov 12:17; 14:25 (*ypḥ*); 19:5, 9). Albright (1955: 9–10) appeals to Ugaritic *mgn*, "to beg, entreat," to explain *magen* in 6:11. But even if this is actually the meaning of the word (see the Commentary), the verse is dependent on 24:34. *Ḥokmot* (see on 1:20) may be a Phoenicianism, though not necessarily an archaic one.

[54] A. Wolter's interpretation of *ṣopiyyah* in 31:27 as a pun on the Greek *sophia* (1985: 580–85) would support a Hellenistic dating. Nevertheless, I find the interpretation (but not the dating) farfetched. At most, the words sound alike, and *sophia* does not fit into the syntax of the Hebrew verse. In any case, 31:10–31 belongs to a series of appendices (chapters 30–31) that were added later, and its dating says nothing about the rest of the book.

TRANSLATION AND COMMENTARY

PART I: PROVERBS 1–9

◆

THE PROLOGUE (1:1–7)

TRANSLATION

The book's goals

1:1 The proverbs of Solomon the son of David, king of Israel,
2 (for use)
in learning wisdom and discipline,
in understanding words of understanding,
3 in absorbing the discipline of insight:
righteousness, justice, and rectitude,
4 in giving the callow cunning,
to the young—knowledge of shrewdness.
5 Let the wise man listen and enhance his instruction,
the astute man gain guidance,
6 in understanding proverbs and epigrams,
the words of the wise and their enigmas.

The motto

7 The fear of the Lord is the beginning of knowledge;
Fools despise wisdom and discipline.

COMMENTARY

The Prologue advertises the book as effective in conveying to children the basic intellectual and ethical virtues and also in enhancing the knowledge and interpretive skills of more advanced scholars. Some of Proverbs' key words and concepts are introduced in the Prologue. For fuller discussion, see "Words for Wisdom" in the Introduction.

1:1. The Title

1:1. *The proverbs of Solomon* [*mišley šᵉlomoh*]: This is the book's title, used also in the Talmud. It is commonly shortened to *mišley*, "proverbs" (actually, "proverbs of"). In the (medieval) Tosefot (commentaries) to *B. Batra* 14b, Proverbs is called *sefer haḥokmah*, "The Book of Wisdom." Among the early Christian writers the book was called variously "Wisdom," "All-Virtuous Wisdom," "The Wisdom Book," and "Wisdom the Teacher" (references in Toy). These designations are not titles (they are not found in any MSS of Proverbs) but rather descriptions of the book's contents.

Proverbs is the book of *m^{e}šalim*. Numerous passages elsewhere in the Bible and other Jewish sources are called *m^{e}šalim*. Yet the texts so labeled are so varied that it is surprisingly difficult to ascertain just what the term means.

The Mašal

The word *mašal* is applied to a great range of utterances, from one-line adages to extended poems. "From evil comes forth evil" (1 Sam 24:13) is a *mašal*, but so is the allegory describing the great eagle (Ezek 17:1–10). It does not designate a single genre or category.

Attempts to find a single feature common to all *m^{e}šalim* (see later) have failed. In my view, this is because the word has two distinct meanings: (a) A *trope*. A trope is a word, statement, or image displaced from its primary, surface meaning so as to represent something else, by virtue of an imputed similarity. (b) A *saying* that has currency among the people. This is its sense in Proverbs (1:1, 6; 10:1; 25:1; 26:7, 9).

(a) A Trope.

As a trope, a *mašal* may be a symbol. For example, the cauldron in Ezek 24:3–5 symbolizes Jerusalem. Or a *mašal* may be an exemplum, meaning that it belongs to the set it represents. For example, a nation can become a *mašal* if it both suffers disaster and is used as a byword to signify others who may suffer the like (Deut 28:37 and often).

When the referent of the trope is difficult to discern, a *mašal* is an enigma. For example, Hab 2:6–12 is (or contains) a *mašal* enigma. Ezek 17:1–10, telling of the great eagle, is both a *mašal* and a *ḥidah*, "enigma." When the people cannot understand what Ezekiel is saying about the "forest of the south," they call him a "maker of *m^{e}šalim*" (Ezek 21:5).

Prophetic visions are *m^{e}šalim* insofar as they are similitudes of the higher reality of which they speak rather than a direct experience of it. Moses alone saw directly. Other prophets see or hear words and images that require interpretation (Num 12:6–8). On this same principle, each of the speeches of Balaam, the foreign diviner, is called a *mašal* (Num 23:7, 18; 24:3, 15, 20, 21, 23).

(b) A Saying.

A saying implies currency among the people. Some *m^{e}šalim* are both sayings and tropes. But there is a difference. Often *mašal* refers to an utterance that has nothing to do with comparison.

David quotes a *mašal* to Saul, "As the *mašal* of the ancients says, 'Wickedness issues from the wicked'" (1 Sam 24:13). This sentence holds no image, metaphor, or comparison. The phrase that introduces the saying says something about the way it is used, not about its form or content. It is the currency of the sentence, past and present, that reinforces its validity and reinforces David's point. The saying "Is Saul too among the prophets?" (1 Sam 10:12) was not a *mašal* on the first occasion it was used (v 11); it subsequently *became* a *mašal* (*hay^{e}ʾta l^{e}mašal*; v 12). This saying too is not a "likeness" of any sort. Furthermore, the quoting formula "therefore they say" or simply "they say" is equivalent to *mašal*, as a comparison of 1 Sam 10:12 with 19:24 and Ezek 18:2 with Jer 31:29 shows.

Although the book of Proverbs contains many tropes (most books do), "likening" is not the feature that explains the title. Rather, the sayings are called *m^e^šalim* because of the presumption or claim that they are well known and in widespread use. By calling the proverbs *m^e^šalim* (rather than simply "words of . . ." as in 30:1; 31:1; and 22:17), the author-editor is implicitly asserting that these sayings are validated not only by their source (a wise man) but also by their use: They are current in public wisdom.

Of the numerous attempts to determine the nature of the *mašal*, I will mention four important studies. Eissfeldt (1913) regards the word as applying haphazardly to six different genres. (This would largely deplete the word of meaning.) McKane (pp. 23–32) defines the *mašal* as a "model, exemplar, paradigm." (But most *m^e^šalim* are general maxims, observations, and admonitions, not exemplars.) D. W. Suter (1981: 198) identifies the essential feature of *mašal* as comparison (in which he includes contrast, misled by the ambiguity of the English word). T. Polk (1983) emphasizes the illocutionary dimension of the *mašal*: what it does "to, with, or for its hearers/readers" (p. 567). The *mašal* is paradigmatic because it works as a model of a broader reality; it is parabolic because it draws the listener into self-judgment (p. 569). (But most *m^e^šalim* do not involve the audience in a self-judgment, and they can be said to "model" a greater reality only in the way that almost any text does.)

son of David, king of Israel: Solomon (966–926 B.C.E.) was the third and last king of the United Kingdom. His reign was remembered as a period of power, prosperity, and peace, but also—without inconsistency—as an era of economic and political oppression. Most important for our purposes, Solomon was remembered as the greatest of sages and as the author par excellence of wisdom.

Several traditional commentators, proceeding from the axiom that there are no wasted words in Scripture, observed that the expansive title does more than identify the author, since Solomon's father and country were universally known. The title, as Naḥmias observes, proclaims that "the prince of the people speaks princely things" (alluding to 8:6). Ramaq says that the phrase "son of David" honors Solomon by mentioning his paternity; he is "a wise man son of a wise man." This proposal is supported by the parallel of some foreign wisdom books, particularly the instructions of Ptahhotep, Amenemope, and Shuruppak (see the Introduction), which detail the titles, posts, ancestry, and position of the teacher by way of commending the book to the reader.

Does 1:1 apply to the entire book or only to chapters 1–9? Since some units are ascribed to persons other than Solomon (24:23; 30:1; 31:1), the title in 1:1 must, according to one opinion, belong only to the first collection (Oesterley). Part I was, however, written as an introduction to the rest of Proverbs (see Essay 1, "The Formation of Proverbs 1–9"). Hence the author must have meant the title to apply to Proverbs in its entirety (at least through chapter 29; the final two chapters may be a later appendix).

In the first instance of redaction-criticism of Proverbs, Radaq (in a preface to his Proverbs commentary) distinguishes between "the scribe who wrote [*katav*] words of the book" (whose own words we read in 1:1–6) and "the author of the book [*m*ᵉ*ḥabber hassefer*]," namely Solomon. (This distinction is already implied in the Greek translation of the title, which speaks of Solomon in the past tense [aorist]: ". . . Solomon, son of David, who ruled in Israel.") Radaq recognizes that the book did not issue in this form from Solomon's pen, though he assumes that the proverbs themselves, unless otherwise ascribed, are Solomon's work.

Solomon and the Title of Proverbs

Historically, it is improbable that many—if any—of the proverbs were written by Solomon. The social background implied by the sayings is quite varied. The proverbs do not usually bespeak the concerns of the royal court and never speak from the perspective of a monarch. Moreover, many of the teachings would not make sense as Solomon's tutelage of his son. Concerns such as the dangers of guaranteeing a loan for another, the threat of public disgrace, and the assumption of monogamy do not seem like the words of Solomon to Rehoboam. A prince would hardly fall in with highwaymen (1:8–18), and 7:6 is not compatible with the location of Solomon's palace.

A number of postexilic Jewish writings claimed Solomon as author: the Song of Songs, Psalm 72 and the Odes of Solomon, the Psalms of Solomon, the Testament of Solomon, and the Wisdom of Solomon.[55] None of these attributions are historically accurate.

Solomon was famed as an author of wisdom. The tradition of his wisdom was not an invention of the redactors of Proverbs; there would be no point in assigning a Wisdom text to a man not known for wisdom. His wisdom is extolled in 1 Kgs 5:10–14, which reports that he wrote 3,000 *m*ᵉ*šalim* and 1,005 songs; that he declaimed on plants and animals, that his wisdom surpassed that of easterners, Egyptians, and Edomites; and that people came from all over the earth to hear his wisdom. The antiquity or accuracy of this tradition is suspect, because the passage has legendary features and some late linguistic characteristics (Scott 1955: 266–69). But even if this passage is post-Deuteronomic, as Scott maintains, it may still be earlier than the title of Proverbs and may have inspired it.

An ancient reading construed the title strictly, as meaning that Solomon himself wrote all of Proverbs, and adjusted the headings throughout the book to fit this assumption. In the LXX, the heading in Prov 10:1 was eliminated altogether. The ascriptions to "the wise" in the original of Prov 22:17[56] and

---

[55]Qohelet, contrary to the usual view, is not exactly identified with Solomon. Instead, he is given Solomon-like traits to make him a suitable figure for the examination of wealth and wisdom that the book reports.

[56]The LXX translates: "To the words of the wise incline your ear, and hear my word, and set your heart, that you may know that they are beautiful" (attaching v 1 to v 2). This translation presupposes a different Hebrew text: *dbry ḥkmym hṭ ʾznk wšmʿ dbry, wlbk tšyt ldʿty*. The correct translation of this text is: "The words of the wise. Incline your ear and hear my words, and set your heart to my knowledge." This reading is original and will henceforth be assumed.

24:23,[57] to Agur in 30:1,[58] and to Lemuel's mother in 31:1[59] were contorted midrashically so that they cease to be headings or ascriptions of authorship. The result is an unambiguous assignment of the authorship of the entire book to Solomon. The Targum and many traditional Jewish commentators achieved a similar harmonization by taking *laḥăkamim* in 24:23 to mean "*to* the wise" rather than "*by* the wise," thus making the wise the audience of the sayings rather than the authors. Likewise, they commonly explained the names Agur and Lemuel as parts of statements, not personal names, or took Agur as an epithet of Solomon who "gathered" (*'agar*) Torah wisdom (*Tanḥuma*).

One modern view understands the notion of Solomonic authorship as a designation of a body or type of traditional Wisdom material, of which Solomon was believed to be the font and preeminent bearer (Plöger; Zimmerli). However, the sages mentioned in other Wisdom texts are supposed to be the authors.

A similar typological interpretation of the title was proposed by W. Brueggemann (1990). He explains the ascription as a reflex of a historical memory of Solomon as initiator of an intellectual enterprise (p. 129). Brueggemann postulates that the rise of the monarchy in Solomon's time brought with it a need for wisdom teachers to function as the intellectual brain trust for policy formation, as ideologues to justify the new social order, and as pedagogues for the young who would inherit the power monopoly (p. 125). However, we cannot determine that it was precisely Solomon's court that introduced wisdom. As for what tradition remembered about Solomon, it certainly did not suppose that Wisdom arose to meet the royalist sociopolitical need for an "intellectual brain trust." In fact, Solomon was not remembered as a patron of a wisdom enterprise or even as the founder of a literary genre (quite the contrary; see 1 Kgs 5:10–11), but rather as an individual author of Wisdom. And though many proverbs teach a royalist ideology, none has a specifically Davidide message. Hence, we cannot say that the putative memory existed, let alone that it is in any way accurate.

Read in the light of the headings in 22:17 and 24:23 (and perhaps 30:1 and 31:1), Prov 1:1 implies that Solomon is the author, but one who not only composed but also gathered and incorporated wisdom from his predecessors.

This notion of authorship has parallels in other Wisdom texts. In the "Instruction of Ptahhotep," the first title reads, "The Instruction which the noble . . . Ptahhotep made" (l. 1). In the preface, Ptahhotep asks for the king's permission to take on a "staff of old age" (a successor) and to instruct him. "Then I may tell him [var.: "instruct him in"] the words of the wise [lit. those who listened], the advice of the ancestors, those who heard the gods [that is, the earlier kings]" (ll. 30–32). The king replies: "Instruct him, then, in the utterances of times past" (l. 37). The author thus claims—proudly—that his teaching incorporates

[57] 24:23a LXX: "These things I say to you wise ones to learn."

[58] 30:1 LXX: "Fear my words, son, and when you have received them, repent. Thus says the man to those who trust in God, and I cease."

[59] 31:1 LXX: "My words have been spoken by God. An oracular response of the king, whom his mother instructed."

teachings of earlier sages. The title of a Ramesside text is "The Beginning of the Educational Instruction According to Old Writings," implying that the maxims were culled from older books. The same notion of authorship appears in the Talmud's explanation of the composition of Psalms: David wrote them down, incorporating the words of ten "elders" starting with Adam (*b. B. Bat.* 14b–15a). There is thus no contradiction between the claim of Solomonic authorship in Prov 1:1 and the ascription of various proverbs to other sages. Solomon was, in the view of later times, a scholar of ancient texts.

The Talmud (*b. B. Bat.* 14b) claims that it was not Solomon but "Hezekiah and his company" who *wrote* Isaiah, Proverbs, the Song of Songs, and Qohelet. This is not a denial of Solomonic authorship for the last three mentioned books (or Isaianic authorship for the book of Isaiah), but a recognition that authorship is to be distinguished from the inscription of the biblical books in their current form. In fact, Prov 25:1 makes it undeniable that the book of Proverbs in its present form is not Solomonic.

1:2–6. The Statement of Purpose

The statement of purpose promotes the book as a textbook in teaching the young and as an aid in an advanced education. The Prologue shows us how one ancient scholar (probably the author of the lectures in Part I) understood the pedagogical function of the book. This understanding is discussed in "Wisdom as Character Education," after the Prologue.

The statement of purpose proceeds in a series of infinitival clauses dependent on the title that describe the goals and functions of the proverbs. (In the translation, I have prefixed "for use" to the series to join it more smoothly to the title.) A mimetic translation will help convey its peculiar structure:

> (1) The proverbs of Solomon the son of David, king of Israel, (2) to know [*lada'at*] wisdom and correction [*musar*], to understand [*l^{e}habin*] utterances of understanding, (3) to receive [*laqaḥat*] the correction of insight, righteousness, and justice and rectitude, (4) to give to the callow cunning, to the young—knowledge and shrewdness. (5) Let the wise man listen and let him increase (his) instruction [*leqaḥ*], the astute one gain guidance [*taḥbulot*], (6) to understand a proverb and an epigram, the words of the wise and their enigmas.

The syntax of this passage—a noun defined by a long series of infinitives of purpose—is without parallel in the Bible. It is later employed in the Rule of the Community from Qumran (1QS I 2–11), probably in dependence on Proverbs.

The closest parallel to this infinitival construction (noun + *lamed* with inf. of purpose) is the inf. with a "*lamed* of respect," as in 1 Chr 12:9; 2 Sam 14:25; and Prov 26:2. But the *lamed* in the construction used in the Prologue does not mean "in regard to." Also similar in syntax but different in meaning is the construction with the infinitive with an imminent sense ("about to"), such as Isa 38:20; Jer 51:49 [IBHS §36.2g]. The author of the Prologue is thus stretching the use of an available syntactic resource.

1:2. *in learning* [*lada'at*]: The verb *yada'* ("know") + a wisdom noun (*ḥokmah, binah, śekel,* or *da'at*) often means "possess" (knowledge) or (denoting the process) "attain" or "learn" it. (Clear examples are Num 24:16; Prov 24:14; 17:27; Qoh 1:17; 8:16; Isa 29:24; and 2 Chr 2:12.) In the present verse, it is parallel to *l^ehabin*, "in understanding" (namely, the teachings of wisdom) and probably means much the same thing.

wisdom [*ḥokmah*]: "Wisdom" here refers to the *message* of the instructions, the teachings themselves; compare 2:1–2, where "wisdom" stands parallel to "my words" and "my precepts" as an object of listening, and Sir 3:29, where it is parallel to "proverbs." *Ḥokmah* in this sense is equivalent to "my *ḥokmah*" in Prov 5:1. *Ḥokmah* means "teachings" in 10:31; 1 Kgs 5:14; and Job 32:7. *Ḥokmah umusar* is a hendiadys meaning "wise instruction"; Rashi accurately paraphrases: "these proverbs."

discipline [*musar*]: *Musar* basically means "correction," whether verbal or physical. It is sometimes "preemptive" correction and means "warning," "admonition." Occasionally, it is broadened to the point of synonymy with "wisdom" or "teaching." In all cases, the content of *musar* is an ethical (rather than, say, practical) teaching. See "Words for Wisdom," §6.

1:3. *in absorbing the discipline of insight* [*laqaḥat musar haśkel*]: *Laqaḥ musar*, lit. "take correction," means to take it to heart, to absorb it and change one's ways. *Musar* as punishment can be inflicted on someone against his will but, as God stresses in Jer 2:30, the *taking* of *musar* cannot be forced. In Jer 7:28, it parallels "hear [that is, obey] the voice of the Lord"; see also Jer 5:3; 17:23; 35:13.

of insight: *Haśkel*, an H-stem infinitive absolute, is one of several terms for wisdom. It apparently means "to have insight" or "give insight, educate."

The inf. abs. *haśkēl* is used as a synonym of *ḥokmah* in Jer 3:15 ("And I will give you shepherds who are in accord with my wishes, and they will feed [*w^era'û*] you on knowledge and *haśkēl*"); Job 34:35 ("Job does not speak in knowledge, and his words are not in *haśkēl*"); Prov 21:16; and Dan 1:17. The distinctive meaning of *haśkēl* is difficult to determine. The root-meaning is "see," hence "perceive," "understand." *Hiśkîl* means literally to "look upon" only in Gen 3:6, where it puns on the notion of becoming wise. Elsewhere it is a metaphorical, intellectual perception; the organ used is the heart, not the eye (Isa 44:18). *Hiśkîl* can also mean "to instruct, enlighten" and "to act perceptively, intelligently," hence "succeed" (note esp. Prov 17:8, where it means "succeed" without necessarily entailing wisdom). Except when it means "succeed," *hiśkîl* always refers to genuine understanding, never to mere cleverness or skill, and it always has a positive moral valence. It almost always refers to perception of God's will and his role in human affairs (Deut 32:29; Isa 41:20; Ps 64:10; etc.). In Ps 2:10, *haśkîlû* is parallel to and synonymous with *hiwwās^erû*, "take a lesson," a verb cognate to *mûsar*. The participle *maśkîl* is nearly synonymous with *ḥākām*, "wise," but without implying an unusual degree of knowledge (e.g., Ps 14:2; Prov 10:5; 15:24; and often). In later texts, *hiśkîl* is associated in particular with teaching and learning. It means "become wise, learned" in Dan 1:4, 17; Neh 8:13; and Ps 119:99, and "teach" in Dan 9:22 and 1 Chr 28:19.

Mûsar haśkēl has been construed in several ways: (1) *mûsār and haśkēl*, supplying a *waw* (Kaspi; Ramaq; cf. Syr). (But can one be said to "take" *haśkēl*?) (2) "To take *mûsār* and *to understand* righteousness, etc." (but this disturbs the pattern of *lamed* + inf. const.). (3) "the teaching of *success*" (McKane; Ringgren). (4) "The teaching *about* [or "in"] insight." Compare *mûsar śēkel*, "the teaching *about* intelligence (Sir 50:27; cf. 34:12; 41:14). (5) "The discipline/correction that *imparts* insight," parsing *haśkēl* as a genitive of purpose. This construction is supported by two close parallels:

mûsar šᵉlômēnû (Isa 53:5), "the correction that brings about our well-being" (Naḥmias, Toy). Compare also Prov 15:33a: *yir'at YHWH mûsar ḥokmāh*, "the fear of the Lord is the discipline of wisdom," meaning that fear of God is the inner discipline or correction (in other words, conscience) that engenders wisdom. (That the relationship between subject and predicate in 15:33a is temporal, hence consequential, is shown by the parallel line, "and humility precedes honor" [v 33b].)

righteousness [*ṣedeq*], *justice* [*mišpaṭ*], *and rectitude* [*meyšarim*]: Rather than demanding these virtues, the Prologue *promises* them. Studying wisdom produces social virtues, the underpinnings of society.

The nouns in v 3b are best taken as appositional to *haśkel*: ". . . the discipline of insight: righteousness, justice, and rectitude." The *musar* of *haśkel*, the "discipline" or "lesson" of insight—that is to say, what *haśkel* teaches—is just and ethical behavior.

The nouns *ṣedeq*, *mišpaṭ*, and *meyšarim* (which appear together again in 2:9) frequently combine in hendiadys and as word pairs. They have distinguishable, if overlapping, meanings, though here they combine to convey a single concept that embraces the entire range of honest and equitable behavior in personal and social relations. For a study of these concepts in their ancient Near Eastern context, see Weinfeld 1995.

Ṣedeq is the principle of right behavior and justice and its manifestation in word and deed.

Ṣedeq and *ṣᵉdaqah* both mean "righteousness." The distinction between them is blurred. According to Licht (EM VI 679–81), Jepsen (1965:78–80), and others, the basic distinction, not consistently maintained, is that *ṣedeq* is an abstract concept referring to the ideal, right situation, and *ṣᵉdaqah* refers to the single act of righteousness, a specific realization of *ṣedeq*, or righteous behavior, i.e., the totality of the acts of the righteous person. A. Ho (1991: 140 and *passim*) says that *ṣedeq* is a broad designation of justice, righteousness, and blessing. *Ṣᵉdaqah* is "*a state of being*, human and divine. It is self-fulfillment according to the ultimate *code of ethics*. It is a set of behavior and actions" (Ho 1991: 140).

Mišpaṭ, "justice," is the right and just condition. Sometimes *mišpaṭ* means "custom," "mode of behavior," the *way things are*, without necessarily implying virtue (such as in 1 Sam 8:11). Most often, it is the right state of affairs or the right mode of behavior. It is an ideal to which individuals and society are obliged to conform.

Meyšarim (from *y-š-r*, "straight") means straightness and levelness, hence "equity," "honesty." Most often, *meyšarim* indicates the quality or result of honest, fair speech or judgment. It is usually the object of verbs of speaking (Isa 33:15; 45:19; Prov 23:16) or judging (Pss 9:9; 58:2; 75:3; 96:10; 98:9; and often in Psalms).

Mêšārîm has both its concrete and abstract sense in Isa 26:7. It is used adverbially to mean "smoothly" in Prov 23:31; Cant 7:10, and probably Cant 1:4. *Mêšārîm* is something done and spoken by persons, but it is not a quality *of* a person; it never takes a poss. sfx., not even when parallelism would seem to call for it, as in Ps 17:2, where *mišpāṭî* parallels bare *mêšārîm*. (The term for the comparable personal quality is *yōšer*.)

1:4. *in giving the callow* [*pᵉta'yim*] *cunning* [*ʿormah*]: The verb *latet*, lit. "to give" (from *n-t-n*), may seem awkward because it describes something the *book* will do, whereas the parallel verbs in the series describe things the *pupil* will do (knowing, understanding, receiving). The same happens in Amenemope's prologue (see "Prologues to Wisdom Books," later in this chapter); some infinitives refer to what the book will do for the pupil (ll. 7–12), and others indicate actions the pupil will learn to do (ll. 5–6).

callow . . . young [*p^{e}taʾim* (pl.) . . . *naʿar* (sg.)]: This is a distributed hendiadys meaning "the callow young." The callow are unformed, gullible youths who are capable of gaining wisdom, but until they do so, they share some of the fool's traits and are susceptible to the same vices.

knowledge of shrewdness: That is, knowledge of how to be shrewd. *Daʿat um^{e}zimmah* is a hendiadys equivalent to a construct, like *daʿat m^{e}zimmot*, "knowledge of shrewdness" (8:12). This verse, too, promises a particular kind of knowledge, the ability to think hidden thoughts and devise one's own plans. The Prologue promises this faculty as a bonus to the diligent pupil.

ʿormah ("cunning") and *m^{e}zimmah* ("shrewdness," "circumspection") both refer to the ability to devise clever, even wily, tactics for attaining one's goals, whatever these may be. (See "Words for Wisdom," §§5, 7.) The neutrality of the terms should not be obscured by infusing them with moral content in translation, such as "prudence" for *ʿormah* (NIV) or "discretion" for *m^{e}zimmah* (KJV, NIV). Though both *ʿormah* and *m^{e}zimmah* are in themselves morally neutral, they usually refer to plans that are hostile and devious. For lack of a precise English equivalent, I translate *m^{e}zimmah* as "shrewdness" to suggest the amoral tone of the word and because "shrewdness" connotes the ability to plan privately and secretly for one's own benefit. "Circumspection" also conveys part of the word's meaning.

It is an audacious move, then, when Proverbs appropriates *ʿormah* and *m^{e}zimmah* for its catalogue of virtues (1:4; 2:11; 5:2). Proverbs assigns all effective mental powers to the realm of wisdom. Lady Wisdom herself has "knowledge of *m^{e}zimmot*" (8:12). The reason for this appropriation is not that "the educational process was more occupied with developing mature intellectual skills than with morality," contrary to McKane (*Proverbs*, p. 265). Teachings of practical skills are intertwined with moral lessons throughout ancient Near Eastern Wisdom literature. Rather, the sages believed that intellectual powers—even pragmatic ones that others might regard as morally neutral—were inherently conducive to morality.

The Prologue wants the reader to know that the book of Proverbs (rather than, say, the wise guys down the street) is the place to turn if you want the prestigious skills of cunning and shrewdness. As Proverbs sees it, the promised skills must be applied to worthy ends, which include legitimate remunerative labors. The particular function of *m^{e}zimmah* is to allow a man to keep his own counsel and to hold to private thoughts. By giving him this autonomy, it will protect him from the temptations of wicked men and women (2:11; 5:2). When they try to seduce him to their ways, he will be able to look inward, maintain independence of purpose, and resist their inveiglements.

ʿormah and *m^{e}zimmah* (for better or worse) typically come with maturity and experience. But how can the callow get experience without the pain and dangers it often entails? "What wisdom proposes on faith to the inexperienced is rather a substitute experience, with the knowledge-value of real experience but packaged quicker, easier, and especially safer" (Perry 1993: 34). "Substitute experience," which is to say, effectively transmitted knowledge, belongs to the essence of education.

the young [*naʿar*]: Hebrew *naʿar* is used of young people (originally of both sexes but in Proverbs only of males) from infancy (e.g., Exod 2:6; 1 Sam 4:21), through late adolescence (e.g., Gen 37:2), and into early adulthood (e.g., 1 Sam 30:17; 2 Sam 18:5; 1 Chr 12:29—these are adult warriors). The period of *neʿurim*, "youth" (abstract), is also the time of marriage (Prov 5:18). (*Naʿar* can also designate servants and retainers irrespective of age, but that usage does not occur in Proverbs.)

In Proverbs, the ostensive listener is imagined as an adolescent. He is old enough to become involved with gangs (1:10–19) and to be sexually seduced (7:7–27, etc.). Indeed, the special intensity of the warnings against sexual seduction (2:16–22; 5:3–23; 6:24–35; 7:5–27) suggests an audience for whom this danger was immediate. The ostensive rhetorical setting is a man who is speaking to an adolescent son about to enter the adult world. The son may be married or about to be, for marriages could be arranged well before adulthood. Adulthood officially began at twenty years for cultic reckoning (Lev 27:3) and was set at twenty-five or thirty years for Levitical and priestly service (Num 8:24 and Num 4:3, respectively). See further "The Listener in the Text," pp. 206f.

1:5. *Let the wise man listen* . . . : This verse interrupts the series of infinitives dependent on the title; hence, some commentators consider it an interpolation (Toy, Plöger). It is, however, a logical continuation of the grand promises of the Prologue: Besides instructing the young in wisdom and ethics, the book will advance the education of those already learned (thus Benjamin ben Judah, Pseudo-Ibn Ezra, Ehrlich, Oesterley). Moreover, this verse is presupposed by the next, which lists activities appropriate to advanced study, not to the education of the immature.

Listen: The verb *šamaʿ*, lit. "listen," "hear," must here mean "pay attention," not literally to listen, for the Prologue conceives of Proverbs as a book. The learned man, unlike the "son" who is the ostensive audience in chapters 1–9, will be studying written wisdom. The Egyptian equivalent, *sḏm*, "to hear," "understand," can likewise have written documents as object ("Satirical Letter," Pap. Anastasi I, 1.7). The books of Kagemeni, Ptahhotep, and Amenemope present themselves as written recordings of teachings that the sages delivered orally.

and enhance (*weyôsep*): Since this form is a jussive, the preceding verb *yišmaʿ* (hear), of which it is a consequence, must also be jussive. Thus 1:5 is an exhortation, not a statement.

(*his*) *instruction* [*leqaḥ*]: This word connotes a quality of verbalized teaching. It inheres in the communication of the message rather than to the knowledge itself. As Ehrlich observes, *leqaḥ* usually (and perhaps always) connotes eloquence and persuasiveness; see esp. Prov 16:23: "The wise man's heart will give skill to his mouth and add *leqaḥ* to his lips." In both 1:5 and 16:23, *leqaḥ* is something the wise man already possesses but hopes to increase. Proverbs 1:5a is offering to enhance the wise man's rhetorical skills in teaching. Ehrlich's paraphrase of 1:5a, "and will make his speech more attractive," brings out this implication, though perhaps it overemphasizes the connotation.

Sometimes the context of *leqaḥ* allows no restriction of meaning beyond the broad notion of "learning" or (when it is spoken) "teaching," "doctrine": Isa 29:24 // *binah*; Prov 4:2 // *torah*; Sir 51:16 (11QPs[a] xxi 14, where Hebrew MS B has *dʿt*); Sir 32:18c [35:14c] (MS B). But in several places, it is possible to detect a special connotation: attractive, persuasive speech. The poet of Deut 32 says: "Let my *leqaḥ* drip like rain, my speech flow like the dew, like light rain on grass, like droplets on plants" (32:2). His imagery conveys fluidity, purity, and refreshment (compare Job 29:23–24). Two proverbs clearly use *leqaḥ* in reference to eloquent, persuasive speech: "The wise of heart will be called astute, and one sweet of speech will increase *leqaḥ*" (Prov 16:21); and Prov 16:23, quoted previously. Job's thoughts are called *leqaḥ* in a context focusing on his speech (11:2–4): Job is an *ʾiš śepatayim*, a "man of lips"—that is, loquacious or articulate. Ben Sira (8:8) speaks of *leqaḥ* as a virtue (rather than a body of knowledge) that will allow one to serve high officials. Most revealing is Prov 7:21, where the teacher says that the seductress enticed the youth "by her great *leqaḥ* (and) led him astray by her smooth speech." Her words are fluent and persuasive. They are called a *leqaḥ*, "teaching" or "lesson," facetiously, to show that they seek to displace the father's teaching.

guidance: *Taḥbulot*, "strategy," "guidance," is the skill that directs actions, and possibly the act of giving advice and direction. The word is a synonym of *ʿeṣah*, "deliberation," "planning," or the verb *yaʿaṣ* (Prov 11:14; 20:18; 24:6). The competencies called *taḥbulot* are not the ones a child needs, but more sophisticated skills. They are not inherently ethical or wise, because the wicked can possess them (12:5). The wise can acquire *taḥbulot* by studying Proverbs. The guidance called *taḥbulot* can be used in directing oneself or others.

1:6. *in understanding proverbs and epigrams*: Verse 6 is consequent upon v 5 (Ramaq): by study of Solomon's proverbs, the learned man will master interpretive skills. Two of the terms designating the literature to be studied are used in the headings elsewhere in Proverbs: "proverbs" (10:1; 25:1) and "words of [the wise]" (22:17; 30:1; 31:1).

understanding: The same verb (*lehabin*) is used of the pupil's activity in 1:2 and suggests a correspondence between the two levels of education. Ben Sira, too, believes that some erudition is a prerequisite for the interpretation of proverbs. Artisans, he assumes, though skilled in their crafts, "will not express perceptive teaching or understand the proverbs of the wise" (38:33).

Ehrlich suggests that *lehabin* is causitive here, meaning "to explicate," a well-attested sense of the H-stem (sim. Malbim, second explanation). However, whenever the causitive use of this verb ("to teach/explain, etc.") governs a single object, this is always the semantic indirect object (the person who receives the teaching), not the semantic direct object (the substance or message taught).

epigrams [*meliṣah*]: The meaning of this word is uncertain. It occurs elsewhere in BH only twice: "Will not all these take up a *mašal* and a *meliṣah* against him, as enigmas about him" (Hab 2:6, a difficult construction); and "With songs, proverbs, and *meliṣah* [LXX: *parabolais*, "proverbs" or "parables"], you [Solomon] stirred up the peoples" (Sir 47:17)—a verse dependent on Prov 1:1. All three occurrences show that *m^{e}liṣot* are not folk adages. They are "epigrams," rhetorically polished, artistic sayings or terse poems (as in 6:1–19).

M^{e}lîṣāh has been explained in various ways:

(1) A matter stated openly, a simple, easily understood saying (Plöger, Mezudat David, and Naḥmias, who compares *mēliṣ*, "interpreter," on the grounds that an interpreter *clarifies* one person's words to another). But a clear saying would not require special study and effort. Also, Habakkuk's *m^{e}lîṣāh* is anything but simple.

(2) A dark saying (Ringgren, Gemser); LXX: *skoteinon logon*, "dark word/saying." This is a surmise based on the collocation with *ḥîdāh*.

(3) A mocking, satirical statement—deriving the word from *l-y-ṣ* "mock" (Oesterley). (This is one meaning of the word in RH). However, *l-y-ṣ* (G and H) almost always reflects pejoratively on the subject and implies arrogance. *M^{e}lîṣāh* would be sayings characteristic of a *lēṣ*, an arrogant scoffer, not a wise man.

(4) A slippery saying, hence "allusion" (Richardson 1955), from *m-l-ṣ*. But *m-l-ṣ* does not connote slipperiness or allusiveness; see Ps 119:103.

(5) A sweet, smooth saying, from *m-l-ṣ* (Benjamin ben Judah, Tur-Sinai 1967: 261). Compare Ps 119:103: "How sweet (*niml^{e}ṣû*) are your sayings [point as pl.] to my palate, more than honey to my mouth!" However, the *q^{e}tîlâh* pattern, used for nouns signifying activities and their results, does not seem to be employed with stative verbs.

(6) "Proverb," "parable" (Syr *pelā'tā'*, "parable, allegory"; the LXX of Sir 47:17 has *parabolais*, the usual rendering of *māšāl*). Toy appeals to the supposed root-meaning "turn/bend," hence a figurative saying. A more likely etymology supporting this interpretation is to derive *m^{e}lîṣāh* from *l-y-ṣ*, as in the H-stem participle *mēlîṣ*, "intermediary/intercessor/translator." This shows that the homonymous root *l-y-ṣ*, "mediate," can form words having to do with facilitating communication. Perhaps *m^{e}lîṣāh* is "a saying that puts things in different words," that is, a trope. Canney (1923: 135–36) proposes that the root means "speak fluently/clearly."

Explanation 6 seems the most reasonable, though it does not distinguish *m^{e}liṣah* from *mašal*. Judging from its few occurrences, however, *m^{e}liṣah* refers to artistic epigrams, never folk sayings, whereas *mašal* is both.

words of the wise: *Ḥăkamim* here seems to designate a specific group rather than simply men who are wise. The wise men mentioned so frequently in the proverbs are all who possess the skills for successful living. The headings in 22:17 and 24:23, however, apply the term to the learned authors of wisdom. Since the narrow sense of *ḥăkamim* as authors of wisdom sayings occurs only in the Prologue and in two headings, it appears that the term was applied to the authors of Wisdom in the latest stages of biblical Wisdom literature. (The headings presumably belong to the stage when the collections were joined because "too" in the heading "these too are by the wise" [24:23] shows awareness of other collections.) Elsewhere in Proverbs, the speech of the wise means either the content and manner of their speech in daily life (12:18; 14:3; 15:2, 7) or the message of their teachings (13:14; 16:23), not the formulations of specific proverbs.

enigmas: A *ḥidah* is an enigmatic, difficult saying that requires skilled interpretation. Often it is a riddle, posing a puzzle in a brief, concentrated form and challenging the audience to solve it, but not all *ḥidot* are riddles. Riddles are a form of play (sometimes serious play), sometimes with a wager, in which there is a winner and a loser, a right answer and a wrong one. Enigmas are a broader concept. In prophetic *ḥidot*, the prophet temporarily hinders communication in order to draw his listeners into his thoughts. Ultimately, however, he does not want to stump them. Likewise, a wise man's enigmas are a form of communication rather than a contest. In Sir 8:8, *ḥidot* is parallel to "the conversation" (*śiḥah*) of the wise. Samson's and the Queen of Sheba's enigmas are the only *ḥidot* in the Bible that are riddles in the narrow sense. This distinction means that we must be wary of assuming that the setting of riddle performance, such as that described in the Samson saga (see, e.g., Camp and Fontaine 1990) is relevant to the *ḥidot* of Wisdom literature. See the excursus on the enigma, later.

Are There Enigmas in Proverbs?

The Prologue promises that the book will teach the readers (at least the ones who are already wise) how to interpret the enigmas composed by the wise. Yet little in Proverbs seems truly enigmatic. A few sentences are cryptic, such as "The scorpion has two daughters, Give! Give!" (30:15) and "Who has gone up to heaven and come down? Who has gathered the wind in his bosom?" and so on (v 4). Some numerical proverbs *might* be riddles, if the original listeners were supposed to supply the final item. But for the readers of the written form of Proverbs, they are less puzzling because the answers are immediately given. The figure of personified Wisdom (1:20–33; 8:1–36; 9:1–6 + 11) calls for "translation" into literal, abstract terms, though the surface message of these passages is quite clear even without such decoding.[60]

On the surface, at least, little else in the book seems to be intrinsically enigmatic, philological and textual difficulties apart. Nevertheless, 1:6 implies that the book of Proverbs holds a fair number of enigmas; otherwise, how could the book teach us to understand them?

Passages elsewhere in the Bible that are labeled *ḥidot* are manifestly puzzling,[61] for example: "From the eater came forth food, from the strong came forth something sweet" (Judg 14:14); the great eagle came to the Lebanon and took the top of the cedar and brought it to the land of Canaan, and he took seed of the land, and so forth (Ezek 17:1–10).

The outstanding feature of an enigma is its immediate obscurity. Its surface meaning is strange and irrational and obviously (or almost obviously) not the author's direct intention. Enigmas require decipherment to make any sense of them, not just to enrich their meaning. Words and images must be read as tokens of entities and events in another domain. An enigma deliberately blocks immediate understanding by ambiguities and obscurities before allowing the audience to push through to a deeper understanding (Crenshaw 1980: 22).

Few commentators have paid much attention to the claim in Prov 1:6. N. H. Tur-Sinai (1947), however, sought to discover and solve numerous unrecognized *ḥidot* in Proverbs. Here is an example of a proverb that Tur-Sinai considers

[60] If my redactional analysis is correct, the Prologue came into the book earlier than the wisdom interludes (A, B, D, and E); see Essay 1, p. 322. Moreover, chapter 30 is probably a later appendix.

[61] Psalm 78, it must be admitted, does not seem very enigmatic.

to be a riddle: *ruaḥ ṣapon t^eḥolel gašem upanim niẓʿamim l^ešon sater* (25:23). The usual translation is "As a north wind brings rain, so a sly tongue brings angry looks." Tur-Sinai (pp. 29–30) reads the same words to mean, "Hide [your] spirit [= emotions] [before your superiors] and you will cause a rain [of good will], [but be careful that your expression does not reveal the way you feel], because an angry face is a language [that can reveal] what is hidden." (The Hebrew does permit this amazing expansion of the terse original.) Even if we accept Tur-Sinai's reading, the proverb is not a *ḥidah* by the criteria observed previously. It is not strange or meaningless on the face of it, and it does not demand decoding. If Tur-Sinai's interpretation is correct, the verse is either an ambiguous proverb (and ambiguity in itself does not make a proverb a *ḥidah*), or it is just an obscure proverb never before fully interpreted. In any case, a large part of Tur-Sinai's decodings are farfetched, often creating hapax legomena by appeal to Arabic and Akkadian or emending the MT unnecessarily—and only by decoding a proverb as an enigma can he know it *is* an enigma. Still, Tur-Sinai's often brilliant and always ingenious exegesis shows that Proverbs holds many deliberate ambiguities not hitherto appreciated.

M. Zer-Kavod (1975) similarly expands the notion of riddles to include coded historical allusions. For example, Prov 27:14 ("He who greets his neighbor in a loud voice early in the morning—it will be reckoned to him as a curse") is supposedly a riddle whose solution is Saul's greeting to Samuel in 1 Sam 15:12–13 (p. 10). Proverbs 13:23 alludes to Naboth's vineyard (p. 11). The medieval Midrash Proverbs took much the same approach. The midrashic hermeneutic explores the potential of a verse for reapplication rather than its meaning. The meaning of a proverb is the entire set of potential applications, not any particular application.

The hermeneutical problem in discovering enigmas is severe, for there is no limit to the number of proverbs that can be applied to something beyond the obvious. Indeed, having been informed in the Prologue that the wise will understand the enigmas to follow, one hesitates to volunteer for the other category by failing even to detect them. Nevertheless, there is reason for skepticism about the Prologue's claim that enigmas are so important in Proverbs that studying the book can teach the reader the skill of deciphering them. If the enigma were truly one of the main genres in Proverbs, we would expect to see an abundance of the earmarks of the enigma—weird images, pointless words, puzzling statements, images that clearly were ciphers—even if many other enigmas were disguised.

The author of the Prologue is asserting the importance of enigmas in the book of Proverbs because wisdom includes the prestigious realm of the esoteric, and he wants us to know that Proverbs, too, holds this sort of wisdom. He indicates that there is more in the ancient collections than meets the eye. In this way, he would pique the reader's interest and encourage careful study.

Ben Sira, too, believes that the words of the wise hold enigmas: "Do not abandon the discourse (*śiḥah*) of wise men, but busy yourself with their enigmas (*ḥidot*), for from them[62] you will gain instruction (*leqaḥ*), so as to stand in the presence of princes" (Sir 8:8). Such discourse can be found wherever wise men hold converse. See also Sir 47:17: "In song, proverb, enigma, and epigram you [Solomon] excited the peoples."

Exaggerated claims to esoteric knowledge have precedents in Egyptian book titles, in particular the Rhind Mathematical Papyrus (Peet 1923) and Onomasticon of Amenemope (Gardiner 1947). (See later, p. 72. Note that the latter is not the Amenemope of the famous instruction.) The authors apparently wished their works to receive the special respect accorded esoterica and mysteries.

The Prologue's assumption that the book holds a significant number of enigmas encourages the reader to seek them out, and this effort may itself *produce* enigmas—as it did for Tur-Sinai and Zer-Kavod. The messages of such "found" enigmas always accord with the basic message of the book and thus reinforce it. When that happens, the enigma then belongs to the act of interpretation, not the moment of composition.

On the riddle/enigma in the Bible, see Tur-Sinai 1924; Müller 1970; Crenshaw 1974: 239–45 and 1980; Camp and Fontaine 1990; see also Polk 1983, many of whose observations on the *mašal* apply more particularly to the enigma.

1:7. The Motto

1:7. *The fear of the Lord is the beginning of knowledge*: that is, the first step to the attainment of knowledge.

The book's motto is syntactically distinct from the rest of the Prologue but is an appropriate climax to it. This verse and 9:10, which gives the same advice, help frame Part I. (If I am right that 9:10 is part of a later insertion [see the comments on 9:7–10], the framing effect is later than the composition of the Prologue.) The initial line (1:7a; 9:10a) occurs in a variant form (with ḥokmah instead of *da*ʿ*at*) in Ps 111:10a. The line is provided with a different parallel in each verse.

There are three main ways of interpreting Prov 1:7a, depending on whether *re*ʾ*šit*, "first," means (1) first in time; (2) principle, essence, chief part; or (3) the best part in quality and importance, a sense supposedly related to *re*ʾ*šit*, "firstfruits." The Greek witnesses are divided on this issue; LXX^{A} (and descendants) has "best" (*aretē*); the other MSS read "first" (*archē*). Becker (1965: 214–15) advocates a combination of meanings 1 and 3, on the (dubious) grounds that, for the ancient Hebrews, the first was always the best (but what about Ishmael? Esau? Jer 11:10?). Delitzsch, Oesterley (p. 70), and Blocher (1977: 15) advocate meaning 2, Toy meaning 3.

The only commentators to understand *re*ʾ*šit* in the temporal sense alone seem to have been a few medievals. For instance, Ps.-Ibn Ezra says, "This means that

[62]The pronoun, masc. sg. in the original, has its antecedent in śiḥah (fem. sg.) + *ḥidot* (fem. pl.) as a single concept.

it [fear of the Lord] is the first thing to know, and afterwards one may learn and know everything else" (sim. Kaspi). This is, I believe, correct. Though the fear of God is undoubtedly excellent, at issue here is not qualitative superiority. Fear of God is not the best part of wisdom, because it is not *part* of wisdom, one component among many. The topic of the Prologue is the value of the book for study, which leads to and enhances wisdom. Likewise, the issue in 1:7, too, is the place of the fear of God in the learning process. This is a temporal priority.

A comparison of Prov 1:7 with 9:10 and 15:33 (in literal translation) supports this interpretation:

> "The fear of the Lord is the beginning of knowledge;
> fools despise wisdom and discipline" (1:7).
> "The beginning of wisdom (*tᵉḥillat-ḥokmah*) is the fear of the Lord, and knowledge of Holiness [= God] is understanding" (9:10).
> "The fear of the Lord is the instruction of wisdom (*musar ḥokmah*), and before honor comes humility" (15:33).

All three proverbs teach that the fear of the Lord is a prerequisite of wisdom. Proverbs 9:10 shows that the relationship is temporal, because *tᵉḥillah*, "beginning," never has a purely qualitative sense, as *re'šit* sometimes does (though rarely: Num 24:20; Deut 33:21; Amos 6:1; Jer 49:35; Ezek 48:14). Proverbs 15:33, too, expresses temporal priority: as humility precedes honor, so is the fear of the Lord a precursor and precondition of wisdom. The fear of the Lord is the *musar* of wisdom—its propaedeutic, the discipline that prepares the way to it. (Comparison with 18:12 also shows that 15:33b is a statement of temporal priority.) Ben Sira (1:14–15) reads 1:7 as an assertion of priority and develops it emphatically: the fear of the Lord was created for the faithful *in the womb*—indeed, "from eternity."

Fools despise wisdom and discipline: The word for "fools" is *'ĕwilim*, the morally perverse (see "Words for Folly," §3). Deep-seated attitudes, rather than lack of raw intelligence, prevent them from gaining wisdom.

McKane believes that 1:7 substitutes piety for educational discipline: "The acquisition of knowledge and wisdom does not now [in the later wisdom] depend on a severe educational discipline in which submission is made to the authority of a teacher and the pupil's attitudes formed by his assimilation of a body of traditional, empirically based wisdom. The context is now one of piety rather than education, and the source of authority is Yahweh" (p. 264). In this way, wisdom is made to hinge on submission to Yahweh and acceptance of his authority (pp. 264–65). McKane is drawing a false dichotomy between fear of God and education. The motto says that the fear of God is the starting point of the educational process, not a substitute for it. One must still actively pursue wisdom (2:1–4) in order to achieve it and to arrive at an understanding of the fear of God (2:5). Piety facilitates submission to educational discipline; it does not replace it.

Though the word *da'at* denotes the entire range of cognition (see "Words for Wisdom," §2), in Proverbs, it is synonymous with *ḥokmah* and refers to wisdom rather than all forms of knowledge. "The fear of the Lord is the first step to *daʿat*" (1:7) and the beginning of *ḥokmah* (9:10). If you absorb the teachings, "Wisdom will enter your heart, and *daʿat* be pleasant to your soul" (2:10). God gives *daʿat*, along with wisdom and good sense (2:6). The pupil is instructed to "take my instruction (*musari*) rather than silver, and *daʿat* rather than choice gold" (8:10). The righteous are delivered from danger by *daʿat* itself (11:9). Knowledge is recognized as valuable everywhere in the Bible, but its moral virtue depends on its object. In Proverbs, knowledge is regarded as inherently and inevitably a virtue; in other words, it is *wisdom* in the English sense of the term.

The Fear of God

It is appropriate, though perhaps not planned, that the theme of the fear of the Lord approximately brackets the present book of Proverbs, appearing both in 1:7 and in 31:30: "A woman who fears the Lord will be praised." Wisdom begins with and leads to the fear of the Lord (1:7; 2:5; 9:10). (Proverbs uses Yahweh ["Lord"] instead of "God," in accordance with its overall preference for the divine name Yahweh.)

Although wisdom and the fear of God are closely correlated, they are not precisely equated (see von Rad 1970: 93). Even Ben Sira, for all his insistence on the bond between the two virtues (1:11–2:18), allows an occasional decoupling: a God-fearing man might be deficient in understanding (*synesis*),[63] and a man of high intelligence (*phronēsis*) may transgress the Law (19:24). (Proverbs never allows for either possibility.) Job 28:28 does identify wisdom and the fear of God, but this is a polemical redefinition of human wisdom, which submerges it in piety.

Proverbs brings the two concepts into close conjunction without equating them. The purpose of the association is, as von Rad (1970: 93) observes, to define the status of wisdom rather than the place of the fear of God. The fear of God is inherently and self-evidently a religious virtue; it is wisdom that has an ethical question mark over it. (Think of the "wisdom" of the Egyptian magicians [e.g., Exod 7:11] or the corrupt royal advisers [e.g., Isa 19:11; 29:14].) The motto in 1:7 states an axiom of the epistemology of Proverbs, though not (as von Rad [1970: 94] believes) of Israelite thought in general. Proverbs 1:7 and similar statements (2:5; 9:10) affirm wisdom's religious validity by subordinating it in various ways to the fear of God. The fear of God is the sphere within which wisdom is possible and can be realized, the precondition for both wisdom and ethical behavior (cf. Nel 1982: 100).

Some scholars believe that in Wisdom literature the emotion of fear is softened into a confident sense of reverence and piety.[64] According to J. Becker, for

---

[63] Greek *synesis*, used in Sir 19:24a (Hebrew not extant), can represent a number of Hebrew words: *binah*, *tᵉbunah*, *daʿat*, *maddaʿ*, *śekel*, and *musar*.

[64] The noun *yirʾah* (fear) and the verb *yareʾ* may refer to everything from dread of danger (1 Sam 12:18) to gentle awe and respect, such as one feels toward the merciful God (Ps 130:4) or for one's parents (Lev 19:3).

example, the fear of God first meant the powerful awe felt in the presence of the divine Other, but this has been turned into an "ethical" concept, in which the attitude is largely depleted of the emotion of fear and becomes an equivalent of our abstract concepts of "religion" and "piety" (*Frömmigkeit*) (Becker 1965: 75, 184–85; cf. TDOT VI: 298; similarly Plath 1963: 68; von Rad 1970: 92; and others).

There is, however, no indication that the concept has become so bland in Proverbs or that it has lost the connotation of real fear. On the contrary, in Prov 14:27, fear of God is parallel to avoidance of lethal snares, which is motivated by dread, not reverence. The emotion in 24:21, "Fear the Lord, my son, and the king" is anxiety before superior powers, occasioned by the fact that both can cause sudden harm (v 22). But the term "fear" allows for a range of pertinent emotions. Proverbs 1:7 does not say anything about the quality of the fear. One person may worry about consequences, another may be uneasy about divine disapproval without thinking about retribution, and yet another may be in trepidation before the otherness of the holy. At the very start, a God-fearing child may simply worry that God will punish him for misdeeds.

At a more advanced stage of development, one attains wisdom, and with it an *understanding* of the fear of God: If you absorb the teachings and seek wisdom eagerly, "then you'll understand the fear of the Lord; and knowledge of God you will find" (2:5). (Likewise in Ps 34:12, the fear of the Lord is seen as something taught and learned.) At this stage, the pupil has progressed from unreflective fear to a cognitive awareness of what fear of God really is, and this is equivalent to knowledge of God. This is fear of God as *conscience*.

The history of the word "conscience"—it derives from Latin *conscientia*, "deep knowledge," and originally meant consciousness or inner, unverbalized thought—nicely points to the cognitive basis of conscience and suggests how fear and knowledge of God can be parallel, as in 2:5. The fear of God, in Dermot Cox's words, is "a form of conscience that calls for an intellectual adhesion to a principle, the divine order, the concept of goodness of life, and this is a guarantee of 'success.' . . . It is a state of mind, not an action; it is almost synonymous with knowledge (especially in Prov 1–9)."[65] Cox's definition is valid for the advanced stage of development. See further the comment at 2:5.

The fear of God is so valued because it motivates right behavior even when socially enforced sanctions do not exist or cannot be effective. A clear example is Gen 20:11, in which Abraham says he worried that he might be killed in Gerar, because "there is no fear of God in this place." No legal authority would have punished the Philistines if they had killed the unprotected stranger; only fear of a divine power might restrain them. Similarly, God knew that Abraham truly feared him when he saw that he did not spare his son (Gen 22:12), although he had no legal obligation to sacrifice him, and even though God did

[65] Cox 1982a: 83–90, esp. 89; similarly Becker, who speaks of the "intellectualizing tendency [*Zug*]" of the fear of God in Proverbs (1965: 217f.).

not reinforce his charge with threats. Thus, too, the Hebrew midwives in Egypt fear God and spare the Hebrew males (Exod 1:17), though no legal constraints force them to do so—quite the contrary! The Holiness Code invokes the fear of God as a motive for kind and respectful actions that belong to individual morality rather than to law (or at least are very difficult to enforce by law), such as honoring the aged (Lev 19:32), not overworking a slave (Lev 25:43), and not mistreating the handicapped (Lev 19:14); compare Lev 25:17, 36. Fear of God works even when fear of man is ineffective.

The power of the fear of God, apart from law and legal sanctions, makes it especially relevant to Wisdom literature. Wisdom deals almost entirely with behavior that is not governed by law or that, like adultery, is usually clandestine. The sages of Proverbs insist on the certainty of punishment, whether divinely enforced or naturally ensuing, yet the connection between act and consequence is usually delayed and far from obvious, especially to the young. Thus there is need for a motivation prior to and deeper than the promised retribution, and this is the fear of God.

The importance Israelite Wisdom assigns to the fear of God in motivating behavior is not paralleled in foreign Wisdom (see Plath 1963: 68–72). Fear of God in Egyptian and Mesopotamian Wisdom is one virtue among many. It is not isolated and identified as the initial step toward wisdom or a deep motive for wise behavior. Its importance in Wisdom literature is an Israelite innovation and shows the rootedness of Israelite Wisdom in Israelite thought generally.

Prologues to Wisdom Books

The Prologue is the first interpretation of the book of Proverbs. It contemplates the book as a whole and tells the reader its benefits and purposes. The present excursus considers the Prologue from the standpoint of its rhetoric and place in the Wisdom tradition. Many features of the Prologue have their precursor in Amenemope:

(1.1) The beginning of the teaching for life,
(2) the instruction for well-being,
(3) all the rules for relations with elders,
(4) the customs for (dealing with) courtiers,
(5) to know how to return an (oral) answer to one who says it,[66]
(6) to bring back a (written) report to one who sends it,[67]
(7) to guide one in the way of life,
(8) to make him healthy on earth,

[66] "It" probably refers to an oral message.

[67] That is, a letter.

(9) to make his heart descend to its shrine,[68]
(10) steering (him) away from evil,
(11) to save him from people's mouths,
(12) that he (instead) be praised in people's mouths,
(13–3.7) which the Supervisor of Fields . . . Amenemope son of Kanakht . . . made (for) his son, the youngest of his children, . . . Horemma-ʾakheru . . . [Extensive honorifics, official titles, and family details follow].[69]

1. Structure

Prov 1:1–6 is structured as a series of infinitives of purpose dependent on the title, with a pair of jussives in v 5 dividing the series into two groups. The concluding principle is an independent sentence (v 7). The only close counterpart to Proverbs' prologue is Amenemope's. Amenemope, too, announces the book's purposes in a series of infinitives syntactically dependent on the title. The formative construction in Amenemope's prologue is *r* + infinitive (*r* is equivalent to English "to"), which corresponds precisely to the Hebrew *l-* ("to") + infinitive in Prov 1:2–6. Amenemope's prologue is a single long sentence, whose complexity suggests a deliberate rhetoric flourish. Egyptian book titles usually consist of a nominal clause or one sentence. Amenemope maintains the form while elaborating it into a detailed and informative preface.

There is nothing quite like this structure elsewhere in Wisdom literature, even in the books with expansive openings. Ptahhotep's inner title uses a different infinitival construction to describe the circumstances of the teaching: "in [*m*] instructing the ignorant in knowledge, etc." (l. 47). The Rhind Mathematical Papyrus, also an "instruction" (*sbʾyt*), states its purpose by a dependent infinitive. The prologue of the Onomasticon of Amenemope[70] defines the book's purposes by a series of three infinitives; these, however, are bound genitivally to the nouns of the title. At the beginning of Anii, a short title is preserved,[71] but the continuation (cols. 13 and 14) is extremely fragmentary, and a prologue may have been lost. What remains is a variety of maxims. The following column (15) begins with an *inner* exordium, which differs from Amenemope's structurally. Nor are there parallels in other biblical books.

In its informational constituents as well, Proverbs' prologue bears a unique resemblance to Amenemope's. Amenemope begins with (a) the title proper, (b) a description of the book's subject matter, (c) promises of rewards, (d) ex-

---

[68]The heart is called "the god in man," and when it goes into its "shrine" (the *r-ib*, belly or torso), it can be effective in steering man in the right path.

[69]Amenemope 1.5–6 refers to oral and written exchanges; see Spiegel 1935: 6–8. The referent of the three masc. sg. pronouns in 1.7–12 is the reader of the instruction.

[70]Not the same as the author of the Instruction of Amenemope.

[71]"The beginning of the teaching of (ethical) instruction [*sbʾyt mtrw*], which the scribe Anii of the temple of Nefertari made."

tended identification of the author (the father), and (e) extended identification of the audience (the son). After a quoting verb ("he says") comes an exordium that demands attention and promises rewards. Proverbs has equivalents to all these elements except the identification of the son (e). Both books separate the prologue, which commends the book for its educational value, from the exordium, which calls the son (and the reader) to attention. One significant difference is that in Amenemope, the exordium is the first of thirty numbered units (chapters), whereas in Prov 1–9, each unit (lecture) has its own exordium.

The unique correlations between the prologues of these two books strengthens the hypothesis that Proverbs is drawing on a tradition that descends specifically from Amenemope rather than from the ancient Wisdom tradition generally. It is not only in 22:17–23:10 that we see its traces but also in scattered verses elsewhere[72] and in the Prologue, which was added late in the book's development. That is not to say that any of the authors of Proverbs knew the book of Amenemope itself, even in a Hebrew form. The nature of the affinities between the two, which lie in formal structure and background assumptions rather than in wording and specifics, points to a more diffuse influence. Amenemope's impress on Israelite Wisdom thus was deep and wide. In other words, Amenemope's book as a whole (and not just a few maxims[73]) entered Israelite wisdom and became a source of ideas and formal usages, and these were recycled and transmitted, eventually influencing authors at some remove.

2. *Author and Speaker, Listener and Reader*

The speaking voice in the Prologue is not that of the father in Part I or of the various sages whose teachings the book preserves. The author of the Prologue speaks as the editor, or at least the transmitter, of Solomon's wisdom. Borrowing a term from 25:1, where a similar distinction is implied, we can designate the author of the Prologue the *maʿătiq*, the "assembler" or "transmitter."

The implied reader of the Prologue is not the son addressed in the lectures of Prov 1–9 but the adult teacher,[74] who is encouraged to use the book both for the instruction of the young and for his own edification. In a sense, the audience of the Prologue is aligned with the father who declaims the lectures, who is the prototype of all parental teachers. The audience of the Prologue is a reader, though the Prologue sees the youngster as the primary audience of the teachings proper. In the lectures, the internal audience (the audience in the text) is a listener, namely, the son. This duality is true in most Wisdom books.

The Prologue of Amenemope has as its implied audience not Amenemope's son Kanakht but future readers, referred to in the third person. The prologue presents the book as an instruction in knowing the rules of courtiers, steering him from evil, and so on, which Amenemope made for his son Kanakht. In other words, the book records teachings *to* Kanakht, in the second person,

---

[72] See the Introduction, p. 18.
[73] As argued by J. Ruffle (1977).
[74] Again, "teachers" include parents as well as schoolmasters.

which the author expects to be of general interest. Again in the epilogue, chapter 30, a dual use is envisioned. The thirty chapters, Amenemope says, "make the ignorant wise. If they are read to the ignorant, he is purified by them" (26.10–12; cf. AEL 2.162). This is precisely the orientation of Prov 1:2–4, which tells the educated reader that the *mᵉšalim* are for use in instructing the young and ignorant, though it is not clear if they are to be read *to* the youth or *by* him under the teacher's supervision.

Amenemope continues: "Be filled with them, put them in your heart, and become an interpreter of them,[75] who interprets them in teaching"[76] (28.13–15). This is precisely the orientation of Prov 1:5–6, which extols the book's value to the wise man, who can thereby enhance his learning and his *leqaḥ*—his teaching.

3. *Speaking and Writing*

These two dimensions of discourse—author to (adult) reader, father to (youthful) son—represent the two fundamental media of teaching: written and oral.

Speech and writing coexist in Proverbs. The lectures in Prov 1–9 consistently (but perhaps fictively) present themselves as spoken discourse. The command to "hear" does not in itself prove orality, but the numerous injunctions to "give ear," "pay attention," and the like pertain best to a dramatic setting of oral counsel. This setting is explicit in 4:3–4: "For when I was a child with my father, a tender darling before my mother, he gave me instruction and said. . . ." Oral communication is presupposed in the instruction to Lemuel (31:1). At the same time, the Prologue obviously has a reading audience in mind. It is an introduction to a book meant for didactic use and for personal study by the wise. The image of wisdom as written appears also in 22:20: "Have I not written for you thirty" (sc., sayings).[77]

Speaking and writing are intertwined also in the self-conception of Egyptian Wisdom. The instructions often indicate an oral setting. Ptahhotep's introduction reports that he spoke the subsequent instructions to his son and successor (l. 51; AEL 1.63). Duachety's instruction was "made" for his son as they sailed together to the palace school. Then he spoke the instructions (3.9–4.1; AEL 1.185). Apparently, we are to understand that he wrote the work in the boat, but *iri sb'yt* does not mean "to deliver a teaching." In any case, there are two phases, "making" the teaching and speaking it, as indicated by the sentence "then he spoke to him," using a verb form which indicates sequential action. Duachety's instruction was delivered orally to his son as they sailed together to the palace school (3.9–4.1; AEL 1.185).

At the same time, there is a concept of Wisdom as written. Papyrus Beatty IV contains an encomium on the *writings* of the ancient sages (vso. 2.5–12; AEL

[75] Lit. "a man of interpreting them."
[76] Others, "as a teacher."
[77] Vocalizing *šᵉlošim*; see the Commentary.

2.176f.). Merikare is instructed to imitate the ancestors, whose words remain in their books (l. 35; AEL 1.99). Duachety's refers to the teaching he has "put before" his son and subsequent generations (11.4; AEL 1.191). In Anii's epilogue, there is mention of a son's reciting the sayings in the books (22.15; AEL 2.144). Note that written literature is *recited*. Amenemope unequivocally describes his teachings as a book he has written (§30; AEL 2.162), yet he also says, "Give your ears to hear the things that are said (§1; cf. AEL 2.149). Anii's instruction was ostensibly declaimed, and it concludes in an oral exchange between father and son.

In Mesopotamian Wisdom, Shuruppak is said to have spoken his teachings to his son in ancient times (ll. 1–8; Alster 1974: 35), and then his wisdom was recorded for posterity (ll. 280–81; Alster 1974: 51).[78]

The epilogue of Kagemeni reverses the expected sequence of oral to written teaching. The vizier gives his children his teachings in writing, and they subsequently read it aloud: "Then he said to them: 'All that is written in this book—heed it just as I have said it.' . . . And they recited it in accordance to what was written" (2.4–5; cf. AEL 1.60). Even in this reversed procedure, the moment of instruction, the reception of the teaching, is supposed to be oral. The teaching is *activated* by oral declamation.

The Wisdom tradition is self-consciously *literary*, but it uses a genre setting (*Sitz im Leben*) that was originally oral, namely, parental advice, the most fundamental form of education. That does not mean that *these* texts were ever declaimed by the authors to their children, but that this setting is the way the authors want their teachings understood. Writing makes the teachings available to all, but it does not cancel out their familial use, for a literate man may write a book for his family's future edification. This is exactly what happened with the medieval Jewish ethical wills.

4. *Wisdom as Character Education*

The Prologue advertises the book's value to pedagogy on two levels. It will help the pupil "learn," "understand," and "absorb" wisdom, and it will impart to him cunning and shrewdness (vv 2–4). Morality is the subject to be taught: "in absorbing the discipline [*musar*] of insight: righteousness, justice, and rectitude" (1:3). The virtues the book will inculcate constitute both the content of the instruction and its rewards. To be sure, wisdom will also bring exterior rewards—life, health, wealth, favor, and well-being—but these are not among the inducements offered in the Prologue.

The Prologue's promise that the book will inculcate wisdom and—consequently, the ethical virtues of righteousness, justice, and rectitude—presupposes

---

[78]Ahiqar addresses his "son" (l. 96). The relation between the auditor of the sayings and Ahiqar's nephew and adopted son, Nadin, who, in the frame narrative, betrays his uncle, is unclear, but it is likely that the Ahiqar's recorded wisdom was what he taught Nadin orally before the betrayal (l. 9). This is the case in the Syriac versions and some others.

that these qualities are something the reader already knows to be desirable. This shows that the Prologue is addressed to the mature individual, the teacher-scholar. Perhaps they were to use the book in school-teaching; if so, this is a re-deployment of a genre that was originally familial.

5. Wisdom as Interpretation

The same book will help the learned reader further his learning (v 5), in particular by developing skills in the interpretation of literary wisdom (v 6). This claim is explicit in 1:6 and implicit in 1:3–4. "Understanding [*l^ehabin*] words of understanding" (1:2) means to interpret them, to penetrate their inner sense. The "words of understanding" (meaning wise, perceptive words) are the teachings of this book and others like it. Elsewhere, mention of the words of the wise has to do either with the content and manner of their speech in daily life (12:18; 14:3; 15:2, 7) or with the message of their teachings (13:14; 16:23), rather than with specific proverbial utterances or writings. The Prologue regards the sayings in Proverbs as *text* that must be studied and interpreted, not just heard and obeyed. This is so both for the youth (vv 2–4) and the educated (vv 5–6). In other words, the *m^ešalim* are viewed as Wisdom *literature*, not just wisdom.

Although the statement of purpose employs some terms drawn from elsewhere in the book, it also introduces new concepts. These pertain to the study of wisdom as literature. The locution *l^ehabin ʾimrey binah*, "in understanding words of understanding" (1:2), is not used elsewhere. The words *ḥidah* ("enigma") and *m^eliṣah* ("epigram") appear in Proverbs only in 1:6. In fact, outside the headings (1:1; 10:1; 25:1), even *mašal* is not a prominent concept.[79] The author of the Prologue is thus *reinterpreting* the book by describing its contents and goals in new terms and from a new perspective.

Elsewhere, references to the book's own teachings, as in chapters 1–9, usually assume that their import lies within the grasp of anyone with good intentions and moderate persistence. To be sure, one must *seek* wisdom, but that means to assimilate the values of the teachings and to *be* wise, not to work hard to get at their message. Basically the father's words of wisdom need only be heard and obeyed, not probed and interpreted.[80] The Prologue alone regards the interpretation of proverbs and enigmas as a goal in itself or views proverbs as an object of explication.

Though the Prologue is one of the latest units of the book, its concept of wisdom as a text that requires interpretation and that trains the reader in hermeneutic skills is ancient and goes back to Egyptian instructions. Amenemope introduces his teachings by urging: "Give your ears to hear the things that are

[79]In Prov 26:7 and 9 (variants of the same proverb), *mašal* refers to folk sayings, for these, rather than ethical-sapiential advice, are what a fool is likely to try to employ.

[80]This is true even when *hebin*, "understand," has wisdom words as object, namely *ʿormah* "cunning" // *leb* "heart" (8:5) and *daʿat* "knowledge" (19:25; 29:7). These phrases mean to gain cunning, intelligence, and knowledge rather than to interpret these things (see comment on 8:5).

said. Set your heart to interpret them" (§1; cf. AEL 2.149). He concludes by charging his son:

> Be filled with [these teachings],
> put them in your heart,
> and you will become one who interprets them,
> who interprets them as a teacher.
>
> (§30; cf. AEL 2.162)

"Interpret" translates *wḥʿ*, lit. "untie," "loosen," hence "explain." This represents a stage beyond "hearing" and "receiving" the teaching and corresponds to Hebrew *hebin*, "understand," "perceive" (Shupak 1993: 47). The ability to penetrate and analyze another's words is necessary for effectively delivering an opinion in council (Ptahhotep 366, 369 [AEL 1.70]; "A Man to His Son" 2.5 [AW 189]). One can *wḥʿ* ("untie," "open," which is to say, "enlighten") the mind itself. The Onomasticon of Amenemope identifies itself as *sbʾyt wḥʿ ib*, "the instruction for enlightening the heart." The intelligent person is called *wḥʿ ib*, lit. "one opened [or disentangled] of heart." Hence, when the Instruction of Amenemope says that the reader should learn to *wḥʿ* his sayings, it does not imply that they are enigmatic but rather that they contain much meaning and can be unfolded or (to use the etymological counterpart) *explicated*.

Pap. Chester Beatty IV regards book-study as a means to understanding wisdom: "When you become skilled [*sšsʾ*] in the writings, you will penetrate [*ʿq*] the teachings" (vso. 4.6; repeated in 4.9). As in Amenemope §30, interpretive skill is seen as a tool for textual penetration and a goal in itself.

Anii's exordium or inner introduction similarly promises to make the pupil "a wise man who can penetrate [*ʿq*] words" (15.4).[81] Later, Anii says that studying books (not only his own) makes one's own speech effective: "When you are skilled in the writings, all that you say will be accomplished. Penetrate the writings, put them in your heart. Then all your words will be effective" (20.4–5). The writings teach eloquence by serving as models thereof.

Qohelet's wisdom included interpretation of *mešalim*: "Furthermore, Qohelet was wise: he constantly taught the people knowledge; and he listened, and investigated, and composed many sayings (12:9). ("Listened," *heʾĕzin*, is literally "gave ear," reminiscent of the charge frequent in Egyptian instructions.)

Ben Sira too considers the wise man an interpreter of texts. These embrace the entire sweep of sacred literature and the wisdom of the ancients, including parables and enigmatic proverbs (39:1–3). For Ben Sira, the *ḥakam* is a scholar as well as a speaker of wisdom (Sir 38:24 + 33b; 39:1–3). "Scholar" is the usual meaning of *ḥakam* in Rabbinic Hebrew as well. Study of words (that is to say, proverbs such as Ben Sira's own) brings wisdom: "Those intelligent in words—they too will become wise, and pour forth precise proverbs" (18:29).

---

[81] Quack (1994: 86) divides the line differently and reads this as an imperative: "Dring in die Worte ein, mach [sie] dir zu eigen" ("Enter in the words, make [them] your own").

All these authors regard wisdom instructions as texts for literary study as well as guides for living. None of the books, however, actually tells *how* to penetrate and interpret the writings. Apparently it is enough to read them, with a desire to comprehend and absorb the message, and the skill will grow by the exercise. This approach resembles the Egyptian practice of teaching mathematics through model calculations.

Lecture I. Avoid Gangs (1:8–19)

TRANSLATION

Hear my teaching

1:8 Listen, my son, to your father's instruction;
neglect not your mother's teaching,
9 for they are a graceful garland for your head,
and a necklace for your throat.

Avoid lawless companions

10 My son,
if criminals lure you,
don't give in.
11 If they say,
"Come with us, let's lurk for blood,
waylay the innocent man without cause.
12 Let us swallow them alive, just as Sheol does,
(swallow) the blameless ones, like those who go down to the Pit.
13 Treasure of all sorts we'll seize,
our houses cram with loot.
14 Throw in your lot with us,
we'll all share one purse"—
15 my son, don't go in the way with them;
don't step upon their path,
16 for their feet run to harm;
they rush to shed blood.

They are self-destructive

17 For "No bird is caught in a net
set out before his eyes."
18 Yet *they* lie in wait—for their very own blood,
set an ambush—for their very own lives.

All sinners are self-destructive

19 This is what happens to everyone who grasps ill-gotten gain:
it robs him who holds it of life.

COMMENTARY

1:8–9. Exordium

Two lines call for attention (8), and two lines (9) motivate the call.

1:8. *Listen* [*šᵉmaʿ*]: A verb for "listen" or a synonym begins each lecture and often recurs. The frequent use of the verb *šamaʿ* does not prove that instruction in Wisdom was predominantly oral (contrary to Gemser); see the comment on 1:5. "Listen" or "hear" can connote both understanding and obedience. In Egyptian Wisdom, love of hearing was recognized as an inherent prerequisite for educability; see esp. the praise of hearing in Ptahhotep ll. 575–97, AEL 1.75.

instruction/teaching [*musar/torah*]: In the introduction to the lectures, these terms designate the lesson about to be delivered. In other words, the verse is not a general admonition to obey one's parents, but an injunction to hear the instruction and teaching in vv 10–19. Each lecture is *an* instruction and *a* teaching.

Outside Proverbs, Hebrew *torah* "instruction" is predominantly for God's Law. This is especially characteristic of the Deuteronomic terminology. *Miṣwah*, "precept" (first used in 2:1), likewise usually refers to God's commandment. Nevertheless, these are basically secular words and carry with them no allusion to divine law.

With regard to Torah and commandments, G. Baumann (1996: 295) observes that outside Proverbs, *torah* and *miṣwah* with the possessive suffix are (with one exception each) always divine. Thus the suffixed forms in Proverbs "transgress or blur the border between human and divine commandments" (Baumann 1996: 295). But theological conclusions cannot be deduced from this incidental grammatic phenomenon. The distribution of the forms has nothing to do with theology, as the exceptions (Jer 35:18; Ps 78:1) and equivalent bound-forms show. There are far more references to divine than to human law and commandments in the Bible, and this gives more opportunity for certain types of usages to appear with greater frequency.

Baumann (pp. 298–99) finds some further parallels between wisdom in Proverbs and law in Deuteronomy: both Yahweh's and the teacher's instructions and commands are to be obeyed; Deuteronomy places love of Yahweh parallel to obedience to his Torah (esp. 6:2–3, 5; 19:9); and Proverbs makes the Wisdom figure the object of love and obedience in Prov 8 (p. 298). These and other parallels in Prov 1–9 imply, in Baumann's view, that wisdom's commandments and instructions are divine in origin (p. 299).

But even if Proverbs and Deuteronomy use similar terms and motifs in speaking of wisdom instructions and Yahweh's Torah, that does not mean that these come from the same source, only that terms of honor learned from the one book are used in the other. Even if Prov 1–9 is appropriating some of the terminology of Deuteronomy,[82] the author is not equating obedience to God with obedience to wisdom. However, there is bound to be some confluence of effects because God's commands are inevitably the wise thing to do.

---

[82]Deuteronomy's affinities to Wisdom were studied in detail by M. Weinfeld (1972: 244–81), who sought to prove the dependence of the former on the latter. The issue of the place of Proverbs in the broader context of Israelite thought will be considered elsewhere.

father's instruction: The setting of father-son education is mentioned in 15:5. It is prominent in Parts I and III and present in the background in Parts IV ("my son" occurs in 27:11) and II (in 19:27).

Fathers as Teachers

The terms "father" and "mother" are sometimes understood as epithets of other persons. Some older Jewish identifications are: "father" = God, "mother" = Israel (*b. Ber.* 35a; *Pesaḥ.* 50b; *Sanh.* 102a); "father" = God, "mother" = Torah (Radaq, Rashi); "father" = written Torah, "mother" = oral Torah (*Midr. Prov.*, Alsheikh). Kaspi (and most modern scholars) also treat the terms as figurative, equating the "father" with the teacher and the "son" with his pupil (Kaspi seems to be the first to suggest this). (The "mother" is ignored in this equation.) Toy believes that the usage "indicates an organized system of instruction" (p. 14). Delitzsch is so certain that the putative father is really a schoolteacher that he psychologizes the paternal terminology: "the teacher feels himself as a father by virtue of his benevolent, guardian, tender love" (p. 59). But even if Proverbs, or just Part I, was in fact composed for school-teaching, the terms "father" and "son" are meant literally. The terms do not display, but—at most—*disguise* a school situation.

The speaker in Prov 1–9 is a father speaking to his son. The parallelism between the mother's teaching and the father's indicates that they are of the same kind, and "mother" can hardly signify schoolmarm. The reminiscence in 4:3 shows family education. Within the text, the speaker is the listener's biological father. This setting may be a fiction for any particular text, but the fiction would make sense only if it reflected a recognized reality.

Most wisdom books are addressed to the author's son or sons,[83] who are identified in the title (see Kitchen 1979: 243–45). The sons are, at least by convention, biological offspring,[84] never unrelated pupils. Some copies of the Ptahhotep identify the author as "Ptahhotep Senior" (*wr*) and the pupil as "Ptahhotep Junior" (*šry*) (Fischer-Elfert 1997: 20). The father-to-son setting is authentic in some books. Amenemope, with the modest station of its author and the circumstantial details about the author's son and wife, is certainly such a case; the instructions of Duachety and Anii too can be assigned to their ostensible authors for similar reasons.

---

[83]The Instruction for Kagemeni is spoken to the old vizier's "children" (*ẖrdw*, male det, pl.) (Epilogue). The "Loyalist Instruction" is addressed to the teacher's "children" (*msw*), written in some manuscripts with male + female + plural determinatives, in others with the male + plural signs only. The inclusion of the female determinative, though possibly a reflex of a common writing of the word, suggests that for some scribes the inclusion of daughters among the auditors was not unthinkable.

According to D. Harrington (1996: 58, 83–84), a fragmentary Qumran text (4Q415 frag. 2, ii 1–9) may address advice to a female, in the 2 fem. sg. imperative. The reading of relevant words is, however, very doubtful.

[84]See note 78.

In Proverbs, the presence of the son is a genre formula that the author continues but does not flesh out, especially outside Part I. The narrator of Qohelet speaks to "my son" (12:12). Ben Sira's true audience is his readership: all the "uneducated" who desire wisdom (51:23–30). In Ben Sira the form is vestigial, traceable only in an occasional reference to the audience as "my son" (e.g., 3:17; 4:1; and often) or "sons" (41:14) and to himself as "father" (3:1a). Yet this book was, as we know, preserved within the author's family, for his grandson received it and translated it.

Very few biblical texts show men involved in raising and educating their children. Sometimes they are shown to be inadequate. Jacob spoiled Joseph and allowed severe dissension in the family (Gen 37). We are told what David *should* have done to his son Adonijah when he was bad: he should have "scolded him" [*ʿăṣabo*] and said, "Why have you done this?" (1 Kgs 1:6). This is the gist of chastisement—calling a person to account for his deeds. Proverbs considers chastisement a vital component of moral education. In legal-homiletic texts, the father is required to interpret sacred objects, rites, and laws in response to his children's curiosity (Exod 12:26–27; 13:8, 14–15; Josh 4:6–7, 21–22). The interpretation is always a reference to God's historical acts of deliverance. In Deut 6:6–7, teaching one's children about God's commands is enjoined as an ongoing duty: "And these words, which I command you today, shall be upon your heart. And you shall teach them to your children and you shall speak of them, when you sit in your house, when you walk in the way, when you lie down, and when you rise up."

Wisdom literature teaches how to educate one's own sons. Ptahhotep tells his son how to raise his own sons: "Make (= raise) a son who pleases god" (197f.).[85] If he is obedient to your teachings, embrace him, but if he is disobedient, he must be punished (197–219). Ptahhotep also counsels: "You should teach your son to be a listener" (566; cf. AEL 1.74). (For Ptahhotep, "listening" epitomizes the essential moral-intellectual virtues.) Absorbing wisdom is an ongoing duty, for a man must be able to instruct his own children. Ptahhotep says that "both [the wise man's] ears hear what is useful for his son" (531; cf. AEL 1.73). Anii tells his son to raise his own children the way his *mother* raised *him*, because if he doesn't, she will be very angry (21.2; cf. AEL 2.141).[86] Ben Sira especially expounds on this duty (30:1–13).

The duty is ongoing. Some Egyptian sages express the hope that their teachings will be transmitted to future generations. If one successfully educates son, says Ptahhotep, then "when he grows old and reaches veneration, he will speak likewise to his children, renewing the teaching of his father. . . . He speaks to (his) children; then they may speak (to) their children" (590–96; cf. AEL 1.75). Ptahhotep himself is teaching in accordance with "the words of those who heard,

[85] AEL 1.66 translates: "If you are a man of worth and produce a son by the grace of God. . . ."

[86] The passage is difficult. We should probably translate: "And set your eye on your child (and) on ⟨*n*⟩ your entire child-rearing, in the same way as your mother did."

the ways of the ancestors" (30–32; AEL 1.63). Duachety likewise wants his words passed on to his descendants (XXXg; AEL 1.191).

Proverbs reiterates the value of paternal discipline and chastisement (13:24; 22:15; 29:15, 17). Prov 22:6 speaks of the importance of shaping character early on: "Educate a child according to his (proper) way, and even when he is old he will not depart from it." The Prologue presents the book in its entirety as an aid to teaching children, "in giving to the callow cunning, to the young knowledge of shrewdness (1:4). Sons, fathers, and sons who will be fathers, are supposed to learn about fathering from this book.

mother's teaching: The father identifies the instruction he is about to deliver as both his own and his wife's (sim. 6:20), even though the mother never speaks. In the present passage, as in 4:3 and 6:20, "mother" serves mainly to provide a parallel term to "father" (thus Haran 1972: 248, who designates it a "poetic automatism"). There is no follow-up to the mention of the mother, and the first-person forms are singular: "my," not "our" (4:2). The speaker of the teachings is the father alone. Nevertheless, the mention of the mother is not a mere formality, for she too is a teacher and a source of authority in the home.

Some commentators (e.g., Ibn Yaḥyah, Delitzsch) distinguish between the father's stricter, disciplinary *musar* (v 8a) and the mother's less stern *torah* (v 8b), which is only verbal. But *musar* is not necessarily harsh, and in any case, both nouns refer to the same teaching, which is about to begin. "Mother" and "father" are a parental unit, and what is said about one here applies to the other. Saʿadia recognizes that *musar* and *torah* form a pair ("It is the Hebrews' practice to ascribe two things to two persons, implying that both things apply to each separately").

Mothers as Teachers

Though inevitably a mother would instruct her children every day in practical, moral, and religious matters, the Bible says little about this crucial role. C. Camp reasonably posits that within the home, the Israelite woman had high status and authority by virtue of her role as mother (1985: 81–82).[87] In the Decalogue, God commands obedience to one's mother as well as one's father (Exod 20:12; Deut 5:16).

A mother undoubtedly would give advice and instruction to her sons, and perhaps even pronounce wisdom instructions in literary form, as does Lemuel's mother (31:1–9). Prov 31:10–31 illustrates the centrality of the woman in the household, and teaching is among her duties and graces: "She opens her mouth in wisdom, and the teaching of kindness is on her tongue" (v 26). But we do not learn more about how and what she would have taught her children.

[87] D. Harrington (1996: 47) says that the Qumran Sapiential Work A (4Q 416 iii 15–19) sees the mother as a source of esoteric doctrine. However, where Harrington translates "they [that is, your parents] uncovered your ear to the mystery that is to be," the verb is actually singular, "he [God] uncovered."

Prov 23:22 tells the reader/learner: "Listen to [or "obey"] your father, the one who begot you, and do not show contempt when your mother grows old." Since "do not show contempt" (*ʾal tabuz*) is the antithesis of "listen to" (*šᵉmaʿ l-*), the form of contempt intended is the ignoring or despising of advice and instruction, synonymous with "do not abandon" (that is, your mother's teaching) in 1:8b and 6:20b.

In some Egyptian instructions, the father charges the son to obey his mother as well as him and identifies her teaching with his own. Duachety concludes his instruction with the words, "Praise God for your father and your mother, who set you on the way of life. See these things that I have set before you and your children's children" (XXXf–g; cf. AEL 1.191). Both parents set the child on "the way of life" (or "the way of the living"), which is what Wisdom literature is all about (see Amenemope §1 [1.7], previously). The specific words of wisdom are the father's, but their substance comes from the mother too. The father in Proverbs is giving expression to the essentials of parental instruction and can thus present his own words as an expression of his wife's teaching.[88] Men and women shared effective power within the Israelite household, which could be called a "mother's house" (*beyt ʾem*[89]) as well as a "father's house" (*beyt ʾab*[90]). It is appropriate, then, to set her alongside the father as a source of educational authority. While the speaker in Prov 1–9 is the father (contrary to Brenner and van Dijk-Hemmes 1993: 113–26; see p. 256), the voice of the teacher is not simply the male voice. It is (at least by its own testimony) the *parental* voice.

1:9. *graceful garland* [*liwyat ḥen*]: This is not primarily a garland that itself looks lovely (though it does). As Ehrlich observes, a *liwyat ḥen* is a garland that *gives* its wearer favor in the eyes of others, just as *ʾeben ḥen* (lit. "a stone of grace") means (as Prov 17:8 shows) a stone that *induces* favor toward its bearer. ("Attractive" suggests the force of the phrase.) The garland and necklace may be a sign of public honor, as suggested by Ibn Yaḥyah; compare the award of a necklace or torque as a mark of honor in Gen 41:42 and Dan 5:7. In other words, wisdom beautifies *you* in the eyes of others.

necklace: "Necklace" is *ʿănaqim*, which means an ornament made up of multiple strands. An *ʿanaq* is a strand or chain, judging from the usage in MH (e.g., *b. ʿErubin* 54a; Yalqut, Psalms §675), in which it means "chain" (*b. B. Bat.* 75a).

Ornament Imagery in Proverbs

The motif of teachings as ornaments for head and neck recurs in 3:3 ("Tie them about your neck, inscribe them on the tablet of your heart"); 4:9 ("[Wisdom

[88]A Ptolemaic Egyptian tomb inscription refers to a woman's written wisdom. Renpet-nefret, as "expert with (her) mouth, sweet in speech, excellent in counsel in her writings" (from the tomb of Petosiris; trans. Fox 1985b: 350).

[89]Gen 24:28; Ruth 1:8; Cant 3:4; 8:2. This is always the nuclear family unit.

[90]Num 34:14; 17:17; Josh 22:14; and often. The *beyt ʾab* is usually an extended family or a dynasty.

will] place a graceful garland on your head; grant you a splendid diadem"); 7:3 "Bind [my words] on your fingers, inscribe them on the tablet of your heart." Similar images are latent in 6:21 ("Bind them always upon your heart, tie them about your throat") and 3:22 ("[The teachings will] give vitality to your throat, grace to your neck"). Ben Sira elaborates the image into an entire set of finery (6:29–31).

The necklace/garland metaphor refers sometimes to learning, sometimes to its rewards. *Learning*: In 3:3 and 6:21, the image signifies the absorption and retention of the teachings. Prov 3:3 and 7:3 also use a tablet metaphor to the same end, and 7:3 speaks of attaching the teachings to one's fingers, apparently as rings. Prov 2:1 has a latent metaphor of memory as storage. Memory metaphors are discussed at 3:3bc. *Rewards*: in 1:9, 3:22, and 4:9 (also Sir 6:29–31), the metaphors signify the benefits of learning and thus bolster the exhortation to pursue and retain wisdom.

Images of ornaments and amulets in Deuteronomy signify remembering and treasuring God's law. Deut 6:6–9 says that the words of God's commandments are to be "on your heart," and "you shall bind them as a sign upon your hand and they shall be for frontlets between your eyes. And you shall write them upon the doorposts of your house and upon your gates." (Compare 11:18–20.) Exod 13:9 says that the dedication of firstlings shall be (figuratively) "a sign upon your hand and a reminder between your eyes, that the law of the Lord may be in your mouth"; similarly v 16.[91] In Exod 13:9, as in Prov 3:3 and 6:21, the objects that (figuratively) are bound to the hands and forehead are mnemonic devices. In Deuteronomy, as in Prov 1:9; 3:22; and 4:9, the objects are symbolic of what is to be remembered. In all these passages, the apotropaic role of the devices and inscriptions is almost entirely displaced by a mnemonic or symbolic function. Only a trace of the apotropaic use is retained in Prov 4:9 and 6:21–22, which speak of the protection the teachings offer, and in 3:22, which says that they give "vitality to your throat."

Kayatz (1966: 107–18) associates the ornaments with particular Egyptian practices. High officials and the vizier wore the icon of Maʿat (Truth and Justice) on a necklace about their throats to symbolize the conformity of their life with Maʿat, and the icon served as an amulet as well. In the mortuary cult, necklaces with Maʿat emblems were used as symbols and amulets. Kayatz also associates the necklaces in Proverbs with the multistranded *wsḫ*-collar, which was ritually laid on statues of gods in their temples (pp. 110–11). She also derives the head garland from an Egyptian cultic device, the Garland of Justification (pp. 111–17). For the dead, this garland symbolizes vindication from accusations and consequently the achievement of eternal life. The Garland of Justification has similar connotations when offered to the sun god and the king.

The Egyptian comparisons do not, however, correlate well with the garland and necklace imagery in Proverbs. The plural *ʿănaqim*, as it appears in this verse,

---

[91] Exod 13:3–16 apparently belongs to a Deuteronomic or proto-Deuteronomic redaction.

means a necklace made up of strands; nothing is said of any pendant *on* the strands. The *wsḥ*-collar was multistrand, but its role was in cult, not in personal life, and it was for the benefit of the *donor*, not its recipient, the god. And the connotation of vindication in the judgment of the dead, essential to the Garland of Justification, is not relevant to the "garland of grace" in Proverbs. In any case, the ornaments must have been a local custom familiar to the reader; otherwise the imagery and the concepts associated with them would be too fuzzy to be effective. A better comparison would be to the wreaths and necklaces worn by the guests in the numerous banquet scenes in Egyptian tombs as well as in Hellenistic banquets. This too does not show a direct connection, but it does exemplify the widespread use of these adornments as tokens of honor and pleasant feelings.

1:10–18. Lesson: Shun Violence

1:10. This verse (and thus the lecture as a whole) looks like an exposition of 16:29: "The violent man lures his fellow and leads him in a way that is not good."

my son: The vocative is given considerable highlighting here by being placed before the conditional. This suggests the earnestness of paternal communication.

criminals: Or "sinners." As the *qattāl* pattern and the use of the word elsewhere show, these *ḥaṭṭa'im* are habitual, dyed-in-the-wool offenders, criminals and not occasional "sinners."

don't give in:

MT *tb'* (*tōbē'*) is an apocopated form of *t'bh* (*tō'beh*), from *'-b-h* "be willing," with elision of the *aleph*. The writing of the final vowel with *-ē'* is apparently an Aramaism; see GKC §75*hh*. The writing *t'bh*, occurring in many MSS, is a normalization. For the replacement of the final *he'* by *'aleph*, compare *yōre'* in Prov 11:25, where, however, the *segol* is maintained.

1:11. *Come with us* [*lᵉkah 'ittanu*]: The robbers' invitation resembles the adulteress's (7:18)—and Lady Wisdom's (9:5).

Niṣpᵉnah (G-stem) is reflexive here; the verb is used similarly in Ps 56:7 and perhaps Ps 10:8.

blood/the innocent man: This is a distributed hendiadys, in which a common word pair or construct phrase (here, *dam nāqî* "blood of an innocent") is broken up and distributed between two parallel lines; cf. 1:18 (*'rb ldm // ṣpn lnpš*) and 12:6. To "waylay blood" means to lie in ambush for a life.

Both *dām nāqî* "innocent blood" and *dam hannāqî* "blood of the innocent" occur elsewhere and are indistinguishable in meaning (cf. esp. Deut 19:10, 13; 2 Kgs 21:16; 24:4). In Prov 6:17, *dām nāqî* is pointed as noun-adjective. Here *nāqî* must be a noun, "innocent man." The existence of *dam hannāqî* suggests that *nāqî* is really a noun, though when the consonantal text allowed it, the vocalizers treated the word as an adjective.

The ground metaphor of this lecture is *going on a path*. The gang urges the boy to *come* with them, and the father tells him not to *go* with them, not to step on their *path*, for they *run* to evil. On related metaphors, see "Paths through Life," after chapter 2.

The gang proposes to carry out a mugging. Such crimes were not peculiar to the Persian or Hellenistic period, when (Toy believes) "Jerusalem and Alexandria sheltered a miscellaneous population, and a distinct criminal class became more prominent."[92] Gangs and robbery were surely a widespread, perhaps universal, phenomenon, and a warning against violence would be appropriate in any era. Psalm 10:8–9 describes a similar mugging: "[The wicked man] sits in ambush in villages, in hiding places to kill a guiltless man. Looking for the unfortunate, he conceals himself [read *yiṣpon*]. He sets ambush in a hiding place like a lion in his thicket; sets ambush to snatch the poor man; snatches the poor man by a yank of his net."

The gang invites the youth to "waylay the innocent man *without cause*." In actuality, a band of thugs would be unlikely to declare that their victim was innocent (how would they know?) or to brand their own act as *ḥinnam* gratuitous. Criminals would be more likely to rationalize their act or at least downplay its heinousness, especially to an outsider. Although committing a pointless crime would help cement the initiate's bonds to the gang by severing his bonds to communal values, the gratuitousness of the act would not be an inducement to an outsider such as the one pictured in this vignette, who is not *seeking* initiation but being enticed to accept it. The purpose of the putative quotation is to implant a moral evaluation of the act in the evildoers' own words, thereby making them at once expose their perverted values and condemn their acts by their own mouths. There are many examples of this rhetorical device. In Jer 7:10, God says: "And you come and stand before Me . . . and say, 'We are saved, so that we may do all these abominations.'" Job quotes the wicked as saying to God: "We don't want to know your ways" (Job 21:14). Similar self-exposure by putative quotations appears in, for example, Jer 2:20; 2:25; 6:17; 22:21; and, most extensively, Wis 2:1–20 (in which vv 10–11 are based on Prov 1:10–11).[93]

We are not to picture the muggers in Prov 1:11–12 as actually using these words, as if they were openly confessing their cruelty. The point is that the sinners' indifference amounts to this assertion; this is their true attitude. Deep down, the wicked really understand the implications of their acts. We hear more about such twisted souls in 2:12–15; see "The Wicked Man," after 2:15.

1:12. *Let us swallow* . . . : Lit. "Let us swallow them alive like Sheol, and the blameless like those who descend to the Pit." The antecedent of "them" is the *naqi*, "innocent man," though that is singular in form; "them" is resumed by the plural *t*ᵉ*mimim* "the blameless." The bandits grandiosely liken themselves to no less a power than Death, the supreme swallower, of whom it is said, "Therefore Sheol has widened her throat [*nepeš*], opened her mouth beyond measure" in Isa 5:14; see also Hab 2:5 and Ps 5:10.

---

[92]"Miscellaneous" population and "criminal class" were early-twentieth-century code words for foreign immigrants.

[93]H. W. Wolff (1937: 43–50) describes the purpose and identifying marks of fictive quotations in the prophets.

the Pit: The underworld is called, among other things, Sheol, the Pit, Death, and Perdition (Abaddon). In Ugaritic mythology, the god Mot ("Death") swallows the living, including Baal. Mot's maw stretches from earth to heaven (CTA 5.ii.2–3); to die is to go down into his throat (CTA 5.i.7). In the present passage, Sheol gulps down people "alive" in the sense that they are alive at the moment he swallows them. The *t*^{e}*mimim* "blameless" are the same as the *naqi* in v 11 (in spite of the change to the plural). They are the morally innocent, not (contrary to Rashi, Delitzsch, Toy) the physically sound. The term is never so used of humans, and in any case, the victims' moral soundness is more pertinent to this tableau than is the state of their health. *T*^{e}*mimim* is commonly understood as an adverbial complement meaning "whole," hence "Let us swallow them . . . whole, like those who go down into the Pit" (JPSV). But *t*^{e}*mimim* does not have that function elsewhere. In 2:21, *t*^{e}*mimim* clearly means "the blameless." That passage denies the murderers' intention and insists that the *t*^{e}*mimim* will *endure* in the earth.

1:13–14. The outlaws promise to get rich and share the booty. To a newcomer, the offer might seem both generous and flattering.

1:14. *Throw in your lot with us*: This sentence, literally translated here, can be heard in two ways: First, "throw in your lot" refers to the actual casting of lots to divide the booty and is thus a promise of reward. Second, *goral*, like English "lot," means fate as well as the die that one casts. "Throw in your lot with us" is thus a proposal to share a life of crime, and not only a single crime. But the "fate" they propose to share is much grimmer than they realize. The first sense is brought out by the next line, which emphasizes equality of profits, but the second sense rumbles ominously in the background.

we'll all share one purse: The band tempts the boy by pledging camaraderie as well as wealth. They will be equals, truly partners in crime. The robbers will also entangle the newcomer by making him a full participant in their guilt. "The purpose of the promise is to cement the newcomer into the group and also seal his lips forever, as well as to bind him to them so that he cannot inform on them without implicating himself. This is a well-known technique of initiation to this very day in city gangs" (DNF).

1:15. *my son, don't go in the way with them*: Lit. ". . . in the way with them." The apodosis, of which vv 11–14 form the lengthy protasis, begins. Verse 15 is consequential to the invitation in v 11a: If they ask you to go with them, do not go "in the way with them," don't go along with them. The "way" of sinners has two meanings: the actual road to the ambush and their way of life. In the latter sense, one can "stand" in the "way" of sinners (Ps 1:1) as well as "go" in it.

1:16. *for their feet run to harm; they rush to shed blood*: This sentence appears in Isa 59:7a, except that Isaiah speaks of *innocent* blood (or "blood of an innocent"). In the absence of this word, the sentence in Proverbs acquires an ironic ambiguity. Though they intended to spill the blood of an innocent man (v 11), it is actually their own blood they are hastening to spill. Both verses may be quoting a common proverb, which is also incorporated in Prov 6:17. Isaiah 59:1–8 draws heavily upon Wisdom usages.

DNF objects that the fem. pl. *raglêhem* should normally govern a masc. pl. verb and proposes an alternative translation: "for they run (with) their feet . . . hasten (with their feet)." In other words, "they run and they hasten (with) their feet." This construes *raglêhem* as adverbial, equivalent to *b*^{e}*raglêhem*, and applies it to both verbs. In actuality, however, the *yiqt*^{e}*lû* form is used virtually as often as *tiqtōlnāh* with fem. pl. nouns in Proverbs (eight and ten times, respectively). The *yiqt*^{e}*lû* is best regarded as epicene. (Examples of the first construction are 3:2, 22; 5:2; and 10:32. The verbs in 1:20 and 8:3 are not really plural; 6:27 and 27:30a are problematic.) On the phenomenon, see GBH §150b. In the present verse, "Their feet" is the natural subject of "run."

Prov 1:16 is missing in the OG (see the Textual Note) and is often considered a later addition to MT. The motive for such an addition is unclear. A pietistic insertion, such Toy and Meinhold think it is, would be superfluous in a passage whose moralistic force is already unequivocal. To be sure, the verse does break the connection between v 15, the exhortation to refuse the robbers' offer, and vv 17–18, which motivate it, but this may be a deliberate technique: setting up an ambiguity (whose blood are they really hastening to shed?) to be resolved in the continuation. The verse works well in context and reinforces the message of the passage, even if v 16 is indeed later.

This verse is to be read in two ways: First, the criminals are hurrying to spill their victim's blood. This is self-evident, since that is their purpose, and as a reason for not joining them, it is tautological. Then the reader realizes that they are actually, but unwittingly, hastening to spill their *own* blood. The latter will be reinforced in v 18.

1:17. "*No bird is caught in a net set out before his eyes*": More literally: "In vain [*ḥinnam*] is the net spread [*m*^{e}*zorah*] before the eyes of every winged creature." This was certainly a preexisting, self-contained adage, whose relevance here is at first unclear. The flow of thought seems to be interrupted, but the interruption is only apparent.

M^e*zōrāh* is of uncertain meaning; three plausible explanations, all with difficulties, are: (1) "Strewn," that is, with seed (Rashi; Winton Thomas 1955: 282). However, the surface upon which something is scattered, such as the ground or a net, is never the dir. obj. of *z-r-h* (G and D) or the subject of the verb in the passive, nor is the semantic dir. obj. (the item scattered) ever omitted. (2) "Spread out," that is, the net (most commentators). However, *zērāh*, like English "scatter," never means to stretch out and spread an indivisible object. (3) Vocalize *m*^{e}*zūrāh*, from an otherwise unattested *m-z-r*, "stretch out" (HALAT II 536), on the basis of Syr *m*^{e}*zar*, "stretch (oneself)"—said of a person. But this creates a hapax on the basis of a word with a different sense in Syriac.

Explanation 2 is preferable, because the act of spreading out the net would warn birds away rather than the strewing of seed, which might not expose the net itself. But the adage has the same import by all three derivations of the word.

We may first ask about the surface meaning of the adage before it is applied to a situation. In itself, the adage declares the uselessness of an attempt to trap a creature (a "silly" one at that) when it is aware of the snare. (Thus *b*$^{e\text{c}}$*eyney-* means literally "in the eyes of" rather than "before.") If we came across this adage in, say, a proverb anthology, we would understand it to say that a ruse that is too obvious will not work, even on a creature of low intelligence. (A bird is silly and gullible [Hosea 7:11 calls it *potah*, "innocent," "gullible"] and unaware of its fate [Qoh 9:12].) A human who is caught in such a trap is even more stupid.

What point does the adage make in this context? Several explanations have been offered. The distinguishing factor is what the birds represent:

1. Birds = the youth and similar innocents. The criminals lay a trap for their prey, but in vain, because they are really going to catch themselves in it (Oesterley). The emphasis is on "in vain."

2. Birds = criminals. Though the snare is laid and baited in their sight, they fall into it (Riyqam, Toy).

3. Birds = birds, simpleminded animals, of whom simpleminded humans are an instance *a fortiori*. If even birds don't let themselves be caught by a clearly visible net, you surely should not be (Delitzsch, McKane). The emphasis is on *ḥinnam*, meaning "to no effect."

4. Birds = dupes. The birds/dupes are undeterred by the danger, even if the net is spread (or strewn with grain) in plain sight of them. They suppose that it is spread for no purpose (*ḥinnam*) (Saʿadia, Rashi).

5. Birds = dupes. It is *not* unjust (*ḥinnam*) when fools are caught in the trap set for them, if they allow themselves to be lured into it. The LXX expresses this by adding a "not." Alternatively, one might also read the sentence as an unmarked rhetorical question.

6. Birds = victims. The verse is a rhetorical question, meaning that it is *not* for naught (*ḥinnam*) that the robbers spread out their nets to catch "birds," because they catch *themselves* (Radaq).

In my view, the proverb *as applied* calls for a double reading:

(1) We are first to compare the birds with the youth. This is the obvious, first-step application. Surely the boy should have enough sense to avoid the obvious trap to which he is being lured, if even a bird has *that* much sense. A youth, like a bird, may be the object of enticement (*pittah*, v 10). The comparison is explicit in 7:23b: The youth follows a seductress "like a bird rushing into a trap: He wasn't aware that he'd pay with his life."

(2) After reading v 18, we are to realize that the adage pertains to the robbers as well, who are more witless than birds. Verses 18–19 in retrospect confirm this reading without invalidating the first reading. It turns out that the muggers, who must have seen the net they themselves spread, step right into it. It is *their* feet that run to harm (1:16), it is they who *rush* to shed blood, just as a bird *rushes* to the trap (7:23). This turns out to be the real point of the adage. (LXX makes it unambiguous.) Its message is driven home by being "discovered" in retrospect.

1:18. *Yet* they *lie in wait*: This verse suddenly makes the thugs the subject of the verbs. The frontally positioned *w^{e}hem* "*they*" points emphatically to them. The phrasing of the verse recalls the ambush they proposed in v 11. It turns out that the smart-guy robbers are less than birdbrained. What could be more stupid than to join them?

1:19. Conclusion: Evil Is Self-Destructive

1:19. The lecture culminates in a grand declaration of the principle of intrinsic retribution: Evildoers destroy themselves by means of the evil that they themselves create. This is the message of the conclusion of Lecture VIII (5:21–23) as well. A similar proverb appears in Job 8:13, where Bildad caps off a similarly structured Wisdom lecture with a similar adage: "This is what happens to (*ken ʾorḥot*) all who forget God; the hope of the hypocrite is lost."

This is what happens to: Lit. "thus are the ways." MT's *ʾrḥwt* is often emended to *ʾḥryt*, "end," "fate" (e.g., Toy, Gemser, BHS), on the grounds that the verse must be describing the consequences of the evildoers' behavior—their *end*—not the behavior itself. However, the similar adage in Job 8:13 also uses *ʾorḥot* in the sense of fate.

The concept of "way" (or "ways") in Hebrew combines "the ideas of action and issue, manner of life and its result" (Delitzsch). Moreover, it signifies what *happens* along one's life course as a concomitant of behavior. (In English, one's "way" or "ways" refers to behavior, not outcome.) Thus, for example, when Job says, "[God] has hedged in my way (*ʾorḥi*) so that I cannot pass, and upon my paths (*nᵉtibotay*—plural) he has set darkness" (19:8) he is not complaining that God has made him behave wrongly, but that he has made his life difficult. The "way" (*ʾoraḥ*) of the wicked in Job 22:15 is what happens to them (v 16).

everyone who grasps ill-gotten gain [*boṣeaʿ baṣaʿ*]: *Beṣaʿ* (from a root meaning "to cut") means "profit" (compare English "a cut"). The word often is used neutrally (Gen 37:26 [*mah beṣaʿ* = "what use is it," "what is the benefit"]; Judg 5:19; Mal 3:14; Job 22:3, etc.). Usually, however, *beṣaʿ* connotes *wrongful* profit, almost always in the form of bribes and peculations (Exod 18:21; 1 Sam 8:3; Isa 33:15; Jer 6:13; Hab 2:9; etc.); this is the case in its other two occurrences in Proverbs (Prov 15:27; 28:16). In the phrase *boṣeʿ beṣaʿ*, *beṣaʿ* always designates illicit profit. Hence the capstone states a principle broader than the situation described in the body of the lecture, implying that the untimely death of cutthroats is paradigmatic for all cheats, even the petty embezzler.

it robs him who holds it of life: Lit. "it takes [*yiqqaḥ*] the life of its possessor" (*bᵉʿalayw*; the plural form often has a singular sense). The term *bᵉʿalayw* is unexpected here because a *baʿal* (or *bᵉʿalim*) is always to the legitimate owner of something, even when it is not actually in his possession (3:27). The *bᵉʿalim* of stolen gold, for example, can only be the person it was stolen from. *Beṣaʿ* is different because the property becomes *beṣaʿ* only when the crook gets hold of it (Naḥmias). Now, as *beṣaʿ*, it is *his*, and like a vicious pet turning on its owner, it will "take his life" (*nepeš*). The implicit image in this locution is of the *beṣaʿ* *taking hold* of its possessor and dragging him off to its own sphere, which is death's domain.

Wisdom and legal texts make unusually frequent use of expressions of the form *baʿal* X. Proverbs employs the pattern in ways foreign to usual BH usage but well paralleled in external sources, particularly RH and Aramaic; see Hurvitz 1986. In the Bible, *baʿal* + an abstract noun (e.g., anger, shrewdness, appetite) is peculiar to Wisdom literature, but it is frequent in rabbinic texts.

The death threatened in vv 18–19 (and elsewhere in Proverbs) is an untimely, violent demise. The death of the righteous will, in principle, come naturally and peacefully.

There is no indication of how the punishment will operate in the present case. Some commentators, e.g., Ibn Yaḥyah and Naḥmias, think in terms of judicial punishment and blood vengeance. There is nothing excluding such outcomes. They would still constitute self-destruction. (The mechanism whereby the adulterer "destroys himself" in 6:32–35 is that the cuckold kills him.) But here the author avoids specifying the mechanism of punishment so as not to obscure the generality of the rule: The gains of sin recoil on the sinner.

The "Deed-Consequence Nexus"

An influential essay by K. Koch (1955) argued that recompense in the Bible takes the form of the *Tat-Ergehen Zusammenhang*, the deed-consequence nexus. This means that an evildoer is punished by falling into the power of his own evil, and a righteous person receives his rewards through his own goodness.[94] Reward and punishment are integrally attached to the deed. The evildoer creates a sphere of evil that then harms *him*. No external interference by God is necessary to complete the process.

It is certainly an exaggeration to claim, as Koch does, that this is the *only* idea of recompense in the Bible, or even in Wisdom literature, where it is more prominent. Studies by P. D. Miller Jr. (1982: 121–39) and L. Boström (1990: 90–140) reveal considerable complexity and variation in the formulation and presuppositions of the passages that are supposed to show the deed-consequence nexus. While the consequences of behavior are often formulated impersonally, in many sayings, God is explicitly active in retribution, though the sentences do not usually indicate just how the consequences will be realized. It is enough to know that God will not let the righteous go hungry (10:3), for he can fulfill this promise in limitless ways. Boström (1990: 90) also observes that Proverbs does not usually speak of consequences of deeds but of one's behavior and character as a whole. He prefers to speak of "character-consequence relationship." This modification is important because Proverbs is not so mechanical as to imagine a precise correlation between every action and its result. The fool will behave in such a way that, overall, his life will be an unhappy one, but the unhappy circumstance may not be the immediate result of the one condemned in a particular proverb.

Nevertheless, Wisdom literature does tend to formulate retribution as an automatic process of cause and effect.[95] Warnings thus formulated are more believable. One need not feel God's immediate presence to get the point: Bad deeds hurt you. Rather than excluding divine judgment, the formulation of retribution as a causal connection, which I would call "intrinsic retribution," emphasizes

---

[94]This article and others responding to it appear in the anthology edited by Koch (1972).

[95]Koch rejected the applicability of the notion of "retribution" (*Vergeltung*) to the biblical concept of reward and punishment, on the grounds that "retribution" requires a juridical process and a decision in accordance with a fixed norm (1972: 132). But this definition is too narrow, and the term is an appropriate designation even for the process he described.

the omnipresence and immediacy of God's justice in human affairs. Since God created a just world and rules it constantly, any deserved consequence can be regarded as divine judgment (thus in Pss 7:11–14; 9:16–17). In other words, God's judgment subsumes natural causality rather than the other way around.

A favorite means of encapsulating the idea of intrinsic retribution is the "pit" topos: "He who digs a pit will fall into it" (Prov 26:27; cf. Pss 7:16, 17; 9:16; Sir 27:25–27). Various images are used to elucidate this principle, such as the net catching the one who spread it (Ps 9:16) and a stone falling down on the head of the one who threw it up (Sir 27:25).

The Design of Lecture I

I. Exordium (8–9)
  A. Hearken to the teachings,
  B. for they are attractive.
II. Lesson (10–18)
  A. *If* robbers tempt you (10–14),
  B. *then* don't succumb (15),
  C. *because* criminals are self-destructive (16–18).
III. Conclusion/Capstone (19): the self-destructiveness of the wicked.

The lesson is a tightly organized syntactic and logical unity: *If . . . then . . . because. . . .*

The Audience

The lectures in Part I have as their ostensive audience a youth who is nearing adulthood and must choose his course of life. Temptations and traps beset him from the start. At this point the juvenile is a *peti*—naive and susceptible to seduction (*p-t-h*, as in v 10). At no time does the father speak to the son as if he were already a sinner. He sees the boy as dangerously near the brink of sin and susceptible to evil influences but still on the firm ground of parental guidance. Forces beckon and tug at the youngster in two directions as he steps into the adult world. On the one side lurks evil: wicked men, corrupt women, and Folly itself; on the other side—using similar language and inducements—stands goodness: one's father, one's own wife, and Wisdom herself.

R. Van Leeuwen calls the invitations in Prov 1–9 "threshold speeches," which are delivered to a youth on the verge of adulthood (1990a: 114). This setting is a "liminal" experience (to use Victor Turner's terminology), in which an adolescent passes the *limen* or threshold into a different social status. At this moment, the definition of boundaries—*limina*—is crucial for the preservation of the communal order. These human boundaries, Part I teaches, have their warrant in boundaries fixed by God (Van Leeuwen 1990a: 119–20).

The development of character—the ethical awareness to make the right choices and the moral fiber to stick with them—is the primary goal of the lectures. The father seeks to foster the right moral stance in the face of inducements to sin. In essence, Part I focuses less on what is right to *do* than on what is right to *choose*.

The Gang

The first circle of associates an adolescent boy must choose is his male companions, and the first danger described is, appropriately, temptation by corrupt men. The entire lecture sounds like a gloss on Prov 28:10, "He who leads honest men astray in an evil path will fall into his own pit, while the blameless will inherit goodness."

The first lecture cautions about temptations from evil men. They form a gang, much like the ones that infest modern cities. They seek to draw in new members and bind them to the group by implicating them in their crime. "The crime chosen is not merely gratuitous but egregious, so as to impress upon the newcomer the spirit in which violence is committed, emphasizing the macho character of the group. It is intended to be as brutal as possible, and the neophyte is forced or persuaded to show his own manhood in the same fashion" (DNF).

The enticement pictured in the first lecture, induction into a gang of cutthroats, is an extreme case, not the sort of dilemma actually faced by most juveniles, and even less likely for those who receive parental wisdom. (This statement must be qualified for some neighborhoods in modern cities.) Wisdom literature rarely dwells on felonious offenses. The Egyptian Instructions do not warn against joining in violent crime. When they do deal with the choice of companions, as in Anii (18.6–9), they caution against consorting with quarrelsome, obstreperous men, not against entanglement with felons. Nor is this a common theme in Israelite Wisdom. The choices before the reader are usually more mundane. Lecture I thus takes a new angle, one perhaps intended to cause surprise, even discomfort. Is life really *that* dangerous?

The author says that it indeed is. Two life courses diverge immediately, one going to life and one to death. The father depicts the second in the starkest terms. He begins with an extremity of evil because he claims that this crime is an analogue to all unjust means of grasping wealth. This is the crime that defines the category. All evil paths, however one may step onto them, lead to the same tragic end. The youth must realize that there are no gray areas, so that he who chooses *any* evil ("everyone who grasps ill-gotten gain") has entered on the road to the same deadly end as these felons are on. See "Paths through Life," after chapter 2.

The bandits hold out two promises: wealth and comradeship; there is much emphasis on *sharing* the loot. But what they will really share is their own disaster.

The youth will hear strong enticements in the years ahead, some beckoning him to wisdom and life, others to folly and death. Since the great challenge lies in identifying and shunning the wrong attractions, the father does not simply warn the son against becoming a robber. He defines the dilemma as one of resistance to temptations: what to do "if criminals lure you." Then he puts the description and even some of the evaluation of the criminal acts in the mouths of the bandits. It is not their crime itself that is attractive; it is their speech. The great danger comes through language.

The criminals' language of seduction, as Aletti shows (1977: 136–39), mirrors that of the wise, including the sage and Lady Wisdom. Key words shared by the inducements of the wicked and the wise are *wealth* (*hon*; 1:13 versus 8:18), *finding* (*m-ṣ-ʾ* 1:13 [translated previously as "seize"]; cf. 7:15; versus 2:5; 3:13; 8:9, 35; etc.), and *filling* (*m-l-ʾ*; 1:13 versus 3:10; 8:21). The gang insinuates that they will enjoy a sort of communal accord, such as Wisdom herself promises and promulgates. The criminals claim to offer the blessings that Lady Wisdom identifies as the rewards of righteousness and obedience (8:17–21). What is more, the robbers seek to undermine wisdom's fundamental principle of recompense by insinuating that the innocent man will be abandoned by God and fall victim to their assault. Temptation thus works by dissociating ends from means, and by subverting language it corrupts the fabric of society itself, which is held together by language.

The father seeks to preempt and defuse the sly rhetoric the youth will soon face, but he does not do so by *proofs*. To understand the rhetoric of wisdom discourse, we should observe that the father has by no means demonstrated his assertion that evildoing rebounds on itself. The adage in v 17 merely highlights the evildoers' stupidity, and the proverb in v 19 extends the principle of the preceding statement in v 18 rather than providing evidence for it. The only argument for the teachings of Lecture I is the speaker's ethos, his personal credibility, and even that is assumed by virtue of his station as father rather than undergirded by reasons. In a discussion of the ideas of wisdom in Prov 1–9, I will consider how this rhetorical ethos is deployed in the inculcation of wisdom. (See Essay 3, "Wisdom in Lectures.")

C. Newsom (1989: 144–45) deconstructs this lecture to expose a hidden agenda: the maintenance of patriarchal authority against the attractions of the son's contemporaries. She suggests that the brigands are a metaphor for the son's peers. These relate to the listener in a "horizontal" mode. "The genuine appeal to younger men of the set of values just described is cleverly defused by associating them with what is clearly outside the law" (p. 144). The warning against joining robbers cloaks an attempt to dissuade younger men from making common enterprise with contemporaries rather than waiting for the deferred wealth of inheritance.

I can see nothing in the text to justify equating the thugs with the entirety of the son's generation. (The principle in v 19 includes *everyone*.) They are robbers and murderers, and we can hardly say that they are ordinary lads who are cleverly "associated" with illegality, since they exist only insofar as they are described in this passage. It is not evident that the thieves are all younger men or that their band is not hierarchical. Their "horizontal" appeal is a ploy, not a social principle, and the initiate might soon find his would-be confreres far from egalitarian. Nor is there any reason for a father to object to the youth's joining in a *legitimate* enterprise with his peers. There is no virtue in waiting for one's patrimony rather than enhancing it. More fundamentally, the father in Part I shows no anxiety for maintaining authority or control beyond having his wise counsels internalized and obeyed. He does not demand filial obedience as a value outside the present learning situation, for when the counsels are taken to heart, they themselves will guide the youth in the right courses.

INTERLUDE A. WISDOM'S WARNING (1:20–33)

TRANSLATION

Wisdom castigates the foolish

1:20 **Wisdom cries aloud in the streets,**
in the plazas gives forth her voice.
21 **At the bustling crossroads she calls out,**
where the gates open into the city,
there she has her say:
22 **"How long, callow ones,**
will you love being callow?
(you) impudent ones treasure scorn?
and (you) dolts hate knowledge?
23 **Turn back toward my reproof!**
See, I pour out to you my spirit,
make you know my words:
24 **Since you spurned me when I called,**
took no heed when I stretched forth my hand,
25 **brushed aside all my advice,**
accepted not my reproof,
26 **I, for my part, will laugh at your downfall,**
mock when what you fear arrives,
27 **when what you fear arrives like a storm,**
and your downfall comes nigh like a gale,
when trouble and torment come upon you."

The fate of the foolish

28 **Then they'll call me, but I won't answer,**
they will seek me but find me not,
29 **because they spurned knowledge,**
and did not choose the fear of the Lord,
30 **did not accept my advice,**
but despised all my reproof.

31 So they shall eat of the fruit of their way,
from their own devices be stuffed full.
32 For the waywardness of the callow will kill them,
and the dolts' complacency will destroy them.
33 But he who obeys me shall dwell in safety,
secure from fear of harm.

COMMENTARY

Interlude A complements the preceding lecture in several ways. To the threats of Lecture I it adds mockery, now directed against both the wicked tempters and the naif who gives in to them. The lecture warned against surrendering to the summons of sinners; the interlude warns against refusing the call of Wisdom (Ramaq). The Vulgate associates the two units nicely by beginning 1:20, "And all the while Wisdom is publishing her message." Nevertheless, these connections are too loose to prove identity of authorship. Essay 1 will argue that Interlude A is probably by a later author who knew Lecture I and built on it.

Wisdom is personified fully in 1:29–33; 8:1–36; and 9:1–6 + 11–12, and personification is suggested but not systematic in 2:3; 3:13–20; 4:8–9; and 7:4. (The last is inchoate personification, discussed in Essay 2, pp. 331f.) The personification of wisdom will be discussed more fully in Essay 2, "The Origins of Personified Wisdom." The present discussion considers only the features of personification relevant to Interlude A. ("Wisdom" will be capitalized when speaking of Lady Wisdom, since that is like a personal name, and kept in lower case for the common noun. But often the distinction is hard to make or unimportant.)

1:20–27. Wisdom Castigates the Foolish

1:20. *Wisdom cries aloud in the streets*: Wisdom is not secretive, confining herself to a coterie of initiates. Quite the contrary, she roams about the busiest parts of the city, demanding attention. Not even study or learning is a precondition for Wisdom's assistance; one need merely respond to her clarion summons. This means that no one can excuse folly by pleading ignorance of Wisdom's demands. In this scene, however—unlike chapter 8—Wisdom is not summoning people to herself. That summons is presumed. Now Wisdom reacts to those who on an earlier occasion scorned her summons.

Wisdom is here called *ḥokmot*, an ostensively plural form but construed with a singular verb because it refers to a single individual. Personified wisdom is called *ḥokmot* also in 9:1 and Sir 4:11, likewise with a singular verb. The same word appears in Ps 49:4, where it means "wise things" and is parallel to the plural *t^{e}bunot* "(words of) understanding."

The form *ḥokmôt* is a puzzle. It has the fem. pl. ending, but the expected pl. abs. of *ḥokmāh* is **ḥăkāmôt*, like *ʿărālôt* from *ʿorlāh* (Josh 5:3) or * *ḥŏkāmôt*, cf. *ḥŏrābôt* from *ḥorbāh* (e.g., Ezek 38:12). Nevertheless, *ḥokmôt* is treated as a plural in Prov 24:7, where it means either wisdom or wise words. The adjectival form *ḥakmôt-* (pl. cst.) occurs in 14:1, where it is again construed with a sg. verb, and should probably be revocalized as *ḥokmôt*.

Ḥokmôt may be a Phoenicianism, from **ḥukmōt*; thus Albright (1955: 8), deriving it from a hypothetical Canaanite * *ḥukmatu*; GKC §86*l* too identifies the ending as fem. sg. (The first *u* would shift to Heb. *o* after borrowing.) This derivation would explain both the retained *-t* and the *ō* of the ending (resulting from the Phoenician shift [*á* → *ā* → *ō*], subsequent to the Canaanite shift). It is no help to call *ḥokmôt* a plural of extension and intensity (Toy et al.), because there is nothing extended or intense about the wisdom designated by this form. Possibly it is a plural of majesty (Hame'iri; Delitzsch; GBH §136*d*). Most likely it is a pl. form treated as a sg. because it refers to a single figure. The pl. forms of *bînāh* and *tᵉbûnāh* function almost exactly like the respective sg. forms, designating both a plurality of sayings and an abstract singular (for the latter see *bînôt* in Isa 27:11 and *tᵉbûnôt* in Ps 78:72); sim. *dēʿôt* in 1 Sam 2:3 = *dēʿāh* "knowledge." Note the parallelism between *ḥokmôt* and the pl. *tᵉbûnôt* in Ps 49:4 (where, however, it means "wise things"). Comparable is the use of *bᵉhēmôt* as a collective sg. (Jer 12:4; Joel 1:20; Job 12:7; in Ps 73:22 the pl. form is semantically sg. as well).

Tāronnāh "shout" (here and in 8:3), is not a fem. pl., which would be *tᵉrunnenāh*. In 8:3, *tāronnāh* has a sg. subject (it appears in 8:1). Rather, it is a 3 fem. sg. (like the parallel verb), with an energic sufformative (*-nā*) (thus, essentially, Riyqam; cf. Judg 5:26; Job 17:16; Isa 28:3).

1:21. *At the bustling crossroads* [*bᵉroš homiyyot*]: Wisdom calls from the busiest places. "Crossroads" are literally "the head of the bustling (roads)," in other words, the point at the city gate from which the roads fan out into the city. *Homiyyot* "bustling, noisy" is a noun only here. It is elliptical for "bustling roads [*dᵉrakim* or the like]."

Hōmiyyôt refers to bustling roads, not cities (contrary to Kaspi, who compares *ʿîr hômiyyāh* in Isa 22:2) or to other busy areas. A road has a "head," a starting point at the city gate (most clearly in Ezek 42:12; cf. Ezek 16:25; 21:24), whereas *areas*, such as cities or plazas, do not. The reading "walls" (*ḥōmôt* or *ḥōmiyyôt*), represented in the LXX, is arguably the original, because Wisdom calls from the "head" of "high places" (*mᵉrômîm*; 8:2) and "the tops of the high places (*mᵉrôm[îm]*) of the city" (9:3). However, a city's walls would probably be called the walls *of* the city (in construct), rather than "in the city."

The phrase "in the city," which may seem superfluous (and which Toy considers a gloss), actually serves to emphasize the conspicuousness of Wisdom's actions (Ehrlich, comparing Amos 7:17).

In ancient Israel, the city gate was the arena of public life. Schools may have been located near the gates. Direct evidence for this is lacking, but Lang (1986: 29–33) compares the Roman forum and the Greek agora, which were loci of both public activities and instruction. The "streets" (*ḥuṣ*, a collective sg.) were the narrow alleys (which is to say, most streets in an ancient city). They were thronging with children at play, animals, stores, beggars, and people going about their business (see Lang's vivid description, pp. 22–23). Jeremiah was sent to prophesy in them (Jer 11:6). The plazas or city squares (*rᵉḥobot*) were the open public places. The city gate and the square before it were the realms of male activity. A woman going through the streets might be suspected of searching for men (Prov 7:12). According to Ezek 16:25, a whore stations herself (builds a *ramah* "pedestal") at the head of a road (*roʾš derek*—reminiscent of *roʾš homiyyot* in Prov 1:21—and *bᵉroʾš mᵉromim ʿăley darek* "atop the heights, near the road" in 8:2). Lady Folly, Wisdom's antithesis, sits "on a chair at the city heights" (*ʿal* *kisse' m^{e}romey qaret*, 9:14). It is, to say the least, incongruous and daring for the dignified Lady Wisdom to be frequenting such places and calling to men.

1:22. *How long*: Wisdom's rhetorical question gives vent to exasperation: How long will fools insist on their folly? "How long" often introduces a word of chastisement (cf. 6:9; Exod 10:3; 1 Sam 1:14; 16:1; 1 Kgs 18:21; Jer 31:22; and often).

Wisdom addresses three kinds of fools: naive, inexperienced youths (*p^{e}tayim*), impudent and scornful people (*leṣim*), and dolts (*k^{e}silim*) (see "Words for Folly"). The *peti* (pl. *p^{e}tayim*) is, in principle, educable, but the ones addressed here have already rejected wisdom and are full-fledged (though perhaps not irredeemable) fools. The *leṣ* is chronically arrogant and cynical, and the *k^{e}sil* is smug and thickheaded. The verse lumps the three together because they are all prone to the complacency condemned in this interlude.

Delitzsch and Plöger believe that only the *peti* is actually addressed in vv 23ff., since he alone is susceptible to correction. But it is hard to read the demand in v 23a as applying to only the first of the three types mentioned. After all, the people addressed and condemned in vv 24–32 have conclusively hated and spurned knowledge (vv 24–25)—which is what the dolts (*k^{e}silim*), not the callow, are said to do in v 22.

Like a prophet preaching to people he knows will refuse to listen (Isa 6:9–13; Ezek 3:7), Wisdom directs her demands at the intractable types too. There is rhetorical logic in this, if not theological consistency. After all, one who is truly impudent or stupid is unlikely to realize that he is, so no reader would identify himself as one of the ostensive addressees. Instead, the speech is an apostrophe to an audience not present. The reader overhears a condemnation of categories of people in which he does not want to be included. If he is guilty of foolish acts, he can choose to repent of his folly and so avoid joining the wisdom-haters and earning Wisdom's aspersions and threats.

treasure . . . hate: Though this cannot be well reflected in translation, the verbs "treasure" and "hate" are in the third person. Only the callow are addressed in the second person, in v 22a. Delitzsch explains this on the grounds that Wisdom expects to find "soonest access" to them. But non-agreement of person is quite common in BH and is not abrasive in that language. Wisdom's chastisement is spoken to all fools. All these fools—including the callow—have at some time heard Wisdom and rejected her call. As 1:20–21; 8:1–5; and 9:1–4 make very clear, Lady Wisdom does not reserve her counsels for the wise. No one can write his transgressions off as mere ignorance.

For a review of the problems in 1:22–23 and the various emendations proposed, see Emerton 1968: 609–14.

Petî is only here used as an abstract ("naiveté," "callowness"); similar formations are *b^{e}kî* "weeping," *m^{e}rî* "rebellion," and *'ădî* "prime" (Emerton 1968: 610). *Petî* is a frozen pausal form.

T'hbw (*t^{e}'ēhăbû*) is a peculiar form, apparently resulting from the progressive assimilation of the two short *e* vowels of *te'ehăbu*; for partial analogues, see GKC §63*m,p*.

1:23. *Turn back toward my reproof* [*tašubu l^{e}tokaḥti*]. This is a brief exordium within Wisdom's speech. The verb *š-w-b* essentially means to turn back in the direction one came from. (I take this as the gist of Holladay's definition in his study of the verb *šub*; 1958: 53.) It does not necessarily mean "return," that is, "*move* back," whether physically or metaphorically. The preposition *l-* "to" indicates the place or a person back toward which one turns. In other words, in this verse, *tašubu* is not a call to repentance, but rather a call to attention.

A very similar phrase is used in concluding a father's rebuke in the Egyptian letter of Menena, a text that draws upon the form and phraseology of Wisdom instructions and calls itself an "instruction."

> Look, turn back (*pnʿ*) to examine my words. You will find my words excellent. Set your heart (lit. "face") to hear my instruction, so as to do all I advise. I'll make you forget all of them [that is, the son's misdeeds described earlier in the letter] that you may become like a *wnb*-flower. Is not one like me, who has provided you with a house, great indeed? (vso. 9–14)

Points of similarity are the call to "turn back" toward the chastiser, the praise of the teacher's words and character, and the reminder of the benefits he offers.

J. Emerton (1968: 614) inserts *petî* before v 23 (supposedly lost by homoioteleuton) because he finds a call to repentance inappropriate here. R. Murphy (1986: 457) too says that the continuation (vv 24–25) is not a way to motivate a call to repentance because it describes the listeners' past infidelity. Hence he translates "you turn away with respect to my reproof," parsing *tašûbu* as an indicative. However, *šûb* means "turn from" only in combination with a preposition meaning "from" (*min, me'aḥărê*); moreover, "turn away with respect to" is an unwieldy notion and represents an unlikely use of the *lamed*. The idiom *šûb l-* means "turn back toward" (literally or metaphorically). *Tašûbû l^{e}tokaḥtî* is a call for attention to the reproof. Compare *ṯṯb bʿl lhwty*, "You will come back to [= heed] my words, O Baal" (CTA 4.vi.2; cf. Dahood 1963: 6; other refs. CML 160).

Though *tašubu l^{e}tokaḥti* is not a call to repentance, there is such a call implicit in Wisdom's words. Her rhetorical question "How long . . . ?" (lit. "until when . . . ?") expresses frustration but also leaves open the possibility, albeit farfetched, that the fools *may* stop loving their folly. The call for attention in "turn back toward my reproof," following immediately upon the "how long" questions, suggests that giving heed to the reproof would indeed bring an end to their perverted values.

Tokaḥat (variant *tokeḥah*) "reproof," "chastisement" is an important educational concept in Proverbs (which has 16 of 32 HB occurrences; Ben Sira has 5 of these). Chastisement is a source of wisdom (Prov 15:10, 31, 32; 29:15). It is expected to be effective unless the recipient actively "hates" and rejects it (5:12; 12:1; 15:10). *Tokaḥat* may take the form of corporal punishment (e.g., 2 Kgs 19:3; Ezek 5:15), but usually it is verbal. A *tokaḥat* is always critical and negative. Though it seeks to change behavior, it need not, and usually does not, include an explicit demand for repentance. Job's reproach in Job 13:6–13 is identified as a *tokaḥat*. In this passage, Job accuses his friends of speaking deceitfully on God's behalf and warns them of God's anger, but he does not demand that they change. *Tokaḥat* (unlike English "reproof") does not always presume a past failing.

See, I pour out to you my spirit [*ruaḥ*]: That is, let you know how I feel. *Ruaḥ* has a range of meanings, including "wind," "breath," "life breath," and "spirit." As a constituent of mind, *ruaḥ* is expressed in emotion more than in intellect and includes feelings, will, faculties, attitudes, and desires. "Temper" is often a good approximation. Hebrew does not draw a dichotomy between emotion and intellect. For the most part, however, *ruaḥ* (when it refers to a component of mind) is usually associated with emotion and matters of the "spirit," while *leb* "heart" is the organ of faculties and thoughts we identify with cognition. See the comment on 2:2.

spirit . . . words: "Words" are her inner words, her thoughts, which she is about to express. This verse introduces Wisdom's quotation of her own words in vv 24–27. S. Harris (1995: 79–86, 95–100) identifies these verses as a quotation of what Wisdom said to another group of people, namely the Jews at the time of the Exile. But we cannot distinguish the ostensible audience so narrowly; all fools in all times and places are included.

1:24. *stretched forth my hand*: This gesture signifies threat and intimidation. Most commentators, however, explain it as a gesture of beckoning or entreaty. Radaq (sim. Meinhold) compares "I spread out my hands" (Isa 65:2). But spreading out the hands is a sign of entreaty (Gruber 1980: 24–33) and quite a different posture from stretching forth (*naṭah*) one hand. Moreover, the Isaiah passage uses a different verb (*paraś*). Meinhold also compares *henip yad*, "raising [*sic*] the hand" in Isa 13:2, a gesture of beckoning (Naḥmias), but there too the verb and the posture are different. "Stretching forth" the hand is invariably a gesture of power or aggression, never a signal to approach. Often the hand holds a staff or a sword, and a comparison of Josh 8:19 with 8:18 or Exod 14:21 with 14:16 suggests that the hand stretched forth is to be pictured as holding, at least metaphorically, a weapon or rod, the rod being an implement of magical or divine power. Only God, angels, Moses (acting as a sort of magician), and Joshua (a warrior) make this gesture. It is never something a prophet does. Riyqam rightly glosses the phrase in Prov 1:24 as "to smite you"; sim. Hame'iri: "to punish you"; Malbim: "to threaten." Stretching forth the hand is like shaking a fist at someone.

Wisdom does not threaten to harm the fools herself, but she does warn them of disaster in a caustic and menacing manner. This is true both of personified Wisdom (as in 8:36) and of the words of wisdom, in which the warnings can be quite intimidating.

1:25. *brushed aside all my advice*: "Brushed aside" is *paraʿ*, lit. "to loosen" (of hair, in Lev 10:6, etc.) or "let go," hence "ignore," "toss aside" (Ezek 24:14; Prov 1:25; 4:15; 8:33; 13:18; 15:32). "Brushing aside" or "letting loose" is the opposite of "holding fast" to advice or instruction. What incenses Wisdom here is not a particular sin that the fools have committed, but the fact that they have ignored her. They have slighted her dignity.

1:26–27. *I, for my part, will laugh at your downfall . . .* : The additive force of "too" (*gam*) applies to the laughing, not the downfall. (For this use of *gam*, see IBHS §39.3.4d, exx. 14–16, where *gam* is translated "in recompense.") The ostensive audience of Wisdom's words includes *leṣim*, the impudent ones who characteristically "laugh" and "mock" words of wisdom. Now wisdom will return their scornful laughter.

Wisdom does not, strictly speaking, vow or predict that disaster will overtake the fools; she *assumes* it. Her response to the impending calamity is schadenfreude; she will jeer at those who earlier disregarded her. This rather unappealing behavior is sometimes considered to imitate God's, for he too mocks his enemies (e.g., Pss 2:4; 37:13; 59:9) and shows contempt for all their powers and plans. In particular, he scorns the scornful—the *leṣim* (Prov 3:34). But not only God behaves like this. Jerusalem will one day deride her enemies (Isa 37:22), and (in spite of Prov 24:17) the righteous too may mock the wicked when their punishment comes (Pss 52:8; 58:11).

"What you fear" translates *paḥdᵉkem*, lit. "your [pl.] fear." (For the idea, see 10:24.) The possessive "your" seems to single out the misfortune each person most dreads.

for my part. This renders *gam* "also." The additive force of *gam* at the head of v 26 applies to the sentence as a whole: The fools showed contempt for Wisdom by rejecting her advice; now she will likewise show them contempt in return. The storm that will sweep away the wicked but spare the righteous is mentioned in 10:25.

The description of disaster builds by chiastic repetition and accretion in vv 26–27 (translating literally):

a . . . at your *downfall* (*'eyd*)
b when what you *fear* (*paḥad*) arrives,
b′ when what you *fear* (*paḥad*) arrives like a storm (*šo'ah*),
a′ and your *downfall* (*'eyd*) comes nigh like a gale (*supah*),
c when trouble and torment (*ṣarah wᵉ ṣuqah*) come upon you.

Clauses a–b set up the two terms of disaster, b′ and a′ elaborate them chiastically by comparison to a storm, and c adds two synonyms meaning disaster. This massing of words, supported by the repetition of the *b*, *d*, and *ṣ* sounds, suggests a relentless snowballing of disasters.

1:28–33. The Fate of the Foolish

1:28. *Then they'll call me, but I won't answer*: This is an "inverse return" to v 24 (Trible 1975: 514), which pronounces the consequences of the action described there.

After quoting what she will say to the fools in the day of disaster—a hypothetical audience—Wisdom turns to the real audience, the reader, as she speaks *about* the fools and draws a lesson from their self-inflicted doom. It is not true, as Newsom claims, that the reader "discovers himself in the text as always, already at fault. And the fault is recalcitrance before legitimate authority" (C. Newsom

1989: 146). The fools are not the readers. Wisdom's address to the dolts and scoffers is a fiction. Although Wisdom's message is public, the fools will never really hear it, in the way that others can hear wisdom by heeding their conscience and upbringing.[96] It is these whom Wisdom is really addressing, desiring them to take this as a warning. The reader does not identify with the fools but views them at a distance, with contempt.

On the day of woe, the simpletons and jerks and scoffers will beseech Wisdom for help, but she will turn away in disdain. This scenario presumes that in their predicament the fools will somehow realize that wisdom is a source of help and that they lack it. This does not mean that they will truly repent of their folly and their earlier repudiation of wisdom. Real fools do not believe that they are repudiating wisdom. They will not, for example, realize that they failed to fear the Lord, to respect their parents, to hold to sexual ethics, and so on, and regret all this. If they did so, that would be a moment of wisdom and a step toward ethical maturity. This is unlikely, but even fools may eventually come to realize that they lack the ability to deal with a crisis and may identify this ability as wisdom. They might desire faculties that belong to wisdom, such as *taḥbulot* ("strategy," "guidance") or *tušiyyah* ("resourcefulness"); but these will not be available.

but find me not: Not letting oneself be "found," that is, refusing to help a supplicant, is something God does in anger. In Hosea 5:15, for example, God says that Israel will one day feel shame and seek him (*šiḥer* as in Prov 1:28b) when they are in trouble (*ṣar* = *ṣarah*, as in Prov 1:27b). God will accept this approach, whereas (according to Hos 5:6) if they seek God merely "with their flocks and cattle" they will not "find" him (*maṣa*ʾ, as in Prov 1:28b). God's refusal to respond when sought is also mentioned in, for example, Mic 3:4; Isa 1:15; and Jer 11:11. In a similar formula of reciprocity, God says, "I spoke to you constantly, but you did not listen; and I called to you, but you did not answer" (Jer 7:13; cf. Jer 35:17; Zech 7:12). Eliphaz upbraids Job with a similar taunt: "Call now. Will anyone answer you? And to whom among the holy beings will you turn?" (Job 5:1).

1:29–30. *because they spurned knowledge . . .* : The fools will not find the wisdom they need because they rejected its foundations: fear of God and knowledge.

1:31. *So they shall eat of the fruit of their way*: Wisdom's discourse, like the father's, issues in a declaration of the principle of intrinsic retribution, the behavior-consequence nexus. Fools will eat what they planted, suffer the effects of their own schemes and deeds (cf. 14:14; 18:20). "Fruit" is implicit in the second line (Hameʾiri), as if it said "and from the fruit of their devices."

1:32. *For the waywardness of the callow . . .* : Like the father's previous lecture, Wisdom's oration culminates in a capstone stating a general principle that encapsulates (but does not prove) the preceding assertions.

---

[96] Isa 6:8 distinguishes one type of "hearing"—the merely auditory—from "understanding." The Eloquent Peasant plays on the two types of hearing in his reproach, "Hearer, you hear not!" (l. 211).

The particle *ki* is most naturally read as a causal connector when it introduces a generalization following upon a conclusion. Verse 32 does not state the reason why v 31 is true but the reason why it is *stated*. This is the "evidential" function of the particle (Claasen 1983: 37).

Waywardness: *m^{e}šubah* is usually translated "backsliding" or "apostasy," but this might imply that the callow began in the right state and went astray. *M^{e}šubah* means the tendency to turn away, namely from right behavior. Wisdom has called them to *turn back* to her rebuke, to hear it again, but the simpletons are afflicted by *m^{e}šubah*, the tendency to turn *away* from wisdom. This *m^{e}šubah* is not so much a deed as an attitude or psychological disposition. This is shown most clearly by Jer 3:22 and Hos 14:5, where God says that he will "heal their *m^{e}šubah*." "Healing" pertains to a spiritual-psychological disorder more than to a sinful deed.

1:33. *But he who obeys me shall dwell in safety*: Wisdom's oration loops back to its opening, vv 20–22. Wisdom went about calling for listeners (though a verb for "hear" or "obey" was not used). She concludes by reminding us of the importance of responding to this call.

The delusive security of the fools is suicidal because it lets them imagine that they can rely on their independent resources, without recourse to wisdom. True security comes only from hearing wisdom and taking it seriously, in other words, in obeying the instructions.

"Safety," *betaḥ*, means both inner and outer security. (*šalwah*, used in 32b, refers only to emotional composure and comfort, though this feeling is naturally attendant on general well-being.) When Toy asserts that security from fear of harm here means merely freedom from outward misfortune and that "the whole tone of the Book makes it improbable that the writer has in mind the inward peace which is independent of external experiences" (p. 29), he has neatly stated the opposite of the truth. Proverbs is directly and deeply concerned with shaping attitudes, beliefs, and feelings for the sake of both internal and external well-being. Plain evidence for this is provided by the teachings emphasizing the value of inner peace, such as Prov 15:16, 17; 17:1 (with *šalwah*); 25:24. More fundamentally, Wisdom's speeches, which give the essence of her demands, describe *attitudes*: on the one hand, stubborn, smug disregard; on the other, love and desire for Wisdom.

The Design of Interlude A

I. Introduction (20–22)
   A. Wisdom calls for attention (20–21)
   B. and demands a hearing from fools (22). She says:
II. Lecture (23–31)
   A. Attend to my reproof (23) (≈ Exordium)
   B. Since you ignored me (24–25),
   C. I'll ignore you (26–27).
   C′. I'll ignore them (28),
   B′. because they ignored me (29–31).

III. Conclusion/Capstone (32–33)
   A. So the fools will die (32),
   B. but those who obey me will be secure (33).

Within the central section, the shift to third person in v 28, reinforced by the CB–B′C′ chiasm, is conspicuous and marks the pivot point. (The third person does appear in v 22b, but there it is less obtrusive and stands outside the chiasm.) The conclusion recalls the exordium in the theme of hearing Wisdom (though the keyword "hearing" is not found in the introduction) and in the echo of v 22 in v 32.

Phyllis Trible (1975) outlines a chiastic structure in which four concentric circles converge at the center of the poem:

A Introduction: an appeal for listeners (vv 20–21)
  B Address to the untutored, scoffers, and fools (v 22)
    C Declaration of disclosure (v 23)
      D Reason for the announcement (vv 24–25)
        E Announcement of derisive judgment (vv 26–27)
      D′ Result of the Announcement, with interruption (vv 28–30)
    C′ Declaration of retribution (v 31)
  B′ Address about the untutored and fools (v 32)
A′ Conclusion: an appeal for a hearer (v 33)

I doubt that many readers have the impression of a precise mirror inversion maintained throughout this passage. The similarities between the passages that are supposed to reflect each other are sometimes too vague to form exclusive links. There is no particular linkage between v 23 and v 31, nor is v 20 more of an "appeal for a hearer" than v 23. There are also correlations that crisscross the design and interfere with it; for example, "hearing" in v 33 is linked to the "calling" in vv 24 and 28 no less than to the calling in v 20. Verse 29 is, as Trible recognizes, an interruption of her schema, but its effect cannot be dismissed as "attention" (p. 515). Rather, its effect is to prevent an unprompted recognition of the design she argues for. There is indeed an inverted structure, but it is prominent only in the central section, and its pivot point falls between vv 27 and 28. Also, the conclusion (vv 32 and 33 together) does, at least loosely, recall the beginning (vv 20–22) and give a sense of closure. Trible does, however, point to some significant cross-connections and echoes, which are reflected in the analysis I proposed.

Interlude A and Jeremiah

Among the numerous historical allusions that the Midrash detects in Proverbs, the one pointing to Jeremiah is especially striking, so much so that actual dependency seems likely. *Mid. Prov.*, commenting on 1:25, says:

> *And would not hear my reproof*—this refers to Jeremiah, for they used to spurn and mock him for each and every reproof which he administered to Israel. Jeremiah said to them, "By your lives, the day (of reckoning) will come! Just as you mock and make fun of me [today], some day in the future I will mock and make fun of you." (transl. Visotzky 1992: 27)

Several modern scholars, including Robert (1934: 172–81), Gemser (p. 23), Kayatz (1966: 122–29) and, most carefully, Harris (1995: 87–109), have traced correspondences with prophetic speech, particularly Jeremiah's (chapters 7 and 20) and Zechariah's (chapter 7). There are numerous similarities in diction and phrasing (listed in Harris 1995: 93–95). For example, Jeremiah complains that everyone "laughs" (*śḥq*) and "mocks" (*lʿg*) him (Jer 20:7)—which is what Wisdom will do to those who turn a deaf ear to her (Prov 1:26). Harris (1995: 87–93) identifies structural and formal similarities as well. The most important parallel is thematic, in God's recurrent complaint that he spoke but they did not listen; that he called but they did not answer (see here on 1:28). This stubbornness seals the fall of Jerusalem. Harris (1995: 95) calls Prov 1:20–33 a "recontextualization" of Jeremiah's words, which is likely, except that the passage may have been influenced by other prophets as well, or perhaps by acquaintance with prophecy in general. This is not to say that the reader is necessarily expected to recall Jeremiah or the disaster he predicted. Wisdom speaks to individual fools about individual punishments, not to the nation about the people's collective failings and impending disasters. Nor does she speak as a prophet or God. Still, the depiction of Lady Wisdom scolding fools draws on the images of the prophet and God and redeploys them in the arena of individual life.

The Message of Interlude A

Lady Wisdom's first discourse deals with people's attitudes rather than deeds. To be sure, attitudes engender deeds, and the latter are the nearer causes of reward and punishment, but the focus here is the inner person. In all of her speeches, rather than explaining what deeds are good or bad, Wisdom demands a basic stance toward wisdom itself: a loving openness to wisdom's message, whether this is sweet or harsh, alongside a dread of the consequences of rejecting it. This attitude is requisite to learning; it motivates effort and enables absorption of the lessons. Without it, even superficial learning is unlikely, and knowledge cannot be translated into action. Other interludes will emphasize the right stance; this one seeks to scare us away from the wrong one.

Lady Wisdom does not threaten to execute the retribution herself. She will not *do* anything to the sinners, not even by means of an intermediary. Rather, she will respond to the fools with an attitude matching their own: scorn for scorn, rebuffing them when they need her, or, more precisely, when they finally *realize* that they need her.

We can transpose the metaphorical personification back to the natural plane: Wisdom's threat (esp. in 1:28–29) means that when a crisis comes upon the fools, they will desperately wrack their brains for a solution, for a clever idea to get them out of their fix, but they won't come up with one. Their cunning will evaporate, their inner resources crumble. No stratagems will come to mind, no plans be at hand. Only the truly wise have access to wisdom's practical resources—*ʿormah, tušiyyah, taḥbulot, mᵉzimmah, ʿeṣah*—because they have earned them in a deeper training, driven by fear of God and love of wisdom.

LECTURE II. THE PATH TO WISDOM (2:1–22)

TRANSLATION

Gaining wisdom

2:1 My son,
if you take in my words,
store up my precepts within you,
2 making your ear attend to wisdom,
directing your heart to good sense;
3 if you call out to understanding,
cry aloud to good sense;
4 if you seek it like silver,
delve for it like treasure;
5 then you'll understand the fear of the Lord;
and knowledge of God you will find.
6 For the Lord grants wisdom,
at his behest come knowledge and good sense.
7 For the upright he stores up resourcefulness—
a shield for those who go with integrity,
8 to guard the paths of justice,
protecting the way of his faithful.

Wisdom's benefits

9 Then you'll perceive righteousness, justice, and equity—
every good course,
10 for wisdom will enter your heart,
knowledge become delightful to your soul.
11 Shrewdness will watch over you,
good sense protect you,

Wisdom will save you from wicked men

12 to save you from the way of the evildoer,
from the man who speaks distortions,
13 who abandons the paths of rectitude,
to walk in the ways of darkness,
14 who delights in doing evil,
rejoices in evil duplicity,
15 whose paths are crooked,
and who is devious in his tracks;

Wisdom will save you from wicked women

16 to save you (also) from a strange woman—
an alien who speaks smooth words,
17 who abandons the mate of her youth,
ignores the covenant of her God.

18 For her path[a] descends to death,
her tracks go down to the ghosts.
19 Of her visitors none return,
or regain the paths to life.

Wisdom will keep you on the right path

20 So shall you go where good men walk,
and keep to the paths of the righteous,
21 for the upright will abide on the earth,
the blameless remain therein;
22 but the wicked shall be cut off from the earth,
traitors torn away from it.

---

[a] *n^etîbātāhh* (MT *bêtāhh* "her house")

COMMENTARY

This rich and well-wrought chapter raises several issues that require extended discussions, namely "Knowledge of God and Fear of God" (after 2:5); "The Wicked Man" (after 2:15); and, following the comments on the chapter, "Paths through Life"; "The Idea of Education in Lecture II"; and "Who Is the 'Strange Woman'?" See further the examination of the Septuagint's interpretation of the Strange Woman in the Textual Note on 2:20.

2:1–11. Exordium

2:1. *if you take in my words . . .* : The father's words are authoritative demands, defined by the parallel *miṣwot* "precepts" or "commandments"; the same word is commonly used for God's laws and commands. The boy must take in his father's words and store them away intact as a treasure. They are to be held in the chambers of the heart (Hameʾiri).

"My words" and "my precepts" do not refer to the teachings of the present lecture. In other words, reading chapter 2 itself does not induce fear of God and protect one from tempters. Rather than giving advice that will preserve the pupil from the dangers described, this lecture describes the consequences of listening to "my words" and "wisdom." Verse 2 refers to the father's words and precepts taught elsewhere in the lectures of Part I, while "wisdom" (v 2) embraces all wise teachings. Lecture II is thus not a self-contained instruction but is aware of and serves as a basis for the larger unit, the layer I designate "Ten Lectures." (See "The Components of Proverbs 1–9" in the Introduction.)

Amenemope too exhorts the son to treasure the teachings in his heart:

Give your ears to hear the things that are said,
Set your heart to understand them.
Valuable it is to put them in your heart,

a woe to him who neglects them.
Make them rest in the casket of your belly,
that they may serve as a doorpost in your heart. (§1; cf. AEL 2.149)

(The heart resides within a "casket," which itself is in the "belly" [Egyptian *ẖt*; more precisely, "torso"].) In one school text, a pupil is told: "Put the writings in your heart" (Pap. Lansing 9.3–4; and see Piankoff 1930: 45). Within the Egyptian Wisdom Instructions proper, the image of storing up the teachings in the heart is unique to Amenemope. This is further evidence for the direct influence of the entire book of Amenemope on the Israelite Wisdom tradition.

precepts [*miṣwotay*]: A *miṣwah* is an authoritative commandment. A *miṣwah* is always issued by a superior in status or power, usually by God (in the Pentateuch, the word is used only for God's commands), a king (e.g., 2 Kgs 18:36; Esth 3:3), or a recognized leader (such as Moses [Josh 22:5]). (Likewise, English "precept" properly means a binding principle, not just advice.) The Rechabites subjugated themselves to the authority of Jonadab their "father" and obeyed his *miṣwah* (Jer 35:14–16). When used of the father's precepts in Proverbs (2:1; 3:1; 4:4; 6:20; 7:1–2), *miṣwah* does not shed its connotation of authority, even though these precepts lack legal status and sanctions for enforcement.

Miṣwāh and *ʿeṣāh*, command and counsel: A scholarly debate was sparked by W. Zimmerli, who argued that wisdom is only counsel, not command. "A command appears categorical; counsel is debatable. It should be considered and pondered. It should be clear before it is transformed into deed" (1933; ET p. 181).[97] But this imposes a dichotomy which is misleading, at least for Prov 1–9. (The tone is less authoritarian in the older proverb collections.) The counsels of Proverbs are not "arguable." The only reflection and weighing they mean to inspire pertain to the means and circumstances of their application, not to their validity. B. Gemser responded by arguing that *ʿeṣāh* is often authoritative (1968: 138–49, at 144–46). P. Nel (1982: 89–92 and *passim*), examining the relation between the admonition and their motivations, argued that admonitions (which are a type of *ʿeṣah*) are indeed authoritative, not by virtue of an external institution or divine command, but by virtue of the truth of the proposition, as judged by human reason. Human reason is authoritative because it operates in conformity to the order established by Yahweh (pp. 96–101). "Order," however, does not itself have normative force. Still, the admonitions of Proverbs are certainly authoritative, even if the word *ʿeṣah* itself does not imply it. Their authority is founded on the ethos and authority of parenthood, the communal will, which undergirds all traditional wisdom, and the divine will, which is implied whenever God's favor or disfavor is mentioned.

2:2. *attend to wisdom*: The father's words are not only the way to wisdom, they are wisdom itself.

The verb *lᵉhaqšib* means to listen attentively and, if the object is a request or a command, to carry it out. Jer 6:17 shows that *haqšib* is more than just hearing.

Most medieval commentators construe the infinitive *lᵉhaqšib* (lit. "to attend to") as a noun-complement defining the substance of "my words" and "my commandments," as if to say, "If you listen to my precepts (which command you) to hearken to wisdom" (thus Ibn Janaḥ, Ramaq, Radaq, Hameʾiri). But this con-

---

[97] "Ein Gebot tritt kategorisch auf, ein Rat is diskutabel. Er soll überlegt und abgewögen sein, er soll einleuchten, bevor er in Tat umgesetzt wird" (1933: 177–204, at 183).

struction would disturb the parallelism with v 2b. Also, the father's precepts enjoin specific actions, not the listening itself. Rather, the infinitive is a gerund, specifying the circumstances of the preceding verb (cf. IBHS §39.2.3e). Though *hiqšîb* is not clearly causative elsewhere (Ps 10:17 is ambiguous), the parallel line supports taking the infinitive as causative: "*make* (your ear) attend."

directing your heart: Lit. "you will incline [*taṭṭeh*, H impf.] your heart." (Infinitive-*yiqtol* parallelism is found also in 2:8 and 5:2; see the comment on the latter.)

Leb "heart" is biblical Hebrew's closest equivalent to our concept of "mind." The heart is the locus and organ of thought and the faculty of understanding (e.g., Prov 2:2; 3:1; 16:1; 18:15; and very often). It is also the organ of psychological experiences that we currently classify as emotions (e.g., trust, 3:5; yearning, 7:25; 13:12; sorrow and happiness, 14:13; 15:13; pride, 16:5). But the intellectual exercise of the mind is not really detached from the emotional, and the modern dichotomy is artificial. The distinction is broken down in a sentence like "the heart knows (*yodea*ᶜ) its own bitterness" (14:10), which applies a verb of cognition to a feeling.

Most frequently, the connotations of "heart" are qualitatively and ethically neutral. Everyone has a *lēb*, even evildoers and fools (e.g., Prov 5:12; 6:18; 7:10). The phrase "wise of heart" (11:29) refers to a *potential* for wisdom, not a static quantity of knowledge; cf. Exod 31:6aβ, "And in the heart of everyone wise of heart (*ubᵉlēb kol ḥăkam lēb*) I have put wisdom"; cf. v 35. Less frequently, "heart" refers to a higher quality of intellect, something a fool lacks (e.g., 6:32; 7:7; 9:4; and often) and that others must strive to "acquire," *qānāh* (15:32; 19:8). (English "intelligence" has the same ambivalence.) Prov 2:2 uses *lēb* in this way, to indicate a valuable intellectual power possessed as a special endowment.

MT's *hābînû lēb* is often emended to *hākînû lēb*, thought to mean "prepare" or "direct" the heart, supposedly with Septuagintal support (see Textual Notes). However, *hēkîn lēb* elsewhere means "be faithful" or "prepare oneself spiritually," which does not fit this context (cf. Ehrlich). Moreover, the parallel *hābînû ᶜormāh* in 8:5a shows that 5b is not a call to attention.

To "incline the heart" (or for the heart to incline) means to desire and choose something, not only to pay attention. This is clear in, for example, Judg 9:3; 1 Kgs 11:3; Ps 119:36; cf. Arad 40,4 (HAHL 3.22), where the idiom *naṭah leb* denotes not only paying attention but also the resulting action. Hence the exhortation in 2:2 is not an appeal for attention only; it is a demand for a certain attitude: an eager receptivity toward the teachings. The exhortation does not, however, demand *understanding*. The elementary stage of education does not require penetrating insight into the wisdom being taught.

Ptahhotep distinguishes two types of hearing (or listening): "He who listens is he who (only) hears what is said, (whereas) it is he who *loves* to hear who *does* what is said" (ll. 553–54; emphasis added).[98] ("Listen" and "hear" render the same Egyptian verb, *sḏm*.) Merely auditory hearing is inadequate. An active desire to grasp and activate the message can alone bring the teachings to fruition.

---

[98] Other renderings are possible. AEL translates, "The hearer is one who hears what is said, / He who loves to hear is one who does what is said" (1.74).

2:3. *call out to understanding*: Yet not even a desire for wisdom is sufficient; the pupil must take the initiative and actively *summon*—"call to"—wisdom. (Kaspi compares the use of *qara'* "call" in 2 Kgs 4:12.)

Whereas the MT vocalizes the consonantal writing *'m* as *'im* "if," a midrashic interpretation in *b. Ber.* 57a reads it as *'em* "mother"; in other words, "for you will call understanding 'Mother.'" This understanding is shared by Tg and widely quoted by the medieval commentators. It was inspired by Prov 7:4: "and call understanding 'friend.'"

The treatment of wisdom in Prov 1–9 wavers between the literal and the figurative. Even outside the passages in which wisdom is consistently personified (Interludes A, D, and E), wisdom may be spoken of in terms appropriate to animate beings, namely in 2:3 (being called to); 2:11 (guarding); 3:18 and 4:8 (being embraced and cherished); 7:4 (being addressed as sister and friend); and 3:16 (having right and left hands). On such incidental or inchoate personification see further pp. 331f. In Hebrew (in which the feminine gender is used for many inanimate objects and abstractions, as well as for females), there is an intriguing ambiguity that disappears in English translation, since we must choose between "it" or "she," while in Hebrew both are possible at once.

2:4. *if you seek it like silver*: Not even "calling out" to wisdom suffices; one must actively *strive* for it, seeking it as eagerly as *maṭmonim*. *Maṭmonim* are treasures that are hidden or buried and thus not easily accessible. There is some ambivalence about the accessibility of wisdom (contrast 8:1–5). In this passage, the need to expend effort on its behalf is stressed.

The three conditional particles in vv 1–4 mark off the phases of the learner's task: he must (passively) *absorb* the father's words; (actively) *call* to wisdom; then take the initiative go forth to *seek* her.

2:5. *then* . . . : This is the apodosis of the three conditionals combined (Ibn Yaḥyah). The delay in the resolution of the conditionals in vv 1–4 creates a suspense that suggests something of the magnitude of the task before the seeker for wisdom. Whereas we would expect the quest for wisdom to culminate in the finding of wisdom, this verse makes an even greater claim. It promises no less than religious enlightenment: the understanding of the fear of the Lord and the knowledge of God.

you'll understand the fear of the Lord: This "understanding" consists in a mature insight into what it means to fear God. At a certain level of development, one can *understand* (and not just feel) the fear of God, for it has cognitive content or "subject matter." Psalm 34:12 speaks of the fear of God as something that can be taught ("I will teach you the fear of Yahweh") and proceeds to inculcate certain principles: Avoid dishonesty; turn from evil; recognize God's omniscience; know that God delivers the righteous and cuts off the wicked. These lessons belong to the content of "fear of the Lord."

When the object of *hēbîn* is a mental state (such as fear of God) or a cognitive faculty, the verb means to *acquire* the designated object in an insightful, cognitive way. For example, "Then you'll perceive righteousness, justice, and equity—every good course" (Prov 2:9). And "understand [impv.] cunning [*ʿormāh*]" (8:5a). In 19:25b, the subject already has enough knowledge to make him a *nābôn*; hence *yābin dāʿat* must mean to acquire more and deeper knowledge. See further the comment on 8:5.

The verb *hēbîn*, like English "understand," always denotes an apprehension (or teaching) of meanings, causes, workings, or implications, and not only a knowledge of facts.

Wisdom both begins with fear of God (1:7; 9:10) and leads to it. If the child does his part—the other parties will obviously do theirs—his fear of God will move to a higher stage, as described in this chapter. The simple fear of divine anger that prompted the first, juvenile steps toward wisdom matures into a reasoned, cognitive conscience. The fear of God at the mature stage is the object of understanding (2:5a) and is defined by the parallel as a form of knowledge (2:5b). Fear of God becomes conscience, an inner sense of right and wrong and a desire to do what is right. See "The Fear of God" at 1:7.

Ben Sira defines different stages in the development of the fear of God. The fear of the Lord is both wisdom's starting point (*archē* "beginning," 1:14; *riza* "root," 1:20), which is imbued in the faithful before birth (1:14), and its culmination (*plēsmonē* "plenitude," 1:16; *stephanos* "crown," 1:18; *synteleia* "completeness," "perfection," 21:11[99]).

knowledge of God: This important concept appears in several forms, verbal and nominal, with "Yahweh," "God," and pronouns. The exact phrase *daʿat ʾĕlohim*, "knowledge of God," is rare (elsewhere only in Hos 4:1 and 6:6), as is the word "God" (rather than Yahweh) in Proverbs. The phrase *daʿat YHWH* "knowledge of Yahweh" never occurs in the Bible, though the concept of knowing Yahweh is widespread. This suggests that *daʿat ʾĕlohim* is a fixed idiom with a generic sense, a type of knowledge ("God knowledge") rather than a specific cognition.

"God" (*ʾĕlohim*) occurs just five times in Proverbs. A special reason can usually be discerned for the use of "God" rather than "Yahweh" ("the Lord"). In 2:5 and 30:9, "God" is required as a synonym variant in parallelism with "Yahweh." In 2:17, "God" is used in "covenant of her God" because "covenant of Yahweh" would inevitably be understood as the Sinaitic covenant, and because the possessive "her" (possible with "God" but not with the personal name "Yahweh") emphasizes that an individual obligation is in view. In 3:4, "God" occurs in a phrase used also in foreign texts and may well be an international cliché (see the comment there). It is unclear why "God" is used in 25:2.

Knowledge of God and Fear of God

"Knowledge of God" (or "knowledge of Yahweh," as well as verbal constructions) is a concept of great importance throughout the Bible, especially in prophecy.

---

[99] "And perfection in the fear of the Lord is wisdom."

Its incorporation in Wisdom literature and its identification with wisdom are among the earmarks, and probably the innovations, of Prov 1–9.

"Knowledge" in this phrase means "consciousness" or "awareness." "Knowing" (*y-d-ʿ*) occasionally has this nuance. For example, if one touches an impurity without knowing it and later *huʾ yadaʿ* "he becomes aware of it" (Lev 5:3, 4); see also the discussion of *daʿat* in "Words for Wisdom."

Proverbs claims that knowledge of God is the goal of learning (2:5), the true wisdom (9:10, using *qᵉdošim*). Yet it is not esoteric. Agur, who declares that he lacks "human understanding" and has not "learned wisdom," nevertheless has "knowledge of the Holy One [*qᵉdošim*]" (30:3, q.v.).

Knowledge of God, in Proverbs as elsewhere in the Bible, is never mere cognition of facts. Like the fear of the Lord, the knowledge of God requires commitment as well. This is an existential stance, insofar as it is prior to prudential calculations. This commitment must be realized in action.

To *know* what God does means to *do* it. "In all your ways know him" (3:6; more freely: "In all that you do, keep him in mind") shows that knowledge of God is a constant background sensitivity to God's will, and that this must permeate all one's actions. Then again, knowledge of God is not essential for good behavior. The statement that the young Samuel "did not yet know the Lord" (1 Sam 3:7) does not impute any misbehavior to him. There is such a thing as a naive goodness, but it is frail.[100]

The fear of the Lord and the knowledge of God have much the same qualities and functions, but there is a difference. Fear of the Lord is essentially an emotion or attitude. Hence it can commence before the attainment of knowledge. A child may have fear of God before he acquires knowledge of him. (This may be true of righteous gentiles [Gen 20:11], though they should come to know him as well [1 Kgs 8:43 and often, see TDOT 5.474–76].) Fear of God does have content and can be learned, but in its elementary form, it requires little learning or understanding. Knowledge of God is in essence an awareness or cognition, though it is inextricably bound to fear of God and righteous action. The pursuit of wisdom engenders and enhances both.

Prov 2:5 shows that the combination of fear and knowledge is the apex of *ḥokmah*, "the highest degree of wisdom and Torah," in Ibn Yaḥyah's words. Becker reads this differently. He says that the terms in 2:5 signify the same reality as "wisdom," "understanding," and the like, and that the temporal separation intimated by "then you will understand" is "purely rhetorical," since in 2:9 this phrase introduces nothing new (1965: 220). On the contrary, "then" in 2:9 marks a stage concurrent with the "then" of 2:5 but subsequent to the process described in vv 1–4. The temporal movement of the passage is carefully paced out by the conditional structure ("if" . . . "then" . . . "then").

---

[100]Proverbs, like most of Wisdom literature, recognizes that some people are born with the inclination to do right (23:24; cf. Ptahhotep ll. 575–97 [AEL 1.75.41–42] and ll. 553–54, quoted at Prov 2:2). But Wisdom's primary concern is with the potential coming to fruition in wisdom. Ben Sira mentions naive goodness in 19:23–24.

Ḥokmah is linked with, but not identical to, fear and knowledge of God. If these virtues were one and the same, the entire passage would be a tautology: If you take in *ḥokmah* you will get *ḥokmah*, which will give you *ḥokmah*. The author has a clear idea of the components of wisdom and how they tie together. Fear of God motivates the search for wisdom, which develops into a more sophisticated fear of God, one in which a moral conscience is fused with knowledge of his will. See below, "The Idea of Education in Lecture II." The components of learning are organized in a complex chain of causality; they are not simply equated. After all, much of the practical advice in Proverbs falls in the range of wisdom without constituting fear of God, such as the advice to provide materially for the future (6:6–11) and to avoid loan guarantees (6:1–5). (Indeed, there is a kind of faith that looks upon such calculations with suspicion—see Matt 6:25–33.) And Agur and others (see there) do not make *ḥokmah* a prerequisite of the deepest faith and piety.

McKane believes that "when v 5 is reached the reader becomes aware that the sense of the preceding verses has been given a sudden and quite violent twist" (p. 281). There is indeed a twist, but not, as McKane thinks, because the vocabulary of "old" wisdom, with its supposed pragmatic bent and moral neutrality, is being reinterpreted. The shift is not in semantics but in epistemology. Great claims are being made for wisdom. The intellectual powers that bring success in everyday life belong to the wisdom that comes from God and culminates in religious consciousness and moral behavior.

2:6. *For the Lord grants wisdom*: Conscience and religious awareness come through wisdom because God is its source. We might capture the emphasis by placing "the Lord" in italics: it is ultimately he and no other who gives wisdom. The belief that God gives people wisdom is well attested for special cases (such as Solomon and the artisans of the Tabernacle). But it is true in ordinary cases as well. God "instructs" the naive (Ps 119:130) and his teachings make them wise (19:8).

at his behest come knowledge and good sense: Lit. "from his mouth—knowledge and good sense." The literal translation makes it seem that God's own utterances are being praised, but v 6a and its context are speaking about the wisdom that God *gives* man. In fact, the verb "gives" in 6a may apply to 6b as well: "from his mouth he gives knowledge and good sense" (DNF). This is, however, uncertain, because the idiom "give from (one's) mouth" is unparalleled.

This verse does not imply verbal revelation. It refers to the endowment of an individual with the spirit of wisdom or the communication of principles not verbally or directly but via the human spirit of wisdom. Meinhold aptly compares Eliphaz's charge in Job 22:22: "Take instruction from [God's] mouth, and set his words in your heart." This "instruction" is an idea, the gist of Eliphaz's message in this chapter, not a specific communication from God, for none is quoted. Job 32:8 is especially instructive. Elihu says, "Indeed there is a spirit in man, a spirit of Shaddai that gives them understanding (*t^{e}binem*)." The intelligent man receives a spirit that infuses him with understanding and wisdom—a *ruaḥ ḥokmah ubinah* "spirit of wisdom and understanding," in the words of

Isa 11:2. For Ben Sira (6:18–37), wisdom is a divine gift consequent upon study: "Meditate on fear of the High One, and reflect always on his commands, and he will give your heart understanding, and teach you (*yḥkmk*) what you desire" (v 37); similarly Sir 11:15.

The Egyptian Wisdom teachings are never directly ascribed to a god. Some Ramesside Egyptian tomb autobiographies, however, mention the teaching one receives from a god. One tomb owner says he is a man

whose god instructed him,
and made him perceptive according to his teaching,
who set him on the way of life,
in order to preserve his body,
whom God already knew as a child:
provisions and treasures were assigned to him. (ÄHG #173)

In an inscription on his statue, the vizier Paser says to Amon-Re, "My limbs are pure; your teaching is in my body" (ÄHG #17); see also Shupak 1993: 33. In Wisdom literature too, God is occasionally identified as the (indirect) source of wisdom: "[God] makes the ignorant (*ḫm*) wise (*rḫ*)" ("A Man to His Son," 4.5); "He [a god] gives instruction and puts insight (*s'w*) in his heart" (Pap. Ramesseum II, vso. 1.8). The god's teaching is not clearly defined. It may be in a general way the moral principles cultivated in Wisdom instructions. The specifics of the teachings are never attributed to God, but the ability to comprehend them is sometimes considered god-given.

Agur's concept of divine communication stands apart from the rest of didactic Wisdom prior to Ben Sira. Agur's injunction not to add to God's pure words (Prov 30:6) shows that these words are verbal communications, which is to say, revealed Torah.

Seeking wisdom (vv 1–4) produces religious understanding, which is the mature, rational piety promised in v 5. Prov 2:6 explains why this is so: God is the source of wisdom, and in seeking it one is in effect seeking him. Enlightenment draws its possessor toward the source of knowledge (2:5).

2:7. *he stores up* [*yiṣpon*] *resourcefulness*: *Tušiyyah* is an inner power that can help one escape a fix. It is not an inherently intellectual faculty, nor is it a moral virtue; in fact, many honest people lack the gift. (After all, the deceitful man *can* cheat and harm honest people.) But the sage insists that God himself imbues the upright with the useful endowment of mental dexterity.

This verse has several concurrent implications that radiate from connotations of the verb *ṣapan* "store away," "hide," "reserve":

a. *Setting aside*: *ṣapan* implies setting something aside for a favored person (this can be oneself), who alone can benefit from it (Ehrlich). To *ṣapan* something *for* somebody implies exclusivity (Job 21:19; Prov 13:22; Cant 7:14). Hence 2:7 is claiming that God reserves this resourcefulness specifically *for the upright*. This is a bold and contestable assertion with a polemical tone, since many crafty but immoral people seem to be quite resourceful.

b. *Preservation:* Since a share of wisdom is stored away for the pupil, he need not worry that his toil will come to naught (Hame'iri; sim. Ibn Yaḥyah). It is there waiting for him.

c. *Concealment*: Since *ṣapan* always implies some sort of concealment and not only storage, the verse implies that God has *hidden* wisdom away. It must be energetically *sought*, as if it were a secreted treasure (v 4). When found, it will be hidden and stored (*ṣᵉpunah*) in the finder's own heart (Naḥmias), available for use but not always on display (10:14). It is not the substance of wisdom—its principles or teachings—that is hidden; these are public and evident. It is the faculty of wisdom that is hidden in the sense of not being easily attained. The form of wisdom mentioned here is *tušiyyah*, but other types of wisdom too require effort.

2:8. *to guard the paths of justice*: According to Kaspi (sim. Rashi), "the upright" is the subject of the infinitive "to guard"; hence we could paraphrase, "so that the upright may behave justly." It is true that the idiom "to guard [or "keep"] a path" elsewhere refers to regulating one's own behavior (Prov 16:17; with synonyms: Gen 18:19; 2 Sam 22:22; Prov 8:32; Ps 39:2; Job 23:11), rather than to protecting others. Nevertheless, the parallel line shows that God is doing the guarding. "Paths" and "ways" must be the life course of his faithful. This does not mean that God protects the righteous from harm. "The paths of justice" signify righteous behavior, not a life of well-being. The verse thus teaches that people are not left to their own resources when they strive to be upright. Once they step onto the right path, God helps them remain on it. He protects them by guarding their behavior.

2:9. *Then you'll perceive righteousness, justice, and equity*: That is to say, what is right, just, and equitable to do. The nouns echo 1:3b, q.v. The verb *tabin* may mean "perceive" (G-stem) or "understand" (H-stem). The verse's syntax overrides the expected balance. Syntactically, *meyšarim* ("equity") belongs to the first line as the third direct object of "perceive," while metrically it belongs to the second line. "Every good course" is in apposition to the three nouns. The MT correctly divides the verse at *mišpaṭ*, giving each line approximately the same length:

Then you'll perceive righteousness and justice,
and equity—every good course.

This is an example of enjambment, rare in Hebrew poetry (see the discussion in Watson 1984: 332–35). For another example of enjambment, with the verb in the second line, see 3:2.

course [*maʿăgal*]: Malbim observes that *maʿăgalim* are the lanes that branch off the main roads (it is never used of a major highway). *Maʿăgal* is never used of the major course of one's life, the way of life or death. The phrase "every good course" shows that there are numerous worthy tracks of behavior (2:9).

2:10. *for wisdom will enter . . .* : The phrase "X enters the heart" (*ba' bᵉleb*) is not used elsewhere in BH. It might mean simply that one has learned the father's teachings (2:1), but since the couplet in vv 9–10 refers to a more advanced stage of wisdom, the phrase probably means that you will have received the faculty of wisdom (v 6), an event that transforms attitudes and perceptions.

This verse motivates the preceding. There is a causal relationship between wisdom's entering one's heart (v 10) and the ability to perceive what is right (v 9). Absorbing wisdom—not just memorizing it but learning to love it—allows one to recognize "every good course." Like the fear of God, the understanding of justice is a stage of development beyond the simple doing of good.

The sages of Proverbs make an essentially intellectual process—learning wisdom—proceed both from and toward piety. They do not explicitly exclude the possibility of a pious simpleton,[101] though they assume that without wisdom one is vulnerable to temptation. But even if an unreflective piety could keep one on the right path, Proverbs proposes to inculcate a higher state of conscience, in which virtue is motivated and assured by an understanding of the right way. Such an understanding, and not just threats of divine wrath, is, after all, what the book teaches.

2:11. *Shrewdness will watch over you . . .* : The teacher turns from wisdom's religious-ethical value to its practical benefits. Those benefits are in themselves an ethical power: the ability to stand up to temptation from whatever quarter it may emanate. Virtue is the first reward of wisdom.[102]

Wisdom encompasses the faculties of *mᵉzimmah* and *tᵉbunah* (see "Words for Wisdom"). *Mᵉzimmah* is private, unrevealed thought, often but not always used in scheming. As the ability to think for oneself and keep one's own counsel, it is especially valuable in withstanding temptation (2:11; 5:2). You will be able to look inward, think independently, and resist their blandishments and wiles. *Tᵉbunah*, practical good sense, will likewise guide you in making the prudent choices.

2:12–19. Lesson: Avoid Wicked Men (12–15) and Women (16–19)

2:12–15. Part A, the First Tempter: The Wicked Man

2:12. *to save*: The lesson is syntactically bound to the exordium by the infinitive of purpose "to save"; compare the way the lessons are introduced in 6:24 and 7:5.

---

[101] Ben Sira recognizes this possibility: "Better one lacking knowledge (*synesis* = *daʿat*?) who is fearful (of God) than one abounding in intelligence (*phronēsis*) who transgresses the law" (19:24; possibly the implied object of "fearful" is "sin"). Rabban Gamaliel, however, excludes the possibility: "The ignoramus (*bur*) cannot fear sin, and an uneducated man (*ʿam haʾareṣ*) cannot be pious (*ḥasid*) (*ʾAbot* 2:5).

[102] Toy disdains the ethics of chapter 2 as a form of "eudaemonism" that "may seem to us ethically defective in several points" (p. 54). Toy's comments on this chapter (esp. pp. 54–55) exemplify the power of selective vision. He believes that Proverbs "makes no direct mention of the function of conscience as moral guide." But this is precisely what this chapter (and most of Part I) is about. Toy's notion that Proverbs' ethics are indifferent to the inner life and concerned only with obedience to "outward law" and tangible rewards typifies a distortion common in an earlier era of Wisdom exegesis.

to save you from the way of the evildoer: This does not mean to save you from direct attacks, but to steel you to enticements, lest you capitulate and share evildoers' fate.

Derek raʿ: Delitzsch parses *raʿ* as an adjective, comparing *derek loʾ ṭob* in 16:29. But the parallel substantives "men" in 12b, and "the strange woman" in 16 makes it likely that *raʿ* too is a noun; hence "the way of the wicked man."

distortions [*tahpukot*]: *Tahpukot* occurs ten times in Proverbs and once in Deuteronomy (Deut 32:20). It is the antonym of straightness and means "perversity," "distortion," or the like. Its precise meaning is hard to determine. The root means "turn," "turn over." The word is used of speech (Prov 2:12; 8:13; 10:31, 32; 23:33) and of scheming (Prov 6:14; 16:30; Deut 32:20; Prov 2:14 and 16:28 are indefinite). *Tahpukut* means, approximately, "unreliability" or "unreliable things" (see esp. Prov 23:33, where the heart of a drunkard "speaks" *tahpukot*—delusive, distorted words).

2:13. *who abandons*: In Hebrew, reference to the evildoers changes from singular in v 12 to plural in vv 13–15. (The immoral woman is singular throughout.) Since the description in all cases is generic, there is no significant difference between the type ("the wicked man") and the class ("wicked men").

the paths of rectitude [*yošer*]: *Yošer* is never used of physical straightness but only of ethical straightness. Nevertheless, the connotation of straightness is near to the surface in the Hebrew. Good behavior is imagined as a straight and safe path (see 4:11).

2:14. *who delights in doing evil*: The wicked not only do evil for the sake of its supposed rewards, they positively enjoy it.

2:15. *who is devious in his tracks*: Actually in the plural: *n^elozim b^emaʿg^elotam*, "who are devious in their tracks." The phrasing suggests that the evildoers themselves are contorted (*n^elozim*) with respect to (*b-*) their paths. Prov 14:2 confirms that *naloz* is applied to the man, not the paths, and 3:32 contrasts the *naloz* with the *y^ešarim*, honest, "straight" men. Hence we should not omit the *bet* of *bmʿglwtm* (Toy, BHS, et al.), although some ancient versions seem to read it thus. Just as he who goes in the straight path is himself straight, so he who walks the crooked track becomes deformed. Or, we might say, you can't walk through mud and stay clean.

The Wicked Man

The wicked man is sketched in broad terms. No specific crime is mentioned, but a single attribute dominates: *crookedness*, in word, thought, and deed.

The first mark of the evildoer is in his speech: It is corrupt and corrupting. He speaks *tahpukot* "crookedness" or "duplicity." He is twisted in behavior as well.

In fact, the evildoer not only does evil, he *delights* in it, just as the wise man takes pleasure in wisdom. The wicked man is a moral pervert. Ptahhotep describes him in similar terms. The fool, deaf to wisdom, is not merely a blockhead, but far worse:

As for the fool who can not listen,[103]
he can do nothing.
He sees knowledge as ignorance,
benefit as harm.
He does whatever is hateful,
so that people are ever angry at him.
He lives on what others die on;
distortion of speech is his bread.
His character is known to the officials,
who say (about him):
"A dead man who is alive every day."
(ll. 575–84 [cf. AEL 1.74])

Foolish, self-destructive behavior stems from a constitutional distortion of moral vision, a twisting of values. The wicked man "lives on" (*ʿnḫ m-*) deadly poison. "Lives on" does not mean that this fare does him no harm, but rather that it is his daily sustenance. (Conversely, the righteous—both humans and gods—are often said to "live on" Maʿat.) The evildoer's poison is perversion of speech. Even when the perverted man is alive, this isn't really life, for "life" in Egyptian (and Hebrew) implies vitality and soundness as well as physical existence. As Lady Wisdom says, "All who hate me love death" (8:36b). The wicked man is a zombie.

2:16–19. Part B, the Second Tempter: The Wicked Woman
Warnings against the sexually predatory female, the "Strange Woman," appear in 2:16–22; 5:1–23; 6:20–35; and 7:1–27; as well as in 22:14 and 23:27,[104] and she provides the traits for the personification of Lady Folly in 9:13–18. I will discuss her identity at the end of this chapter and consider the broader questions to which the figure gives rise after chapter 7. I follow the standard practice and refer to the *ʾiššah zarah* as "Strange Woman," without predetermining the kind of strangeness. In my view, however, the Strange Woman is another man's wife; she is not a foreigner or a mythological or allegorical figure.

Various early Jewish commentators construed the Strange Woman as an allegory of religious defection. In the Talmud (*b. ʿAbod. Zar.* 7a), Prov 2:19 is applied to heresy, from which there is no adequate repentance. Rashi (on 2:16) identifies the woman as "the congregation of disbelief, which is heresy" (*kᵉnesiyyah šel ʾepiqorsut, wᵉhiʾ hamminut*), by which he means Christianity. Malbim explains the woman in Prov 2 as both fornication and apostasy. See further "Allegorical-Symbolic Interpretations," pp. 254f. On the Septuagint's interpretation, see the Textual Note on 2:20. Ibn Yaḥyah is unusual in construing the male as well as the female figures allegorically. The deceitful men of 2:12–15, the traitors of v 22, and the woman of 2:16–19 (whom he also identifies as an adulteress) are all ciphers for heresy. (In one manuscript, a church censor has

[103] Lit. "who has no listening" (*iwty sḏm.f*); in other words, has no listening ability.
[104] See also Sir 9:1–9 and 4Q184 ("4Q Wiles of the Wicked Woman"; García-Martínez 1994: 379).

crossed out the crucial words in these sentences, showing that he interpreted references to "heresy" as allusions to Christianity.)

2:16. *to save*: The warning against the seductress is introduced by an infinitive and is dependent on v 11 (noted by Pseudo-Ibn Ezra), as is the warning against wicked men in v 12 and the seductress in 6:24 and 7:5. This construction—"Shrewdness will watch over you, good sense protect you . . . to save you, etc."—indicates that wisdom is the best prophylactic against seduction.

smooth words [*heḥĕliqah*]: lit. "makes her words smooth" or "slippery." The woman's allure lies less in her looks (mentioned only in 6:25) than in her words (2:16; 5:3; 6:24; 7:5, 21; cf. 22:14). Though the sages hold elegance and sweetness of speech in esteem (16:21, 24; 29:9), "smoothness" of speech (with various derivates of *ḥ-l-q*) is deplored, whether in man or in woman. Smooth, slippery speech is flattering and ingratiating (Ps 55:22; Prov 28:23; 29:5). It sets a trap (Prov 29:5) and brings ruination (26:28). It is hypocritical and may conceal malice (Ps 55:22). It is often a quality of deceits (Isa 30:10; Ezek 12:24, etc.), for these must be made attractive. In the Dead Sea Scrolls, the opposing party (Pharisees?) speaks and expounds *ḥălaqot* "smooth things" (*Hodayot* 2.15, 32; 4.10).

Whereas the wicked man's speech is tricky and full of *tahpukot* "distortions" (a word contrasting with straightness and suggesting bumpiness and unevenness), the woman's is distinguished by its *smoothness*. Her art of deception is on display in 7:13–20. (Its deep insidiousness is well analyzed by Aletti 1977; see the Commentary on chapter 7.) Her invitation there is unctuous and insidious. Nevertheless, it is not false or, on the surface, even dishonest. It is, in a sense, quite direct and to the point (7:18!). It is her eloquent "teaching" (*leqaḥ*) rather than a falsehood as such that traps the youth in 7:21. But even truth can mislead by shading and incompleteness. Like her speech, so her paths—in contrast to her male counterpart's—are not rugged and winding, but rather are sloped, inclining down to death (2:18; 7:27).

As Carol Newsom observes, Prov 2 "construes the world as a place of conflicting discourses" (1989: 146–49). In a sense, this is true of much of Wisdom literature, because the sages, like modern humanists, were men of letters, trained in discourse and fascinated by its powers.[105] But I do not agree that the primary concern of chapter 2 is with discourse as such, whether man's or woman's. The issue is the moral content and the effects of a particular discourse.

Nor can I agree with Newsom that the evil man of vv. 12–15 "simply serves to signify whatever stands over against 'us,' the group of the father's discourse" (1989: 148). This reading in effect reduces a description of wicked men, a category whose reality and dangers can hardly be denied, to rhetoric in service of in-group snobbery. It is the evildoers' behavior that defines them as standing "over against us," not their otherness that defines their behavior as evil. In any case, the contrast with "us" is not stated. As for the Strange Woman being a symbol of the "Other," see "The Strange Woman," esp. pp. 257ff.

[105] For a discussion of Egyptian ideas of rhetoric, see Fox 1983.

2:17. *the mate* [*ʾallup*] *of her youth*: *ʾallup* means "friend, companion." The phrase connotes intimacy and affection and thus sounds a note of pathos.

ʾallûp has been understood in three ways, of which the third is best.

(1) *ʾallûp* = leader. Thus Aq *ēgemona*, Vul *ducem*, and some commentators, e.g., Hameʾiri. *ʾallûp* = "commander" in Gen 36:15; Exod 15:15; etc. But *ʾallûp* in that sense is a homonym, deriving from *ʾelep* "thousand" (a military unit) and is used only of a clan leader.

(2) *ʾallûp* = teacher. Thus Syr *mrabbyānāʾ* "foster-father," "one who raises." McKane proposes that *ʾallûp* n^{e}*ʿûrûm* means "paternal educator of youth," that is, the woman's father. His main evidence for this usage is a reference to Jer 3:4, where Yahweh's people address him as "my father, *ʾallûp* of my youth." But in Jer 3, Israel is a faithless wife and Yahweh her first husband; hence an epithet of God as the *companion* (husband) of Israel's youth is appropriate.

(3) "Mate," "companion." In Prov 16:28 and 17:9, which teach that a gossip "estranges companions" (*ʾallûp*, a collective), the context requires a word connoting more than ordinary acquaintance: "*even* close companions." In Jer 3:4, the ostensibly penitent Israel recalls the intimacy of her bond with Yahweh, her former "husband," and speaks of him as *ʾallûp* n^{e}*ʿuray* "the companion of my youth." In Mic 7:5, the intimacy implied by *rēaʿ* in the first line is raised to a higher degree by *ʾallûp* in the second: don't trust *even* your *ʾallûp*, your best friend. In Ps 55:14, *ʾallûpî* is collocated with m^{e}*yuddāʿî* "my (close) acquaintance." *ʾallûp* n^{e}*ʿûreyhā* in Prov 2:17 has its female equivalent in 5:18, where a man's first wife is called *ʾešet* n^{e}*ʿûreykā* "the wife of your youth." *ʾallûp* n^{e}*ʿuray* in Jer 3:4 recalls *ḥesed* n^{e}*ʿûrayik* in Jer 2:2, where likewise former intimacy and affection are invoked.

ignores [*šakeḥah*]: The woman is not only betraying a personal bond with a human, but a legal bond prescribed by God himself (Saʿadia; cf. Ibn Yaḥyah). The verb *šakaḥ*, as Ehrlich observes, does not here mean to forget something once known but to put it out of mind. This woman is not absentminded but insolent, deliberately scorning the covenant of her God.

the covenant of her God: A covenant is an agreement, whether a bilateral compact or a one-sided promise. The covenant in this verse has been explained in three ways.

(1) A covenant, perhaps a marriage agreement, whose guarantor is a pagan god (Alsheikh and, apparently, Hameʾiri), the deity of the supposedly foreign woman. The locution "her God" instead of "Yahweh" or simply "God" is sometimes thought to show this (e.g., G. Boström 1935: 103–4). Preuss believes there is deliberate ambiguity in this regard.

This is most unlikely. Nowhere in the Bible do we find the notion that foreigners had covenants with their gods, and it is doubtful that they did. In any case, a Yahwist such as the teacher of Proverbs would consider it meaningless, and he would hardly be troubled by a violation of a contract with a nonexistent party. "Her God" must be Yahweh.

(2) The covenant at Sinai (Radaq, Meinhold; cf. McKane). LXX's rendering "the covenant of God" exhibits this understanding. That covenant, to be sure, forbids adultery, but the Sinaitic covenant would probably not be called "the covenant of *her* God," since it was made with the entire people. Also, reference to the Sinaitic covenant in Proverbs would be unique and unexpected.

(3) The marriage agreement between the woman and her husband (Saʿadia, Riyqam; Ibn Yaḥyah; see esp. Hugenberger 1993: 296–302). This is the best interpretation. Although marriage is rarely designated as a covenant in the Bible,

Hugenberger (1993) shows that some biblical authors promoted the ideal of marriage as a covenant (the main evidence is Mal 2:14; Hos 2:18–22; Ezek 16:8, 59, 60, 62; Prov 2:16; and cf. 1 Sam 18–20). Hugenberger defines covenant as "an elected, as opposed to natural, relationship of obligation established under divine sanction" (p. 215). The marriage covenant morally bound the husband as well as the wife to sexual fidelity (Hugenberger 1993: 313–38).

The marriage covenant is said to be *God's* insofar as he is its witness and guarantor (cf. Gen 31:44), just as an oath sworn in his name is called an "oath of God" or "Yahweh" (cf. 2 Sam 21:7). The marriage covenant is said to be of *her* God to underscore the fact that this woman is violating her own personal bond.

Likewise, as Saʿadia observes, a man who treats his wife unjustly is violating the covenant that God has witnessed between him and his wife. Saʿadia (like most commentators) compares Mal 2:14–16, which reads:

> (14) And you say, "Why [does God reject our offerings]?" Because the Lord has witnessed (*heʿid*) between you and the wife of your youth (*ʾešet neʿureyka*), whom you have betrayed, though she is your mate and the wife of your covenant (*ʾešet beriteka*). (15) . . . [obscure] . . . do not betray [read *tibgod*] the wife of your youth, (16) for [God] hates divorce. . . .

Malachi is rebuking Jewish men for divorcing their Jewish wives and taking foreign brides. The covenant in Mal 2:14 is the marriage agreement, written or oral.[106] (See further the thorough treatment of Mal 2:14–16 by Hugenberger 1993: 13–47.) That a marriage agreement may be called a *berit* is shown by Ezek 16:8, the parable in which Yahweh "marries" the maiden Israel and says "and I made a promise to you and I entered into a covenant with you."[107] Even a patriarchal marriage (such as envisioned in Ezekiel's parable) requires of both parties personal commitments and formal obligations, sanctified before and by God.

2:18. *For her path descends to death*: Corrected from MT's "For her house inclines down to death." This introduces the reason why it is important to get wisdom, which saves its possessor from the Strange Woman. "Death" is a name for Sheol, the realm of the dead. (In Ugaritic, it is the name of the god of death, a usage with echoes in the Bible.) "Her path" is the path *to* her. Whoever steps on that path slides helplessly down the incline to death.

MT's *byth* should be emended to *ntybth* (to be pointed *netîbātāhh* sg. or *netîbôteyhā* pl.—fem. pl. nouns often govern sg. verbs). The presumed original *mwtntybth* became *mwtbyth* by partial haplography and metathesis: *b-y* for *y-b*. From the standpoint of both sense and grammar, it is awkward to say "her house [m. sg.] inclines down [fem. sg.]." (*šāḥāh* is fem. sg. from *š-ḥ-ḥ*.) The emendation

---

[106] The use of a written document, a "bill of divorcement" (*seper keritut*; Deut 24:1, 3; Isa 50:1; Jer 3:8) at least sometimes in divorce makes it likely that marriage was sealed contractually.

[107] This verse is complicated by the fact that God's actual covenant with Israel is called *berit*, but Ezekiel is here speaking of events within the narrative, and on this level the *berit* is between the husband and the wife.

provides a fem. subject for *šāḥāh* and a better parallel to "her tracks." The image of the woman's house sinking down to the underworld is not found elsewhere, whereas the image of paths or steps leading down to death appears in 5:5; 7:27; 14:12; and 16:25; cf. 12:28b, but the text is uncertain. MT's *beytahh* may be influenced by 7:27, where the word is grammatically feasible (the subject of *yōrdôt* is *darkê-*). Emerton (1979) proposes *šuḥāh ʾel māwet* a "pit (leading) to death" but offers no good parallels to a noun clause of this sort.

ghosts [*rᵉpaʾim*]: "Ghosts" or "shades" are the spirits of the dead. In Ugaritic mythology, the *rpum* seem to be chthonic deities, denizens of the underworld; it is uncertain whether they are dead humans. In Hebrew terminology, the *rᵉpaʾim* are the spirits of the dead (frequently parallel to *metim* "dead"). (See Isa 14:9; 26:14, 19; Ps 88:11; Prov 2:18; 9:18; 21:16; Job 26:5.) They are not demonic. (These *rᵉpaʾim* should not be confused with the ancient nation of Rephaim mentioned in Gen 15:20, etc.) The underworld is a land of silence, darkness, marginal existence, and liminal consciousness. The dead are, at best, in a condition of honorable repose (Isa 14:18). At worst, they are in a state of disgrace, rot, and discomfort (v 19), a condition due to lack of proper burial, not death itself. To go to Sheol is not in itself a misfortune, since that is everyone's fate. The threatened misfortune is a *premature* death.

The *rᵉpāʾîm* are the "weak ones" (from *r-p-ʾ*, a by-form of *r-p-h* "be loose," "weak"). Ramaq aptly compares *taḥăluʾeyha* (Deut 29:21; from *ḥ-l-h*) for the formation and Job 14:10–12 for the concept. Similarly, in Egypt the dead were called *nnyw*, the "weary ones," because the dead (prior to revivification) were envisioned as in a state of extreme weakness, like Osiris, the god of the dead. In Israel too the dead were thought to recline in the underworld in an enervated stupor (Job 3:13–18; Isa 14:9–11). Others derive *rᵉpāʾîm* from *r-p-ʾ* "to heal," thus "the healed ones," used as a euphemism, and in fact the word may be a significant pun on the two contrary meanings. In most of the Bible, the Rephaim are not a separate class of beings, but rather the ordinary dead. Isa 14:9, however, may preserve a memory of the Rephaim as originally dead kings or heroes. See further ABD V 674–76 and the bibliography there.

The underworld and its denizens are vividly depicted in the Babylonian poems "The Descent of Ishtar to the Netherworld" and "Nergal and Ereshkigal" (BTM 1.403–28), as well as in Homer's haunting account of Hades in book XI of the *Odyssey*, which seems to accord in all respects with Near Eastern conceptions.

2:19. *her visitors*: lit. those who come to her. "To come to" a woman in Hebrew is often a euphemism for sexual intercourse (e.g., Gen 6:4; 16:2; Prov 6:29). Her visitors "come to" her in both senses.

the paths to life: There are many paths leading to life, as there are to death (7:27).

2:20–22. Conclusion

2:20. *So shall you go where good men walk*: Lit. "so that you may go in the ways of good (men)." The verse is a purpose clause (introduced by *lᵉmaʿan*) dependent on the two infinitives ("to save") in vv 12 and 16. (Rashi links v 20 with v 12, Ehrlich with v 16, Benjamin ben Judah with both.) Alternatively, the verse may be dependent on v 11, wisdom's guarding you (Naḥmias); or on vv 1–5, the advice to get wisdom (Radaq). The last option provides the most logical basis for the purpose clause: Gain wisdom, so that it may keep you from the path of the wicked and on the path of the righteous. The conclusion thus circles back to the exordium.

2:21–22. The lecture is capped off by a pair of complementary proverbs recapitulating the two paths—life and death—and reinforcing the gravity of the right choice. Like the capstone of Lecture I, this extends the principle beyond the cases exemplified in the lesson proper.

These verses were probably preexisting proverbs and recognizable as such. They occur elsewhere in different forms, from which we can abstract a *topos*. (A topos is an idea or a verbal formula that can be assumed to receive common consent and can be reused in new forms and contexts.) The topos of 2:21–22 is "the righteous will abide in the land, and the wicked be cut off from it." The topos appears in Prov 10:30. Ps 37 (a Wisdom psalm dealing with the success of the wicked) is built around this topos, mustering it repeatedly as a given in proving a difficult proposition (vv 9, 11, 22, 28b, 29, 34b, 38b).

Prov 2:21 bears on the question of whether Wisdom literature draws upon the particular beliefs of Yahwism and traditions of Israel.

the upright will abide on the earth [*ʾereṣ*]: *ʾereṣ* (*haʾareṣ* = "the earth") means both world and land (namely, of Israel). This ambiguity allows for four interpretations:

(1) *ʾereṣ* = the land of Israel. The righteous of the nation shall remain in the land of Israel, while the wicked are sent into exile. Toy, Gemser, McKane, Plöger, Meinhold, and probably most modern commentators read these verses as an allusion to God's covenantal promise of the land of Canaan to the people of Israel, alongside a warning of exile should they fail to keep his law. The background of this promise is considered specifically Deuteronomic (Gemser, Plöger, Steiert 1990: 252–53). (Gemser refers to Deut 4:10; 5:16, 33; 6:18; 11:9; 15:4–5; 16:20; 17:20; 22:7; 25:15; 32:47; and Jer 46:27f.) Plöger, who sees Prov 2:21–22 as a reference to the Land of Canaan, considers the quatrain as a later addition intended to round off the chapter. Plöger suggests that the purpose of the addition was to be an admonition to the entire people of Israel to examine its way of life.

(2) *ʾereṣ* = a portion of the physical land, in particular a family's ancestral portion. The righteous will live in security on their ancestral land and bequeath it to their offspring (Radaq).

(3) *ʾereṣ* = the next world, eternal life. The righteous will live forever, while the wicked are consigned to final destruction or to Gehenna (Naḥmias, Kaspi, Rashi, Saʿadia [comparing Arabic *dār*, which can refer to this world or the next]).

(4) *ʾereṣ* = this world. The righteous will live (long), the wicked will die (prematurely). This is, I believe, correct.

Concern for the Land of Israel is absent from biblical Wisdom literature, as is the belief in an afterlife. The theme recurrent in Proverbs is (long) life for the righteous, (early) death for the wicked. Lecture II maps out two roads, the one of life, leading to life, the other of death, leading to death. "The earth" rather than "the Land (of Israel)" is appropriate to the metaphorical geography. Moreover, sayings that use this topos always refer to individual life and death.

Deuteronomy promises enduring possession of the Land as a reward for obedience, and national exile as punishment (e.g., 28:63). This topos elsewhere, however, envisages individual reward and punishment. The fates described in Prov 10:30 are allocated individually, namely: "The righteous man never totters, while the wicked shall not abide in the earth" (*lōʾ yiškᵉnû ʾāreṣ*). "Never tottering" is not a national destiny (cf. Ps 15:5).

Psalm 37 uses the topos as a variable refrain (vv 9, 11, 22, 28b, 29, 34b, 38b). Closest to 2:21–22 are Ps 37:29 for the positive ("The righteous will inherit the earth [*ʾereṣ*] and abide [*yiškᵉnû*] forever upon it") and v 9 for the negative ("for evildoers will be cut off"). The promises sometimes include the progeny of the righteous and wicked in their fate (vv 28b, 37–38; cf. Ps 25:13[108]). That does not mean that *ʾereṣ* is family property (contrary to interpretation 2); it never is elsewhere. Rather, the implication of *yiyrᵉšû ʾāreṣ* in Ps 37:29 is that the righteous man's descendants will live and continue his line. The Psalm makes no reference to the Land of Israel, but throughout assigns reward and punishment in accordance with individual merits. The topos is reused in Isa 60:21, apparently in the sense of national possession, though the sense of long lifespans is also possible.

One problem with interpretation 1 is that exile is a national punishment, a judgment on the people as a whole (certainly so in Deuteronomy), whereas the warning in v 22, as in Psalm 37, distinguishes individuals within the nation and promises them appropriate fates. The prophetic concept of the "righteous remnant" is not applicable here. That concept envisions a communal desolation, then, as an afterthought, allows for the survival of a small remnant composed of the righteous (1 Kgs 19:18; Zeph 2:3; Isa 6:13bβ [a gloss]; 10:19–21; Ezek 9:4; and, most consistently, Ezek 18). More significant is the idea that the remnant of Israel will be purified and *become* righteous (e.g., Isa 1:24–38; 10:20–21; Ezek 20:37–38). The idea of the righteous remnant certainly does not assume that all righteous people survive the disaster.[109] In Zech 13:8, which uses language similar to Prov 2:21, the third part that are left in the land after the others are killed off are no more righteous than the others, and they will continue to suffer. Nor does this concept envision a continuous process that sifts out sinners (licentious youths, for example) for exile.[110]

the blameless remain [yiwwatᵉru] therein: The verb translated "remain" means more precisely "be a residue, be left over," rather than "endure." The verb thus presupposes the next verse as its context. Hameʾiri observes that "this is said with respect to what follows." Rashi glosses, "when the wicked go down to Gehenna." We might translate v 22a: "*when* the wicked are cut off from the earth. . . ."

2:22. *cut off [yikkaretu] from the earth*: The wicked will be severed from the land of the living. It is possible that this means that they will leave no lineage behind them (DNF). Various sins against God, particularly in the priestly legislation, are punished by *karet*, lit. "cutting off," to use the rabbinic designation. The rabbis viewed *karet*, correctly, as a penalty executed by God for sins not punished by humans. Milgrom (1991: 457–60) sees two possible meanings, which are

---

108 The phrase *zarʿô yiyraš ʾāreṣ* means that his descendants will live, rather than that they will inherit his land, which would call for *ʾadmato* or *naḥălato*.

109 Ezekiel makes this claim in chapter 18, but even he does not suppose that all victims are wicked; see esp. 21:8–9. In the Elijah story, God promises to save a remnant of seven thousand faithful in the future, but masses of loyal Yahwists have already been slaughtered (1 Kgs 18:13). In Gen 18:22b–33, ten righteous men (if there had been any) would not have constituted a "righteous remnant" because the destruction of the collectivity would have been averted.

110 Moreover, in Deuteronomy, which is, according to interpretation 1, the source of the theme of living long in the land, the promise refers to long lifespans for individuals (Deut 5:16, 33; 22:7). Even when the nation as a whole is addressed (16:20; 32:47), the long life they are promised on the land (*ʾădamah*, not *ʾereṣ*) is the lifespan of individuals, not the persistence of the nation in the Land (which, if the people are righteous, will not be merely long, but eternal).

not mutually exclusive: (1) *Karet* is the extirpation of one's lineage (thus Ibn Ezra on Gen 17:14). (2) *Karet* is severance from one's ancestors in the afterlife (the opposite of "being gathered to one's kin").

torn away [*yissᵉḥû*] *from it*: The verse may be using vocabulary from imprecation formulas. Except for Prov 15:25, the verb *nsḥ* (in Aramaic and Hebrew) appears only in imprecations.

Compare Ahiqar 156 (obj. = "his tongue") and 211, as well as KAI 225, 10–11 ("[The gods] will tear away [*ysḥw*] your name and your place from the living and kill you with an evil death and destroy your seed"); KAI 228A, 14; Ps 52:7 (G-stem); Ezra 6:11 (Gt); and Deut 28:63 (N).

Yissᵉḥû: The G of *n-s-ḥ* is elsewhere transitive (Prov 15:25; Ps 52:7; likewise in Aramaic, see above). *Yissᵉḥû* is unlikely to be a G intransitive from this root (contrary to Naḥmias and Hameʾiri), esp. as the context requires a true passive sense, which is not expected in G intransitives. One possibility is to point *yussᵉḥû*, a G passive of *n-s-ḥ*. The MT vocalization apparently intends an indefinite G plural (Ramaq and Delitzsch; see GKC §144g), which may be correct.

The Design of Lecture II[111]

Prov 2, a self-contained unit in the first collection (Prov 1–9), is doubly peculiar. First, the exordium (the call to attention), which is usually introductory to a specific counsel, extends through fully half the chapter (vv 1–11). Second, the body of the lesson gives no explicit advice. To be sure, practical counsels are easily and legitimately deduced from the praise of wisdom, but these are implicit, not stated. The imperatives usually heaped up in the other lectures are absent here, as are the warning ("lest") clauses that commonly reinforce the precepts.

These features have led some commentators to deprecate this lecture as diffuse and unstructured. Its peculiarities might indeed be flaws if it were attempting to do the same thing as the other units of Prov 1–9, but it is not. Prov 2 has a different purpose, namely, to encourage the pupil in the search for wisdom. In so doing, it unfolds a theory of learning unique in ancient literature.

Lecture II comprises an exordium (1–11), a lesson (12–20), and a capstone (21–22), the last composed of a proverb pair that drives home the message. The movement of thought in the chapter proceeds according to the following design:

I. Exordium (1–11)
  A. *If* you attend to my teachings (1–4),
  B. *then* you will attain true piety (5),
    1. *because* it is God who gives wisdom (6)
    2. and this will protect you (7–8);
  C. *then* you will know the right behavior (9)
    1. *because* you will have received wisdom (10),
    2. and this will protect you (11)

[111] "Composition" refers to the historical process of literary formation, the way the present text came to be. This will be discussed only in units where a strong claim has been made for historical layering. "Design" refers to the disposition of the text in its Masoretic form.

II. Lesson (12–20)
  A. *in order to* save you from wicked men (12–15) and
  B. *in order to* save you from the wicked woman (16–19),
  C. *so that* (consequent upon exordium) you will go on the right path (20),
III. Conclusion/capstone (21–22)
  for that is the salvation of the righteous.

The syntactical-logical movement of the lecture, marked by the italicized words, proceeds independently of the standard tripartite literary division (exordium, lesson, and conclusion). This double weave preserves the literary structure of the other lectures while making it serve a different end.

The lecture proceeds in a single chain of thought: If you take in my teachings and seek wisdom, you will gain wisdom, which will bring you to fear of God and righteousness, which will protect you and keep you away from wicked men and women, so that you may enjoy a long life. In fact, Lecture II can be read as a single conditional sentence, and is so translated by Meinhold. The sections of the lecture are fused syntactically. The lesson comprises two long result clauses dependent on the exordium: vv 12–15 and vv 16–19. These two sections are highly congruent. Each comprises four couplets; both are introduced by the same word, *l*ᵉ*haṣṣil*ᵉ*ka* "to save you," both begin the second verse with the participle *ʿozeb* (m. pl. and fem. sg.) "who abandon(s)"; and both continue with a characterization of the sinners and their perils.

D. Pardee (1988) has used this chapter as the basis of an analysis of the interworkings of the various types of parallelisms used in Hebrew poetry. The purpose of his study is to test different ways of describing parallelism as a poetic principle, but in so doing he reveals a complex network of echoes, some of which link lines at a distance. Parallels in distant distribution strengthen the cohesiveness of the unit (p. 151).

About half the verses in this chapter (1, 4, 5, 7, 8, 9, 12, 15, 16, 17, 18, 20) display a striking chiasm, not all of which can be rendered smoothly in English. Two clusters, vv 4–9 and 15–20, have a high concentration of chiastic structures. The effect of the string of chiasms may be likened to walking forward in a zigzag.

Meinhold (1991: 43–47) calls this chapter a "teaching program" or "syllabus" (*Lehrprogramm*) for Prov 1–9. The chapter lays out the themes in the order in which they will be treated in the remaining chapters. (On Meinhold's structural analysis, see pp. 322f.) The connections he draws are, however, forced. The contents and structure of this lecture are not governed by the thematic development of the following chapters but by the rhetorical disposition of the educational message that Lecture II propounds; see later, "The Idea of Education in Lecture II."

P. Skehan (1947a: 9–10) describes this chapter as a nonalphabetic acrostic. It has twenty-two verses, the number of letters in the Hebrew alphabet. In Skehan's analysis, stanzas 1, 2, and 3 (vv 1–4; 5–8; 9–11) begin with *aleph*, and stanzas 4, 5, and 6 begin with *lamed* (vv 12, 16, 20). Skehan's method is procrustean. He grants that we must ignore *b*ᵉ*ni* at the start of v 1 and *ki* in v 3. He also ignores the *lamed* of v 8 and the *aleph* of v 15, which violate his schema. At any rate, in the absence of a *taw* ending for the chapter, these letters are insignificant.

D. N. Freedman (1997) also identifies this chapter as a nonalphabetic acrostic. He notes that Lam 5 has twenty-two verses, like the indisputably acrostic poems that precede it. He considers the nonalphabetic acrostic as a recognized poetic form with a fixed metrical pattern (8 + 8 = 16 syllables, with considerable variation). Still, the notion of "acrostic" is of dubious value here. Poems that do not follow the alphabet or spell out words are definitely *not* acrostics. Perhaps the tradition of alphabetical acrostics created a *mold* of twenty-two verses. But since the lectures in Prov 1–9 vary in length from eight to thirty-one verses,[112] it does not seem that a length of twenty-two verses would cue the reader into its special nature, unless (as is the case in Lam 5) the proximity of clear acrostics gives the number 22 special significance and alerts the reader to it.

The Redaction History of Proverbs 2

Some scholars believe that Prov 2 grew to its present scope through a series of additions and elaborations, and furthermore that the stages of growth correspond to a historical development in the idea of wisdom and religion. Such theories apply to the entirety of Prov 1–9, whose composition will be addressed in Essay 1.

With regard to this chapter, C. H. Toy excises 2:5–8 as an editorial expansion by an editor "who thought that the central idea of these discourses, the *fear of Yahweh*, ought not to be lacking here" (p. 34). He also places v 20 after v 9. Interestingly, Toy assumes that the *idea* of the fear of Yahweh is original to the discourses, although it is secondary in this context. It is true that redaction history need not correspond to a greater intellectual history but may arise from individual ideas and preferences. In the present case, however, piety and ethics are central to the chapter's essential concerns, and the primary author may have introduced this theme for the very reasons that Toy thinks motivated a redactor to add.

R. N. Whybray (1965b: 40–41; 1966: 482–96) argues that in this chapter, as throughout Prov 1–9, an original, pragmatically oriented wisdom discourse has been expanded (if not distended) in order to infuse the lectures with Yahwistic piety. In Prov 2, the original discourse comprised vv 1 + 9 (the "introduction") and 16–19 (the instruction proper). This "genuine," skeletal, instruction was practical (rather than theological in purpose) and not repetitive. Whybray rightly observes that two points of view, Yahwistic piety and wisdom teaching, intersect in Lecture II. There is, however, no disharmony. The viewpoints are synthesized, and that synthesis is at the heart of the author's intention. Features that Whybray ascribes to the putative editors (such as emphatic repetition and intensification of the theological message) can better be assigned to the author; see further p. 322.

D. Michel (1992) traces four stages of development in chapter 2: (1) The original teaching, based on the deed-consequence nexus (2:1–4, 9–15, 20). This was elaborated by three interpretive, "actualizing" supplements. (2) A supplement introducing the idea that wisdom leads to fear of Yahweh, that is to say, religion (vv 5–8). (3) A supplement introducing the "Strange Woman," who (in Michel's view) had come to symbolize evil in itself (vv 16–19). (4) A conclusion, formulated under the influence of apocalyptic circles, promising of a final judgment. Michel's schema requires reading the Strange Woman as an allegory, although there is nothing in the text to justify that type of reading. The putative addition, read allegorically, would use a vivid image to produce an

---

[112] I = 12 vv; II = 22 vv; III = 12 vv; IV = 16 vv; V = 9 vv; VI = 10 vv; VII = 8 vv; VIII = 23 vv; IX = 16 vv; X = 27 vv.

unbalanced promise: Wisdom will save you from harm at the hands of wicked men (12–15) *and* from evil in itself. Michel's argument for the apocalyptic reading of vv 21–22 is that if the evildoers were obliterated in the here and now, they would not present the danger described in vv 5–8. The answer is that the wicked are threatened with a premature death as individuals, as always in Proverbs. That leaves plenty of time for them to be wicked and plenty of young evildoers to take their place. The fates described in Prov 10:30, for example ("The righteous man never totters, while the wicked shall not abide in the earth"), are assigned individually and do not await the final judgment.[113]

According to McKane (pp. 278–81), the shape of the chapter resulted from a slackening of structure in which "the imperative has disappeared and crisp, authoritative Instruction has given place to diffuse preaching organized in a series of protases and apodoses" (p. 7, cf. 278). Quite to the contrary, the design described previously shows that this lecture is by no means rambling. The absence of imperatives is indeed striking; see p. 133.

The scholars mentioned in this sketch agree that this chapter underwent some sort of religious expansion. Yet it is improbable that the tightly knit structure of Lecture II would have resulted from multiple intrusions. The unusual expansiveness of the exordium is due not to editorial bloating but to the inherent demands of the theme of the lecture. The true subject is not the danger of sin but Wisdom pedagogy itself (discussed later), and the exordium is elaborated because that is the section that deals with teaching and learning. Other lectures become expansive in *their* areas of interest. Lecture V (4:1–9) is entirely an extended exordium. Lecture X devotes the entire lesson (vv 6–23) to a lengthy description of the encounter with the adulteress.

There were indeed intellectual developments within Wisdom, of which this chapter is the product (see Essay 3, "Wisdom in the Lectures"), but there is no reason to place the developments *after* the author of the lectures. They may be the creation of prior sages or of the author himself. But whatever its history or prehistory, Lecture II now forms a meaningful, well-structured literary and conceptual unity.

Paths through Life

BEHAVIOR IS A PATH[114] is the *ground metaphor* of Prov 1–9, or, as N. Habel (1972) designates it, the "nuclear symbol" that unifies its teachings. A ground

---

[113] Proverbs throughout promises long life and speedy death in accordance with individual merits. The promise sometimes includes the progeny of the righteous in their fate (e.g., 11:21; 13:22; 14:26; 20:7; cf. Ps 25:13). The proverb formula is reused in Isa 60:21 in a promise for the future, apparently in the sense of national possession of the Land of Israel, though the sense of long lifespans is also possible. The eschatological use should not be retrojected onto other occurrences.

[114] The convention of capitalizing metaphors is taken from Lackoff and Johnson's *Metaphors We Live By* (1980). Their study demonstrates how metaphors infuse and guide our thoughts and take on a life of their own.

metaphor is an image that organizes other perceptions and images and conveys a way of perceiving the world.[115]

Several words—*derek, maʿgal, ʾoraḥ, nᵉtib*, and *nᵉtibah*—are used to designate the paths in this metaphor. (In this commentary, no distinction is intended between "way" and "path," but "way" is sometimes ambiguous, as in "way of life," so "path" is often preferable.)

BEHAVIOR IS A PATH implies that an action leads somewhere. Action is not its own goal. It is not static, but has consequences that sometimes lie beyond the horizon (14:12; 16:2; 20:24). This same metaphor suggests that once a person enters onto this path, he is likely to follow it to the end. It becomes his natural course and, in spite of its difficulties, is easier to stay on than to leave. The metaphor of life's PATHS also allows for a "map"—guidance as to which paths lie where—whereas if life were a trackless wasteland, it would be very hard to know where to go. Wisdom literature provides the map.

The underlying metaphor of PATH takes two distinct forms: MANY PATHS and TWO PATHS.

1. There are MANY PATHS or ways of behaving, some leading to life, others to death, others (of less interest in Proverbs) to nowhere in particular. (*Maʿgal* "course" usually has this neutral sense, one path of many.) The injunction "in all your ways know him [namely, God]" (3:6) can only refer to all that you do, for it would be a tautology to say, "in your Way of Life know him." In the aphorism "a man's mind calculates his way" (*darko*) (16:9), "way" can refer only to whatever type of action one chooses. "Make straight the course (*maʿăgal*) you go on, and all your ways will be secure" (4:26) makes sense if "the course you go on" can refer to whatever type of life one chooses. The innocence in the heart of the righteous man will make his path—his behavior—straight (11:5). Only when one's life course is made straight will it be a "Way of Life."

2. Another way of thinking of our movement through life is by the metaphor of TWO PATHS. While in one sense we can go on a limitless number of "paths," from another perspective there are really only two paths, or types of path, of fatal importance. The path that wisdom teaches, the one the righteous take, is the WAY OF LIFE (*ʾoraḥ ḥayyim* in 5:6 and 15:24; *derek ḥayyim* in 6:23) or (with no significant difference) the "Ways of Life" (*ʾorḥot ḥayyim*, 2:19). The WAY OF LIFE is the way *to* life, and it is so formulated in 10:17 (*ʾoraḥ lᵉḥayyim*). Any reference to the way of the righteous and wise belongs in this category.

The opposite path is the WAY OF DEATH. The term occurs only in the plural, "ways of [i.e., to] death" (14:12; 16:25) or "ways of [to] Sheol" (7:27). But

---

[115]For Prov 1–9, R. Van Leeuwen (1990a) proposes two coordinated ground metaphors: the two roads and the two women, both based on the even more fundamental metaphor of boundaries or limits. Limits, however, seem to me an abstraction rather than a metaphor. Nor are limits as important as WAYS in organizing the thoughts of Part I. I agree with Habel that the polarity of the two ways is most fundamental and provides the pattern for the other polarities, notably the two hearts and the two women. Women (real and figurative), like men, are on one of these paths.

all wicked, foolish ways lead to the same end and are really one and the same. Any behavior that leads to life is *a* WAY OF LIFE, and conversely for those that go to death.

In spite of the importance of the TWO PATHS dichotomy, the author does not picture life as a landscape with two highways running through it and instead has a much more complicated map in mind. There are a vast number of paths ("lifestyles" in the current cliché) crisscrossing the landscape. Even within the TWO PATHS metaphor, there are a plurality of "paths of life," actions and types of behavior that lead to life (2:19); these are the "ways of the righteous" (2:20). Likewise, a single sinner takes many roads on his way through life, but each one leads to death. It requires wisdom to recognize which path leads to which end.

The WAY OF LIFE is straight, flat, and well-lit. No one stumbles in it. This road, the way taught by wisdom, is, as Habel (1972: 137) observes, not secretive or esoteric, but open, well-lit, and public. It is the *natural* route to choose. Every track the wicked go on, in contrast, snakes erratically through rough and dark territory. A person inevitably stumbles and stubs his toes walking along it. Its meanderings are erratic, but its end is certain: death.

The WAY OF LIFE is important in Egyptian Wisdom of all periods. It sums up the ethical behavior inculcated by Wisdom literature. The author of Beatty IV says, "I spread out before you a teaching, instruct you in the way of life" (vso 6.3–4). Amenemope proposes to direct the reader "in the way of life" (§1; 1.7). (In Egyptian literature, "life" means both this world and the next, and it may be read both ways in the latter sentence.) It is synonymous with the "way of God," the way on which God leads man, which is also the way to success (Shirun-Grumach 1972: 10, 14). Amenakhte calls his teachings "the utterances of the way of life" (l. 1). (For further examples, see the comment on 2:6.) The Egyptian sages do not refer to the other path; therefore, the image of the "way" is not inherently polar. The polarity of the TWO PATHS is a deliberate development in Proverbs.

Corresponding to the TWO PATHS there are two classes of people. Proverbs splits the world along a moral fault line that runs between two classes, the wicked/foolish and the righteous/wise. The first class is the source of all evils and dangers; the second is innocent. The two remain apart, each type pursuing his own path. There is little thought of a wise man degenerating or a wicked man repenting, but sometimes, particularly at the transitional stage of adolescence, one comes to a fork in the road. What is required for life and well-being is to enter and remain on the right branch, lest one fall into the irredeemably wicked. These are the Other, not because they are women or socially marginal groups (the Strange Woman is *not* socially marginal), but because they stand as the Other vis-à-vis the righteous/wise, to whose number people of all social groups and both sexes may belong.

This dichotomy oversimplifies the difficulty of moral choices confronting one in any particular moment. One sees ahead a confusing variety of behavioral paths. Wisdom allows one to classify each path and deduce its end point from its quality at point of entry. Education in wisdom is needed to enable a person to do so, and to this end the sages developed an idea of what education must do and how this is best achieved.

The Idea of Education in Lecture II

Education in ancient Israel commonly is pictured as a harsh and mindless affair: demands for obedience to rules learned by rote and drummed in by incessant rebukes, simplistic promises, and, above all, zealous thrashings, but directed by little thought or principled methodology. Lorenz Dürr's authoritative study of education in the ancient Near East (1932) devotes a mere page and a half to the "Principles and Methods of Education and Instruction in the OT" (pp. 114–15). On the basis of an etymology of *musar* and the proverbs praising the rod, he asserts, grimly: "Thus too in the 'Wisdom texts,' rigor and discipline ("Strenge und Zucht") are demanded to the extreme" (p. 114). This, he says, applies to education in both home and school. H. van Oyen says, "Moreover, in general the idea predominated that starting very early the soul of the child was possessed by a demonic power and only a merciless opposing force of harshness and stringency could protect the soul from total ruination" (1967: 155). C. Westermann (1990: 38–40; ET 26–28) draws a similar picture, but only for postexilic schools.[116] Sayings that express a certain distaste for corporal punishment (17:10) and greater sensitivity to individual needs (18:19; 20:11; 22:6) he locates in an earlier, oral stage of proverb making. Sayings that endorse the rod (13:24; 19:25; 22:15; 29:15, 17) he ascribes to the postexilic school and reads as the self-justifications of the schoolmaster to the parents for using corporal punishment. That is the setting Westermann sees for Prov 1–9 as well.

Though beatings and scoldings were undoubtedly a staple of discipline in both school and home, what is missing in this picture is any thought about pedagogy itself: how a child learns, what the possibilities and limits of learning are, what constitutes learning, and where it leads. The sages were not oblivious to these issues.

Lecture II aims at encouraging the neophyte in the search for wisdom by leading him through the logic of the educational process. This aim explains the unusual length of the exordium. The exordium usually introduces the lesson by urging the son to hearken to the father's wisdom. Here it is the exordium that bears the central message of the chapter, while the lesson's main function is basically to illustrate the exordium's message.

[116] In my review of this book (Fox 1992), I criticize Westermann's schematic early-late dichotomy in Wisdom literature and education.

Some medieval Jewish commentators recognized the pedagogic thrust of Lecture II. Saʿadia Gaon, who is throughout his commentary alert to the book's pedagogy and psychology, identifies the purpose of this chapter thus:

> The theme of this chapter is that learning begins with acquisition [*qᵉniyyah*; cf. 4:5] and culminates in thought and analysis. Therefore [Solomon] begins, "My son, if you take in my words" [v 1], and then says, "if you seek it" [v 4], and next says [in so many words]: "If you who seek wisdom and do these two things, then you will understand the fear of the Lord, etc." [v 5]. Without learning from a teacher [vv 1–2], reflection will avail nothing, and likewise learning without reflection and analysis [vv 3–4] will avail nothing. But by joining these together the goal may be attained. (Introduction to chapter 2)

In other words, education has two main phases. It commences with the father's teaching and its rote incorporation by the child, complemented by the learner's own thought and inquiry. *Then* God steps into the picture and grants wisdom. God's grant of wisdom, Saʿadia goes on to observe, has a prerequisite in the labor invested in study, just as his gift of bread (Ps 136:25) requires and responds to the human labor of farming. Education is thus a cooperative effort of child, parents, and God.

But, Saʿadia says, there is a possible hitch in the process. To attain wisdom the novice must persevere in an effort toward goals whose benefits he cannot really grasp in advance:

> [Solomon] informs us afterwards that the soul takes pleasure in wisdom just as the body takes pleasure in what it senses, as he says, "and knowledge will become a delight to your soul" [10b]. . . . But there is a difference between the pleasure of wisdom and the pleasure of the senses. The senses enjoy what they are accustomed to, and therefore all nature aspires to these things, whereas man takes pleasure in wisdom only after reflection and inquiry, for which reason [wisdom] is not universally desired. (Introduction to chapter 2)

The neophyte has not yet tasted the pleasures of wisdom. Therefore, he needs immediate encouragement and reassurance in his task:

> Accordingly, the sage wrote this chapter to reassure the seeker of wisdom [to the following effect]: "Do not suppose that at the start of your inquiry [in wisdom] you will gain its benefit and enjoy it. Rather, be patient, for its beginnings are wearisome, but if you work through them, you will later arrive at lasting satisfaction and joy and happiness. (Introduction to chapter 2)

To provide this encouragement—and not merely to force the child to obedient attention—is the intent of Lecture II. The tone of the exordium is accordingly sympathetic and supportive. Several other medieval commentators were alert to this tone (see also Hameʾiri and Ibn Yaḥyah on 2:7), but it seems to have escaped the notice of modern exegetes.

The thrust of the exordium is not: "seek wisdom!" but rather: "if you seek wisdom you *will* find it."[117] The threefold conditional of vv 1–4 (which replaces the expected imperatives) conveys the earnestness of the reassurance. The declaration "for the *Lord* grants wisdom" (v 6a), with its emphatic frontal positioning of "Lord," reinforces the assurance: Do not fear failure, for the guarantor of success is God himself, who gives wisdom to those who labor for it. Father, mother, and God cooperate with the youngster himself in the shaping of moral character, which will provide reliable guidance and protection throughout his life.

In the context of the cycle of lectures of Prov 1–9, Lecture II is the main exposition of a well-thought-out idea of the learning process: (1) Elementary moral conscience (fear of God) motivates one to seek wisdom (1:7). (2) One seeks wisdom diligently (2:1–4 and other exordia). (3) God grants wisdom (2:6). (4) Wisdom brings with it a higher level of moral conscience (2:5a) and knowledge of God (2:5b), so that (5) one can better discern what God wants in all circumstances (2:9; 3:6).

The search for wisdom proceeds not through esoteric inquiries or even through religious devotions, but rather through eager absorption and pursuit of earthy, practical wisdom, such as the father is teaching. Yet while parental teaching is sensible advice about good behavior, it is also the path to the loftiest religious knowledge.

Admonition as well as reassurance has a place in pedagogical rhetoric. A child must *fear* the peril presented by evildoers. The danger is not so much that he will fall victim to the wicked as that he will bring calamity upon himself by consorting with them. The father, in Prov 1–9 at least, is not himself an object of fear. His wrath and punishment are not among the dangers threatened.[118] Indeed, the father never even rebukes the child in Part I, though he praises chastisement in 6:23 and makes God its source in 3:11.[119] The dangers are all external to the teaching relationship, all lurking outside the home.

Wisdom, for the author of Part I, is not simply knowing what is good to do, such as maintaining sexual virtue and avoiding loan guarantees. Wisdom is a disposition of character, a configuration of knowledge, fears, expectations, and desires, that enables one to identify the right path and keep to it. Wisdom means not only knowing but also *desiring* to do what is right. This desire will keep one from sliding into sin and suffering its tragic consequences.

This idea of wisdom is a naturalistic equivalent of Jeremiah's concept of the new covenant written on people's hearts (31:31–34) and Ezekiel's idea of the heart of flesh (11:19), by which they mean a rectified psychology, which will make the Israelites *desire* to obey God's commandments. The prophets, however,

---

[117] Even Ben Sira, though harsh in depicting the pains and difficulties of education (4:17; 6:22–27), assures the novice that success awaits the persistent (4:16, 18; 6:28–33; cf. 32:14–16).

[118] Likewise Lady Wisdom, though severe and menacing in her rebukes of fools (1:22–33; 8:36), never threatens to harm them herself, not even by means of an agent.

[119] Lady Wisdom's rebukes in 1:20–33 (Interlude A) are, in my view, by a different author than the lectures; see Essay 1, "The Formation of Proverbs 1–9."

expect God to intervene and bring about the change for all Israel, whereas the sage of Prov 2 believes that education, with God's help, can achieve this rectification individually, in the present. This is pedagogy as *musar*, the training of moral character.

Who Is the "Strange Woman"?

The *ʾiššah zarah*, the "strange woman" who is the villain in four passages (2:16–22; 5:1–23; 6:20–35; 7:1–27), has been understood in six ways: (1) a foreign, secular harlot, (2) a foreign devotee of a foreign god, (3) a foreign goddess, (4) a social outsider, (5) a native prostitute, and (6) another man's wife.[120] In my view, the last identification alone is correct. She may also be motivated by money, but this is not clearly indicated. The Strange Woman (to use the conventional but misleading designation) is a type-figure representing any seductive, adulterous woman. The allegorical interpretation, which most commonly understands the woman as a cipher for foreign philosophy, introduces an additional level of meaning and does not compete with these other explanations on the plain-sense level. (Several commentators, such as the midrash Avot deR. Natan, equate her with both a prostitute and heresy.) The allegorical interpretation is discussed after chapter 7.

The present excursus inquires into the identity of the Strange Woman. An excursus after chapter 7 examines how the Strange Woman is portrayed and how she has been interpreted.[121]

1. A Foreign Woman, Secular Relations

The Strange Woman is often thought to be a foreigner. Alsheikh (on 2:17) identifies the *nokriyyah* with the foreigner while equating the *zarah* with the Israelite adulteress (sim. Ibn Yaḥyah, Malbim, et al.). According to Delitzsch, the designation *nokriyyah* (which appears in synonymous parallelism with *zarah*) denotes a foreigner and indicates that she is a foreign prostitute. In the opinion of some commentators, foreign women are nonconformists, inclined to looseness, and especially attractive to young men. Oort (1885; summarized in G. Boström 1935: 32–34) also assures us that heathen women were known for their imprudence and infidelity.

---

[120]For a summary of nineteenth- and early-twentieth-century interpretations, see G. Boström 1935, chapter II. For a useful survey and assessment, see B. Lang 1972: 87–99.

[121]The recent study by C. Maier, *Die "Fremde Frau" in Proverbien 1–9* (1995), takes a feminist, sociological approach. Her conclusions include the following:

There are numerous allusions to other biblical texts in the Strange Woman passages. Prov 2:5–8, 20–22; 5:15–19, 21–23 are expansions anchoring the figure more closely in Jewish ethics. Prov 1–9 belongs to the Persian period. The Strange Woman represents both the Israelite adulteress (*zarah*) and the foreign woman (*nokriyyah*). Maier dates Part I as a whole to the Achaemenid period, after the middle of the fifth century B.C.E.; see the introduction to Part I.

Maier's feminist interpretation overlaps the ones discussed in "Feminist Readings of the Strange Woman" (pp. 256ff.).

H. Washington (1994a) identifies the Strange Woman as a foreigner who presents the danger not of promiscuity but of exogamous marriage. Such marriages would imperil the system of landholdings during the Persian period. But this hardly fits the scene in the Strange Woman passages, where the seductress is assumed to be already married (2:17; 5:10; 6:24 [emended], 29, 34–35; 7:19–20). She is looking for a one-night stand (7:18), not marriage.

In a passage often thought to support the identification of the Strange Woman as a foreigner, the Egyptian sage Anii cautions against the wiles of an "outsider":

(13) Beware of[122] a woman who is an outsider,[123]
who is unknown in her town.
Do not stare at her when (14) she passes.[124]
Do not know her wrongly.
She is a deep water, which cannot be crossed—
a woman far from her (15) husband.[125]
"I am smooth"[126] she says to you constantly—
when she has no witnesses.
She sets a trap—(16)
a great abomination, deadly
when it is heard,
although you were not aware.[127]
One may be saved (17) from any abomination,
except from this one alone.

(16.13–17; cf. AEL 2.137)

Anii is speaking of a woman from another town, an outsider but not a foreigner (there are other, unambiguous designations for non-Egyptians).[128] She may be from elsewhere, but she is a long-term resident, since she is located in "her town." Her being "unknown" means either that she lacks a proper reputation[129] or is reclusive and unsociable.[130] The writer sees the danger not in her stranger status as such but in her distance from her husband. Perhaps it is he who is "away," since she is, after all, in *her* town. Being "unknown" and without witnesses, she can pursue her illicit desires boldly. To this extent, there is a parallel with 7:19–20.

---

[122]Variant: "Protect yourself from."

[123]Lit. "from the outside" (*m rwty*).

[124]Reading *sni.s*. Quack (1994: 93) translates the line: "Zwinkere ihr nicht hinter dem Rücken ihres Gefährten zu! ("Do not wink at her behind the back of her companion!").

[125]Variant: "She is a deep water. A wife cannot be kept hidden (when she is) far from her husband."

[126]Implying smooth of skin, as well as gentle and amorous.

[127]Uncertain; cf. Quack 1994: 95.

[128]See Buchberger 1989–90: 9, 17–18, and Quack 1994: 156.

[129]Quack 1994: 93 translates "nicht angesehen ist" ("is not regarded" or "noticed").

[130]Ptahhotep uses the reverse of this phrase in speaking of a wife "who is joyful and known by her town" (l. 500; AEL 1.73). This is not a foreigner or stranger, but a woman whom the man being addressed might marry.

2. A Human Seductress Based on a Foreign Goddess
Here we mention the theory of R. J. Clifford (1993), which combines features of foreign religion with a secular interpretation. In his view, the Strange Woman isn't a foreign goddess, but she is derived from one. She and her behavior are based on a type-scene in epic literature.

The kernel of the scene is a goddess's deceitful offer of life to a young hero. Clifford finds this in Gilgamesh (VI.i.1–79), Dan'el (KTU 1.17.5), and, in attenuated form, the Odyssey (V.202–9). The common components are that the goddesses offer marriage or a long-term relationship; the young man's choice means life or death; and the goddess's offer is recognized as deceitful and is spurned (p. 68).

The differences, however, overwhelm the similarities. (1) In the supposed type-scene, the hero rejects the offer; in Proverbs, the boy accepts it. (2) In Gilgamesh, Ishtar proposes marriage; in Proverbs, the Strange Woman proposes a brief encounter—before her husband returns. Nor is Lady Folly (9:13–18), who is a personification based on the Strange Woman, urging a (metaphorical) marriage, but only "stolen waters." Her meal is hardly a "marriage banquet," as Clifford (1993: 72) calls it. *All* foolish men are invited. They are her guests, not her husbands. (3) Neither the Strange Woman nor Lady Folly even pretends to offer life, temporal or eternal, and the latter is in any case not within Proverbs' purview. Moreover, Anat's offer of (eternal) life to Aqhat and Calypso's to Odysseus are not spurious.

3. A Foreign Cult Prostitute
G. Boström (1935: 103–55), like advocates of the allegorical reading, believes that ordinary fornication would not warrant such a massive warning. In an interpretation that has often been cited but rarely accepted, Boström identifies the Strange Woman as a foreign resident who is a devotee of Aphrodite-Astarte (the counterpart of Babylonian-Assyrian Ishtar). This woman seeks to lure the youth into fertility rituals, which involved sacral prostitution and the "sacred marriage" on the new moon. The teacher is warning young men against participation in heathen rites.

There is, however, nothing to suggest that the woman's actions are a form of sacral prostitution (see the survey and arguments of Lang 1972: 91–95 and ABD 5.507–9). There is no evidence of foreigners practicing such rites in Israel, though foreign women (such as Solomon's wives, 1 Kgs 11:1–6) might worship their own gods. If the words *qadeš* (masc.) and *q^{e}dešah* (fem.) do refer to cult prostitutes, as is usually believed,[131] then the Bible does forbid and condemn cultic prostitution (male and female), which is seen as a foreign practice (Deut 23:18; 1 Kgs 15:12; 2 Kgs 23:7; Hos 4:14, etc.), but it identifies the sponsors and participants as *Israelites*. The advocates of the cult-prostitute hypothesis do not, however, choose to identify the Strange Woman as an Israelite, for the interpretation of

---

[131] Gruber (1986) argues that *q^{e}dešah* is a poetic term for "prostitute" and does not imply a cultic function, although the root *q-d-š* implies sacredness.

zarah and *nokriyyah* as foreign is crucial to the theory. In any case, the most likely term for cult prostitute, *q^e dešah*, is absent from the Strange Woman passages.

Nothing in the Strange Woman's words associates her with a cult or devotion to a love goddess. Supposed parallels between the Strange Woman passages and the Ishtar myth, such as the expressions "beloved of her youth" and the "land without return," are too vague to show a dependency on the figure of Ishtar, especially since the "beloved of her youth" is the Strange Woman's husband, whom she is forsaking, not the lad she is seducing, whereas Inanna-Ishtar's beloved, Dumuzzi-Tammuz, is her husband. Moreover, the Strange Woman's actions entail abandoning the "covenant of her God" (2:17), whereas a cult prostitute would be *fulfilling* her god's demands.

Prov 7, which is the proving ground for Boström's theory, hardly depicts a woman involved in sacral prostitution or sacred marriage. She tempts the boy with sensual pleasures, not religious exaltation or fertility. If this were the *hieros gamos*, a sacred marriage, the youth would be enacting the role of the king or a fertility god and would not require deceptive lures. Were she a priestess of Ishtar or Aphrodite, she would not need to skulk about the streets seeking a paramour, and her husband's absence would not be required for the tryst. Most important, if the teacher wished to caution the boy to avoid foreign sacral prostitution, he would be doing a poor job of it by being so elusive about a deadly sin.

The Babylonian *Counsels of Shuruppak* admonishes, "Do not marry a prostitute whose husbands are legion,/A temple harlot who is dedicated to a god,/A courtesan whose favors are many" (BWL 102–3). But, as McKane (339–40) observes, this is quite a different matter from the situation in Prov 7. The Babylonian instruction does not admonish against involvement in a fertility cult, but against marrying a cult prostitute, for she will prove a miserable homemaker and companion. Observe also that the activities of this prostitute are presumed to be public knowledge.

The teacher in Proverbs warns against an individual ethical offense and threatens individual punishments. One of these is vengeance by the husband (6:34–35). Yet a husband would probably know about and accept sacral prostitution. Moreover, the youth's sin is contrasted to sexual loyalty to his wife, with no mention of fidelity to Yahweh. It is unbelievable that the teacher would describe pagan cultic acts while overlooking the danger of national apostasy from Yahweh. Num 25:1–9 certainly is not hesitant to name the sin of religious apostasy in excoriating cultic sex.

4. A Social Outsider

The Gesenius-Buhl lexicon glosses *zarah* as *fremd* ("strange") in the sense of "illegitim, ausgeschlossen durch Sitte od. Gesetz . . . von einem buhlerischen Weibe" ("illegitimate, excluded by custom or law . . . [said] of a wanton woman"). Snijders (1954: 89–104) says that *zar* and *nokri* can refer to an outsider, one who "steps out of the (divine) order"; hence the *zarah* is "a 'loose' woman" and a *nokriyya* is "someone living in a world strange and unknown to the pious and upright (ii 8, 20f.)" (p. 92). She "leaves the community and the rules in force there" (p. 96). Such a woman (Snijders believes) is uninhibited and especially attractive to young men. McKane too regards the Strange Woman as a social outsider, but without excluding foreignness. She is "a type or paradigm of any woman who spurns the conventions of the society in which she lives" (p. 185).

Radaq (on 2:16) has an unusual interpretation of the Strange Woman, which explains her "strangeness" as a quality of character: "She is strange in that her ways and behavior are different (*zarim*) from the behavior of good women, and she is an outsider or alien (*nokriyyah*) who alienates (*m*ᵉ*nakkeret*) her heart by the smoothness of her lips. That is to say, her heart is evil and her words are smooth and she is alien to all good morals."

5. *A Prostitute, Not Necessarily Foreign*

Wisdom literature, like the rest of the Bible, does not seem much troubled by prostitution in itself. Prov 6:26 (see the Commentary) contrasts an ordinary harlot with a married woman and emphasizes the far greater danger of the latter. The reason that Prov 29:3 gives for its warning against consorting with prostitutes is just that it's a waste of money. Ben Sira too cautions against the harlot because it can deprive one of his wealth (Sir 9:6). He downplays the relative severity of consorting with a whore: "A woman for hire is reckoned as naught, but a married woman is reckoned as a trap of death to those who consort (with her)" (26:22).[132] Adultery, with or without payment, is far deadlier and more disruptive.[133]

An adulteress may also be a harlot.[134] In 7:10, the Strange Woman is said to be "in harlot's garb," though that might mean only that she is veiled to obscure her identity.

One motivation for prostitution could be to get money to pay a vow to the Temple. K. Van der Toorn (1989: 198) argues that the woman in Prov 7 is selling herself for that reason. The argument for this requires translating *sillamti* in 7:14 (tendentiously) as "I must fulfill" rather than "I paid." If this surmise is correct, the act of prostitution is still secular in character, not sacral. If the woman is married, the real sin involved is adultery, not prostitution. The proposed interpretation, however, supposes too narrow a circumstance as the occasion for the warning. The author of the Strange Woman passages is damning adultery in whatever guise, and the woman's motives are merely illustrative of the situations that can give rise to the transgression.

A *zarah*, even a promiscuous one, is not necessarily a prostitute. Ben Sira distinguishes four types of dangerous women, who are clearly not one and the

---

[132]"Naught": thus Syr, which has *kryq*. Gk reads *krwq*, "as spittle." LXX's *pyrgos* is a misrendering of *mṣwdh* "trap" as the homographic "tower."

[133]In 19:2, Ben Sira seems to take a stronger stance on consorting with prostitutes, but the original text is uncertain.

[134]The MT of Prov 23:27 (q.v.) places *zonah* "prostitute" parallel to *nokriyyah*. But the right reading is probably LXX's *zarah*. Prov 23:27a is a variant of 22:14a, which has *zarot* "strange women" instead of *zonah*.

same: the *'iššah zarah*, the harlot (*zonah*), musicians, and virgins (9:1–6). To be sure, prostitution is the usual situation in which a married woman debauches a youth. G. Boström (1935: 39) complains that many interpreters equivocate over whether the Strange Woman is a prostitute or adulteress, but the alternatives are not exclusive. She is certainly an adulteress; she may be a whore, but that is incidental to her status as *zarah*. The issue is adultery.

6. Someone Else's Wife

Mezudat David neatly glosses the *zarah* thus: "She is a married woman who is strange (*zarah*) to you (*lak*)"; cf. Saʿadia. Most commentators understand "strange" in this sense. The LXX conveys this accurately by rendering *'iššah zarah* as "one who is not your own" (*tēs mē idias*) in 5:20b; as "a married woman" in 6:24; and as "base woman" and "harlotrous woman" (a doublet) in 5:3 (though the latter may reflect an underlying Hebrew *znh*). For a thorough examination of terminology, see Humbert 1937 and 1939.

Both "strange" and "foreign" are misleading translations of *zar* (fem. *zarah*). *Zar* means something that does not properly belong to or in a situation—an "other," though not with the current ideological overloading of the concept of the Other. The definition of "stranger" in English legal terminology can apply precisely to Hebrew *zar*: someone who, with respect to the transaction or set of occurrences in question, has no legally cognizable relationship to the parties or to the subject of the transaction or to the set of occurrences. This is regardless of the degree of acquaintance.

A lay Israelite is a *zār*, an outsider or alien, in situations permitted to priests alone; for example, the consumption of offerings (Exod 29:33) or entry into the sanctuary (Num 1:51). In the levirate law (Deut 25:5), an *'îš zār* is a man belonging to another family. In Lev 22:12, the *'îš zār* is a nonpriestly Israelite, who is an outsider only in the sense that he does not belong to the caste in question. Tobit warns his son against taking a *gynaika allotrian [= Heb 'iššah zarah] hē ouk estin ek tēs phylēs tou patros sou*, "a strange woman (wife) who is not from the tribe of your father" (Tob 4:12). The context defines "strangeness" as belonging to another Israelite clan.[135] In Prov 5:17, *zārîm* are other men besides oneself; sim. 14:10; 27:2, etc. In the Aramaic Panammuwa I inscription from Zinjrli (800–750 B.C.E.), there is a distinction between "you will kill him" and "you instruct an *'š zr* to kill him" (KAI 214, 30–34). *Zr* and *'š zr* can only mean the same thing as *'aḥer*, "another" (Humbert 1939: 262).

Nokri usually refers to foreigners and is probably marked for foreignness in a way that *zār* is not (e.g., Exod 18:3; Deut 14:21; esp. 1 Kgs 11:1 [*našim nokriyyot*]). Nevertheless, *nokri* too can by extension be used of locals or indigenous people who are alien to the relationship in question—exactly like *zar*—especially when in parallelism with the latter. There may be a note of intensity or hyperbole in this use. I translate *nokriyyah* as "alien," to be understood in this sense.

---

[135] Gk *allotrios*, the standard LXX equivalent for *zār*, means "other" in this sense. In the Gk of Sir 9:8, *kallos allotrion* corresponds to *ypy l' lk*—"beauty that does not belong to you," referring to another man's wife.

Laban's daughters protest that he has treated them like *nokriyyôt*, in other words, as if they were not of this family (Gen 31:15). The word expresses their vehemence. In Jer 2:21, the vine is "alien" in the sense that it is not the vintner's own. In Ps 69:9, *nokrî* means "stranger" (// *mûzār*). When Job (19:15) complains that his maidservant treats him as *zār* // *nokrî*, the problem is not that she regards him as a foreigner (a non-Edomite?), because one might treat a foreigner with respect, but that she treats him disdainfully, as if he were an outsider, not her master. Cf. *ʾîš nokri*—"another man," any man besides the toiler—in Qoh 6:2. In Prov 5:10, the *zārîm* // *nokrî* are simply other people. Both terms are equivalent to *ʾăḥērîm* "others" in v 9. The nationality of the people who receive the sinner's wealth is irrelevant. Similarly, *nokrî* parallels *zār* in warnings against giving surety for another's loan (Prov 20:16).[136] *Nokriyyāh* is parallel to "a neighbor's wife" in Prov 6:24 (where we should point *ʾēšet rēʿekā*). *Nokrî* undoubtedly means "another person" in 27:13, for the proverb could not be advising that you let a *foreigner* praise you. Therefore, the epithet *nokriyyāh* is no reason for ascribing foreignness to the Strange Woman.

Nothing whatsoever in any of the lectures indicates that the Strange Woman is a foreigner or even a social outsider. The antithesis of the *zarah-nokriyyah* is not an Israelite woman or a woman of proper social standing, but rather one's own wife (5:15–20). Every wife is an *ʾiššah zarah* to all men but her husband. Likewise, men are *zarim* with respect to other men's wives (5:17). Ezekiel's use of *zarim* in Ezek 16:32 shows this: God calls the female personification of Judah *haʾiššah hammᵉnaʾapet, taḥat ʾišahh tiqqaḥ ʾet zarim*, a "woman who commits adultery, taking other men instead of her husband.[137] To be sure, these men personify foreign nations, but within the narrative of the parable, they are not foreigners but any men who resort to the adulteress (who personifies Jerusalem). In other words, they are any men other than the woman's husband (Yahweh). Thus the *ʾiššah zarah* has her counterpart in the *ʾiš zar*, and an instruction aimed at a young woman might well warn against consorting with the *ʾiš zar* and *nokri*—the Strange Man, anyone besides her husband.

In fact, Ben Sira mentions the Strange Man as a sexual offender, along with his female counterpart, the Strange Woman. In 23:22–27, Ben Sira, drawing upon Proverbs' Strange Woman passages,[138] describes an ordinary Jewish adulteress, who is violating God's law and will be judged before the assembly. Through her treachery she gives her husband an heir from *another man*—Greek *ex allotriou* (22b) or *ex allotriou andros* (23d). *Allotrios* is the standard equivalent of *zar* in Ben Sira.[139] The Hebrew of this passage (not extant) undoubtedly spoke of the

---

[136] G. Boström (1935: 100) must posit that the terms were used because trade was largely in foreigners' control—a strained and ad hoc supposition.

[137] Not to be emended to *ʾetnānîm* (BHS), for this harlot gives payment rather than taking it (v 33).

[138] Note these correspondences:

Sir 23:22a	(abandoning the husband)	Prov	2:17a
23a	(law/covenant of God)		2:17b
23b	(sinning against the husband)		2:17a
24	(judgment before the *ekklēsia*)		5:14

[139] Sir 8:18; 40:29; 45:18. In Sir 11:34 (MS A: *zryw*) and 32[35]:18 (MSS B and E have *zd*), the translator undoubtedly read *zr*. In 36[33]:3, *allotrios* corresponds to *nkr(y)*. In 9:8 it accurately renders *lʾ lk*, "(beauty) that is not yours."

zar and the *ʾiš zar*, the man who is "strange" in the same way his mistress is: he is not married to her.

The Strange Woman in Proverbs is married (see 2:17; 6:26, 29, 34; 7:19; possibly 5:10 as well). An unmarried woman would probably not be called an *ʾiššah zarah* in a sexual context, since *zarah* implies belonging to another person sexually, and an unmarried woman is sexually out of bounds to everyone. In Sir 9, the *ʾiššah zarah* (v 3) is in a different category from the *bᵉtulah* "virgin," "unmarried woman" (v 5). In fact, *ʾiššah* itself usually designates a married woman, outside certain stereotyped constructions. *ʾešet zᵉnunim* in Hos 1:2 means a married prostitute. Consorting with an unmarried harlot would fall under less severe strictures.

An *ʾiššah zarah* might be the wife of one's best friend, not a stranger at all. Indeed, the term *iššah zarah* may refer to a godfearing Jewish woman, though that is not the sort of *iššah zarah* depicted in the Strange Woman passages. It is not what a Strange Woman is but what she does that can make her a vicious snare. Rather than the passage from Anii quoted above, §1, I would compare the Strange Woman warnings with admonitions in Ptahhotep (ll. 277–88; AEL 1.68), Pap. Ch. Beatty IV (vso. 1.13; AW 223), and Phibis (§9; Pap. Insinger 7.20–8.20; AEL 3.191–92). These remonstrate against adultery and even against being overly familiar with the women of another household. Compare also the Syriac Ahiqar S_1 7 (= S_2 5), which admonishes against coveting a beautiful woman, and Syriac Ahiqar S_2 6, which warns against adultery (quoted at 3:7 and 5:16).

Much has been written about the Strange Woman as foreign, or socially marginal, or symbolic of the Other, but all these forms of otherness are beside the point. There is no stigma inherent in being a *zar(ah)* or *nokriyy(ah)* in itself, no taint (or allure) to foreignness, marginality, or "Otherness." The taint adheres only to the illicit relations between her and the men who are *zarim* to her.

LECTURE III. THE WISDOM OF PIETY (3:1–12)

TRANSLATION

Keep my teachings in mind

3:1 My son, forget not my teaching;
let your heart retain my precepts,
2 for length of days and years of life
and peace they'll add to you.
3 ⟨Let kindness and constancy not forsake you!⟩
Tie them about your neck,
inscribe them on the tablet of your heart,
4 and you'll gain the favor and high regard
of God and man alike.

Piety

5 Trust in the Lord with all your heart
and rely not on your own understanding.
6 In all that you do, hold him in mind,
and *he* will keep your path smooth.
7 Do not reckon yourself wise,
but fear the Lord and shun evil,
8 and there will be health to your flesh[a]
and vigor to your bones.
9 Honor the Lord from your wealth,
with the firstfruits of all your produce,
10 and your barns will overflow with abundance,
your vats burst with new wine.

Suffering as discipline

11 Do not, my son, reject the Lord's discipline,
nor despise his chastisement,
12 For the one whom the Lord loves—him he reproves,
as a father does to a favored son.

---

[a] *šeʾērekā* or *šērekā* (MT: *šorrekā* "your navel").

COMMENTARY

3:1–4. Exordium

3:1. *forget not*: To "forget" (*šakaḥ*), as Hameʾiri observes, usually refers not to the natural slippage of memory (as in Prov 31:7) but to willful neglect and diversion of attention (as in Prov 2:17). This latter sense is clear when God threatens to "forget" something, as in Hos 4:6, "And I, for my part, will forget your sons." Hameʾiri believes that both kinds of forgetting pertain here, but the parallel with *yiṣṣor* (from *naṣar* "retain") favors the active sense.

retain [*yiṣṣor*]: "Retaining" or "guarding" (*naṣar*) is likewise a deliberate act. The word is used of protection, maintenance (Deut 33:9), nurture (Deut 32:10), and cultivation (Isa 27:3), rather than just vessel-like containment. The father demands continued attention to the teachings, not merely passive retention or rote memory. *Naṣar* is antonymic to verbs implying deliberate retention—*naṭaš* "abandon" in 6:20, and *naṭah min* "turn aside from" in 4:5b. The injunctions in other exordia support the active notion. The exordium of Lecture III does not mention the hearing of the teachings, just their retention and, like Lecture IV, is describing a more advanced stage in the learning of Wisdom. The father is teaching the need for persistence and diligence, which must continue even when (basic) wisdom has been acquired (Hameʾiri).

teaching, precepts: Like *miṣwah* (see 2:1), *torah* in Proverbs does not refer to law or legally enforceable ordinances. Nevertheless, a *torah* always consists of authoritative injunctions, never of suggestions or recommendations that one is morally free to weigh and dismiss. Unlike *ʿeṣah* "counsel," *miṣwot* and *torot* are never given to superiors or equals.

In spite of 3:1b, there are no true *miṣwot* ("precepts," "commands") in this lecture. This exordium thus shows awareness of the other lectures, which do contain precepts. The appeal to retain the *miṣwot* would make no sense in an originally independent text consisting of 3:1–12 or even 3:1–20. The call to obey the father's precepts is evidence that Part I is not a "collection" (as it is usually called) of independent instructions. The Ten Lectures were composed as a unity; see Essay 1, "The Formation of Proverbs 1–9."

3:2. *length of days and years of life and peace*: The father's teachings bring long life (3:22; 4:10) (as do wisdom itself [3:16, 18] and the fear of God [10:27]). The verse is enjambed or run-on, with "peace" belonging syntactically with the other direct objects of "add," whereas metrically the verse divides after "life"; compare 2:9.

life: The word *ḥayyim* "life" in Proverbs is widely thought to imply "life in the full sense of the word . . . *vita vitalis*" (Delitzsch), "a fullness of life" (Cosser 1953–54), a life of well-being and peace (Gemser, and many). Hameʾiri defines *ḥayyim* in 8:35 as *haḥayyim haʾămitiyyim* "authentic life." *Life* may often hold these qualities, but it is hard to prove that the word *ḥayyim* bears these connotations. Sometimes *ḥayyim* means health, as in 4:22, where it parallels *marpeʾ* "healing" or "balm." Often, the author is quite clear in promising wisdom's adherents life in the literal, quantitative sense—"length of days," "years of life"—while threatening sinners with a very literal early death. Wisdom gives one a long life by steering him away from life-threatening follies (2:19). Saʿadia explains that "life" means security from premature death at man's or God's hands. Life is promised in Egyptian Wisdom too (see the prologue to Amenemope, quoted on pp. 71f.), where it refers to this life and sometimes alludes to the next as well.[140] Several medieval commentators (Saʿadia, Radaq, et al.) explain the double promise in Prov 3:3bc (and similar promises of life elsewhere) as alluding to life in this world and in the next. I find no evidence that "life" in Proverbs ever implies immortality; see the discussion at Prov 12:28 in vol. 2.

peace: The teachings also bring *šalom*, a state of wholesome, peaceful well-being, primarily realized in relations among people. Amenemope calls his book, "the teaching for life, the instruction for well-being"[141] (1.1–2).

DNF suggests that *yôsîpû lāk* and *ʾal yaʿazbûkā* are parallel and are both predicated of *ḥesed weʾĕmet*. He argues that if the subject of *yôsîpû* "they'll add" is *tôrātî* "my teaching" and *miṣwôtay* "my precepts," there would be gender incongruity. But the syntax of the sentence as he parses it is awkward and violates parallelism. In regard to the frequent use of the *yiqṭᵉlû* form with fem. pl. subjects, see the comment on 1:16.

---

[140] In the "Loyalist Teaching" (§1, 8), one version (the stele) says that the teaching is a plan "to pass life in peace," while the other versions read, "to attain the state of a Venerable," meaning the blessed state of a properly interred dead person.

[141] Egyptian *wḏ* = Hebrew *šalom*.

3:3a. *Let kindness and constancy not forsake you*: This sentence is introduced by the negative volitive particle *ʾal* and is formally jussive. For this reason, the sentence is usually taken as a further injunction: You should not stop (showing) kindness and constancy. Nevertheless, the sentence is virtually consequential: Forget not my teaching (1), *so that* kindness and constancy not forsake you (3a). This sentence is a second promise, alongside the assurance of long life (2).

Volitionals are often used to express consequence and promise (which amount to the same thing here); e.g., Prov 3:4, 25; 28:17; and Ps 41:3b (these three examples use the volitive *ʾal*); see IBHS §34.4c; GBH §114k.

The *ḥesed* in this line can only be God's kindness toward the pupil, not the pupil's toward others. As a person's own virtues, *ḥesed* and *ʾĕmet* would not be said to "abandon" him. (The failure would be for *him* to abandon *them*.) However, divine kindness might "abandon" a person, if he deserved it. More fundamentally, if *ḥesed* were a virtue of the listener, it could be only kindness directed at fellow humans (which is how most commentators understand it), but that would not be relevant to anything else in this lecture. The kindness cannot be the pupil's attitude toward God, for *ḥesed* is always conferred by a superior upon an inferior (in status or power).

Ḥesed is kindness (whether as an act or an attitude) that is *not mandatory*. (Riyqam observes that there are rewards for performance of *ḥesed* but not punishments for their omission.) It is always the *right* thing to do, never a mere gift and certainly never an unfair partiality. *Ḥesed* is *charity*, in the sense of gracious benevolence, correctly translated *eleos* "mercy" in the LXX. The particular kindness in view in this context is God's gift of a long life, which is at once a divine grant and a natural outcome of human wisdom, and yet is not something that God is *obligated* to bestow.

This understanding of *ḥesed* runs counter to the widely accepted theory of N. Glueck (1927), who defined *ḥesed* as covenantal loyalty. In my view, *ḥesed* has no covenantal reference, nor is it essentially loyalty. (There is no covenantal relationship, let alone loyalty, between, e.g., the Josephite scouts and the man they came upon at Beth El (Judg 1:24), or between the chief eunuch and Daniel (Dan 1:9). *Ḥesed* within a covenantal relationship is a benefit not mandated by the terms of the covenant. In a study of Jer 2:2, which I interpret as referring to *God's ḥesed*, not Israel's, I argue briefly that *ḥesed* is always a one-sided boon (Fox 1973: 443f.). K. Sakenfeld (1978) shows that the relationship implied by *ḥesed* is not essentially covenantal and that it indicates an imbalance in status or power. However, she imports too much theological information from the word's various contexts into the meaning of the concept itself. A semantic analysis by E. Kellenberger (1982) shows that *ḥesed* is not "covenantal loyalty" but is something unusual and outside the concept of order. *Ḥesed*, unlike *bᵉrit* ("covenant") and *ṣedeq* (righteousness), exceeds norms (Kellenberger 1982: 41, 185f. and *passim*).

ʾĕmet signifies "the validation or fulfillment of a definite intention" (Kellenberger 1982: 98). When manifested in speech, *ʾĕmet* means "truth," "something validated." With respect to attitudes and actions, it means "constancy," "loyalty."

Ḥesed weʾĕmet is a common word-pair meaning "reliable kindness." (It is hard to know if it is, strictly speaking, a hendiadys, since both words are separately applicable in every occurrence.) "One who does *ḥesed* opens himself up to another and goes toward him helpfully. Such a spontaneously established relationship is always at risk and may at any time, instead of being realized ever anew, come to a dead end. *Ḥesed we'ĕmet* indicates that this relationship will be effectively maintained in spite of all risks" (Kellenberger 1982: 185).[142] Although kindness is not obligatory or contractual, it can be relied on. This word-pair is used of God's kindness in Gen 24:27, for example, which says that God has not *abandoned* (*ʿazab*, as here) his faithful kindness toward Abraham; sim. Ruth 2:20.

While kindness and constancy often pertain to relations between covenanted parties, these qualities are not inherently covenantal. Covenantal relationships are necessarily described partly in terms of free personal relations, and not the other way around. The present verse does not allude to a covenant, neither the one at Sinai nor (as McKane thinks) Jeremiah's new covenant (31:33). Nevertheless, Lecture III (and Proverbs as a whole) is thoroughly "Yahwistic." Yahwism is the framework for various covenants, but it is not coextensive with them.

As it stands, the promise in v 3a is a monostich connected (though loosely) with v 2 rather than with the rest of v 3. Monostichs are rare in Part I (1:23a; 4:4a; 5:19a; 8:13c). This line is, moreover, syntactically awkward, intruding between the pronoun "them" in v 3b and its antecedents ("teaching" and "precepts") in vv 1–2. Also, the word *ḥesed* appears only here in Prov 1–9. Prov 3:3a is probably a gloss on v 2 (thus Meinhold [1987: 472] and Plöger). While thematically pertinent, it adds a new message: You should look upon the blessings that come with piety as the bounty of God's grace rather than as simply your own deserts.

DNF, while granting that v 3a may be a gloss on v 2, argues for a strong unity in vv 1–3. Vv 2–3a belong together, with *ḥesed we'ĕmet* serving as the subject of the verbs in both verses. It is *God's* kindness and faithfulness which produces the benefits listed in these lines. Vv 1 and 3bc form an envelope around vv 2–3a, with the combination explaining the relationship between requirements and performance on the one hand and, on the other, kindness and grace on the part of God, the latter being the actual source of benefits. However, the teaching ("wisdom") is said to produce benefits in a number of places, including 3:22; 4:6, 8–9, 22; and 6:22–23.

3:3bc. *Tie them about your neck*: As 6:21 and 7:3 show, the antecedent of "them" is the teaching and precepts, mentioned in vv 1–2 (Plöger), rather than kindness and constancy (Delitzsch, Toy, and most). The teachings are to be (figuratively) worn as a necklace or garland (1:9 [q.v.]; 3:22; 4:9; 6:21).

According to 7:3, the teachings are also to be tied to one's fingers. As argued at 1:9, the necklace in this metaphor is an adornment, not primarily an amulet.

inscribe them on the tablet of your heart: Hold them permanently in your memory; make them an indelible part of your character. "Tablet of the heart"

[142]"Wer ḥäsäd tut, öffnet sich von innen heraus dem Andern und geht hilfreich auf ihn zu. Eine so spontan begründete Beziehung ist zugleich stets gefährdet und kann, statt sich immer neu zu aktualisieren, schliesslich jederzeit versanden. *ḥäsäd wä'ämät* drückt aus, dass diese Beziehung trotz aller Gefährdung wirklich durchgehalten wird."

occurs in 7:3 and Jer 17:1. It probably means the tablet *which is* the heart ("genitive of association"; for the construction, see IBHS §9.5.3h).

Engraving on a tablet signifies permanency, as in Isa 30:8: "Now come, write it on a tablet with them, and inscribe it on a book, and it shall be for later times, as a testimony [*lᵉʿēd*] forever." Jer 31:33b ("and I shall write it [God's law] on their heart, and I shall be a god for them, and they shall be my people") shows that being inscribed "on the heart" connotes not just retention in memory but, more importantly, the indelible definition of character. Jeremiah's point is not only that the Jews will remember God's law but also that they will internalize it, *incorporate* it, so that they will be instinctively aware of its demands and will naturally desire to fulfill them (v 34). Jeremiah 17:1 also mentions the tablet of the heart: "The sin of Judah is written with an iron stylus, engraved with an adamant point on the tablet of their heart and on the horns of their altars." The problem is not Judah's *memory* of its sins but its inability to extricate itself from them. The metaphor of the tablet of the heart thus epitomizes the notion of education as character formation, developed first in Lecture II; see "The Idea of Education in Lecture II," after Prov 2.

Couroyer (1983; sim. Ehrlich) argues that the tablet here and in 7:3 is not the heart but rather an actual school tablet tied to the neck and hanging down onto the chest. This image, however, would be expressed by *luaḥ ʿal libbam* (cf. Exod 28:29, 30), not *luaḥ libbam*. Moreover, the existence of this practice in Egypt is not known for certain. A similar image in Jer 31:33 implies that the heart itself is the tablet: "I will place my law in their midst and write it upon their heart." Although something placed "on the heart" might be external, something *written* "*on* the heart" would not be, just as words "written on tablets of stone" (Deut 4:13) are not written on tablets hung on stone. But even though the tablet is not a school tablet (literally or metaphorically), the background of the image may be a command to a pupil to write the teachings from dictation.

A similar concept is reflected in an Egyptian instruction, which cites the idea in order to reject it: "Beware of saying, 'Every man is in accordance with his character, the ignorant and the wise alike. Shay and Renenet [fate and destiny] are engraved on one's character [*biʾt*] in the writing of God himself'" (Pap. Beatty IV, vso. 6.6). As in Prov 3:3, a person's nature is metaphorically "engraved" on his character. (Note that "character" is the equivalent of "heart" in Prov 3:3c.) The authors of Prov 1–9 and this Egyptian text would agree that the person does his own "engraving," with moral education as guide. It is not done by God prior to birth. Other Egyptians did hold this view; see "Who Can Learn, and How?" after 9:10. Ben Sira too inclines, though inconsistently, toward predetermination of character; see Sir 1:14–15.

There are various ways of conceiving of the mysterious process of memory, all of them requiring metaphors.[143] Memory can be thought of as STORAGE, the permanent and intact containment of treasures. Amenemope tells his son

[143] Here capitalized; see n. 114.

to place the teachings in the "casket of the belly" (§1, see here at 2:1); a similar metaphor is implicit in the command to "store up my precepts within you" in Prov 2:1. Alternatively, memory may be imagined as RECORDING AND RETRIEVAL. The tablet is suggestive of this. But this is not the entirety of the process, for wisdom is not just a chunk of information. The possessor must still "read" the message on the tablet and let it affect him. The teaching must be activated. The teachings are preserved in writing—both metaphorically in the heart and actually in Wisdom literature. The written teachings are mnemonics that communicate to the pupil and remind him of his duties. Another image for memory is STIMULUS. The necklace in 3:3b and in 3:21–22 is a mnemonic device. Rather than being stored away or "hidden" in the heart, it is always on display, drawing attention to itself by its proximity and attractiveness. Prov 4:21 speaks of memory as both STORAGE and STIMULUS.

Together, then, the imagery of 3:3bc teaches that wisdom is to be possessed externally, as if it were a necklace, and internally, as if it were written on the heart; that is to say, it is preserved and realized in action and thought (Riyqam).

3:4. *the favor and high regard of God and man alike*: Lit. "you will find favor [*ḥen*] and good regard [*śekel ṭob*] in the eyes of God and man."

Favor (*ḥen*) is an additional reward for incorporating the precepts. This is the approbation others feel toward its possessor. For example, in Joseph's case, "his *ḥen*" consisted of the warder's favorable feelings toward him (Gen 39:21). A *liwyat ḥen* (1:9) is an "attractive garland" in the sense that it attracts favor *to* its possessor.

High regard [*śekel ṭob*]: Lit. "good view" or "good opinion." *śekel* sometimes means "perspicacity" or "intelligence"; on that usage, see "Words for Wisdom." Here *śekel* (similar to *ḥen*) indicates the way others see you, *their* perspective or attitude.

The root-meaning of *śēkel* (var. *śekel*) is "vision," "perception." It almost always refers to (1) perception from the standpoint of the perceiver. The possessor of *śēkel* sees a situation clearly and is consequently discerning and circumspect. Sometimes *śēkel* refers to (2) perception from the standpoint of the object, i.e., the way *others* see a person. Thus Hameʾiri, who considers (2) a semantic extension of (1); sim. Ibn Janaḥ, *Sefer Hašorašim*. Abigail was *ṭôbat śekel wîypat tōʾar* "good to look at and lovely of visage" (1 Sam 25:3). In various permutations of this phrase, *marʾeh* ("sight," "appearance") is used instead of *śēkel*; cf. Esth 2:7; Gen 29:17; 39:6; and see Weinfeld 1982: 93. Ps 111:10 (probably based on Prov 3:4) promises a *śēkel ṭôb* "good regard" for all who obey God's commandments. In Sir 32 [35]:2, *tśʾ śkl* clearly means "receive favor, good regard."

The language of the promises in vv 2 and 4 is based on a widespread formula, (to receive) "favor in the eyes of god(s) and man," which Weinfeld (1982) argues is Egyptian in origin. It is closely paralleled in the Phoenician inscription of Yeḥaumilk, king of Byblos (5th–4th c. B.C.E.):

> May the Mistress of Byblos bless Yeḥaumilk king of Byblos and keep him alive and prolong his days and his years over Byblos, for he is a righteous king. And may [the Lady], the Mistress of Byblos, grant him favor [*ḥen*] in the eyes of the gods and in the eyes of the people of this land! (KAI 10, 8–11)

Similar wording appears in another Phoenician inscription (KAI 48, 9), this one found in Egypt: "May God give them favor and life [*ḥn wḥym*] in the eyes of the gods and men." A very similar formula occurs earlier in Egyptian epistles, starting in about the eleventh century B.C.E. The writer wishes that the gods would give his correspondent life, health, peace, length of days, and a ripe old age and that they would grant him favor (*hswt*) before the gods and men (Černý 1939, nos. 1, 3, 6, etc.) A somewhat different formula, praying for "mercy and peace in the sight of gods and men," is found in Assyrian and Babylonian letters and prayers. The fact that Prov 3:4 employs a widespread international formula can explain why it uses "God" (only five times in Proverbs) instead of the usual "Yahweh"; see the comment on 2:5.

3:5–12. Lesson: Have Faith in God

3:5. *Trust in the Lord with all your heart*: Hameʾiri connects this verse to the exordium: the attainment of wisdom (presumed in the exhortations of the exordium) should not make you overly confident in your intelligence (v 5) or arrogant about your wisdom (v 7). Lecture III tempers the enthusiastic commendations of wisdom in Lecture II and elsewhere in favor of a less intellectualized faith. It recognizes that knowledge is not inevitably tantamount to piety and righteousness.

Trusting in the Lord does not require resignation and passivity. (One may, for example, trust in the Lord *and* make war; 1 Chr 5:20). Rather, it means trusting God to guide your life aright—after *you* do the right thing. It means believing that all that happens in your life, including suffering, is God's will and that it is motivated by his kindness, because it allows you a chance to reform (3:12).

This verse is one of very few in Proverbs that concedes the possibility of an intellectual power that is not ipso facto virtuous, hence not intrinsically wise or conducive to wisdom. More in line with the book's usual viewpoint is Prov 16:20, which equates "one who is perceptive in a matter" with "one who trusts in the Lord." By the usual assumptions of the book, a mental faculty employed without trust in God could not be called *binah*. This is also the only place in Proverbs where a wisdom word has a second sg. suffix. (In 23:4, *binnat*^{e}*ka* means "your staring.") Elsewhere the wisdom words refer either to the father's knowledge or to wisdom itself, whether personified or abstract.

Wisdom may "enter your heart" (2:10), but it is not, strictly speaking, your own. Prov 28:26 similarly draws a distinction between "walking in wisdom" and trusting in one's mind (*leb*). A mind holds true understanding only insofar as it conforms itself to the real wisdom, which is conveyed by the father's teaching and, ultimately, granted by God.

To "trust in" (*baṭaḥ b-*) God does not mean faith as assent to a theological proposition. All derivatives of *b-ṭ-ḥ* imply a feeling of security and confidence in the fulfillment of expectations. To trust in something is to believe that it can and will do what it is supposed to do. Trusting almost always implies that some danger or threat lurks in the background, against which one expects protection and help. "Trust" is the antonym of "fear" (Prov 14:16; 28:1; 29:25)—except when the object is God. To trust in riches or fortifications or princes is to have confidence that these will help and protect you when the need arises. One who trusts in princes supposes that they will provide deliverance (Ps 146:3). Prov 28:26 presumes a situation of danger, since the hope is to *escape*: "He who trusts in his mind is a dolt, while he who walks in wisdom—*he* will escape." The implication is that one who trusts in and relies on his own intelligence expects to evade trouble. Such a person is a *k^esil*, an overconfident, smug dolt.

The charge to trust in God is found in various forms in Proverbs (16:20; 28:25; 29:25). There is no reason to identify this message as particularly connected with Wisdom thought (contrary to TDOT II, 93); trust in God is valued throughout Psalms (e.g., 9:11; 31:7, 15; 55:24; 84:13) and elsewhere (e.g., Jer 39:18; Isa 12:2; 50:10). It is also arbitrary to view its appearance as a later development in Wisdom, contrary to McKane. The idea is attested in the earlier collections of Proverbs, as well as in Egyptian Wisdom.

and rely not on your own understanding: The warning against depending on one's own intellect does not deny the ability of the human intellect to analyze and comprehend the ways of the world. Contrary to McKane, the warning does not imply that "clarity is certainly not achieved by a severe educational discipline, but through religious illumination," for Proverbs does not concern itself with communication or enlightenment directly from God. Rather, 3:5 cautions against the presumption that a man can predict the outcome of his deeds. In Riyqam's paraphrase, "A man should not say, 'I know that I will prosper in this enterprise,' 'I know how to succeed in this matter'; but trust in the Lord in all regards." Saʿadia (comparing Deut 8:17 and Isa 10:15) similarly identifies the flaw as imagining that one can manage events by one's own wits and produce success by one's own powers, without divine providence. This is the message of several proverbs as well, in particular 16:1, 9; 20:24; and 21:31.

A popular Egyptian maxim, repeated in various forms, warns against confidence in one's ability to plan for the future, often using the same terms as Prov 27:1, q.v. (and see the Textual Note to 3:28). Sayings such as Prov 3:5 and 3:7 are not a new kind of wisdom, or a "Yahwistic" reinterpretation of an old, practical wisdom (contrary to McKane [1965: 50–51; 1970: 292]), or even a "special possession of Israel" ("israelitische Sondergut"), as argued by Gese 1958: 45–50. Ptahhotep taught, "Do not be proud about your knowledge" (52), which a later scribe glossed as, "Do not rely on the fact that you are learned (L_2, 53).

3:6. *In all that you do, hold him in mind*: Lit. "in all your ways, know him [*daʿehu*]." As Hameʾiri says, "This is a noble saying, small in quantity but great in quality." The tenet that knowledge of God must permeate all one's behavior is at the core of the message of Prov 1–9, fusing knowledge, piety, and action into one principle. Knowledge of God must be realized in a person's ways—his behavior—not merely in cognition and certainly not in theological erudition. Knowledge of God is an attitude, awareness of what he wants as well as a desire to do it. To "know God in all your ways" means giving constant attention to the divine will and presence (Hameʾiri). See "Knowledge of God and Fear of God," after 2:5.

and he *will keep your path smooth* [y^e*yašer*]: Or, "make straight." This can mean leveling as well as straightening horizontally, and perhaps only the former. Some commentators interpret this to mean that God will keep you honest, by clearing away the stumbling blocks of temptation. Radaq quotes the rabbinic saying, "He who comes to purify himself receives help." But even though "making smooth" or "straightening" (*yiššer*) one's own path means to behave righteously (e.g., Ps 119:128; Prov 9:15; cf. 2:14), to do so to someone *else's* path means to make his progress smooth, to help him reach his goal by removing difficulties, and that is probably the intention of this verse.

In Isa 40:3, "to make (God's) way smooth/straight" obviously does not mean making God behave righteously. It means to prepare a smooth and easy road, as for a royal procession. That "make straight" refers to horizontal leveling rather than preparing a route in a straight line is shown by the next verse, "Every valley shall be lifted up, and every mountain and hill made low. And the rough ground will become a plain, and the crags become a valley." In Isa 45:13 the idiom means that God will give Cyrus success, not that it will make him righteous. In Prov 11:5 it means that the righteousness of the honest man will protect him, the opposite of falling into one's own evil. The antithesis between falling into a (metaphorical) pit (11:5b) and "keeping straight" supports understanding the straightness as horizontal leveling and smoothing.

This verse promises a safe and prosperous life (Toy). Moffatt paraphrases nicely: "Have mind of him wherever you may go, and he will clear the road for you."

3:7. *Do not reckon yourself wise*: Even when you acquire wisdom, you must hold to humility and not allow confidence in your own intellect and learning to displace the demands of religious conscience and faith. It is best to be wise but not to think you are. Isaiah declares: "Woe to those who are wise in their own eyes, and who see themselves as understanding" (5:21). Jeremiah expands on this theme:

Thus says the Lord,
Let not the wise man take pride in his wisdom;
let not the mighty man take pride in his might;
let not the rich man take pride in his riches.
But let him who would feel pride take pride in this:
discerning and knowing me.
For I am the Lord who practices kindness,
justice and righteousness in the earth,
for these are what I delight in.
An oracle of the Lord.

(9:23–24)

Jeremiah is not condemning all wisdom or the wise, but only the cleverness and learning of those whose knowledge makes them smug and self-righteous.

Speaking of Jeremiah's debt to the wisdom teachers, von Rad says that "Jeremiah has correctly interpreted the deepest insights of the teachers and has given to them their keenest or finest expression" (1972: 103). But there is no reason to credit this insight to the teachers of Wisdom alone. McKane reverses the direction of dependency and describes 3:7 as "strongly reminiscent of the prophetic attack on old wisdom and its insistence that the intellectual self-determination on which the sages set such store is illusory." But the notion of "intellectual self-determination" never characterized Wisdom literature at any stage. The frailty of human intellect is recognized in sayings in the early collections of Proverbs (16:9; 19:21; 20:24), as well as in Egyptian Wisdom; see the comment on 3:5. Ptahhotep, for example, says, "Do not be arrogant about your wisdom" (l. 52). A later copyist rephrased this to read: "Do not let your heart be overconfident because you are wise."

The Syriac Ahiqar has similar advice: "My son, do not consider yourself wise when others do not consider you wise" (S_2, 2:30). This formulation means that one must not consider himself wise if he alone thinks he is. We should perhaps understand "in your own eyes" in Prov 3:7 similarly.

3:8. *flesh*: MT *šor* "navel" should be emended to *bšʾrk* "your flesh."

Some commentators justify MT's *l^ešorrekā* on the grounds that the navel's centrality makes it an appropriate synecdoche for the entire body (Saʿadia, Plöger). But "navel" is never used in this way, and the notion of "health" for the *navel* would make little sense. Driver (1951: 175) posits the existence of a noun *šōr* "health," from *š-r-r* "be strong." McKane follows this explanation, translating "health" (sim. Gemser). Sir 30:15, where *šr* is rendered *hygieia*, does seem to support the existence of a noun *šr* with this meaning. Interestingly, that noun has the marginal variants *bśr* and *šʾr* in Sir 30:15 and *šʾr* in v 16. Nevertheless, health/bones is not a word pair, whereas flesh (*bāśār*)/bones is standard; e.g., Gen 2:23; Ps 38:4; Job 33:21; Prov 14:30. Also, "give health to your health [*šōr*]" in the present verse would be tautologous. We should read *lišʾērekā* or possibly *libśārekā*, both meaning "to your flesh," with LXX. The former assumes only the loss of an *ʾaleph*. Also possible is a defective writing: *šēr* for *š^{eʾ}ēr* "flesh."

Moist, lubricated bones were thought to be a source and sign of vitality and health (Isa 58:11; 66:14; Prov 15:30; Job 21:24; etc.), whereas hot and dry bones were deemed a severe systemic ailment (Ps 102:4; Prov 17:22; Job 30:30).

3:9–10. *Honor the Lord . . .* : God will reward gifts to him (v 9) by enhancing the giver's own prosperity.

Honor (*kabbed*) sometimes implies giving gifts or benefits (e.g., Num 22:37; 24:11; Judg 9:9; perhaps Prov 14:31), but it never lacks its usual signification of showing respect and even homage.

from your wealth: Ezek 27:12, 18, 33 define *hon* as valuable metals and other merchandise. *Hon* is movable wealth and is probably distinct from real estate and one's own crops and husbandry. (When they are traded, they become *hon* for the merchant; Ezek 27:33.) Agricultural yield is *t^ebuʾah* "produce." This verse, then, advises contributing offerings to the temple from the entire range of his property.

C. Cohen (1997) argues that the *m-* of *mēhônekā* is comparative ("more than" rather than "from") and translates, "Honor the Lord more than your wealth and more than your choicest income" (p. 140). The difficulty with this interpretation is that one is not said to "honor" (*kabbēd*) wealth, a construction implicit in the sentence as he translates it. Not only is the specific construction lacking, but the concept of "honoring" wealth—which means holding it dear—is an unlikely one.

abundance: The word *śabaʿ* ("satiety," "abundance") in collocation with *tiroš* ("new wine") probably denotes grain. The same combination in Phoenician, *śbʿ wtrš*, apparently means "grain and new wine" (Karatepe A III 7–9 [KAI 26];

Dahood 1963: 9). Avishur (1975) notes several features in Prov 3 that give this chapter a Phoenician coloring.

This is the only verse in Proverbs that recommends donations to the temple cult, but its presence is not out of place in Wisdom literature. Merikare is told: "Richly provide and increase the offerings; give abundantly for the daily offering, for this is valuable for him who does it" (XXIV; P 65ff. [cf. AEL 1.102]). He is also urged to celebrate the festivals (XXIII B; cf. XLV; AEL 1.102, 106). Pap. Beatty IV teaches: "Offer to (your god) with a loving heart, that he may grant your provisions as his gift" (4.11). Anii advises: "Celebrate the festival of your god and repeat it at its set times. God is angry at him who neglects it" (16.3–4; cf. 4–9 [cf. AEL 2.136]). The Babylonian Counsels of Wisdom (ll. 135–47; BTM 330) prescribes daily offerings and prayer. There are also admonitions about proper comportment in the temple and festivals. Wisdom in no way repudiates the sacrificial cult, though, like the prophets and the Psalms, it gives priority to ethical behavior (21:3; 21:27; sim. Qoh 4:17b; 8:10), a ranking that even priests could accept.[144] Perdue's comprehensive study, *Wisdom and Cult* (1977), shows that cultic worship has a more significant and positive role in Wisdom literature than earlier believed. Nevertheless, such concerns are not prominent in Proverbs.

3:11. *Do not, my son, reject the Lord's discipline . . .* : The MT marks a new section (*pisqaʾ*) here, beginning the verse on a new line. In terms of content, there is undoubtedly a certain shift in topic, but unless we take vv 11–12 as a stray epigram or a later addition, it must be joined to Lecture III. Having spoken about the prosperity that comes with piety, the author now puts suffering in a religious perspective.

Sometimes suffering is divine discipline, a gracious warning intended to spare you greater punishments. Job's friends hold this idea. Eliphaz (Job 5:17–18) uses nearly the same terms as Prov 3:11–12: "Behold, happy is the man whom God chastises (*yokiḥennu*), so do not reject (*timaʾs*) Shaddai's discipline (*musar*). For he hurts (*yakʾib*) but binds up; he smashes—but his own hands give healing." Elihu repeats this teaching in 33:1–22. Deut 8:5 uses the same simile.

3:12. *as a father* [*wkʾb*] *does to a favored son*: For *wkʾb*, many commentators read *wykʾb* (*w*ᵉ*yakʾîb*) "and afflict" (note the use of this verb in Job 5:18, quoted previously). But in the emended text, the "son" in the simile would be God's instead of an indefinite father's, and, as Ehrlich observes, individuals are not called "sons" of God. Only the people of Israel and the king ex officio are so called. Perhaps the original text had both words—*wykʾbw kʾb*—one of which was lost by haplography. Verse 12b would mean "and he afflicts him, as a father (does) to a son he loves"; see Textual Note. This emendation (DNF) results in a neat chiasm of verb forms but is not necessary.

The juxtaposition between "faith and wealth" in 3:9–10 and "faith and difficulty" in 3:11–12 is a paradigm of Proverbs' worldview, not a violation of it (cf.

[144]Toeg (1974, esp. 13–14) shows that Num 15:22–31 propounds the theological principle that the sin offering is not effective for intentional transgressions. On the ethical foundation of the Priestly Code, see Milgrom 1991: 21–26.

Van Leeuwen 1992: 34–35). The withholding of the promised benefits does not prove that a person is wicked or that God is unjust. Suffering as well as good fortune can flow from God's love. This doctrine shows that Wisdom (even as expounded by Job's doctrinaire friends) did not hold to a mechanical balance sheet notion of retribution or a simple and immediate causal link between sin and commensurate retribution. Much in Proverbs contradicts the oversimplified view that Wisdom held to a mechanical retribution concept (see Van Leeuwen 1992: esp. 28f.; Fox 1989: 132–37). It begs the question to create a Wisdom dogma by isolating the supposedly mechanistic sayings as the book's true dogma and then explaining the non-mechanistic observations as reactions to dogmatism or as evidence for the breakdown of the dogma. To say, for example, "Once the sages acknowledged exceptions, their entire scheme became problematic" (Crenshaw 1989b: 30–32) is to assume that their scheme did not include exceptions from the start. But the vicissitudes of fortune were well known to the predecessors of Proverbs,[145] and there is no reason to expect a greater blindness among Israel's earliest sages.

The author of Prov 3:11–12, unlike Elihu, is not rationalizing suffering; he is inculcating the right attitude toward it. One must accept suffering as an act of divine love, not repudiate it and rebel against one's condition. This verse reformulates the principle of relying on God rather than on one's intellectual resources (3:5).

The final two verses are on a different topic and stand apart. In view of its parallels in Job 5:17 and Deut 8:5, v 12 may well be a quoted maxim or turn of phrase. Lecture III lacks a conclusion summing up the lesson, but the declaration in v 12 has the effect of a caesura and brings the unit to a proper close.

The Design of Lecture III

This highly symmetrical lecture proceeds by pairs of injunctions + promises.

I. Exordium (1–4): four quatrains, with an inserted monostich (3a)
  A. Retain my teaching (double injunction, literal) (1)
  B. then you'll have long life and peace (double promise) (2).
     Added promise [phrased as impv.]: favor with God and humans (3a)
  A′. Retain my teaching (double injunction; metaphorical) (3bc)
  B′. then you'll receive favor and regard, divine and human (double promise) (4).

II. Lesson (5–12): four quatrains, each with advice + reason
  A. Trust God, not yourself (5);
     then he will smooth your path (6).

[145] Compare the "ignorance of the morrow" topos in Anii (21.4–10; AEL 2.142; Ptahhotep (339–50, esp. 343, 345; AEL 1.69); Amenemope (§18 = 19.11–15; AEL 2.157); O. Petrie 11 (vso. 5); and Pap. Ramesseum I (A 18). The authors of Wisdom did not imagine that one can guarantee his prosperity by right behavior.

B. Do not think yourself wise, but avoid evil (7);
then you'll have good health (8).
C. Give offerings to God (9);
then you'll enjoy affluence (10).
D. Do not reject divine chastisement (11),
for God does this out of love (12; ≈ conclusion).

III. Conclusion: lacking

Piety and Wisdom

If we were to encounter Lecture III in isolation, we could classify it as a pietistic homily rather than a Wisdom instruction. It nowhere requires wisdom and mentions it only within a negative admonition (3:7). The message of this lecture is the importance of piety. The lecture preaches humility, faith in God, fulfillment of cultic duties, and loving submission to divine chastisement. It does not say that *wisdom* will produce these virtues, or even that they will promote wisdom. (The Wisdom of Solomon does this: "Those who trust in [God] will understand truth, and the faithful will abide with him in love" [3:9a].) Moreover, none of the lecture's teachings require special intelligence, penetration, or intellectual effort to carry out.

The present (and probably secondary) collocation of Lecture III and Interlude B suggests a connection between faith and wisdom. This may have been the intention of the interpolator of Interlude B, but the connection is not made explicitly and is absent from Lecture III. The thrust of the lecture is not, however, anti-intellectual. It does not exist on its own, but develops one aspect of the greater message, which is to be gathered from the lectures in their totality.

Lecture III is primarily concerned with shaping attitudes. The imperatives enjoin feelings and mental dispositions rather than deeds: "trust," "rely not," "hold in mind" (lit. "know"), "do not reckon" (lit. "be not . . . in your eyes"), "fear," "honor," "do not reject," "do not despise." Only "shun" (lit. "turn aside from") is strictly in the realm of action, and this verb is more a consequence of the preceding imperative than an independent exhortation. These attitudes will inevitably lead to the right actions, but the present lecture focuses on attitudes and moral character. The pious frame of mind that the lecture would inculcate, together with the resulting morality, is enough to ensure a fortunate and happy life.

Egyptian Wisdom, in its later stages, developed an attitude known as personal piety. It came to flower in the Eighteenth Dynasty (with some precedents) and became prominent in the Ramesside period. It left its imprint on many genres of literature, including Wisdom. Personal piety grew out of and expressed a sense of individual frailty, isolation, and sometimes even angst. Its characteristics were a conviction of complete dependence on God and a surrender to his will, a belief in an immediate contact between a man and his god, and a confidence that God hears prayers, grants forgiveness, and saves people from distress. Retribution proceeds directly from God rather than by natural processes.

The ideal type is the "silent man," who excels not only in tactical reticence and self-control (as in earlier Wisdom) but in repose, resignation, and humility. On personal piety, see esp. Assmann 1979 and LÄ IV 951ff.

The contrast between the classical Wisdom of the Old Kingdom and the Wisdom of the New Kingdom should not be overdrawn. Some of the features of personal piety, especially the belief in human dependency on God and the opacity of the future, are present in classical Wisdom and other types of texts. Feelings of anxiety and isolation are attested as well, especially in "The Dispute between a Man and his *Ba*" (AEL I 163–69). Even in Ptahhotep, with its robust Old Kingdom setting, "there is an undercurrent of assertions that the world is uncertain and full of social mobility, social competition, instability, and complexity" (Parkinson 1997: 248).

Moreover, it may be that the attributes of personal piety seem so predominant in NK Wisdom only because of the special attention that Amenemope commands in modern study. These features are less prominent in Anii and absent from Pap. Beatty IV, and if we had a broader sampling of Wisdom texts, the theological profile of NK Wisdom might be different. As M. Lichtheim's comprehensive study of Egyptian autobiographies concludes, "Wisdom and piety were partners in the endeavor to formulate and teach the right kind of living" (1992: 100), though piety did receive greater emphasis in the NK and beyond.

Piety in Proverbs, even in Part I where it is most prominent, is quite distant from the Egyptian personal piety of the NK. Proverbs lacks both the underlying anxiety and the intimacy of religious communion that we find in Egypt. Although the sages were quite aware that retribution is not a perfect balance sheet, they usually display a robust confidence—well encapsulated in 3:10—in their ability to ascertain the right stance in life and to secure God's blessings through it. Proverbs calls for reliance on God, not resignation or quietism. God's forgiveness and mercy (*raḥămim*, as distinct from his kindness, *ḥesed*), which are central to personal piety, have no role in Prov 1–9 and are scarcely mentioned elsewhere in Proverbs (16:6; 28:13). Absent too is the sense of almost inevitable human sinfulness. In Proverbs, *fools* are sinful, not *us*.

Personal piety in the Egyptian form is thus foreign to Proverbs. In fact, it was largely strained out of the sections of Amenemope incorporated in Proverbs (see Römheld 1989 and the discussion in the Commentary on 24:22 in vol. 2).

INTERLUDE B. IN PRAISE OF WISDOM (3:13–20)

TRANSLATION

Love of wisdom

3:13 **Happy the man who has found wisdom,**
the man who obtains good sense!

14 For better her profit than the profit of silver,
her yield than that of fine gold.
15 More precious is she than rubies;
no valuables[a] can match her.
16 Long life is in her right hand,
in her left—wealth and honor.
17 Her ways are pleasant ways,
and all her paths are peace.
18 A tree of life is she for those who grasp her;
and those who hold her are deemed fortunate.[b]

God himself uses wisdom

19 By wisdom the Lord founded the earth,
established the heavens by skill.
20 By his knowledge the waters of the abyss gush forth,
and the skies drip down dew.

---

[a] *ḥăpāṣîm* (MT *ḥăpāṣeykā*) [b] *meʾuššārîm* (MT *meʾuššār*)

COMMENTARY

3:13–18. Love of Wisdom

3:13. *Happy* [*ʾašrey*]: On this exclamation, see the later excursus on "The Macarism," a genre used in extolling a certain virtue or experience by exclaiming on the good fortune of its possessor.

has found . . . obtains [*maṣaʾ . . . yapiq*]: Saʿadia distinguishes "finding" wisdom—that is, procuring it by one's own efforts—from "obtaining" it—that is, receiving it as a gift. Ramaq, more accurately, observes that *yapiq* (H-stem of *p-w-q*) means "bring forth," whether from oneself or another source. Thus *yapiq* too implies a deliberate action—the active *taking* rather than the passive reception of wisdom.

3:14. *her profit* [*saḥrahh*] . . . *yield*: A person's *saḥar* is neither her value nor her trading activity, but what she earns; see Isa 23:18 ("her *saḥar*" is her income); 45:14; Prov 31:18 (Isa 23:3 is unclear). In Prov 3:14, then, the comparison is not between the value of wisdom and that of precious metals, but between the profits that each can produce (cf. Ehrlich). For similar comparisons with different emphases, see Prov 8:10 and 16:16.

3:15. *no valuables*: Lit. "desired objects." The noun *ḥepeṣ* (pl. *ḥăpaṣim*) first means "desire" or "thing desired." In the present verse, *ḥăpaṣim* intensifies the parallelism: Not only treasures, but *whatever* one might desire cannot compare with wisdom (Ramaq, Ehrlich). Most of the medieval commentators believe the point of the contrast is that wisdom, unlike wealth, is not diminished by use or disbursement to others. But the superiority of wisdom is not limited to that one feature. A variant of this verse appears in 8:11.

MT's *ḥăpāṣeykā* "your desirable things" should be emended to *ḥăpāṣîm* "desirable things"; see the Textual Note. The emended form (as in LXX) has the advantage of not introducing a lone second sg. address into a unit otherwise lacking it.

Although *ḥepeṣ* sometimes refers to possessions or to business activities in classical BH, it does not seem to lose the connotation of volition or desire until quite late, as in Qohelet (3:1, 17; 5:7; etc.) and in MH, when it means "matter" or "affair."

rubies: The meaning of *pᵉninim* is uncertain; perhaps "corals" or "pearls," which is the later sense of the word.

3:16. *right hand*: Wisdom is pictured as a woman in this verse and perhaps vv 14–17 as well.

honor: *Kabod* usually means "honor," but sometimes it means "wealth." (The underlying meaning of *k-b-d* is weightiness, substance. In English, "substance" can refer to material wealth.) Clear examples of *kabod* = "wealth" are Gen 31:1; Isa 10:3; and 61:6. *Kabod* may always have this sense when collocated with *ʿošer* "wealth" (e.g., 2 Chr 17:5; 32:27; Qoh 6:2). The occasional synonymity of *ʿošer* and *kabod* is shown by the way the terms can combine in either order in construct (Esth 1:4 and 5:11) and by the fact that whenever the two share a verb, it is always singular. Since wealth tends to bring honor (or at least prestige), it is often hard to determine which sense is intended. In the present verse, since one hand is said to hold *ʿošer wᵉkabod*, the pair of nouns probably designates a single concept (parallel to "life," in her right hand)—perhaps "substantive wealth" or "honorable wealth." LXX adds a verse; see the Textual Notes.

Ch. Kayatz (1966: 105) proposed that the image in 3:16 is Egyptian in origin. Many figures of Maʿat (the goddess of truth and justice) portray her with one hand holding an *ʿanḫ* emblem, which represents life, and the other holding a *waʾs* scepter, representing (according to Kayatz) wealth and honor. In fact, however, Maʿat sometimes holds the *ʿanḫ* in her *left* hand, the *waʾs* scepter in her right (e.g., Kayatz, fig. 13), so the iconographic resemblance is not precise. A fair number of gods are portrayed in this way, and there is no justification for singling out Maʿat as the background image of Prov 3:16. Furthermore, the *waʾs* scepter symbolizes happiness and prosperity generally, as well as dominion, and it is tendentious to explain its signification as "Reichtum und Ehre" ("wealth and honor"). Nevertheless, the Egyptian practice of depicting gods holding symbols for their powers and blessings may be in the background of the picture of Lady Wisdom. See "A Canaanite Goddess?" in Essay 2.

3:17. *Her ways*: This phrase and the like may be understood in three ways: the paths *to* wisdom, the paths wisdom prescribes, or the paths (personified) Wisdom goes in, in other words, the way she treats her adherents. For 3:17, the third interpretation is favored both by the next verse (in which Wisdom promises rewards to her faithful) and by 8:20–21 (according to which Wisdom goes in righteous paths to benefit her devotees).

are peace: That is, peaceful. A predicate noun can function adjectivally in Hebrew (e.g., Ps 19:10; 109:4; Jer 10:10). This may create an intensification similar to what occurs in English when we say, "Her paths are peace itself." "Peace,"

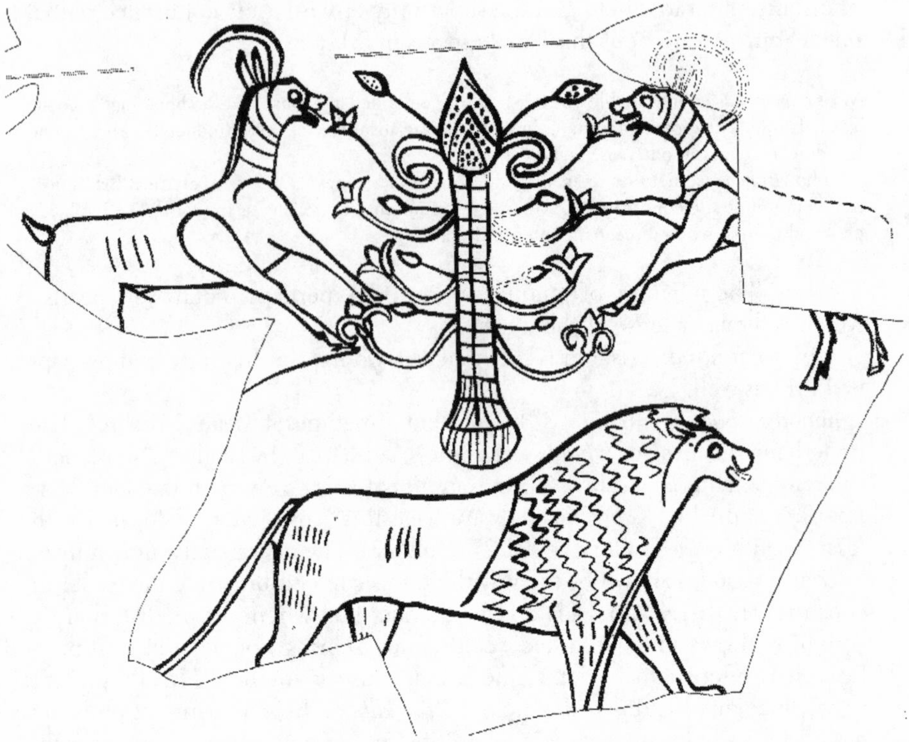

A *"Tree of Life" (Prov 3:18) from Kuntillet ʿAjrud, ninth–eighth century* B.C.E.

šalom, means harmony and well-being as well as absence of strife among people. DNF, however, suggests that "peace" is elliptical for "paths of peace."

To a youngster forced to study, sometimes prodded on by scoldings and spankings, the pleasantness and peacefulness of the path to wisdom may not be immediately apparent. Ben Sira describes it in rather grim terms (4:17; 6:18–31).

3:18. *tree of life*: Other things called trees of life in Proverbs are a fulfilled desire (13:12), a gentle tongue (15:4), and the fruit [read "mouth"?] of the righteous (11:30). These all impart vitality and good cheer.

The tree of life originally belonged to mythology, and life sometimes meant eternal life. In Gen 3:22, the tree of life affords immortality to those who *eat* its fruit. In Egypt, certain trees, in particular the sycamore, are dispensers of eternal life (noted by Kayatz 1966: 105–6). The expression "tree of life" occurs in Egyptian starting in the late period (which was not, however, necessarily later than our passage). A common motif in tombs, starting with the Eighteenth Dynasty, shows the deceased being nourished by the goddess of the sycamore. The idea of the tree of life belongs to the common culture of the ancient Near East, though the term "tree of life" in this sense is not common.

Drawings of a stylized tree were widespread throughout the Near East. (For a discussion of the "sacred tree" as the iconographic background of the Tabernacle Menorah, see C. Meyers 1974: 95–122 and *passim*.) Though not so labeled, these depictions probably represent the tree of life. The tree is commonly flanked by divinities, humans, or animals (ibexes), who hold up their hands or front legs or touch the tree in veneration. The ibexes sometimes seem to be eating from the tree (which shows that this is not the so-called "world tree," a different mythological motif). Ezekiel (47:12) prophesies the growth of a literal tree that will provide nourishment and healing. The mythological associations of the tree of life survive in Jewish Hellenistic literature (Marcus 1943) and attach themselves to the Torah, which inherits the epithet "the tree of life."

In Proverbs, the tree of life is devoid of mythological significance and serves only as a figure for vitality and healing. Marcus (1943) identifies the referent of the metaphor as a medicinal, life-giving plant, equivalent to MH *sam ḥayyim* "life-giving remedy." The image in Prov 3:18 does not, however, imply a medicinal plant, because it is to be (metaphorically) "grasped" rather than eaten.

and those who hold her: The sacred tree in ancient iconography is commonly shown being touched by the beings flanking it. "Holding" or "grasping" the tree was apparently a source of life and strength.

deemed fortunate [*meʿuššar*]: This verse links up with v 13 to bracket the macarism: those who find wisdom (v 13) and hold on to it (v 18) are deemed happy or fortunate (*ʾašrey-*, *meʾuššar*). Ramaq observes that the Dp of *ʾ-š-r*, like the D, is declarative and means to be called or deemed (rather than simply *being*) fortunate.

Tōmkeyhā meʾuššār: A sg. predicate with a preceding pl. subject is often thought to have a distributive sense, meaning each and every one of those who grasp it (thus, e.g., Ramaq, Naḥmias, Delitzsch, GKC §145*l*). The justification for this assumption is unclear. Possibly the construction treats the noun as a collectivity.

3:19–20. God Himself Uses Wisdom

3:19. To the macarism proper, the poet adds two verses that give human wisdom cosmological significance (Meinhold). The crowning proof of wisdom's glory is that God himself uses it. The shift in themes between the macarism and vv 19–20 may indicate that the author is quoting an older saying. Psalm 104:24 too declares that God performs all his works in wisdom.

wisdom, skill (*ḥokmah* and *tebunah*): the same terms as used in 3:13. *Tebunah* is practical know-how and is best translated "good sense" in reference to human relations (as in 3:13) but "skill" in reference to craftsmanship.

In physical terms, the "founding" (*ysd*) of the earth means setting the solid, habitable world on "the pillars of the earth" (*mosedot tebel* [Ps 18:16] or *mosedey ʾereṣ* [Prov 8:29, etc.]). These pillars are perhaps to be imagined as mountains. The "establishing" of the heavens means fixing the sky like a cupola on columns, which are called *ʿammudey šamayim* "the pillars of heaven" (Job 26:11). On the Hebrew conception of the physical universe, see the Commentary on 8:24–29.

3:20. *By his knowledge*:

For *bᵉdaʿto* we should probably, but not necessarily, read *bᵉdaʿat* "by knowledge" without the suffix (= LXX), parallel to *bᵉḥokmāh* "by wisdom" because the aim of the passage is to praise wisdom (= knowledge) as such rather than to extol specifically *God's* wisdom. Also, *daʿat* has a possessive genitive only once elsewhere in Proverbs (22:17—but not in the LXX).

the waters of the abyss gush forth: Lit. "the abyss waters [*tᵉhomot*] are [or were] split [*nibqaʿu*]." This refers to opening of channels through which waters can rise from the subterranean seas. The waters themselves are not split, but *spill out* of split rock (Hameʾiri, Ehrlich; for *nibqaʿ* in this sense, see Isa 35:6; 58:8). The unruly waters of the abyss were imprisoned at creation (Job 38:8–11) and are ever straining against their bonds. An excessive release of abyss waters causes catastrophic flooding (Gen 7:11; Hab 3:9b), but a controlled opening of channels is a blessing (Judg 15:19; Isa 35:6).

the skies drip down dew: God's blessings also come from above. During the summer, dew is an important source of moisture for certain plants. Dew is formed by condensation from the moist west wind, but it seems to drip from the clouds like rain (see ABD 4.124–25). Though the welling up of springs and the descent of dew were events in the original creation, these processes continue as ongoing providential deeds that recall and renew creation.

Malbim compares 3:19–20 to Prov 24:3–4, "By wisdom a house is built, by skill it is established. By knowledge rooms are filled with all sorts of precious and pleasant wealth." Both passages describe two stages: creation (3:19; 24:3) and provisioning (3:20; 24:4). The first stage employs *ḥokmāh* and *tᵉbûnāh*, the second, *daʿat*. Malbim believes this choice of terminology is significant, but it is likely that any of the terms could be applied to either stage. The first stage itself has two steps, "founding" or "laying down foundations" (*y-s-d*), perhaps equivalent to "building" in 24:3, and "establishing" (*k-n-n*), which Malbim explains as the completion of a structure by an overhead covering, namely a roof or sky, but the evidence for this distinction too is insufficient.

The Design of Interlude B

All of vv 14–20 may be considered a motivation of the macarism in v 13. This unit is like an extended motivation in an exordium.

A. Usefulness for man
   1. The good fortune of him who finds wisdom (13)
   2. Its incomparable value (14–15)
   3. Its gifts of long life, wealth, and honor (16),
   4. and pleasantness and peace (17)
   5. The good fortune of him who finds wisdom (18)

B. Usefulness for God
   1. God's use of wisdom, in creation and always (19–20)

The Message of Interlude B

Interlude B, with its spirited encouragement to study wisdom, nicely complements Lecture III, which extols piety alone and even expresses a certain caution about relying on one's own intellectual powers (3:5). There is no actual contradiction in this, because piety is tantamount to wisdom. The difference between the units is one of emphasis. The balance and interdependence of these two virtues is a central theme in Prov 1–9.

The idea that God created the world by wisdom is ancient. It was hardly an invention of Deutero-Isaiah (contrary to McKane). It appears in the Memphite Theology (a Twenty-fifth Dynasty text with origins in the Old Kingdom), which says that Ptah created the universe through his heart (intelligence) and tongue (speech) (AEL 1.51–56). In Israel, the idea is found in Ps 104 (v 24), a hymn with Egyptian background, and Jer 10:12 and 51:15; and compare Isa 40:12–17. Usually the purpose of such statements is to praise God, either directly or by celebrating his works. Prov 3:19–20 alone employs this idea in praise of wisdom itself. Later, God's creative wisdom, identified with Torah, becomes an important theme in Jewish thought, starting with Sir 24 and the Midrash, particularly *Gen. Rab.* 1:1.

The Macarism (ʾašrey)

Interlude B is a macarism, extolling a certain virtue by exclaiming the good fortune of its possessor. (This form is often called the "beatitude.") The exclamatory word is *ʾašrey,* lit. "The good fortune (of so-and-so)!" or "How fortunate is so-and-so!" The word is close in force to *baruk* "blessed."

Biblical examples are Isa 56:2; Ps 1:1–3; 32:1–2; 40:5; 41:2–4; 84:5–6; 89:16–18; 94:12–15; 112:1–3; 119:1–3; 128:1–4; Prov 3:13; 8:32, 34; 28:14; Job 5:17; Sir 14:1–2; 14:20–15:1; 25:8–9; 28:19–23; 31:8–11; 48:11; 50:28–29. Examples in later literature include Qumran (4Q525; Puech 1991) and the NT (Matt 5:3–12; Luke 6:20–23). 4Q525 praises the man who speaks the truth and who "attains wisdom, and walks in the law of the Most High." Related forms use *ʾašrey* in different positions and constructions (Prov 14:21; 16:20; 20:7; 29:18; Qoh 10:17).

The macarism is predominantly represented in Wisdom literature, and it is often thought that the macarism originated there. The formula is, however, well represented elsewhere, particularly in Psalms, including some of the oldest of them (Lipiński 1968: 326).

There are cross-influences among different genres. Wisdom themes and diction appear in some psalmodic macarisms. (Pss 1, 112, and 119 show strong Wisdom influence.) Conversely, Prov 3:13–20 shows dependence on the hymnic style (Lipiński 1968: 359–60).

Macarisms may have served a didactic function within the temple service, similar to the query formula, "Who . . . ?" (Pss 15:1; 24:3; 25:12; 34:13), which likewise lauds the virtuous and fortunate man. The macarism has no role in Egyptian Wisdom literature but is frequent in Egyptian mortuary banquet scenes, in which singers declare the good fortune of the deceased in songs beginning, "How fortunate (*wʾḏ.wy*) is this good prince."

Lecture IV. The Wisdom of Honesty (3:21–35)

TRANSLATION

Keep my teachings

3:21 My son, let not (my words) escape your eyes;
retain competence and shrewdness.

They give life and security

22 They'll give vitality to your throat,
grace to your neck.
23 Then you'll go your way securely
and never stub your toe.
24 When you sit down[a] you'll have no fear,
when you recline, your sleep will be sweet.
25 You will not fear the sudden terror,
the calamity of the wicked, when it comes,
26 for the Lord will be your trust,
and keep your foot from the snare.

Treat others fairly

27 Don't deny a benefit to the one to whom it is due,
when you have the ability to do it.
28 Don't say to your fellow,
"Go away and come back,
and tomorrow I'll give it to you,"
when you have it all along.
29 Don't devise harm against another person,
when he dwells in trust with you.
30 Don't quarrel with a man without reason,
if he has done you no wrong.
31 Don't envy the lawless man,
and don't choose any of his ways,
32 for the Lord loathes the crooked man
but with the honest he is intimate.

God's favor and disgust

33 The Lord's curse is in the house of the wicked,
but he blesses the abode of the righteous.
34 As for the scornful—them he scorns,
but upon the humble he bestows favor.
35 The wise inherit honor,
while dolts gain[b] only contempt.

---

[a]*tēšēb* (MT *tiškab* "lie down") [b]*m^erîmîm* (MT *mērîm*)

COMMENTARY

3:21–26. Exordium

3:21. *let not (my words) escape your eyes*: ("My words" is added in the translation.) The verb "escape" (*yaluzu*) lacks a subject. Riyqam, Hameʾiri, Naḥmias, and other medieval commentators identify the subject as the wisdom mentioned in vv 19–20. But it would be incongruous to say that the wisdom God used in creation should not escape your eyes or that it should be kept in your heart (for your own use rather than as a reminder of God's greatness). It is likewise forced to extract the subject from the following line (Ralbag). In any case, an exordium must start with a command to listen or remember. It is likely that a verse was skipped in copying (an error perhaps occasioned by the insertion of Interlude B), and we should restore a couplet along the lines of 4:20: "My son, hearken to my words, incline your ear to what I say." The near identity of 4:21a and 3:21a supports this restoration. Toy and BHS transpose lines 22a and 22b (except for "my son"), but the example of 4:21 supports MT's order.

escape [*yaluzu*]: This is an unusual verb, used in this way only here and in the nearly identical 4:21. Derivatives of *l-w-z* elsewhere convey the notion of twisting or straying (see esp. Sir 31[34]:8, *nlwz ʾḥry* = "go astray after") and connote moral perversity on the part of the subject, but this cannot be the case here. The verb may suggest that the teachings have a tendency to slip away and can be retained only with resolution.

competence [*tušiyyah*] and *shrewdness* [*m^ezimmah*]: The father identifies his teachings with two eminently practical faculties. *Tušiyyah* is an inner resource, not specifically intellectual or moral, that can help one deal with a crisis; *m^ezimmah* is private, unrevealed thought, hence "circumspection" or "discretion"; see "Words for Wisdom," §§6, 9.

3:22. *vitality to your throat*: or "life to your soul" (*ḥayyim l^enapšeka*). *Nepeš* refers to (a) the physical throat or, more specifically, to the windpipe and the breath within it; (2) the "spirit" of man, in the sense of personality and emotions; and (3) the individual life itself. (The second and third aspects are implied by English "soul," which is often a valid translation.) All three are relevant here. The parallel in v 22b, with its reference to the "neck" and the promise of attractiveness (*ḥen*, as in 1:22; 4:9; cf. 3:4), activates the necklace metaphor in 22a. See the comments on 1:9 and 3:3. LXX adds a verse; see the Textual Notes.

3:23. *and never stub your toe*: lit. "foot." Stubbing the toe is a figure for a minor mishap; e.g., Ps 91:12 (Ehrlich; cf. Riyqam). We could translate, "and not even stub your toe."

3:24. *sit down*: MT's *tškb* "lie down" in 24a arose by *b-k* dittography. LXX confirms *tēšēb* "sit down." This reading reveals a sequence of actions in 23–24: walking, sitting down, going to sleep. All are done without pain or fear. God will protect you when you sleep (Ps 4:9). You will not have nightmares (contrast Job 7:14).

3:25. *You will not fear* [*ʾal tiraʾ*]: lit. "do not fear." An imperative can serve as a negative final clause to a preceding imperative.

the sudden terror: Suddenness in biblical usage implies unexpected timing and is almost always associated with disaster (Daube 1964: chapter 1). The sinner's calamity comes without warning.

the calamity of the wicked: Or "storm" (*šoʾah*), thus translated at 1:27. This is not simply a misfortune that comes upon the wicked; it is *their* calamity, stored in readiness for their day of judgment. Job 38:22–23 and Isa 47:11b speak of punitive storms in similar terms. The wicked are imagined to be at least vaguely aware of what is coming and to live in gnawing foreboding of its advent (1:27). Only the timing of their fate is unknown, which makes the anxiety all the more oppressive.

3:26. *the Lord will be your trust* [*b^{e}kisleka*]: A *k^{e}sil*—dolt—is characterized by *kesel* "trust," "confidence," which is probably the word's derivation. The fool has confidence, but of a pernicious sort. His *kesel* is a delusion (Ps 49:14; Job 8:14; cf. Job 31:24), whereas the wise man's *kesel* is God himself, not man (Prov 3:26).

Dahood (1965: 330), Hamp (*TDOT* IV, 444), Meinhold, and others accept Jerome's translation of *b^{e}kislekā* as *in latere tuo* "at your side" (sim. Syr, Tg) because the *bet* of *b^{e}kisleka* seems to mean "in" or "at." This is, however, a *beth essentiae* (GKC §119 *i*), exactly as in *b^{eʿ}ezri* in Exod 18:4.

and keep your foot from the snare: This assurance reinforces the promise of walking safely through life (v 23). The motifs of trap and unexpected disaster are paired also in Ps 35:8, "A calamity [*šoʾah*] of which he is unaware will come upon him, and his net, which he hid, will ensnare him. He will fall into it in a storm/calamity [*b^{e}šoʾah*]."

The righteous escape such fates. Nevertheless, life, even for the righteous, is a narrow path through rough and perilous territory full of pitfalls, snares, rocks, and storms. A judicious fear of the dangers on the way can encourage obedience to the teachings of wisdom and reliance on God, and this will keep one on the safe path. In this way, the righteous person fears, and this promotes genuine security and inner repose, whereas the fool lives in "confidence"—a smug overconfidence that blinds him to real dangers and makes him blunder blithely into hazardous paths and life's pitfalls. Therefore, paradoxically, "Happy is the man who fears always, but he who hardens his heart will fall into evil" (Prov 28:14).

3:27–32. Lesson: Treat Others Fairly

3:27. *Don't deny a benefit* [*ṭob*] *to the one to whom it is due* [*b^{eʿ}alayw*]: *B^{eʿ}alayw* (a pl. in a sg. sense) is lit. "its possessor." A *baʿal* (or pl. *b^{eʿ}alim*) is one who possesses something by right, not someone who needs or wants it. Even if the *baʿal* does not currently hold the item, it is still rightfully his. See also the comment on 1:19. The expression *baʿal(ey) ṭob/ṭobah*, lit. "possessor of something good," is implicit in this verse and Qoh 5:10.

The infinitive *laʿăśot* "to do" in v 27b has as its object *ṭob* in 27a and thus implies the clause *laʿăśot ṭob* "to do good." One is obliged *laʿăśot ṭob* to *baʿăley ṭob*. A *ṭob* ("good," "benefit") must be a type of activity, since it is something someone *does*.

To identify *baʿăley ṭob* as the poor (LXX, Rashi, Ramaq, Radaq, and many others) misses the point. Verse 27, like Lecture IV as a whole, preaches fairness and honesty, not charity or kindness. An example of "doing good" (though that term is not used in the passage) is helping someone raise up an ass which has collapsed under its burden (Exod 23:4). If you can help this man, you are obliged to do so *even if he is your enemy.* The ass's owner has a *claim* upon that assistance. We may say that he is the *baʿal* of that assistance, that he "possesses" it. Such moral claims and their corresponding duties are essential to the cohesion and sound working of society, perhaps even more so than acts of mercy and kindness.

to do it (namely, "good"): "Perform" or "do" good (*laʿăśot ṭob*) sometimes means to do someone a favor or a benefit, without a necessary implication of ethical or charitable behavior; e.g., 1 Sam 24:19; 2 Sam 2:6.

An Aramaic letter from Elephantine (Cowley 1929: 107–11; Hempel 1929: 150–51) gives us a clearer idea of what *baʿal ṭôb* and *ʿāśāh ṭôb* can mean in practice. Both phrases have their precise Aramaic equivalents in *bʿl ṭbh* and *ʿbd ṭbh*. A man writes his mother, Kawiliah (a Jew), concerning a shepherd called Napna who is coming to market in her town, Syene. This Napna, the son says, is *bʿl ṭbtkm*, lit. "possessor of your [pl.] good." The son says to his mother, *hn tʿbdn ṭbh yʿbd ly [k]n)* (lit.) "if you do his good [i.e., treat him well] he will treat me thus." Napna is by no means a poor man or a supplicant—the writer expects reciprocity. In this letter, *bʿl ṭbtkm* means approximately "someone who has a claim on your [household's] good graces" or "someone toward whom you had or have obligations." The phrase *bʿly ṭbh* appears in conjunction with *wrḥmyk* "those who love you" in Cowley (1923: 30.23–24). By my understanding, the Jews are not telling the governor merely that they are his "well-wishers" (as Cowley translates it), but reminding him that they have a claim upon his attention and assistance, as their complaints in 17–22 likewise imply.

3:28. *Don't say to your fellow . . .* : A variant of the previous admonition. This warns against temporizing when someone comes to you to claim something rightfully his. This item may be any of a number of things: money or something of value lent, valuables deposited in pledge for a loan, goods held in safekeeping (an important practice when there were no banks), or wages owed him (*b. Bab. Meṣiaʿ* 110b), which according to Lev 19:13 must not be held even overnight. The admonition has nothing to do with giving alms, for that would require a reference to the poor rather than the more inclusive "your fellow." Also, the precondition for giving charity would not be worded, "when you have it all along" (lit. "and it is with you"), for this implies a specific object in your holding that really belongs to the other person.

your fellow: This verse and the next speak of one's *rēaʿ*. This does not mean precisely "neighbor," as the word is traditionally rendered, but, more broadly, any person in one's category or sphere of interaction as defined by context (cf. HALAT 1169b; D. Kellermann in TWAT VII 546–57, 786–91; Fichtner 1955). (This is closer to the older usage of English "neighbor.")

Rēaʿ (var. *rēʿeh*; fem. *rēʿāh*, *raʿyāh*, *rᵉʿût*) often refers to an intimate, whether a friend (e.g., Deut 13:7) or a lover (e.g., Cant 5:16). But it can also refer to another person with whom there is no personal attachment (1 Sam 15:28; Esth 1:19). In Proverbs, a *rēaʿ* may be a friend (14:20; 17:17; 18:24;

27:10), but he may also be anyone in the vicinity (18:17; 24:28, etc.). *Rēaʿ* does not imply a proximity of dwelling.

Rēaʿ generally excludes foreigners, but only because of their distance. If one lives among foreigners, they too are *rēʿîm*. Thus *rēaʿ/rᵉʿût* is used of the Israelite's Egyptian neighbors (Exod 11:2).

The semantic range of *reʿa* can be more narrowly defined. It probably includes only one's social peers (the king, for example, would not be your *rēaʿ* unless you belonged to his circle of intimates; 1 Chr 27:33). *Rēaʿ* does not seem to be used of blood relations (except in the reciprocity idiom, *ʾîš ʾet rēʿēhû*, etc.); Deut 15:2 assumes a distinction between *ʾāḥ* (here, "relative") and *rēaʿ*. However, the teachings about treatment of one's *rēaʿ* would presumably apply to blood relatives as well.

Zār and *rēaʿ* are not antonyms; one person can be both a *zār* and a *rēaʿ*, as in 6:1.

3:29. *Don't devise harm . . . when he dwells in trust with you*: It is especially nefarious and underhanded to scheme to injure someone who trusts you. That is not to say (Saʿadia emphasizes) that it is permitted to scheme against people in other circumstances.

"Dwells in trust with you" does not mean that this person lives in your residence; he may be anyone in your acquaintance. "With you" modifies "in trust" rather than "dwells" (Ramaq glosses "he trusts you"). That is to say, he trusts *you*. The phrase *yošeb labetaḥ* means to live confidently, with a sense of security (see Judg 18:7; Isa 47:8; Ezek 38:11; etc.). Confidence is the theme of the exordium (3:23–26).

another person: Or "your fellow"—*reaʿ*, as in v 28. There is a sound play between the words *reaʿ* and *raʿ* ("another man"–"harm").

3:30. *quarrel . . . without reason*: Unlike v 29b, v 30b should be read restrictively, implying that while you may not quarrel without reason, you may do so *with* reason, with adequate justification (cf. Radaq, Toy). If someone has done you wrong, you need not turn the other cheek, for "quarreling" or "struggling" (*rib*) may be legitimate verbal contention or litigation. Prov 25:9 allows for legitimate contentions: "Have your dispute with your fellow, but do not reveal the secret of another."

3:31. *Don't envy the lawless man*: That is to say, one who prospers. His prosperity is fleeting. This is the message of lengthy meditations in Psalms 37 and 73. The sages of Wisdom literature were quite aware that the wicked could flourish. The usual solution to this problem was to insist on the inevitability of the punishment awaiting them. God's abhorrence of evildoers guarantees this.

3:32. *for the Lord loathes* [*toʿăbat YHWH*; lit. "the abomination of the Lord is"]: The concept of God's *toʿebah* (commonly rendered "abomination"), though found in various types of literature, has special importance in Proverbs. The root-meaning of *t-ʿ-b* is "disgusting," "loathsome," not necessarily on ethical or religious grounds. Sometimes *t-ʿ-b* just signifies simple disgust, with no ethical connotations. For example, shepherds are *repulsive* to the Egyptians (Gen 46:34). Job thinks of himself as so filthy that his own garments are disgusted with him (Job 9:31, D-stem). Sick people find food *repulsive*, that is, nauseating (Ps 107:18, D-stem). Although many of the things that God loathes are cultic offenses, the concept is not essentially or originally cultic. There is a range of disgusting things, some of which we may classify as cultic matters, others as ethical.

In Proverbs, *toʿebah* is used particularly in reference to offenses in speech: falsity in thought or words. *Toʿebah* is exactly equivalent to Egyptian *bwt nṯr* "abomination of God." Particularly in Wisdom literature, it is used in condemning moral offenses that God finds especially loathsome. Amenemope applies the term to hypocrisy (§10; AEL 2.154) and dishonesty in writing (§13; AEL 2.155). Proverbs employs *toʿebah* (and the cognate verb) in condemning offenses in situations where discovery is unlikely or redress is difficult to obtain, as well as to rebuke antisocial (but not necessarily illegal) attitudes and deeds.

There is no intrinsic distinction between *toʿebot* "of the Lord" and *toʿebot* without further definition (compare 15:8 with 21:27), since behavior that God finds loathsome is inevitably what offends the authors. *Toʿebot YHWH* is intensive. A sense of what disgusts God is essential to the fear of God. See Clements (1996) on the function of the concept in Proverbs and Humbert (1960) on the word's history and uses.

but with the honest he is intimate: He is friendly with them and stays near them. *Sod* is intimate converse or a circle of intimates. This is the opposite of God's loathing (*toʿebah*) for the perverse man, which sets a distance between them. (Tg appropriately translates *toʿebah* as *mᵉraḥaq*, lit. "distant," "alien.") When Job says, "All the men of my *sod* are disgusted by me (*tiʿăbuni*)" (Job 19:19), he is bringing together the two extremes, *sod* and *toʿebah*. To be in the *sod* of God is no small thing; the angelic council itself is called God's *sod* (Job 15:8). In addition to fellowship, *sod* implies counsel and conversation, sometimes private and confidential. This is clearly the sense in Prov 15:22 (// counselors); 11:13 ("to reveal *sod*" = to reveal secrets; likewise 20:19; 25:9); Ps 25:14 ("God's *sod* is with those who fear him, to inform them of his covenant"). Hence the present verse implies immediate, personal communication between God and honest people.

The five admonitions of 3:27–31, all of which begin with *ʾal* ("do not") share the same structure and the same general theme. Nevertheless, they are not so closely interlinked as to indicate that they were written from scratch to form a unit. It appears that the author selected five proverbs that served his purpose and that share certain obvious formal features. The admonitions' demands are modest enough: ordinary decency in everyday relations and the avoidance of thoughts that can induce evil deeds. Quarreling (probably in litigation) and even devising harm are not categorically forbidden. Granting a benefit or paying an obligation are (as Meinhold observes) required only within the scope of one's ability. One need not be a saint to be wise.

3:33–35. God's Favor and Disgust

The Conclusion consists of three aphorisms contrasting the consequences of wisdom and folly. The beginning of the conclusion is best set at v. 33 because v 32b, though a generalization similar to the aphorisms of vv 33–35, motivates the admonition in v 32a and is inseparable from the lesson. Verse 35 is the capstone. It is set apart by its reversal of the order bad/good in the antitheses of vv 32–35, by the lack of reference to God, and by the mention of wise and the foolish for the first time in the lecture. The last feature brings out the basic tenet of Part I: it is wise to be righteous, foolish to be wicked.

3:33. *The Lord's curse*: God's "curse" (*mᵉʾerah*) is not just the pronouncement of a malediction but the unhappy situation itself (Prov 28:27) that God "sends" (Deut 28:20; Mal 2:2) as punishment.

The fact that when the evildoer's house is cursed, his wife and children will suffer with him goes unnoticed. Throughout the Bible, a man's wife and children are regarded as an extension of him and share the consequences of his actions. (A few illustrations of this mentality are Esth 8:11; Josh 7:24–25; and Num 16:32. Ezek 18 deliberately rejects this principle.) The family is a unit, for better or worse. This is undoubtedly objectionable theologically, but in reality it is usually true that a man's family suffers or prospers along with him.[146]

3:34. *As for the scornful*: The *leṣ*—the "scorner" or "impudent"—is insolent and cynical and refuses to take rebukes seriously (13:1; 15:12). See "Words for Folly," §5.

In *ʾim lallēṣîm*, the conditional particle *ʾim* is usually considered problematic and often emended; for example, to *ʿămal lēṣîm* (Ehrlich) or *ʿim lēṣîm* (Wildeboer, BHS). Others take *ʾim* as a conditional particle. Naḥmias designates v 34b as the apodosis, identifying the *waw* with Arabic *fa-*, which can serve that function; in other words: If (God) scorns the scornful, he all the more surely will show favor to the humble. McKane similarly translates, "Though [*ʾim*] he pours scorn on scoffers, yet he shows favour to the humble." But the second line is in no way contingent on the first, and a concessive clause in v 34a would be meaningless.

ʾim l- (not *ʾim* alone) means "in regard to." This is clearly so in Job 9:19. This usage may derive from an elliptical conditional: "If it is scoffers (we are speaking of)," or the like. Compare the use of Egyptian *ir*, meaning both "if" and "in regard to," the latter marking a noun in anticipatory emphasis. The dir. obj. "them" (namely, *lēṣîm*), is ellided.

them he scorns [*yaliṣ*]: Some earlier commentators sought to circumvent the not too exalted notion of God treating the scornful in kind. Saʿadia explains *yaliṣ* as declarative: God will *class* the scoffers among the *leṣim*, will show them to be *leṣim* (sim. Hameʾiri); but this is tautologous. Mezudat David parses the verb as causative: "make them be mocked (by others)"; sim. Malbim. Such measures are clearly apologetic. Radaq rebuffs them by insisting: "It is *true* that God mocks the mockers!" There are many examples in prophetic literature of divine mockery, in which God details, with a certain schadenfreude, the calamities that will befall the wicked. These are probably examples of *laṣon*, though they are not so labeled. God derides and laughs (*yilʿag, yiśḥaq*) at the rebel nations (Ps 2:4). In Ps 18:26–27 [Eng. 25:25–26] (= 2 Sam 22:26–27) God is said to treat people in accordance with their actions: "With the kind he shows himself kind, with the guileless he shows himself guileless, with the pure he shows himself pure, and with the perverse he shows himself wily." Similarly, in

---

[146]There is a certain egalitarianism in the fact that a foolish or wicked woman's family likewise suffers for her folly (Prov 14:1a) and, more happily, a virtuous woman's household shares in her blessing (Exod 1:21; Prov 14:1b; 31:10–31).

Prov 1:26–27, Lady Wisdom herself derides fools, including the insolent (*leṣim*, v 22), referring to her mockery by the verbs *laʿag* ("mock") and *śaḥaq* ("laugh at"). The author of Prov 1–9 did not consider it undignified for God and the lofty Lady Wisdom to mock and sneer at people who deserve it. In the present verse, God's *laʿag* is the antithesis of bestowing favor (*ḥen*) upon the humble.

he bestows favor: One's *ḥen* is the approval and favor others feel toward him (see 3:4). To "give (*natan*) favor" means to make someone attractive to others. When God promises Moses, "I will give the *ḥen* of this people in Egypt's eyes," he means that he will make the Egyptians show them favor (Exod 3:21; fulfilled in 11:3). "A good perception (*śekel ṭob*) gives *ḥen*" (Prov 13:15) means that this virtue makes others esteem its possessor. Hence when God grants the humble *ḥen*, he makes them pleasing to others, namely to himself and man (3:4). This idea is restated in the next verse: The wise (who are inherently modest) attain the honor that the haughty vainly strive for.

3:35. *The wise . . . dolts*: The capstone sums up the fate of the two types.

mērîm (*mrym*) is difficult because it is a sg. verb adjacent to a plural noun that appears to be its subject and because the usual sense of *hērîm* (*r-w-m*) "to lift up" does not fit this context well. Winton Thomas (1955: 282–83) explains *mērîm* as "heighten," "increase," but the verb does not mean that elsewhere. To be sure, *mērîm* is loosely parallel to *rab* in Prov 14:29, but there *rab* is equivalent to "has much" rather than "increases." Various emendations have been proposed, most of them rather arbitrary. Examples are *maddām* "their garment" (G. R. Driver 1951: 177); *marbîm* "increase" (Graetz 1884: ad loc.); *hryš* = *hōrîšû*/*yrš* = *yōrîšû* (*sic*; supposedly meaning "get possession"; Toy); *pārîm* "propagate" (M. Scott; *piryām* "their fruit is" would be better); Perles (1922: 66) emends to *mrwm* "height"; and more. Shadal takes *qālôn* as the subject and reads the sentence as a sarcasm: disgrace "exalts" fools, meaning that they think it does, while it actually debases them; but this is forced.

A solution is suggested by the fact that *hērîm* means not only "raise" but also "separate," "remove," always in the sense of removing something from its current position (e.g., Lev 6:3; Ezek 21:31 [// *hāsîr* "remove"]; Dan 8:11). In Prov 14:29, *mērîm* means, approximately, "get," "acquire": *ûqᵉṣar rûaḥ mērîm ʾiwwelet* ("And the impatient man gets folly"). If we apply this notion to the present context, we can imagine a metaphorical division of an inheritance in which the wise sons inherit the honor (14:29) while the foolish ones walk away with society's contempt (3:35). In this vein, Mezudat David glosses the line as "separates out [*maprîš*] contempt as his portion." To be sure, *hērîm* does not elsewhere refer to taking something away for one's own use, but this proposal requires only a minor semantic extension of a well-attested meaning. The functional equivalence of *hērîm* and *nāḥāl* "to inherit" is suggested by the fact that both can have *ʾiwwelet* as dir. obj. without distinction of sense (14:18, 29).

Numerical disagreement between a subject and an adjoined participle (*kᵉsîlîm mērîm*) is awkward but possible (thus Ramaq; cf. 3:18b). Still, we should probably emend to *mrymym* (haplography). The versions cannot be used as proof either way, since they had no choice but to use a pl. verb.

The Design of Lecture IV

- I. Exordium (21–26)
  - A. Retain my teachings (21)
  - B. and you will receive blessings (22–25),
  - C. because God will protect you (26).
- II. Lesson (27–31): *five admonitions, all beginning with ʾal "don't"*
  - A. Don't withhold benefits (27)

B. Don't temporize in giving back what you owe (28)
C. Don't devise to harm another unjustly (29)
D. Don't quarrel unjustly (30)
E. Don't envy the lawless man (31)

III. Conclusion/Capstone
A. The wise/righteous are blessed, the foolish/wicked cursed (33–34).
B. Capstone: just retribution v 35.

The general theme of the lecture is good social relations. Sections II A and B form a subunit on the improper withholding of things due another person. II D and E form a subunit on disturbances in human relationships. II C, structurally the pivot point, relates to both topics.

The admonitions of the lesson are only loosely bound to the promises of the exordium. (Plöger thinks that the looseness of 3:27–35 shows it to be a collection of sentences added later.) The exordium promises life, favor, and, especially, security. The lesson teaches fair and generous treatment of other people. The linkage would have been stronger and more distinctive if the exordium had prepared the way for the social ethics of the lesson by promising, say, social and commercial success.

This lack of concern for a tight fit between deed and result is common in Proverbs, especially Part I. It runs contrary to the theory of the "deed-consequence connection"—the notion of tit-for-tat recompense—which is thought to be the essence of the Wisdom doctrine of retribution; see "The Deed-Consequence Nexus," after 1:19. Intrinsic retribution does figure into many sayings, but it is part of a larger picture, in which wisdom as a whole brings about the total array of blessings. Wisdom is like a fractal pattern in which the whole is replicated in every segment, so that each area implies the entire pattern of reward. Wise behavior of any and every sort is rewarded by a happy life in all regards. One who gains wisdom not only knows and does wise things but also *is* wise, and any segment of his behavior entails the reward of a blessed life.

Chapter 3 as a Whole

There is general agreement that chapter 3 is a composite, not an integral unit. (There is no significance to the fact that they are numbered in the same chapter.) But the possibility arises here and elsewhere that a redactor gave thought to creating a new unit with its own message, one richer than the sum of its parts. Meinhold (1987: 477) argues that this is the case: Originally independent units—(1) 3:1–12; (2) 3:13–20; (3) 3:21–35—were joined editorially to create a "theological summa." The effect of the addition of 3:13–20 was to imbue the themes of human piety (3:1–12) and ethical social behavior (3:21–35) with a cosmic dimension, to show that the man who stands in the right relation with God and man is in harmony with creation (p. 477).

Meinhold exaggerates the redactor's control. A redactor could choose a suitable spot for the insertion but would be unlikely to create an integrated unit by placement alone. Interlude B does balance Lecture III nicely, and the two together do convey the message that Meinhold recognizes, but the relation of Interlude B to Lecture IV is looser. The interlude's message—the value of wisdom—is so broad and fundamental that, had it been inserted almost anywhere in Prov 1–9, an interpreter could easily have found some tie-in. If it were located next to chapter 7, for example, we might say that it counterpoises the true desirability of wisdom to the spurious attractions of the temptress.

It is likely that the "redactor" of chapter 3 was the author of Interlude B, who sought to enrich the lectures' teachings by adding a paean to piety in an existing book, which I designate "Ten Lectures." (See Essay 1, "The Formation of Proverbs 1–9.") Further redactional activities are not evident in the arrangement of the chapter, and an ingenious overenrichment of the message only obscures the goals and achievements of both the original author and subsequent contributors.

LECTURE V. LOVING WISDOM, HATING EVIL (4:1–9)

TRANSLATION

Hear my teaching

4:1 **Hear O sons a father's instruction,**
listen to learn understanding!
2 **For I give you a good lesson;**
forsake not my teaching.

I learned this from my own father

3 **For when I was a child with my father,**
a tender darling before my mother,
4 **he gave me instruction and said to me:**

Cherish wisdom

"Let your heart hold my words;
keep my precepts and live.
5 **Get wisdom, get understanding,**
do not forget, do not stray
from the words of my mouth.
6 **Don't desert her—then she'll keep you,**
love her and she'll guard you.
7 **The first step to wisdom is: get wisdom!**
With all you possess, get understanding.
8 **Cherish her and she'll exalt you,**
she'll bring you honor if you embrace her.
9 **She'll place a graceful garland on your head;**
grant you a splendid diadem."

COMMENTARY

4:1–4a. Exordium

4:1. *Hear O sons*: The teaching is addressed to "sons" in the plural in vv 1–2. The plural address to "sons" appears in 4:1; 5:7; 7:24; and 8:32–33. In 4:1; 5:7; and 7:24, the plural is intrusive because the units in which they appear are otherwise addressed to a singular "son." Naḥmias (citing the phrase "sons of the prophets" in 1 Kgs 20:35) says that the speaker is now addressing students. Naḥmias is not identifying Proverbs as a school text (in the terms of the current debate) but rather observing that the text holds two levels of discourse: father to son and teacher to students. For Naḥmias, the father-instructor is Solomon, the teacher of us all.

The author seems indifferent to the grammatical number of his addresses to the audience. This is undeniable in 9:4–5, where Lady Folly speaks in the plural to a simpleton. Such fluctuations show that the father-son address in Proverbs is a generic convention. A father is ostensibly speaking to his son, but through him the author is actually addressing all boys.

In the original body of Ben Sira's book (chapters 1–38), the author consistently addresses a singular "son," occasionally with the vocative "my son." In the appendices, however, beginning with chapter 39, second plural and second singular in the vocatives are intermixed. Sir 39:13 (Greek) addresses "pious sons" and continues in the hymnic plural (sim. 43:30). In 41:14a, he addresses "children" (*šmʿw bnym*), but slips into the sg. by v 17, and in 42:11 says, "my son." His autobiographical acrostic (51:13–30) is addressed to a plurality—people generally. This mixture suggests that for Ben Sira too addressing a son is a genre formula. He has in mind the entirety of his potential readership (as revealed in 50:28–29).

Most Egyptian instructions address a single son. An exception is the instruction to Kagemeni. In the body of the instructions, the speaker uses the second masculine singular, but in the epilogue, the vizier gives his teachings to his children. A teaching intended for several people can speak to each one individually. In the "Loyalist Teaching," the speaker addresses his children and consistently uses the second plural (in §1, 2: *msw*, with the male and the plural determinatives; some exemplars have female determinative as well). The tomb autobiography of Amenemhet Priest of Amon is labeled "a teaching for his children" and uses the second plural. The Egyptian instructions do not seem to show the inconsistency seen in Prov 1–9 and Ben Sira, probably because the father-son setting was not, for the most part, a fiction in Egyptian Wisdom.

a father's instruction [*musar ʾab*]: Elsewhere, the speaker refers to himself as "your father" (or "I"). *Musar ʾab* is generic—paternal instruction. Although the teaching was originally the grandfather's, the father can designate it "my teaching," because *he* is now delivering it. The term suggests earnestness: The teaching is given by someone who *cares* about you, who places your best interests foremost.

The transmission of wisdom from father to son is the setting of almost all Wisdom literature. Occasionally, as here, the transmission over more than one generation is also in view. Brenner (1993: 117–19), however, proposes an "alternative reading," according to which the narrator (the speaking voice encompassing the others) is the mother, who tells the sons to listen to their father (vv 1–2), whom she then quotes as he speaks briefly quoting *his* father (starting in v 3). Brenner offers no reasons for such a convoluted supposition other than its bare possibility. Throughout Prov 1–9 (and virtually everywhere in Wisdom literature), when the speaker's sex is identifiable, it is male. "A father's instruction" in 4:1 is identical with the lesson that "I" am giving you (v 2), which is a quotation from "my" father (v 3), and there is no quoting phrase or anything else to distinguish the "I" of v 2 from the "I" of v 3, as there is in v 4a, which introduces the grandfather's words.

4:3. *For*: The *ki* is causal: The fact that the speaker was educated by his father heightens his own authority and the value of his teachings by showing him to be a transmitter as well as a creator of wisdom.

when I was a child with my father: Lit. "For I was a son to my father." This is a tautology whose purpose is to set the scene: when I was a child living with my father and under his tutelage. His young age at that time is emphasized by the next sentence.

a tender darling before my mother: Lit. "delicate (*rak*) and alone (*wᵉyaḥid*) before my mother." *Rak* "soft," "delicate" sometimes signifies youthfulness (1 Chr 29:1; Ezek 17:22), though not necessarily denoting early childhood, since the young King David can use it of himself, with some exaggeration (2 Sam 3:39). *Yaḥid* (lit. "alone," "unique") connotes being especially precious and "beloved," as the LXX renders the term several times. A lone child has all his parents' attention and focused affection. Hence even when a child is not actually an only child, he may be called "alone" to emphasize his dearness (Naḥmias et al.), as in the case of Isaac, for example (Gen 22:2; etc.).

The presence of the mother in this scene undermines the assumption that "father" means schoolmaster. The author depicts instruction in a family setting. Mention of the mother may have been prompted by the need for a parallel to "father," but it would not have provided a good parallel to "father" if the latter meant schoolmaster.

Several medieval commentators discerned tones of empathy and encouragement as well as authority in the emphasis of the youthfulness of the father when he heard these words. Naḥmias paraphrases Solomon as saying, "Let not the beginnings be too difficult in your eyes, for I too was like you, and likewise was 'soft' with respect to my father and the 'only one' with respect to my mother, and had I not commenced (my studies) and toiled and exerted myself, I would not have arrived at the high degree of wisdom. You too do this, and you will become wise, after being neophytes [*talmidim*]" (sim. Saʿadia, Hameʾiri).

4:4bc–9. Lesson

4:5. *Get wisdom, get understanding*: G. Boström (1935: 155–56) and Meinhold think that wisdom is personified as a bride, to serve as an antithesis to the Strange

Woman. To be sure, the verb *qanah* "acquire" is used of taking a wife in MH, but it is not so used in the Bible. Gemser says that the crown and garland are reminiscent of the wedding scene in Cant 3:11; but these images appear also in 1:9, where a reference to weddings would be inappropriate. Nothing in the present passage alludes to marriage.

Kuhn proposes placing v 5a after v 5b, so that v 5b would continue the demand of adherence to the father's words and 5a would be contiguous to vv 6–9, for which it provides the antecedent, "wisdom." Toy believes we must omit either 5b or *wḥyh* + 5a, but the fem. sg. verbs in v 6 require the presence of v 5a. Gemser omits the end of 4 and 5a (*weḥyeh q^eneh ḥokmah q^eneh binah*) and reverses vv 6 and 7 in order to supply the antecedents for v 6. But the changes are not necessary, because the speaker equates his teaching with wisdom (see esp. 2:1–2), so that the mention of "my words" in 5b is not really intrusive and the antecedent of v 6 is wisdom.

Do not forget: The object of *tiškaḥ* "forget" is "the words of my mouth."

The *m(in)* ("from") prefixed to *ʾimrê pî* is governed by the verb *ʾal tēṭ* ("do not stray") alone. There is no point in positing a homonymous verb *šākaḥ* meaning "slacken" and translating "flag not" (Dahood 1963: 11), which is inappropriate in the present verse. The exordia typically reiterate the demand to *remember* the father's words.

do not stray: This command intensifies the preceding: Do not forget (unintentionally) and certainly do not stray (deliberately) from my commands (Saʿadia). "Stray," "turn away" (*naṭah*) is used of intentional apostasy or misdeeds, while "forgetting" can be either intentional or not.

4:6. *she'll keep you . . . and she'll guard you*: The relationship between pupil and wisdom is portrayed as that between man and woman. Nevertheless (contrary to modern stereotypes of ancient attitudes), it is the (metaphorical) woman who is the protector, the one who "keeps" and "guards" and "shields" her protégé.

love her: It is not enough to *do* wise things; one must *love* wisdom. The teacher wishes to shape attitudes and feelings, and he therefore *demands* certain sentiments and emotions; see "The Idea of Education in Lecture II," esp. p. 133. We might wonder how the Bible can command love, whether the object is wisdom, one's fellow (Lev 19:18), or God (Deut 6:5, etc.). To be sure, Deuteronomy's charge to love God may echo treaty language and mean to maintain loyalty rather than *feeling* love (Weinfeld 1972: 81, 333). Nevertheless, verses such as Deut 6:5 show that Deuteronomy is demanding a genuine emotion as well as obedience in deed. Certain emotions are commanded or prohibited often enough that we may conclude that the Israelites believed that they were normally within a person's control. Thus one must avoid *desiring* ("coveting") another's wife and possessions, and not only refrain from stealing them; one must control his *temper* ("spirit"; Prov 16:32), and not only refrain from outbursts; and so on. The inchoate personification of wisdom in 4:6–8 is a step on the way to the fully developed personification in Interludes A, D, and E; see pp. 331f.

4:7. *The first step to wisdom*: Or "the beginning of wisdom" (*re'šit ḥokmah*). On the meanings of *re'šit*, see the comment on 1:7. In 4:7, even more clearly than in 1:7, *re'šit* means "first" (in time), "beginning."

The verse presents difficulties. The imperative "get wisdom!" is an awkward predicate in a nominal sentence. The imperative clause must be understood as a quotation of the rule about how to start on the way to wisdom.

It is tautologous to identify the *beginning* of getting something with getting it, as this verse seems to do. This can be resolved by drawing a distinction: The first *ḥokmah* mentioned is wisdom of the sort possessed by a wise individual, the second is the content of the knowledge being taught. In other words: the first step toward becoming a wise man is to imbibe the teachings, even before understanding and applying them. The possession of this knowledge is not fully wisdom, but it will start you on the way to intelligence and judiciousness in thought and action.

Saʿadia observes that at the start, before the child recognizes the value of wisdom, he should simply acquire it—in other words, absorb the teachings by rote—whereupon the desire for wisdom will grow and increase. This is indeed the best hope for development in all types of education. Radaq draws a different distinction. The first step is fear of the Lord (1:7; Ps 111:10; sim. Hame'iri). Then, when one is practiced in the Torah and the fear of God, he may turn to other branches of learning (*ḥokmot*).

Verse 7 is absent in the LXX and might be a scribal addition. It interrupts the exhortations to hold (v 6) and cherish (v 8) wisdom. Nevertheless, the structure as it stands forms a chiastic:

A Get wisdom (5).
B Keep wisdom and she'll reward you (6).
A′ Get wisdom (7).
B′ Keep wisdom and she'll reward you (8).

4:8. *Cherish her* [*sals*ᵉ*leha*]: The hapax *salsel* is a reduplicated D-stem from *s-l-l*, whose root-meaning is apparently "be/make high" (thus Naḥmias, after a thorough discussion of alternatives), hence "exalt," "cherish," a synonym of the following *t*ᵉ*romemka*.

Ehrlich explains *salsēl* as "*eng anschmiegen*" ("cuddle closely"), on the basis of MH usage. He refers to *Tos. Sota* 5,7: *hamm*ᵉ*salselet* "she who cuddles (?) her young son," cf. *nāšîm hamm*ᵉ*sôl*ᵉ*lôt* [poel] *zô b*ᵉ*zô* "women who cuddle each other" (*b. Sota* 65a). According to *b. Rosh Hashana* 26b, "the rabbis did not know what *sāls*ᵉ*lehā ût*ᵉ*rôm*ᵉ*mekkā* meant until they heard the maidservant of Rabbi say to a man who was turning [*m*ᵉ*happēk*] his hair, "How long will you curl *m*ᵉ*salsēl* your hair?" From which the rabbis concluded that the verse tells us to "turn over" the Torah and study it constantly. Syr (= Tg) translates "love her." The verb may derive from *slsl* "intertwine," "curl," hence "dandle," "show affection." The notion of cherishing can be derived from either etymology.

4:9. *graceful garland . . . splendid diadem*: In 1:9, the garland metaphor signifies the benefits of learning; sim. Sir 6:29–31. A graceful or "attractive" garland (*l^{e}wiyyat ḥen*) is one that adorns its wearer and thus is attractive to others. Malbim compares Prov 3:4, "you'll gain the favor and high regard of God and man alike." The garland itself may be a token of favor. In the Greek of Ben Sira's description of a feast ("symposium"), he says that satisfied guests will give the banquet leader a *crown* (*stephanon*) (32:2 [35:3]); in the Hebrew Ben Sira uses *śekel*, "(good) regard."

grant you: The verb *t^{e}maggen^{e}ka* holds a double entendre: *grant* (from the verb *miggēn*) and *shield* (a denominative from *māgēn* "shield." Wisdom will grant you a splendid diadem *and* shield you. Wisdom provides protection (2:7, 11; 6:22a; etc.) and is called a shield in 2:7. Diadems and other head ornaments had apotropaic functions.

On the basis of various cognates, esp. Ugaritic *mgn* "bestow" and Akkadian *magannu* "gift," as well as the uses of the verb in Gen 14:20 and Hos 11:8 ("give into," "give up"), Heb *miggēn* can be derived from the root *m-g-n* "give" (HALAT 517a, and most; thus already Riyqam). But *t^{e}maggēn* could also be a denominative from *māgēn* "shield," as most commentators understood it until recently.

a splendid diadem: The diadem, *ʿăṭarah*, was made of metals: gold (2 Sam 12:30, etc.) and silver (Zech 6:11, 14). An *ʿăṭeret tip*ʾ*eret* (the phrase used here) is worn by celebrants in Ezek 23:42. Zion was an *ʿăṭeret tip*ʾ*eret* to God (Isa 62:3). Kings wear an *ʿăṭarah* (Cant 3:11; Jer 13:18; 1 Chr 20:2), as does a high priest (Sir 45:12). In Esth 8:15, a gold diadem is part of royal attire. The diadem thus betokens honor and nobility. The reward wisdom offers here is public esteem. "The diadem of the wise is their cunning" (Prov 14:24, as emended).

The Design of Lecture V

I. Exordium (1–4a; 3 couplets + transition line)
II. Lesson (4bc–9): The grandfather's teaching (5 couplets + tristich)
III. Conclusion: lacking

Though the location of the boundary between Lectures V and VI is uncertain, it is best set after v 9, because v 10 is an exordium, and the subsequent verses move to a new topic. It is possible, however, that the grandfather's speech extends to v 18 or even v 27. Lecture V lacks a clear tripartite division because the substance of the grandfather's call to embrace wisdom resembles an extended exordium. There is no well-marked conclusion, though v 9 does wrap things up nicely. The departure from the expected pattern may be due to the use of extensive quotation, which moves the discourse off the usual track.

The Message of Lecture V

Unique to this lecture is the ascription of a teaching to the speaker's own father. This ascription strengthens the authority of the exhortation. Two other quotations in the lectures—the words of the robbers in 1:11–14 and the seductress in 7:14–20—are also words of persuasion. (The fourth is of a fool lamenting his folly in 5:12–14.) The grandfather's quotation is the only one without negative content. Contrary to Meinhold, however, it is doubtful that this peculiarity highlights the central purpose of this lecture.

The essence of paternal education, oral and written, lies in the son's "incorporating the character of the father."[147] This must happen from generation to generation. The concept of transmission of wisdom from father to son is prominent in the Egyptian instructions. Almost all the instructions are spoken by a man to his son or sons. Moreover, there are several references to family transmission in subsequent generations. The father in "Loyalist Teaching" says, "Practice the rules that I have made. Then you [pl.] may speak (them) to your children. The mouth instructs from the time of the god [= creation]" (7.7–8.2). In his epilogue, Ptahhotep says, "When [the obedient son] grows old and reaches veneration, he will speak likewise to his children, renewing the teaching of his father. . . . He speaks to (his) children so that they may speak to their children" (ll. 590–96; cf. AEL 1.75). Duachety says, "See these things that I have placed before you and your children's children" (XXXg; cf. AEL 1.191). Duachety, like the speaker of Lecture V, declares that *his* father instructed him, and that the son, his auditor, should do the same for his own sons. The *Kemit* says:

> Oh, open your books [and read], that you may from the start become a son[148] who is educated in the useful writings. My father instructed me earlier in the effective writings of his predecessors. (XV)

The author of the *Kemit* mentions the instruction he received from his father in order to confirm his own wisdom and authority.

McKane describes the relation between tradition and authority as follows:

> . . . whether [its provenience] is home or school, the same kind of authority is envisaged in either case, and this is radically different from the concept of religious authority represented by *mūsar YHWH*. What is said about this instruction is not that it bears Yahweh's authority, but that it is validated by tradition and empirical testing. (p. 303)

This strong statement is wrong on three counts. First of all, the teacher appeals less to tradition than to a particular origin for the teachings. In other words, it is the fact that the teaching came from his father that is important and

[147] In a short school text, which seems to be in the form of a letter to the writer's father, the youth quotes his father as having said to him, "You cannot incorporate [lit. "bring in"] the character of your father by coming-and-going in incompetence" (ODeM 1219; Fischer-Elfert 1997: 10). The first clause shows by negation what a son should do. The "Loyalist Teaching" exhorts the son: "Emulate my character, do not neglect my words. Practice the rules which I have made" (§7.6; cf. §8.5). See further Fischer-Elfert 1997: ad loc.

[148] The expression *iri.k sꜣ* does not mean "make a son" or "take a pupil" (contrary to Brunner AW: 368). The context is speaking of learning, not teaching. The verb *iri* (usually "do") can mean "become," as in the phrase *iri sš* "become a scribe" (e.g., Pap. Lansing 7.5, and very often).

that somehow validates, or at least reinforces, its truth. He does not *in this context* claim that the teaching is a tradition descending from the former generations (as in Merikare[149]) or that the ancients testified to its verity (as asserted by Bildad in Job 8:8–10). He does not *deny* that the teaching is an ancient tradition, but he does not make that claim here.

Second, the speaker does not imply that the teaching was observed or proved "empirically." The status of the teaching is axiomatic, prior to and independent of observation. Validation comes from the fact that the grandfather *said* these things, not that he *saw* them.

Third, the authority of the father is *not* radically different from the religious authority represented by *musar YHWH*.[150] Parental authority is a channel for communication of God's will. The two sources of authority reinforce each other, and in places where only one is mentioned, the other is not thereby excluded. The father's wisdom is clearly identified with God-given wisdom in 2:1–6.

The grandfather's message is an extended exordium. As in Lecture II, the exordium of Lecture V is not only preparation for the message, it is its heart.

The speaker's father instructed him to love and cherish wisdom, here described metaphorically as a woman. Wisdom *cares* about your affection and loyalty, and will match your love with graciousness and protection. To embrace wisdom means to *obey* her. Wisdom is an authority figure, but a kindly and loving one. In this passage, Wisdom is not pictured as a lover (contrary to G. Boström, pp. 156–57) but as a powerful patroness who rewards her faithful protégés (thus McKane, Plöger). Lady Wisdom has the features of a mother figure. She gives the garland that is bestowed by the parents in 1:9. Ben Sira understood this and introduced a passage in which Wisdom is personified with the heading "Wisdom teaches her sons" (4:11a).

Lecture VI. The Right Path (4:10–19)

Translation

Hear my teaching

4:10 Attend, my son, and take my words,
that the years of your life may increase.

Choose the way of wisdom

11 I guide you in wisdom's way,
lead you in routes of rectitude.

---

[149]"The truth comes to [the intelligent man] (fully) brewed, in accordance with [or "according to the manner of"] the sayings of the ancestors" (Merikare §IX; P 34–35).

[150]Actually, the phrase *musar YHWH* in Prov 3:11 (as well as *musar šadday* in Job 5:17 and, probably, *musar YHWH* in Deut 11:2) refers to divine chastisement, not to education in general.

12 **In walking, your stride won't be hobbled,**
and if you run you will not trip.
13 **Hold fast to discipline, don't let go,**
guard it, for it is your life.

Shun the way of evil

14 **Enter not on the way of the wicked,**
nor tread on the path of evildoers.
15 **Shun it, pass not upon it;**
veer away from it, then pass on.
16 **For they cannot sleep unless they've done harm;**
they're robbed of sleep if they've made no one stumble,
17 **for they feed on the food of evil,**
drink the wine of lawlessness.

The two paths

18 **But the way of the righteous is like the glow of dawn,**
shining ever brighter till the day sets in.
19 **The way of the wicked is as the murk:**
they know not on what they may stumble.

COMMENTARY

4:10. Exordium

4:11–17. Lesson

4:11. *guide you* [*horeytika*] . . . *lead you* [*hidraktika*]: *Horah* means "guide," "inform," hence "teach." It is the verb from which *torah* ("teaching," then "Law") is derived. Though *torah* in Proverbs is not law, it is authoritative. It comprises "directions for the road of a mandatory kind, that is, directives" (McKane, p. 308). The verbs in this sentence, translated here in the present tense, may alternately be present-perfects, to be translated "have guided" and "have led," with reference to teachings in the past.

wisdom's way . . . routes of rectitude [*maʿgley yošer*]: Wisdom is honesty. Devious cleverness is not wise, though in other books, the word *ḥokmah* can refer to cunning of that sort. McKane prefers to translate *maʿgley yošer* as "straight tracks" because that better accords with the imagery of v 12 and because "tracks of uprightness" is too "emphatically moralistic." It *is* "emphatically moralistic," as is the entire lecture. *Yošer* is never used of actual physical straightness, but only of moral rectitude: honesty, equity, and the like.

4:12. *In walking . . . if you run*: According to Ehrlich, these are metaphors "for grasping and pursuing in daily life, for exertions in the struggle for existence"; see Isa 40:31 and esp. Hag 1:9. Verse 12b means "not *even* when you run," when you are the more likely to fall (cf. Naḥmias). Verses 11–12 together show that the ethical path alone is the safe one.

your stride won't be hobbled: Lit. "straitened." Narrow, impeded steps are an affliction typical of old age, when a man's "(formerly) strong steps are hobbled" (Job 18:7). A "broad" stride means security (Ps 18:37). Here the difficulty is not caused by the infirmity of the walker but by the path itself, which may be pictured as uneven and broken (McKane). If you behave wisely and honestly, you will move through life smoothly, in confident comfort, without stumbling even when you must "run," that is to say, work hard.

4:13. *discipline*: *Musar* is treated as feminine in the second line (*niṣrahh, hiʾ*). This happens also in Sir 6:22 (MS A). In these cases, *musar* is equivalent to wisdom, and the feminine gender of *ḥokmah* is maintained in speaking about *musar*, though that word is formally masculine. "Hold fast to" (*haḥăzeq b-*) and "life" recall wisdom as the tree of life (3:18), and the carryover of this particular image suggests that *musar* is being used as a name of wisdom. Wisdom (even in the form of *musar*, which is not always pleasant) is life itself and must be embraced with the same passion.

4:14. *the way of the wicked*: Toy believes that the writer was probably "thinking of a class of men that was numerous in the great cities of that period, unscrupulous government agents, revenue farmers, grasping and desperate men of all sorts, some of whom are described by Josephus." This reveals both Victorian smugness and a strange periodization of Jewish history. For some reason, the reference to the righteous does not inspire Toy to characterize the "period" (apparently the entire Second Commonwealth) as particularly honest and just. In Prov 1–9, there are two archetypal ways, the way of life and the way of death. They are both timeless realities, and to historicize the reference is to miss this central point.

Radaq observes that the verse does not say *ʾal telek* "go not" in the way of the wicked, but rather *ʾal taboʾ* "enter not" (or "come not") into it. "Entering" (*bwʾ*) indicates the moment one comes into a space rather than continuous movement ("going") within that space. Radaq takes the line to mean that one should not join in the abominable customs and activities of the wicked. Radaq cites *ʾoraḥ kannašim* "the way (that is usual with) women," in Gen 18:11 to show that *ʾoraḥ* can mean *minhag* ("custom," "ordinary situation") as well as "way."

Radaq paraphrases the second part of the verse as "Do not stride in their ways, lest you learn from their actions or arouse suspicion in their company, for even if you do not do as they do, people will suspect you of evil." Radaq is distinguishing going in the "ways" of the wicked, which he understands to mean being in their company, from the actual commission of a crime. The second danger Radaq mentions, namely the arousing of unfounded suspicion, does not come into the purview of Prov 1–9, for the author does not seem to conceive of the possibility of avoiding actual villainy once one has joined the company of the wicked. The danger may, however, be avoided at the last minute, as the next verse teaches.

4:15. *Shun it, pass not upon it; veer away from it, then pass on*: The path of the wicked is not somewhere off in the distance, far from the path of the righteous. Somehow, their path zigzags through the territory of life. You are in danger not only if you choose to seek it out; you may come upon it willy-nilly as it crosses or nears your own life course. When that happens, it is not enough just to continue on your way. You must actively "shun" (*paraʿ*) the evil path and "veer aside" (*śaṭah*) from it without tarrying (Saʿadia). Sometimes we find ourselves willy-nilly on the verge of evil and must actively change our life course in order to avoid it.

The verb *śāṭāh* literally means to swerve aside from the expected or right path. Elsewhere it is used only in reference to sexual transgressions, namely the acts of an unfaithful wife (Num 5:12, 19, 20, 29; Sir 42:10 [MS M]) and a male fornicator (Prov 7:25). The word may be deliberately incongruous in the present context.

4:16. *they cannot sleep* . . . : According to Mic 2:1, the wicked lie awake planning wicked deeds; thus too in Ps 36:5. Here also, the evildoers presumably devise evil machinations while lying awake. But their wakefulness is involuntary (McAlpin 1987: 128). They lie awake not in order to do evil (as in Micah and Ps 36) but because they have *not* done it. The wicked have a need to cause harm; their "peace of mind" depends upon it. They are not merely morally lazy, indifferent, or greedy for gain. Their corruption is deep-rooted, their characters warped to the core. Just as wild animals cannot lie down until they have taken prey (Num 23:24), so the wicked are compelled by nature and habit to do harm (Saʿadia).

The wicked constitute a separate category of humanity. Hence the danger envisioned in Part I is not precisely *being* one of them so much as it is being induced (as a *peti*) into joining their company, thereby becoming a *victim* of their blandishments. There would be no point in warning an inherently evil person against evildoing, because he could neither understand nor change his nature, nor would he desire to do so. On the ingrained perversity of the evildoer, see "The Wicked Man," after 2:15.

if they've made no one stumble: Their goal is not merely to amass wealth. They must also make others stumble into iniquity and behave as they do, and they are not satisfied until they succeed in this. In Lecture I, the wicked try to draw a youth into their schemes even though this does not promise them any apparent material gain. Theirs is a maliciousness deeper than greed. They have a strange need for corruption for its own sake.

4:17. *the food of evil* . . . *the wine of lawlessness*: That is to say, they feed on evil itself (Toy; McKane); cf. Job 15:16; 34:7. In Radaq's words, "[Solomon] compares their learning and habits to bread and wine and says that they grew up on bad habits and became accustomed to doing what is lawless and wicked, for which reason they are unable to refrain from doing evil." Ptahhotep describes the corrupt man in almost exactly the same way: "He lives on what others die on; distortion of speech is his bread; he is 'a dead man who is alive every day'" (ll. 582–84; cf. AEL 1.74). In other words, he "lives on" evil—gets his "sustenance" from it—even though it is a poison that will ultimately kill him.

Another interpretation of v 17 identifies the food and wine as provisions *purchased by* lawless gains (Ramaq, Hameʾiri, Malbim, Delitzsch). This would not, however, explain why the evildoers cannot sleep. By the first interpretation, this verse, like the preceding, describes the desires and needs of the evildoer's soul.

4:18–19. Conclusion

Two aphorisms in antithesis together constitute the capstone. Radaq observes that "the later is earlier," that is to say, the expected sequence is violated in vv 18–19, for we would expect the threat to the wicked (v 19) to follow immediately upon the description of their behavior (vv 16–17). Toy (also BHS) simply inverts the order of vv 18–19 to "secure a natural sequence," but such adjustments are editorial, not text-critical. The present sequence places a caesura after the description of the way of the wicked and marks off vv 18 and 19 as a distinct unit. This allows the lecture to culminate in a statement of the fate of the wicked, and it is they, rather than the righteous, who are in focus in this lecture.

McKane regards 4:18–19 as an addition, "a heavy underlining of the theme of the two ways rather than a precise continuation of the topic of vv. 14–17" (p. 309). In fact, "heavy underlining" is precisely the function of a conclusion and, even more, of a capstone. The conclusions of other lectures too are not direct extensions of the topic of the lesson. Prov 1:19 tells how illicit gain harms those who take it, rather than warning against joining with criminals. Prov 2:20–22 is joined somewhat artificially to the preceding. Prov 3:34–35 states a generalization about disgrace and honor rather than extending the advice on social integrity. Prov 5:21–22 pronounces a theological principle about deeds and punishment rather than developing the admonitions on sexual fidelity. Without 4:18–19, Lecture V would be incomplete.

4:18. *the way of the righteous*: Here "way" is not a type of behavior but the course of one's life, imagined as linear movement. The life course of the righteous becomes ever brighter. Hence they do not stumble or suffer harm, and they know increasing joy, for which light is a frequent metaphor.

the glow of dawn [*nogah*]: *Nogah* is a derivative luminescence or radiance, not the light itself. (Hab 3:4 implies a distinction between *nogah* and *'or* "light.") Fire radiates *nogah* (Ezek 1:13, 27; Isa 4:5), as do stars (Joel 2:10), the moon (Isa 60:19), lightning (Hab 3:11), and God's glory (Ezek 10:4). In RH and Targumic Aramaic, it means "Venus" (the dawn star), hence "dawn." This seems to be its reference in Isa 62:1 as well. In the present verse, *'or nogah* is the light radiating from the glow of dawn.

shining ever brighter till the day sets in [*n^{e}kon hayyom*]: Most commentators explain the day's "setting in" as noontime (Sa'adia, Riyqam, Radaq, Delitzsch et al.), on the grounds that the light diminishes in the afternoon. But the dawn's light does not, in fact, go on increasing till noon. Rather, *n^{e}kon hayyom* refers to the moment in the morning when the day has fully dawned (Ehrlich, Toy). The image is thus dynamic: The life course of the righteous grows ever brighter—from the moment of appearance until full day. This dynamism suggests the education and moral growth of a youngster.

The form n^{e}*kôn* ("sets in") is difficult. An infinitive (not a ptcp.!) is expected (cf. Gen 8:7; 32:25), but the inf. abs. are not supposed to appear as *regens* (GBH §123^c) or undergo vowel reduction. The form n^{e}*kôn* may be a noun derived from the inf. abs. Similar formations, but using the inf. cst., are n^{e}*ṭôt hayyôm* and *ḥănôt hayyôm* in Judg 19:8–9.

4:19. *The way of the wicked is as the murk* [*ka'ăpelah*]. Or "as in the murk," with the *bet* suppressed after the comparative *kaph*. Not only will the wicked meet with future disaster, but even before it arrives they suffer gnawing uncertainty and anxiety about what dangers lie ahead. Even if they do get some sleep (perversely, when they have caused trouble; v 16), their composure is a delusion, never real serenity.

Light and dark are metaphors for the happiness and good fortune that grace the righteous life and the misery and disaster that afflict the wicked one, respectively. They also serve as metaphors of the mental and moral qualities of the two types. Just as the teaching is light (6:23), the dark may be ignorance and moral blindness. Plöger (p. 48) calls this "the darkness of their moral irresponsibility surrounding them" ("das Dunkel ihrer Gewissenlosigkeit, das sie umgibt").

on what [*bameh*]: namely, on what stumbling block (Delitzsch), rather than "*into* what."

The Design of Lecture VI

I. Exordium (4:10)
II. Lesson (11–17)
  A. The way of wisdom (11–13)
  B. The way of evil (14–17)
III. Conclusion/capstone (18–19): the Two Paths

The Message of Lecture VI

The point of this lecture is: Choose the right path and avoid the evil one. It provides no specifics as to what to do or avoid. It praises the course of rectitude but does not exactly lead the pupil upon it. When the father says, "I . . . lead you [or "have lead you"] in routes of rectitude" (v 11), he does not refer to what he is about to do in this particular lesson, but rather alludes to all the teachings of the lectures—the ones spoken so far and perhaps also those that follow. The substance of the lecture is thus encouragement to obey the directives taught *elsewhere*. This is further evidence for the unity of the lectures in Part I; see Essay 1, p. 325.

Here, as often in Part I, especially in the exordia, the speaker seeks to create an attitude of receptivity to wisdom rather than to specify wise and foolish actions. This receptivity is almost more important than the actions themselves, because if one has an eager openness to wisdom and starts upon its path, wisdom itself will provide guidance in the choices along the way.

The teaching of the Two Paths concerns not only the destinations of the paths (life and death) but also the experiences of the journeys on them, describing how it feels to walk upon these paths. (See "Paths through Life," after chapter 2.) On wisdom's path, one can stride boldly and walk in confidence, alertness, and security, inner and outer. Walking on the evil path means a life in the shadows of dissatisfaction, gloom, and anxiety about what lies ahead on the darkened road.

Lecture VII. The Straight Path (4:20–27)

TRANSLATION

Keep my teachings

4:20 Attend, my son, to my words,
incline your ear to my sayings:
21 Don't let them escape[a] your eyes;
keep them within your heart,
22 for to those who find them they give life—
healing to their whole body.

Be honest

23 Above all else, guard your heart,
for it is the source of life.
24 Remove from yourself crookedness of mouth,
and banish from you deceit of lips.
25 Keep your eyes looking forward,
your gaze straight ahead.
26 Make level the path you travel,
and you'll walk steady wherever you go.
27 Swerve neither to right nor left;
Keep your feet from evil.

---

[a]*yālûzû* (MT *yallîzû*)

COMMENTARY

4:20–22. Exordium

4:21. *escape your eyes*: The same sentence appears in 3:21a.

"Escape" is written *ylyzw* and vocalized *yallîzû*, as if it were an H-stem from a geminate root (GKC §72*ee*). We should emend to *ylwzw* (*yālûzû*), a G-stem, as in 3:21, since the root is consistently treated as II-w elsewhere and an intransitive meaning is required. Hame'iri does read *yallîzû* as transitive and supposes an ellipsis of a subject: Do not allow *inciters* to remove my words from before your eyes, which is to say, your thoughts. But the introduction of another party is not warranted by the context.

In 14:2, *nᵉlôz dᵉrākāyw* is the antithesis of *hôlēk bᵉyošrô* "one who walks straight"; sim. 2:15; 3:32. In Sir 31[34]:8, *nlwz ʾḥry* means "go astray after."

4:22. *for to those who find . . .* : Lit. "for they are life to those who find them, and healing to all his flesh." The singular "his" refers back to the plural "those." Toy says that one of them must be changed. BHS seems willing to change both. But numerical disagreement is not uncommon and should be recognized as a feature of biblical style.

4:23–26. Lesson

4:23. *Above all else, guard your heart*: Lit. "More than every [other] guarding [*mišmar*] guard [*nᵉṣor*] your heart." The heart must be guarded more zealously than anything else—not to protect it but to govern it, lest it utter inappropriate words.

Mikkol mišmār is sometimes understood as a passive notion, meaning "more than anything else that is guarded," that is to say, treasures (Hameʾiri [first explanation], HALAT, Meinhold). In BH, however, *mišmār* only means a unit of guards (or possibly the act of keeping guard), and by extension it is used of other duties at fixed times. It never conveys a passive notion ("something guarded/kept"); that is expressed by *mišmeret*. Moreover, the entity upon which a *mišmār* is placed is almost always a creature that must be restrained (e.g., a prisoner [Lev 24:12, etc.], a dragon [Job 7:12], or a daughter [Sir 42:11]), rather than a valued item that is to be protected. An exception may be a city's *mišmār* [Neh 4:16, etc.], but even in that case the guarding involves control and restraint of potentially harmful forces.

heart: To "guard [or "keep"] your heart" means to be careful in your *speech*. The phrase is synonymous with "guard your mouth" in Ahiqar §15 (l. 98), which is virtually the same saying as Prov 4:23: "More than any keeping, guard your mouth [*mn kl mnṭrh ṭr pmk*], and be discreet [*hwqr lbb*] about what you have heard."[151] The Babylonian "Counsels of Wisdom" urges: "Let your mouth be controlled and your speech guarded [*nāṣir*]. Therein is a man's wealth—let your lips be very precious [*šuqûra*]" (ll. 26–27; BWL 101). The word *šuqûra* is the precise equivalent of Aramaic *hwqr* and might be translated "make discreet." Similarly, Ptahhotep teaches, "Master[152] your heart, control your mouth" (l. 618; cf. AEL 1.75). In the present verse, "guard your heart" means to be circumspect, to be careful about the thoughts you express, and thus to avoid running off at the mouth.

---

[151]Lindenberger (1983: 75) interprets *hwqr lbb* to mean "harden the heart," "be stubborn." Tg Onkelos uses *yqr lb* to translate Heb *hikbid leb*, "harden the heart" (sc. of Pharaoh). Alternatively, Lindenberger proposes, *hwqr* may be related to *yqyr* "precious." The latter is preferable, because the A-stem is not used in the idiom cited, and because this provides a better parallel to "guarding." The phrase *hwqr lbb* means "treat as precious," in other words, guard carefully.

[152]Egyptian *ḥrp*, lit. "submerge," as in water, hence "suppress" or the like.

The theme of concealing one's thoughts and controlling speech is prominent in Egyptian Wisdom. Amenemope connects the heart and speech: "Put [my words] in the casket of your belly,[153] so that they may be as a lock in your heart. When a storm of words arises, [the teachings] will be a mooring post for your tongue" (§1; cf. AEL 2.149). Wisdom "locks up" one's heart so that he can control his tongue and thus be a "truly silent" man. This verse, then, is an admonition about discretion in speech, which is the theme of the next verse also.

The phrase *nāṣar lēb* (as well as the presumably synonymous *šāmar lēb*) is found elsewhere only in Prov 7:10, where the harlot is called *n^{e}ṣurat lēb*, lit. "guarded of heart." This surely does not mean that she preserves her intellectual powers, but that she is secretive and circumspect, a quality manifest in her dress, for she is wrapped in a harlot's veil.

for it is the source of life: Lit. "for from it are the outgoings [*toṣ^{e}ʾot-*] of life." "It" refers to the heart. Toy identifies "it" as the "guarding" (*mišmār*, v 23b), but that refers not to the guarding of the heart, but to *other* instances of guarding, to which the former is given preference.

Heb *tôṣāʾôt* means "outgoings." In 20 of its 22 occurrences, *tôṣāʾôt* is a geographical term meaning "extremities," "outskirts," a sense inappropriate here. This verse designates the heart as the source of the "outgoings." Context requires understanding the word as the process or action of departure. In other words, life proceeds from the heart; the heart is life's source. This sense fits the obscure Ps 68:21, in which *lammāwet tôṣāʾôt* means, "death has its outgoings"; that is to say, there are ways of escaping death (Tate 1990: 168).

The heart works its power in tandem with the tongue. The heart is the source of life, and it sends up the thoughts that the tongue utters. Therefore, "Life and death are in the power of the tongue" (Prov 18:21a). Sir 37:17–18 expands on this idea: "The root of designs is the heart, and it sprouts four branches: good and evil, life and death. But the tongue rules them entirely."[154] This means that the heart is the source of *taḥbulot*, which is used of illegitimate as well as legitimate schemes. (It may also be translated "guidance"; see "Words for Wisdom, §9.) As such, it produces four powers, two good and two bad, but the tongue is in control of them all. In other words, even dangerous thoughts need not be destructive, for one can suppress them.

4:24. *and banish from you deceit of lips* [*l^{e}zut ś^{e}patayim*]: Some medieval commentators thought that the verse cautions against provoking hostile reactions to oneself. Rashi paraphrases: "Do not do something which people will despise and for which they'll make a sour face at you" (lit. "twist their mouths"); sim. Malbim. Naḥmias, however, correctly applies the expressions "crookedness" and "deceit" to one's own speech: one should not be stubborn (*ʿiqqeš*) with one's

---

[153]The belly (*r-ib*) is the casket or shrine (*qrsy*) of the heart.

[154]Reading the following eclectic text: *ʿqr tḥbwlwt lbb ʾrbʿh šbṭym ypryḥ; ṭwb wrʿh wḥyym wmwt wmwšlt bm klyl lšwn*.

mouth or have duplicity (*lazut*) on one's lips (in our idiom: speak out of both sides of the mouth). Hence, as Kaspi explains, Solomon is not advising timid avoidance of *others'* contempt. The meaning of the hapax *lāzût* is uncertain; context and the parallel suggest "duplicity," "deceit," or the like.

lᵉzût- (presumably *lāzût* in the absolute state): Hameʾiri connects *lᵉzût-* with *hizzîlûhā* (Lam 1:8), from *z-l-l,* and with the anomalous *zullût* "contempt" (Ps 12:9). He understands it to mean contemptible words (whether spoken by or against oneself). But the etymology is impossible. Riyqam identifies the root as *l-z-h,* a by-form of *l-w-z,* as in *yālûzû* (3:21). He compares the interchange of the roots *b-w-z* and *b-z-h* (sim. Ramaq). Saʿadia plausibly connects *lᵉzût-* with *nālōz* (3:32) and defines it as *nᵉlôzût,* that is, the quality of being a *nālōz,* one who departs from the right direction (Prov 2:15; 3:32; 14:2; as an abstract, Isa 30:12). Bauer and Leander (1922: §61) and the lexicons parse it as a construct form from (an unattested) *lāzût* (root: *l-w-z*), with anomalous reduction of a stable *â.* See earlier on *yalûzû* (3:21). The other occurrences of this root connote slipperiness, dishonesty, and the like.

4:25. *Keep your eyes looking forward*: Looking straight ahead is an external expression of unswerving directedness toward a goal. Temptations lie on both sides, and one must not even glance at them. Squinted eyes and sidelong glances were supposed to be a symptom of unreliability and guile (Prov 6:13; 10:10; 16:30). The same sequence of "crookedness of the mouth" and eye gestures appears in 6:12–13.

your gaze [*ʿapʿappeyka*]: The literal meaning is probably "eyeballs."

The LXX and Syr, as well as some recent translations, translate *ʿapʿappayim* "eyelids," but the evidence for this sense is vague. According to Naḥmias it means the pupil of the eye. Tg Jonathan to Jer 9:17 translates it *glgly ʿynnʾ* "eyeballs." The word is commonly parsed as a reduplicated form of *ʿ-w-p* "fly," hence "flutter." Most likely it is a derivative of *ʿ-y-p* "to glimmer, shine," a metathesis of *y-p-ʿ,* as proposed by Ibn Janaḥ. The connection of eyes with shining fits well with the image *ʿapʿappê šāḥar* "glimmerings of dawn" (Job 3:9; 41:10; JPSV), for healthy eyes were thought to shine of their own accord, from within (1 Sam 14:29; Ps 13:4; Prov 29:13; etc.; Gruber 1980: 583–98).

4:26. *Make level* [*palles*] *the path* [*maʿăgal*] *you travel, and you'll walk steady wherever you go*: Lit. "make the path of your foot level, and all your ways will be established [*yikkonu*]." Kaspi regards *yikkonu* as a jussive, "let (them) be established," making the line synonymous with v 26a rather than consequential. This is possible, but a jussive would normally precede its subject (GBH §155*l*).

Heb *pallēs,* whose basic sense is "make level," sometimes means "weigh" (from the idea of making the arms of the scale level), hence "consider carefully," as in Prov 5:21, a meaning that Ramaq applies to 4:26 as well. Akkadian *palāsû* has this sense (HALAT). In any case, the son is not being exhorted "weigh"—that is, think about and decide—which path to choose, but only to go where and how he is instructed. Dorsey (1991: 235) suggests that *peles* is the pointer that shows when the scales are balanced; hence the verb means "align," "make straight." This etymology, though uncertain, would support the word's meaning as defined here: both "make level" and "weigh," "assess."

The verb *pallēs* may mean "go straight," as in Prov 5:6 and Isa 26:7, or "make straight," as in Ps 78:50. The latter sense is appropriate in the present verse, since the consequence of this act (v 26b) is that the paths are established or made firm (*yikkōnû*). The procedure for straightening a road is described in Isa 40:3–4, where the verb *yaššēr* is used.

One's life course, as understood here, is not laid out in advance; rather, one must level and "pave" it himself as he moves along, removing obstacles to moral progress.

4:27. Conclusion

4:27. *Swerve neither to right nor left*: One must also stay on the straight and level path. The imagery of vv 26 and 27 implies that a person chooses a path early in life (v 26). Then—if it is the right path—he must then stick to it (v 27), because to step off it even for a moment is to blunder into the muck of evil. The right path is not like the Greek golden mean or the Confucian Middle Way, contrary to Malbim and Plöger. The golden mean lies midway between extremes, such as arrogance and self-denigration. The path of wisdom *is* an extreme: the opposing pole to folly. One is either on this narrow path or off it.

The Greek adds two verses reinterpreting v 27; see the Textual Notes.

The Design of Lecture VII

I. Exordium (20–22)
  A. Hold my words (20–21),
  B. for they give life (22)
II. Lesson (23–26): Behave carefully and honestly
III. Conclusion (27): Walk straight ahead

Verse 27 is not well demarcated as a conclusion because the entire lesson has a generalizing character. Still, the final verse does encapsulate the lesson and may function as a conclusion.

Prov 4:20–27 constitutes a separate lecture. Its beginning is well marked by an exordium, while its end is marked by the unmistakable start of the next lecture in 5:1–2. Some commentators doubt that a new unit begins in v 20. McKane believes that there is no real change in subject in vv 20–27. There is, however, a change in imagery and topic starting in v 20. Lecture VI warns against entering on the path of the wicked. The lecture's governing image is the metaphor of the Two Paths, according to which there is a good path ("wisdom's way"), which is, ipso facto, straight and level, and an evil path, which is crooked and full of pitfalls. Lecture VII, by contrast, envisions a single path, a person's life course. It instructs the reader to *walk straight ahead*. Temptations lie on each side, requiring you to keep your eyes before you and to walk without deviating to either side. This single path must be *made* straight and smooth. (See "Paths through Life," pp. 128ff.)

Lecture VII seeks to shape the student's moral self-image by framing it in physiological terms, describing the right demeanor in terms of parts of the body: the ear (20b), eyes (21a, 25a, 25b), heart (21b, 23a), mouth (24a, 24b), and feet (26a, 27b). An inner sense of straightness is to permeate all one's thoughts, words, and actions. Although the imagery is of body organs, only the act of looking straight ahead could receive actual physical expression. The body-posture imagery seeks rather to encourage in the youth's incorporation of a certain self-image, an inner carriage, a sense of being straightforward and unequivocal.

LECTURE VIII. ANOTHER MAN'S WIFE AND ONE'S OWN (5:1–23)

TRANSLATION

Hear my teaching

5:1 My son, attend to my wisdom,
give ear to my good sense,
2 so that you may keep shrewdness
b and your lips guard knowledge,
c {to keep you from the strange woman,
from the alien who speaks smooth words.}[a]

The deadly delights of the Strange Woman

3 For the strange woman's lips drip honey;
her palate is smoother than oil.
4 But her aftereffect is as bitter as wormwood,
sharp as a two-edged sword.
5 Down to Death-Land go her feet;
she holds fast to Sheol's path.
6 She refuses to go straight in the path of life;
her courses wander but she knows it not.

The wages of debauchery

7 So now, my sons, listen to me;
depart not from the words of my mouth:
8 Distance yourself from her,
approach not the door of her house,
9 lest you yield your vigor to others,
and your years to a ruthless man;
10 lest strangers sate themselves with your strength,
and your toil end up in an alien's house;
11 and in the end you groan,
as your body and flesh waste away,
12 and you say:
"How I hated discipline,
and my heart did scorn reproof!
13 And I heeded not my teachers' voice,
nor to my instructors gave ear.

14 Quickly I fell into all sorts of trouble,
within the assembly and congregation."

Stay loyal to your wife

15 Drink water from your own cistern,
liquids from your well,
16 lest[b] your springs disperse outward,
through the plazas, as channels of water.
17 Let them be yours alone,
no strangers joining with you.
18 Let your fount be blessed,
take pleasure in the wife of your youth:
19 a loving doe, a graceful gazelle—
let her lovemaking[c] ever slake your thirst,
lose yourself always in her love.
20 Why lose yourself, my son, with a stranger,
or embrace an alien's bosom?

The sinner dies by his own devices

21 For a man's ways are before the Lord,
and he assesses all his paths.
22 His (the evildoer's[d]) iniquities will trap him,
in the cords of his sin he'll be seized.
23 He will die for lack of discipline,
and be lost in the greatness of his folly.

---

[a]Conjectural restoration based on 7:5; see the Commentary. [b]Prefix *pen*. [c]Point *dōdeyhā* (MT *daddeyhā* "her breasts"). [d]*ʾet hārāšāʿ* ("the evildoer") is probably a gloss.

COMMENTARY

5:1–2. Exordium

5:1. *my wisdom . . . my good sense* [*ḥokmati, tᵉbunati*]: Elsewhere in Proverbs the speaker does not call *ḥokmah* or *tᵉbunah* his own ("my wisdom," "my good sense"). Moreover, *binah* "understanding" is never thus modified, and *daʿat* "knowledge" has the first-person suffix only in 22:17. This shows a tendency to present as universal the wisdom being taught: It is wisdom itself. However, words for the specific teachings (*miṣwot* "precepts"; *torah* "teaching"; *ʾămarim* "words"; *dᵉbarim* "words") have appeared with the possessive suffix. For the most part, then, the author wishes to imply the universality of the wisdom he is teaching (it is not his alone), while claiming possession and authorship of the words and instructions whereby the wisdom is conveyed.

5:2. *that you may keep* [*lišmor*] *shrewdness and your lips guard* [*yinṣoru*] knowledge: Lit. "to keep shrewdness, and your lips shall guard knowledge."

lišmōr // yinṣōrû: The parallel between the infinitive and the finite verb (jussive) seems awkward and is necessarily smoothed over in translation. Various emendations have been proposed, all of them rather distant from the MT. But emendation is unnecessary. Parallelism between infinitives and verbs in the imperfect does appear in similar contexts; for example, in 2:2; 8:21; and 2:8 (where the verbs *šamar* and *naṣar* are used). The contrast is purely formal, as both infinitives and imperfects may head purpose clauses. Such skewed parallelism may be a stylistic fillip to avoid monotony.

M^e^zimmah (here in the pl.) is private, unspoken thought (see "Words for Wisdom," §5). This faculty provides a shield against the wiles of wicked people, according to 2:12 and 2:16. *M^e^zimmah* together with *daʿat* will allow the youth to keep his own counsel and resist the enticements of the adulteress.

For one's lips to "guard" or "keep" (*šamar*) knowledge means that he is to speak knowledge alone. The closest parallel is Mal 2:7, "The lips of the priest keep [*yišm^e^ru*] knowledge, and (people) seek instruction from his mouth" (*šamar* is a synonym of *naṣar*). The priest "keeps" knowledge by *speaking*, specifically when instructing the people. A variation of this idea appears in 22:18, which says that the teacher's knowledge (v 17) should "remain firm" (*yikkonu*) on the listener's lips, meaning that this is what he must always speak. The present verse insists on harmony of thought and speech, as does 4:23–24 (Plöger).

[5:2c. *to keep you from the strange woman, from the alien who speaks smooth words*]: I have added this couplet to fill a logical gap between vv 2 and 3 (similarly Toy, R. B. Y. Scott, Whybray [1994: 23], and others). Though conjectural, the addition is justified because the motivation in v 3 ("For the strange woman's lips drip honey") does not in itself provide a reason for the exhortation to listen to wisdom and hold fast to it in vv 1–2. All the other Strange Woman passages follow up the exhortation to gain wisdom with a couplet promising protection from the woman's temptations: "To save you (also) from a strange woman—an alien who speaks smooth words" (2:16); "to guard you from another man's wife, from the smooth talk of the alien" (6:24); "to guard you from a strange woman, an alien who speaks smooth words" (7:5, literally). These are all formulated with an infinitive. I use 7:5 for the restoration, because the loss of such a verse could be explained as parablepsis from *lšmrk* to *lšmr* (v 2). If we do not emend thus, we must fill the gap mentally.

5:3–20. Lesson

5:3–6. The deadly delights of the Strange Woman

5:3. *For the strange woman's lips drip honey*: Lit. "stranger" (fem.). The delight of her pleasures is deceptive. Once the confection is tasted, the sweetness turns to wormwood (a bitter plant) and the smoothness to an eviscerating sword. The reason that your lips must guard knowledge (v 3) is that the Strange Woman's lips are so alluring (v 5). Speech is both the danger and the antidote.

The "stranger" (*zarah*) is another man's wife; see p. 139. She is assumed to be a prostitute by all the medieval plain-sense commentators and almost all the modern ones (e.g., Toy and McKane). The LXX apparently read *znh* "harlot" instead of *zrh* ("stranger") in its Hebrew text of v 3. This reading could be a scribal change motivated by the same assumption rather than original. In my view, the Strange Woman is another man's wife, whose transgression is thus adultery. She is not a prostitute but a wanton amateur of the sort who "opens her quiver for every arrow," as Ben Sira puts it (26:12; and see pp. 138f.).

The adulteress works her wiles more by speech than by beauty (though she may be beautiful; see 6:25) or by physical stimulation (she begins with just a hug and a kiss; see 7:13). Her honeyed words are described in a lovely assonance, which intimates the dripping of the honey by its very sound:[155]

(a) *ki nOfet tiṭṭOfnAh śiftEy zarAh*, (b) *w^e^ḥalAq miššEmen ḥikkAhh*. Verse 3a strongly resembles, and may be based on, Cant 4:11a, *nOfet tiṭṭOfnah śiftotAyik kallAh*, "your lips drip honeycomb, (my) bride." Presumably, the felicitous wording originated as praise of a beloved woman rather than as a description of decadent lures. To Prov 5:3b, compare Cant 5:16a, "His palate is sweet drink," as well as 7:10a and 4:11b. The unctuous deceptiveness of a male evildoer's speech is similarly described in Ps 55:21: "The flatteries of his mouth were smooth, but his heart was (set) on war. His words were softer than oil, but they were (actually) drawn swords." Prov 7:14–20 quotes an example of the seductress' wiles, also in language strongly reminiscent of the Song of Songs.

5:4. *her aftereffect* [*ʾaḥărit*]: Lit. "her end." Compare 23:32: "[Wine's] aftereffect bites like a serpent." The teacher in Prov 5 is concerned not with the end awaiting the woman—that would be no deterrent to the audience—but with the bitter fate she brings upon the youth who gives in to her lures.

The Greek and Syriac translations have the comparative degree: "more bitter than" and "sharper than." These readings are probably later than MT's, since a later scribe would be more likely to heighten than to diminish the intensity of the comparisons.

This sword is the *ḥereb piyyôt*, lit. "sword of mouths," which is mentioned in Judg 3:16. A *ḥereb* is any bladed instrument, including a knife (e.g., Josh 5:2, 3; Ezek 5:1; Exod 20:25). The blade of a sword is thought of as a "mouth" that "eats" its victims. Being intended for fighting, a double-bladed sword would be kept especially sharp. Saʿadia observes a progression in the punishments: from bitter taste, to slashing, to death, to Sheol.

5:5. *Death-Land*: Lit. death, viewed as a location, which is to say, Sheol.

she holds fast to Sheol's path. Lit. "They [her feet] hold fast to Sheol." Possibly "death" is Mot, the Canaanite god of the underworld (DNF). Elsewhere, *tamak* "hold fast" is used of feet staying on a path only in Ps 17:5, where it is the opposite of tottering. Here the use of *tamak* suggests that the woman is deliberately proceeding with firm, secure strides to Sheol. Eventually, she too will fall, but for now she sticks to her path.

5:6. *She refuses to go straight* [*pen t^e^palles*]: Lit. "lest she go straight." Verse 6a, with its independent "lest," subtly imputes negative volition. The adulteress *wishes* to avoid going on the path of life. She does not merely blunder onto

---

[155] The stressed vowels are capitalized.

Sheol's path; she chooses it and holds to it resolutely (*tamak*), in order not to go on the path of life. Verse 6a looks into the adulteress's mind, exposing motives she herself is unaware of, just as v 6b tells us what she does not know. Though she may not realize that she has chosen the fatal road, her deeper purpose is to avoid the path that leads to life. Her twisted desire is an expression of her depravity. The death-loving wicked man has similar perverted values; see the excursus on "The Wicked Man," after 2:15.

The conjunction *pen* ("lest," "so that not") usually introduces a subordinate clause that states an undesired event, but in this case the main clause is lacking. To emend *pen* to a negative particle used with the indicative (*lōʾ* or *bal*) (e.g., BHS) is an expedient that blurs the special character of the sentence. Occasionally *pen*-clauses lack a main clause, leaving an ellipsis to be supplied from context (e.g., Gen 26:9b; 38:11; 42:4; see BDB). Most such cases are introduced by *ʾāmar* "say" in the sense of "say to oneself." GBH (§168 g[3]) explains the independent *pen*-clause as an ellipsis of *hiššāmēr*, "guard yourself." However, that verb does not always fit the context; e.g., Gen 3:22; 38:11; Exod 13:17. A better explanation is that since *to do* X *lest* Y implies that Y *should not* happen, *pen* itself comes to provide the negative optative. The ellipsis in v 6a can be supplied from 5b: The reason the Strange Woman holds fast to Sheol's path is that she wishes to avoid the path of life. Although the main clause of 6a is implicit in 5b, we should not join the two lines in a single sentence, because that would leave 5a and 6b syntactically severed from their parallel lines.

go straight [*tᵉpalles*]: The verb *pilles* means "make straight," hence "go straight" (see the comment on 4:26). The Talmud (*b. Moʿed Qat*. 9a) and most of the medieval commentators understand it to mean "weigh," "assess," as in 5:21. Radaq paraphrases: You will be unable to weigh properly the path of life because of her flattery. But this sense works poorly here. "The way of life" is not whatever way one lives his life, but *the* way to life, which need not be "weighed."

her courses wander [*naʿu*]: The paths of her life—that is, the way she behaves—meander and twist about (cf. 2:15). Their end point is death, but because of their crookedness, this is not superficially obvious.

but she knows (it) not [*lo tedaʿ*]: The verb "know" lacks a direct object in the Hebrew. Just what doesn't she know? The implicit direct object of "knows" is probably the fact that her paths wander. For examples of the unstated object of *yadaʿ* ("know") being the fact stated in the preceding clause, see Job 8:9; 9:5; 14:21; and 37:5.

Tur-Sinai identifies that the direct object of *tēdāʿ* as *ʾōraḥ ḥayyîm*, "path of life" (1967: 6.13). He compares Isa 59:8, which says that the wicked "do not know the way of peace" (*derek šālôm lōʾ yādāʿû*). In the present verse, however, another noun ("her paths") is closer to the verb, and the reader could not be expected to skip over it to a farther dir. obj.

The verbs *tᵉpalles* "go straight" and *tedaʿ* "know" can be parsed either as third fem. sg. or second masc. sg. Hence a possible rendering is, "You will not go straight in the path of life. Her paths wander, but you will not know"; that is, you will not know enough to beware of her ways (Radaq); cf. 7:23. At this point, however, the woman is being described without reference to her victim, and there has been no clear change of grammatical subject, so the subject is probably still the woman.

The woman's obliviousness is not due to naiveté or true ignorance of guilt. She knowingly chooses evil courses, but she is not giving thought to where they are heading. She wanders about like one lost in the woods but still unaware of the fact. Evildoers do not see where they are going—"they know not on what they may stumble" (4:19). Prov 12:15a makes the same point: "The way of the fool is straight in his own eyes." The immoral woman is ignorant of where she will end up, but it is a willful ignorance because she has freely chosen the evil way. She is a self-destructive fool, as is whoever follows her.

5:7–14. The wages of debauchery

5:7. *So now, my sons*: The teacher warns young men to shun her fatal attractions. The call to attention is reiterated, as in 8:32. The teacher addresses "sons" here, putting the verbs in the plural too, though in vv 1–2 he spoke to his "son" and used the singular, and in v 8 he reverts to the singular. The audience is plural also in 4:1 and 7:24. The plural indicates that the instruction is actually intended for all young men. They are usually represented within the text by the speaker's "son"; see the comment on 4:1.

5:8. *Distance yourself from her*: Lit. "keep your way far from her."

approach not the door of her house: As the young fool in chapter 7 belatedly discovers, the door of the Strange Woman's house is death's portal. "Door" (*petaḥ*) is literally "opening" and may also allude to the vagina (Alter 1985: 182).

5:9–10. *lest you yield your vigor [hodeka] . . . your years [š^{e}noteka] . . . your strength [koḥ^{e}ka] . . . your toil [ʿăṣabeyka]*: What will the youth be forced to turn over to others to own and enjoy? There are two main possibilities, (1) his property and (2) his sexual vigor. If it is his property, there are further alternatives as to how the loss might occur: he might (a) be exploited by the woman and her husband (thus Toy); (b) be forced to pay compensation to the injured husband (thus Gemser); or (c) be compelled to forfeit his wealth in judicial confiscation (Hameʾiri). If it is his sexual vigor he is losing, the meaning would be that he surrenders his offspring and the wealth they will produce to the man whose wife he impregnates. The cuckold will possess the adulterer's children as his own and benefit from their labor. The four nouns specifying the types of loss are open to different interpretations.

(1) "Vigor" (*hôd*), usually translated "honor" or "majesty," is a power of some sort. It is not primarily the respect and honor others feel toward its possessor, but rather an inner power that inspires these feelings. It is usually ascribed to God or majestic individuals, but it appears that everyone has some *hôd*, at least in the later usage. When Daniel is overpowered by a vision, he reports that "strength [*kōaḥ*] did not remain in me, and my *hôd* was ruined,[156] and I retained no strength [*kōaḥ*]" (10:8). The consequence of Daniel's losing *kōaḥ* and *hôd* is that he collapses. Hosea ascribes *hôd*—vigor and vitality—to Israel, imagined as a plant (14:7). In the present verse, *hôd* is a suitable designation for youthful generative power, though it never has that exact sense elsewhere.

Toy emends to *hônekā* "your wealth", BHS to *ḥêlekā* "your strength" or "wealth." Neither emen-

[156] Lit. "turned into corruption" (*mašḥît*).

dation is supported by Syr's *ḥylk*, which correctly understands *hôd* to mean "strength." The LXX seems to have read *ḥyyk* "your life." MT's *hwdk* is early attested by the paraphrase *hwdy* in Sir 51:17 (11QPs[a] xxi 15).

(2) "Your years" (*šᵉnōteykā*, written *šntk*) is commonly understood to mean years of life. (LXX's "your life" reflects this understanding.) MT's "yield [or "give"] . . . your years" seems difficult because although one could *lose* years of his life at the hands of an angry cuckold (thus Radaq), he could not *give* them to him. Ehrlich renders "und dein Glanz," comparing *šānî* "scarlet"; but this is etymologically forced. Winton Thomas (1937b) similarly renders "dignity," but derives this from a hypothetical root *š-n-h* = Arabic *sny* "raise." But the existence of this root in Hebrew is doubtful, and all the passages where it supposedly appears can be better explained in terms of the recognized root *š-n-h* "change," "repeat," and so on. Riyqam follows Yosef ben Zebara in interpreting "years" as a metonymy for the *earnings* of one's years; thus too Toy, Meinhold.

(3) "Your strength" (*kōḥᵉkā*) can mean your sexual vigor. (Jacob calls Reuben, "my strength [*kōḥî*] and the first product of my vigor [*ʾônî*]"; Gen 49:3.) Alternatively, "strength" may allude to wealth, as in Job 6:22. Hosea (7:9) says, "Others will eat your strength," that is, your wealth, a threat comparable to this verse. "Your strength" may also allude to the wealth one's son produces, which *should* stay in the family but will now belong to the adulteress's husband.

(4) "Your toil" (*ʿăṣābeykā*) means pain or painful labor (cf. *ʿeṣeb* in Prov 10:22; 14:23; and Ps 127:2). It may also refer to the product of toil, that is to say, wealth.

I suggest reading the terms as two pairs in hendiadys equivalent to *hod šᵉnoteyka* = "the (sexual) vigor of your years" and *koaḥ ʿăṣabeyka* = "the strength (i.e., produce) of your toil." In this way, we will not have to assign unexampled uses to any of the terms. The first pair must refer to the dissipation of youthful sexual vigor, which is wasted on a union that will bear the violator no fruit (v 9). The second pair refers to the loss of the adulterer's earnings (v 10).

It is not clear how the latter loss will occur. Radaq thinks that the woman is a prostitute whose services are ruinously expensive (cf. Prov 29:3), and after a man wastes his wealth on her (v 9), he will have to sell or pawn chattels to a stranger (v 10). Perhaps the adulterer will give his wealth to the woman, whose husband will be the real beneficiary. A third possibility is that the adulterer will end up paying a large *koper*—appeasement money—which is mentioned in 6:35. To be sure, that verse asserts that the husband will not accept it, but the teacher is concerned with heaping up scary threats, and a logical inconsistency between two perils in different lectures would not impede this purpose.

to others [*ʾăḥerim*] . . . *a ruthless man* [*ʾakzari*] . . . *strangers* [*zarim*] . . . *an alien* [*nokri*]: These are synonyms meaning another person, one not in your family; they do not denote foreignness with respect to nationality. (On *zar* and *nokri*, see pp. 139f.) The connotations of *ʾakzari*, meaning "cruel," "harsh," or the like, tint its parallel nouns: this stranger is ruthless; he will give no quarter on the day of vengeance (6:34). The singular *ʾakzari* is sometimes a collective; cf. Jer 50:42.

The fluctuation in number between "others" and the two singular nouns suggests that the author's thoughts fluctuate between the cheated husband and the latter's family. They are "other" with respect to the listener's family. If one keeps his wealth, its stays within his lineage rather than going to "others." The adulterer sacrifices this blessing.

The desire to have one's sons marry within the family or clan so as to keep its property intact is reflected, for example, in Tobit's instructions to his son to take a wife "from the seed of your ancestors" rather than taking "a strange woman [*gynaika allotrian* = *ʾiššah zarah*] who is not of your father's tribe" (Tob 4:12; cf. Num 36:1–9).

The themes of sexual vigor and wealth are central in other passages in Wisdom literature too.

1. Job 31:9–12, in a conditional self-curse, describes the consequences of adultery in terms similar to Prov 5:9–10. Job declares:

(9) If my heart has been seduced after a woman,
and I lay in wait at the door of my neighbor,

(10) let my wife "grind" for another,
and others crouch over her.

(11) For it is a vile offense,
a criminal iniquity.

(12) For it is a fire that consumes down to Abaddon,
and takes root[157] in all my produce [*t^{e}buʾati*].

Job envisions a scene in which he surrenders to temptation (*niptah*) and lurks near the door (*petaḥ*) of his neighbor (*reaʿ*; cf. Prov 5:8), perhaps waiting till the neighbor departs. Job calls down upon himself a double punishment, should he be guilty. First, another man (or men) will couple with *Job's* wife, supposedly a tit-for-tat punishment. Second, Job's adultery, as a destructive fire, would somehow destroy his produce. The word "produce" (*t^{e}buʾah*) first of all means agricultural harvest. If Job has harmed another man's possession, his own possessions should be harmed. It also alludes to his offspring: By violating another man's family line, his own would ultimately be damaged ("roots" = lineage, family stock; cf. Isa 11:1, 10; Dan 11:7; Tob 5:15 [MS ^{S}: *ek rhizēs*]).

2. A passage inserted in Ben Sira (26:19–21[158]) restates the moral of Prov 5:9–10 in this way:

(19) My son, keep the prime of your life sound,
and do not give your strength to strangers.

(20) Seek out a fertile portion from the entire field,
and sow your seed there, confident in your good lineage [*eugeneia*].

(21) So your offspring [*genēma*] will surround you,
and will grow up confident in their good lineage.

Ben Sira is using agriculture as a metaphor for procreation. Greek *gen(n)ēma* "offspring" usually corresponds to Hebrew *t^{e}buʾah* in the LXX and is used of both agricultural harvest and human progeny. This passage reflects a text close to Prov 5:9–10 and is certainly dependent on it.[159]

---

[157] Point *tašrēš* or *t^{e}šōrēš*.

[158] Sir 26:19–27 is preserved only in a later stratum of the Greek (GII) and the Syriac, but it is probably of Hebrew origin; see the commentaries of Segal (p. 161) and Di Lella (p. 346).

[159] The Greek of Sir 26:19b, *kai mē dos allotriois tēn ischun sou* "and do not give your strength to strangers," can be retroverted to *w^{e}ʾal titten l^{e}zarim koḥăka* (or *ḥeyleka*) "and do not give your strength to strangers." The verse conflates Prov 5:9a and 10a (which in the LXX reads *hina mē plēsthōsin allotrioi sēs ischuos* "so that strangers not be sated from your strength."

3. In Prov 31:3, Lemuel's mother admonishes him: "Do not give your strength (*ḥayil*) to women." *Ḥayil* means wealth and power. It probably does not mean sexual vigor in standard BH, but in Prov 31:3, with its Aramaizing features, it may be a calque on Aramaic *ḥaylāʾ*, the exact equivalent of *kōaḥ*, which Syr translates *ḥaylaʾ* in 5:10a. "Your ways" in the obscure 31:3b is apparently a euphemism for sexual activity; cf. 30:19b. Lemuel's mother warns him not to allow women to deprive him of his *hayil*, meaning either his physical strength or his wealth or both.

4. Ptahhotep plays on the agriculture-procreation double entendre. The section begins, "If you plow and there's growth in the field, which God gives into your hand," do not boast of your wealth (ll. 160–62). At first, this seems an unambiguous warning to an actual harvest, but the same unit goes on to admonish against boasting about one's children in the presence of a childless man (169–74).

Allusions to offspring and wealth, in particular agricultural produce, intertwine in these four passages. The ambiguity in Prov 5:9–10 too is probably a deliberate play on the two types of "strength." The most natural reading of this passage is that adultery threatens both types of productivity. In an agrarian society, a man's sons had economic value for him and provided him with security in old age. Wealth generated by an adulterer's sons would accrue to the cheated husband's benefit. To have one's offspring reckoned as another's means losing some very concrete benefits.

The sons of one's youth were considered especially valuable. A firstborn is the "first of (a man's) vigor" (*reʾšit ʾono*; Deut 21:17; Gen 49:3; etc.) and is presumed to be "preeminent in distinction and preeminent in power" (Gen 49:3). But all sons conceived in one's youth are a special blessing, a source of strength to their father (Ps 127:4).

5:11. *in the end* [*beʾaḥăriteka*]: Lit. "in your end." This does not necessarily mean the end of life. It could refer to the future generally. But the next clause suggests that the adulterer will be wasting away from disease, and v 23 too speaks of his imminent death.

as your body and flesh waste away: The phrase refers to disease (cf. esp. Job 33:21). In this context, disease might be hyperbole for exhaustion; still, venereal disease comes to mind. Various genital maladies were recognized in the ancient Near East, some of them associated with sexual contact. One ailment was known in Akkadian as "the disease of coitus." Its symptoms include fever, weariness, slackness of flesh, loss of appetite, jaundice, and heat in the penis and abdomen, the latter affliction being ascribed to "the hand of Ishtar" (*RA* 2.221). There are also references to "the disease of Ishtar," which is the precise equivalent of "venereal disease." Gonorrhea is mentioned in Lev 15:1–15, but it may be nonvenereal (see Milgrom 1991: ad loc.).

5:12. *and you say*: The sinner belatedly realizes that he should have obeyed the teachings and taken chastisement to heart. Proverbs emphasizes that chastisement is a positive educational force, a way to wisdom (12:1; 15:5, 31, 32; 29:15), life (6:23; 10:17; 15:31) and honor (e.g., 13:18). Accepting chastisement is difficult because it requires humility and acknowledgment of weakness, but one cannot improve without recognizing his inadequacies.

5:13. *my teachers* [*moray*] . . . *my instructors* [*melammeday*]: The Greek treats these nouns as singular. This is only a matter of different interpretation of the consonantal text, but the choice of the singular suggests that the translator understood the "teacher" to be the father, and this may well be correct. Elsewhere in Proverbs, chastisement comes from the father (e.g., 15:5), Lady Wisdom (1:23, 25, 30), God (3:11), and acquaintances (27:5, cf. 6).

Even if MT's plural is the original intent, "teachers" (*morim*, sg. *moreh*) and "instructors" (*m*^{e}*lamm*^{e}*dim*, sg. *m*^{e}*lammed*) are not necessarily schoolteachers. The word does not assume the existence of schools and surely not "incipient universities such as appear in the second century B.C.," as Toy believes. The terms may refer to all who teach moral wisdom and piety, including the father (e.g., Prov 4:4, 11; Deut 11:19; Ps 51:15) and society generally (Jer 31:34). Qohelet is described as a wise man who taught wisdom (*limmed da*ʿ*at*)—not to pupils in a school setting, but to the people as a whole (12:9; cf. 2 Chr 17:7, 9). The noun *m*^{e}*lammed* means teacher, but not necessarily schoolmasters, in Ps 119:99: "I have become wiser than all my teachers [*mikkol m*^{e}*lamm*^{e}*day hiśkalti*], because your ordinances are the object of my thought." In the next verse, the psalmist compares himself favorably to "elders," suggesting that the "instructors" of v 99 are a broader group than professional tutors. They are all who gave the psalmist instruction, formally or otherwise. In sum, the semantic range of "teach(er)" and "instruct(or)" is too broad to justify limiting the reference in the present verse to schoolmasters. But even if that were the author's intent, that would show only that such teachers existed (which is quite likely anyway), not that they are the authors of the book of Proverbs.

5:14. *Quickly* [*kim*ʿ*aṭ*]: The assumption that *kim*ʿ*aṭ* means "almost" caused earlier commentators (Delitzsch, Toy, etc.) some difficulty, since the fool has already fallen into misery. Some traditional commentators took *kim*ʿ*aṭ* to mean "for a trivial thing" (e.g., Rashi, Malbim, based on Ps 105:12), but that would require *bim*ʿ*at*. *Kim*ʿ*aṭ* means "soon," "quickly," as in Pss 2:12; 81:15; and Isa 1:9.

within the assembly and congregation [*qahal w*^{e}ʿ*edah*]: That is, the "assembled congregation" (JPS) or the public assembly. The adulterer's punishment is both public (v 14) and private (vv 9–11).

Public shaming was a powerful means of social control and served as a sanction both informally and in the judicial forum (see Bechtel 1991). Ben Sira speaks of both settings of shaming. Informal disgrace (alongside judicial punishment) is the lot of the fornicator. Though he imagines that his sin is clandestine, he is seen by God. Consequently, his punishment is, appropriately, public shame, and he will unexpectedly be exposed and "known in the streets of his city" (Sir 23:19–21; cf. Prov 5:21). Even the man who is insufficiently severe in disciplining his daughter will suffer disgrace before the assembly of the gate (*ʿdt šʿr*) because of her behavior (Sir 7:7). This disgrace is informal, for he would not undergo judgment for his daughter's promiscuity. Hypocrisy too can result in shame before the assembly (Sir 1:30). Then again, forensic judgment is the context of disgrace in the case of the woman who abandons her husband and gives birth to children by adultery. She will be "brought forth to the assembly" (*ekklēsia* = *qahal*) (Sir 23:24a; Gk).[160] Similarly, Susanna is judged for adultery (and acquitted) by the assembly (*synagogē*), which is also called "the people" (Sus 34–41).

ʿēdāh "congregation" is an ancient term for the entirety of the Israelite community and, more specifically, for the assembly of adult males in tribal times. The *ʿēdāh* carried out the stoning in capital cases (Lev 24:16; Num 15:35). The term fell into disuse and was replaced by the synonymous *qāhāl*. (Ezekiel uses only *qāhāl*, and Chronicles substitutes it for the older term. See Milgrom 1991: 242–43.) The appearance of *ʿēdāh* alongside *qāhāl* in Sir 23:24a and Prov 5:14 is a revival of old terminology.

In Ezek 16:40, stoning of an adulteress is carried out by a *qāhāl* (not *the qāhāl*). An *ʿēdāh* is sometimes whoever is assembled, not necessarily a formally constituted assembly. (Hence there can be an *ʿēdāh* of evildoers [Ps 22:17] or bees [Judg 14:8].) Likewise, *qāhāl* can refer to informal gatherings, such as the *qāhāl* of peoples (Gen 28:3:) or of ghosts (Prov 21:16).

Both shame and death are punishments for adultery. In this passage, the author leaves the form of the retribution indefinite: the youth finds himself in "all sorts of misfortune" (*bᵉkol raʿ*). This allows the reader's imagination to fill in the unpleasant details. To a youngster, the threat of public disgrace might seem the more immediate and disturbing danger.

5:15–20. Stay Loyal to Your Wife

This is the positive advice: Enjoy your wife's sexuality. Several figures refer to the young man's wife. These form an extended riddle resolved only in v 18b (Alter 1985: 180).

5:15. *water from your own cistern, liquids from your well:* A woman's sexuality is compared to a source of water in 5:18 and (probably) 16. Drinking is a metaphor for sexual pleasure in 9:17. One's wife is a well of fresh flowing water (*nozᵉlim*). The lover in the Song of Songs uses very similar words in speaking of his beloved, calling her "a spring sealed" (4:12b) and "a garden spring, a well of living water, liquids [*nozᵉlim*] from Lebanon" (4:15). The image suggests cool, limpid refreshment for hot desires, which are slaked by "drinking," that is, lovemaking; see the comment on 5:19.

Formally, there is a distinction between a *bor* ("cistern"), which is a reservoir or container, and a *bᵉʾer* ("well"), which is a source of water continually replenished by underground springs, *nozᵉlim* (see, e.g., Hameʾiri). This distinction does not, however, seem to be active in the present verse, which uses different synonyms for the same metaphoric vehicle. Hameʾiri interprets the continual flowing of water as an allusion to the constant "daily renewal and increase of love between him and her."

your well: A man's wife is "his" well. In the Song of Songs, the girl speaks of her body in the same sentence as "my garden" *and* "his garden" (4:16), for she

---

[160] There will be also be "visitation" or "punishment" (*episkopē*) for her children, meaning that her sins will be visited upon them (cf. Exod 34:7), and they will be barren (v 24b).

belongs to her beloved as he does to her (6:3). A well is a source of refreshment and fecundity.

5:16. *lest your springs disperse outward, through the plazas, as channels of water*: The MT lacks "lest" (*pen*). Interpreting v 16 as a threat requires reading the sentence as a negative (a vetitive or negative purpose clause).

The LXX has a negative particle, but that is for the sake of the translation and is not evidence for a negative in the source text; see the Textual Notes. Some commentators take the sentence as an unmarked rhetorical question (Toy, Meinhold, etc.), but there would have to be some mark, syntactical or semantic, of a sharp disjunction between vv 15 and 16 to signal an implicit negative. Some add *lō'* or *'al*. It would be better to prefix *pen* "lest" (BHS), because that is a prominent way of introducing warnings in this chapter (vv 9, 10, cf. 6), and because the loss of the letters *pn* can be explained as a near dittography with *pw* of *ypwṣw*.

The sense of the couplet is realized by combining the lines: "Lest your springs disperse as channels of water outward through the plazas." There are three main ways of understanding this sentence.

1. As a reward. If we translate "Let your springs, etc.," the verse describes a reward. The husband's sexual fidelity will be rewarded by numerous legitimate children of his own (thus the Qimḥis and Hame'iri). These will be reckoned to his name (thus Immanuel of Rome). Furthermore, just as channels of water branch out, so will his offspring proliferate (Radaq).

The "springs" could be the male reproductive powers, specifically the semen. Men too have "springs." Ehrlich compares *Gen. Rab.* §26, which says that God blocked up Noah's spring (*ma'yan*) so that he could no longer beget children. Ehrlich notes that *ma'yan* used literally refers not just to the wellspring but to the water issuing from it; cf. Joel 4:18. "Springs" may thus stand for sperm (cf. Isa 48:1, "the waters of Judah," and Num 24:7).

"Spring" (and synonyms) might be an allusion to begetting children. This is probably the way the LXX understood 5:16a ("Let not the waters be spilt by you from your spring"), though it construes 16b affirmatively: "but let your waters go through your [own] plazas". But this interpretation does not provide a good contrast with the next verse.

2. As an admonition. If we read the sentence as a negative of some sort or add *pen* "lest," the verse warns the youth against squandering his seed in promiscuity (Snijders 1954: 93; McKane). The "springs" allude to male sexuality (as noted previously).

Although a precept of this sort does appear in vv 9–10, the present passage concerns the benefits of fidelity rather than the penalties of infidelity. Moreover, by this interpretation, "Let them be yours alone" in the next verse would imply that the damage of adultery is in making the adulterer *share* his offspring with others, whereas the actual risk is that strangers will possess them entirely.

3. As a threat. If one violates another man's wife, others will violate *his*. A number of considerations support this interpretation. The "water" of a man's own wife is the topic in both the preceding and the following verses, and there is no sign of a sudden shift in referent. Also, "disperse outward" (v 16) has its antith-

esis in "let them be yours alone" (v 17a). Since the second eventuality is desirable, the first must be undesirable.

We can add P. Kruger's observation (1987: 67–68) that the passage contrasts private property, namely wells and cisterns (v 15; cf. 2 Kgs 18:31; Jer 38:6), with common property, namely the streets and plazas (v 16). Moreover, the street and the plazas are the arena of the Strange Woman (cf. esp. 7:12), not of the proper wife. (Kruger believes that 5:16 refers to the Strange Woman, but nothing indicates a sudden shift in topic.) To be sure, wisdom too is to be found in the streets and plazas (1:20), but this is because she is offering herself to others, which is something a wife cannot do legitimately.

The image of "scattering abroad" suggests an undesirable loss of control rather than the fortunate enhancement of a valuable asset that remains in one's possession. The scattering of the springs does not imply an increase of "water" (children), but a spilling of valuable water from the cistern or well to the city streets, where it is wasted. Once the waters are scattered about the city, they *cannot* be "yours alone." Ben Sira uses the dispersal of water as an analogy to giving an untrustworthy woman her rein: "Do not give water an outlet (*diexodon*), nor to a bad woman (her) freedom (*parrhēsian*)" (25:25).

Words from *p-w-ṣ*, in its various stems, refer to scattering and dispersion, almost always with consequent disorganization, rather than to an increase of objects still maintaining organization. Thus the builders of the tower of Babel fear being scattered (G and H-stems; Gen 11:4, 9). The tribes of Levi and Simeon are to be punished by being scattered (H-stem; Gen 49:7) in Israel, which will result in their decrease. Israel is punished by being scattered (H-stem; Deut 28:64; etc.). In its sixty-four occurrences, only once, in Zech 1:17, is the root used of a desirable increase, namely of cities.

The same warning appears in the Syriac Ahiqar: "My son, do not commit adultery with the wife of your neighbor, lest others commit adultery with your wife" (S_2 2:6). Similarly, Job says that if he is guilty of adultery, others should "crouch over" *his* wife (31:10; see the comment on 5:10). In both cases, the idea behind the threat is that the sexual defilement of one's own wife is an appropriate, tit-for-tat punishment for violating another's wife. The wronged wife's motive, whether it is spite or sexual frustration, is not stated, nor are we told whether she will be acting voluntarily. The only relevant agents are male.

5:17. *Let them be yours alone*: Let your wife's sexuality belong to you alone. The reproductive resources of an adulterer's wife will (according to interpretation 3 of v 16) ultimately be shared by another man—a *zar*, as in v 10 (Hameʾiri and Radaq, the latter identifying the "strangers" as other lovers). Naḥmias construes the verse as a reference to legitimate children, who will be recognized as yours alone, in accordance with interpretation 1.

5:18. *Let your fount be blessed*: Let her womb be fruitful (Saʿadia). The word for "fount" or "source"—*maqor*—is used of the source of menstrual blood in Lev 20:18; sim. 12:7. It refers to the female procreative organs here too. Perhaps metaphors have more specific referents, with the "cistern"/"well" being the vagina and the "fount" or "source" (*maqor*) being the womb. A man's wife's reproductive organs may be said to be "his" (and referred to as "your fount") since, in the biblical view, he alone has the right of access to their fruits and pleasures.

The term "blessed" (*baruk*) shows that the reward promised in v 18 is fertility rather than erotic pleasures (contrary to Toy), for *blessing* (*b-r-k* in its various forms) refers to prosperity, success, and well-being. The fruit of the womb is a blessing (Deut 28:4), and a man who fears the Lord will be "blessed" with a fruitful wife and many sons (Ps 128:3–4). "Blessing" (*b*ᵉ*rakah*) is "the power decreed by God which effects fertility and prosperity" (Wehmeier 1970: 76). The word never refers to the gratification of sensual desires of any sort, including sexual.

The clause *y*ᵉ*hi . . . baruk* is a jussive and, as often with volitives, indicates the consequence of the preceding verb (cf. Ramaq). Thus: Let your wife be blessed with fertility (v 18) by staying loyal to her (v 15). "Blessed" (*baruk*) has both a passive and an active implication: it means both blessed by God and a source of blessings (cf. Deut 28:4–5; Jer 20:14; Mitchell 1987: 124, who, however, interprets Prov 5:18a as promising sexual joy rather than fertility).

take pleasure in [*ś*ᵉ*maḥ me-*] *the wife of your youth*: Enjoy erotic pleasures from your wife alone. Words derived from *ś-m-ḥ* often refer to sexual pleasure, and this (rather than general marital happiness) is clearly the intent in 5:18 (G. Anderson 1991: 36). The imperative *ś*ᵉ*maḥ* "enjoy" is a virtual future: As a consequence of fidelity, you will receive pleasure from your wife (cf. Hameʾiri).

The verb *śāmaḥ* elsewhere always governs *b-*, except in Qoh 2:10 (where there is textual evidence for a variant with *b-*) and 2 Chr 20:27 (where the phrase has a different sense). In Ugaritic, *šmḫ m-* seems to have a sense close to what is required in Prov 5:18: *wum tšmḫ mab* "May (my) mother receive pleasure from (my) father" (CTA 2.16.10–11 [= *UT* 1015]; see Dahood 1963: 12). This translation tries to suggest the force of "from," but the well-attested variant *śmḥ b-* (see Textual Notes) may be original.

The Talmud (*b. San.* 22a) understands "the wife of your youth" to be the first of possibly several wives. Though that may pertain in Mal 2:15, it is too restrictive here. The author can speak of a man's current wife as the wife of his youth without implying a contrast with others, just as the phrase "the mate of her youth" in 2:17 in no way implies that the woman has or will have additional husbands.

5:19. *a loving doe, a graceful gazelle*: The father depicts his son's wife as ipso facto graceful, lovely, and *sexy*. Let the youth make *her* the object of his desire.

Gazelles and does connote grace, tenderness, and affection in the Song of Songs, where the girl speaks of her lover running like a gazelle and a deer (2:9, 17), and he compares her breasts to fawns of the gazelle (4:5). The phrase *ʾayyelet ʾăhabim* a "loving doe" (lit. "a doe of lovemaking" or "love-doe") has strong sexual connotations. The word *ʾăhabim* designates a sexual relationship. This is shown by the fact that *ʾăhabim* (var. *ʾŏhabim*) in Hos 8:9 and Prov 7:18 signifies loveless sex. The relationship in the present verse is undoubtedly a loving one, but the word *ʾăhabim* refers only to its sexual aspect.

let her lovemaking ever slake your thirst: For MT's *daddeyhā* "her breasts" (more precisely, "nipples"), we should vocalize the consonantal *ddyh* as *dōdeyhā* "her lovemaking"; see the Textual Note.

Dodim "lovemaking," always refers to physical lovemaking, from kisses and caresses to sexual intercourse, whether or not accompanied by affection. It can even refer to harlotry, as in *miškab dodim* in Ezek 23:17. The word *dd* occurs as a Semiticism in Egyptian, where it is written with the phallus sign as the determinative and usually alludes to sexual intercourse. Given these connotations, the advice in Prov 5:19 is quite explicit.

The expression "drink *dodim*" occurs in Cant 5:1b, *šᵉtu wᵉšikru dodim* "Drink yourself drunk on caresses!" In Cant 4:10, the youth tells his beloved, "Your *dodim* are better than wine." Decisive in favor of the pointing *dōdeyhā* in 5:19 is Prov 7:18, where the temptress says *lᵉkah nirweh dodim ʿad boqer* "Come, let's drink of love till dawn," using *rwh ddym* as in this verse.

While "lovemaking" is the most appropriate way to construe *ddyh* here, the idea of a woman's breasts slaking her lover's sexual thirst is not bizarre. This is implicit in Cant 8:1–2 and explicit in an Egyptian song, where a girl says to her lover, "Take my breasts, that their gift may flow forth to you" (trans. Fox 1985b: 166). Moreover, the stranger's "bosom" in v 20b seems to be a counterpart of the wife's breasts. Since both senses are supported by context, *ddym* may be a deliberate pun, but its primary sense is lovemaking. Likewise, to "embrace an alien's bosom" (v 20b) means having sex with her.

lose yourself [*tišgeh*] *always in her love*: The verb *šagah* literally means "go astray" and almost always connotes moral error. It is used disapprovingly of alcohol abuse in Isa 28:7 and Prov 20:1. Some medieval commentators read the verse as a grudging concession to sexual needs: One who is too involved in loving his wife goes astray, because it distracts him from the service of God, but better to do so with one's own wife than with another's (thus Naḥmias, Ramaq). G. R. Driver translates *yišgeh* as "be wrapped in" (1947: 410), on the basis of Arabic *sajâ*, one of whose senses is supposed to be "wrap (a corpse) in a shroud." But this etymology is farfetched and unsupported biblical usage.

In my view, *šagah* does mean "go astray" here, but without connoting imperfection or impropriety. The word sets up a contrast with the next line. Instead of simply being admonished never to stray, the youth is encouraged *to do so*—but only with his own wife. The term connotes no disapproval here, but perhaps it bears a slightly "naughty" overtone by suggestions of "straying" deliciously dazed in the ecstasies of lovemaking. In the marriage bed, inhibitions may be left behind. The lovers in the Song of Songs are urged to "get drunk on lovemaking" (5:1). In an Egyptian love song, a girl says, "Your liquor is your lovemaking" (*dd*) (trans. Fox 1985b: 10), in other words, the intoxicant you offer is lovemaking.

The son is not merely allowed to "lose" himself in connubial sex as a concession to weakness; he is positively encouraged to do so—"ever" (*bᵉkol ʿet*) and "always" (*tamid*). This is not the exclusionary "always," as if to say, if you make love, it must be *only* with your own wife. The father does make that demand, but that's not his point here. The phrase *bᵉkol ʿet* (lit. "in every moment") means "constantly," "on a regular basis" (see, e.g., Prov 6:14; 8:30; Qoh 9:8). *Tamid* means "always" in the sense of regularly, continually (cf. Isa 60:11; 62:6, e.g.), rather than "for all time to come." The usage in Prov 5:19 is exactly paralleled in Ps 34:2, where *tamid* and *bᵉkol ʿet* are parallel. The psalmist is not saying that whenever he praises gods, he will praise only Yahweh, for other divinities do not come into the purview of this psalm. He is declaring that he will praise him continually.

According to Ehrlich, *riwwah* ("slake") and *šagah* ("get lost") express ability or possibility: Your wife *can* satisfy you at all times, because she will be always available. But this ignores the imperative modality of vv 15–18 taken as a whole, as well as the celebration of the young wife's beauty in v 19a. She is not merely accessible, she is desirable. The youth *should* enjoy her charms.

5:20. *Why lose yourself, my son, with a stranger* [*zarah*]: Verses 19 and 20 pivot on the word *tišgeh* "lose yourself" or "stray." Why go astray with another man's wife, when you have your own woman to "stray" with?

5:21–23. Conclusion

The conclusion comprises three distinct sayings that together remind the audience that God is omniscient and guarantees justice. The third saying is a capstone summing up the principle of the lesson: the sinner is self-destructive.

The broad principle asserted in the conclusion is true of every sin, not just adultery. The verses of the conclusion stand apart from the lesson also because, as McKane observes, they "present a concept of *musar* (v. 23) into which there enters a theology and moralism conspicuously absent from the remainder of the chapter" (p. 313). But the distinctiveness of vv 21–23 does not justify McKane's inference that they are a "Yahwistic addition." It is the function of a conclusion to summarize on the level of theological generalization. Since each verse in the conclusion is self-contained, they may have existed as independent proverbs before being combined and applied to the lesson at hand, but that does not mean that they are an *addition* to the lesson.

5:21. *For a man's ways are before the Lord*: The conclusion reinforces the lesson in its entirety: every deed is exposed to God's eyes; therefore, every sin is punished, even adultery, though it is committed in secret (Job 24:15). Ben Sira elaborates this theme in 23:17–21.

and he assesses [*mᵉpalles*] *all his paths*: God weighs and judges all that a man does. The wording recalls v 6, where *pilles* is used in a different sense: The Strange Woman "refuses to go straight in the path of life."

5:22. *His (the evildoer's) iniquities will trap him*: The sinner is self-destructive; see 11:5, 18, and often. Verses 21 and 22 combined show that God's awareness of a person's actions brings about the punishment, even as the sinner brings it upon himself. The author does not explain the mechanism of divine retribution. It is enough to affirm that God is intimately and directly involved in the entirety of man's life, so that the natural consequences of one's actions are God's doing. See "The Deed-Consequence Nexus," after chapter 1.

"The evildoer's" (*ʾet haraša*) is an epexegetical gloss explaining the object of "trap him," but it is not really necessary, since *anyone's* iniquities trap him. The original would have said "his iniquities will trap him," meaning that any iniquities that a man (v 21) may have will trap him.

The sentence *ʿăwônôtāyw yilkᵉdûnô ʾet hārāšāʿ* presents two peculiarities: The third masc. sg. sfx. *-nô* is unique with the *yiqtol* but occurs with the impv. in *qobnô* (Num 23:13). The word *ʾet-hārāšāʿ* is an explanatory gloss to the third masc. sg. suffixes, as is shown by its awkward placement as well as its absence in the LXX and Syr.

5:23. *He will die for lack of discipline*: *Musar* here is not disciplinary instruction, but rather internalized teaching—moral discipline and self-control. Unable to guide himself aright, the fool goes astray and perishes.

be lost: For the third time, the author plays on *šagah b-*, lit. "go astray in" (or "with" or "through"). In vv 19 and 20, it means to distract oneself in delights, but in the latter it also connotes moral error. Here it means to stray from the safe path and hence to perish. The verb is used similarly of lost sheep in Ezek 34:6, and compare how *ʾabad* means both to get lost and to perish.

folly [*ʾiwwelet*]: *ʾiwwelet* is parallel to *ʾeyn musar*, "absence of discipline." The type of fool called the *ʾĕwil*, the possessor of *ʾiwwelet*, is morally perverse. He does not lack the intellectual capacity to attain discipline; he lacks the moral capacity to want it. (See "Words for Folly" §3.) The youth may begin as a *peti*, a gullible and naive fool (7:7), but if he succumbs to seduction, he becomes, or proves himself to be, an *ʾĕwil*.

The Design of Lecture VIII

I. Exordium (1–2): Attend to my teaching.
II. Lesson (3–20): Avoid the licentious woman and stick to your own wife.
  A. The Strange Woman is deadly (3–6).
  B. Avoid her, or you'll pay a severe price (7–14).
  C. Rather, take your sexual pleasures with your wife (15–20).
III. Conclusion (21–23)
  A. God sees all (21),
  B. so wickedness is punished (22–23 = capstone).

Lecture VIII is the first of three preachments against adultery, (VIII) 5:1–23; (IX) 6:20–35; (X) 7:1–27. Prior to the insertion of Interlude C, these three lectures formed an unbroken sequence on this theme, which is introduced in 2:16–20 but amplified only here.

Lecture VIII focuses on the dangers of the adulterous woman. The lesson opens and closes with the theme word *zarah*, while the conclusion plays upon the verb *šagah* in expressing the different ways of "losing" oneself. The rhetoric of the lecture, as Plöger and Meinhold observe, is carefully structured and coherent. The lesson proceeds logically, describing the negative (forbidden sex and its consequences) and the positive (permitted sex), and concludes with sayings that underscore the religious message. Its images work as a unit in exposing the two sources of sexual allure, while a narrative line describes an action and its multiple consequences. For an enlightening exposition of the complex and multifaceted poetic design of Prov 5, see Alter 1985: 179–84.

In spite of these signs of deliberate artistry, various commentators have found the unit in such disorder as to require major relocations. R. B. Y. Scott (1965) ends the present unit at 5:14 and makes 5:15–19 + 6:22 + 5:20 the first of the independent discourses in the next chapter. Skehan (1946: 291) places 6:22 (which he reconstructs according to the LXX) after 5:19. Goldingay (1977: 80–87) separates out three stages of composition: (1) original two paragraphs: (a) 5:1 + 20 + 3–6, and (b) vv 7–14; (2) a Yahwistic addition: 5:21–23; (3) the insertion of vv 15–19 (at which time v 20 was relocated to be near vv 19 and 23, which also use *šagah*). Whybray (1994: 23) reconstructs three stages of composition: an original instruction (5:1–6, 8, parts of vv 21–23) and miscellaneous expansions concerned with marital fidelity (vv 9–14, 15–20).

Dissections like these presuppose arbitrary rules for unity and fragment any unit that does not meet them. They assume that a literary unit must be highly homogeneous, with all sections speaking about the same narrow topic in the same way. This assumption does not allow an author to develop different aspects of a single theme, which is what happens in this lecture.

The Listener in the Text

One of the reasons Whybray considers 5:9–14 a later addition is that he believes that the section is concerned "not with seduction but with the fate of the adulterer: not the inexperienced, unmarried boy or young man but the unfaithful married man" (1994: 24). The oppositions Whybray sets up are misconceived. The scene depicts seduction *and* adultery, and the listener is both young and inexperienced *and* married.

We should picture the youth addressed in Lecture VIII (and probably in Part I in its entirety) as an adolescent married or on the verge thereof. The type of man depicted in the dramatic scenes and presupposed as the audience of the admonitions against adultery is young but sexually mature, for the most severe temptation he faces throughout Part I is sexual. He is also presumed to be married, because Lecture VIII speaks of the erotic delights offered by the listener's own wife as a tempting and available alternative to forbidden sex. The issue of fornication would make little sense to a young child. For the teaching to be relevant and effective, the situation of the ostensible audience must be congruent with that of the intended readers or listeners. Even if vv 15–19 are understood as relating to a future wife, that does not change the setting the audience is to imagine: At the time the youth confronts the seduction, he will have an alternative in a wife of his own.

Marriage often took place at an early age in the ancient Near East (and, indeed, in many places even in modern times), but marriage was not necessarily connected with maturity or independence from the parents for either sex.[161] In

[161] Little is known about the typical age of marriage in the ancient Near East. According to the chronologies in 2 Kings, Josiah and Amon married at 14, Jehoiachin at 16. The marriageable age in Egypt has been calculated at about 12 years for girls, 15 for boys. Pirqey Avot (5:21) advises men to marry at 18. The Ptolemaic Egyptian Anchsheshonq (11.7) advises boys to marry at age 20. These counsels may show a tendency toward later marriage in Hellenistic times and should probably be

one genre of Egyptian letters popular in scribal instruction, a father writes to his son, who is a young scribe and student, and chides him for laziness and dissipation, including sexual licentiousness. (Most such letters are fictional but presuppose the realities of adolescent behavior.) In one letter, a father lambastes his son for getting drunk and disporting himself in a brothel (LEM 48).

Occasionally, the marital status of the recipient of the scolding is evident. The *Kemit*, a model letter copied in Egyptian scribal academies for centuries, describes a scribal student as a married man. The text is difficult, but the treatment of similar topics in other paternal letters help clarify what is going on. It appears that a scribe named Au, in his third year of training, is dressing extravagantly and generally living it up. "When as a cadet (Au) visited a dancing-girl, she said, 'Go, Au, and see to your wife. How bitterly she weeps for you! Because of your (catching) fish by night and your (snaring) fowl by day, she is constantly weeping for you'" (transl. LAE 16). Au's "fish" and "birds" are undoubtedly girls he is chasing, because actual fishing and fowling would not make his wife weep. In the Egyptian love songs, fishing and bird trapping are frequent metaphors for ensnaring someone by love (see Fox 1985b: 10, 18–21). Au takes the scolding delivered by the dancing-girl (his mistress?) to heart and invites his wife to join him.

Marital Fidelity

This is the only passage in the Bible that celebrates the pleasures of marital sex, with the partial exception of the Song of Songs. Though the lovers in the Song are not yet married, they intend to marry and view their passion as undying and fiercely exclusive (see Fox 1985b: 230–32; 313–15).

It is noteworthy that Lecture VIII, in arguing for marital fidelity, does not confine itself to warnings against the temptations of illicit sex. Nor does the lecture merely concede the legitimacy of conjugal relations, along the lines of "better to marry than to burn" (some of the medieval commentators read it this way). Rather, it addresses the male reader and positively encourages him to take his fill of legitimate erotic pleasures, depicting their delights in lush, provocative terms: "drink"—satisfy your sexual desires; from your wife's "well"—her vagina. She is not just your lawful and proper mate; she is a graceful gazelle, a "love-doe." Let her lovemaking slake your sensual thirst. "Lose yourself" in her erotic delights.

---

understood as encouraging later marriage than reporting the norm. See the references in Fox 1985b: xii.

In traditional Chinese society, and even today in India, marriage is commonly arranged between adolescents (or even children), who continue to grow up in the boy's house, under the tutelage and domination of his parents, especially his mother.

On the other hand, M. Roth (1987, esp. 737) calculates that in Neo-Babylonian and Neo-Assyrian rural households, the age at first marriage for women was about 14 to 20 years and for men 26 to 30. It is hard to know if these late ages were typical elsewhere.

While this discourse is an engaging celebration of marital love, its rhetoric is inspired less by a concern for marital bliss or personal gratification of either partner than by practical considerations. First of all, the father praises the charms of the son's wife in order to remind him that he has recourse to *her* sexuality, which is all that he needs. That is why the praise culminates in the rhetorical question, "Why lose yourself, my son, with a stranger"? (v 20). Second, the rather fervid praise of the attractions of the young wife (who represents all young wives) betrays an awareness that the son (who is paradigmatic of young husbands in similar circumstances) may not necessarily be enthralled with his new mate. Youthful marriages were commonly arranged between the families rather than inspired by love. Against this background, the father in Lecture VIII might be trying to convince his son that the wife he was assigned is as sexy as any woman out there.

In making the case for marital fidelity, Lecture VIII appeals to emotions—fears, desires, interests, and sympathies—rather than to law. It does so for two reasons. First of all, the author is trying to persuade a young man to stay faithful to his wife. To the temptations of illicit sex, the speaker counterpoises the lush and dizzying potentials of married sex. Second, the legal obligations to one's wife do not include sexual fidelity. Loyalty to her is a personal commitment and has to be encouraged on that level.

In biblical terms, adultery means intercourse between a married or betrothed woman and a man other than her husband or fiancé. The deed damned in the Strange Woman passages is an offense against the other woman's husband. Proverbs does insist on marital fidelity for men, though not with the same vehemence with which it condemns violations of other men's marriages. Malachi too demands male constancy: "Do not betray [read *'al tibgōd b-*] the wife of your youth," for "she is your companion and your covenanted wife" (2:14). Malachi is denouncing divorce rather than adultery, but the underlying principle is that marriage obligates men to constancy. In Proverbs, arguments against infidelity do not adduce the harm it causes the cheated wife. At most, this is softly evoked in the pathos of the phrase "the wife of your youth."

Adultery was absolutely intolerable in ancient Israel because it threatened the social structure, which depended on the stability of the family (Camp 1985: 114). Moreover, promiscuity throws patrimony into uncertainty, denying a man confidence that his heirs are his own offspring. Lecture VIII, however, does not speak of these injuries, mentioning neither the destabilization of the youth's own marriage nor the violation of the betrayed husband's honor and lineage. (The adulterous woman's treachery toward her husband is recognized in 2:17.) In fact, what might be regarded as a violation to the integrity of the cuckold's lineage is paradoxically seen as *advantageous* to him (5:10, 16). Nor does the author give thought to the pain and humiliation that the adulterer's wife suffers. Rather, adultery is conceived of as a folly of individual men and women that violates personal loyalties and harms those who commit it.

This perspective is not determined by a peculiar social viewpoint but by rhetorical needs. The author is seeking to convince young men to control fierce urges, to shun the allure of the exotic and forbidden in favor of lawful pleasures. He must make the dangers of the forbidden and the attractions of the permitted immediate, striking, and personal.

Although both men and women are obliged to avoid adultery, the admonitions against infidelity in Proverbs are directed only to men. Toy believes that this is chiefly because "in the OT it is only men that are had in mind, the moral independence of women not being distinctly recognized" (p. 103). On the contrary, Proverbs does recognize the "moral independence" of women, as demonstrated by the bad case, the adulteress who brings about her own downfall and is responsible for her own fate, as well as by the good case, the pious and benevolent wife described in 31:10–31. The admonition about sexual morality is addressed to men because the entire book (including 31:10–31!) is addressed to men. Even in third-person passages, the implied audience is male. That does not mean that similar ethical demands were not made of females. Girls, however, did not receive their moral instruction in writing.

Allegory in Lecture VIII?

The Talmud (*b. ʿAb. Zar.* 17a), the midrash (*Mid. Prov.*, ad loc.), and almost all the traditional commentators read 5:3–20 allegorically. The medievals recognized the literal message about sexual morality but focused on the allegorical. In the Talmudic discussion, too, 5:3 is applied to an actual harlot. The allegorical interpreters identified the Strange Woman most often as *minut* "heresy" (*b. ʿAb. Zar* 17a). In the Talmudic discussion (ibid.), the heresy in question is Christianity. The woman is also equated with *ʾepikorsut* "skepticism" (Rashi). Ralbag suggests a double decoding: sensual desire and also the imaginative faculty (*hakoaḥ hadimyoni*), which sows confusion about ultimate causes. The legitimate wife is the Torah, which is a well of truth and life. If one "drinks" from it alone, he will become a teacher and his own teachings will "spread abroad" (cf. Rashi et al.).

The allegorical reading allows for variation in interpreting the details of the chapter. On the one hand, Saʿadia identifies the well or fount (vv 15, 18) as the Jewish teacher, noting the metaphor of "fount" for speech in 10:11; 13:14; and 18:4. This fount, he says, enables one to produce his own wisdom (5:16). On the other hand, Saʿadia believes that the attractions of the forbidden woman are exemplary of all worldly pleasures that promise immediate enjoyment. Rashi equates the "others" who will obtain the fool's honor (v 9) with foreign gods, and the "strangers" who will receive his wealth (v 10) with idolatrous prophets. Hameʾiri accepts the warning against licentiousness as the surface level, then deciphers all the details of the lecture as an allegory with a special philosophical message. The Strange Woman's temptations are "the claims of antagonistic dissenters" (at 5:6), probably alluding to Christianity. These claims must be ignored in favor of the Torah, which is likened to a well and a gazelle. A Jew's duty is to invest his faith in Torah without expecting rational proof. Thus *pen tᵉpalles* in v 6 means that one should *not* try to weigh or verify the principles and laws of the Torah.

Along similar lines, the early Christian interpreters identified the Strange Woman as folly, sensuality, or heresy (see Delitzsch, p. 122).

Various modern readings too are allegorical in part. Meinhold's, for example, without denying that the Strange Woman is a human type, sees her also as a symbol of folly, while the love for one's one wife is an analogy (*Vergleich*) to the proper relationship to wisdom.

INTERLUDE C. FOUR EPIGRAMS ON FOLLY AND EVIL (6:1–19)

TRANSLATION

Epigram i. Loan guarantees

6:1 My son, if you've provided surety to your neighbor,
shaken hands for a stranger,
2 (if) you have ensnared yourself by your own words,
trapped yourself by your own words,
3 do this, then, my son, and save yourself
(for you have fallen into your neighbor's hands):
Go and grovel, and badger your neighbor.
4 Allow your eyes no sleep,
your eyelids no snoozing.
5 Escape like a gazelle from a hunter,[a]
like a bird from the fowler's hand.

Epigram ii. Sloth and industry

6 Go to the ant, you loafer!
Observe its ways, and wise up.
7 It has no leader,
no chief, no ruler,
8 yet it prepares its bread in the summer,
stores up its food at harvest.
9 How long will you lie there, loafer?
When will you get up from your sleep?
10 A bit more sleep, a bit more snoozing,
a bit more lying with folded arms,
11 and penury will come upon you like a vagabond,
and poverty like a man of arms.

Epigram iii. The good-for-nothing

12 It's a worthless man, a man of iniquity,
who goes about with crooked mouth;

13 **who squints his eyes,**
shuffles his foot,
points his finger;
14 **with perversity in his heart,**
he crafts trouble,
constantly foments strife.
15 **That's why his ruin will come abruptly,**
he'll be shattered all at once, beyond cure.

Epigram iv. What the Lord Loathes

16 **Six things there are that the Lord hates,**
seven his soul does loathe:
17 **arrogant eyes, a lying tongue,**
hands that spill innocent blood,
18 **a heart that crafts wicked plans,**
feet that hasten to run to evil.
19 **a lying witness who breathes out deceits,**
and a fomenter of strife among brothers.

---

[a]*miṣṣayyād* (MT *miyyād* "from a hand")

COMMENTARY

6:1–5. Epigram i: Loan Guarantees

6:1. *your neighbor* [*reʿeka*]: Most commentators identify the *reaʿ* (in this context, a "neighbor" or "acquaintance") with the borrower, but this understanding does not accord with the text. Verse 3 warns against falling into the power of "your neighbor." But a guarantor does not become dependent on the borrower's good will but on the creditor's. Why would a guarantor attempt to escape the trap by begging and badgering his neighbor (v 3b) if the latter were the borrower? Only the lender could release the surety, and he would not agree to do so at the borrower's request. It makes more sense to identify the "neighbor" as the lender and the "stranger" as the borrower. This is the configuration presumed in 20:16: "Take his garment for he has given surety for a stranger! Seize it in pledge, for (he has given surety) for aliens!"[162] The reason why one would give his pledge to an acquaintance on behalf of a stranger is explained later.

---

[162]These words are not spoken to the reader. Rather, they dramatically quote what the lender, or someone in authority, would demand on the occasion of a default and thus indirectly warn the reader against giving surety for a stranger. For *nkryh* "strange woman" (*qere*) read *nokrîm* "strangers" (*ketiv*).

6:1. *neighbor . . . stranger*: A *zar* is anyone outside the sphere of affiliation relevant to context (see pp. 137f.). A *rea'* is another person within the pertinent sphere of affiliation (see pp. 165f.). In this case, a *rea'* is an acquaintance, probably someone living in the proximity, as opposed to a *zar*, who is a stranger and needs someone to vouch for him. In Prov 20:16, *zar* is paralleled by *nokrim*, which definitely means "strangers," "unfamiliar persons," though not necessarily "foreigners." In the present context, the conventional renderings "friend" or "neighbor" for *rea'* and "stranger" for *zar* are appropriate, although the *zar* on whose behalf one is making a commitment need not be a complete stranger or a foreigner.

L. Snijders (1954: 82–84) identifies the *zār* as a social outsider, in this case a neighbor who is a social misfit. McKane says that the *zār* is a foreigner. But neither social adjustment nor foreignness is an issue in any of the proverbs about going surety. For Delitzsch and Toy, the *rēa'* and the *zār* (to be translated "another") are the same. It is true that in some contexts, a *rēa'* can be a *zār*—an "outsider" to a specific sphere of relationships. But here the context provides no relationship to be "outside" except the one between "you" and "your neighbor." Moreover, in 20:16, *zār* is paralleled by *nokrîm* (ketiv), which definitely refers to people who are strange and alien, though not necessarily foreign.

provided surety to your neighbor: The verb *'arab* means "take responsibility" or "make a commitment"; see Gen 43:9; 44:32; Ps 119:122. Here it refers more narrowly to giving surety for a loan. Malbim applies the broader definition—"make a commitment"—here too. An example of such a commitment would be a promise to sell someone a house or a field. However, the parallels in Prov 20:16; 22:26; 27:13; Sir 8:13; and 29:14–20 (the latter dependent on Prov 6:1–5) clearly concern loan surety.

The verb phrase *'arabta lᵉ-* has been understood to mean either give surety *for* (JPSV: "stood surety for your fellow") or give surety *to* (NRSV: "given your pledge to your neighbor"), that is to say, on another's behalf. The latter is the more likely. Though *rea'* and *zar* are different persons, the parallel lines refer to the same event.

Syntactically, *'ārab* governs the beneficiary of the surety as an accusative. For example, "Your servant took responsibility for the lad [*'ārab 'et hanna'ar*] to [lit. "from"] my father [*mē'im 'ābî*]" (Gen 44:32; Gen 43:9). In Ps 119:122, the Psalmist asks God to "take responsibility for" or "vouch for" him "for good" [*'ărōb 'abdĕkā lᵉṭôb*]. The item given as security can also appear as an accusative: Neh 5:3; Jer 30:21. The verb *'ārab* does not govern *zār* in the present verse, though it does so in Prov 11:15 and 20:16 (= 27:13), which offer basically the same advice. The precise locution *'ārab l-* (here: *'arābtā lᵉrē'ekā*) does not occur elsewhere in a sense appropriate to the present verse, but in 17:18 the neighbor's role is unambiguous: "A senseless man strikes a bargain [lit., "strikes the hand," as here], giving surety before a neighbor [*'ōrēb 'ărubbāh lipnê rē'ēhû*]." The preposition "before" shows that the neighbor is the recipient, not the beneficiary, of the guarantee. The guarantor takes responsibility for the borrower's loan *in the presence of* or *to* the latter.

shaken hands: The idiom *taqa' kap* (or *yad*), lit. "striking the hand," signifies concluding an agreement. "Striking the hand" is parallel to *'arab* "go surety" in

Prov 17:18; 22:26; 11:15 (where *toq*ᵉ*ʿim* is used elliptically and abstractly in the sense of "making agreements"); and in the difficult Job 17:3. The idiom is not used outside Wisdom literature, but that may be due to a the overall paucity of commercial terminology in the Bible. In our sources, *taqaʿ yad* always refers to going surety, though the gesture probably had a broader implication of friendship or accord. The same gesture is called "hand to hand" in Prov 11:21; 16:5, where it signifies assurance or personal commitment by the speaker.

This epigram, as Hameʾiri observes, gives advice on how to extricate oneself ex post facto from the self-imposed obligation, as if the author assumes that one is likely to go surety on occasion. Though the conditional formulation implies a warning against the practice, the author does seem to recognize surety as a predicament that one may bumble into from time to time. See "Design and Purpose," later.

6:2. *(if) you have ensnared yourself*: If the "stranger" defaults on the loan, *you* will have to pay. This verse possibly belongs to the protasis of the conditional begun in v 1, with the apodosis starting in v 3: "Do this, etc."

by your own words [*b*ᵉ*ʾimrey piyka*] (twice): Lit. "by [or "in"] the words of your mouth." The Syriac apparently read "by the word of your lips" (*bidbar ś*ᵉ*pateyka*) in v 2b (see Textual Notes), which seems less awkward than the MT's repetition. The surety agreement seems to be entirely oral and sealed by a handshake rather than a written contract. (Contracts in the ancient Near East were essentially records of oral agreements.) The author takes it for granted that such an agreement locks one in as effectively as a written document.

6:3. (*for you have fallen into your neighbor's hands*): The versions, assuming that the logical danger is falling into *hostile* hands, add "evil men" (LXX) and "your enemy" (Syr). The author of the Hebrew text, however, does not regard the danger as hostility or wickedness in the other parties to the loan agreement. Rather, the danger is inherent in the practice of surety, even if the lender is one's neighbor. The neighbor is not hostile: He may, after all, be moved by entreaties. But once you have gone surety, the earlier relationship of equality (implied by *reaʿ*) is warped because you have given your neighbor, the lender, power over you.

Go and grovel, and badger your neighbor: The only recourse is to abase oneself and appeal to the lender's pity.

The verbs translated "grovel" and "badger" are rare, but their meaning is deducible from etymology and context. "Grovel," *hitrappēs*, is from *r-p-s*/*r-p-ś*, "to tread, trample down" (thus HALAT), whence "trample oneself down," "abase oneself" in the Dt (Riyqam, Ramaq, et al.). (The other occurrence of the Dt, Ps 68:31, is unintelligible.)

"Badger," *r*ᵉ*hab*, is from the root *r-h-b*, which conveys the notion of agitation and alarm. The agitation may manifest itself in arrogance (Sir 13:8; Isa 3:5), pride (Ps 138:3; H-stem) or even pleasant confusion (Cant 6:5; H-stem). The use of the H-stem for the causitive in the last example (and cf. Syr *ʾarhēb* "disquiet," "trouble") suggests that the G-stem is intransitive (as in Sir 13:8; Isa 3:5). Consequently, the D (impv. *rahab*) is expected here, and we should perhaps so emend.

6:4. *sleep* [*šenah*] . . . *snoozing* [*t*ᵉ*numah*]: *T*ᵉ*numah* seems to refer to a light or intermittent sleep (see later). Thus the second line is an intensification: even a bit of snoozing or drowsing can do this to you.[163] Compare Ahiqar's advice: "Do not take a heavy loan, or (take one) from an evil man. But if you borrow a loan, give yourself no peace until [you have repaid] it" (ll. 130–31).

Malbim distinguishes between *šēnāh* as regular sleep and *tᵉnûmāh* as occasional (*ʿărāʾî*); in other words, sleeping and snoozing. McAlpine (1987: 66–68) glosses *nûm* as "doze off" and observes that it occurs in contexts where one should be on guard (and thus avoid even *tᵉnûmāh*, let alone *šēnāh*). Words from *n-w-m* seem to indicate sporadic, shallow sleep rather than nightly repose.

6:5. *escape* . . . : The imperative may be understood as consequential to the preceding advice.

A trapped animal writhes and thrashes about desperately in order to free itself, often injuring itself in the process. If it succeeds, it races away. So too, a guarantor's escape from the commitment may be painful and costly, but it is still imperative.

from a hunter: MT has "from a hand," which Naḥmias takes as elliptical for "from the hand of a hunter," but this is rather ad hoc. A minor change yields "from a hunter."

The original reading was probably *miṣṣayyād* "from a hunter" for *miyyād* "from a hand," with the mistake (*myd* for *myṣd*) due to the similarity of *y* and *ṣ* in the archaic script. Possibly we should read *miyyād ṣayyād* "from the hand of a hunter" (DNF, ascribing the error to a double homeoteleuton), though this makes the line rather long. See the Textual Notes.

The Design and Purpose of Epigram i

A. Circumstance: if you have gone surety (6 lines) (6:1–3b)
B. Advice: beseech your neighbor to release you (5 lines) (3c–5)

Epigram i is a monitory discourse with affinities to the lecture form. It addresses the son as in the lectures, but without the introductory call to attention. It uses imperatives extending a conditional, as in Lecture II. Toy is probably right in detecting an "eager, semi-humorous" tone, esp. in v 3.

A number of proverbs warn against going surety. Guaranteeing another's loan is always risky (17:18; 22:26), but most dangerous is when one does so on behalf of a stranger (6:1; 11:15; 20:16 = [27:13]). The situation envisioned in this epigram (and in other proverbs on surety) is that one man (the addressee) has given surety *to* a neighbor *on behalf of* a less familiar person (a "stranger") to enable the latter to borrow from the former. A creditor naturally prefers to

---

[163] J. L. Kugel described the phenomenon of heightening as the essence of biblical parallelism (1981: 49–58 and *passim*). In parallelism, the B-line has an emphatic, "seconding" character, carrying the A-line further, echoing it, defining it, restating it, or contrasting with it. In the couplets in Proverbs, the B-line usually intensifies the first, commonly by negating the reverse.

receive a commitment from an acquaintance rather than a stranger. If one gives such an undertaking, he has fallen into his neighbor's power, for the stranger may renege on his commitment with little concern for the personal consequences and leave the guarantor to make good the loss.

Several procedures were available for securing loans in ancient Israel. A borrower could deposit an item of value as collateral for his own loan (see Deut 24:6, 10–13, 17; Exod 22:25–26). He could pledge his houses and fields (Neh 5:3) or even his children (v 2; read *ʿrbym*). Alternatively, a borrower could have the loan guaranteed by someone else, whose possessions in their entirety would be vulnerable to seizure. The proverb "Take his garment, for he has gone surety for a stranger" (27:13a),[164] shows that a guarantor was liable to loss of possessions down to his very *beged*, the large cloak which provided protection against the nighttime chill. He might even be susceptible to indentured servitude ("debt slavery"), an outcome that is not stated but perhaps alluded to by the repeated image of being trapped.

For all its riskiness, surety is necessary in money lending, and loans are essential in commercial economies and often required in agricultural transactions as well. Ben Sira grants the necessity of the practice and gives more realistic advice: Do not give surety beyond your means (*yoter mimmᵉka*), for guaranteeing a loan is tantamount to paying it yourself (8:13). Ben Sira expounds upon the topic in 29:14–20, going so far as to teach that a good man goes surety for a neighbor (*reaʿ*) (v 14) and that there is even a moral obligation to do so. Conversely, a borrower must be grateful to the guarantor's kindness (v 15). Yet, because giving pledges can be destructive, Ben Sira adds, "Give surety for your neighbor (only) in accordance with your ability, and keep yourself from collapse" (v 20). Hameʾiri interprets Prov 6:1–5 similarly. The author, he says, is not asserting that one must refuse to give surety altogether, since this may be an act of kindness. If, however, one has taken on an obligation that impinges upon his familial inheritance, he must beg to be released.

A man might go surety as an act of friendship, but why do so for a "stranger"? It could be an act of charity, but Epigram i gives no sense that the stranger is needy or that the guarantor has acted meritoriously. The likely motive for vouching for a stranger would be to receive a fee for the service. Ben Sira alludes to this practice: "A wicked man falls through a pledge, and he who pursues contracts [*qibbolet*] falls into judgment" (29:19). (In the Mishna, *qibbolet* refers to contractual undertakings, specifically for labor.) The motive must be financial, for a wicked man would not risk his money to perform a kindness. Remunerative surety is the likely background in Proverbs as well. Going surety may seem like an easy way to make a profit, for he will (he hopes) be compensated just for giving a verbal assurance. But this hope may be a perilous delusion.

---

[164]See n. 162.

While various proverbs offer prudential advice about giving surety, Epigram i seems to push the concern to an extreme and to display a high anxiety about its dangers. Perhaps the heightened uneasiness reflects a growth in the frequency of money lending in an increasingly commercial society and a corresponding temptation to exploit such transactions for quick gain.

The teacher advises the guarantor: Debase yourself and implore your neighbor to release you from your obligation. Pester him day and night (v 4) until he wearies and gives in. The real point of the epigram does not lie in this degrading advice. After all, the groveling could easily prove ineffective. One's neighbor is as likely to resign himself to loss of friendship as to let his acquaintance default on the commitment. And the pathetic spectacle of a man humbling himself to squirm out of a monetary obligation hardly accords with the ideal of independence and self-reliance advocated in the next epigram. Why doesn't the father urge the son to make every effort to stand by his commitment? He could say, as Ben Sira does: If you go surety, you might as well figure on paying off the debt. That fate is hardly comparable to the doom awaiting an ensnared gazelle. The point of Epigram i is, rather, to paint the consequences of going surety in such dire and demeaning terms that the reader will beware of stepping into the trap.[165]

6:6–11. Epigram ii: Sloth and Industry

This epigram (in vv 10–11) cites the quatrain in 24:33–34 and incorporates it in a more expansive admonition against laziness. Since the quatrain is fit into a larger context in the present passage, this is probably the borrower.

6:6. *Go to the ant*: The sluggard is directed to consider the ant as a paragon of enterprise. The real audience is the pupil or reader, whether or not he is actually lazy, who is thereby warned against such behavior by listening in on the chastisement of a sluggard. An intelligent person can learn from another's chastisement; see 19:25.

6:7. *It has no leader* . . . : The poet is impressed by the apparent self-motivation of the ant and argues a fortiori: If the ant, a lesser creature, performs its tasks without coercion and supervision, humans can and should do no less (Hame'iri, aptly comparing Isa 1:3).

6:8. *yet it prepares . . . stores up*: V 8a = 30:25b. Perhaps 6:8 also echoes 10:5, "An intelligent son stores up [*'oger*] (food) in summer; the shameful son sleeps in harvest time." Prov 10:5 shows that "storing up" (*'oger*) in 6:8 is not the consequence of the ant's summertime efforts but another instance of its diligence. The verse is, in reality, an anthropomorphic construction of the ant's activity, but the author is adducing the behavior as a self-evident fact.

[165] Anii 18.15–19.1 seems to be a warning against going surety for an untrustworthy superior, which may result in losing all you own. The text, however, is ambiguous. (It is left untranslated in AEL 2.139); see the discussion in Quack 1994: 166–67.

At this point the LXX introduces an engaging but irrelevant essay on the bee, praising its diligence and productivity; see the Textual Note.

6:9. *How long*: The hectoring tone is that of a *tokeḥah*, a rebuke. Rebukes are introduced by "how long?" (*ʿad matay*) in Prov 1:22 as well as Exod 10:3; 1 Sam 1:14; 16:1; 1 Kgs 18:21; Ps 82:2; Sir 51:24; and more.

6:10. *a bit more* [*m^{e}ʿaṭ*]: Lit. "a bit of." Not only is excessive lethargy harmful, but even a *bit* of it can bring on disaster. The threat of impoverishment ever looms in the background, and only constant diligence and preparedness can stave it off. The verse is a doublet of 24:33.

sleep . . . snoozing: Compare 6:4. This verse intensifies the warning by placing the lighter form of sleep second: *even* a bit of *t^{e}numah* (snoozing or nodding off); see on v 6.

lying with folded arms: Lit. "to lie down, the arms being folded" (also 24:33). (*Ḥibbûq* is a passive noun-formation serving as a genitive of specification [C. Rabin 1948].) The infinitive *liškab* loosely indicates purpose: The inactivity is for the sake of lying abed a bit more. The intensification progresses from line to line: Regular sleep, even snoozing, *even* just lying around can bring on poverty. Qohelet says that this complacent and apparently peaceful posture is self-destructive: "The fool folds his arms together and eats his flesh" (4:5).

Delitzsch, among others, reads this verse as the words of the sluggard, who is begging for a little more sleep (sim. Ehrlich, who places it before v 9). But the shift of voices would be abrupt and unsignaled.

6:11. *like a vagabond* [*kimhallek*]: Lit. "like one who walks about." The duplicate proverb in 24:34 has "will come (as) a *mithallek*" (with no *kaph* of comparison). Many traditional commentators explained *m^{e}hallek* as elliptical for "walks fast" (e.g., Rashi). Albright (1955: 10) identifies *mithallek* with Akkadian *muttalliku* "wanderer," "vagabond" (sim. Margalith 1976: 517–18). A vagrant's visits are unpredictable and accompanied by the danger of theft. Toy's gloss, "highwayman," conveys the nature of the danger, but the *m^{e}hallek* is probably an opportunistic rather than a vocational robber. "Vagabond" is intensified and given more precise definition in the next line.

The variant in 6:11, *kimhallēk*, is a normalization of the archaic term and somewhat awkward syntax in 24:34a. The result is somewhat limp (lit. "your poverty will come like one who walks about"). The Greek paraphrases "evil wayfarer."

like a man of arms [*k^{e}ʾiš magen*]: Lit. "man of shield," a difficult term which has been explained variously.

ʾîš māgēn may be: (a) An image of speed. Rashi paraphrases: Like a man who walks *fast*, like a shield bearer who comes quickly to defend his lord; sim. Radaq, Hameʾiri. Loretz explains "shield bearer" as a soldier who is fast but unskilled (1974: 477); but the latter quality would be irrelevant here. (b) An image of power or hostility. Ibn Ezra paraphrases: like a man who comes with a shield to defeat another; sim. Ramaq, Toy, Ringgren. (c) An image of impermanence. Ralbag says that the comparison is to a man with a shield who does not tarry anywhere but goes to his war. (d) An image of mendicancy. Ehrlich points *maggān*, which, in view of Arabic and Syriac cognates, he translates "die milde Gabe" ("the kind gift") hence *ʾîš maggān* = beggar; sim. Albright (1955: 9–10), comparing Ugaritic *mgn*, which probably means "to beg, entreat."

Connotations of power and hostility as well as unpredictability are most appropriate to a threat, as this verse is. "Shield bearer," or "man of arms," allows for both. The vagrant is not, contrary to McKane, a "jolly [!] beggar," but an armed, socially marginal vagabond who is as apt to steal and rob as to beg. Job pictures the displaced poor as forced to live in the desert like wild asses, without clothing or shelter, and to glean food from the fields and vineyards of the wicked (= rich?) by night (24:5–8). The other explanations of *ʾîš magen* are less appropriate. Poverty does not beg or supplicate; it attacks suddenly, and it is not transient.

The Design and Purpose of Epigram ii

A. The ant's behavior and its consequences (6 lines) (6–8)
B. The sluggard's behavior and its consequences (6 lines) (9–11)

The genre of Epigram ii is, as Hameʾiri terms it, *tokeḥah*—rebuke or chastisement. The author addresses someone (a type figure) who is already implicated in the blameworthy behavior. The example of the ant is ostensively intended to shame the lazy man. "How long" (*ʿad matay*) is a formula of rebuke; see comment on 6:9. The actual purpose of this rebuke is to divert the reader from foolish behavior by describing its consequences. The epigram does not use imperatives, except in v 6, in which "go" is a rhetorical imperative meaning "consider."

The passage is not an animal fable or parable, for these tell a story about anthropomorphized animals to illuminate human behavior. Rather, it describes the ant's natural behavior for the sake of contrast: If even the little ant does his job without being forced, why can't *you*? (In Prov 30:25, it is the ants' powerlessness that makes their providence so impressive.) The tone of the epigram is wry and biting.

Contrary to the influential theory of A. Alt (1951), this passage is not an example of "nature wisdom" (*Naturweisheit*), which attempts to understand the natural order by observing patterns of animal and plant behavior. Nature wisdom observes and compares analogous phenomena in order to discover hidden patterns and principles. Nature wisdom, according to Alt (1951) is mentioned in the praise of Solomon's wisdom in 1 Kgs 5:13. But authentic nature wisdom, as Alt says, observes nature for its own sake and not to illustrate truths for human lives (1951: 91; ET p. 103). (Alt regards Job 38–41 and Prov 30:15–31 as nature wisdom.) The sage in Epigram ii is not seeking to make discoveries about ant behavior; he does not even describe the results of the ant's efforts. He adduces accepted notions about the ant to exemplify a form of good behavior and to shame the indolent listener by the contrast.

The lazy man resembles the loan guarantor—if the latter is indeed motivated by a fee for service—inasmuch as both want to get along without effort.

Anii advises,

(13) Set your eye on your property,
that you not end up a beggar,
a man rich in slackness
amounts to nothing (?).
Let yourself be praised as a man of affairs (18.13–14; cf. AEL 2.139).[166]

Pap. Ch. Beatty IV advises "Avoid being lazy, so that you may establish all your affairs" (vso. 1.5). The Brooklyn Wisdom Papyrus advises, "Be energetic so that your sustenance comes about (5.9–10); cf. Anchsheshonq 23.17–18. In the school letters, the father or teacher frequently scolds a pupil for idleness.

6:12–15. Epigram iii: The Good-for-Nothing

6:12. *It's a worthless man*: Lit. "A worthless man, a man of iniquity, goes about, etc."

The idiom for "worthless man" has various synonymous forms: *ʾadam bᵉliyyaʿal* ("man of *bᵉliyyaʿal*") or *ben/bat bᵉliyyaʿal* ("son/daughter of *bᵉliyyaʿal*") or simply *bᵉliyyaʿal*. It is used of a wide variety of evildoers, including rapists (Judg 19:22), perjurers (1 Kgs 21:10, 13; Prov 19:28), apostates (Deut 13:14), drunks (1 Sam 1:16), political malcontents and ne'er-do-wells (1 Sam 10:27; 2 Chr 13:7), and all-around louts, such as Nabal (1 Sam 25:17, 25) and the sons of Eli (1 Sam 2:12). The idiom indicates a quality of character apart from particular pernicious actions. The rabble at Gibeah are called "sons of *bᵉliyyaʿal*" prior to the rape (Judg 19:22), and the men who were to slander Naboth were chosen because they had the reputation of being "sons of *bᵉliyyaʿal*" (1 Kgs 21:10). Being a "son/daughter of *bᵉliyyaʿal*" ("Belial") is to be of shoddy moral character, prone to wickedness and simple nastiness, and devoid of good sense and moral compunctions. The quality is not precisely *wickedness*, because one can be a drunk (such as Hannah was mistaken for) or a boor (like Nabal) without committing evil deeds.

Since the term has such a wide usage, we should think of the present passage not as an attempt to describe the man of *bᵉliyyaʿal*, as if he were an unknown character, but rather as a censure of certain behaviors by ascribing them to the man of *bᵉliyyaʿal*. The translation "It's a worthless man . . . who . . ." seeks to convey this focus by making "the worthless man // the man of iniquity" the predicate of the description.

bᵉlîyyaʿal. The etymology and exact meaning of the word (which occurs 27 times in the HB + 1 in the Heb Sira [11:32b]) are uncertain. See the surveys by D. Winton Thomas (1963a) and T. Lewis (ABD 1.654–56). The traditional derivation, still widely accepted, is "without" (*bᵉlî*) + "usefulness" (*yaʿal*), in other words, "worthless," "good for nothing." This is the most likely explanation. Nominalization of

[166] Variant: ". . . as a man capable of perseverance."

bᵉlî (which, like most prepositions, is essentially substantival) occurs in the syntactically equivalent *bᵉnê bᵉlî šēm* "sons of a no-name" (Job 30:8); similarly *bᵉlî-māh* "non-thing" (Job 26:7). For the concept, compare *lōʾ yôʿîlû,* "things that do not profit" (also nominalized), referring to pagan gods (Jer 2:8). The noun *yaʿal* is not attested independently, but in the compound it is easily derived from the root *y-ʿ-l* "profit," though the root is used otherwise only in the H-stem. Others derive the word from *ʿ-l-h* "go up," hence "without arising," or from *b-l-ʿ* "swallow," hence "the Swallower," i.e., Death (Winton Thomas 1963a: 18–19). These are unlikely morphologically.

In later Jewish literature, Belial was regarded as the prince of wickedness, the chief of demons. This might have biblical antecedents. The parallelism in Ps 18:5 (= 2 Sam 22:5) suggests that *bᵉlîyyaʿal* is an epithet (perhaps a satirical distortion) for death, alluding to the Canaanite god Mot. Note the parallel between "Baal" and "things that do not profit" (*lōʾ yôʿîlû*) in Jer 2:8.

with crooked mouth [*ʿiqqᵉšut peh*]: Lit. "in crookedness of mouth," meaning that he speaks deceit. The phrase refers to fraudulent speech (cf. 19:1). At the same time, it describes a physical contortion, a twisting (*ʿ-q-š*) of the mouth that, like the gesticulations in the next verse, is thought to reveal an underlying moral distortion.

In the Bible (and elsewhere in world literature), a triad of body zones (heart + eyes; mouth + ears; hands + feet) implies the totality of personality (thus B. de Geradon 1974: 14–32 and *passim*). The eye is the point of entry to the will, whose organ is the heart; the hands and feet put the will into action, and the mouth gives expression to thought and will, and this utterance is received by the ears. Prov 6:12–20 organizes manifestations of evil in accordance with these three zones.

6:13. *squints* [*qoreṣ] his eyes*: Or "eye" (qeré). The verb *qrṣ* means "pinch together," hence "squint." "Squint" is a better rendering than "wink" the eye, since one can be said to *qrṣ* the lips (Prov 16:30) and to *qrṣ* clay with the fingers (Job 33:6), both of which actions are more than momentary compressions. Also, a variant of this proverb in Prov 16:30 speaks of the scoundrel as "*closing*" (read *ʿoṣēm*) his eyes.

Squinting the eyes was considered a symptom of hostile thoughts. It reveals malicious pleasure (Ps 35:19) and causes unhappiness (Prov 10:10). One who plans deceit is said to "close his eyes" (Prov 16:30). Job says that his enemy "sharpens [*yilṭoš*] his eyes against me" (16:9). Since there are not many gestures the eye can make, this too must refer to some sort of squinting, making the eyes "sharp" like knives. According to Ben Sira, "He who makes hints [*dianeuōn* = *qrṣ*] with the eye devises evil, and those who know him will avoid him. In your presence he speaks sweetly and admires your words but later he will twist his mouth [*diastrepsei to stoma autou* = *yʿqš pyw*], and with your own words he will place a stumbling block" (Sir 27:22–23, Gk). Even today, a certain type of squinting gaze is construed as hostile. Squinting is thought to indicate a dishonest personality, perhaps because the squinter is shifty-eyed and does not look at others in a straightforward way. The virtuous keep their gaze straight ahead (4:25).

The Greek translators understood *qoreṣ ʿayin* (and the other gestures in 6:13) to be a hint or signal to others, but this does not seem right. In v 13, squinting or winking is not a conspiratorial sign, because there is no confederate in the present context and because the other movements are not signals. They are probably all symptoms of a personality disorder.

The description of the knave's shifty look is a condensation of 16:30, with the verb (*qoreṣ* "pinch," "squint") taken from v 30b and the noun (*ʿeynayw* "his eyes") taken from v 30a.

shuffles [*molel*] *his foot*: Or "feet" (qeré). *Molel* = "scrapes," a hapax in BH, but existing in RH in the sense of "rub" or "scrape" (thus too Aq, Sym, Vul). Riyqam regards the gesture as a signal to a confederate, but such signs would be useful in very few circumstances. The notion that the worthless man is drawing patterns with his feet (McKane) has no etymological support, and in any case this would be very difficult to do. The movement is best understood as a restless shifting and shuffling, a sign of inner disquietude.

points his finger: Lit. "fingers." *Moreh* is probably from *y-r-h* "show," "point." A derivation from the homonymous *y-r-h* "throw," "shoot" (cf. 2 Sam 11:24, qeré), as suggested by Radaq, is also possible. Compare the use of the synonymous *šalaḥ* "send forth" in Isa 58:9. Is this a nervous gesticulation or a purposeful gesture? The Greek understands the latter, rendering "teaches [*didaskei*] with hints of his fingers." This interpretation might find some support in Prov 16:29 (in a passage which influenced Epigram iii), which says that the lawless man entices his comrades and leads them on an evil path. In the present passage, however, the miscreant does not seem to be enticing others to join him in his misdeeds so much as entangling them in conflicts with others. "Sending forth"—that is, sticking out—the finger is condemned alongside "speaking wickedness" (*ʾawen*) in Isa 58:9, where the gesture may indicate derision or accusation. Finger pointing may express derision in the present verse too (Radaq).

6:14. *perversity* [*tahpukot*]: Lit. "turnings over," the opposite of *meyšarim* "straightness," "rectitude"; see at 2:12.

he crafts: Not only does the worthless man craft or "design" (*ḥoreš*, from a verb meaning "engrave") plans that harm an individual but he also causes (lit. "sends") discord among others (cf. 16:28a). His nastiness infects others and spoils relationships all about him.

6:15. *That's why his ruin will come abruptly*: It is abrupt and sudden (*pitʾom*) insofar as it is shocking and unexpected, though a wiser person could predict it. In the HB, suddenness is usually associated with disasters and intensifies their severity (Daube 1964: 5 and *passim*).

A step is elided in the logical connection between the villain's perversity and the suddenness of his ruin, such as human antagonism or divine anger (Radaq supplies the latter). But for the sages, the misbehavior itself is adequate assurance of the punishment's inevitability and suddenness, and the worse the behavior, the more certain and violent the downfall. They rarely attempt to *demonstrate* the principle that wickedness leads to punishment, but seek only to impress its truth on the reader and to turn the recognition into action.

The Design and Purpose of Epigram iii

A. The scoundrel (6:12a)
B. His behavior (12b–14)
C. His punishment (15)

Epigram iii is a reflection, meaning that it describes a reality without explicitly extracting a norm from the observation. It does, however, have a practical goal. The enumeration of the outward marks and evil effects of the worthless man implies a warning to avoid him and the danger he presents (Naḥmias). It is not a warning to avoid *being* this sort of person, for a man of Belial is innately and incurably worthless and corrupt, and the audience is presumed not to belong to this hopeless category.

The Composition of Epigram iii

Epigram iii (6:12–15) extracts sayings and phraseology from other parts of Proverbs and embeds them in a new poem. (With regard to the direction of influence, see later "The History and Composition of Interlude C.")

6:13 ≈ 16:30 (Part IIb).
6:14 ≈ 16:28a (Part IIb)
6:15a = 24:22a (Part III)
6:15b = 29:1b (Part IVb)

Epigram iii (as well as iv) draws particularly upon Prov 16:27–30, which is an epigram about three kinds of scoundrels: *ʾiš beliyyaʿal* the "worthless man," whose earmark is vicious talk; *ʾiš tahpukot* the "perverse man," also called the agitated man,[167] who provokes strife; and *ʾiš ḥamas* the "lawless man," who leads others astray. These three types are really one and the same; Prov 16:30 seems to refer to them as one. Prov 6:12–15 fuses the three types into one person, designated *ʾadam beliyyaʿal // ʾiš ʾawen*, the wicked good-for-nothing. This miscreant betrays his malicious thoughts and intentions by nervous, twitchy gesticulations. He devises evil and causes discord. Therefore, the epigram concludes (using a phrase from 29:1b), "he'll be shattered all at once, beyond cure" (6:15b).

6:16–19. Epigram iv: What the Lord Loathes

6:16. *six . . . seven*: The graded numerical sequence (discussed by Roth 1965) is a frequent rhetorical device in Hebrew poetry, as in ancient Near Eastern poetry generally. It sets a number parallel to the next integer (x // x + 1). The

[167] Reading *nirgāz* for MT's *nirgān* in 16:28b.

number pair is best conceived of as a word pair distributed between parallel lines (Haran 1972: 238–41). The gist of 6:16 is "There are six or seven things the Lord hates." Sometimes a number pair may intend the first of the two numbers, but the examples of this are few and uncertain. Usually, only the second number is relevant to the verse (Haran 1972: 256–57; cf. Ramaq). The present epigram has a full itemization. Other examples (according to Haran 1972: 257) are Prov 6:16–19; 30:15–17, 18–19, 21–23, 29–31; Job 5:19–22; Sir 23:16–17; 25:7–11; 26:5–6, 28; and 50:25–26; also *b. Nid.* 16b (ascribed to Ben Sira); CTA 4.iii.17–21 (UT 51); and Ahiqar (6.92–93). The pattern thus seems to be characteristic of Wisdom literature.

Several traditional Jewish interpreters, following Leviticus Rabbah (§16), regard the seventh item in this epigram, namely "fomenter of strife" (v 19), as its climax and as the feature called *toʿăbat napšo* "what his soul loathes." The last item does seem to be the climax, though it is artificial to restrict the object of loathing to "fomenter of strife" alone (*šebaʿ* [v 16b] means "seven," not "seventh"). Epigrams iii and iv both make the provocation of strife the ultimate offense, for, as Malbim observes, "It destroys the entire (social) collectivity."

In Epigram iii, the seven disgusting things are: (1) arrogant eyes, (2) a lying tongue, (3) hands that spill innocent blood, (4) a heart that crafts wicked plans, (5) feet that run quickly to evil, (6) a lying witness, and (7) a fomenter of strife among brothers. The first five items are body parts, proceeding from top to bottom. (The hands or arms—*yadayim* includes both—may be regarded as located at the shoulders.) Items 6 and 7 are types of persons and break the homogeneity of the series.

there are [*šeš-hēnnāh*]: The syntagm noun + indep. pronoun is a typically MH way of predicating existence; e.g., *ʾarbaʿah raʾšey šanah hem*, "there are four new year's days" (m. *Roš Haš* 1:1). It is also found in Cant 6:8.

his soul does loathe. Read with the ketiv, *tôʿăbôt napšo*, lit. "the loathings [or "abominations"] of his soul," that is, the things he loathes. On *toʿebah*, see at 3:32.

6:18. *feet that hasten to run to evil*: The idiom "run to evil" appears in 1:16 and Isa 59:7, signifying eagerness and alacrity. The worthless man not only does evil, he does it with zest.

6:19. *a lying witness who breathes out deceits* [*yapiaḥ kezabim ʿed šaqer*]: Lit. "one who breathes out deceits—a witness of lying" (the phrases are in apposition). "Breathes out" is an etymological rendering of *yapiaḥ*, which as a verb means "blow," hence "utter." The noun *yapiaḥ* means "witness" and is always collocated with *ʿed* "witness." This, in apposition to "a lying witness," constitutes the sixth abomination. The testimony of the lying witness can be either forensic, in a court proceeding, or informal, that is to say, everyday lies about other people.

The form *yāpîaḥ* can be either a verb (H-stem), as here, or a noun (a "patiens"). The basic meaning of *hēpîaḥ* (*p-w-ḥ*) is "to blow" (Cant 4:16), whence it comes to indicate a hostile action, perhaps "snort at" (Ezek 21:36; Ps 10:5) or "blow (the flames)," "provoke" (Prov 29:8). In Hab 2:3 and Prov 14:5, the verb means "to witness," which may also be derived from the notion of blowing = uttering, though that etymology is uncertain. *Yāpîaḥ* is a noun meaning "witness" in Prov 12:17; 14:25 (*ypḥ*); 19:5, 9; and "one who snorts at" (?) in Ps 12:6. The word is a noun from *y-p-ḥ* (a by-form of *p-w-ḥ*), attested in Jer 4:31; and see UT glossary 1129. The pattern is precisely paralleled by *yārîb* "antagonist" from *r-w-b/y-r-b*. All the occurrences of *yāpîaḥ* as a noun in Proverbs are in construct and should be pointed *yᵉpîaḥ-*. The vocalization *yāpîaḥ* shows that the Masoretes construed the word as a verb throughout, as the LXX and many later interpreters have done.

fomenter of strife [*mᵉšalleaḥ midyanim*]: Lit. "one who sends forth strife," using the same locution as in v 14b and 16:28a, *šlḥ mᵉdanim/midyanim/madon*. The two types of person in this verse are not entirely distinct. In Amenemope §13, a chapter warning against giving false testimony culminates in praise of social harmony, because that is the first casualty of deceit.

The Design and Purpose of Epigram iv

A. What God hates (6:16)
B. Five organs (17–18)
C. Two kinds of people (19)

Epigram iv, like the preceding, is a reflection, describing a reality without explicitly offering advice. Its practical purpose is to align the reader's attitudes with God's. Awareness of what disgusts God can motivate personal conscience and ethical behavior, even in matters where the law does not apply and society cannot consistently enforce its norms (see the comment on *toʿebah* at 3:32).

The Composition of Epigram iv

Epigram iv employs motifs found in Epigram iii, which locates immoral qualities in certain physical organs. In Epigram iii, the physical organs were mentioned as locations of the body language of the scoundrel. Now the organs that "speak" or communicate this language are topics in themselves: mouth-tongue (vv 17a and 12b), hands-fingers (vv 17b and 13b), heart (vv 18a and 14a), and feet (18b and 13a). Other topics are carried over too: the "crafting of wickedness" (*ḥrš ʾawen*) (vv 18a, 14a) that characterizes the man and his deeds (vv 18b, 12a). The lists in both epigrams culminate in the fomenting of strife (vv 19b, 14b), for this sums up the effect of all vices.

In the following comparison, thematic but nonverbal similarities are indicated by ≈ (the "nearly equals" sign).

16:27–30:	*parallels in 6:12–19*
(27) The worthless man (*ʾiš bᵉliyaʿal*)	the worthless man (12a)
is a furnace of evil, and on his lips is scorching fire.	≈ crooked mouth (12b), lying tongue (17a)

16:27–30:	*parallels in 6:12–19*
(28) The man of perversities	perversities (14a)
(*tahpukot*) provokes strife,	provokes strive (14b, 19b)
and the agitated man separates friends.	≈ foments strife among brothers
(29) The lawless man (*ʾiš ḥamas*) misleads his friend, and guides him on a path not good.	
(30) He closes (read *ʿṣm*) his eyes to plan (*ḥšb*) perversities (*tahpukot*).	squints (*qrṣ*) his eyes (13a), plans (*ḥrš*) perversities (14a; cf. 18a)
He purses (*qrṣ*) his lips (and) carries out the evil (*raʿah*).	squints *qrṣ* (his eyes) (13a) (plans) evil (*raʿ*) (14a; cf. 18b: *raʿah*)

6:19a has a duplicate in 14:5b, "A lying witness blows lies."

Since Epigram iv continues to mine components from 16:27–30, as did Epigram iii, the two epigrams probably had the same author. In Epigram iv, he thematizes the physical organs mentioned incidentally in vv 12–14 by making them the subjects of the predications in the first four abominations.

The History and Composition of Interlude C

The four epigrams of Interlude C fall into two groups: i–ii, concerning folly; and iii–iv, concerning evil. The first two epigrams are admonitions, second-person warnings to avoid certain behaviors. They are interconnected loosely by the underlying theme of behavior conducive to poverty. They share some phraseology: a repeated vocative (vv 1, 3 and 6, 9); "sleep" and "snoozing" (vv 4 and 10); and animal comparisons (vv 5 and 6–8). The second pair of epigrams comprises observations, descriptions of corrupt types of persons and qualities. The evidence noted previously indicates that iii and iv were composed sequentially by the same author in dependence on other units of Proverbs.

Little unites the two pairs of epigrams of Interlude C besides the loose theme of undesirable behavior. (Saʿadia says that they all describe elective actions that a man takes upon himself and then regrets.) The four epigrams are built around sayings and ideas extracted from the other parts of Proverbs. The author of Interlude C is using the book of Proverbs in much the same way that Ben Sira did, shaping miscellaneous sayings into well-structured proverb-poems.

Interlude C is not an original component of Part I. Its structure is very different from that of the lectures, which begin with an exordium calling for the son's attention, then proceed to give counsel in the lesson, and then (usually) conclude with a summary proverb. Prov 6:1 does address "my son," but, unlike the exordia, does not do so to call his attention to the father's wisdom or to praise the value of the teachings. Nor is the audience urged to seek and hold to wisdom. Verse 6 addresses the sluggard. This seems to be a sort of "apostrophe," a fictive address to someone not present that is really meant for edification of the audience.

Whereas the lectures all give advice on fundamental issues of morality and inculcate the value of wisdom, the first two epigrams in Interlude C offer specific prudential advice on two types of behavior (surety and sloth), which are unwise but not immoral. The second two epigrams, which describe a type of person and seven types of behavior without relating them to the addressee or reader, are also unique in Prov 1–9.

I do not see any literary explanation for the location of Interlude C. One can find a few associations with the preceding lecture: 5:1–23 ends with reference to the evildoer, who is described (by a different name) in 6:12–19. Interlude C describes folly, mentioned (by a different name) in 5:23. Prov 6:1–5 and 5:10 describe impoverishment caused by a "stranger." (Wildeboer, Plöger, and Meinhold place importance on these connections.) But such connectors are trivial, and the features that are supposed to motivate the disposition of the units are frequent in Proverbs. Interlude C could just as well have been placed after 1:10–19 (scholars would then note the shared "trap" imagery, the animal similes, and the feet running to evil) or after 16:27–30 (that unit, after all, describes the worthless man in almost identical terms). The placement of Interlude C seems to have been adventitious, with the interpolator giving little thought to its location, except insofar as he inserted the interlude on the boundary between two units.

S. Harris (1995: 111–34) argues for the unity and deliberate editorial placement of 6:1–19. In addition to affinities between epigrams i and ii and between iii and iv, Harris sees connections that reach beyond these pairs, such a "family point of view" in vv 1–5 and 19 (reference to discord among brothers); the emphasis on speech (vv 2, 12, 13, 17, 19); references to "man" in several places; and the danger threatened by a "hand" in vv 5 and 17. But such motifs are frequent throughout Proverbs, and the similarities proposed are too loose to constitute a principle of organization.

Harris also argues that the unity of 6:1–19 is manifest in the use of the Joseph story as the background for the entire passage. The relationship is created by intertextual allusions in three themes: going surety (Prov 6:1–5, alluding to Gen 43:9); agricultural preparations (Prov 6:6–11, alluding to Gen 41:47–49 and 43:22); and relationships among brothers (Gen 37—esp. Judah's role in vv. 26–27—alluding to Prov 6:19, "fomenting strife among brothers"). Harris finds other allusions as well, but they all are too nebulous to direct the reader of Prov 6 to the Joseph story. Nor would the suggested cross-references "assist the parent in making his/her case to the son," as Harris believes they are meant to do (p. 155). "Sending strife among brothers" has nothing to do with Judah's selling of Joseph. (It might be said that it was Jacob who fomented the fraternal strife.) Judah's offering himself as surety for Benjamin was commendable, not something he should have extricated himself from, as the son is urged to do in Prov 6:5). The extraordinary measures taken during the famine have no bearing on the advice to store up food in harvest time. The midrash (Genesis Rabbah) saw connections between the passages, as Harris notes (pp. 153–54), but it is in the nature of midrash to interrelate all parts of the Bible, with farfetched applications a sign of homiletical virtuosity.

Interlude C borrows and embeds sentences and locutions from other parts of Proverbs.[168] That this is the direction of the borrowing is shown by the fact that the interlude, in particular in 6:12–19, has duplicates and echoes in most of the other collections, and even contains one proverb compounded of lines from two collections (6:15 = 24:22a [in Part III] + 29:1b [in Part IV]). The reverse hypothesis is farfetched: that three or four redactors would independently descend on this short unit and pick lines and phrases out of it, or that the redactor of Part IV would (at 16:27–30) take the description of the worthless man from 6:12–14 and distribute its components among three character types, whose distinctions are in any case artificial. An alternative hypothesis, that the other redactors and the poet of this unit were drawing independently on a nonextant source or sources, or just on the reservoir of folk sayings, would be gratuitous and fail to explain why so many duplicates and echoes are concentrated in this one unit. Far more likely, the author of Interlude C has borrowed materials from elsewhere in Proverbs in constructing four epigrams, then inserted the result in Part I. This means that Interlude C belongs to the latest stage of the book's redaction.

LECTURE IX. ADULTERY KILLS (6:20–35)

TRANSLATION

Keep my teachings

6:20 Keep, my son, your father's precepts,
forsake not your mother's teaching.
21 Bind them always upon your heart,
tie them about your throat,

They will guide you through life

23[a] For the precept is a lamp and the teaching a light,
and disciplinary reproof is the way to life.
22 When you walk about it will guide you,
when you lie down it will watch over you,
when you wake up it will converse with you,
24 to guard you from another man's wife,[b]
from the smooth talk of the alien.

[168]In sum:

6:8a	= 30:25b	6:15a	= 24:22a
6:10	= 24:33	6:15b	= 29:1b
6:11	= 24:34	6:19a	= 14:5b
6:13	≈ 16:30	6:19b	= 6:28a
6:14	≈ 16:28a		

See the Comments and the table on pp. 224f.

Avoid the adulteress

25 Don't desire her beauty in your heart,
or let her take you in with her glances.
26 For a whore costs but a loaf of bread,
but a married woman hunts for a precious life.
27 Can a man scoop up fire in his lap
without his clothes getting burnt?
28 Can a man walk on glowing embers
without his feet getting scorched?
29 So too with him who approaches another man's wife:
None who touches her goes unpunished.
30 People don't despise a thief
if he steals to fill his belly when starving.
31 Still, if caught, he'll repay sevenfold—
even surrendering all the wealth of his house.
32 An adulterer lacks sense;
a self-destroyer—he's the one who does this.
33 Wounds and insult are all he gains,
and his disgrace will not be expunged.

A husband's jealousy cannot be appeased

34 For jealousy enrages a man;
he'll not relent in the day of vengeance.
35 He'll accept no ransom, however large,
nor be appeased, however big your bribe.

---

[a]Verses 22 and 23 reversed for clarity; see comment. [b]*ʾēšet rēʿekā* (MT *ʾēšet rāʿ*).

COMMENTARY

6:20–23. Exordium

6:20. *father's precepts* [*miṣwot*] . . . *mother's teaching* [*torah*]: Both "precepts" and "torah" apply to both parents (Riyqam, Hameʾiri). Though the LXX draws a certain distinction between the mother's and father's instructions (see Textual Note to 1:8), the Hebrew text does not reserve different words for each parent's teachings. The one other mention of the mother's teaching in Part I (1:8) speaks of her *torah*, but the father too is said to speak *torah* (3:1; 4:2; 7:2) as well as *miṣwot*. A mother's teaching may include *musar*, for Prov 31:1 says that Lemuel's mother *yissᵉrattu* "instructed him," that is to say, taught him *musar*. (Both words are from the root *y-s-r*.)

6:21. *Bind them always upon your heart . . . throat*: That is, tie them like a pendant or amulet on a string around your neck, so that they may always be close to your heart; cf. Exod 28:29 and Cant 8:6. The metaphor also suggests amulet-like protection. (P. Miller [1970: 130] emphasizes the apotropaic implications of the imagery.) This does not mean that the teachings *are* an amulet, but that they are a *substitute* for one. See further the comment on 3:3. The verb *ʿnd* (only here and Job 31:36) is a metathesized by-form of *ʿdn* (e.g., *maʿădanot*; Job 38:31) (Riyqam).

6:23. *For the precept* . . . : Toy transposes vv 22 and 23, and perhaps that was the original order. But even without changing the text, we can transpose the verses mentally (and in translation) so as to convey the logical progression of the passage (thus Moffatt). In its present position, v 23 is parenthetical, explaining how wisdom guides a person (v 22a), while v 24 resumes v 22's promise of guidance and protection and extends it into the lesson.

lamp . . . light: The underlying metaphor is life as a journey through a dark and pitted landscape. Wisdom is often figured as the straight and lighted path, but here it is the lamp that allows its possessor to see and avoid lethal pitfalls (see "The Paths through Life," after chapter 2). One pitfall is the seductress, who is a "deep pit" (22:14; cf. 23:27). The alliteration of *torah* and *ʾor* ("teaching" and "light") can be nicely imitated in Latin *lex* and *lux* (Crenshaw 1980: 25). Ps 119:105 applies these words to the divine *torah* revealed to Israel.

disciplinary reproof: *tokeḥot musar* (lit. "reproofs of discipline") is a construct of synonyms (in Hameʾiri's phrase, "a doubled noun"), in other words, "*tokaḥot* which are *musar*." *Tokaḥat/tokeḥah* can be constructive admonitions and warnings such as the following lesson, as well as chastisement for misdeeds already committed; see the comment on 1:23. *Musar* is moral chastisement and admonition; see "Words for Wisdom," §6.

6:22. *it will guide . . . watch over . . . converse with you*: The fem. sg. "it" (which can also be translated "she") has no fem. sg. antecedent. The "precepts" and "teachings" together constitute wisdom, which is the implicit subject of the verbs in this verse.

Wisdom, which here refers to the internalized parental principles, is described in terms suggestive of personification: Wisdom is your friend, protector, and teacher. She will accompany you at all times, protect you from harm, and provide you with worthy and valuable thoughts. Make her—and not the temptress—your companion.

In naturalistic, non-metaphorical terms, the verbs "guide," "watch over," and "converse" allude to the internal dialogue that goes on constantly in the mind. Internalized wisdom is a kind of superego or conscience, a voice felt as somehow separate from oneself (for it can be ignored) but also distinct from the moral precepts one has been taught (for these have been generalized as principles that can be applied unconsciously). This voice, then, is like a faithful companion whom we must keep near us at all times, who will guide us in the right direction and warn us away from dangers.

converse with you [*teśiḥeka*]: The verb *śyḥ* means to utter, whether inaudibly, in thought, or audibly, in speech. The verb seems to be used only of quiet utterances (thought being the quietest of them). Hence *teśiḥeka* is suggestive of

Wisdom speaking gently in one's ear, your counselor and confidant—but only if you bring her with you on life's path.

The exordium resembles Deut 11:18–20:

> (18) And you shall set these words upon your heart and upon your soul [or "throat"—*nepeš*], and bind them as a sign upon your arm, and they shall be as amulets [*ṭoṭapot*] between your eyes. (19) And you will teach them to your sons, to speak of them when sitting in your house, when walking in the way, and when lying down, and when rising up. (20) And you shall write them upon the doorposts of your house and upon your gates. (Compare Deut 6:7)

Whether we ascribe the similarity between these passages to a shared wisdom tradition or to the influence of one text on the other is a moot point. Whatever its source, Prov 6:20–22 formulates a commonplace of education: the teachings must permeate your entire life. If you keep them (Deut 11:22) they will keep you and watch over you (Prov 6:22).

A Talmudic homily often cited by traditional Jewish commentators distributes the three activities of v 22 among different phases of existence: "'When you walk about, it [the Torah] will guide you'—in this world. 'When you lie down, it will watch over you'—this is the day of death. 'And when you wake up, it will converse with you'—in the world to come" (*b. Soṭa* 21a).

6:24–33. Lesson

The lesson warns against extramarital entanglements by describing the shame and pain they bring on the perpetrator.

6:24. *to guard you from another man's wife*: The focus is narrowed to protection from the married woman, who is "alien" (*nokriyyah*) in the sense that she is another's wife. The author argues on the basis of the mortal peril she poses, rather than the youth's moral obligations, because the rhetoric of the lesson is designed to scare the youth away from this hazard.

another man's wife: MT reads *ʾēšet rāʿ* "a woman of evil." Though she certainly is that, emendation brings the verse in line with the usual usage and the parallel word *nokriyyah* "alien."

MT's *ʾēšet rāʿ* "a woman of evil," with the noun *rāʿ* functioning attributively, is grammatically possible (Naḥmias aptly compares *ʾēšet midyānîm* in Prov 21:9). But this is not the usage with the noun *raʿ* elsewhere in Proverbs, and it does not produce a good parallel. The LXX's *gynaikos hypandrou* "married woman" implicitly vocalizes the phrase as *ʾēšet rēaʿ*, lit. "the wife of a neighbor" (see the Textual Note). This makes good sense, esp. since v 26 refers to *ʾēšet ʾîš* and v 29 to *ʾēšet rēʿēhû*. Elsewhere, however, the phrase meaning "neighbor's wife" has a suffix, and bare *rēaʿ* (without an article or suffix) is not used in the sense of "another man." The expected form is *ʾēšet rēʿekā* (cf. Exod 20:17). The final *kaph* could easily have been lost by haplography with the similar-looking *mem* of the next word. The absence of the *kaph* is probably what led to the MT vocalization.

smooth talk: lit. "smoothness [or slipperiness] of tongue."

As Naḥmias observes, MT's *lāšôn nokriyyāh* must mean "a foreign tongue." We should vocalize *lᵉšôn nokriyyāh*, "tongue of an alien, strange woman." On *nokriyyāh* in the sense of "not your own," see pp. 139f.

McKane argues effectively against G. Boström's view that vv 20–26 concern the foreign cult prostitute whereas vv 27–35 warn against adultery with a neighbor's wife. McKane believes that the woman in question throughout the passage is the wife of a neighbor who happens to be a foreigner. But while a foreigner who settled in Israel *might* be called one's *reaʿ* (this is uncertain), resident foreigners with licentious wives could not have been so common as to justify devoting three of the ten lectures to this particular group. Nor is there any reason for the author to worry less about native married sexual tempters than foreign ones. In fact, the author is indifferent to the woman's nationality.

6:25. *Don't desire . . . let her take*: The clauses can be read as consequential: Don't desire her beauty *so that* she does not capture you with her glances. The youth is, as always, warned to avoid being seduced; he is never admonished to avoid being a seducer.

her glances: lit. "eyelids." Rather than modestly diverting her eyes downward as she ought, she looks about with coquettish winks and bold stares. Ben Sira says, "A woman's harlotry is (revealed) by her looking up [lit. the rising of her eyes], and by her eyelids it is made known" (26:9).

This admonition has been rephrased in the Syriac Ahiqar (S_2 2:72): "My son, let not your eyes look upon a woman who is beautiful; and do not inquire into beauty that is not yours. For many have perished through the beauty of woman, and her love is like a fire that burns."

6:26. *For a whore costs but a loaf of bread*: In 1 Sam 2:36, a loaf of bread plus a small amount of silver (an *ăgorah*[169]) constitutes a subsistence wage for a priest. A loaf seems like a low fee for a prostitute—certainly much less than the goat kid that Judah was willing to pay (Gen 38:17). The author seems relatively untroubled by prostitution (which is not forbidden by biblical law) and is willing to downplay its cost in order to make the contrast more dramatic. Ben Sira rephrases this principle: "A woman for hire is reckoned as naught, but a married woman is reckoned as a trap of death to those who consort (with her)" (26:22; see Di Lella on the text). Though, like Ben Sira, the author of Lecture IX does not condone prostitution, he does insinuate that it is safer to resort to harlots than to married women. See further p. 138.

Many commentators read this verse as describing the consequences of a single sin and take *ʿad* as meaning "is reduced to," "comes down to" (the Qimḥis, Hame'iri, and most earlier Jewish commentators, as well as Delitzsch and others). KJV follows this reading: "For by means of a whorish woman *a man is brought* to a piece of bread." An interpretation found first in *b. Soṭa* 4a and cited

[169] Some (e.g., DCH) gloss *ʾăgorah* as "payment." Even so, it could not have been much silver, because the context requires a trivial payment, one small enough to make a loaf of bread a significant supplement.

by traditional commentators explains *ʿad* this way but draws a distinction between the two lines: by consorting with the "strange woman," a man will be impoverished until he has to beg his bread (*ʿad* = "brought down to"), but by consorting with a *married* harlot one is brought to death or hell.

The literal translation of 6:26a is "because for [*beʿad*] a harlot—up to [*ʿad*] a loaf of bread." Though difficult, this makes sense as an ellipsis for "Because for a harlot (one pays only) as much as a loaf of bread." M. Scott (1927) emends *beʿad* to *ʿerek* "value," citing LXX *timē* (Lev 5:15, 18; 27:2); but context alone could produce this LXX rendering without a different source text. In any case, *ʿerek* means "value" or "estimate," whereas the verse is concerned with expenditures not values. G. R. Driver (1954: 244) emends *beʿad* to *baʿad* or *bāʿad* "price," but the nominal use of the word is unexampled, and in any case the prepositional *beʿad* "for," "in exchange for" is unproblematic (cf. Job 2:4). In the second phrase, *ʿad* means "up to," hence "as much as" (e.g., Esth 5:6). The word downplays the significance of the cost of a prostitute for the sake of the contrast, as if she might cost even less.

but a married woman hunts for a precious life [*nepeš yeqarah taṣud*]: or "precious soul." The *nepeš* is not a detachable, "spiritual" soul, but (with a few exceptions) the living person in his or her entirety or an integral part thereof. *Nepeš* is "soul" in the sense of the living, desiring, feeling personality, but not in the sense of a spiritual entity separable from the body and potentially immortal. One's *nepeš* is his life. Thus, for example, *hikkah X nepeš*, lit. "smite [someone] *nepeš*," means to smite him mortally (Gen 37:21; Deut 19:11; Jer 40:15), and "take my *nepeš*" (1 Kgs 19:4) means "deprive me of my life." David complains to Saul, "you are hunting my *nepeš*, to take it away" (*ʾatta ṣodeh ʾet napši laqahtahh* (1 Sam 24:12), meaning that Saul is trying to kill him.

The phrase "to hunt (*ṣwd*) a *nepeš*" has additional connotations. In Ezek 13:17–23, witches (called "prophetesses") are accused of *hunting souls* (*leṣoded nepašot*). The exact nature of their activity is unclear, but it involves a magical apparatus to hunt souls. Ezekiel calls this "putting to death persons who should not die" (v 19a), yet it is not actual homicide because the victims are trapped and can be released (v 20). Ezekiel says that the witches do this "for handfuls of barley and bits of bread" (v 19), which is even less than the wages assigned the harlot in Prov 6:26. Both statements are hyperbolic. The image of the adulteress "hunting souls" (or "lives") is thus suggestive of sorcery. The woman is not only a murderer; she wishes to *trap* and bind the boy's life, as the witches in Ezekiel do their victims. The "precious soul" is not just an incidental victim of the seductress, it is her "kill," the profit of her hunt.

The phrase "precious life" (*nepeš yeqarah*) means a valued life. For a *nepeš* to be precious in someone's eyes means that he holds that life dear; see 2 Kgs 1:14; cf. v 13 and 1 Sam 26:21; Isa 43:4. "Precious life" refers to everyone (Hameʾiri) and not only to an eminent man (thus Malbim) or "a person of substance" (thus Gemser, McKane, et al.). After all, the temptress is deadly to *everyone*, including an anonymous adolescent.

The adulteress is a murderer who is said to *hunt* lives, as if she were deliberately seeking her lovers' deaths and not only her own sexual gratification. She is portrayed not only as sluttish and immoral but also as almost demonic. In this sense, she is indeed the Other—the "other side," as Satan's realm was called in Jewish Aramaic.

P. R. Berger (1987, at 99–100) explains the verse as a single sentence: "Denn nur hinter einer Frau, bereit zu huren noch für einen Rundlaib Brot, /oder aber der Frau eines Mannes, einem kostbaren Wesen, jagst du doch her!" ("For you are either (merely) hunting a woman who is ready to go whoring even for a loaf of bread, or for a man's wife, an expensive creature"; p. 101). Berger explains: "To cause her unpleasantness through undesired pursuit would be a shabby injustice. It is distasteful to pursue these women, in the first case because of [the woman's] lack of value, in the second because of [her] high value" (p. 101)—as if sexual harassment were the issue. Berger believes that this understanding is based on the Masoretic accentuation, which has an *ʾatnaḥ* at *ʾēšet ʾîš*, which Berger believes is the major disjunctive. In the Three Books, however, the major disjunctive is not the *ʾatnaḥ* but the *ʿôleh wᵉyôrēd*, which in the present verse is placed on *kikkar lāḥem*, as expected. In any case, the prepositions do not fit this interpretation.

6:27–28. *Can a man . . . ?*: Verses 27–28 do not ask "impossible questions," nor do they have any affinity with riddles, contrary to Crenshaw 1980: 20–22 (who, however, correctly describes the rhetorical function of these questions as an appeal to consensus [p. 23]). They are rhetorical questions asking about the obvious, which call for the answer: "Of course not!" The reader is to recognize in them the rule that one cannot avoid the natural consequences of his actions. At the same time, these questions leave the reader with memorable images with which to imagine the deed described: Adultery is playing with fire (cf. Job 31:12). Just as touching fire hurts, so touching another man's wife hurts. The line's assonances and alliterations (especially in *ʾîš ʾeš*) are evocative of the hissing and crackling of fire: *hăyaḥteh ʾîš ʾeš bᵉḥeqo*.

Saʿadia draws a distinction between the two analogies. In the first (v 27), a man brings fire into contact with his garment. This corresponds to merely caressing a woman (= "whoever touches her" in 29b). One who does this does not escape punishment altogether (*loʾ yinnaqeh*). In the second (v 28), a man comes into direct contact with the fire. This is like having intercourse (cf. *baʾ ʾel* "approaches," in v 29a, understood as coitus). The perpetrator cannot escape the fire of hell. Although this exact distinction is not supported by context or coordinated with v 29, Saʿadia has rightly noted an intensification in the imagery from indirect to direct contact, with the climax coming in the next verse, the most excruciating burn of all.

There is apparent noncoordination between the (usually) masc. *bᵉgādāyw* and the fem. verb *tiśśārapnāh*. But Lev 6:20 and Ezek 42:14 provide some evidence (albeit uncertain) for the occasional treatment of *beged* as fem.

6:29. *approaches* [*baʾ ʾel*]: or "comes to." This is frequently a euphemism for intercourse, but that might not be its implication here. Given the parallel with "touches," the locution "approaches" may be intended more delicately, which makes the admonition all the more uncompromising: Don't even go *near* her.

another man's wife: Lit. "the wife of his neighbor" (*reaʿ*), see the comments on 6:24 and pp. 165f. This phrase makes it clear that the "Strange Woman" is strange in the sense of belonging to another man, not in being foreign or socially marginal.

goes unpunished [*yinnaqeh*]: lit. "be clean," that is, get off scot-free or (in legal contexts) "be acquitted" (e.g., Exod 20:7).

6:30. *People don't despise a thief*: Though people can understand and sympathize with the motives of a man who steals bread, society still exacts punishment.

Many interpreters have been puzzled by v 30, for *shouldn't* people despise a thief? As Ben Sira asserts (Sir 5:14b), shame was "created for" the thief. Saʿadia[170] reads the statement as relative: People do scorn a thief, but not *as much as* they do an adulterer. This may be the social reality, but the verse does say that people do *not* do scorn a thief. Another proposal is to read v 30a as a question—"Is not a thief despised?" (McKane, Meinhold, et al.). (The latter sense would be more clearly expressed by reading *hl'*, a minor emendation proposed by Wildeboer and others and recently supported by C. Cohen 1997: 146–52.) By either interpretation, the verse is an argument a fortiori, but construing v 30 as a rhetorical question (and thus a negative) weakens the contrast between the lesser and worse evil. The text itself rhetorically heightens the contrast by exaggeration, denying (improbably) that a thief suffers public disgrace. If a wrongdoer is punished severely even when his deed elicts some sympathy, how much the more so when it is a crime that arouses universal revulsion (6:33).

The Egyptian story of "The Eloquent Peasant" shows a similar leniency toward a thief who steals because of poverty: "Stealing by a thief is the misdeed of one who is needy. He should not be blamed, for this is just a matter of seeking (necessities) for himself" (B 121–24; cf. AEL 1.174).

6:31. *if caught* [*wᵉnimṣa'*]: *Maṣa'*, usually translated "find," sometimes means "seize," "catch"; see Iwry 1966.

he'll repay: The thief has the possibility of making monetary compensation, perhaps to avoid being sold into debt slavery (Exod 22:2).

sevenfold: This is not a judicial imposure. While sevenfold restitution is not implausible,[171] the extant Israelite laws set a lower limit. The Covenant Code stipulates reimbursement plus punitive damages of 100% for theft or negligence if the animal is recovered (Exod 22:3, 8) or, if the stolen animal is killed, fourfold and fivefold compensation (21:37). "Sevenfold" in the present verse is not necessarily a precise figure. It is probably a way of saying "a great deal" (Saʿadia, Ehrlich, et al.). The next line heightens this to "all the wealth of his house." The thief is willing to pay massively to exculpate himself, and (as "he'll pay" implies) will be allowed to do so. The adulterer, whose motives are indefensible and behavior loathsome, will not be able to buy his way out of physical harm or death and will suffer indelible ignominy (vv 32, 33, 35).

---

[170] Saʿadia, incidentally, was familiar with Ben Sira (see Segal 1958: 43), though there is no sign of influence in this case.

[171] In the Code of Hammurabi, penalties for theft, depending on the circumstances and persons involved, include restitution of three or five shekels for theft of certain tools, punitive compensation ranging from ten to thirtyfold, and death (see §§6–13, 22, 23, 25, 259, 260, 265).

even surrendering all the wealth of his house: Lit. "He will give all the wealth of his house." Justice is ineluctable, and even he who steals from hunger must pay heavily. He, however, at least *can* pay, whereas no monetary payment can get the adulterer off the hook (v 35).

On the basis of a comparison with the treatment of theft in the Code of Hammurabi, R. Westbrook (1988: 124) argues that the restitution in Exod 21:37 is, in principle, a fixed ransom in lieu of the death of the thief. This means that the payments mentioned in v 31 are to be understood as ransom, which v 35 says would be spurned.

6:32. *An adulterer lacks sense*: Lit. "one who commits adultery with a woman [*noʾep ʾiššah*] lacks heart." The superfluous *ʾiššah* "woman" is added for better quantitative balance with the B-line. The flaw in focus here is not the adulterer's sin but his stupidity, his lack of "heart," as evidenced in his self-destructiveness.

a self-destroyer . . . : Lit. "One who destroys himself, he does it." The destruction envisaged is not immediate death, since the adulterer, at least in the short term, suffers insults and wounds (v 33), indicating that he is not killed at once. Still, the principle that the sinner destroys himself (cf. 5:22–23) stands, because he has set himself on the path to death.

Mašḥît napšô hûʾ yaʿăśennāhh: The word *mašḥît* has two basic senses: (1) "Destruction" (e.g., Exod 12:13). In Dan 10:8, *mašḥît* refers to psychological distress; in 2 Chr 22:4, it means "corruption" or "corruptive force." (2) "Destroyer" (e.g., Exod 12:23; 1 Sam 13:17), including a weapon (e.g., Prov 18:9; Ezek 21:36) and a military unit, a "commando" (e.g., 1 Sam 13:17; Jer 22:7). As an extension of this usage it can mean "trap" (Jer 5:26).

Correspondingly, the verse can be translated two ways. (1) "The destruction of his life—he himself does it." In this case, the antecedent of the fem. sfx. "it" is *mašḥît*. That word, however, is masc. (2) "One who destroys himself—he is the one who does it," namely, commits adultery, the antecedent of the indefinite fem. sfx. being implicit in the preceding sentence. In either case, the indep. pronoun *hûʾ* between obj. and verb is very emphatic: "he himself does it."

6:33. *Wounds . . . insult . . . disgrace*: Though vv 34–35 seem to speak of blood vengeance, or perhaps judicial proceedings with the husband as plaintiff, the adulterer's afflictions as described here are not immediately fatal. The word for "wound" (*negaʿ*) includes diseases, plagues, injuries, and afflictions of all sorts, but never corporal or capital punishment by the judiciary. In Deut 17:8 and 21:5, the *negaʿ* happens in physical altercations between individuals. Canings imposed by the judiciary are called *makkot* (Deut 25:3). The fornicator will be thrashed, certainly by the husband but perhaps by others as well, and publicly and eternally humiliated. An Egyptian instruction too uses shame as a sanction for adultery: "Do not approach a married woman, lest your name stink" (Pap. Ch. Beatty IV, 18.13).

6:34–35. Conclusion

6:34. *For jealousy enrages a man* [*ki qinʾah ḥămat geber*]: Lit. "for jealousy is a man's fury" or "for a man's fury is jealousy." As Prov 27:4 observes, "Fury is cruel and anger is a torrent, but who can stand before jealousy?" The word for "man," *geber* (rather than the more generic *ʾîš*), has the connotation of strength and is related to *gibbor* "warrior."

Some emend *ḥmt* "fury" to *tmt* = *tāmît* "kill": "for jealousy kills a man" (Ehrlich, BHS, and many), comparing Job 5:2, *ûpōteh tāmît qinʾāh*, "and jealousy kills the naif." But, as comparison to that verse shows, "man" in the present verse is the one who harbors the jealousy, and he is not the one to be killed. Ehrlich recognizes this and claims that "kill" means, in effect, "drives the man to extremes," but he brings no similar cases.

relent [*yaḥmol*]: or "spare." The verb refers primarily to the act of sparing someone from expected injury. See, for example, 1 Sam 15:15, where Saul does not feel *compassion* for the best of the flocks (he intends to slaughter them), but he does *spare* them; sim. 2 Sam 12:4; Jer 50:14.

6:35. *ransom . . . bribe* [*koper . . . šoḥad*]. In the normal course of events, gifts can assuage anger (21:14), but not when a man's marriage has been violated.

The punishment here is not judicial. Compensatory ransom or blood money belongs to the realm of private blood vengeance, and "wounds" and "disgrace" (v 33) are not judicial punishments for adultery. The retribution pictured in vv 33–35 is a physical attack by the wronged husband. In contrast, in vv 30–31, the context of punishment seems to be judicial. The pivot between the two kinds of retribution is v 32, which says that the adulterer destroys *himself*. The adulterer brings about his own ruin with or without the intervention of judicial punishment. In the normal course of events, it might be difficult to prove adultery, for there would be no witnesses. But that is no reason for the adulterer to feel safe, for a husband's suspicions would be enough to provoke a violent assault. As Anchsheshonq warns, "Do not make love to a married woman. He who makes love to a married woman is killed on her doorstep" (AEL 3.177).

The clause *lōʾ yiśśāʾ pᵉnê kol kōper* is peculiar because elsewhere the genitive in the idiom *nāśāʾ pᵉnê* X is not an inanimate object, but only a person or God. It is the accused man and not the compensatory payment that must receive favor, lit. have his "face raised." Ehrlich emends to *pnyk lkpr*, translating "He will not favor you with respect to a bribe." On the consonantal level, this involves only a different word division. Still, the MT makes sense as a synecdoche: the bribe for the briber.

Though the quatrain in vv 34–35 does not summarize or justify the message of the lesson, it serves as the lecture's conclusion by moving to a higher level of generality, giving the reason for the preceding assertions, and returning to the second person of the exordium.

The Design of Lecture IX

I. Exordium (20–24)
  A. Keep wisdom with you at all times (20–21),
  B. *because* it is a light (22) and will give guidance to you (23),
  C. *so as* to save you from the Strange Woman (24).
II. Lesson (25–33): adultery destroys its perpetrator.
  A. Avoid the adulteress (25–33)
    1. Don't let the Strange Woman catch you (25),

2. *because* she is lethal (26),
3. *because* (proving her lethalness) (27–33)
   a. dangerous deeds naturally have painful consequences; thus too adultery (27–29); and
   b. if even a crime that arouses sympathy has harsh consequences, how much the more inescapable is punishment for adultery (30–33).

III. Conclusion (34–35): Punishment is guaranteed by the husband's anger.

Lecture IX continues the theme of chapter 5, the adulteress. Before the intrusion of Interlude C, Lectures VIII–X formed an uninterrupted block of lectures on this topic.

The Message of Lecture IX

The lesson presents a single and cohesive argument whose main point is the *inevitability* of the adulterer's punishment: do not imagine that you can evade punishment for adultery, though it is the most secretive of sins.

The warning is blunt: Keep away from a man's wife, or he'll beat the hell out of you, maybe kill you. No mention is made of ethical and religious motives for avoiding this sin, such as its moral taint, the loathing God feels for it, or the anguish (and not only anger) that it can cause the husband. That is not to say that the author was indifferent to these matters, but rather that he chose a harsh and easily imagined scenario to put a scare into young men. The teaching must, after all, compete with the relentless demands of raw adolescent lust. When faced by the slippery temptress, reflection on ethical and religious principles is unlikely to be as compelling as the gut fear of facing a fuming husband and sneering neighbors.

Lecture IX is unique in its form of argumentation. While other lectures assume and declare the inevitability and severity of retribution for sin, this one seeks to derive the consequence logically as natural effect from cause. Thus 6:27–29 argues from the consequences of morally neutral but immediately painful behavior. Prov 6:30–35 argues *a minori a maius* using the analogy of another criminal act. Prov 6:34–35 seals the case by appeal to psychology: Nothing can placate a cheated husband. In this way, physical and social analogies reinforce each other in demonstrating the inescapability of retribution.

Lecture X. Beware the Seductress (7:1–27)

Translation

Make wisdom your companion and protector

7:1 My son, keep my words,
store my precepts within you.

2 Keep my precepts and live—
my teaching, as the pupil of your eye.
3 Bind them on your fingers,
inscribe them on the tablet of your heart.
4 Say to wisdom, "You are my sister,"
and call understanding "friend"—
5 that she may guard you from a strange woman,
an alien who speaks smooth words.

The seduction

6 For once, through the window of my house,
through my lattice, I was gazing down,
7 when I saw among the callow, spied among the youngsters,
a lad devoid of sense,
8 passing down the street, by her corner,
toward her house he strode,
9 at dusk, when evening was falling,[a]
in the dark of night and gloom.
10 And now: a woman comes toward him,
in harlot's garb, her intent hidden.
11 Rowdy and defiant is she,
her feet stay not at home,
12 now in the street, now in the plazas,
in ambush at every corner.
13 She seized him and kissed him,
and with brazen face she said:
14 "I had to make well-being offerings:
today I paid my vows.
15 That's why I have come out to you,
to seek you eagerly—and I found you!
16 I've decked my bed with covers,
dyed drapes of Egyptian linen.
17 I've sprinkled my bed with myrrh,
with aloes and cinnamon.
18 Come, let's slake our thirst on love till dawn,
take our delight in lovemaking!
19 For the man's not at home,
he's gone on a journey afar.
20 A purse of money he took in his hand;
he'll not return till mid-month."

The fool's fate

21 She enticed him with her soft[b] "instruction,"
misled him with her smooth speech.
22 Impulsively he followed her—
like an ox going to slaughter,
like a stag bounding to bonds,[c]

23b like a bird rushing to a trap:
c He wasn't aware that he'll pay with his life—
a till an arrow split his liver.[d]

A *warning*

24 So now, my sons, listen to me,
give heed to the words of my mouth.
25 Let not your heart veer to her ways,
stray not upon her paths.
26 For many a victim she's laid low,
numerous are those she has slain!
27 Her house is the way to Sheol,
descending to the chambers of Death.

---

[a]point *baʿărōb yôm* (MT *b^{e}ʿereb yôm*). [b]*b^{e}rōk* (MT *b^{e}rōb*). [c]*ûk^{e}ʿakkēs ʾel môsēr ʾayyāl* (MT *ûkʿekes ʾel mûsar ʾĕwîl*). [d]Line transposed from start of verse.

COMMENTARY

This is the last of four lectures dealing with the Strange Woman (II: 2:16–22; VIII: 5:1–23; IX: 6:20–35; X: 7:1–27). This one focuses on her seductive power, which she wields through her sinuous and flattering words.

7:1–5. Exordium

7:1. *keep* [*š^{e}mor*] . . . *store* [*tiṣpon*]: The parallelism with *ṣpn* "store" shows that *šmr* here means "keep" in the sense of "hold," "retain," rather than "obey"; and see 4:4, 21 and the image in 7:3. The exordia typically exhort the boy to absorb and *retain* the precepts. With rare exceptions (perhaps 5:7b and 8:33), they do not tell him to *do* what is commanded, for that is assumed to be the inevitable consequence of learning and remembering the teachings.

7:2. *Keep my precepts*: Verse 2 repeats the keywords "keep" (*š^{e}mor*) and "my precepts" (*miṣwotay*) from the preceding verse, now joining them as verb and object. This creates a staircase parallelism, which is extended by a simile in 2b.

pupil of your eye: lit. "eyes." The pupil (*ʾiyšon*) of one's eye is always before and near him, in the center of his vision. It is dear to its possessor, who will reflexively protect it from attack, and as such it is the epitome of something protected diligently (Deut 32:10; Ps 17:8). As the organ of sight, it is the physical medium of knowledge, alongside the ear.

The word translated "pupil," *ʾîšôn*, is probably a diminutive of *ʾîš* "man," hence "little man," referring to the image one sees reflected in the pupil of another's eye; cf. "daughter of the eye" in Ps 17:8 (Naḥmias; HALAT; and most). As the black of the eye, *ʾîšôn* comes to refer to the dark of night (Prov 7:9; 20:20 [ketiv *ʾĕšûn*]). The etymology is complicated by the fact that the qeré in 20:20 (*beʾĕšûn*) points to a different word meaning "time" (HALAT), but this would not apply to the other occurrences. Given the uses in Deut 32:10 and Ps 17:8, an emendation to *ʾwšwn* "foundation, depth"

(Nebe 1972) is not called for, even though in 4Q184, 6–7, *b'w/yšny* is parallel to *mwsdy 'p[lwt]*, "foundations of gloom."

and live: The imperative "live!" is consequential upon the preceding imperatives. Life is used in the "fuller," qualitative sense to connote abounding vitality (McKane), but the author first of all means it literally, for neglect of the precepts leads to actual death (7:27).

7:3. *bind them on your fingers*: A number of things are said to be bound to the *yad* "arm" (including the hand) as a "sign" (*'ot*), a "reminder" (*zikkaron*) or "amulets" (*ṭoṭapot*), namely the unleavened bread (Exod 13:9); the dedication of the firstborn (Exod 13:16); and God's commandments (Deut 6:8; 11:18). The sign on the hand is a mnemonic device. In Exod 13:9, 16, and Prov 7:3, the sign is figurative, since one can hardly bind unleavened bread to the hand. In Deut 6:8 and 11:18 too, this is probably the case, though Jews have traditionally understood these verses as commanding the actual use of phylacteries. Prov 7:3 is certainly figurative: No one has ever tied these words (all of Prov 7?) to his hand. The underlying image may be a signet ring; cf. Cant 8:6a, "Set me as a signet on your arm." The problem (as noted by Meinhold) is that *qašar* "bind," "tie," does not seem the appropriate verb for something slipped on. Also, the plural of "fingers" does not accord well with the ring image. Some medieval commentators explain it as a string tied around the finger as a reminder (Saʿadia, Ramaq, Naḥmias). But a string so used is meant to recall something else, whereas the precepts are what are supposed to be remembered. Perhaps there is no specific practice underlying the metaphor, but only the notion of tying something to oneself.

the tablet of your heart. Prov 3:3 uses the tablet-of-the-heart metaphor similarly; see the comment there. The image represents the heart itself as a tablet and memory as inscription upon it. As well as being memory itself, the "inscription" also "labels" and defines one's character; see the comment on 3:3 and the remarks on ornament imagery at 3:3bc.

The triad of eyes-fingers-heart represents personality as a whole; see the comment on 6:12.

7:4. *Say to wisdom, "You are my sister,"* . . . : The verse speaks of wisdom as if she were a person. The "as if" is maintained in the wording, in contrast to chapters 8–9, where wisdom is consistently treated as a person. This verse tells us to relate to wisdom as to a person, but it does not picture her as one. The point of comparison is the nature of the relationship itself. "Sister" in the Song of Songs (and in the Egyptian love songs) is a term of endearment for the beloved. "Sister" in this sense would stand in a sharp counterpoint to the illegitimate erotic relationship described in the rest of the chapter. Nevertheless, "sister" may express intimacy and affection without connoting erotic attraction.

friend (*modaʿ* [masc.]): lit. "one known." In Ruth 2:1 (qeré) *modaʿ* refers to Boaz without erotic overtones. The feminine *modaʿat* is also used of Boaz (3:2) and is apparently epicene, as it is in RH. The question is whether the form *modaʿ* can refer to a female acquaintance (thus Toy), making it a better parallel to "sister"—or whether it is only masculine and refers to a male friend (Saʿadia, Ramaq, Naḥmias, and other medievals). (The synonymous parallelism does not decide the question because it does not indicate strict identity, as v 3 shows.) In the absence of other evidence, the probability is with the latter. If so, the femininity of wisdom is not essential in these verses, in which it is not fully personified, and both friendship with a man and affection for a sister can be used as analogies, just as inanimate objects provide the similes in vv 2–3.

Whether "sister" means sibling or beloved, and whether the "friend" is male or female, the metaphors in this verse imply an egalitarian relationship between the reader and wisdom. (The sociological fact of a brother's authority over his sister is not a relevant connotation here, for there is no thought of *supervising* wisdom.) This differs from the asymmetrical relationship between the exalted Lady Wisdom and human beings in passages where she is fully personified (1:20–33; 8:1–36; 9:1–6).

7:5. *that she may guard you*: lit. "to guard you" (*lišmorka*). An infinitive of purpose provides the transition from exordium to lesson, as in 2:12 and 5:2.

speaks smooth words [*ʾămareha heḥliqah*]: lit. "(who) makes her words smooth" or "slippery." "Smooth" speech entices (Prov 2:16; 5:3; 7:5, 21) or flatters (Prov 28:23; Ps 12:3–4). The idiom (which appears in various forms using the root *ḥ-l-q*) always refers to insincere talk (or glances, in Ps 36:3), though the "honey and milk" of the beloved's speech in Cant 4:11 implies an honest smoothness. See the comment on 2:16. Except for an embrace and kiss (v 13), the seduction in this chapter is entirely verbal, as v 21 says. Prov 7:5 ≈ 2:16.

7:6–23. Lesson

The speaker recounts an event he purportedly observed: the seduction of a youth by a married woman.

The medieval commentators agree that the scene is imaginary. Its fictitious quality is evident from the way the speaker claims to have seen the couple in the dead of night and to have heard the woman's words. Hameʾiri explains that the warning is put in narrative form for the sake of verisimilitude ("to strengthen the truth of the matter for the listener and so that he will believe [the author] as if he himself had seen it"). Saʿadia calls the passage a *mašal* and argues that the narrative reports progressively worse actions and describes how the woman seduces the boy by appealing to all five senses.

On the allegorical level, according to Saʿadia, the chapter describes the enticements of this world, which is compared to a whore. For example, this world, like the harlot, is noisy and full of changes and vicissitudes. It is also dark—for fools, who live in darkness and confusion. Just as the harlot deludes the boy about her husband, so the evil impulse (lust) deludes people about divine punishment; and so on. According to Maimonides, the hidden message is the rule that we must "abstain from excessive indulgence in bodily pleasures." The author compares the body, which is the source of all sensual pleasures, to a married woman who at the same time is a harlot. All human deficiencies are to be traced to the body alone (*Guide to the Perplexed*, Introduction, pp. 7–8). Maimonides explains that this chapter is an allegory in which the entirety represents a certain reality but whose details cannot be decoded individually. Naḥmias, however, undertakes an item-by-item decoding. Malbim again identifies the Strange Woman with foreign philosophy.

7:6. *lattice*: Windows were enclosed with trelliswork, through which one could peer without being seen (Radaq; Toy).

I was gazing down [*nišqapti*]: The verb means "look down" (from a height), as from a mountain (Num 21:20) or heaven (Ps 85:12; Cant 6:10) (the H-stem has the same use). Moreover, all occurrences seem to indicate extended watching (e.g., Num 21:20; Judg 5:28) rather than a brief glance. This suggests that the speaker was spending time peering down from his upper-story window in curiosity or (as in Judg 5:28) in expectancy. Though looking through a lattice is typically a feminine posture, it is not exclusively so, and we need not imagine that the speaker—elsewhere the father—is a woman here; see pp. 256f.

7:7. *callow . . . youngsters*: The parallelism equates youngsters (*banim*, lit. "sons") with callow, untutored boys (*p^{e}ta'im*). Among them is one who (as will eventuate) is worse than the others; he is devoid of sense—"lacking a mind" (*ḥăsar leb*)—and therefore is not only ignorant but lacks the faculty for grasping and holding wisdom (cf. Prov 17:16). Yet he is culpable, for the defect is remediable. It is within one's power to "get a mind" (19:18).

Verses 6 and 7 have an unusual rhythm (stressed syllables in boldface):

6 *ki b^e**ḥallon bey**ti // b^e**ʿad** 'ešnab**bi** + niš**qap**ti*

for through the window of my house // through my lattice
+ I was gazing down,

7 *wa'**ere'** bapp^{e}ta'**yim** // '**abi**nah babba**nim** + **na**ʿar ḥăsar-**leb**.*

when I saw among the callow // spied among the youngsters
+ a lad devoid of sense,

Rather than comprising two couplets of two balanced lines each, each verse is composed of two short parallel phrases (two stress units each) plus a phrase standing outside the parallelism. The last phrase is the predicate and the focal point. The asymmetry creates a certain suspense that draws the reader's attention forward to the scene about to be described.

7:8. *passing down the street, by her corner, toward her house*: This verse may give the impression that the youth is deliberately heading to the woman's house (thus Hame'iri). But the fact that she finds it necessary to come out toward him and implore him to enter shows that he had not set out to visit her. He is, after all, being seduced. Danger lurks even when one does not seek it out.

Her corner *pinnāhh*: the masc. form (for the expected *pinnātāhh*) appears only here and Zech 14:10. Examples of similar structures are *middāhh* (Job 11:9) and *niṣṣāhh* (Gen 40:10).

he strode: The verb for "striding," *ṣʿd*, suggests a bold and deliberate step. Malbim distinguishes three stages: walking down the street at evening, then turning at her corner, then heading to her house when it is dark. But these distinctions do not seem to be marked in the text, and they imply a longer span of time than the actions would require.

7:9. *dusk*: *nešep* is twilight, either before night (as here) or before dawn (Job 3:9).

when evening was falling:

MT points *b*[e]*ʿereb yôm* "at the evening of day" (sim. LXX). For a more natural phrasing we should vocalize *baʿărōb yôm* (BHS), lit. "when the day was becoming evening."

dark of night: *ʾiyšon laylah*. The *ʾiyšon* usually is the pupil of the eye (see at v 2). In 7:9 and 20:20, it means "dark," a transferred sense based on the blackness of the pupil; see the comment on 7:2.

Verse 9a places the events at twilight, while 9b speaks of the dead of night. Both times seem relevant to the setting. The first line refers to the time when people are still circulating in the streets. The second line gives the circumstance of the meeting, namely deep darkness, when people think they can remain concealed or unrecognized: "The eye of the adulterer watches for twilight, thinking, 'No eye will see me,' and he cloaks his face" (Job 24:15). But darkness descends quickly at the latitude of Palestine, and evening and night may be set in parallelism to imply the passage of a short interval (Plöger). The darkness also evokes the special dangers of night, one of which is now approaching the boy. The Shulammite too seeks her beloved at night (Cant 3:1–4; 5:2–8).

7:10. *And now: a woman comes toward him*: This sentence, with *hinneh* + noun clause, is the equivalent of the English historical present, used for vividness in recounting a past event. This vividness is heightened by the particle *hinneh* (traditionally translated "behold"), which marks participant perspective: at this moment, the speaker sees the woman approaching, and we view the event through his eyes. The narrative as a whole, however, is set in the past.

in harlot's garb [*šit zonah*]: This may refer to any garment or a specific one. The only item of clothing that seems to have marked a prostitute was a heavy veil (*ṣaʿip*, Gen 38:14). The Strange Woman might be wearing one in an attempt to hide her identity. In Job 24:15 (quoted previously), the male adulterer, creeping about at night, "cloaks his face" (lit. "puts on a face-concealer," a *seter panim*). Prov 7:10 does not say that the Strange Woman *is* a harlot or even that she intends to look like one, but that her harlot-like garb gives her a harlotrous appearance. Judging from her self-description, she is actually an outwardly respectable, well-to-do woman, the wife of a merchant. To say that she looks like a whore expresses derision.

(1) By form and parallelism, *šît* can be the G masc. pass. ptcp. of *š-y-t* "to put." The verb *š-y-t* refers to putting on ornaments in Exod 33:4 and Ps 73:6. If the subject of the ptcp. is the woman, it must mean something like: "(she is) put on as a harlot," which could be an indirect, elliptical locution

for being dressed as a harlot. The masc., however, is inappropriate, especially since the following participle, *n^e^ṣurat-*, is feminine. (2) Alternatively, *šît* may also be a noun, a garment of some sort, as in Ps 73:6. In the present verse, *šît* functions adverbially, meaning "in a garment of" (Radaq, Hameʾiri).

her intent hidden [*n^e^ṣurat leb*]: lit. "guarded of heart." The Strange Woman keeps her designs to herself; she is always dissembling and crafty. (G. R. Driver [1950: 250] mentions examples in various languages of the semantic development from "guarded" to "crafty"/"sly"; for example, Heb *ṣānûaʿ* "guarded," "reserved" and Syr *ṣnîʿ* "crafty, sly.") Reserve is not inherently a character flaw. In 4:23, "guarding" (*nṣr*) one's heart is a virtue, namely the ability to keep one's thoughts to oneself and control one's mouth. But this same ability makes one all the more dangerous when his or her thoughts and intentions are evil. The Strange Woman "is of a hidden mind, of a concealed nature; for she feigns fidelity to her husband and flatters her paramours as her only beloved, while in truth she loves none, and each of them to her is only a means to an end, viz. to the indulgence of her worldly sensual desire" (Delitzsch).

7:11. *Rowdy and defiant is she*: The narrator can penetrate the woman's inner character (v 10b), just as he knows the youth's mentality (v 7b), even before either has taken action. Though she is not making noise at this time (she is skulking about the dark streets), she is by nature *homiyyah*, noisy, boisterous, and unsettled—like Lady Folly (9:13)—rather than quiet and composed, as a proper woman (and man—see 17:27, etc.) must be. The speaker sees into the woman's soul and reports character traits not on display on this occasion.

Hāmāh, whose root-meaning is "utter" or "moan," is used of buzzing or humming noises, including the buzz and clamor of cities and the busy places in them (e.g., Isa 22:2; Prov 1:21; 1 Kgs 1:41), the growling of bears (Isa 59:11), the roar of the sea (e.g., Isa 51:15), the groaning of one's innards (e.g., Cant 5:4—in longing); and the cooing of doves (Ezek 7:16). The word may be applied in a transferred sense to the inward groaning of a disturbed soul (Pss 42:6, 12; 43:5).

The woman is also *soreret*—rebellious or defiant. G. R. Driver believes that *soreret* must mean "restless" or "fickle" as well as "rebellious," like the Akkadian *sarāru*, on the assumption that rebelliousness is "off the point" (1932a: 141–42). But this is very much the point. *Sorer* is always used of a person incorrigibly defiant to proper authority, such as a parent's authority (Deut 21:18), God's (Isa 30:1; 65:2), or an owner's (Hos 4:16). The authority the woman is defying must be that of her husband.

Soreret is from *s-r-r*, a by-form of *s-w-r* ("turn aside," "stray") and reminiscent of that word (see the wordplay *sarey sor^e^rim* in Jer 6:28). "She turns aside and is inclined to go in crooked paths hither and yon" (Hameʾiri). The connotation of straying is reinforced by the next line.

her feet stay not at home: lit. "her house." This reveals her insubordination and her restlessness.

7:12. *now in the street, now in the plazas*: Again, her behavior is a perversion of the Shulammite's search for her beloved in the Song of Songs, "in the streets and in the plazas" (3:2).

now [*pa*ʿ*am*]: lit. "once." *Pa*ʿ*am* also means "foot," and v 12a could also be rendered, "A foot in the street, a foot in the plazas" (Ehrlich). In other words, her feet are all over town. This would be a double entendre, reinforced by the previous verse.

in ambush [*te*ʾ*ĕrob*]: lit. "she lies in ambush." This is an aggressive action, one expected of a hunter, a lion, an army, a robber, or the like. This woman is rapacious, a predator of young men.

As in v 11, the speaker seems already familiar with the Strange Woman, as he refers to behavior not described in the present scene. She is a type-figure, who comes into the scene with certain predefined features. The speaker describes her behavior as habitual. This is not the only time she has gone on her licentious pursuit, for she characteristically goes "now" to one place, "now" to another. She seems to have a gnawing and incessant need for sexual satisfaction.

7:13. *with brazen face* [*he*ʿ*ezah paneyha*]: lit. "she makes her face strong." To have a "strong" or "hard" face (ʿ*-z-z panim* in various locutions) means to be devoid of proper human sensibilities, such as the capacity for mercy (Deut 28:50), humility (Qoh 8:1, cf. 2a), and shame (Prov 7:13). A hard forehead similarly connotes obduracy and callousness (Ezek 3:7–9; Sir 8:16). A harlot, living in defiance of social mores, is inured to public contempt: "You had the forehead of a harlot: you refused to be ashamed" (Jer 3:3). The impudence of the woman in our passage is manifest in her speech in its entirety (vv 14–20) and not only in the claim in v 14 that she has offerings available. Her brazenness is needed for the lewd and shameless display that began with the embrace and kisses. To behave thus even in a legitimate love requires a boldness verging on impropriety. In the Song of Songs, the girl knows that public kissing is likely to arouse scorn (Cant 8:1). Nevertheless, she embraces her lover when she finds him at night (Cant 3:4) and determines to bring him home, so that their union may find acceptance.

There are two anomalies in vocalization: *hē*ʿ*ēzāh* (from ʿ*-z-z*) without a dagesh in the *zayin*; and *wattōmar*, the pausal form (penultimate stress) being used (instead of *wattōmer*), though it is not joined by a maqeph to the following word.

7:14. *I had to make* . . . : lit. "well-being offerings (were) upon me" (ʿ*alay*), indicating obligation. For the construction, compare Num 30:7, 9, 15; Ps 56:13.

well-being offerings [*š*ᵉ*lamim*]: Having made these offerings earlier, she now has meat available for a festive meal, which the youth can join in. The sexual implications of the invitation will soon be unmistakable, but at this point, the boy may believe—or allow himself to believe—that he is being invited to innocent feasting. As Saʿadia observes, the pleasures the woman describes are progressively immoral. She leads the boy forward step by step. She speaks "with guarded intent."

The meaning of *š*ᵉ*lamim* is disputed; it is commonly translated "peace offerings," "well-being offerings," or "communion offerings." These are a type of *zebaḥ*, the broader term for "sacrifice." They were offered and cooked by the lay public in the outer area of the temple, which is called "the entrance to the Tent of Meeting" in the Tabernacle ordinances (Lev 3:2; 8:33; Num 6:18).

today I paid my vows [n^e*daray*]: Earlier that day, she paid her vows, that is, made votive offerings (n^e*darim*, sg. *neder*). Vows may be paid by *š*^{e}*lamim* (Lev 7:16). Votive offerings are one of the three types of *š*^{e}*lamim*. According to the Priestly Code, animals intended for lay consumption were to be offered as *š*^{e}*lamim*. Most of the meat would revert to the offerer (Lev 17:15) and could be eaten on the day of the sacrifice and the next day (Lev 7:16). These offerings were of a celebratory character and expressive of joy. See further the survey by G. Anderson in ABD 5.878–79.

Since the woman could not eat the sacrificial meat in a state of ritual impurity (Lev 7:19–20), she may also be implying that she is not menstruating and is thus sexually available. We may wonder why this would matter to either party, since they are involved in a sin incomparably worse than violation of ritual purity. But people may be punctilious in ritual and taboo while shabby in ethics.

C. Camp (1991: 21) maintains that the woman in Prov 7 (though an unrealistic stereotype) is an Israelite who proposes to defile the sacred offerings by eating them in the state of impurity consequent upon intercourse, contrary to the law in Lev 7:19–20. However, the couple would be in a state of impurity only if they had sex *before* eating the sacrificial meat, and since the woman suggests debauchery "to dawn," it is not clear that any technical desecration would be involved. They could purify themselves by ablutions if they wished to continue to eat the *š*^{e}*lamim* the next evening. At any rate, there is no reason for the boy to find a solicitation to ritual desecration in any way tempting.

The reference to vows and *š*^{e}*lamim* has sometimes been thought to imply that the woman's sexual invitation involved a temple ritual and cultic prostitution. (This view was promoted mainly by G. Boström 1935: chapter 4, esp. 106–7.) This is surely unwarranted. The woman does not invite the boy to join in a cultic action or even to participate in a sacrifice. She claims that the offering was brought earlier in the day. (To translate *šillamti* ["I paid"] as a simple future, as Boström does, is contrary to Proverbs' usage.) The nondevoted portion of the meat is now available for dinner. The woman baits her trap with food, not religion. She uses the cultic details as an embellishment for her actual desires, thereby covering them in a thin religious veneer (Plöger).

7:15. *That's why I have come out to you, // to seek you eagerly—and I found you*!: lit. "eagerly to seek [l^e*šaḥer*] your face." Her explanation for being in the street ("that's why") is patently hollow. The fact that she paid her vows is no reason for her to have gone out looking for this youth. She flatters him by pretending that she went out in search of him specifically, as though she were attracted to him as an individual. In reality, as we know, she habitually roams about looking for sexual prey.

The two lines of this verse are not parallel but sequential, comprising two sentences. She came toward (*liqra't*) him in order to *seek* (l^e*šaḥer*) him. The verb *šḥr* means "to seek for" and also "to beseech" and connotes diligence and intensity of desire. With the added *paneyka* ("your face" or "presence"), it implies making a request. The skilled seducer plays to the boy's ego by claiming intense longing for him, him alone (cf. Alsheikh). She perverts the motif of seeking the beloved, which, in the Song of Songs, epitomizes the legitimate and pure longings of the Shulammite, who braves nocturnal dangers to seek her beloved until she finds and embraces him (Cant 3:1–4).

The verb *šḥr* (D-stem) is usually used of earnestly seeking God (e.g., Isa 26:9; Hos 5:15; Ps 63:2) and wisdom (Prov 1:28; Prov 8:17). Other uses too connote intensity of desire and diligence in the quest, as when used of wild asses seeking food in the desert (Job 24:5) or of God seeking Job after his death in Job 7:21, whose point is that no matter how zealously Job's friends seek him, they will not find him. The idiom *l^ešaḥēr pānîm* "to seek the face"/"presence" is a hapax. However, the synonymous *biqqēš pānîm* occurs eight times, always with reference to a fervent appeal to God (e.g., Hos 5:15; Ps 24:6, 27:8 [2×]; 105:4) or a ruler (Prov 29:26). The idiom *biqqēš pānîm* means not only "look for" but also "to seek favor." This is clear in Prov 29:26, "Many seek the face [= seek the favor] of the ruler, but a man's justice comes from the Lord"; sim. Hos 5:15. The idiom in the present verse, *l^ešaḥēr pānîm*, thus conflates two locutions, one (*šiḥēr*) implying eagerness and intensity, the other (*biqqēš pānîm*) an appeal or solicitation.

7:16. *I've decked my bed with covers*: The sexual innuendos of the invitation become unmistakable, though still oblique. The woman describes her bed with its expensive, imported coverlets, creating an air of sumptuous indulgence. The boy can picture himself luxuriating in her plush, fragrant bedding, all his senses pampered.

The covers, *marbadim*, are layered carpets laid on the *ʿereś*, the bed frame (see Deut 3:11). The *ʿereś* seems to have been used only as a bed, not as a divan for reclining at meals (that is a *miṭṭah* "couch," "divan"). The lovers in the Song of Songs call their "bed" under the trees their *ʿereś*, by which they mean the grass and leaves they are lying on, for it is "verdant" (1:16).

The root *r-b-d* is a by-form of *rpd* (Cant 3:10; Job 17:13).

dyed drapes of Egyptian linen [*ḥăṭubot ʾeṭun miṣrayim*]: The "drapes" are embroidered or multicolored cloth (cf. HALAT). Both *ḥăṭubot* and *ʾeṭyn* are hapax legomena, suggesting that the textiles were rarities in Israel.

There is no need to emend *ḥăṭubôt* to *hiṭṭîtî* (BHS), even if that was indeed read by LXX and Syr. The verb *hiṭṭāh* "stretch out" is not used of spreading coverings. *ʾēṭûn* is a loanword, from Egyptian *idmy* "red linen."

7:17. *myrrh, with aloes and cinnamon*: She now appeals to his olfactory imagination. Fragrant spices are an important motif in the Song of Songs (1:13; 3:6; 4:6, 11, 14–16; 5:5, 13) and the Egyptian love songs (e.g., nos. 8, 9, 20F in Fox 1985b). They are evocative of the sweet delights, emotional and physical, of love. The three spices the Strange Woman mentions are among the fragrances of the "garden" that is a metaphor for the girl's body in Cant 4:14. Myrrh, aloes, and cinnamon were imported from Arabia and the Far East and were very expensive. Spices were kept in the royal treasury (2 Kgs 20:13) and sprinkled on the royal couch (Cant 3:6–7). Literally to sprinkle them on a bed would be an extravagance, and the Strange Woman's claim might have been recognizable to the original readers as an exaggeration or an outright lie.

7:18. *Come, let's slake our thirst on love* [*nirweh dodim*]: Her invitation to sex is now unambiguous. The words in this verse, discussed at 5:19, allude to sexual intercourse. *Dodim* "love" always refers to physical lovemaking, from caresses to sexual intercourse. The idiom "to drink love" (with *šth* rather than *rwh* for "drink") occurs in Cant 5:1b, *šᵉtu wᵉšikru dodim* "Drink yourself drunk on caresses!" "Eating" alludes to sexual satisfaction in Prov 30:20. The noun *ʾŏhabim* (= *ʾăhabim*) "lovemaking" seems to mean coitus, not necessarily with emotional involvement; cf. Hos 8:9 (noted by Malbim). In Prov 5:19, it refers to marital sexuality. Likewise, the verb *ʾahab* "to love" can refer to simple lust; cf. 2 Sam 13:1.

7:19. *For the man's not at home*: lit. "in his house." The stark phrasing, "the man" (*haʾiš*) rather than "my husband" (*ʾiši* or *baʿăli*) seems to have a dismissive tone (Ramaq). The phrasing "his house" too is suggestive of alienation and emotional distance, for a woman's husband's house is normally called "her house" (e.g., Gen 39:14; Josh 2:15; Prov 31:21, 27) or "your house" (e.g., Josh 2:3; 1 Sam 25:35). Indeed, the narrator refers to the Strange Woman's home as "her house" in Prov 7:11.

Rashi, basing himself on *b. San.* 96b, identifies "the man" as God, who has removed his Shekinah from Israel. This gives an interesting picture of sin set in an atmosphere of national desperation, as in Ezek 8:12. While the national scope is irrelevant here, the insight that the woman feels deserted and neglected seems pertinent.

7:20. *A purse of money*: She indicates that her husband is on a long journey, for business in the neighborhood would not require carrying silver (Ehrlich).

The Strange Woman reassures the foolish youth that he won't get caught with her. Her remark calls to mind the risk of the husband's wrath, mentioned in 6:34–35. If she were a professional harlot, her husband would not attack her customers and jeopardize her intake, nor would it be to her advantage to remind them that there *is* a danger of getting caught.

mid-month: The *keseʾ* (= *kēseh* in Ps 81:4) is the day of the full moon. (The medievals, however, identify it as an appointed time or the new moon.) The deep darkness of the night of meeting (v 9) suggests that it is now on or near the new moon. Thus the woman is indicating that her husband will be away for another couple of weeks (Meinhold). There is no justification for associating the new moon with sacred marriage (*hieros gamos*), as G. Boström does (1935: 123–24). Certainly the woman is not proposing marriage, sacred or otherwise, but if she were, she would not have to deceive her lover, who would be taking the role of the goddess's husband.

7:21. *enticed* [*hiṭṭattu*] . . . misled [*taddiḥennu*]: Both verbs mean "cause to turn aside," "to sidetrack," that is, to deflect someone from the right path. The second verb retains the connotation of a physical shove.

with her soft "instruction": *leqaḥ* is elsewhere used of teaching or doctrine, as in 1:5 (q.v.). The word should not be assigned a unique meaning in this one occurrence, such as "seductive speech" (NRSV) or "eloquence" (JPSV). Rather, it is used in its usual sense—"doctrine," "instruction"—but said in a facetious tone. The words of seduction are, as it were, the Strange Woman's "doctrine," the negative counterpart of wisdom's teaching. The word *leqaḥ* often connotes (but does not denote) verbal fluency and persuasiveness (note esp. Prov 16:21b). See the comment on 1:5.

The words *liqaḥahh* ("her instruction") and *ḥeleq* ("slipperiness") are alliterative. In fact, they are transpositions of the same letters: *lqḥ—ḥlq*. Verse 21b resembles 26:28b, which condemns smooth talk generally: *upeh ḥalaq yaʿăśeh midḥeh* "and a smooth mouth causes stumbling."

smooth: This is an emendation of MT's *bᵉrob* "by the greatness of" to *bᵉrōk* lit. "by the smoothness of" (Tur-Sinai, p. 100).

The graphic difference (*b/k*) is minuscule in many scripts. The emendation makes better sense because it is not the quantity (*rōb*) of the woman's words that seduces the boy, but rather their soft, slippery quality (*rōk*). (*Leqaḥ* always denotes the words or substance of a teaching, not its quality, so that "great eloquence," though making sense in English, is misleading.) The equivalency of *ḥlq* and *rk* is shown by Ps 55:22, in which *ḥālᵉqu maḥmāʾôt pîw* (lit. "the flatteries of his mouth are smooth") is parallel to *rakkû dᵉbārāyw miššemen* ("his words are smoother than oil").

7:22. *Impulsively* [*pitʾom*]: lit. "suddenly." The ox and, especially, the stag and bird bound along to their death quickly and rashly and in ignorance of their fate. When Jeremiah says that he was like "a tame lamb led to slaughter" (11:19a), he means that he was ignorant of what was happening to him ("And I did not know that they were planning evil against me"; 19b). The suddenness with which the fool lurches toward sin is not incidental to his guilt. Aletti observes that "because seduction comes by means of the word, a gap always remains between the word and the act—a distance, that is to say, the possibility to reflect, to resist, even to desist" (1977: 140[172]). The fool rushes over the gap.

like a stag bounding to bonds: The MT is incomprehensible. The various attempts to translate without emendation are along the lines of the KJV: "or as a fool to the correction of the stocks." Radaq and other traditional commentators gloss *ʿekes* as "chain" and paraphrase: as they bring a fool running to prison [*musar*] and put him in chains. Malbim: "as a snake goes to afflict a fool"; that is, he is dangerous but makes a warning noise. But all such proposals are forced and unwarranted by the Hebrew. By a widely accepted emendation, supported by the LXX, we can translate "like a stag bounding to bonds." This is in harmony with the other similes and need not be deleted as an interpolation.

For MT's *ûkᵉʿekes ʾel mûsar ʾĕwîl* read *ûkᵉʿakkēs ʾel môsēr ʾayyāl*. The verb *ʿakkēs* appears in Isa 3:16b and 11QPs^a 22, 5. It means "gambol," "bound" (rather than "jangle," a denominative of *ʿekes* "anklet"). Both verses speak of a merry, lighthearted movement. The verb thus suggests that the stag is bounding along mindlessly and blithely. G. R. Driver (1932a: 143) points *kᵉʿăkōs*, from an unattested verb *ʿākas* "to tie." However, the phrase "as a stag is tied to a cord" would not reinforce the other images of

[172] "Parce que la séduction vient de la parole, un écart demeure toujours entre parole et exécution; une distance, c'est-à-dire la possibilité de réfléchir, de résister, de se désister même."

movement and suddenness. Also, the other two similes refer to the animals' behavior, not what happens *to* them.

7:23. The three lines in v 23 seem out of order. As it stands, v 23a refers to the trapped stag mentioned in v 22. However, v 23a interrupts the sequence of three similes. Nor does it make good sense to compare a fool rushing to death to "a stag bounding to bonds, till an arrow splits his liver," for the trap is irrelevant if the stag is shot down on the way to it. Moreover, a *trapped* stag would be butchered by a knife, not an arrow. Meinhold suggests that v 23a is a later insertion, though it is hard to see why the interpolator would have considered it necessary or helpful. It is likely that v 23a was displaced from the end of v 23 (Hitzig, Delitzsch, etc.). With v 23a at its end, the verse effectively culminates in the boy's death pictured in a dramatic image. Mention of his death is otherwise lacking from this section. Other images for the death of fools are a storm (1:27), a sword (5:4), and ropes (5:22).

7:23b. *like a bird*: A bird is the epitome of mindless gullibility (Hos 7:11) and of obliviousness to one's fate; see Prov 1:17. For Qohelet, all humans are "like birds caught in a trap" because they do not know the time of their death (9:12). For the sage of Prov 7, bird-brained folly means ignorance of knowable consequences and is not an inevitable human condition.

7:23c. *He wasn't aware that he'd pay with his life*: lit. "He did not know that it was by his life [*ki b*^e^*napšo hu'*]." "Pay" is implied by *b*^e^*napšo*, with the *bet* of price. The subject is the youth, not the bird, which is a feminine noun in Hebrew (Ps 102:8 is possibly, but not necessarily, an exception). Compare how Jeremiah likens himself to a lamb brought to slaughter and then explicates the simile by stating his own ignorance: *w*^e^*lo' yada'ti ki* "but I did not know that (Jer 11:19; see at v 22). The youth in the events of Prov 7 is as ignorant of where he is heading as these dumb animals are, but it is not an innocent ignorance. Fools are ignorant because they spurn wisdom. In contrast, the youth addressed in this lecture is gaining the knowledge that will save him, if he holds it in his heart. The assumption is that one who knows the ramifications of his sin will avoid it.

7:23a. *till an arrow split his liver*: This is distinct from the metaphors of slaughter and trapping. It is a figure for the death of the fool, who is one of those slain by the Strange Woman (7:26).

7:24–27. Conclusion

7:24. *So now, my sons*: After the long lesson, the father reiterates the call to attention. The plural "sons" is at variance with the singular "son" of v 1 as well as the singular forms in the next verse. An intrusive plural appears in 4:1 and 5:7 as well; see the comment on 4:1. The speaker fluctuates for no evident reason between the singular "son" of his ostensive audience and the plurality of youths who will learn from his words. Ramaq explains that "the people [of Israel] are like (Solomon's) sons."

7:25. *stray not upon her paths*: Judging from Gen 21:14; 37:15; and Ps 107:4, *ta'ah b-* means to wander or be lost *in* an area, rather than to stray *into* an area.

Hence v 25b is sequential: If you are attracted to her ways (25a), you will wander about in her crooked paths (25b), until you plunge into death (26–27).

7:26–27. Capstone. The Strange Woman's Danger.

7:26. *For many a victim she's laid low*: lit. "for many are the victims (that) she has cast down," with elision of the relative adjective. *Ḥălalim*, "victims," lit. "pierced ones," are casualties of violent death, usually in battle. The wording in this verse echoes the metaphor of death by arrow in v 23a, if that line refers to the adulterer, as proposed.

numerous: *ʿăṣumim* means both "numerous" and "mighty." The first sense is reinforced by v 26a, but the second also is relevant to the warning.

(that) she's laid low . . . slain: The Strange Woman is not only the occasion of death, she is the killer. She is not merely going astray with her victim, as his partner in befuddlement, but actively causing his death. She is leading him to slaughter like the butcher an ox, or pursuing his life like the hunter a stag, for she "hunts for a precious life" (6:26).

7:27. *Her house is the way to Sheol*: lit. "ways." Delitzsch renders: "A multiplicity of ways to hell is her house." The plural "ways" is used in reference to the collectivity of behaviors that characterize a person's life (see "Paths through Life," after chapter 2). The point is, if you enter her house, you are heading to death. Wisdom's house (8:34; 9:1) stands in contrast (Meinhold).

chambers of Death: "Death" = Sheol, the underworld, or (to the same effect) Mot, the Canaanite god of the underworld, of whom literary traces remain in the Bible. Sheol is divided into separate provinces or "chambers," sometimes numbered as seven. It is unclear who resides where, but the "depths" of Sheol (Prov 9:18) is considered the worst, and the uncircumcised seem to have their own chamber, in which they may be joined by the unburied casualties of battle (Ezek 31:18; 32:19, 21, 24; 32:25–26).

The Design of Lecture X

- I. Exordium (7:1–5)
  - A. Keep the teaching (1–3)
  - B. Make wisdom your companion, that she may protect you from the Strange Woman (4–5)
- II. The Lesson (7:6–23): The seduction of the simpleton
  - A. Encounter: What the teacher observed (6–13)
    1. The setting (6–9)
    2. The woman (10–13)
  - B. Seduction: What the woman said (14–20)
    1. The attractions at her home (14–17)
    2. The proposition (18–20)
  - C. Submission: What the boy did (21–23)
- III. Conclusion (24–27): The adulteress is deadly
  - A. Resumed exhortation: Listen to me, not to her (24–25)
  - B. Reason (capstone): Because she is deadly (26–27)

The lesson is subdivided with unusual regularity. The exordium consists of a six-couplet strophe + a two-couplet strophe. The lesson comprises five strophes (6–9; 10–13; 14–17; 18–20; 21–23), and the conclusion has two strophes of two couplets each (24–25; 26–27).

The Form of Lecture X

The lesson is in the form of a first-person narration, with a fairly long prologue (vv 6–13) setting the scene and describing the characters. A similar device is used in 24:30–34, where the teacher describes how he passed by the field of a lazy man and saw it overgrown with thorns, from which observation he draws a moral, namely an observation on the effects of laziness.

The lesson of Lecture X sets the scene and mediates the events through the perceptions of an observer rather than simply recounting them in a third-person report. The effect of this mediation is a heightened vividness. The reader is introduced into the scene and sees it with eyes of imagination. Moreover, the eyewitness report gives the observations the heightened validity and authenticity of something "seen with the eyes" rather than merely "heard with the ears" (as Job 42:5 puts it). We are invited to join in the narrator's voyeurism as he peers out the window on the dark street. Through his eyes we see the furtive assignation, and through his ears we hear the woman's lush and lewd inveiglements.

The little drama is lurid and alluring. The audience (which is to say, the male reader who is the assumed audience of the book) is lured into imagining the erotic delights offered the youth in the story: the kisses, the banquet the woman has prepared, her silky plush bedding, the sensual intoxication of a night of sex, passed in deceptive security in the husband's absence. The reader can surrender to fantasy, enjoy the titillation, relax into the vicarious eroticism, and imagine himself in that bed. Then, when his guard is down, reality slaps him in the face. He learns that the fool, whom the reader has joined in fancy, is actually lurching not to bliss but to butchery, rashly and mindlessly like a dumb animal.

The speaker does not see or report the results. The slaughter mentioned in v 22 lies in the future. He declares the inevitable disaster as something that can be taken for granted without observation or proof. The focus of this lecture is the seduction itself, whose powerful allure is described so that the reader may know what to beware of.

The Strange Woman

I. The Character of the Strange Woman

Much has been said about the mythological proportions of the Strange Woman, how she is a stereotype of women's evil and a symbol of vast chaotic and destructive powers and how she epitomizes "the Other." All this, in my view, is an egregious, if productive, overreading. The narrative in Lecture X displays the Strange

Woman in her particularity and human frailty. She is indeed dangerous, but at the same time rather pathetic.

Only in Lecture X is the Strange Woman portrayed as a personality and endowed with some suggestion of feelings and motives. To recognize that this portrayal is a deliberate characterization, we should consider that the personality of the woman in 7:6–23 is not the only one possible. The author might have shown a languorous, sultry femme fatale waiting for her prey; or a friendly neighbor concealing her seductive plans till the time is ripe; or a desperate nymphomaniac, who snatches at sex like Potiphar's wife; or a harlot, promising copulation without complications. The Strange Woman in Prov 7 is quite different. The author depicts a particular type of person, and even in his abhorrence for her he reveals a certain sensitivity to the forces that drive such a one to sin.

The woman's actions bespeak a deep disquiet, not a simple physical lust. Verse 11, which encapsulates her demeanor generally, and not only what she does during the seduction, states that she is *homiyyah*—noisy, turbulent (v 11)—and *soreret*—defiant and rebellious, presumably against the authority of her husband. She roams about the city incessantly—"now in the street, now in the plazas," lurking at *every* corner, like a hungry animal (v 12). Thus the seduction this night is but one of many. The woman's agitation may be sensed also in her overeager lurching from ambush (implied by the verb *ʾarab* in v 12b) to grab and kiss the boy even before exercising her verbal powers.

The woman seems desperate in her search for sexual satisfaction. Perhaps she is not getting it at home (v 19). But her relentless pursuit of sexual gratification suggests that she is not finding it in promiscuity either. Her husband's lengthy absence may contribute to her feeling of alienation from "the man" (v 19a) and push her on in joyless pursuit of gratification through sex.

The woman's long entreaty, with its inflated offer of all delectations, has an overwrought tone that seems driven by a need deeper than physical desire. And the statement of her husband's absence (vv 19–20) is longer and more insistent than necessary to allay the nervousness of the youth, who is, after all, being invited to spend a night, not half a month.

But understanding is not yet sympathy. Although the portrayal of the Strange Woman intimates some awareness of the distress and yearnings that might explain the woman's behavior, the author views her with unqualified repugnance. He does not envision the possibility that she might desist from her promiscuity and repent, nor does he care about the grievous consequences of her behavior for *her*. His motive for the subtle portrayal seems more rhetorical than humane. In order to make the danger realistic and memorable, he creates a plausible seduction scene and a believable seducer.

The Strange Woman emerges as a character in her own right, not merely a personification of sins and dangers. To be sure, in the conclusion (vv 26–27), the woman is described in nearly superhuman terms, as a mass murderer and an affiliate of the underworld. We should note, however, that the woman described in the conclusion is not quite identical to the one depicted in the narrative. The one the audience is told to beware of is someone *you*—the reader—might meet, not the woman in the exemplary tale of vv 6–23, who met the senseless lad. More precisely, the woman in the conclusion is the Strange Woman in the abstract, the paradigm of all adulterous tempters, of whom exemplars abound in real life. The hyperbole of the warning in the conclusion thus does not override the verisimilitude of the characterization in the lesson. Beneath her sensuous veneer and sumptuous promises, the Strange Woman in chapter 7 is sad and shabby—but no less a menace for that.

II. Allegorical-Symbolic Interpretations

One ancient hermeneutic still in vogue treats the Strange Woman as a cipher for other, more abstract dangers. This was especially popular among rabbinic commentators. They recognized the literal meaning, but were usually more interested in the figurative. Hameʾiri in particular carefully distinguishes the literal from the "hidden" meaning (*hannistar*).

The following allegorical correlations have been proposed for the Strange Woman or her qualities:

1. Folly and Wicked Counsels Generally

In the LXX of chapter 2, the "Strange Woman" disappears from v 16, while a reference to "evil counsel" appears in v 17. The evil counsel signifies the urgings of wicked people; see the Textual Note on 2:19.

At 5:5, the LXX identifies the woman as *aphrosynē* "folly." Meinhold offers a similar reading (see the comment on 5:3), and compare Newsom's interpretation (p. 257).

One of the Qumran covenanters, probably during the first century B.C.E., drew on the Strange Woman passages for a new poem that gives her truly mythic dimensions. She is called a prostitute, but the erotic nature of her seduction is muted in favor of her danger as a provocateur and rebel against God and a peril to the covenanted community, the *yaḥad*. Apparently she embodies all ideas to which the sect was hostile (4Q184).

2. Heresy, with Reference to Christianity

This is probably the most popular interpretation in traditional Jewish sources, starting with *b. ʿAb. Zar.* 17a, where the heresy in view is Christianity. R. Eliezer (*t. Ḥul.* 2:24) reads Prov 5:8 and 7:26 similarly.

Rashi identifies the *ʾiššah zarah* with "the heretical church" (*kenesiah šel ʾepiqorsut*), that is, Christianity, and also with heresy generally. He defends the allegorical reading by asking rhetorically, "What would the excellence of the Torah [wisdom] be if [Solomon] said here that it would save you from the adulteress alone and not from other transgressions?" In other words, avoidance of the adulteress is too narrow a benefit for what the context seems about to promise, whereas defection from Judaism encompasses all transgressions.

3. Foreign Wisdom

An addition to LXX in 9:12a–12c prepares the reader to perceive the "foolish woman" of 9:13–18 (who is identified with the Strange Woman in the LXX) as barren foreign territory, which should probably be understood as foreign doctrines and beliefs. Following the "Lady Folly" passage, a second addition, 9:18a–18d, identifies that same figure as foreign waters, which is a metaphor for gentile culture. These additions are discussed in the Textual Notes on 9:12 and 18. Cook maintains that this is the intention throughout the LXX's treatment of the Strange Woman (CSP 138, 285, 329, 332).

In the same spirit, Malbim identifies the Strange Woman with foreign philosophy, and M. Friedländer (1904: 68–76) equates her more specifically with Greek philosophy. Friedländer advocates an allegorical reading because he finds it strange that the wisdom teacher would launch such a powerful attack against a mere whore—"no longer in the first bloom of youth," no less—and set such a paltry figure in antithesis with Wisdom herself (p. 68).

M. Fishbane (1974: 44) construes 6:20–35 as an "inner-biblical midrash on the Decalogue," in which the foreign woman symbolizes the seduction of false wisdom; see the comment ad loc.

Several Church Fathers applied the figure to Greek education (Clement, *Strom.* I 5, 29, on Prov 5:3; sim. Clement, *Paedag.* III, 2, 9; Origen, *c. Cels.* IV, 44).

4. Material Pleasures or the Body (see at 7:6–23)

Some medieval interpreters associated the Strange Woman with aspects of materiality: physical, worldly, sensual pleasures (Saʿadia) or the body itself (Maimonides), which is beset by physical limitations and lusts for physical, material pleasures. Ralbag equates her with sensual desire—but also with the imaginative faculty. Hameʾiri pursues this hermeneutic most consistently. In his preface to Prov 6:20–7:27 and elsewhere, he says that the surface ("revealed") meaning of the Strange Woman passages is a warning against the prostitute, while the figurative ("hidden") meaning is an injunction to shun the attraction of worldly, material pleasures.

Similarly, Alsheikh explicates the Strange Woman as a cipher for the evil inclination, which basically means the sex drive. Cook (CSP 136–37) claims that the LXX implies this allegorical interpretation in Prov 2; see the Textual Note on 2:16–17.

5. The "Other"

Feminist interpreters have revived a form of the allegorical interpretation by decoding the Strange Woman as a symbol of the "radical other" or of "a variety of marginal discourses" (Newsom 1989: 149, 155). This approach is discussed in the next section.

See further the comments on the various Strange Woman passages.

Many commentators have enriched the homiletical signification of the Strange Woman by construing her as a symbol of a different or more extensive evil. But the very richness and pliancy of the allegorical hermeneutic is also its weak point: The Strange Woman can easily be expanded into a symbol of any evil one may wish. Nothing in the text controls the direction of expansion, which shows that the expansion is not continuous with the author's intention.

III. Feminist Readings of the Strange Woman

Feminist scholarship, starting in the late 1970s, has brought new perspectives and aims to Bible study. Among the various goals it has defined for itself are the unmasking of patriarchy, the recovery of suppressed female voices, the rehabilitation of biblical woman's image, and the evaluation of biblical mores and practices in the light of modern women's interests. Feminists eschew claims of objectivity and muster their scholarship in deliberate advocacy of women's interests.

Feminist interpreters have undertaken a reappraisal of the figure of the Strange Woman. She is one of the few female figures to receive extended portrayal in the Bible, and as the object of hostility for her sexual behavior, she seems to be a locus of gender conflict. I will discuss three vigorous and original feminist readings of the Strange Woman, particularly as she is portrayed in Prov 7.

1. A. Brenner and F. van Dijk-Hemmes, *On Gendering Texts* (1993)

Van Dijk-Hemmes and Brenner wish to recover the "F (female) voices" in the Bible. These are the traditions and cultural voices of women that can speak even through male-authored texts. Van Dijk-Hemmes and Brenner propose that the speaker in parts of Prov 1–9, and specifically in chapter 7 (not only in vv 14–20), is a woman.[173]

Their combined arguments (van Dijk-Hemmes's on pp. 57–62, Brenner's on pp. 117–26) are: (1) The mother's instruction is mentioned in 1:8 and 6:20, so the speaker in chapter 7 *could* be the mother. (2) Women sometimes give counsel elsewhere in the Bible (Gen 27; 2 Chr 22:2–3; 1 Kgs 21; Prov 31:1–9). (3) Looking out the window is a practice usually ascribed to women (2 Sam 6:16; 2 Kgs 9:30; Judg 5:28; and depicted in the Samaria ivories). (4) The speaker in Prov 7 remains inside the house, whereas "one suspects that a male teacher, less bound to societal conventions, would have rushed outside to get a closer look" (p. 120).[174]

Having recovered this "F voice," Brenner censures it for internalizing patriarchal values. The mother has traveled "the road from acceptance to rationalization, then ultimately to enforcement. . . . It appears that we read here not just complicity with androcentric values, not simply voiced conformity, but also overzealousness in protecting those values" (p. 125). She believes that "F self interest is silenced through identification with M interest" (p. 125), and that the "F voice" adopts the "M ideology" by recommending "control over fe-

[173]Brenner proposes (but does not actually argue for) the possibility that the entirety of Prov 1–9 is framed in an "F voice." She asks, "What if we adopt the readerly privilege of denying the 'father's instruction to son' genre for Prov 1–9 and 31?" (115). That is her privilege, but she offers no positive arguments for the denial. Brenner concedes that her proposal is not "'more correct'" (118) than the usual view, but given the reasons for regarding the frame speaker as male (see p. 258), it must be judged incorrect.

[174]Brenner and van Dijk-Hemmes might have added that the Septuagint identifies the person looking out the window as a woman, but as the Strange Woman, not the teacher (see the Textual Note to 7:6).

male sexuality" (p. 126). Van Dijk-Hemmes, however, proposes a deconstruction that (from the feminist standpoint) mitigates this subservience. She says that the F voice, having internalized androcentric discourse, "deconstructs its own position" by calling to mind negatively presented biblical figures who looked through windows, namely Michal, Jezebel, and Sisera's mother (p. 62).

2. Carol A. Newsom, "Woman and the Discourse of Patriarchal Wisdom" (1989)

The role of speech serves as the key in Newsom's exposure of the patriarchal worldview of Prov 1–9. For her reading of other passages, see the Commentary on 1:10–19, 20–33; and 2:1–22.

"Woman qua woman," according to Newsom, is the quintessential "other." She is a persistent irritant. "The strange woman figures the irreducible difference that prevents any discourse from establishing itself unproblematically." She is "the symbolic figure of a variety of marginal discourses" (pp. 148–49).

The father shows deep anxiety toward female sexuality: "In the father's phantasm the danger is that behind the reassuring smoothness, that visible absence of the phallus, there lurks something 'sharp as a two edged sword' (5:4)" (p. 153). The woman's potency is castrating, threatening to reverse the body symbolism on which the father's authority is established.

The Strange Woman has symbolic significance beyond her realistic image; she is an allegory of folly. She embodies many of the values that the wisdom tradition repudiates, and verses 24–27 expose her monstrous, mythic dimension.

3. Claudia Camp, "What's So Strange about the Strange Woman" (1991)[175]

In an earlier work, *Wisdom and the Feminine* (1985, esp. 112–20, 265–71), Camp argued that the Strange Woman symbolizes both an adulteress who threatens family stability and a foreign national who presents the danger of exogamy. The interpretation of *zarah* as "foreign," Camp conjectures, may have emerged with the arrival of Ezra and Nehemiah (p. 270).

In "Wise and Strange" (1988), Camp suggested that the trickster figure of folklore has been split between Lady Wisdom and the Strange Woman. The conclusions of the 1985 and 1988 studies are partly modified in her 1991 article.

Camp's main contention in "What's So Strange" is that the Strange Woman can be better understood as a metaphor: WOMAN IS A STRANGER. Woman-Stranger in Proverbs "is a full-blown force of evil, an evil that manifests death in sexual form" (26). She symbolizes forces deemed destructive to patriarchal control of family, property, and society.

The aim of Proverbs is social control of women's sexual behavior. The Strange Woman is a stranger in that she acts in ways that are alien to the family structure,

---

[175] J. E. McKinlay (1996, chapter 4 and *passim*) combines Camp's interpretation with the other feminist readings summarized here and seconds them. In the Strange Woman passages, "social boundaries are used to symbolize religious ones" (p. 97). But there is no symbolism in this regard. Marriage is a social boundary and at the same time a religious one, and not only a symbol thereof.

namely prostitution and adultery. "Because control of women's sexuality is a sine qua non of the patriarchal family, it is no accident that the forces of 'chaos' are embodied in a woman who takes control of her own sexuality" (p. 27).

Neither the Strange Woman's infidelity nor her cultic violations, Camp believes, are actual activities. The depiction of the woman is polemical, "an expression of male anxiety as one generation attempts to pass its ideology of control to the next" (p. 29).

4. Critique

Though diverging in some regards (such as the identity of the speaker in Prov 1–9), these three studies, as well as other feminist interpretations, share some essential viewpoints and may be commented on together.

a. Recovering the Female Voice. Brenner's and van Dijk-Hemmes's arguments on behalf of a woman speaker in Prov 1–9 presuppose some peculiar stereotypes about how men and women behave. In reality, men as well as women can look out windows, and men are no more likely to run into the street to get a closer look at a curious sight. In Gen 26:8, Abimelech looks out the window on Isaac and Rebekah "sporting" but does not run out and stare at them.

It is true that a woman *could* have spoken the very words of Prov 7. After all, mothers care no less than fathers about their sons' sexual behavior. But that does not mean that the speaker *is* a woman. In the entirety of extant Wisdom literature, with the exception of Prov 31:1–9, whenever we can determine the sex of the speaker, it is male (see pp. 83ff.). In Prov 4:1–4, the speaker is certainly a man quoting his own father (see comment to 4:1). The precedence of "father" to "mother" in parallelism (1:8; 6:20) shows that the speaker is identifying himself as the former and adding the latter for emphasis. The title in 1:1 ascribes at least chapters 1–9, and probably the entire book of Proverbs, to Solomon. There is no way the reader could be expected to recognize a sudden and unmarked switch to an unprecedented "F voice" in Prov 7 or anywhere else in Part I.

Although the discovery of a female teacher (besides Lady Wisdom) in the androcentric book of Proverbs would be most welcome, Newsom's judgment is more realistic:

> All readers of this text, whatever their actual identities, are called upon to take up the subject position of son in relation to an authoritative father. . . . The familiar scene, a father advising his son, is important. . . . *Ḥokmot* (personified wisdom) as an extension of the cultural voice that speaks through the father can be seen in the complementary authoritative position she occupies. (1989: 145–46)

b. Masculine Versus Feminine Interests and Values. The authors reviewed here share the belief that the Strange Woman passages seek to enforce specifically masculine, patriarchal values over female interests. Now there can be no dispute that the sages of Proverbs were androcentric and unabashedly patriarchal. But that does not mean that they are programmatically enforcing male supremacy and female subordination and marginality (hardly at issue for the ancient sages) or that they were in any way striving to silence women's voices.

There is no reason to classify the values motivating the author's antagonism to fornication as specifically masculine. Brenner assumes that there are certain invariable and universal feminine interests to which she, but apparently not the putative "F voice" in Prov 7, is privy. In my view, there is no way in which a woman speaker of Prov 7 (assuming that identification is correct) would be violating her self-interest as a female. Neither as mother nor wife would she benefit from male adultery. What broader female interests would be served if her son followed the example of the fool and went off with the adulteress? Is female promiscuity a trans-temporal feminist value? Feminine solidarity did not keep Lemuel's mother from warning him against dissipating his wealth on women (31:3).

Brenner's feeling that the speaker's loathing for adultery is excessive is an individual value judgment. But it is strange to ascribe concern for sexual ethics to men alone, or to assume that if women accept these and the other moral norms of their society, they do so as dupes of patriarchy (Brenner 1993: 125).

It is interesting that assigning the speaking voice in Prov 7 to a woman accomplishes little, since, as Brenner sees it, the recovered F voice ends up speaking M sentiments. Van Dijk-Hemmes's deconstructive reading is too convoluted to help much, since it presumes that the (male?) author has created a female persona as an advocate of androcentric positions, but then made her self-destruct and subvert this advocacy. In any case, the (very slender) association of the speaker with others who looked out windows—an act never considered illegitimate—hardly taints the speaker's reliability.

c. Woman as Other. Among feminist interpreters there is currently a consensus that Proverbs (like other biblical texts—and men generally) regards woman as the quintessential Other. "Woman Is a Stranger" is Camp's provocative summation of the patriarchal mentality. In my view, however, this mind-set is foreign to the book of Proverbs. There are a great many "others" to all of us. To each sex, the other sex is in some regards inevitably "other," but *woman's* otherness is not a special concern in Proverbs.

In Proverbs, there is indeed an essential Other: evildoers (and some kinds of fool) of both sexes. These are "the Other Side," as a rabbinic phrase calls the satanic realm). *This* Other is beyond influence and redemption, possessing an inverted and incorrigibly perverse set of values.

Women are not the "other" in such a radical sense. Though a man's own wife is "other" in the obvious sense of belonging to the other sex and having different social rights and roles, in the Bible she is, more significantly, his *own*. She is called "*your* well," "*your* source," "the wife of *your* youth" (Prov 5:16–18). From the woman's standpoint, her husband is "the companion of her youth" and partner to "the covenant of her God" (2:17). The Song of Songs epitomizes the relationship by the formula of mutual possession: "My beloved is mine and I am his" (Cant 2:16a). To a woman, any man besides her husband is a "strange man," an *allotrios andros* as Ben Sira calls him, translating *ʾîš zar* (23:23a; see pp. 140f.). To a man, other men's wives are all "strange" or "other" in the sense that *zarah* is used here, but women are hardly condemned for this "strangeness." Only a woman who fornicates is anathematized, not for being strange or "other" but for her decadent behavior.

This dichotomy has nothing to do with the "whore or goddess" syndrome often imputed to patriarchal thinking. For one thing, the wife is not necessarily saintly; for another, the dichotomy that Proverbs does pursue—fundamentally decent and proper people versus the indelibly wicked—embraces men no less than women.

Nor should the dichotomy be decoded as a class struggle. A Strange Woman may be poor or, like the one in Prov 7, well-to-do.

d. Sexual Anxieties and Hostilities. Female sexuality in itself is not problematic in Proverbs. As intriguing as Newsom's Freudian deciphering of 7:5 may be, these lips are on the Strange Woman's *mouth*, and her menace lies more in *exciting* than in spoiling masculine potency. Woman's sexuality, enjoyed within the marriage covenant, is not a menace but a blessing and joy (5:18).

e. Male Control of Female Sexuality. Feminist hermeneutics indefatigably discovers a single subtext throughout biblical literature: the reinforcement of patriarchy and the domination of female sexuality. That reading seems less strained in Prov 7 than in most places because the issue *is* sexuality and its control. Nevertheless, the author is not trying to control female sexuality. The Strange Woman (like the male evildoers in Prov 1:10–19; 2:12–16; 6:12–19) is beyond control, and the teacher makes no attempt to reach her sort. What's more, Proverbs makes no attempt to inculcate female chastity.[176] All discourse in Wisdom literature is directed at males, and it is their behavior that the authors of Proverbs wish to control.[177] We may be sure that many people—mothers, fathers, brothers (Cant 1:6), and husbands—tried to regulate female sexuality, but the book of Proverbs does not.

The moral evaluation of the Strange Woman's behavior (particularly in Camp's and Brenner's essays) is puzzling. It trivializes adultery to call the Strange Woman's promiscuity "[taking] control of her own sexuality" (Camp, p. 27) and "opting out" of the boundaries of male-controlled sexuality (p. 28), as though she were a proto-feminist rather than just dissolute. She does indeed threaten the patriarchal family; she threatens *every* kind of family. This is no less true of

---

[176] Ben Sira, by contrast, does offer counsel on controlling female sexuality: Keep a close watch on your daughter, pen her up in a windowless room, and don't allow her to converse with married women, lest she learn about sex from them (42:11–12b). Anii, interestingly, advises the reader not to control his wife, if she is reliable (AEL 2.143). The issue there, however, is not sexual.

[177] Even for males, admonitions about sexual behavior are infrequent outside Prov 1–9. Ptahhotep too warns his son against sexual transgressions: Do not approach the women of another household (§18; ll. 277–97; AEL 1.68) and avoid homosexual relations (§32; 457–62; omitted in AEL). The term used in the latter admonition is lit. "woman [f.]-child [m.]," that is to say, a catamite. Anii cautions against intimacy with a strange woman and counsels his son to have children while young (16.2–3; AEL 2.136). Chastisement for debauchery is a theme of Egyptian epistolary literature; see p. 207.

the man who indulges in adultery—and in Proverbs it is really he who is condemned.

It is true that Proverbs pays "no attention to the dangers to which women and their sexuality are subject in a patriarchal society" (Van Dijk-Hemmes, p. 61).[178] There are many meritorious things that Proverbs does not do.

The symbolic readings of this figure begin at least as early as the Septuagint; clearly something in the Strange Woman evokes this type of reading. But the feminist symbolic reading is subject to the same objections as other allegorical decodings, discussed previously. It is true that by the intensity of his description of the woman's evil the author comes very close to the boundary between literal and allegorical and prepares the way for symbolic interpretations, but that is not his intention. Allegory or symbolism is not *within* the text.

The Strange Woman represents the class of women who behave like her, and nothing indicates that she is a trope for some other disruptive and chaotic force or for all such forces. An ordinary adulteress is quite destructive enough. Other evils are not imputed to her, and to overgeneralize her meaning blunts the edge of her significance.

Certainly the Strange Woman is not a portrait of "every sexually liminal woman" (Camp 1985: 116), for, as Camp herself observes (pp. 113, 118), she is not a common harlot, but rather an adulteress, who is not "liminal"—on the border—but *over* the border. She is a type figure, representing any woman who behaves in her fashion. And, contrary to what Camp seems to believe, some do.[179]

f. Another Criticism. A more trenchant feminist critique might take its departure from the fact that Proverbs does *not* attempt to control female sexuality. No condemnation is addressed to the Strange Woman and her ilk, for it is assumed that such people are inherently and indelibly dissolute. Even more troubling is the way the authors of Proverbs neglect the control of the "normal" woman's sexuality. Proverbs never admonishes girls to avoid fornication or to be wary of seductive males. When Ben Sira takes up the topic (42:9–14; see n. 178), rather than demanding that females control their deportment, he instructs his son on how to regulate the sexual behavior of his wife (7:26; 25:13–26:18, *passim*, esp. 26:10–12) and daughter (7:24–25; 42:9–14), making no appeal to their own willpower and conscience. Pseudo-Phocylides (215–17) similarly advises the reader to lock up his virgin daughter.

Granted that Proverbs addresses males, the sages could still have informed young men of their responsibility in the moral education of *their* daughters, in

---

[178] Ben Sira does this, though not in a way that most of us would find satisfactory. He says that the dangers facing a daughter are that she may be sexually defiled and get pregnant before marriage, she may remain unmarried, or, if married, she may be barren or prove unfaithful to her husband (42:9–12).

[179] Against Camp's and other interpretations that introduce the issue of exogamy (see p. 48), we must note that the youth envisioned in chapter 5 is already married, as is the Strange Woman herself. Even if she is lying (in a twist on what we'd expect an adulterer to claim), her proposition would be a peculiar way to get the boy to marry her.

the way they charge them to educate their sons (Prov 19:18; 22:6; 29:17; cf. Ptahhotep ll. 564–74 [AEL 1.74]; 590–95 [AEL 1.75]; Duachety [Pap. Sallier II 11.4; AEL 2.191]). Taking people seriously as moral agents means making ethical demands of them and, when necessary, chastising them for failures. It is the neglect to do this for young women, and not the damning picture of the licentious female, that is most revealing of the sages' androcentrism.

IV. Overreading Is Misreading

Common to the allegorical interpretations, as well as to the foreign cult interpretation and some feminist readings, are certain presuppositions of a rather academic character: that "mere" fornication or even adultery is too incidental or narrow or banal a danger to warrant such solemn and extended admonitions, or that an ordinary slut would be an inadequate antithesis to Wisdom herself. Against the first assumption, we must note that sexual transgression is a very immediate and alluring danger facing young (and not-so-young) men, who are more likely to be led astray by desire for sex than by desire for a foreign philosophy or an indigenous heresy. The menace of sexual trespass is sufficiently grave to warrant the intensity of the warning it receives.

Contrary to the second assumption, the Strange Woman is the negative counterpart of the human wife, not of personified Lady Wisdom. The female antitheses in Part I are twofold:

(1) the Strange Woman	versus	one's own wife
↓		↓
(2) Personified folly	versus	personified wisdom

The vertical relationship is not personification, for Lady Folly (9:13–18) does not embody fornication but folly in its entirety, and Lady Wisdom is not a trope for qualities abstracted from the good wife. Rather, the vertical relationship represents the source of some of the features used in portraying imaginary entities.

In my view, the allegorical readings only blur the image's focus. It would be unconvincing to paint the lures and perils of heresy or Greek philosophy and the like in erotic terms because that is just not the way they are felt, nor would the warnings have impact if the dangers are to be read allegorically. A reader can easily see how adultery could cost him his life and can picture the raging husband or the contemptuous community. He can also understand, and feel, the sensuous tug and tickle of the woman's enticements: good food, silky bed covers, a safe and hidden tryst. All these vivid details must be overlooked (as Maimonides would do) or laboriously decoded (as Naḥmias does) when the Strange Woman passages are translated into a more abstract or intellectual evil or broadened to encompass evil and folly and chaos in their entirety. Still, the allegorical hermeneutic is legitimate as a homiletic strategy. It reuses biblical material in creating a new and distinct text with its own values.

INTERLUDE D. WISDOM'S SELF-PRAISE (8:1–36)

TRANSLATION

Wisdom traverses the city

8:1 Listen! isn't it Wisdom calling,
Good Sense raising her voice?
2 Atop the heights near the road,
at the crossroads, she takes her stand;
3 near the gates at the city entrance,
at the portals she cries aloud:

Wisdom's call

4 "To you, O men, I call,
my voice is to mankind.
5 Learn cunning, you who are callow,
and you dolts—put some sense in your heart!
6 Pay heed, for I have candid things to say,
the opening of my lips is rectitude,
7 for it is truth that my mouth declares,
and my lips loathe wickedness.
8 All the words of my mouth are in righteousness,
not one is contorted or warped.
9 The discerning man sees that they're all honest,
The knowledgeable know they are straight.
10 Take correction,[a] not silver,
and knowledge rather than choice gold,
11 for wisdom is better than rubies;
no valuables can match it.

Wisdom's character

12 I am Wisdom. I inhabit cunning;
knowledge of shrewdness I find.
13a ⟨The fear of the Lord means hating evil.⟩[b]
13b Pride and arrogance and wicked behavior,
13c and duplicitous speech do I hate.

Wisdom grants power

14 Mine are counsel and competence,
I am Understanding, power is mine.
15 By me kings reign,
and governors decree righteous laws.
16 By me princes rule,
so too nobles, all the judges of the earth.[c]

Wisdom grants wealth

17 I love those who love me,
and those who seek me find me.
18 Wealth and honor are with me,
enduring riches and righteousness.
19 ⟨Better my fruit than finest gold,
my yield than choice silver.⟩[b]
20 I walk in the way of righteousness,
within the paths of justice,
21 to grant wealth to those who love me,
their storehouses to fill.

Wisdom's beginnings

22 The Lord created me at the beginning of his way,
at the start of his works of old.
23 In primeval days I was formed,[d]
at the start, at the world's origin.
24 When there were yet no deeps I was born,
when there were yet no springs, sources of water.
25 Before the mountains were set down,
before the hills I was born,
26 ere he made the earth and the ground,
the land's first lumps of soil.
27 When he established the heavens, there was I,
when he inscribed a circle on the face of the deep,
28 when he secured the clouds on high,
when he strengthened[e] the founts of the deep,
29 when he marked the bounds of the sea,
that the waters transgress not his command,
when he firmed up[f] the foundations of the earth.
30 And I was near him, growing up,
and I was his delight day by day,
frolicking before him at all times,
31 frolicking in his habitable world.
And *my* delight is in mankind.

Her love for humanity

32 And now, my sons, listen to me.
Happy are they who keep to my ways!
33 Heed correction and become wise;
brush it not aside.
34 Happy is the man who listens to me,
keeping vigil at my doors day by day,
watching the posts of my portals!
35 For he who finds me finds life,
and obtains favor from the Lord.

36 But he who offends against me harms himself;
all those who hate me love death."

---

[a]*mûsār* (MT *mûsārî* "my instruction"). [b]Probably a later addition. [c]*ʾāreṣ* (Leningradensis, Aleppo, MSS, read *ṣedeq*). [d]*nᵉsakkōtî* (MT *nissaktî*). [e]*bᵉʿazzᵉzô* (MT *baʿăzôz*). [f]*bᵉḥazzᵉqô* (MT *bᵉḥûqô*).

COMMENTARY

8:1–3. The Setting: Wisdom's Public Call

This chapter stands in deliberate contrast to the preceding. Wisdom's invitation is opposed to the invitation of the Strange Woman. Chapter 7 declares the evils of the Strange Woman, who is to be shunned, while chapter 8 speaks in praise of Wisdom, to whom one should draw near (Naḥmias). Whereas the Strange Woman speaks in hushed tones in dark corners (a paradox, because she is rowdy), Wisdom proclaims her message in a bold voice in the most public of venues (Malbim).

The meaning of the wisdom personification is discussed in "Wisdom in the Wisdom Interludes" (Essay 4 at the end of this volume).

8:1. *Listen! isn't it Wisdom calling . . . ?*: The rhetorical question (with *haloʾ*) implies that an affirmative answer is obvious. The positioning of "wisdom" (*ḥokmah*) and "understanding" (*tᵉbunah*) before the verbs is emphatic: It is *Wisdom* calling. In other words, the sentence premises that *something* is calling, some voice is heard. But whose? It is, the author declares, surely Wisdom whose voice we hear everywhere, loud and clear—unless we perversely choose to stopple our ears. In naturalistic terms, wisdom's call is the power of reason, heard within the mind. "And man senses this voice in the depths of his soul, and he calls to understanding and brings her forth from his mind" (Malbim).

Good Sense (*tᵉbunah*) is another name for Wisdom. In v 14, she calls herself *binah*, intellectual penetration or insight.

8:2. *Atop the heights near the road* [*bᵉroʾš mᵉromim ʿăley darek*]: lit. "at the head of high places upon the road." These are the hills or high ground within the city (Radaq, Hameʾiri), the same place as *gappey mᵉromey qaret* "the tops of the city heights" (9:3), where Wisdom sends her maids to call from, and *mᵉromey qaret*, "the high places of the city," where Folly sits before her house (9:14).

"Heights *mᵉrômîm*: Some commentators (e.g., Meinhold) identify the *mᵉrômîm* as the city walls; others believe it means thoroughfares (Toy). But *mᵉrômîm* (used literally) denotes only natural high spots—hills or the heavens—not constructed high objects such as highways and city walls. While one can speak of the *mārôm* ("top") of a man-made structure (see Jer 51:53), only natural objects are themselves called *mᵉrômîm*). The phrase *rōʾš mᵉrômîm* is probably to be distinguished from *rōʾš derek*, the beginning of a road, which is usually where several roads converge, as in Ezek 21:26.

at the crossroads [*beyt nᵉtibot*]: lit. "between the paths" (or, literally, "house of the paths"). This refers to the same place as v 2a. "Between the paths" may be the point where several lanes diverge from the main road. A prostitute would station herself at a busy intersection (Ezek 16:25). Lady Wisdom gives herself the same visibility and exposure.

A *n^{e}tîb*, according to Malbim, is a secondary lane leading off the main roads. This definition is suggested, though not required, by some of the uses of the word in BH. Jer 18:15 rephrases *n^{e}tîb* as *derek lōʾ s^{e}lûlāh*, "a road not built up," i.e., not raised and leveled as major thoroughfares would be.

As the ancient versions recognized, *bêt* here is the equivalent of Aram *bêt* "between," "within." This usage is attested in Hebrew most clearly in Job 8:17; Ezek 41:9; and 2 Kgs 11:15. Wisdom is standing at the crossroads, where the paths converge; cf. Syr *byt ʾwrḥtʾ$^{pl.}$*, rendering *diexodoi tōn hodōn* in Matt 22:9 (some MSS). Those who understand *bêt* as "house" (Delitzsch, Meinhold) conjecture the same meaning for the phrase.

8:3. *near the gates* [*l^{e}yad š^{e}ʿarim*] *at the city entrance* [*l^{e}pîy qāret*]: This location is not the same as the city heights mentioned in v 2, for the gates would inevitably be farther down the hill or mound. Verse 3 speaks of places near the gates but outside the city walls, whereas v 2 refers to areas within them (Meinhold). The city gate, with benches and side chambers, was the center of social, commercial, and legal activity.

Qeret, a rare word for city (9:3, 14; 11:11; Job 29:7), is a Phoenician or Aramaic borrowing. *Peh* (lit. "mouth") is not used elsewhere for a gate entrance but is easily understandable in that sense.

at the portals [*m^{e}boʾ p^{e}taḥim*]: lit. the entry of the openings; in other words, not within the gate passageway or chambers, but at the outer opening of the gateway, where everyone entering or leaving the city or conducting business in the gate would hear the speaker. Both *l^{e}piy qaret* "at the city entrance" and *m^{e}boʾ p^{e}taḥim* "at the portals" describe the gate from an external perspective. "Openings" (*p^{e}taḥim*) are the apertures giving access to the gate proper, the *šaʿar*. This is where Absalom stood when he sought to curry favor with the populace. He stationed himself *ʿal yad derek haššaʿar*, "next to the road of the gate," and whenever someone came by with a dispute to present to the king, Absalom would call him over and ingratiate himself (2 Sam 15:2). Jeremiah is told to stand in "all the gates of Jerusalem" and address "the kings of Judah and all Judah and all the inhabitants of Jerusalem who enter these gates" (17:19–20).

Prov 8:2 elaborates on 1:21a (*b^{e}roʾš m^{e}romim* ≈ *b^{e}roʾš homiyyot*), and 8:3 reworks the phraseology of 1:21b (*l^{e}yad š^{e}ʿarim l^{e}piy qaret, m^{e}boʾ p^{e}taḥim taronnah* ≈ *b^{e}pitḥey š^{e}ʿarim baʿir*).

she cries aloud [*tārōnnāh*]: We might translate "crieth," since the form seems to be archaistic; see at 1:20. Zeraḥiah b. Shealtiel sees an interesting connection between this verb and 1 Kgs 22:36, "and the *rinnāh* [fem.] passed [masc.!] through the camp." Zeraḥiah says "this is the herald who proclaims matters of state." This comparison implies that in 8:1–3 (and 1:20–21), Wisdom is acting the part of a royal herald.[180]

---

[180]Zeraḥiah's proposal agrees with LXX's *stratokēryx* "army herald" for *hrnh* in 1 Kgs 22:36, on the basis of which some scholars (see BHS; HALAT) vocalize *hārōneh* "the caller." Possibly, however, *hārinnāh* is a metonymy with that sense.

If these identifications of locations are correct, Lady Wisdom is not delivering her speech in a single spot. Rather, she preaches in two distinct areas of similar character: at the high places within the city, whence the lanes branch out, and outside the city wall, at the entries to the gates. (Note the plurals, and compare the plural in Jer 17:20.) This means that the chapter is describing not a unique incident or sequence of events but an ongoing, typical occurrence. The scene and events are atemporal: Wisdom addresses mankind in all cities, inside and outside the city walls, in high places and low grounds, repeatedly and forever. Her city represents every city, and even the entirety of the inhabited world. Ancient Near Eastern mythology often represented the cosmos as a city, and some cities were regarded as microcosms of heaven and earth (L. Perdue 1994: 86).

Wisdom, as McKane notes, delivers her message where the competition is fiercest, not competition from other orators but from the everyday distractions of business, politics, and disputes. Far from being esoteric or academic, Wisdom plunges into the midst of this hustle and bustle to reach people where *they* are. The same accessibility is claimed for God's commandments in Deut 30:11–14.

8:4–11. Exordium: Wisdom's Precious Words

Wisdom's speech has four sections: (I) 4–11; (II) 12–21; (III) 22–31; and (IV) 32–36. The first section is a long exordium. It elaborates and radically reshapes the features of standard exordia to fit Wisdom as the speaker as well as the topic of the speech. Wisdom *addresses* the listeners, in this case all mankind, including the callow and the obtuse (v 4). She *exhorts* them to pay attention (vv 6, 10, renewed in 32–33), and she *motivates* the exhortation by praising wisdom, which is to say, herself (most of vv 6–21). In fact, the motivation of the exordium may be regarded as extending through v 31, since the self-praise of Wisdom continues, though in a very different way. The exordium, which normally lauds wisdom as a prelude to a specific lesson, is expanded into the dominant theme of the chapter. The same happens in Lecture II (chapter 2).

8:4. *To you, O men*: The frontal positioning of "to you" (*ʾălēykem*) is emphatic, making it the semantic predicate of the sentence. In other words, the issue is *to whom* Wisdom calls rather than *what* she does. Her audience is humanity in its entirety. However lofty her origins and status, Wisdom cares about people, even the less worthy, and seeks them out.

men [*ʾîšîm*] . . . *mankind* [*bᵉney ʾadam*]: On the basis of Ps 49:3, where the terms are parallel to "rich and poor," traditional commentators distinguish *ʾîšîm* and *bᵉney ʾadam* as the rich and the poor (Ramaq), or the more honored and the less (Hameʾiri and many), or the learned in Torah and the uneducated masses (Alsheikh). Though Isa 53:3 and Ps 141:4 disprove such distinctions, the two expressions together do connote totality. The pair "men" and "mankind" (lit. "sons of men") encompasses all nations and classes and demonstrates the universality of Wisdom, "who seeks her disciples among Jews and Greeks, learned and unlearned" (Toy). The breadth of this audience is similar to that in Psalm 49:3, which is an exordium in the wisdom mode in which the speaker promises to declare *ḥokmot* and *tᵉbunot*, "wise things" and "understanding things."

The rare plural *ʾîšîm* "men" appears only in those verses just mentioned. This seems like a Phoenicianism, since the standard plural in Phoenician and Punic is *ʾšm*.

8:5. *you who are callow* [*pᵉtaʾim*] . . . *dolts* [*kᵉsilim*]: (The Hebrew has simply "callow," "dolts.") Wisdom first addresses all mankind (v 4), then the gullible and thickheaded, without thereby restricting the audience to the latter. In Interlude A (1:20–33), these two types, along with the impudent (*leṣim*), are the ostensible audience, and they are presumed to have already rejected Wisdom's call. In Interlude D, the callow and dull (but not the impudent) are included in the wider audience and admonished to learn good sense. This may indicate that, in principle, they are not beyond redemption (Meinhold). But perhaps Lady Wisdom, like a prophet, is morally obliged to deliver her message even to those who will not or cannot absorb it (cf. Isa 6:8–10; Ezek 2:3–5; 3:7).

Learn cunning [*habinu ʿormah*]: lit. "understand cunning." On *ʿormah*, see "Words for Wisdom," §7, and the comment on 1:4. It is precisely *ʿormah* that the *peti* lacks (1:4; 19:25). This faculty, even without deep wisdom, would enable an inexperienced and unsophisticated youth to avoid thoughtless and harmful behavior.

put some sense in your heart [*habinu leb*]: The closest English equivalent to Hebrew *leb* is "mind," which is the organ of cognition and memory as well as the locus of emotion. See the discussion at 2:2. The verb *hebin* in this verse does not have its usual meaning of "understand." Delitzsch explains: "Apprehend . . . what wisdom is and . . . what understanding is." But to say that the callow boy must "understand" or "apprehend" cunning or heart would imply that the untutored youngster is to pursue the study of epistemology, which is surely not his task at this stage. Nor, given the parallel with *habinu ʿormah*, is the verb in v 5b causative in the sense of "make (someone) understand," "teach" (Hameʾiri's first explanation). Rather, the listeners are exhorted to *acquire* cunning and intelligence ("heart") in an understanding, perceptive way, with the direct object "heart"/"mind" indicating the substance of the teaching.

When the dir. obj. of *hēbîn* is an intellectual-spiritual faculty, the verb means to *acquire* or *possess* its object in a perceptive, intelligent way. Prov 29:7 says that "the wicked man does not 'understand knowledge' [*yābîn dāʿat*]"; his failure lies not in lacking a grounding in epistemology but in lacking knowledge itself. In 19:25, *yābîn dāʿat* is parallel to the internal H-stem *yaʿrîm*, "become clever"—a change within the subject rather than a change that the subject effects in something else; compare *mᵉbînê maddāʿ* (lit. "those who understand knowledge") in Dan 1:4. Other verbs of cognition behave similarly. *Yādaʿ bînāh* means to *have* understanding, not to "know" understanding (Job 38:4; Prov 4:1; Isa 29:24; 1 Chr 12:33; 2 Chr 2:11 [+ *śēkel ûbînāh*]; 2 Chr 2:12). *Yādaʿ daʿat* is similar; see most clearly Num 24:16; Prov 17:27; and Dan 1:4. *Yādaʿ ḥokmāh* means to *get* wisdom; see esp. Prov 24:14, where "knowing" wisdom is equivalent to "finding" or "attaining" it (*māṣāʾ*). When *ḥokmāh* refers to the teachings themselves, however, as in Prov 1:2, then *yādaʿ* or *hēbîn ḥokmāh* means to understand or learn them.

8:6. *candid things*: N^{e}gidim (only here in this sense) means honest or forthright things, things that are directly before (*neged*) a person. This is supported by the parallel with *meyšarim* and the fact that vv 6–9 are entirely concerned with the honesty and truth of wisdom rather than with its nobility.

The rendering of *n^{e}gîdîm* as "candid things" (which is similar to Syr's *šryrtʾ* "truth") assumes a semantic analogy: *n^{e}gîdîm* is to *neged* as *n^{e}kōḥîm* "honest" (v 9) is to the preposition *nōkaḥ*, which, like *neged*, means "opposite," "in front of." The original vocalization was probably *n^{e}gādîm*, the pl. of *neged* (Grollenberg 1952: 41). MT's *n^{e}gîdîm* parses the word as the pl. of *nāgîd* "prince." Most commentators, medieval and modern, likewise derive the word from *nāgîd* "leader," "prince," hence "princely things"; so too, apparently, LXX's *semna* "august things." This could be supported by the analogy of *nādîb* "noble" and *n^{e}dîbôt* "noble things," the latter being the object of *yāʿaṣ* "counsel" in Isa 32:8. Hameʾiri derives the word from Aramaic *n^{e}gād* "pull"; hence *n^{e}gîdîm* are words that *attract* the heart. However, *n^{e}gîdîm* is a stative formation.

the opening of my lips is rectitude: "Opening," judging from 1 Chr 9:27 and the noun pattern of *miptaḥ*, means the place of opening rather than the act of opening. At the very point where Wisdom's lips part, truth is to be found.

8:7. *for it is truth*: This motivates the call to attention in v 6a. "Truth" (*ʾĕmet*) is in the emphatic frontal position, placed, so to speak, in italics: What wisdom speaks is *truth*, nothing else. The basic senses of *ʾĕmet* are "reliable" and (by extension) "true." Given that *ḥokmah* (and certainly its neighbor *ʿormah*) can designate amoral cleverness, the claim of this verse is by no means self-evident. It is axiomatic in Proverbs that genuine intelligence is inherently and inevitably honest. The equation of truth and wisdom does, however, have parallels, as in Ps 51:8 [Eng. 6], "Behold, you desire truth in the inward parts, so teach me wisdom in secret."

my lips loathe wickedness: Lit. "the abomination of my lips is wickedness." This is a vivid figure for the incompatibility of wise speech and evil words. Compare the ascription of emotion to the palate in Job 6:30.

The LXX's "My abomination is wicked lips" reflects Heb *twʿbty śpty ršʿ*. Toy et al. emend to this. (BHS's emendation to *w^{e}tôʿēbāh lî śiptê rešaʿ* is contrary to normal construction.) On the one hand, LXX's reading may seem more logical, since lips do not have feelings, and that "logic" may have produced the reading. Favoring MT, however, is the fact that the purpose of vv 6–9 is to motivate Wisdom's call for attention, and thus it is more pertinent to praise the speech of Wisdom (MT) than of humans (LXX).

8:8. *are in righteousness*: that is, are spoken in righteousness.

not one is contorted [*niptal*] *or warped* [*ʿiqqeš*]: The roots *p-t-l* and *ʿ-q-š* are paired also in Deut 32:5 and 2 Sam 22:27 (= Ps 18:27). "Contorted" (*niptal*) in a physical sense means twisted or braided, like strands of a cord (a *p^{e}til*). Twisting is an image of trickiness. Wily men are *niptalim* (Job 5:13), and God himself can be tricky with the warped man, the *ʿiqqeš* (2 Sam 22:27). The word *ʿiqqeš* means bent or crooked, as a road may be (Prov 2:15; 10:9; 28:6), hence warped or perverse. This is also used of the heart (Ps 101:4; Prov 11:20; 17:20) and of the mouth and lips (4:24; 6:12; 19:1). The physical imagery of ethics throughout

Prov 1–9 is consistent: Honesty is bright, straight, directly to the front. Dishonesty is dark, crooked, and off to the side—a departure from the right and bright path.

A comparison between Job 5:13 and this verse highlights the distinctiveness of Proverbs' concept of wisdom. Eliphaz says that God "captures the wise (*ḥăkamim*) in their cunning, and the plans of tricky men (*niptalim*) are dashed." Eliphaz (whose discourses have many sapiential features) can place *ḥăkamim* and *niptalim* in synonymous parallelism in referring to the same type of people: those whose plans can offend God. (More precisely, *niptalim* narrows the scope of *ḥăkamim*: those wise men who are tricky.) In Prov 8:8, in contrast, Wisdom insists that she speaks only true, straight things; never a contorted word. And as Wisdom speaks, so do the wise, all of them.

8:9. *The discerning man sees that they're all honest*: lit. "They are all honest (*nᵉkoḥim*) to the discerning man (*mebin*)." The preposition *nokaḥ* means "opposite," "straight ahead." The adjective/substantive *nakoaḥ* is almost always used metaphorically in the sense of forthright and honest. "Honesty"—*nᵉkoḥah*—is another name for personified truth (*ʾĕmet*) in Isa 59:14. Isa 30:10 contrasts prophecies that are "honest" (*nᵉkoḥot*) with "slippery things" (*ḥălaqot*) and "illusions" (*mahătallot*).

the knowledgeable [pl.] *know they are straight*: lit. "and (they) are straight to those who find knowledge [*moṣᵉʾey daʿat*]." Knowledge is not innate; to have it requires "finding" it. Wisdom herself "finds" knowledge (8:12), and those who seek wisdom "find" her (v 17). But one must undertake the quest with the proper root values—the fear of God and the desire for wisdom and righteousness—even before being tutored in them.

The real issue in this verse is not so much the truth of Wisdom's words (which is declared in vv 6–8) as how they are to be perceived. Riyqam points out the gist of the verse by stating its obverse: "But in the eyes of the fool they will seem contrary and contradictory to one another." In Toy's words, "The world is divided into the two classes of the wise and the fools, and whether one will understand the truth depends on which class he belongs to." This, he says, is "a direct insight of the conscience." Conscience, in Proverbs, is an intellectual faculty (see 1:7), hence a property of the discerning and knowledgeable.

8:10. *Take correction*: "Take" (*qaḥ*) means both "choose" (Ehrlich) and (especially in the idiom *laqaḥ musar*) "take to heart"; see the comment on 1:3. *Musar* means corrective instruction. Here its application is extended to moral instruction generally; see "Words for Wisdom," §6.

LXX's reading *mûsār* provides a better parallel to the undetermined *daʿat* "knowledge" than does MT's *mûsārî* "my instruction," which is probably a *y/w* dittography.

silver . . . choice gold: Essentially the same comparison appears in 3:14; 8:19; and 16:16. By form, v 10a is an elliptical vetitive introduced by *wᵉʾal* "and do not," but its sense is comparative: "rather than" or "above" silver. The verse does not teach the avoidance of wealth but sets it above legitimately valued items—silver and (even) fine gold.

8:11. *for wisdom is better* . . . : A variant of 3:15, q.v. "Valuables" (*ḥăpaṣim*) are, literally, "desired objects." In Hame'iri's paraphrase, "Even if you acquire all that you desire in the world, it is worth nothing in comparison with wisdom."

This verse praises wisdom in a passage spoken *by* Wisdom. This apparent circularity has led some to excise it as an interpolation (Skehan 1979: 368; Meinhold). But the verse works well as a proverb cited to support the preceding advice and to cap off the first section of Wisdom's speech. Since variants of vv 10–11 appear elsewhere, these verses give the impression of being existing apothegms incorporated into Lady Wisdom's speech.

8:12–21. Wisdom's Benefits to Society and Individuals

After introducing herself and proclaiming her powers (vv 12 + 13bc), Wisdom commends herself as the fount of statecraft, thus of ordered society itself (vv 14–16), and as the source of wealth for her followers (vv 18–21). The second and third strophes are introduced by general affirmations of Wisdom's qualities—her practical intelligence (vv 12 + 13bc) and her generosity (v 17).

8:12–13. Wisdom's Character

8:12. *I am Wisdom*: Or "I, Wisdom, inhabit cunning." The second rendering is the usual one. The first, which is adopted here, resembles the self-identification in numerous royal inscriptions and divine declarations, such as "I am Kilamuwa son of Hayya"; "I am Azitawadda, blessed by Baal"; "I am Isis the divine." Meinhold compares the self-revelation formula, "I am Yahweh" (Exod 6:2; Lev 19:18; etc.). And indeed, Wisdom's speech has several features in common with divine self-revelation texts; see later "Models for Wisdom: The Goddess Isis," pp. 336ff.

inhabit cunning: Wisdom does not say that she *is* cunning, but that she "inhabits" cunning; in other words, she has an abiding connection to it but is not precisely equated with it. Wisdom has, as it were, moved into the territory of *ʿormah* and made it her own. Similarly, Wisdom "finds" shrewdness (*m^ezimmot*) (v 12b)—meaning that they are related but distinct.

I inhabit cunning: *šakanti ʿormah*, with no preposition. The verb *šākan* + accusative elsewhere means "inhabit," i.e., dwell *in* or *at* (e.g., 2:21; 10:30; Isa 33:16; Job 4:19), not *nearby* or *with* (the obscure Ps 68:19b is a possible exception). For MT's *šākantî*, Ehrlich, Kuhn, BHS, et al., propose *šĕkentî*, "my neighbor." This is possible but not preferable because the rest of the section speaks only about wisdom, not about other entities in relation to wisdom. By the emended reading, cunning too is personified, which seems extraneous.

Saʿadia defines *ʿormah* here as understanding and cleverness in obedience to God. This pietistic, ad hoc interpretation of *ʿormah* reemerges in renderings like "prudence" in KJV, JPSV, and NRSV. On *ʿormah* see "Words for Wisdom," §7.

knowledge of shrewdness: Shrewdness, *m^ezimmot*, is the "thought hidden in the heart" (Ramaq). It can be manifested as desirable circumspection as well as devious scheming; see "Words for Wisdom," §5. The Prologue promises cunning and knowledge of shrewdness to those who study the book.

I find [*ʾemṣaʾ*]: Or "attain." We might expect a statement of possession rather than attainment. After all, wasn't Wisdom *born* shrewd? But *maṣaʾ* is an ingressive verb, marking the beginning of an action or state. It does not mean "possess," which is an enduring (or constative) action with no reference to the starting point. Wisdom is describing herself in terms of a wise human being, and an attribute of the wise is that they can gain or "find" knowledge. The wise are those who have "found knowledge" (8:9). "Finding" knowledge of various sorts is the consequence of the learning process, according to Prov 2:5; 24:14; and Sir 51:16.

The revocalization of *ʾemṣāʾ* to *ʾemmāṣēʾ* "am found" (HALAT et al.; cf. BHS) may seem to provide a better parallel to *šākantî*. However, the N-stem of *m-ṣ-ʾ* requires *šām* (Isa 35:9) or *b-* when indicating location (e.g., Deut 17:2; Jer 5:26; Isa 51:3; Prov 10:13).

8:13a. *The fear of the Lord means hating evil*: lit. "is hating [*śᵉnot*, infin.] evil." Verse 13a is probably a pietistic insertion intended to counterbalance the possibly amoral overtones of cunning and shrewdness. The line interrupts the connection between vv 12 and 14, which speak of the excellence of wisdom, and it has nothing to do with the rest of the interlude, which does not aim at inculcating the proper attitude toward God. Some commentators excise v 13 in its entirety (e.g., Toy, Meinhold), but v 13bc is probably original (Plöger).

This couplet actually belongs to Wisdom's self-praise, as she is commending her own moral standards. Camp (1985: 95) believes that v 13, as well as the words "[the woman] who fears the Lord" in 31:30 (where LXX reads *nbwnh* "understanding") are later additions by an editor who saw parallels between Lady Wisdom and the Excellent Woman. The more likely motive of the addition in 8:13 is to strengthen the identification of wisdom with piety. This identification is emphasized in 9:10, which is also a later addition.

8:13bc. *Pride and arrogance*: The paronomastic cognate pair *geʾah wᵉgaʾon* connotes totality: "every sort of pride."

wicked behavior: "Behavior" (*derek*) is literally "way," that is, a way of living.

and duplicitous speech do I hate: lit. "and I hate the mouth of turnings-about" (*tahpukot*; see the comment on 2:12). The verb is delayed till the end of the sentence, after the four direct objects (cf. 3:2). Having claimed the morally ambiguous faculties of cunning and shrewdness, Lady Wisdom quickly disavows the duplicity that often accompanies them.

8:14–16. Wisdom's Contribution to Statecraft

8:14. *Mine are counsel* [*ʿeṣah*] *and competence* [*tušiyyah*]: Radaq paraphrases nicely: "With me are the ability and precision of observation to give good advice, and I have the potency and the advantages wherewith to bring (people) profit." The latter part of the sentence is a good gloss on *tušiyyah*, which denotes clear, efficient thinking in the exercise of power and practical operations, as distinct from thinking as an intellectual act. "Counsel" (*ʿeṣah*) is not only advice, but the capability for deliberation and planning.

I am Understanding [*ʾăni binah*]: ("Understanding" is a noun.) This can be translated either "I, Understanding, have . . ." or "I am Understanding. I have. . ." (compare v 12). Wisdom identifies herself between two statements of possession, *li ʿeṣah wᵉtušiyyah* "Mine are counsel and competence" and *li gᵉburah* "I am Understanding, power is mine."

ʾănî bînāh: Various measures have been suggested to make this a statement of possession. Toy, following LXX and Syr, emends *ʾănî* to the rather distant *lî* (BHS) and translates "understanding is mine." Plöger parses *ʾănî* as a proleptic subject: "ich—ich besitze Einsicht und Kraft" ("I—I possess insight and power"). These measures, however, overlook the fact that *bînāh* is not in the same category as the other three qualities. Counsel, competence, and power are faculties that wisdom possesses and embraces, whereas she *is* Understanding. Wisdom is called *bînāh* in 2:3 (in which wisdom is implicitly personified); 4:5; and 4:7 (note that *ḥokmāh* and *bînāh* together form the antecedent of the singular pronouns in vv 6 and 8).

Counsel, competence, and power are the faculties of statecraft, wielded by effective rulers to achieve their goals. They are not inherently ethical attributes, though they may and should be employed justly. The ideal king is described in similar terms in Isa 11:2: "And there shall descend upon him the spirit of the Lord, the spirit of wisdom and understanding, the spirit of counsel and power, the spirit of knowledge and the fear of the Lord." ("Spirit" *ruaḥ* could be translated "faculty.") Plöger observes that in Prov 8, wisdom stands in place of the gift of spirit.

Cazelles (1959: 515) appeals to Isa 11:2 in arguing that Wisdom presents herself as specifically royal wisdom. But though the faculties listed there are desirable in a king, they are not confined to royalty and are not in themselves marks of kingship. Job ascribes wisdom, counsel, power, and practical sense (*ḥokmah, ʿeṣah, gᵉburah, tᵉbunah*) as well as competence (*tušiyyah*) to God (12:13, 16), who wields them aggressively (vv 14–21).

The martial efficacy of wisdom is asserted in Prov 21:22 as well: "The wise man went up against the city of the mighty (*gibborim*) and brought down its strong fortresses"; similarly Qoh 7:19. The faculties of *ʿeṣah* and *gᵉburah* overlap insofar as in war one should deliberate and employ stratagems as well as use force (Prov 20:18).

McKane locates the terms of v 14 in the "old wisdom," in accordance with his dichotomy between the old, practical wisdom of statecraft and the later, religious wisdom of Yahwistic piety. In my view, these are simply different aspects of wisdom and not time-bound. In any case, the passage is not giving advice about statecraft but praising wisdom for its contributions to that realm.

8:15. *kings reign*: The clause *bi mᵉlakim yimloku* is paronomastic.

and governors decree righteous laws: The exact meaning of *rozᵉnim* ("governors" or the like) is unknown. The word is always parallel to "kings," except in Isa 40:23, where it parallels "judges of the earth" (*šopᵉtey ʾereṣ*, as in Prov 8:16b). It always refers to foreign officials. "Decree" *yᵉḥoqᵉqu* probably refers to the promulgation of written ordinances, since the root-meaning of the verb is "to engrave," "inscribe," and *ḥ-q-q* is three times parallel to "write" (Job 19:23; Isa 10:1; 30:8). "Righteous laws" is lit. "righteousness" *ṣedeq*.

8:16. *By me princes rule*: The clause *bi śarim yaśoru* is paronomastic. In the quatrain in vv 15–16, the author couples lines that are paronomastic (vv 15a, 16a) with ones that are not (15b, 16b), thus linking the couplets without producing a distracting jingle.

so too nobles, all the judges of the earth: Hebrew *nadib*, like English "noble," can mean either a man of the ruling class (as here) or a person who is generous and gracious. A "judge" *šopeṭ* has duties in public administration and leadership as well as in forensic judgment. All the earth's judges embraces all types of governors.

earth (*ʾāreṣ*): Leningradensis, Aleppo, and most printed editions have *ṣedeq*, "righteousness." Cod. Hillel and some editions have *ʾāreṣ* "earth" (= LXX, Vul). The latter is an inner-Masoretic variant (see the Textual Note). "Earth" is preferable from the literary standpoint because the parallel words in vv 15–16 are not terms for *righteous* officeholders. "Righteous" may be a deliberate modification to avoid attributing wisdom to gentile princes, because "judges of righteousness" could be understood as confined to Israelite rulers. The phrase *šōpṭê ʾereṣ* appears in Isa 40:23 (// *rôzᵉnîm*); Ps 2:10 (// *mᵉlākîm*); and Ps 148:11 (// *malkê ʾereṣ*, collocated with *śārîm*).

Verses 15–16 are not claiming that all kings and princes actually rule wisely or mandate righteous laws—no one would suppose that—but rather that wisdom is the principle of rulership, and effective governance depends on it. Thus the verb *malak* "reign," parallel to "decree *righteous* laws [*ṣedeq*]," must be understood here in a positive sense: not merely to exercise power, but to do so effectively and justly. (Ehrlich says that *yimloku* has *ṣedeq* as its complement, but this is dubious syntax, and the parallelism in itself can have the same adverbial effect on the first verb.) Nor is the intent to advise rulers to employ wisdom; the interlude offers no specific counsels and is not addressed to rulers. Rather, the quatrain is a continuation of Lady Wisdom's declaration of the benefits of which she is the conduit.

The universalism of 8:12–16, which is implicit throughout the interlude, is remarkable. The author recognizes that the potentates of all nations have access to wisdom and can exercise it in ruling justly. Whereas according to Ben Sira 24 and Baruch 3, wisdom finds no home among the gentiles and so takes up residence in Israel, the author of Prov 8 makes no such restriction. Contrast too the hostility toward gentile rulers (called *mᵉlakim* and *rozᵉnim*, as here) expressed in Ps 2:1–2: "Why do the nations make an uproar, and the peoples utter emptiness, the kings of the earth take a stand, and the governors take counsel together, against Yahweh and his anointed?" Although not assuming that all rulers are righteous, the author of Interlude D does flatter gentile potentates to the extent of assuming that the principle of their rule is wisdom.

Another peculiarity of the book of Proverbs is prominent in this passage: The principle of righteous rulership is under the dispensation of wisdom, which disposes of the practical political faculties as well. Other books do not assign precedence to wisdom over either ethical merit or practical intelligence. In

Isa 11:2, the faculty of wisdom is one of several qualities and powers to be bestowed on the king; it is not the primary category subsuming the others. Isa 32:1–8 does not assume that rectitude in governance is an inevitable concomitant of wisdom. This is in spite of that passage's affinities with Wisdom literature, including the use of some of the same vocabulary as Prov 8:15–16 in describing the ideal future monarch: *hen lᵉṣedeq yimlok melek, uśarim* [MT *wlśrym*] *lᵉmišpaṭ yaśoru*, "Behold the king shall reign by righteousness, and princes rule by justice" (Isa 32:1). Job includes wisdom among God's powers (12:13, 16), but only as one of several divine forces. In contrast, the author of Prov 8 subsumes all political virtues and faculties to wisdom by making it their fount and possessor.

8:17–21. Wisdom's Material Benefits

8:17. *I love* . . . : Like Prov 2 as a whole, this verse offers encouragement to the neophyte. Radaq paraphrases: "Let no one say, I strove but did not find." Hameʾiri elaborates: "The intent of the statement is that man should not slack off from study, fearing lest he not succeed because of the weight of the burden in the task of study, which requires much time and lengthy preparations." He who goes toward wisdom may be confident that learning will become progressively easier, for his mentality will conform itself to wisdom and come to absorb it more easily. "Love" is the emotion that embodies this process because, as Hameʾiri observes: "It is known that the definition of love is the convergence and uniting of minds, that is, their concurrence in a single opinion."

I love those who love me: The love that binds wisdom to her adherents is a notable theme in Proverbs, particularly in Part I (elsewhere only in 12:1 and 29:3, but implicit in several verses). This theme is given great prominence in Ben Sira but is scarcely attested in foreign Wisdom literature.

ʾēhāb "I love" is first sg., with elision of the radical *ʾaleph* and contraction of the first two vowels (GKC §68*f*). Radaq says that the *aleph* was dropped for ease of pronunciation. And indeed, the line, nicely rhythmic and alliterative as it stands, would sound like stuttering in the expected grammatical form, *ʾăni ʾōḥăbay ʾeʾĕhāb*.

Reciprocal Love in Proverbs

The authors of Proverbs, especially but not exclusively in Part I, require that we do more than simply obey the teachings or learn wisdom for utilitarian advantage alone. They insist on an emotional commitment, a desire for learning. This love propels one to seek the unknown and allows learning to impress itself on character. Without love, knowledge is inert. Hence we are required to love wisdom (4:6; 7:4; 29:3; cf. 8:34).

For Proverbs, love and hate are not two emotions among many. They are the polar mind-sets that define the basic shape of a person's character. The wise are typified by love of wisdom and hate of deceit, fools by their perverse loves and hatreds. Fools hate wisdom (1:29). They despise its chastisement (1:30) and instruction (5:12). The callow soul "loves" his callowness (1:22). The cynic delights in his own cynicism (1:22). Those who hate wisdom love death (8:36). A lazy man is not merely weary but loves sleep (20:13). A contentious man is not just irascible but "loves" transgression (17:19). To be wise is not only to know wisdom, but to love it and seek it (see the comment on 8:30c–31a), and this love is met by wisdom's own, the attraction of like for like (8:21).

To love wisdom means to crave knowledge and draw deep satisfaction from attaining it. But in what sense does wisdom feel a corresponding emotion—a desire to be *taken*, as it were? Proverbs does not provide the answer, but its insistence (reiterated more explicitly by Ben Sira) on wisdom's amenability to being learned supports the following reflection. To the neophyte, knowledge in any area appears massive, fragmented, and unmanageable. As one progresses in learning, the vastness of knowledge is even more evident, but lines of organization begin to appear, and interconnections emerge that facilitate memory and comprehension. Eventually, one assimilates these structures so that they seem natural, almost self-evident, and what once seemed a great obstacle to knowledge (Hebrew verb forms, for instance) now seems to offer the line of least resistance. In other words, a learner may have the sensation that the field of knowledge is cooperating in clarifying itself, at least in the territory one has already traversed. While such an abstract formulation would have been foreign to the sages, they are expressing a similar experience of learning in terms of the reciprocal love of wisdom and the wise.

Behind the concept of the mutual love of wisdom and humanity may lie the theme of reciprocal divine-human love. While the theme of mutual divine-human love is biblical (especially prominent in Deuteronomy), the formula of reciprocal love is not. There are, however, strong Egyptian parallels. Kayatz (1966: 98–102) quotes the formulas on heart scarabs, such as "Khonsu loves him who loves him"; "Isis loves the one who loves her." Kayatz believes that the qualities of loving and being loved are particularly characteristic of Maʿat, the goddess of justice and truth (see pp. 335f.). This reciprocality formula, however, is used of a variety of deities.

and those who seek me find me: It is not even enough to be receptive to wisdom; one must actively pursue it (2:4; 15:14; 18:15). Wisdom will be found by those who seek it earnestly. A less-than-wholehearted aspiration to wisdom will not bring one to it. Nor is wisdom accessible to the cynic, the *leṣ*, who may want to possess learning but will not obey its dicta (Prov 14:6), to the dolt who thinks he can buy it (17:16), or to the fool who belatedly grasps for it in desperation (1:28); cf. Sir 15:7–8.

Seeking and Studying

What does it mean in practice to seek wisdom? First of all, one must give attention to the words of one's teacher and of other sages. For Ben Sira, seeking wisdom means studying both wise sayings and the sacred books of Israel, above all the Law (see esp. Sir 6:32–37; 14:20–15:10). It is less clear what it means for

Proverbs, though textual study is certainly within the purview of the Prologue. Does seeking wisdom include book learning, as in the first chapter of Daniel?

The Egyptian sages encouraged the study of all the scribal literature, especially the Wisdom instructions. Anii says: "Penetrate the writings, put them in your heart. Then all that you say will be effective" (20.4–5; cf. AEL 2.140). Pap. Beatty IV praises the ancient scribes at length (vso. 2.5–4.6 [AEL 2.176–77]) and exhorts the reader: "Be a scribe! Put it in your heart. Then it will be thus with your name" (vso. 2.13; cf. AEL 2.177), meaning that the reader too will gain renown. The author is urging the study of the ancient books; this study is preparatory to the understanding of ethical wisdom: "(Only) when you are learned in the books will you penetrate the instruction" (4.6, 9). Duachety promises to teach his son love of book learning, and he praises the scribal office for which it is a prerequisite: "Nothing surpasses book learning [lit. "books"]; it is like being on the water" (that is, "sailing" successfully through life) (IIc; cf. AEL 1.185). Amennakhte counsels: "Be a scribe, frequent the House of Life [the library and scriptorium joined to large temples], for that means becoming like a book-box" (l. 12). (To "be a scribe" could be translated "become literate.")

Like the Egyptian sages and Ben Sira, the authors of Proverbs, especially of Part I, may well be including the study of ancient books (minimally, the book of Proverbs itself) when they urge the reader to seek wisdom. Proverbs, however, does not isolate the components of wisdom. Wisdom is to be sought in its totality, in speech and writing, in this book and in the entirety of literature.

8:18. *Wealth and honor are with me*: The pair is a hendiadys meaning "honorable wealth." Wisdom holds both wealth (*ʿošer*) and honor (*kabod*) in her right hand (Prov 3:16), symbolizing their association. Note too how the extra gift of "wealth and honor" that Solomon receives in 1 Kgs 3:13 corresponds to "wealth" alone in v 11. The construct pairs *ʿošer kᵉbod-* (lit. "the wealth of the honor [of his kingdom]"; Esth 1:4) and *kᵉbod ʿošro* (lit. "the honor of his wealth"; Esth 5:11) show that the concepts are sometimes interchangeable, since riches usually bring prestige. However, *kabod* is not an exact equivalent of *ʿošer*, for a person can have one without the other, and the two stand in opposition in Prov 11:16. *Kabod* refers to wealth and not honor in, e.g., Ps 49:17–18 and Isa 66:11–12. Not all wealth brings honor, but the wealth possessed (and granted) by wisdom does.

enduring riches and righteousness [*hon ʿateq uṣᵉdaqah*]: As in "wealth and honor" (18a), the second noun defines the quality of the first. Ehrlich paraphrases: "exceedingly great property gained justly" ("überaus grosses, auf rechtlichem Wege erworbenes Vermögen"). Wisdom's benefits are all attained honestly. In vv 15, 18, and 20, the author takes care not to exalt power and wealth apart from moral values.

enduring riches [*hôn ʿātēq*]: *ʿātēq* (= *ʿātāq*) is usually understood to mean "old" (Malbim) or "venerable" (Delitzsch), equivalent to *ʿattîq* "ancient," hence "enduring." Both *ʿattîq* and *ʿātēq* are adjectival forms from *ʿ-t-q*, so the equation is reasonable. The ability to endure, demonstrated by something's antiquity, is transposed into the future. The word has also been understood as "great." Naḥmias, for example, glosses *rāb wᵉgādôl*. In Job 21:7, which is thought to support the latter,

ʿāt^eqû actually means "grow old," parallel to "live." In Isa 23:18, *ʿātîq* is predicated of a garment and traditionally translated "stately" or "venerable," but this is conjecture.

righteousness [*ṣ^edāqāh*] refers to wealth gained righteously and honestly. Some explain *ṣ^edāqāh* here as "wealth" or "prosperity," a cause-for-effect metonymy. Toy: "the *just measure of fortune* which is meted out to man," hence "the *good fortune* awarded him." Similarly, "success" (JPSV) and "prosperity" (NRSV). The parallel between *ṣidqātām* and *naḥălat-* "inheritance of" in Isa 54:17b might be thought to support this. There, however, both nouns refer not to material prosperity but to vindication (17a). In Ps 112:3, *ṣidqātô* parallels *hôn wāʿōšer* "riches and wealth," but the second line may be supplementary rather than not synonymous. Note that *w^eṣidqātô ʿōmedet lāʿad* in Ps 111:3 is recapitulated as *t^ehillātô ʿōmedet lāʿad*, "his *praise* endures forever," later in the same psalm (v 10). Thus there is no need to ascribe a special sense to *ṣ^edāqāh* in Prov 8:18.

8:19. *Better my fruit* . . . : In the present text, Wisdom takes a precautionary step away from her enthusiastic promise of material blessings to remind us (in an echo of v 10) that wealth is still inferior to the fruits of wisdom, which are intellectual and ethical, not only material. Yet the antithesis between Wisdom's wealth and fruit is not really appropriate here, since Wisdom has just declared that her fruits include wealth (v 18). Moreover, the relative depreciation of wealth—though certainly consonant with the author's belief—weakens the promise of affluence in the next verse. This verse is probably a pietistic precaution based on 8:10 and, especially, 3:14, which has the same chiasm reversed.

finest gold: *Ḥārûṣ* and *pāz* are two unidentified types of gold used synonymously. They reinforce each other to form a superlative of value. *Kesep nibḥār* "choice silver" is the antonym of *kesep nimʾās* (Jer 6:30), which means silver that is rejected, not to be chosen (Ehrlich).

8:20–21. *I walk in the way of righteousness* . . . : Wisdom bestows her wealth only in honest ways, meaning that the wise themselves take honorable paths to prosperity.

walk: The D-stem *m^ehallek* means to go about habitually, referring here to a mode of behavior.

to grant wealth: The verb *l^ehanḥil* "to give as an inheritance" means to transfer ownership permanently, so that it may be passed on in inheritance. Compare the promise in 13:22a, "The good man bequeaths [*yanḥil*] his wealth to his children." Lady Wisdom's promise of prosperity is framed in terms connoting habituality (*m^ehallek*) and permanence (*l^ehanḥil*). Wealth gained improperly, in contrast, will not endure (20:21; 23:4–5; 28:8, 22).

The word for wealth, *yēš*, is a noun meaning possessions only here and in Sir 42:3 (*nḥlh wyš*). The phrase *wʿl yš lh* "and upon that which is hers" in Sir 25:21 shows the intermediate step between *yēš* as an existential particle and as a noun meaning possessions. The pairing of *yēš* with *nḥlh* in Sir 42:3 suggests that *yēš* is enduring, stable property, and not just any valuables.

to grant // (to) fill (*l^ehanḥîl // ʾămallēʾ*): Compare the inf.-yiqtol parallelism in, e.g., 2:2, 8, and see the comment on 5:2. No special semantic significance is discernible.

Throughout 8:12–21, Wisdom extols the benefits of which she is the means and the facilitator. In doing so, she is boasting of her own prowess and prestige. The endowments so highly cherished by man—cleverness, power, dominion, and wealth—are in her control. She moves in the most esteemed circles, among the rich and the powerful, for whom she is a majestic patron and benefactor. Indeed, as we are about to learn, she is an intimate of God himself. For him, however, she is a darling little girl.

The LXX adds a verse (8:21a) introducing the next unit; see the Textual Notes.

8:22–23. Wisdom the First Creation

8:22. *The Lord created me* . . . : This verse has inspired extensive theological and homiletical exposition since ancient times, with each word being probed for its exact and full meaning.

created me [*qanani*]: Since ancient times, interpreters have been divided as to whether *qanah* denotes *acquisition* (and thus possession) or *creation*. The former interpretation ("acquired me" or "possessed me") is reflected in a Greek variant and the Vulgate. Interpreting thus (and looking at this verb alone) allows for the possibility that wisdom was preexistent and coeval with God. The latter interpretation ("created me") is represented by the main Septuagintal tradition and the Syr and presupposed by Ben Sira's paraphrase: "Before all things, wisdom was created [Gk *ektistai*]" (1:4: cf. v 9). This is accepted by the medieval Jewish commentators and most modern translations and interpreters (JPSV, NRSV, Toy, McKane, etc.). By this interpretation, v 22 declares both Lady Wisdom's derivation from Yahweh and her subordination to him.

The debate between these two interpretations became acute in early Christianity. In the New Testament, Sophia was equated with and replaced by the Logos, which was for its part identified with the Christ, whose preexistent eternality was a matter of dispute. According to John 1:1–2, the Logos was with God from the beginning and apparently uncreated. According to Col 1:15–16 (a passage clearly dependent on Prov 8), the Christ is the "firstborn" (*prōtotokos*) of creation, through whom all was created (cf. Heb 1:3). In the fourth century, Prov 8:22 became a *crux interpretum* that pivoted on the question of whether Christ was coeval with the Father (Athanasians) or was his creation (Arians). See the Textual Note.

In my view, the question is moot. The word's *lexical* meaning, the semantic content it brings to context, is "acquire," no more than that. But one way something can be acquired is by creation. English "acquire" implies that the object was already in existence, but this is not the case with *qanah*. To avoid misunderstanding, the better translation in context is "created."

While both "created" and "acquired" are legitimate contextual translations of this verb, "possessed" (Vul, KJV) is not. Though this mutes the theologically difficult implication that prior to creation God did not have wisdom, it does not really fit the context. The verbs in vv 22–25 relating to Wisdom's genesis describe a one-time action, whereas possession is continuous. Subsequent possession may be assumed, though prior possession is indeed excluded. God acquired/created wisdom as the first of his deeds. Wisdom "was born" (vv 24, 25) at that time. She did not exist from eternity. Wisdom is therefore an accidental attribute of godhead, not an essential or inherent one.

"Acquire"/"create": In the great majority of its occurrences (eighty-three in the G and N stems in the HB + nine in Ben Sira), *qnh* (G) indisputably means "acquire" (most often by purchase). The question is whether *qnh* ever refers to creation. Irwin (1961) and Vawter (1980) argue that nowhere does *qnh* definitely mean "create," while Humbert (1950) allows for six occurrences. The following cases seem to me unambiguously to refer to acts of creation or production: (1) Parent-child: Gen 4:1 (what Eve does to Cain can mean "acquired by giving birth to." Asherah is called *qnyt ilm* "creator of the gods" because she gave birth to them. (2) God-Israel: Deut 32:6 (the parallel verbs, "made you and established you," show that *qānekā* refers to God's creating Israel as his peculiar possession). (3) God-individual: Ps 139:13 (*qānîtā* "created my kidneys" // *tᵉsukkēnî* "wove me." The sentence does not describe the father's act and must refer to the special creation of the individual). (4) Human-inanimate object: *qānāh* never has this function in BH, though *qn* does in Phoenician (KAI 25,1). (5) God-world: No unambiguous examples. The epithet *qōnēh šāmayim wāʾāreṣ*, usually translated "Creator of heaven and earth" (Gen 14:19, 22), is ambiguous, since God both created and acquired the world. (Note that *qōnēh* in Gen 14:19, 22 is translated by Aramaic *mrh* "master" in Gen Apoc 22.16, 21). The Phoenician-Punic parallel *ʾl qn ʾrṣ* (KAI 26 A III 18 and 129, 1) is likewise ambiguous.

The verb *qanah* is chosen to designate divine acquisition of wisdom to show that this is the prototype of human acquisition of wisdom, even though they gain wisdom in quite different ways. *Qanah* is used of human acquisition of wisdom in Prov 4:7a: "The beginning of wisdom is: get (*qᵉneh*) wisdom!"; also 1:5; 4:5; 15:32; 16:16; 17:16; 18:15; 19:8; 23:23. At the same time, since *qanah* can refer to the parent's role in procreation (no. 1, above), this verb introduces the theme of *begetting* as the governing metaphor in describing this act of creation.

the beginning of his way [*reʾšit darko*]: *Reʾšit* can be understood in three ways: (1) The best or most important thing (e.g., Amos 6:1; Jer 49:35; advocated by Irwin 1961: 140). (2) The first *thing* temporally, in apposition to "me" in "created me" (e.g., Exod 23:19). "First" can simultaneously imply excellence (e.g., Gen 49:3; Ps 105:36). (3) The first *stage* (e.g., Mic 1:13; Prov 4:7; Job 8:7; 42:12). This is the best explanation. Radaq accurately paraphrases *reʾšit darko* as *bitᵉḥillat maʿăśayw* "at the beginning of his deeds." Explanation no. 3 is favored by the parallel *qedem*, which only means a prior time period.

Unlike *rēʾšît*, *qedem* never has a qualitative sense, "best" (1). Nor does *qedem* mean "first" as a noun, the earliest thing in a series (2). In other words, an entity could not be called "a *qedem*." In line with sense 3, however, *qedem* in its temporal sense means "ancient/beginning time," as in *yᵉmê qedem*, "ancient days" (Ps 44:2) or *minnî-qedem* "from ancient times" (Ps 78:2). (*Qedem* also means "east," which is not relevant here.) *Qedem mipʿālāyw* is the era called *qadmê ʾāreṣ* in Prov 8:23. In Prov 8:22, *qedem* (and thus *rēʾšît*) functions adverbially: "*at* the beginning," "*at* the start." Compare the adverbial use of *qedem* in Ps 119:152 and esp. 74:2, where it modifies *qānāh* (*ʿădātᵉkā qānîtā qedem*).

his way: What is God's *way*? A "way" or path" (*derek*) can signify a collectivity of actions—a pattern of behavior or a course of action. The course of a person's life is a "way" or "path"; here it is parallel to plural "works." God's "way" and "works" include but do not end with the creation of the world. The verse seems to think of God as having a history, a series of connected events beginning with the creation of wisdom and stretching on through time.

The noun *darkô* has occasioned some tortuous interpretations. Savignac (1954: 431) claims that *derek* means "model, ideal image" and translates "Le Seigneur m'a produite comme sa manifestation première, les prémices éternelles de ses oeuvres." Irwin (1961: 140) defines *darkô* as "what is expressive of his essential nature" or "attributes." These heavily theological explications seek support in Job 40:19. (Behemoth is *rēʾšît darkê ʾēl* "the first of God's ways"), but the same uncertainty exists there. Some ascribe to *derek* the meaning "reign," "dominion," or the like (Albright 1955: 7; J. Bauer 1958), on the grounds that Ugaritic *drk* appears parallel to *mlk* "rule" (see UT Glossary no. 702). This meaning, however, is contextual. *Derek* refers to rule when the "way" or behavior in question is rulership, which is not the case here.

Pointing *dᵉrākāyw* (plural) with LXX and Sym is stylistically attractive but unnecessary. *Derek* means deed or deeds as a collectivity; note the parallelism in Ps 145:17: "The Lord is righteous in all his ways [*dᵉrākāyw*] // and kind in all his deeds [*maʿăśāyw*]"; cf. Deut 32:4 (*dᵉrākāyw* // *poʿŏlô* "his work"); Jonah 3:10 (*darkām* = *maʿăśêhem* "their deeds"); and 2 Chr 13:22 (where *derek* refers to Abiah's behavior throughout his reign).

8:23. *In primeval days* [*meʿolam*]: or "from the start of time." This is the same as *meroʾš* "at the start." There are two great aeons: past and future. They are both called *ʿolam* and extend indefinitely in both directions; see, for example, Ps 90:2.

I was formed [*nissaktî*]: MT means "I was poured out," which is difficult. By a different vocalization, *nᵉsakkōtî* (*s-k-k* N), the word means "was woven," "formed." Wisdom speaks of her formation, her "being woven together," during her figurative gestation. The same verb is used of God's crafting an embryo by interweaving bones and sinews in Ps 139:13b (G-stem) and Job 10:11 (Dr [*polel*]). This sense accords best with context.

Nissaktî has been explained in four ways: (1) "Anointed," lit. "was poured out" (*n-s-k* N-stem), alluding to the pouring of oil to anoint a king; cf. Ps 2:6 (G). (2) "Made princess," as denominative from *nāsîk* "prince." Thus Radaq: "given the station of prince/princess [*nᵉsîkût*]"; sim. Ramaq, Naḥmias. (3) "Placed," "appointed" (so too in Ps 2:6), assuming that *nāsak* can have this sense without reference to anointing (Delitzsch, Toy). Thus Aq: *katestathēn* "set down," "appoint." But the existence of this root is doubtful. (4) "Was woven" = was formed. This requires either vocalizing *nᵉsakkōtî* (*s-k-k* N-stem) or construing MT's pointing as reflecting a by-form from the root, *n-s-k*; cf. *nᵉsûkāh* in Isa 25:7.

8:24–29. The Physical Universe

The change in perspective from the universal present to the far past is marked by the shift from "before" clauses in vv 24–26 to "when" clauses in vv 27–29. These two stanzas, together with vv 22–23, emphasize Wisdom's priority in creation. Her own genesis is the topic in vv 24–26, while her presence during the construction of the world is in focus in vv 27–29. The six creative actions in vv 27–29 are in "when" clauses subordinate to Wisdom's statement, "there was I" (as noted by Ramaq). This shows that creation is described not for its own sake or to praise God, but in order to underscore Wisdom's presence throughout creation and thus to celebrate her preeminence.

The poem now surveys the phases of creation, moving generally upward and then downward: from the deeps (v 24a) to the springs that lead to the earth's surface (v 24b), to the mountains, whose foundations are in the abyss (v 25), to the land (v 26), to the sky (v 27a) and horizon (v 27b), to the clouds (v 28a), then downward to the wellsprings (v 28b) and sea shores (v 29ab), and finally to the foundations of the earth, which are also in the abyss (v 29c). This systematic movement (noted by Meinhold) impresses on the reader creation as a coherent panorama rather than just an assemblage of phenomena.

The following (somewhat oversimplified) sketch of the ancient Israelite conception of the world may help clarify the assumptions of this passage. The physical universe is constructed on three levels: the underworld (*š*^{e}*ʾol*), the earth (*ʾereṣ*), and the heavens (*šamayim*). Pillars, perhaps pictured as mountains, support each level. The mountains and earth themselves rest on bases or "supports," known as "supports of the mountains" (*mos*^{e}*dey harim*; Ps 18:8) and "the pillars of the earth" (*mos*^{e}*dot tebel* [Ps 18:16] or *mos*^{e}*dey ʾareṣ* [Prov 8:29, etc.]), the former possibly included among the latter. These supports are also called pillars, *ʿammudim* (Ps 75:4; Job 9:6). Upon these props, the habitable land (*tebel*) lies like a griddle. Around and beneath the *tebel* (and, according to Gen 1:7, above the entire earth), there is the *t*^{e}*hom*, the primeval ocean or abyss, which is sometimes identified with the underworld, Sheol. (Ordinary seas partake of this same water but are distinguished from the *t*^{e}*hom* by being gathered and contained by land; see Gen 1:10.) Wellsprings serve as conduits connecting the underground waters to the earth and feeding the seas from the abyss, while floodgates in the sky control the upper waters (Gen 7:11). The sky is a dome or cupola, a two-dimensional "firmament," resting on "the columns of the sky" (*ʿammudey šamayim*; Job 26:11). Separating the sky from the flat surface (earth + seas) there is a visible border (namely, the horizon), which is called both "the circle of the sky" (*ḥug šamayim*; Job 22:14) and "the circle of the earth" (*ḥug haʾareṣ*; Isa 40:22). See further Cornelius (1994), who reconstructs the physical world in accordance with ancient Near Eastern iconography, and the bibliography there, esp. works by Stadelmann and Keel.

8:24. *When there were yet no deeps*: or "abysses" *t*^{e}*homot*. The abyss, *t*^{e}*hom*, is the primeval ocean, which, according to Gen 1:2, preceded creation. In Gen 1, it does not belong to the process of creation, because creation there means giving form and structure, while the *t*^{e}*hom* is chaotic and formless. In Prov 8, however, their formation is a step in creation, apparently the first after wisdom's. Another possibility is that the *t*^{e}*homot* here are the deeps of the ordinary seas (cf. Exod 15:5; Isa 63:13; Ps 106:9; thus Emerton 1965: 126, q.v. for further discussion). But Prov 8 exhibits some unusual notions and need not be assimilated to other biblical texts.

I was born [*ḥolalti*]: The verb *ḥolel* (from *ḥ-y-l*, "to writhe in pain") usually refers to birth. To be sure, this verb, and even the more explicit *yalad*, can be transferred to other forms of production. Both are used of God's creating the earth (Ps 90:2) and Israel (Deut 32:18). In this chapter, however, the metaphor of parenthood is reinforced by v 30.

Usually, and fundamentally, the verb (in G and Dr) designates the mother's birth labors (Isa 13:8; 23:4; 45:10; 51:2; etc.). It is twice applied to God (Deut 32:18; Ps 90:2), but never to human males. Though we cannot say for certain that *ḥolel* could not be said of actual fathers, from the attested usages it appears that God is being given a female role, though figuratively and allusively (insofar as he must be the tacit subject of the passive "was born"). Since divine productivity is not really sexual, tropes for this activity need not be governed by the constraints of human reproduction.

sources of water: MT has *nikbaddey mayim*, using a word, *nikbad*, that usually means "honored." Most commentators explain *nikbad* as indicating a large quantity and compare Gen 13:2, "Abram was very *kabed* 'weighty' in cattle, etc."; and Job 14:21, "His sons *yikbᵉdu* grow great and he knows not"; sim. Num 20:20 (other renderings are possible). The parallels are not exact and in any case belong to a different stem, the (stative) G rather than the (passive) N. An emendation to *nibkê* "sources," "wellheads," is warranted (Landes 1956: 31–33; BHS). These are the sources from which the underground waters feed the seas and rivers (Job 28:11) and are synonymous with *maʿyanot* "springs."

The N-stem of *k-b-d* never refers to quantity, literally or figuratively, but only to the reception or possession of honor and esteem. Moreover, this chapter shows no interest in the size or majesty of the natural phenomena. For *nibkê* "fountains of," see Job 38:16, *nibkê yam*, "fountains of the sea" and 1QHod 3,15, *nbwky mym*. The word is apparently equivalent to *mibbᵉkê-* "sources" (of rivers) in Job 28:11 = Ugaritic *mbk*; cf. *npk* "well" (Keret 216).

8:25. *Before the mountains were set down* [*hoṭbaʿu*]: The verb *hoṭbaʿu* ("set down," "sunk") refers more precisely to the sinking of the mountains' *pillars* in their sockets. The author of this poem seems to imagine the pillars as set in the abyss or in the underworld. The author of Job seems to recognize the logical problem involved. God asks Job rhetorically, "Upon what are its sockets sunk (*hoṭbaʿu*)?" (38:6), referring to the sockets that hold the earth's pillars. The paradoxical answer was given earlier: God "suspends the earth upon no-thing"—*bᵉli-mah* (26:7).

before the hills: The verb "were set down," is to be supplied from the preceding line.

8:26. *ere*: lit. "while . . . not."

ʿad lōʾ is a hapax (in Isa 47:7, *ʿad* actually belongs to the preceding clause). This conjunction is common in Syriac (*ʿad-lāʾ*) and may be an Aramaism here. The phrase *ʿad ʾăšer lōʾ* appears in Qoh 12:1, 2, 6, and *ʿad šellōʾ* is common in RH.

the earth and the ground [*ḥuṣot*]: *Ḥuṣot*, lit. "outsides," does not have its usual sense of city streets, since these were not part of God's primeval creation. Most commentators understand it to mean fields (compare Aramaic *bar*, which means both "outside" and "fields" and cf. Job 5:10; Ps 144:13, though these too are ambiguous). Ramaq and Naḥmias take *ḥuṣot* as a metonymy for buildings, apparently by contiguity with streets. The LXX draws the opposite conclusion, translating "uninhabited places," while Syr guesses "rivers." In my view, *ʾereṣ* and *ḥuṣot*, as well as *roʾš ʿaprot tebel*, all refer to the ground, the soil of the earth; hence the balance is exact. A word may be used to designate one aspect of the totality it denotes. In English, for example, we can speak of moving or piling up "earth" when we mean the soil. Though *ʾereṣ* usually refers to the earth as a whole or to a land within it and *ḥuṣot* to city streets, here the focus is on the soil.

DCH 1.396 lists likely cases of *ʾereṣ* in the sense of ground/soil, noting that this usage is generally difficult to distinguish from *ʾereṣ* in the sense of land/territory. Good examples of the former include Jer 17:13 ("written in the *ʾereṣ*"); Ps 143:10 (*ʾereṣ mîšôr* "flat ground"); 1QHod fr. 7.2.4(mg.) (*kwšly ʾrṣ* "those who stumble on the ground"); Ps 7:6, "trample on the *ʾereṣ*" (// *ʿāpār* "dirt"); and esp. 2 Sam 22:43 ("dirt of the *ʾereṣ* ground" // "mud of the *ḥûṣôt*"). See also Isa 51:23b and Job 5:10.

the land's first lumps of soil: The phrase *roʾš ʿaprot tebel* (lit. "the head of the dirts of the land") signifies the soil in some regard, but its exact sense is uncertain.

The word *rōʾš* "head" can mean "best," "chief." According to an explanation cited by Radaq, the "best of the soil of the earth" is the Garden of Eden. The word can also mean "highest part," "top." In that case, the verse refers to the emergence of the top (*rōʾš*) from the receding waters, as described in Gen 1:9; cf. Gen 8:5 (Malbim); sim. KJV: "the highest part of the dust of the world." Others explain *rōʾš* as totality, mass (HALAT; Gemser: "die Masse der Schollen des Erdreichs"—"the mass of the clods of the soil"). But the evidence for this use is poor. The temporal meaning "first" is supported by the chapter's emphasis on wisdom's chronological precedence (Toy, Meinhold; most translations).

ʿaprôt- [sic]: If the pl. is to be distinguished from the sg. *ʿāpār*, it may mean "layers" (HALAT; Meinhold: *Erdschichten*) or "clumps" (JPSV), or regions of the earth (thus Ramaq, who says that there are seven of these). "Clumps" is supported, though not proved, by Job 28:6, where *ʿaprōt* apparently refers to gold ore (rather than gold dust, since the passage is speaking of gold as it is mined).

In Ps 90:2, the psalmist says to God: "(a) Before [*bᵉṭerem*] the mountains were born [*yulladu*] (b) and you brought forth [*tᵉḥolel*] the earth and habitable land [*tebel*]—(c) from eternity [*meʿolam*] to eternity [*ʿolam*] you are God." Prov 8:25–26 seems like an expansion of the statements in Ps 90:2a and 2b respectively, sharing vocabulary and giving priority to the mountains over the dry land, possibly because the former would have emerged first from the receding waters. Prov 8 starts from the indisputable commonplace that God existed before the start of time and ascribes the same precedence to wisdom.

8:27. *the heavens, there was I*: In Hebrew this is highly alliterative: *šamáyim šám ʾáni*.

there was I: that is, present in that event and the others mentioned in vv 27–28. "There" is a situation, not a location.

For *šām* referring to a situation or set of events, see Isa 48:16b, "From the time it came to pass, *šām ʾānî* there I was," meaning that he (God) was present in the events. It is doubtful that *šām* ever has a simple temporal sense, "at that time," "then."

inscribed a circle: This is the horizon, the border between earth and sky that God inscribed or engraved (*bᵉḥûqô*, from *ḥ-q-q*, but lacking the expected dagesh) on the surface of the abyss. The essence of creation is separation and the marking of boundaries (see esp. v 29a). This circle marks the great division between the two realms of heaven and earth.

8:28. *when he secured* [*bᵉʾammᵉṣo*] *the clouds on high*: The word for clouds, *šᵉḥaqim* (from a root meaning "rub," "pulverize"), also means "fine dust" (Isa 40:15) and thus suggests the clouds in their wispy, insubstantial aspect. There is a paradoxical quality in the notion of "securing" the wispy clouds, one which heightens the wonder of God's acts. The *š^eḥaqim* are probably the high cirrus clouds (Stadelmann 1970: 98), which seem to be in proximity to the firmament and thus closely associated with the sky (*šamayim*) or used as a metonymy for it (see, e.g., Ps 89:7; Deut 33:26; Ps 78:23). The verb *ʾimmeṣ* "strengthened," "secured," means to infuse something with vigor or courage; an exception is 2 Chr 24:13, where the verb has the extended sense of reconditioning and reinforcing a building. "Securing" the clouds in the present verse does not mean that God fixed them in place, but that he gave them the power or, we might say, the energy to remain suspended above the earth (Naḥmias).

In Job 38:9, God subdues the sea by wrapping it in clouds as swaddling cloths after it burst forth from its "womb." Likewise in Prov 8:27–28, the juxtaposition of securing or "strengthening" the clouds and marking the sea's boundary, which at first seems haphazard, may reflect the notion that these are sequential acts of creation.

when he strengthened the founts of the deep: He gave them the power to surge up in perpetuity (Naḥmias). The founts of the deep (*ʿiynot t^ehom*) may be the same as the springs (*maʿyanot*) in v 24b, though possibly v 24b refers to the fountains on land and 28b to the ones that feed the seas.

MT's *baʿăzôz* (G, intrans.), "when the founts of the deep grew strong," provides a poor parallel to God's creative act in v 28a. Emend to D-stem following LXX: either *b^eʿazz^ezô* or *b^eʿazzôz*, with the suffix implicit.

8:29. *when he marked the bounds of the sea*: lit. when he placed for the sea its law (*ḥuqqô*, cognate to *ḥûqô* "incised" in v 27b). The boundary God set for the unruly sea (Ps 104:9), namely the sand (Jer 5:22), may also be imagined as a barred door (Job 38:8, 10).

that the waters transgress not his command: lit. "his mouth." This command is quoted in Job 38:11a: "And I said, 'you may come this far and no farther.'"

when he firmed up: MT has *b^eḥûqô* "when he inscribed"; but that is not how foundations are laid. Emend *bḥwqw* to *bḥzqw* (*b^eḥazz^eqô*) "when he strengthened," with the LXX (BHS and many), a *z/w* interchange.

8:30–31. Wisdom between God and Man

8:30. *And I was near him, growing up* [*waʾehyeh ʾeṣlo ʾamon*]: This verse has provided one of the great puzzles of the Hebrew Bible because of its theological implications. (For the history of interpretation, see H.-P. Rüger 1977.) The most important explanations of *ʾamon* may be grouped into three categories: (1) artisan, (2) constant(ly), and (3) ward/nursling. According to a variant of the last, which I favor (3c), Wisdom is declaring that while God was busy creating the world, she was near him, growing up in his care and giving him delight. A. Cooper (1987: 73–75) wishes to leave the ambiguity unresolved. He understands *ʾamon* as a child in v. 30c, as an artisan in 31a, and as a nurse or teacher in 31b.

(1) *Artisan* and related concepts

(1a) Emending *ʾāmôn* to *ʾommān* "artisan" (or construing the word in this way without emendation). Syr and Vul, and perhaps LXX (see Textual Notes), understand the word thus, as does Wis (7:21; 8:6), which speaks of wisdom as the *technitis* "artificer" of the world.

ʾāmôn is frequently taken as a loanword from Akkadian *ummānu* via Aramaic. The Akkadian word basically means artisan, but the term may be used more broadly. Greenfield identifies *ʾāmōn* with the *ummānē* (pl.), the postdiluvian sages, and the latter with the *apkallū*, the divine antediluvian sages who brought the arts to the world (1985: 17–20). The title *ummānu* covers a broad spectrum of occupations, including scribe, scholar, master craftsman, officer (p. 17). Cazelles (1995: 45–55) notes that one Aḫuaqari is called an *ummānu* in a tablet from the Seleucid period. Pointing to Wisdom's role as royal counselor in 8:15–16, Cazelles says that Wisdom is to be understood as a steward or high-ranking scribe in 8:30, and as an artisan only in 9:1.

Lady Wisdom is, however, shown in none of these roles during creation, and only in that setting is she called *ʾāmôn*. (It would be different if Wisdom said she was an *ʾāmôn* with kings and princes.) Moreover, the parallels in v 30bc emphasize that Wisdom was *playing* constantly. Even in Prov 3:19, according to which God created the world "by" (or "in") wisdom, wisdom is an instrument, not an agent. She was certainly not bringing the civilized arts to humanity during the time when she was "with" God, namely at creation![181]

Furthermore, MT's *ʾāmôn* is not compatible phonologically or orthographically with *ummānu*. The attested Hebrew cognate (possibly a loanword) is *ʾommān*. The analogy with *ummānu* requires an emendation, but the only justification for the emendation is the analogy, which is not a close one.

(1b) *Uniting, organizing*—emending to *ʾômēn*, which supposedly means "binding [all] together," "uniting"; thus R. B. Y. Scott (1960 and AB commentary), for which he appeals to LXX, Vul, and Syr. But this too goes contrary to context and syntax and assumes an unattested meaning for the verb *ʾmn*.

(1c) *Instrument*. R. Hoshaya states simply: *ʾmwn ʾwmn*, "*ʾāmôn* means artisan" (*Gen. Rab.* 1.2). However, he goes on to describe wisdom not as the artisan but as the "instrument" or "tool" (*kly ʾwmntw*) of God:

> The Torah is saying (in Prov 8:30): "I was the instrument (*kly ʾwmntw*) of God." In this world, it is the custom that when a mortal king builds a palace he does not build it from his own knowledge alone but uses the knowledge of a craftsman. And the craftsman does not build it from his own knowledge alone, but has scrolls and tablets so that he may know how to make the rooms and how to make the doors. So too did God look in the Torah and create the world. (*Gen. Rab.* 1.2)

In this Midrash, God is both the king and (more relevantly) the architect. The Torah (Wisdom) is like a blueprint, a static repository of information.

Saʿadia similarly explains that wisdom was the means whereby all things were initiated and put into operation.

(2) *Constant(ly), faithful(ly)*, or the like, deriving the word from *ʾ-m-n* "be faithful," etc.

(2a) Symmachus and Theodotion translate *estērigmenē* "set firm."

(2b) Parsing *āmôn* as an inf. abs. used adverbially and translating *beständig* "constantly" (hesitantly proposed by Plöger). Ehrlich: *vertrauten Freund* ("trusted friend") or *beständiger Gast* ("constant guest"). Targum: *mhymntʾ* "trusted one."

This explanation runs up against the fact that the root *ʾ-m-n* "be firm" is not productive in the G-stem (it appears only in the frozen form, *ʾāmēn* "Amen!"). Moreover, the N-stem would be expected in the proposed sense.

---

[181] Soon after the midrash in *Gen. Rab.* 1.2 identifies wisdom as the instrument of God's artistry, it goes on (in 1.4) to insist that God had no "partner" (*šutap*) in creation, but did the work entirely on his own.

(3) *Nurturing* or *raising* (a child), deriving the word from *ʾ-m-n* "to nurture," "serve as ward (to a child)," etc.

(3a) *Pedagogue*. This gloss (using the Greek word) is suggested by R. Hoshaya (early third century) as one valid interpretation among several (*Gen. Rab.* 1.1). He cites Num 11:12, "as an *ʾōmēn* carries an infant." The *pedaigogos* was not a schoolmaster but a household slave who took children to school and was responsible for their upbringing. Gal 3:24 offers a permutation of this reading: *ho nomos paidagōgos hēmōn gegonen eis christon*, "The Law was our *pedagogue* till Christ came."

"Pedagogue" could be justified morphologically by parsing *ʾāmôn* as a rare (or Aramaizing) *nomen agentis* of the *qātōl* pattern. But the picture of Wisdom either carrying or instructing (whom?) during creation has no place in Prov 8.

(3b) *Ward, one who is raised/nurtured*, or the like, vocalizing (or understanding) *ʾmwn* as *ʾāmûn*, a passive ptcp. Thus Aq *tithēnoumenē* "nursed," "nursling" (fem.). If so, *ʾmwnn* must be taken as an unattested epicene noun, "ward," "nursling," because if it were functioning as an adjective, the pass. ptcp. would be in the fem. The masc. pl. adj. *ʾĕmûnîm* appears in Lam 4:5.

(3c) *Growing up with*, parsing *ʾāmôn* as an inf. abs. serving as an adverbial complement. Hence: "I was with him growing up" ("*ʾāmôn*-ing," as it were). This, I believe, is the solution to the puzzle. It requires no emendations and accords with the morphology of the Hebrew word.

This explanation combines insights of Ibn Janaḥ (*Sefer Hariqmah* 323.16) and Ramaq. Ibn Janaḥ identifies *ʾāmôn* as a (G) inf. abs. serving as an adverbial complement. For the sense, he cites Esth 2:7, "And he [Mordecai] was raising (*ʾômēn*) Hadassah." The syntax is correct, but the example (which others adduce in favor of explanation 3b) is problematic. It shows that the G-stem of this verb is transitive, and in the case of Prov 8:30 this would imply that Wisdom was doing the child rearing, which is impossible. Ramaq offers a better example, Esth 2:20b, "just as it was *bᵉʾomnāh ʾittô* when she was growing up with him."[182] This verse shows that the G-stem of *ʾ-m-n*, at least in the inf., can be intransitive and refer to the child's role as well as the guardian's. (The G inf. is, in any case, indifferent as to voice.) It also shows that the verb in this sense can govern a preposition meaning "with," for *ʾēṣel* "with"/"next to" is a near synonym of *ʾēt* as a preposition of proximity (cf. the interchange of these prepositions in 1 Kgs 20:36). On the inf. abs. as adverbial complement, see IBHS §35.3.2; some examples are Gen 30:32; Exod 30:36; Num 6:5, 23; Jer 22:19. The last also displays the passive use of the G and H infinitives.

I was (his) delight (*waʾehyeh šaʿăšuʿim*): Lit. "I was delights" (pl. of abstraction). ("His" is supplied in this translation, as in the LXX, but it is implicit in the Hebrew.) To be one's *šaʿšuʿim* is to be a *source* of delight to him (cf. Isa 5:7; Jer 31:20; Ps 119:24). God, rather than Wisdom, is the one experiencing the delight here. Wisdom has the role of *yeled šaʿăšuʿim* "child (that gives) delight," which is the position Jeremiah assigns to Ephraim (31:20) and similar to Judah's role as *netaʿ šaʿăšuʿayw* "planting of his [God] delight" (Isa 5:7). The cognate verb is used (metaphorically) of a child being dandled on the knee and of a child's thoughtless play (Isa 66:12). The poet of Ps 119 favors this verb in describing his pleasure in the contemplation of God's law.

8:30c, 31a. *frolicking* [*mᵉśaḥeqet*] . . . : Or "playing." God gets amusement from his creatures; compare Ps 104:26b, "and Leviathan, whom you formed to play with [*lᵉśaḥeq bo*]" and Ps 104:31b, "May the Lord take pleasure [*yiśmaḥ*] in his works" (Hameʾiri).

---

[182] The form *bᵉʾomnāh* can be parsed as inf. + third fem. sg. suffix, "when she was being raised" (for the "softening" of the mappiq see GKC §91*f*), or we may simply add the mappiq as a minor emendation. In either case, it is an infinitive, not a hapax noun, contrary to the lexicons.

Keel (1974) derives the motif of Wisdom's playing before Yahweh from the theme of the Egyptian goddess Maʿat playing before the High God. Keel adduces many examples of various sorts of play in Egyptian iconography, but none of them in any way supports the identification of Lady Wisdom with Maʿat, especially since Maʿat herself is never shown doing this. If any Egyptian goddess is associated with diversions (music and dance), it is Hathor, not Maʿat. Nevertheless, the broader theme of playing for the amusement of a god, as in cultic processionals, is well attested and may belong to the background of the present verse.

The keywords in vv 30b–31c are highlighted by chiasm, *šaʿšuʿim/meśaheqet/ meśaheqet/šaʿšuʿim*. Together with the statement that Wisdom was playing "at all times," the emphasis on play and delight makes the stanza seem an almost deliberate repudiation of the idea that Wisdom served as craftsman or architect in creation (see comment on 8:30). In Prov 8, during creation Wisdom only frolicked about and gave pleasure to her divine guardian.

Wisdom's play, according to Nahmias, is symbolic of the play of the wise, which is "the joy of understanding" (*śimhat hahăbanah*). Nahmias's apt proof-text is Ps 119:92: "Were your law not my delight (*šaʿăšuʿay*), I would have perished in my misery." Verses 16, 24, 47, 77, 143, and 174 make a similar point. Nahmias and the psalmist knew the joy of study and immersion in words of wisdom. For them, however, the relevant wisdom was Torah.

8:31b. *and my delight is in mankind:* lit. "and my delight (*šaʿăšuʿay*) is with (*ʾet*) the sons of man." This line is an isolated monostich, but not for that reason a later addition (*pace* Toy). It serves as a coda to the section and prepares for the next by introducing Wisdom's relation to mankind.

Who is feeling the pleasure called *šaʿăšuʿay* "my delight"—Wisdom or mankind? Supporting the former is the fact that elsewhere in the HB the possessive suffix of *šaʿăšuʿim* (seven of ten occurrences have a suffix) refers to the one who feels the pleasure. For example, "your testimonies are my *šaʿăšuʿim* (Ps 119:24) means that the testimonies give *me*—the psalmist—delight. By this measure, Prov 8:31b says that the source of the pleasure Wisdom feels is mankind: Just as God takes pleasure in her, so she takes pleasure in them. However, the usual phrasing for this idea would be nominal predication: *ubeney ʾadam šaʿăšuʿay*. The unusual syntax of the present line allows for the second interpretation: the delight I *give* is found with (*ʾet*)—felt by—humans.

Most commentators are not clear on which construction they accept but seem to favor the first. Some medieval commentators choose the second reading and identify the *šaʿăšuʿim* as the joy that comes from Torah. Saʿadia, for example, says that v 31b explains the figure (*mašal*) in vv 30–31a: It is not really Wisdom herself, but her possessors, who rejoice. However, the usual meaning of "my" (or "his") *šaʿăšuʿim* favors the first interpretation. Wisdom seems to be setting up an analogy: As God delights in Wisdom, so Wisdom delights in mankind.

This gives an extraordinary picture of Wisdom—the noble, ancient sage, the stern disciplinarian and teacher—frolicking like a little child near her divine paternal guardian as he goes about his great work. But *how* does Wisdom play and what does this signify? McKane believes that it alludes to "the delightful confidences and reminiscences which Wisdom can share with Yahweh, just because she saw the world coming into existence, and because in this respect her experience is unique" (p. 358). The words *šaʿăšuʿim* and *mᵉśaḥeqqet*, however, connote a lighter form of amusement, and there is no hint of intellectual dialogue between the young Wisdom and her guardian. Moreover, since Wisdom's playing takes place *during* creation, she and God could not be discussing that aeon in retrospect.

As Saʿadia recognized, Wisdom's play expresses the joy of intellect: exploring, thinking, learning. To be sure, it is (contrary to Saʿadia) Lady Wisdom rather than mankind who is feeling the delight mentioned in v 31c. Still, because Wisdom herself is wise, she typifies the experience of wise humans. The wise, as the author of Psalm 119, Ben Sira (esp. 14:6), and later scholars testify, are not only performing a solemn duty; they are savoring the grandest of pleasures in their studies. They are *playing* before God.

8:32–36. Wisdom's Appeal to Mankind

In this section, but beginning already in v 31b, Wisdom speaks of a different stage in her life, her "maturity." She addresses mankind as "sons" and takes on the persona of an owner of a house where people gather as supplicants or disciples. At creation, Wisdom was God's delightful foster-daughter. Now that humanity is on the scene, *she* is the guardian: "And *my* delight is in mankind" (31b).

The message of an exordium—listen to wisdom—is the substance of Interlude D in its entirety. As a teacher urges his disciples to listen to wisdom—meaning his teachings—that they may live and prosper, so Lady Wisdom appeals to mankind, her "sons" and pupils, to listen to her teaching. The grand celebration of Wisdom—the exaltation of her righteousness, power, gifts, antiquity, transcendence—all leads to the practical conclusion that it is good to seek and obey her.

There is a certain incongruence between the two lines of v 32, since we expect the imperative of the first line to be matched by one in the second. Proceeding from the fact that LXX locates v 32b after v 34a, Whybray (1966: 492–96, cf. 1994: 42–43) proposes that the original order was 34a/32b; 34bc; 35a/36a. He omits the "metrically deficient" v 33 and excises 32a as an interpolation. He has thus, he believes, uncovered three couplets, "all manifesting impeccable parallelism of sense, structure, and vocabulary" (1966: 493). In my view, such rearrangements may create a neater text, but this chapter is not composed entirely of neat couplets, and the MT in this section is meaningful and well designed as it stands. Verse 32a recapitulates the exordium and recalls the opening, in which Wisdom proclaimed her excellence. Verse 32b motivates the appeal in 32a. Verse 34b does seem rather long, but there is no reason to ascribe such a "deficiency," if that is what this is, to an editor rather than to the author, especially since there is no apparent motive for the posited interpolation.

8:32. *And now, my sons, listen to me*: ("My" is added in translation.) Wisdom, speaking as a teacher, resumes the exordium, as the teacher does in 5:7 and 7:24, using the same words. Wisdom addresses her audience in the plural, as 5:7; 7:24; and 4:1–2, q.v. The call to attention in 8:32a is motivated in vv 32b–36.

"And now" (*w*ᵉ*ʿattah*) sometimes has a consequential sense and can be translated "therefore" or "consequently"; see H. Brongers (1965: 293–94).

Happy are they who keep to my ways! This line motivates the first. Since the *ʾašrey* exclamation belongs to another genre (the macarism, on which see p. 161) and seems grammatically out of place here, v 32b may be excerpted from an existing poem. Prov 3:13 may be the immediate influence.

8:33. *brush (it) not aside* [*ʾal tipraʿu*]: The verb *prʿ* (G) means "release," "let loose," hence "ignore." It is parallel to *loʾ ʾabitem* ("you did not accept") in Prov 1:25 (see comment). The dir. obj. of "brush aside," supplied from v 33a, is *musar* "correction." Compare 13:18 and 15:32, both of which show that the *musar* in question is chastisement.

8:34. *Happy* [*ʾašrey*] . . . : another brief macarism.

keeping vigil . . . watching the posts . . . : The devotee of wisdom keeps a diligent watch at her door. There are different ways of picturing the guiding image of this action. (1) The devotee may be like a supplicant waiting at a queen's or a prominent lady's door to petition for a benefit. But a wise man does not receive wisdom's gifts by entreating for favors. (2) The pursuer of wisdom may be pictured as an attendant in the palace of a royal mistress, waiting to do her service (Plöger). Yet the obedience Wisdom demands is not service to her, but rather a fulfillment of her counsels. (3) The pursuer of wisdom may be viewed as a disciple waiting at the master's door for instruction (McKane). On behalf of this, we may observe that Lady Wisdom often speaks like a teacher. Then again, pupils would not need to wait outside her house when wisdom is readily available and, according to 9:4, invites everyone in. (4) The aspirant to wisdom may be pictured as a lover waiting to catch a glimpse of an influential lady, mistress of the house or palace (Meinhold). This option is favored by the way Job describes the adulterer: "If my heart was seduced by a woman, and if I lay in wait at my neighbor's door" (31:9). Moreover, in Prov 5:8, the youth is admonished to avoid approaching the door (*petaḥ*) of the Strange Woman. Prov 8:34 implies a contrast between waiting at Wisdom's door and that of a seductress. The attraction of wisdom is erotic in its power, and the wise pursue her as ardently as a lover does his beloved.[183] It must be admitted, however, that this image is not prominent. When Ben Sira develops the motif of keeping vigil at Wisdom's house, he seems to have no consistent guiding image. He describes the disciple as following Wisdom about, peeking through her windows and listening at her doors, camping next to her house, and (shifting metaphors) taking shelter in her foliage (14:20–27).

day by day: This phrase harks back to v 30b and suggests a parallel between the persistence of the wise man's attendance upon Wisdom and the constancy of Lady Wisdom's presence throughout the work of creation.

---

[183]The erotic nature of the love for wisdom becomes prominent in Wis 8:2–16 and esp. Sir 51:13–19 (Hebrew in 11QPs[a]; Sanders 1967: 115).

8:35. *For he who finds me finds life*: Here the finding of wisdom calls to mind the finding of a beloved woman. The present verse sounds like a reapplication of Prov 18:22: "He who finds a wife finds goodness [*ṭob*], and obtains favor [*raṣon*] from the Lord." To find life is equivalent to finding goodness. (The motif is reversed in Qohelet's complaint that he sought but did *not* find a woman; Qoh 7:28.) In the Song of Songs, the Shulammite goes out in search of her beloved (Cant 3:1–4 and 5:2–6:2) and she "finds" him in 3:4; cf. 8:1.

8:36. *But he who offends against me* [*ḥoṭeʾi*]: Some commentators (e.g., Hameʾiri, Delitzsch, Toy) understand *ḥoṭeʾ* in its etymological sense of "miss the mark," mainly because of the antithesis to "finds me." But this verse is decrying a more pernicious offense than just "missing" wisdom. After all, the fool and sinner are not aiming at wisdom to start with. The failure in v 36a is comparable to hating wisdom (v 36b). Moreover, *ḥ-ṭ-ʾ* means "miss" only in the H-stem, whereas the verb here is in the G-stem. *Ḥoṭeʾ* and *ḥaṭṭaʾ* mean "offender" and "one who is offensive." The offense is usually an ethical violation, but not always. See, for example, Exod 5:16, in which the Israelites fret that they have become offensive to Pharaoh. They are not confessing a sin against him. Similarly Qoh 2:26; 1 Kgs 1:21; Prov 20:2 (one who angers a king offends against himself).

Wisdom is not speaking of moral sins but describing a personal, "emotional" relationship: love and devotion versus offensiveness and hatred. "Offends against" is an antonym of "finds," because the latter here connotes uniting with a beloved person (namely, Wisdom). Those who hate Wisdom are not just stupid, they are depraved. Though they might not realize it, down deep they love not the life that flows from wisdom, but death itself. Compare the description of the wicked man, who, in Ptahhotep's words, "lives on what others die on" (l. 581; see pp. 117f.).

harms himself: The principle that evildoing brings on its own punishment is reiterated in 1:19; 5:22; 6:32; 15:32; 29:24, and elsewhere.

The Design of Interlude D

I. Introduction (1–3): Setting, Wisdom calls
II. Exordium (4–11)
  A. Exhortation: listen to Wisdom (4–6)
  B. Motivation (7–9)
  C. Exhortation: get wisdom (10–11)
III. Wisdom's present state (12–21)
  A. Wisdom's practical intelligence (12 + 13bc)
  B. Wisdom's gift of power (14–16)
  C. Wisdom's material benefits (17–21)
IV. Wisdom's past (22–31)
  A. Wisdom's priority (22–26)
    1. Wisdom was created first (22–23)
    2. *before* the world was created (24–26)
  B. Wisdom's presence *during* creation (27–29)

C. Wisdom is God's darling and mankind hers (30–31)
V. Exordium renewed (32–36): Wisdom and man

Interlude D not only has exordia, it is itself a sort of extended exordium. It comprises an address to the audience (v 4), an exhortation to listen (vv 4–6, 8–10, 32–36), and an extended motivation praising wisdom (vv 12–31). The praise of wisdom's benefits, which is the way the exhortation is motivated in all the exordia,[184] is here elaborated into a long oration in the self-praise form.

After the mise-en-scène in vv 1–3, Wisdom's discourse proceeds in a symmetrical and hierarchical envelope structure, with V corresponding to I and IV to III. Wisdom's call in Section I is echoed in the resumed appeal in V. Within this frame, Wisdom's description of her present glory in III is matched by her report of her past glory in IV. Sections III and IV serve also as motivations for the exhortation.

Interlude D exhibits balance and symmetry. There is considerable agreement among commentators about the points of subdivision, even when they differ in analyzing the overall structure.

Skehan (1979), after excising vv 11 and 13a, divides the chapter into seven uniform stanzas of five lines each: vv 1–5; 6–10; 12–16; 17–21; 22–26; 27–31; 32–36. Skehan's arrangement breaks down, however, at v 4, which shifts to Wisdom's voice, and v 5, which surely belongs with the parallel exhortation in v 6.

McKane (pp. 351–53) holds that the cosmological dimension of vv 22–31 presupposes a more sophisticated audience than the preceding and thus points to different authorship. This section, he says, is "a reorientation, enrichment and supplementation" of vv 12–21 (p. 352). This is an apt characterization of Section IV, but we should not assume that just because one passage in a poem says something new it must have a different origin.

Whybray (1994: 40–43) divides the chapter into five sections, as previously, but does not trace substructures. He regards vv 22–31 as an originally independent poem whose innovation is to introduce Yahweh and show wisdom's total dependency on him. On Whybray's rewriting of vv 32–36, see the comment on those verses.

Yee (1982) suggests a different but also symmetrical and hierarchal structuration of vv 22–31 alone. Her major subunits are vv 22–26; 27–30a; 30b–31. She argues for the existence of envelope structures (inclusios) enforced by various distant echoes.

The Purpose of Interlude D

The primary purpose of the interlude is indicated by the underlying structure of Wisdom's speech in its entirety, which is that of an extended exordium, namely: (a) address (v 4), (b) exhortation to listen (vv 5–6, 8–10, 32–36), and (c) an extended motivation praising wisdom (vv 12–31). This structure shows that the chapter is meant to be edifying and practical as well as reflective. Like an exordium, Interlude D aims to move the reader to listen to and obey wisdom. In this case, however, the object of attention is not the father's teachings but wisdom generally, or wisdom in and of itself.

[184]A motivating sentence should probably be supplied after 5:2; see the commentary.

The interlude is a didactic discourse, not a theoretical treatise. Everything in the chapter serves the rhetorical goal of influencing the reader to desire wisdom. The reason the author declares that the earth's potentates avail themselves of wisdom is to make *you* want to bring this mighty and renowned resource into your own life. It will bring *you* wealth and honor. Even the grand survey of creation is subordinated to the pedagogical goal. That is why the survey is formulated in subordinate clauses that define the time before which Wisdom was created or during which she was present. The description of creation, which is just an elaboration of v 22, adds no new information. Its purpose is to heighten Wisdom's grandeur by describing the glorious works *to which God gave her precedence.* But granted this rhetorical thrust, the poem still conveys an unusual conception of wisdom and makes powerful claims for this entity, and these may also be read from a theoretical or philosophical perspective.

In Prov 8, Wisdom is portrayed as an entity proceeding from God (according to 2:6, from his *mouth*) and intermediate between him and the world. In Hellenistic Jewish philosophy (most distinctively Philo [*Leg. All. 1.65* et al.]), this concept of wisdom came to be identified with the *logos*, the divine word or spirit that pervades the world. This was in turn identified with Christ, in John 1:1. For an orientation to this vast topic, see ABD 4.348–56 and B. Mack, *Logos und Sophia* (1973).

Personified Wisdom in Proverbs 8

The background and meaning of the personification of wisdom is discussed in Essays 2 and 4 (see pp. 331–45 and 352–59). The following observations pertain in particular to chapter 8.

1. Human Wisdom Is External

When you use your mind, you are not just initiating and developing your own thoughts. You are opening yourself to an objective wisdom that permeates the universe, and you become wise to the degree that your thoughts conform to this greater wisdom. You will approach Understanding itself, which is distinct from the notions that are merely *binatᵉka* "your (own) understanding" (Prov 3:5), and even distinct from the particular teachings that will convey you to wisdom itself.

2. Wisdom Is a Unity

The device of personification teaches the reader to think of the multifarious and largely independent ideas and precepts of wisdom—such as are assembled in the book of Proverbs—as a unity. This transcendent, unified wisdom is not a blanched philosophical abstraction. It is infused with the concreteness and specificity of the woman metaphor. (For a discussion of the literary-rhetorical function of personification, see Camp 1985: 209–22.)

3. Wisdom Speaks Wisdom, not God's Word

She is *not* the medium of something else—an *Offenbarungsträger* or "bearer of revelation" (G. von Rad 1970: 213). She is more like a person raised and trained well (Prov 8:30a), who gives her father joy (v 30b; compare 10:1) and who can then be trusted to operate as an autonomous thinker and teacher of wisdom.

4. Wisdom is Energy

Since the creation of wisdom was the first deed of God's "way" and prior to his other "works," the implication is that before he created wisdom, he had no "ways" or works. Though the author may not realize it, the underlying assumption is that prior to creation God was in stasis, his power only potential. He brought his power to actuality by acquiring wisdom. He acquired wisdom by creating it, drawing it from within, from the infinite potential for being that is inherent in Godhead. There is nowhere else he could have gotten it. That is why God's acquiring (*qnh*; 8:22) wisdom is figured in terms of giving birth (*ḥll*; v 24, q.v.).

5. Wisdom is Fun

God set the example by taking delight (*šaʿăšuʿim*) in young Wisdom's play, at the very time he was busy creating the world. Wisdom's only function during creation seems to have been to give God pleasure. God is the supreme and quintessential artist (note that *ḥokmah* includes artistry), and he feels the joy of the creative act, just as he savored the goodness of his handiwork in Gen 1.

While commentators have recognized Wisdom's pride, few have remarked on her *exuberance*. She delights in all aspects of her life: her history, the privilege of being present during creation and watching the divine artistry at first hand, her playfulness as the work proceeded, her delight in humanity.

Reading this mythos in naturalistic terms, it means that the delight of intellect suffuses all that wisdom embraces: the artisan's pleasure in his or her craft, the counselor's satisfaction in working through a dilemma, the author's elation in the success of effort, and the scholar's exhilaration in partaking of the lore and learning of tradition, in exploring the unknown, and in growing in knowledge. Perhaps the joy of learning is what the author primarily has in mind, since he is directing his words in the first instance to young men who need encouragement in their pursuit of learning.

The message for the reader is that seeking wisdom—study, memorization, thought—is not a dreary grind (contrary to Sir 6:23–25), but a pleasure, a "graceful garland" (Prov 1:9), delightful to the soul (2:10).

But the delight reaches even higher. God himself takes pleasure in wisdom. As M. Greenberg (1995: 22) describes the concept of Torah in Ps 119, the psalmist believes that closeness to God through the study of Torah is the most precious experience he can have. "From this," Greenberg says, "it is but a step to the talmudic conception of God and his court studying Torah in the heavenly yeshiva (e.g., *b. B. Meṣ.* 86a). Here the Torah is an absolute value as an embodiment of divine wisdom, in which all the celestials can delight." Following the process one step back brings us to Prov 8:30.

6. Wisdom Loves Humanity

Lady Wisdom is attracted to humans and they to her by the energy of eros—the "spiritual-intellectual eros" (*der geistige Eros*), as von Rad calls it (1970: 217).

The description of the reciprocal attraction between humanity and wisdom draws on language used in the description of the allures of the wife and the temptress. Wisdom resembles a lover who seeks and is sought by her beloved (8:17, 34–35; cf. Cant 3:1–4; 5:2–6:2; and see R. E. Murphy 1988). The sexual connotations in Wisdom's portrayal are more muted than is sometimes thought, but, in Prov 8, at least, they are there in the background. Eros is the yearning for completion by filling a lack in oneself. In this sense, all statements of the reciprocal love between wisdom and mankind proclaim this "intellectual eros."

That the wise love wisdom is a truism. It is surprising, however, to learn that Wisdom loves the wise. The motif of Wisdom's emotions is not confined to this interlude. Elsewhere we are told that Wisdom exalts and honors those who embrace her (4:8). She takes the trouble to prepare a banquet and invites everyone to her house (9:1–5). Her pique at those who spurn her call (1:24–33) suggests a need for love.

INTERLUDE E. TWO BANQUETS (9:1–18)

TRANSLATION

Lady Wisdom's banquet

9:1 Wisdom has built her house,
set up[a] her pillars seven,
2 slaughtered her cattle,
mixed her wine,
set her table.
3 Having sent forth her maids, she cries
at the tops of the city heights:
4 "Whoever is callow—let him come over here!
Whoever is senseless—to him I'll say:[b]
5 'Come, dine on my food;
drink of the wine I have mixed.
6 Abandon callowness and live;
walk in the path of understanding,[c]
11 for through me your days will increase,
and years be added to your life.' "[d]

Lady Folly's banquet

13 The foolish woman is boisterous—
callowness itself! She knows nothing at all.
14 She sits at the door of her house,
on a chair at the city heights,
15 calling to those who pass by,
who are going straight ahead.

16 "Whoever is callow, let him come over here!
Whoever is senseless—to him I'll say:[e]
17 'Stolen water is sweet,
secret food a delight.'"
18 But he knows not that ghosts are there,
that her guests are in the depths of Sheol.

Two insertions:
Advice to the adviser

9:7 ⟨He who chastises an impudent man receives insult,
he who reproves an evildoer gets hurt.
8 Don't reprove an impudent man lest he hate you;
reprove the wise and he'll love you.
9 Give (reproof) to the wise, and he'll grow even wiser.
Instruct the righteous man and he'll enhance his learning.
10 Wisdom begins with the fear of the Lord,
and understanding—with the knowledge of the Holy One.⟩

Wisdom's value

9:12 ⟨If you grow wise, you benefit yourself,
but if you are impudent, you bear it alone.⟩

---

[a]*hiṣṣibāh* (MT *ḥāṣ^{e}bāh*). [b]*ʾōm^{e}rāh* (MT *ʾām^{e}rāh*). [c, d]Verses 7–10 (see pp. 306ff.) and v 12 (see pp. 317f.) are probably later additions. [e]*w^{e}ʾōm^{e}rāh* (MT *w^{e}ʾām^{e}rāh*).

COMMENTARY

Interlude E picks up the motif of Wisdom's invitation to her house (8:34) and elaborates it into a figure of two contrary invitations.

9:1–6 + 11. Lady Wisdom's Banquet

Lady Wisdom builds a house (v 1), prepares a feast (v 2), and issues an open invitation (vv 3–5). She then explains the meaning of her invitation (v 6) and reinforces her exhortation (v 11).

9:1. *Wisdom*: The apparent plural form *ḥokmôt* is used, as in 1:20; see the comment there. Verses 1–3a supply antecedent information and set the scene. The "present tense" of the scene proper begins with *taronnah*ʾ ("cries aloud") at the end of v 3. The syntax might be rendered accurately, though awkwardly, by a series of circumstantial clauses: "Wisdom, having built her house, . . . and having sent forth her maids, (now) cries at the top of the city heights."

The long sentence, extending into v 3, begins with a clause consisting of the noun *ḥokmōt* + six *qatal* verbs. This is an initial compound nominal clause giving antecedent information. It reports events prior to the narrative. Thus the new information (as far as the author is concerned) begins only with the verb "cries." On this construction see Niccacci [1990: §§6, 15]. Niccacci's observations concern prose but often apply to poetry as well, especially in narrative passages.

set up: MT has *ḥāṣᵉbāh* "has hewn out." The reading *hiṣṣîbāh* "set up," well attested in the versions (see the Textual Notes) and involving a very minor change in consonants, *ḥṣbh* to *hṣbh*, provides a better parallel to "building" a house.

her house . . . : This verse applies to Lady Wisdom what is said about wise human women in 14:1a: "The women's wisdom builds her house."[185] Another verse in the background is Prov 24:3, "By wisdom a house is built, and by good sense it is established." Both these verses use "house" in the sense of "home" or "household." Prov 9:1 reapplies these proverbs to the construction of a building.

Vattioni (1967a) mentions an interesting parallel, the Assyro-Babylonian designation of Apsu as "the house of wisdom" (*bît nimêqi*). Apsu, the sweet-water mass under the earth, is the realm of the god Ea-Enki, one of whose epithets is "Lord of Wisdom" (*bēl ḫasisi*). Perhaps the notion of wisdom's house predates Prov 9:1, but if so, it has been reappropriated and demythologized, for here Wisdom's house is purely figurative, like Folly's.

her pillars seven: This rendering imitates the Hebrew word order. (The numeral following a determined noun is a feature of late biblical Hebrew [IBHS 278, n. 12].) "Seven" is a round or typological number (Ramaq; Hameʾiri; Toy), similar to "a dozen" in English. It seems to connote completeness or appropriateness. If we are to picture the pillars as belonging to an inner room facing a courtyard, the number would indicate spaciousness and elegance. Houses with seven pillars are attested, but the particular number may be coincidental, since other houses have different numbers of pillars. Still, it seems significant that the Akitu sanctuary in Assyria had two sets of seven pillars, and the pillars of Solomon's temple had seven meshwork decorations (1 Kgs 7:17). For a review of the relevant archaeological data on the function and number of pillars in an Israelite dwelling, see Lang 1986: 90–93.

The details of the scene are not significant individually, but together they show that wisdom has much to offer and is eager to do so. To listen to Wisdom, to live within her house, to partake of her food and wine, are different ways of envisioning a lifetime of learning.

Many commentators interpret the number seven symbolically. Identifications include: the seven means of perceiving the Creator (Riyqam); the first seven chapters of Proverbs (Hitzig [1858]; thus too Skehan [1947a], who argued that they were inscribed in seven written columns); the seven antediluvian sages (*apkallū*) of Babylonian mythology (Greenfield 1985[186]); the seven firmaments or the seven lands (*Midr. Prov.*); the seven planets or the seven days of creation (*b. San.* 38a); the seven sacraments of the church; the seven gifts or virtues of the Holy Spirit (Delitzsch); the seven liberal

---

185 We should probably vocalize *ḥakmôt nāšîm* "wise ones [f. pl.] of women" as *ḥokmôt nāšîm* "wisdom of women," with *ḥokmôt* being the sg. abstract. See the comment on 1:20. "Wisdom" is an abstract-for-concrete trope equivalent to "wise women."

186 Greenfield emends *ḥṣbh* to *hṣb*, which he vocalizes *hiṣṣîbû*, and translates v 1b as "the Seven have set its foundations." On the *apkallû*, see the comment on 8:30.

arts (!) (Heidenheim). For the older Christian interpretations, see the survey in Delitzsch, ad loc. All such decodings are arbitrary and unsupported by context.

9:2. *slaughtered her cattle* [*ṭabᵉḥah tibḥahh*]: lit. "slaughtered her slaughtering." Meat was a luxury reserved for special occasions. The verb *tabaḥ* (unlike *zabaḥ*) does not imply ritual sacrifice and is always used of secular slaughter (of humans as well as animals). It may include the act of cooking; cf. *haṭṭabbaḥ* = "the cook" in 1 Sam 9:23–24 (Hame'iri).

9:3. *sent forth her maids*: In her eagerness to invite everyone, Lady Wisdom dispatches messengers to the high ground of the city, the prominent area mentioned in 8:2 (see comment there) and 9:14. Some have construed the maids as symbols—of chastisements, for example (Ramaq), preachers (Radaq), or students (Hame'iri). But all the maids do is transmit the invitation and seem to have no significance in themselves.

There is some disagreement as to whether it is Wisdom or the maids who are calling. It is clearly the former in the MT. Messages were formulated as the sender's words, not the messenger's. In v 3, the verb *tiqra'* "cries" is singular, and in v 4 Wisdom is the speaker. Moreover, the call to come "here"—that is, to Wisdom's house—shows that the invitation is phrased from the standpoint of Wisdom, not the maids. The maids convey the message, but the message is Wisdom's and is spoken in her voice. Thus there is no real incoherence in this passage, contrary to McKane (p. 362), who excises vv 2 and 4 so as to have Wisdom alone addressing mankind.

at the tops of the city heights: Wisdom chooses the most public setting for her invitation, as does her rival, Lady Folly.

Wisdom's repast, following immediately upon the construction of her residence, may celebrate a house dedication (Meinhold). This banquet is not a unique event but an ongoing occurrence in the ever-present time of myth and parable. Wisdom is always and forever building her house, preparing her feast, and inviting people in.

9:4. *Whoever is callow*: In the preceding chapter, Wisdom addressed all mankind (8:4), then focused her attention on the callow and stupid (*pᵉta'im, kᵉsilim*; 8:5). Now she appeals to the naif (the *peti*), who is susceptible to seduction, and to the senseless man (*ḥăsar leb*), who is an empty vessel, but no distinction is drawn here between the two types. Though they are both unpromising material, there *is* hope that they will "abandon callowness" (*pᵉta'yim*) (v 6). The Prologue's promises, which include "to give the callow cunning," resonate in Wisdom's invitation.

Whoever is senseless: lit. "devoid of heart." The "whoever" (*mi*) of v 4a (with the interrogative *mi* serving as an indefinite pronoun) applies to this clause as well.

to him I'll say: MT has "to him she says" (*'amᵉrah lo*), awkwardly switching to the third person within first-person discourse. A minor change in vocalization to the first person (cohortative) *w'ōmᵉrāh* (= Syr) yields a smoother sentence. The cohortative form conveys volition or determination: "I will surely say to him." Although the sentence is structured as if one invitation were being issued to the callow (v 4a) and another to the senseless (v 4b), the two combined constitute a single call.

9:5. *Come, dine on my food* . . . : The word for food, *leḥem* (used also in v 17b), is usually translated "bread" but (like English "bread" in an earlier usage) means solid food of all kinds.

In a Ugaritic myth, El gives a banquet and invites the gods in similar words: "Eat, gods, and drink. Drink wine unto satiety, must unto drunkenness!" (KTU 1.114.2–4).

Wisdom is the sustenance of the soul. (Compare "Man does not live by food alone"; Deut 8:3.) The metaphorical invitation in Isa 55:1 to eat and drink without cost is explained in the next two verses as listening to the prophet's teaching. Ben Sira says that when a man fears the Lord, Wisdom will "feed him the bread of perspicacity [*leḥem śekel*] and give him the water of understanding [*mey* t^e*bunah*] to drink" (Sir 15:3). In contrast, the (spiritual) bread and wine of evildoers is wickedness (Prov 4:17).

I have mixed: Strong, thick wine was typically cut by adding water, which may be the intention here. In this context, however, we would expect a detail embellishing the luxury of the feast—namely that she has mixed her wine with spices (Meinhold; cf. Cant 8:2).

9:6. *Abandon callowness*: This demand suggests that callowness is a condition that its possessor is deliberately embracing rather than merely the absence of a quality not yet gained (such as learning or sophistication). This is confirmed by 1:22, which scolds the callow for *loving* their callowness. The view of callowness as a discardable impediment (which probably applies to folly of other sorts as well) perceives wisdom as a natural condition, which one reaches by first shucking off psychological encumbrances.

and live: This is meant literally, for "the waywardness of the callow will kill them" (1:32), meaning that they will die prematurely. But, additionally, *life* in Proverbs connotes a fortunate, vital condition, and not only the avoidance of death (see comment on 3:2).

walk in the path of understanding: Underlying this injunction is the metaphor of folly as a path or, perhaps, a pathless wasteland. The callow are to abandon it and enter onto the path of understanding, which is the straight road. The verb *ʾišru* "go," "walk forward," or "walk in a path" (G-stem; the D has a similar sense in 4:14) may, by sound association with *yašar* "straight," connote "walk straight"; compare *ham*^{e}*yaššerim ʾorḥotam*, lit. "make their ways straight," in 9:15b.

9:11. *for through me* . . . : This verse directly reinforces v 6 and was its original continuation.

and years be added to your life: lit. "and they'll add to you years of life."

This verse combines phrases from earlier chapters:

(9:11a) "for through me your days will increase"	(4:10b) "that [years of life] may increase for you"
	(+ 3:2aα) "for length of days"

(9:11b) "and they'll add to you years of life"	(≈ 3:2b) "they'll add to you" (+ 3:2aβ) "years of life."

The verb *yôsîpû*, translated perforce as a passive, is actually a transitive, "will add," with no subject available. The form has been transferred rather mechanically from 3:2b, where *yôsîpû* has as its subject "my teaching/precepts" in the preceding verse. Emending in 9:11b to the N-stem *yiwwās*ᵉ*pû* (Ehrlich, BHS, and many) smooths out the syntax but does not account for the difficult syntax of the MT.

9:13–18. Lady Folly's Banquet

The Septuagint begins this section with a long allegorical insertion about going astray in alien fields, 9:12a–c (Addition 1). See the Textual Notes.

Lady Wisdom has her antithesis in Lady Folly. Though less vigorous than her rival, Folly too presents herself to the public and invites passersby to enjoy her treats. Death, not life, awaits those who do her bidding.

Lady Folly is a literary personification with no mythological roots. The author is less interested in her than in Wisdom and depicts her in pallid colors, with little narrative development. The motive for the creation of this personification is rhetorical, to create a symmetry between wisdom and folly. Lang (1986: 168) aptly compares the classical device of *synkrisis* or *comparatio*, in which two persons or points of view are set in confrontation.

9:13. *The foolish woman*: *ʾešet k*ᵉ*silut*, lit. "woman of folly." This must be translated "foolish woman" (cf. 11:16, "woman of grace" = "gracious woman"; sim. 12:4; 21:9, 19; 25:24, etc.), not "folly" or "woman folly." Nevertheless, we are constrained by context to understand this "foolish woman" as the personification or embodiment of folly rather than as a human fool. First of all, the antithesis between her and personified Wisdom is deliberate: They are both stationed at the city heights and invite passersby to their houses. They address the callow and senseless in the same words. Wisdom brings life, and folly death. Moreover, in v 13b the "foolish woman" is called "callowness" (*p*ᵉ*tayyut*), an abstraction. Lady Folly represents all folly, and "foolish woman" is her epithet, as if Lady Wisdom had been called "wise woman" rather than "Wisdom."

Driver (1951: 178) calls *ʾēšet k*ᵉ*sîlût*, lit. "foolish woman," a periphrasis for "foolish," on the grounds that Hebrew has no fem. for *k*ᵉ*sîl*. But the form *k*ᵉ*sîlāh* could have been produced as easily as *k*ᵉ*sîlût*. Delitzsch says that the genitive is appositional, i.e., "the woman folly" (*Frau Torheit*), comparing *bat ṣiyyôn* "Daughter Zion." But the epexegetical genitive does not occur with *ʾēšet-*.

Traditional Jewish exegesis usually regarded this figure as a foolish human woman. She was also explained as a *mašal* (in this case, "figure") of a variety of entities: a babbling fool (*šotah*) (Radaq); idolatry and false prophecy (cited by Radaq); Eve (*Midr. Prov.*); the fool's body, which seeks ease (Ralbag); the scoffer mentioned in vv 7–8 (Naḥmias); unworthy materiality, which tempts a man to sensual pleasure (Hameʾiri); an inadequate teacher, who attracts unprepared students and confuses them with stolen and contradictory discourses (also Hame-ʾiri). No one seems to have explained her as the *mašal* of folly itself.

boisterous: Lady Folly is *homiyyah*, loud and agitated, like her human counterpart (7:11a). Wisdom too cries aloud, but Folly makes muddled or strident noises (*hamah* means "murmur" or "roar") rather than a lucid, stately proclamation.

callowness itself [*pᵉtayyut*]: "Itself" has been added in translation to suggest the use of an abstraction to characterize the essence of a human personality. In the present text, *pᵉtayyut* is a nominal predicate of "foolish woman."

In v 13b, Ramaq suggests *pᵉtayyût* is short for *ʾēšet pᵉtayyût*; but this would disturb the syntax of the line. The abstract noun *pᵉtayyût* is best taken as a nominal predicate used adjectivally to express the essence of an attribute: "callowness itself." For similar cases, see the comment on 3:17 and cf. GBH §154e. The expected vocalization is *pᵉtiyyût*.

It is ironic that Lady Folly is herself gullible—a *pᵉtiyyah*, we might say, just like her "guests," the *pᵉtaʾim*. (*Pᵉtayyut* cannot have an active sense, "seductive" [Plöger, Meinhold]; that would require a denominative or ptcp. from the D-stem.)

knows nothing at all: As Lady Wisdom is wise and knowledgeable, so is Lady Folly foolish and ignorant. Seducers and deceivers think they are shrewd and hold their victims in contempt, but they too are ninnies and ignoramuses. Prov 4:19b; 5:6b; and 7:23b speak of their "not knowing."

Ehrlich proposes an alternative explanation worth considering: "Folly utters callowness and knows no shame." Ehrlich deletes *ʾšt* as a dittography of *tśʾ* at the end of v 12 and follows the LXX's reading *klmh* (*kᵉlimmāh*) "shame" for *mh* at the end of v 13. (Words from *k-l-m* can designate the mortification one feels or should feel when guilty of wrongdoing; e.g., Ezek 16:52; Jer 3:3; and Jer 8:12 [with *ydʿ*].) The word *hmyh* (which he vocalizes *hōmᵉyāh*) is to be treated as a verb, "utters," with *pᵉtayyût* as its object (thus already Hameʾiri). The sentence thus construed makes a nice contrast with 8:7, "for my palate utters [*yehgeh*] truth"; compare also Ps 37:30: "The mouth of the righteous utters [*yehgeh*] wisdom."

9:14. *sits at the door of her house*: This may be one way that a prostitute presented herself in ancient times. Folly has no counterpart to Wisdom's building her house before her feast, because building one's house is an act of wisdom, whereas folly destroys it (14:1).

on a chair at the city heights: Like Wisdom, Folly seeks a public venue and appears in much the same places as Wisdom. They are often in proximity, proposing alternative choices in many circumstances.

Wisdom invested energy and care in preparing her banquet, in contrast to Folly's indolence. Wisdom is energetic, effective, and clever, like the Excellent Woman of 31:10–31 (Meinhold). Folly neither makes preparations nor sends out messengers, but merely sits at her door summoning passersby. The food she provides is, after all, stolen.

9:15. *going straight ahead*: lit. "who are making their way straight" (*hammᵉyaššᵉrim ʾorḥotam*). Idioms meaning "going straight" always connote moral virtue. This implies that the passersby Folly hopes to ensnare are not the wicked, who, after all, require no further enticement. Folly calls to ordinary people who are going about their business and are presumed honest. She hopes to sidetrack some gullible and witless souls among them.

9:16. *Whoever is callow. . . . Whoever is senseless*: As in v 4 (q.v.), MT reads "she says" (*wᵉʾāmᵉrāh*) but revocalization to *wᵉʾōmᵉrāh*, following the LXX, produces a smoother text: "I will say" or "may I say." Folly mimics Wisdom's call in v 4 but to the opposite effect, for Folly wants to exploit the failings that Wisdom would remedy.

9:17. *'Stolen water is sweet . . .'*: Folly is telling the truth, but her message has two faces. The wise recognize her words as an unintended warning to be wary of sweet pleasures, for the sweetness is just a coating for their poison. The foolish hear the same words as encouragement to taste illegitimate pleasures, for these will prove sweet. Neither Folly nor her human counterpart, the Strange Woman, tells actual falsehoods. Both lure and trap their quarry through truths craftily told. The net lies spread in plain sight (1:17), and the fool cannot claim that he was tricked by falsehood. Folly dupes her victims by showing them what they want to see.

Water can allude to sexual intercourse, as in 5:15–20, and that is the first illicit indulgence that comes to mind here too. But Folly's allure is not confined to the sexual, and her statement applies to illicit gratifications of all sorts—greed, say, or pride. Thus these too pick up undertones of lewdness.

Folly insinuates that legitimate pleasures, such as sex with one's own wife, are somehow deficient. Stolen, clandestine pleasures have a special tang because they give a feeling of surplus of possession, of having more than is one's due. There is also a special sense of power to be had from defying authority and transgressing boundaries, and in that way furtively imposing one's will on a corner of the moral economy. The man who yields to this temptation is therefore not simply driven by lust or blinded by naiveté. Though naive, he is not really an "innocent" (as *peti* is sometimes rendered). He is guilty and relishing it. If he surrenders to the seduction, he is impelled by a measure of depravity or perversity that makes his sin all the more titillating for being sinful.

When the Strange Woman mentions her husband and his absence (7:19), it is not just to assure the boy that they would not be caught in the act. She is also adding a dash of spice to her bait. When the muggers coax a youth to join them, they do not appeal to his greed alone. They dangle the very injustice of their act before the newcomer as an added attraction, as they invite him to "waylay the innocent man *without cause*" (1:11).

9:18. *But he knows not that ghosts are there*: Wisdom imparts life (v 11), Folly death (v 18). Folly's house, like the Strange Woman's (2:18; 7:27), is at once the path to death and the place thereof. It is the netherworld itself.

depths of Sheol: The deepest parts of the netherworld are the worst (cf. Ps 86:13; Ezek 26:20; 31:14–18; 32:24, using derivatives of *t-ḥ-t* rather than *ʿ-m-q*, as here).

Folly's banquet for the ghosts (or "shades"), the Rephaim, may allude to a mythological motif known from Ugarit. In a group of poorly understood texts, the high god El invites the "shades" (*rpum*, perhaps pronounced *rapiuma*) to a feast at his palace:

> Come to my banquet.
> Set off to my house, O shades.
> Into my house I bid you,
> I beckon you into my palace.
> (CTA 21.ii (A) 9–11; transl. T. Lewis 1996: 129; brackets omitted)

The "shades," elsewhere called "shades of the underworld," are also called *ilnym* "divine spirits" and "the warriors of Baal"/"the warriors of Anat." They come and feast for seven days. In Ugarit, the shades seem to be dead heroes, whereas in Israel they include all the dead, and they are depleted of the vitality ascribed to them in Ugarit. Their meal is a spectral, pallid affair, held in the underworld, not (as in the Ugaritic texts) a lively feast in the high god's palace.

The LXX adds an epigram here; see the Textual Notes.

The Design of Interlude E

- I. Wisdom's banquet (9:1–6 + 11 = 7 verses; 15 lines)
  - A. Setting (1–3)
    - 1. Preparations (1–2)
    - 2. Location and issuance of invitation (3)
  - B. Invitation (4–6)
    - 1. Summons to passersby (4)
    - 2. Offer of "food" (5–6)
  - C. Reason to accept: life (11)
- II. Folly's banquet (13–18 = 6 verses; 12 lines)
  - A. Setting (13–15)
    - 1. Description of hostess (13)
    - 2. Location and issuance of invitation (14–15)
  - B. Invitation (16–17)
    - 1. Summons to passersby (16)
    - 2. Praise of her "food" (17)
  - C. Reason to refuse: she is lethal (18)

THE BACKGROUND OF THE TWO BANQUETS

In his influential cultic interpretation of the female figures in Prov 1–9, G. Boström (1935: 156–61) argues that *ʾešet kᵉsilut* (whether translated "the foolish woman" or emended to "folly") is modeled on a cultic prostitute who offers herself to strangers as a sacral act. The "water" and "bread" in 9:17 represent the entire forbidden cult, including the sacrificial meal and associated sexual activity. The woman personifies the immorality of the cult of Astarte, goddess of love. Lady Wisdom was secondarily created as an antithesis to the Strange Woman and possesses her lineaments in reverse (pp. 156–59). McKane (pp. 360–65) accepts much of Boström's analysis while adding that Wisdom is inconsistently portrayed as both the love goddess and her devotee. Along similar lines, L. Perdue believes that folly is personified as a fertility goddess, an "Ishtar, Asherah, or Anat." Her solicitation may be an invitation to participate in fertility rites, which offer life and well-being (1994: 98–100).

Such identifications have no anchoring in the text. Lady Folly has none of the characteristics of these goddesses. She does not hold forth fertility, but only sweetness and pleasure, evanescent gains with no promise of productivity or prosperity.

Lady Folly may well be modeled on a prostitute, but there is nothing cultic about her act. The essence of cultic prostitution is the woman's consecration to, and possibly representation of, the love goddess, and there is no hint of that here. The text, whose main purpose, according to Boström, is to warn against cultic immorality, fails entirely to convey that message. Neither banquet in chapter 9 has the trappings of cult. (If they did, the women would be receiving the meat, not offering it to their guests, and the food would be designated by terms appropriate to oblations.) Boström's explication of the details of the two banquets by reference to the cult of Aphrodite is based largely on his speculations about the latter.

Taking a fresh approach to the possibly foreign background of Folly's background, R. Clifford (1993), turns to ancient literary texts for the literary prototype of Folly's banquet and finds it in an epic type-scene of rebuffed seduction. This scene he believes to be exemplified in Ishtar's proposition to Gilgamesh (VI.i.1–79), in Anat's request of Dan'el, in 2 *Aqhat* (CTA 17.5.26–55), and in Calypso's proposal to Odysseus (*Odyssey* V 202–9; cf. Circe's proposition in book X). The type-scene has three defining features: (1) At issue is marriage or a long-term relationship, not merely a one-time escapade. (2) The young man's choice means life or death. (3) The hero recognizes the offer as deceitful and spurns it (Clifford 1993: 68–69). (This type-scene supposedly influenced chapter 7 as well.) Prov 9 modifies the type-scene by incorporating it into Wisdom literature and by introducing a third character, Wisdom, who unmasks the deceptive offer, while the man is left silent (pp. 69–70). In the light of this prototype, Clifford reads the Strange Woman passages as a warning not against promiscuity so much as against a "false marriage or relationship" (p. 72).

It seems, however, that Clifford's comparisons effectively *eliminate* the relevance of these scenes to Prov 9. All they have in common is the "spurious or deceitful offer" by a female. Anat is not seeking marriage or sex. Calypso's offer is genuine. Lady Folly is not proposing marriage, just furtive and transient thrills with no obligations or commitments. (The relationship will, ironically, be permanent, but this is hardly the feature that attracts her guests.) Contrary to the supposed type-scene, the passersby do not all reject Folly's offer. Nor is it true that Lady Wisdom exposes the danger of Folly's solicitations, for v 18 is in the author's voice, not Wisdom's.

There is no need to look elsewhere to trace the literary background of Folly's banquet. The banquet motif is an expansion of the "feast" to which the Strange Woman invites the gullible youth in 7:14–17. Wisdom's banquet is an alternative to the Strange Woman's, and Folly's invitation provides a negative counterpart to Wisdom's. The banquets in chapter 9 are not private, like the one in chapter 7, but open to many participants.

LIFE AS A BANQUET

To the root trope of PATHS THROUGH LIFE (see pp. 128ff.), Interlude E adds another metaphor for life's choices: food. People are offered two repasts. Both are savory and enticing (on the sweetness of wisdom's food, see 24:13–14), but one is life-giving, the other toxic. These images have antecedents in earlier metaphors, namely the fruit-bearing tree of life (3:18; 8:19[187]), the Strange Woman's proffered meats (7:14), and the evil bread and wine of the wicked (4:17).

With the aid of hints and statements about wisdom and folly elsewhere, we may form a picture of the two banquets. These banquets resemble the Hellenistic *symposium*, which was a practice among Jews as well and is vividly described by Ben Sira (31:12–32:13 [34:12–35:17]). The Hebrew for "feast" is *mišteh*, lit. "drinking." Greek *symposion* literally means "drinking together." In Sir 32:7 [35:5] and Esth 7:7, *mišteh* (or *mišteh yayin*) is translated *symposion*.

The Greek symposium was a ceremonial gathering mainly for drinking, sometimes held in a religious fraternity or (later) a philosophical school. Wine was mixed in a krater for distribution. (According to the LXX of 9:2, Wisdom "has mixed her wine into a krater.") It was commonly accompanied by music, poetry, and other forms of entertainment, sometimes degenerating into inebriation and sexual license. The banquet and its procedures were directed by a *symposiarch*, sometimes called "king." In Sir 32[35]:1, the Greek calls this person *hēgoumenon* "leader," which Segal (1958) retroverts to Hebrew *śar* "prince." See further Segal's discussion ad loc. of Jewish references to this practice. Some Greek symposia were attended by *hetaerae* (courtesans or concubines). Similar banquets were well known in the ancient Near East. In Ugarit, a social organization known as *marzaʾu* (= Heb *marzeaḥ*) held drinking feasts (and compare El's invitation, quoted in the comment on 9:5). A "*marzeaḥ* of recliners" is mentioned in Amos 6:4–8. (For descriptions of Greek symposia and their oriental counterparts, see von der Mühll 1976, Murray 1983, and the essays in Slater 1991: esp. pp. 1–6, 7–24, 152.)

Banquets are everywhere, and drunken follies not rare. But there are also banquets of the wise. The notion of a banquet of the wise, implicit in Lady Wisdom's invitation, recalls one (by no means universal) Greek practice and ideal: the symposium as an occasion for philosophical discussion, of which Plato's symposium was the most eminent example.

---

[187] Ben Sira says that Wisdom offers "the bread of intelligence and the water of good sense" (15:3).

Especially from the fourth century B.C.E. on, symposia were the setting for displays of poetry, wisdom, and erudition (Murray 1983: 270–71). Ben Sira describes such a banquet in the Jewish world (Sir 32[35]:1–13). He praises fine words (*dbrym ypym*) at a wine feast (*mišteh hayyin*, translated *en symposiǭ oinou*) (v 5b, Hebrew only). He informs older men that it is appropriate for them to display their wisdom (*tithakkem* = *sophizou*) at symposia (see the Greek of v 5), though not during the music, when they should "hide" their intellect (*śekel*) (v 3). The *Letter of Aristeas* (vv 186–294) also describes a banquet of the wise. The Jewish sages who will translate the Bible into Greek are invited by King Ptolemy to a seven-day symposium, during which he probes their wisdom by posing queries on philosophical topics. One of the topics is wisdom (v 236), and when the king asks, "How ought one to conduct himself at symposia?" the answer is, "By inviting men of learning, who are able to remind him of matters advantageous to the kingdom and the lives of the subjects" (v 286).

We do not have enough details about Wisdom's banquet to fit it securely in the context of Hellenistic symposia, but given the prevalence of this institution in the Hellenistic world, including among Jews, Wisdom's banquet may be envisioned as a symposium of philosophers. The wise eat and drink, listen to wisdom, and discourse upon it. Wisdom sits as symposiarch. As her guests recline on couches and converse on wisdom, they dine on the food and drink of life. Accepting Wisdom's invitation thus does not mean a life of grim self-denial, even if the preparatory stages seem that way (Sir 6:23–25). On the contrary, a life of wisdom is blessed by satisfaction and happiness.

Folly's banquet too is a symposium, for symposia were commonly an occasion for drunken and lewd carousals. Picture Folly's feast: a true *mošab leṣim*, "company of the insolent" (Ps 1:1), with fools lounging about, silly, licentious, lazy, and raucous—just like their hostess. As they gorge on forbidden meats and relish evanescent confections, they feel quite pleased with themselves, thinking themselves clever guys indeed. But in truth, they are nitwits, pathetic and ludicrous, blithely unaware that they sit in the house of death, surrounded by ghosts, to whose number they will soon belong—in a sense, already do. They are the living dead.

9:7–10. Advice to the Adviser

This passage is undoubtedly an addition. It interrupts Wisdom's speech and is inappropriately interposed between the injunction in v 6 and its natural sequel in v 11, which gives the reason (introduced by causal *ki*) for the injunction. The later scribe who inserted these verses apparently doubted that the "callow" and "senseless" are the right recipients of the invitation to wisdom, and so introduced a caveat. The passage does not echo the vocabulary of the preceding section and does not confront Wisdom's invitation directly; it speaks instead to the issue of effective chastisement. It appears, then, that the present passage originated as an independent epigram and was subsequently inserted as a response to Wisdom's summons of the ignorant.

Even within the unit 9:7–10, v 10 seems to have originated separately from vv 7–9. If 9:7–10 is read without its present context, v 10 seems abrupt and isolated, for the practical advice in vv 7–9 does not prepare the way for the definition of wisdom in v 10. In the context of Wisdom's summons, however, v 10 converts the entirety of vv 7–10 into a comment on the moral-religious preconditions of education. Verse 10 has the appearance of a citation of a principle added to vv 7–9 at the time these were inserted after 9:6.

Almost all modern scholars remove 9:7–12 as secondary and regard these verses as a diverse compilation. Toy is typical in regarding 9:7–12 as a "little group of aphorisms, belonging in the body of the Book" (i.e., chapters 10–29), which comprise four independent segments: vv 7–9, 10, 11, and 12. McKane believes that vv 7–12 were added to elaborate on Wisdom's role as a teacher, which is otherwise confined to v 6. Goldingay (1977: 87–93) regards vv 1–6 + 11 as the original core of chapter 9. Verse 10 is a "Yahwistic re-interpretation," while vv 7–9, 12, and 13–18 are later elaborations on the theme of *lāṣôn*, as is LXX 12a–c. Lang (1986: 88) conjectures that vv 7–10 formed the original conclusion of the chapter and were later transposed to their present position. Meinhold suggests that vv 7–12 are a compound of several sayings appended as a conclusion to chapters 1–9. The passage, he says, is transitional and points back to chapter 1 while previewing the subsequent collections. However, no transitional function is evident in 9:7–12. On the contrary, chapter 8 would have filled that function more effectively if Part I had ended there.

9:7. *He who chastises an impudent man* [*leṣ*] *receives insult*: The *leṣ*, arrogant and contemptuous of others, cannot tolerate rebuke. Such a man will react with ire and contempt to any affront to his self-image. Acceptance of criticism requires the wisdom of humility, meaning a recognition of one's own limitations.

he who reproves an evildoer [*rašaʿ*] *gets hurt* [*mumo*]: This line intensifies the warning of the first, for a *rašaʿ*, who is evil in deed, is worse than a *leṣ*, whose offenses are in thoughts and words. Consequently, chastising a *rašaʿ* may bring upon the rebuker physical as well as verbal abuse (*mum*).

In eighteen of twenty occurrences, a *mûm* (= *meʾûm*) is a physical blemish or injury. A *mûm* may be damage caused (*ntn*) by another (Lev 24:19–20). When *mûm* refers to moral blemish (Deut 32:5 and Job 11:15 only), it means *guilt*, which is not something caused by a hostile act of another. Hence in Prov 9:7, *mûm* should be understood as a physical wound, such as a broken tooth (Lev 24:20).

Saʿadia reads this verse as a limited statement—*sometimes* a rebuker ends up hurt and insulted, but not always. This happens when one takes a wrong approach to chastisement, such as speaking out of malice, rebuking in public, or providing inadequate reasons for the censure. But, contrary to this interpretation, the author believes that scorners and sinners reject chastisement, however delivered.

9:8. *Don't reprove an impudent man . . . reprove the wise*: A transition verse to the topic of the wise in v 9.

9:9. *Give (reproof) to the wise. . . . Instruct the righteous man*: "Give" lacks a direct object in the Hebrew, but a noun, *toḥekah* "reproof" or *musar* "discipline" (Ramaq), can be inferred from v 8.

One must instruct those who are by nature open to improvement, namely the wise and righteous. The equation of these two is a peculiarity of Proverbs, for which wisdom is a matter of moral character, which is the sine qua non of intellectual and personal growth.

enhance his learning: lit. "will add instruction," the knowledge he can teach [*leqaḥ*]. See 1:5.

9:10. *Wisdom begins with the fear of the Lord*: lit. "The beginning of [*t^{e}ḥillat-*] wisdom is the fear of the Lord." This reiterates the great principle of Prov 1:7, "The fear of the Lord is the beginning of knowledge." Here the principle provides the rationale for the foregoing counsel: It makes sense to educate only the righteous (9:7–9) because wisdom can grow only on the fertile soil of conscience and piety (v 10). The starting point of education is an awareness of God's presence and a concern for what is right and wrong, even prior to absorbing the particulars of religion and ethics. Intellectual growth leads to a divine grant of wisdom and to a higher form of reverence and knowledge of God (2:5–6). But the goal, wisdom, must be latent in the beginnings, embedded in untutored attitudes and qualities.

Verse 10 situates the observations of vv 7–9 in a larger conceptual framework. While vv 7–9 focus on chastisement (a frequent topic in Proverbs), v 10 turns the passage into an observation on the religious relationship between intellect and moral character and gives the entire passage this scope.

Early in the history of Wisdom literature, Ptahhotep identified moral character, which he epitomized as the ability to *listen*, as the precondition of learning. The son who "loves to listen" (l. 554) can absorb the teachings and prosper. His opposite cannot listen, for he is morally obtuse: "As for the fool who cannot listen, he can do nothing. He sees knowledge as ignorance, benefit as harm" (ll. 575–76). See the excursus on "The Wicked Man," after 2:15.

and understanding (begins with) the knowledge of the Holy One [*w^{e}daʿat q^{e}došim binah*]: This line could be translated as a predication of identity: "And understanding is the knowledge of the Holy One." But since the first line defines the initial step toward wisdom (*t^{e}ḥillat ḥokmah*), we are probably to read *binah* in v 10b as elliptical for *t^{e}ḥillat binah* "the beginning of understanding." Construing thus, the translation is, literally: "and the knowledge of the Holy One is the beginning of understanding." The phrase *daʿat q^{e}došim* "knowledge of the Holy One," in synonymous parallelism with "fear of the Lord," designates an attitude or aptitude—religious awareness—rather than cognitive knowledge about the deity. The formally plural *q^{e}došim* is probably an epithet of God.

A comparison with Prov 2:5, in which *yirʾat YHWH* strictly parallels *daʿat ʾĕlōhîm* ("knowledge of God"), shows the equivalence of *q^{e}dôšîm* and *ʾĕlōhîm* in this locution. Compare also *q^{e}dôšîm // ʾēl* in Hos 12:1. *Q^{e}dōšîm* is usually explained as an honorific plural with reference to God. The word may alternatively be explained as a plural of abstraction meaning "holiness." (Saʿadia seems to intend this by comparing *q^{e}dôšîm* to *šimmûrîm* "keeping," *kippûrîm* "atonement," and *millûʾîm* "installation [of priests].") It can then be used as an abstract-for-concrete epithet of God. (For examples of this trope, see Isa 3:25; Obad 8; Job 32:7; Qoh 10:6a.) This usage is comparable to the honorific "His Holiness" in reference to the pope.

Knowledge of God is first of all a mind-set, an innate *consciousness* of God in one's life. This important concept was discussed previously in "Knowledge of

God and Fear of God" at 2:5. In 30:3, *daʿat qᵉdōšim* stands in contrastive parallelism with *ḥokmah*. Agur says that though he is the most ignorant of men and has not "learned wisdom" (v 3a), he nevertheless does possess "knowledge of the Holy One" (*daʿat qᵉdošim ʾedaʿ*). Such knowledge is thus not erudition, but an untutored awareness of divinity—God's presence, will, and works. Prov 9:10 also distinguishes between knowledge of the Holy One and wisdom, but makes the former a prerequisite to the latter.

WHO CAN LEARN, AND HOW? A DEBATE IN ANCIENT PEDAGOGY

The authors of Wisdom literature were teachers, whether in the school or in the home, and as such they gave thought to the means and possibilities of education. This excursus examines three ancient ideas on innate learning ability and its relation to learning, as these are expressed in Proverbs and in Egyptian Wisdom literature.

At issue is the way the ancient sages defined the scope of god-given (in modern terms, innate) learning capacity. In both traditions, opinions varied as to who is capable of learning and how moral education can best be pursued.

Three views come to expression in both Wisdom traditions:

(1) Some people are closed to learning, and there's no point in trying to teach them.
(2) Learning is always possible, because teaching is the imposition of will on resistant material.
(3) Learning is often problematic, but it is always in principle possible, given the right approach.

These three views do not follow in historical progression but emerge at various stages in the history of Wisdom literature and can coexist in a synchronic dialectic.

A. In Egypt

The dispute about the possibilities of learning emerged first among Egyptian sages, in a dialogue extending through many centuries. This dispute has invariably been construed as the clash between determinism and free will—the "nature or nurture" debate[188]—but the argument is more nuanced than that.

---

188 The standard study of the issues discussed here is Hellmut Brunner's *Altägyptische Erziehung* (1957; esp. 112–16 on "The Consciousness of the Possibilities and Limitations of Education," see also Brunner 1991: 35–36. Similarly Quack 1994: 186–93), though he translates the passage quite differently.

There are three viewpoints, and although one of them can be called "deterministic," this is not meant as a philosophical or theoretical category but as a label for the implications of the attitude in question.

1. Some People Cannot Learn

Some Egyptian sages believed that obtuseness is innate and indelible in some people, not because of stupidity but because of ingrained moral perversity. This is not a statement on human nature generally but an observation about individuals. This belief was born not of theory or philosophy, but of a teacher's frustration at the impenetrability of some pupils, who may be intellectually capable of improving but refuse to do so. This frustration is revealed in the exclamation of the teacher in the NK Pap. Lansing (LEM 101–2), who is stymied by his inability to force his pupil to learn: "If only I knew another way of doing it! Then I would do it for you and you would listen" (2.8). But he cannot think of one.

The most elaborate exposition of the deterministic viewpoint is in the Instruction of Ptahhotep, mainly in the conclusion, ll. 534–607. Ptahhotep contrasts two types of people: those who listen and those who do not. "Listening" or "hearing" is the precondition and means of moral growth. Ptahhotep's purpose is to encourage the reader to be a "listener," but in doing so, he reveals his assumption that this crucial faculty must be infused in an individual's character at birth: "He whom god hates does not listen" (l. 546; cf. AEL 1.74). The morally deaf man, Ptahhotep says earlier, has a congenital inability or "impediment" (*sḏb*): The hateful son is "one for whom an impediment was assigned (already) in the womb" (l. 217; cf. AEL 1.67). (A later manuscript (L_2) reformulates this as "one into whom God has driven an impediment [already] in the womb.") The handicap is virtually physical: "It is the heart [the mentality, we might say] that makes its possessor into a listener or a non-listener" (ll. 550–51; cf. AEL 1.74). Within the "hearing" group, there is still much scope for wisdom and ignorance, but nothing can be done for the congenitally obtuse man other than to reject him—as the gods manifestly have done—and make him into a virtual slave, whose every action is commanded by others (ll. 206–19; AEL 1.67).

About a millennium later, O. Petrie 11 echoed this view: "Do not straighten out what is crooked; then you will be loved [compare Prov 9:8b!]. Every man is compelled [lit. "dragged"] by his character just as by his limbs" (rco. 4).

In Pap. Lansing, a teacher castigates his pupil for his refusal to listen and for his dull heart. Even animals, the writer says, can learn, but "even if I beat you with a stick of whatever kind, you do not listen" (2.4–3.3; cf. AEL 2.189). The rod *should* be effective in enforcing education, so when it fails in this, one looks for an explanation in prior disposition.

This view comes to clear expression in Pap. Beatty IV, which quotes it in order to repudiate it:

> Beware of saying,
> "Every man is in accordance with his character,
> The ignorant and the wise are the same thing.

> Shay and Renenet[189] are engraved on one's character
> with the writing of God himself.
> Every man is as he is made,
> and his lifetime is (run) within an hour."
> (vso. 6.5ff.; cf. AW 216)

Belief in the predetermination of moral character was maintained into Hellenistic times. Phibis (Pap. Insinger) urges the reader to persist in instructing his son, yet recognizes that "It is the god who gives the heart, gives the son, and gives the good character" (LEWL 206).[190] Anchsheshonq (in language closely resembling Prov 9:8) warns: "Do not instruct a fool, lest he hate you. Do not instruct him who will not listen to you" (7.4–5; LEWL 72).

2. Everyone Can Be Taught

One way of conceiving of education is as the imposition of the teacher's will on the student, a process epitomized in images of forcing and bending. This is not a statement about individuals but an assumption about human nature generally: It is malleable. The practical motive for this view is to rebut a pupil's excuse that he cannot learn, that the task is beyond him. Model letters addressed to students and copied in the schools dismiss this rationalization, using, among other arguments, the cliché that even animals can be trained:

> Pay attention and listen to what I have said, that it may be of use to you. Apes can be taught to dance; horses can be tamed; a kite can be put in a nest; a falcon can be pinioned. Persevere in seeking advice and do not weary of it. (Pap. Anastasi III, 4.1–4; LEM 24)

This topos occurs several times in the school miscellanies.[191] Education is training, and this includes character education as well as booklearning. And children are fundamentally similar.

The scribe Anii, in the dialogue with his son discussed later, insists vehemently that neither human limitations nor the difficulty of the teachings is an excuse for failure to learn. Learning can be forced on everyone. Anii spins out a long series of analogies, many of them mustered for use in the "imposition and training" topos attested elsewhere, to show that anyone can be made to learn.

The fact that everyone *can* learn does not mean that everyone *will*. After all, Anii does not assure his son that he *will* learn but rather gets angry at him for saying he cannot. "Oh heart that cannot think! Do you desire wisdom, or are you corrupt (23.14–15)?" There is a certain inconsistency here, since resistance to learning *is* possible. The assumption is that human nature allows for learning, just as equine nature allows for training, so if someone resists, that can only be

---

[189] Gods who determine an individual's destiny.

[190] Lichtheim (LEWL, esp. 184–96) shows that West Asian influence on Egyptian Wisdom is likely in the Hellenistic period, and this saying in Anchsheshonq seems to be one such case.

[191] E.g., Pap. Sallier I, 7.1–8.2 (LEM 85) and Pap. Bologna 1094, 3.9–10 (LEM 3–4).

evidence of deliberate perversity. But what makes a person perverse if not constraints of innate character? This brings us back to the first view. Down deep, they share an underlying view of character and intellect, which is pessimistic at the core.

3. Teaching Requires the Right Approach

The author of Pap. Beatty IV (whose repudiation of the deterministic view was quoted on pp. 310f.) rejects the doctrine that one's character is fixed at birth and that his life is too short to allow significant change. But this author does not assume that the cure for sluggish learning is simply greater rigor in teaching. Rather, he goes on to say:

> Instruction is good,
> when (the pupil) does not weary of it.
> (Then) a son will speak out
> with the saying of his father.
>
> (vso. 6.7–8; cf. AW 229)[192]

I take this to mean that good instruction is pleasant and does not require the pupil to weary himself. When it succeeds, the son can respond in conformity to what he was taught.

The third view emerges most clearly, and somewhat earlier than Pap. Beatty IV, in the epilogue of Anii (22.13–23.17).[193] This epilogue is a lengthy debate between view 2, represented by Anii, and view 3, advocated by his son Khonsuhotep, the recipient of the instruction. Rather than asserting that the teacher's mold can be forcibly impressed on the pupil's raw material, the epilogue holds that gentler methods alone can shape character. This is a profound innovation in pedagogical thought.

The epilogue is probably a later addition to Anii's instruction. It differs from the epilogues of other Wisdom instructions by recording a debate of principle rather than reporting the reception and transmission of the instruction. Also, the scribe of the instruction proper (Anii) would not compose a dialogue in which he himself was effectively challenged and possibly bested, or at least not decisively victorious. Since Wisdom instructions were sometimes transmitted within the family,[194] the epilogue may have been written and appended by Khonsuhotep himself, in order to express his own ideas on learning and teaching. He does seem to get the better of the argument.

---

[192]The relation between the last two clauses is ambivalent. It may be temporal (". . . when a son answers") or jussive (". . . let a son answer").

[193]The dialogue may be found in AEL 2.145–46.

[194]See Ptahhotep ll. 30–32, 590–96; Duachety (XXXg = Pap. Sallier II, 11.4); and the ending of Kagemeni, in which the old vizier transmits his teaching in writing to his children. See "The Authors and Their Social Setting," in the Introduction (VI).

Khonsuhotep protests that his father's teachings are too difficult for him to master. He quotes the proverb "Every man is compelled by his personality [*inw*, lit. 'complexion']" (22.14f.).[195] Anii assumes that Khonsuhotep is reiterating the deterministic excuse that one who lacks the right predisposition *cannot* learn (= view 1), and he disputes this by insisting that education can indeed be imposed on anyone, for the teacher's willpower can subdue inborn refractoriness (= view 2). But Anii has not heard his son correctly and does not get his point. The dispute proceeds through four exchanges of opinion.

Khonsuhotep believes that everyone can learn, but not because everyone can be forced to learn. At issue is method, not metaphysics. Khonsuhotep invokes the constraints of inborn character not to assert that some people are unable to learn, and that is that, but to say that people must be taught *in accordance with* their character. As the means of overcoming barriers to learning, Khonsuhotep advocates pleasantness and moderation in instruction rather than mere pressure to memorize and recite, for the ability to iterate the teachings does not assure their performance: "A youth does not carry out the ethical instructions [*sb'yt mtrt*] (if) books have (merely) appeared upon his tongue" (22.17). The books must also be *received* (*šsp* = Heb *lqḥ*) in the heart, to which end they must be communicated pleasantly and in right measure (22.16).

Anii replies by reiterating the tiresome commonplace that everyone can be compelled to learn. Education "conquers" character: Wild animals can be tamed, dogs and geese trained, foreigners taught Egyptian (22.17–23.7). Again he misses the point.

Khonsuhotep's reply (23.7–11) is an extraordinary move in the history of educational thought:[196]

> (7) Do not make your strength overbearing. (8)
> I am wronged by your arguments.[197]
> Has there never been a man who relaxed his arm,
> so as to hear an appropriate response?
> Men are the likenesses [*snw*][198] (9) of God:

---

[195] Or, "toward [*r*] his personality," that is to say, drawn after it, as if by a rope.

[196] There are a number of uncertainties and textual corruptions in this passage and the translations differ. Quack's rendering (1994: 123–27) differs from the above in several respects. He translates *sn* as "Gefährte" ("companion," "associate") rather than "image" (of God).

The present translation assumes certain emendations, for which see Quack (1994: 123–27), and implicitly supplies some determinatives. Some pronouns have been replaced by their referents in translation. In spite of these uncertainties, the gist of the passage is clear.

[197] The word used is *sḫrw*, apparently referring to Anii's comparison of Khonsuhotep to animals and foreigners.

[198] Egyptian *sn* means "likeness" or "second," not (physical) "image." ("Gefährte," as Quack prefers to translate *sn*, places man and God too much on the same plane.) Humans are God's *snw* by virtue of resembling him, in particular in the possession of reason (B. Ockinga 1984: 139). Khonsuhotep relates wisdom to divinity when he calls his father *p'y.f mitt p' rḫ tnr m ḏrt.f*, "His [God's] semblance, wise man with strong arm" (23.15f.; Ockinga 1994: 87–88).

their practice is to hear a man with his statement.[199]
It is not only the wise man who is his (God's) likeness,[200]
while the masses have all become cattle.
It is not the wise (man) alone (10) whom (God) teaches,
so that (only) one man becomes a possessor of a heart,[201]
while all the multitude are stupid.
All you say is excellent indeed. (11)
It is judged (so?) by the spirit (?).
Say to the god who gave you understanding:
"Set them [namely, my children] upon your path." (23.7–11)

The old analogy of animal training fails, Khonsuhotep says, because to teach is to imitate God[202] and it is godly to listen before answering. That is, after all, how God receives prayer. In other words, let the God-worshiper model replace the master-beast model. And not only should a son listen to his father, as all the sages said, but *a father should listen to his son*. Indeed, a man is godlike when he listens patiently to another who has something to say, in particular a pupil.

Moreover, it is not only the elite who are able to learn. The mass of men can do so, given the right approach, for the real teacher of all is God. So, Khonsuhotep urges his father, give instruction in gentle, moderate words, and ask God for help in setting your children on the right path.

Anii, unmoved, comes back with another analogy: Straight sticks can be bent into an axle (23.14). Why, then, does Khonsuhotep resist? "Do you desire to comprehend, or are you corrupt?" (23.15).

Khonsuhotep answers:

"See," he said, "(you) [God's] likeness,
wise man with strong arm:
The infant who is in his mother's bosom,
his desire is to suck." (23.15–16)

---

[199]"Statement" = *wšbt*, which commonly means "response" or "charge." The verb *wšb* usually means "answer, response" but, like Hebrew *ʿanah*, sometimes means "speak up"—responding not to a question but to a statement or situation (cf. Job 3:2). Khonsuhotep has himself in mind in the first instance. His statements, as well as his father's, are introduced by *wšb* "responded."

Learning to give the right "response" is a goal of Wisdom instruction. Anii teaches that excelling in one's "responses" protects him from punishments (15.8–9 [not in AEL]), and that one should choose the right "response" from the ones stored in his belly (20.10). P. Beatty IV says, "Instruction is good, without wearying of it, (and then) a son responds [or "speaks out," *wšb*] with the saying of his father" (vso. 6.7–8; cf. AW 229). Good "responses" are often praised elsewhere.

[200]Or "Does not one (man) know his fellow?"

[201]Possibly "Does not one (man) know his teaching, so that one becomes a possessor of a heart?" i.e., intelligent.

[202]See also 23.11, quoted later.

Of course, Khonsuhotep wishes to learn—even an infant in arms craves what nourishes him.[203] The desire to learn is innate; the question is how to stimulate and satisfy it.

The final sentence reads:

> "Look," said he, "when [the child] finds his mouth [= learns how to speak] what he says is, 'Give me food.'" (23.16–17)

These words could be a continuation of Khonsuhotep's speech, reiterating his principle with a new model. It is, however, more likely that Anii is speaking here, since there is a new *verbum dicendi* (though indefinite), and the preceding sentence, though it too lacks specification of speaker, is clearly Khonsuhotep's. If so, Anii has in the end been persuaded. However, the sentence is ambiguous, and Anii might be understood as saying that Khonsuhotep should use his mouth to ask for intellectual nutrition rather than complaining that he cannot digest it. Or, perhaps, he means that his son should seek "solid" food, such as Anii has been trying to provide.

Throughout the epilogue, Anii's response to his son's modest demurral sounds harsh, but in fact Anii is insisting on a democratic notion, that all are educable, no one is beyond hope. Khonsuhotep takes a new tack, denying that learning can be *imposed*, but not because character is predetermined and unalterable. Rather, pushing the pupil too hard is self-defeating. It is better to respond to the innate desire to learn and to choose methods that nurture character.

B. In Israel

1. Some People Cannot Learn

The scribe who inserted 9:7–10 does not believe that fools *can* be educated, at least not if their ignorance is rooted in arrogance and vice.[204] He uses more severe terms for fools than does the author of Wisdom's invitation, as if to say: You might attempt to educate the *naive* and *mindless* (though even this is probably a hopeless task), but if you go further and try to straighten out a *leṣ* or (what is worse) a *rašaʿ*—the very ones who most need the correction—you will only bring harm upon yourself.

The epigram agrees with Prov 13:1b and 15:12, which warn that an impudent man will not heed a rebuke. Other proverbs (15:5; 23:9; 27:22; cf. Sir 22:9–10)

[203]Quack (1994: 193) understands this to mean that the teaching is *inappropriate* to an infant, who is interested only in his mother's milk. Hence, by analogy, it is too hard for Khonsuhotep himself. But it would not be reasonable for Khonsuhotep, who is at least an adolescent, to compare himself to a baby who is oblivious to wisdom. Khonsuhotep never says that he lacks a desire to learn, but only that he finds it impossible to do so under the present conditions. The sentence must mean that just as a babe desires nutrition, so anyone (Khonsuhotep, in this context) naturally craves (intellectual) sustenance.

[204]See the Textual Notes on the Syriac to 8:5.

agree that it is futile to try to educate the scornful and other types of fools. As Ben Sira puts it, "Teaching a fool is like gluing a broken pot" (Sir 22:9). In what could be an echo of Prov 9:8, the Hellenistic Egyptian sage Anchsheshonq cautions: "Do not instruct a fool, lest he hate you. Do not instruct him who will not listen to you" (7.4–5).

Prov 19:25 grants that the *peti* can learn from the beating the *leṣ* receives but holds out no hope for the *leṣ* himself: "Smite an impudent man (*leṣ*) and the callow (*peti*) will gain cunning. Reprove an astute man, and he will gain knowledge"; sim. 21:11. That is to say, *even* the raw and ignorant youngster can learn from watching the beating, whereas the impudent one remains closed to discipline even in this vigorous form. The purpose of these sayings is not so much to assert a pedagogical tenet as to warn the reader that to resist chastisement is to be a fool.

The epigram in 9:7–11 expresses the viewpoint prevalent in Proverbs. There are two types of person: the teachable, who may not yet be wise but *can* progress in learning, and the foolish, who are incapable of learning. The *peti* is, in his present condition, foolish and empty-headed (Prov 7:7), but he is still malleable and can learn (1:4; 19:25; etc.). The teachings are addressed to those who presumably can learn, and there is little hope for the others.

2. Everyone Can Be Taught

In the personification interludes (A, D, and E), Wisdom summons fools as well as the wise. In 8:5, she urges both the callow and dull-minded (*pᵉtaʾim* and *kᵉsilim*) to "get smart" (*habinu leb, habinu ʿormah*). In 1:22, she speaks not only to the callow but also to the impudent and the dull-minded (*leṣim* and *kᵉsilim*). In 1:22, she addresses them in order to excoriate them, but in 1:24 we learn that she had earlier appealed to them to repent.

Wisdom's calls to the foolish (1:22; 8:5; 9:4) are not necessarily a theoretical assertion of the educability of such types. When Wisdom speaks in 1:22, she already knows that the fools ignored her call. Nevertheless, in 8:5 the callow and the dull-minded, and in 9:4 the callow and the mindless, are being invited to learn wisdom. The call to the callow is not problematic, because the *peti* is defined as the primary audience of the book in 1:4; the mindless are similar. As for the pernicious sorts of fools—the *leṣim* (1:22) and the *kᵉsilim* (8:5)—the author may believe that the wise man has a duty to urge them to repent and gain wisdom, just as the prophets preached to the wicked with little expectation of success.

No saying in Proverbs asserts programmatically that everybody can learn, but Prov 22:15 declares confidence in the efficacy of beatings to purge a lad of folly: "Folly [*ʾiwwelet*] is bound to the heart of a lad, but the rod of discipline will remove it from him." A young person starts with a measure of folly, though he is not necessarily a dyed-in-the-wool fool, an *ʾĕwil* whose perversity is probably indelible.

3. Teaching Requires the Right Approach

The third view is that education is possible but demands the right method. This is expounded at length in Prov 2. Even for the educable, the path to wisdom is a difficult one. Prov 2 does not exactly assert that everyone can learn. Instead of coming down on one side of the dichotomy, it gives thought to the process itself. It recognizes that moral education is a difficult process, but it encourages the learner in the search for wisdom by explaining how the process can succeed.

Education, it says, begins with the father's teaching and its rote incorporation by the child (2:1–2), but this must be complemented by the learner's own thought and inquiry—"calling," "digging," and "seeking" (vv 3–4). *Then* God steps into the picture and grants wisdom (v 6)—not the words or propositions of wisdom teaching, but the faculty of wisdom, realized as moral character. Prov 2 assures the pupil that if he seeks wisdom earnestly he will surely find it.

The author of Prov 2 saw the learning process in much the same way as Khonsuhotep: The combined efforts of parent, child, and God bring one to wisdom. Education commences with the father's teaching and its rote incorporation by the child, but this must be complemented by the learner's own thought and inquiry. *Then* God steps into the picture and grants wisdom. This then provides sure guidance and protection throughout his life. See further "The Idea of Education in Lecture II," after chapter 2.

The similarity in the formulation of the three viewpoints in Egypt and Israel is not sufficient to show a direct or genetic connection. It does, however, present a significant analogy: Both Wisdom traditions debated basic questions of the potentials and processes of education. There was, and could be, no simple resolution of the dispute in ancient Wisdom, nor is there one today.

9:12. A Later Addition

Verse 12 was probably added separately from the large insertion in vv 7–10. Whereas that passage addresses the question of who is capable of learning, this verse identifies the recipient of wisdom's benefits, which is a separate issue. The proverb could have been attracted to this location merely by association with the words *ḥakam* and *leṣ* in 9:7–10.

9:12. *If you grow wise . . .* : Wisdom profits its holder while impudence and arrogance hurt their possessor alone. The conditional in 9:12a does not mean that wisdom benefits *only* its possessor. That unlikely notion would require *l^{e}badd^{e}ka* "you alone," as in v 12b. But to prevent the sentence from being read thus, the LXX adds "and for your friends" to 12a. The importance of using one's wisdom to benefit others as well as oneself is emphasized in Sir 37:22–23; cf. 24:34.

According to Saʿadia, the verse admonishes against feeling proud of one's learning, because one pursues it for one's own benefit. He compares Avot 2:49, "If you have learnt much Torah, do not hold it to your credit, because for this were you created." This interpretation, however, does not accord with the parallelism.

you bear (it) alone: The Hebrew lacks an object for "bear" (*tiśśa'*). We may implicitly supply an "it," with reference to the guilt *ʿawon* (Saʿadia) or "the (consequences of) cynicism [*leṣanut*]" (Ramaq).

Following 9:12, the LXX adds an epigram (9:12a–12c, Addition 1) on the futility of straying in foreign territories, meaning alien doctrines. See the Textual Notes.

"The first part of the book of seeking wisdom is here completed. The second part consists of proverbs and words of instruction in disconnected utterances" (Saʿadia).

ESSAYS AND TEXTUAL NOTES ON PROVERBS 1–9

◆

ESSAYS ON PROVERBS 1–9

◆

These essays consider the formation and meaning of Prov 1–9. The first two examine issues of development: (1) the history of the literary formation of the unit and (2) the background and evolution of the figure of personified wisdom. The second two essays examine the idea of wisdom in (3) the lectures and (4) the interludes, as well as the interplay of these ideas in the present text.

Essay 1. The Formation of Proverbs 1–9

A close examination of Prov 1–9 shows that it was not written by a single author but rather grew in several stages. Identifying them and tracing their development, insofar as this is possible, will give us an idea of the historical depth of Wisdom literature and show us how ancient wise men interpreted and built on the achievements of their predecessors.

Modern scholars have seen different degrees of cohesion in Prov 1–9, ranging from fragmentation to unity, from numerous, uncoordinated stages of collection, expansion, and revision, to an all-embracing structure and a single set of ideas.

Fragmentation: At the one extreme, B. Lang calls the unit "an unsystematically compiled piece of school literature without a planned structure, without unity of thought, and without progression in content" (1972: 28).

R. N. Whybray (1994: 11–61) too opts for multiple components and little thematic organization in the final placement of the instructions. He tries, however, to explain the mechanisms and rationale of the growth of the resulting units. He dissects chapters 1–9 into numerous components. The first stage was ten originally independent instructions, namely: (I) 1:8–19; (II) 2:1, 9, 16–19; (III) 3:1–2, 3bc, 4–10; (IV) 3:21–24, 27–31; (V) 4:1–4bα, 5b; (VI) 4:10, 12, 14–19; (VII) 4:20–27; (VIII) 5:1–6, 8; parts of 21–23; (IX) 6:20–21 (or 22), 24–25 + (possibly) 32; and (X) 7:1–3, 5, 25–27. The rest of the material is expansion, including a sporadic series of "wisdom additions," which associated the father's teaching with personified wisdom (2:2–4, 10–15; 4:5–9, 13; 7:4) and an unsystematic set of "Yahweh additions," which associated the father's teaching with Yahweh (2:5–8; 3:26; 5:21). Further additions are the wisdom poems (containing *parts* of 1:20–27, 32–33; 3:13–20; and 8:1–36); chapter 9 (originally 1–6, 13–18) and 6:1–19, comprising four independent poems. The Prologue itself is composite, with 1:1–4 the original core.

In assigning the instructions to different authors, Whybray (pp. 26–32; 56–58) brings as evidence both their similarity to one another (a single author, he believes, would not repeat himself so much; p. 27) *and* their diversity in theme and style (p. 32). (Some of the similarities he ascribes to influence, which he calls "plagiarism"! [p. 35].) The ten instructions, he says, "can hardly be said to constitute a compendium or educational 'syllabus,' since they are manifestly both incomplete and repetitious" (p. 57).

Whybray's procedure is procrustean. He assumes that the instructions—though supposedly by different authors—were extremely uniform to start with. Then he pares down the instructions until they all fit a preconceived primitive mold by excising virtually everything that seems to him to be redundant or emphatic or to change the topic.

Neither repetitiveness nor diversity is evidence for different authorship. Repetitiousness is hardly foreign to educational tracts. Identifying additions and separating compositional layers requires locating the seams: syntactic roughnesses and incompatibilities in conception that run counter to the purpose of the unit as a whole.

Unity: At the other end of the spectrum, Meinhold (pp. 43–46) traces a careful and intricate design that organizes the totality of the first nine chapters, though it is the work of a redactor rather than of an author. Its components are ten *Lehrreden* (= the lectures, in my terminology), four *Weisheitsgedichte* (Interludes A, D, and the two passages of E), and three *Zwischenstücke* (3:13–20 [B], 6:1–19 [C], and 9:7–12). These components he believes to be interwoven in a meaningful pattern, a progressive program whose design is introduced in a "Lehrprogramm" in chapter 2: (a) the right relation to God (2:5–8 and 3:1–12); (b) right relations with other men (2:9–11 and 3:21–25); (c) warnings against wicked men (2:12–15 and 4:10–19 + 20–27); and (d) warnings against the Strange Woman (2:16–19 and 5:1–23 + 6:20–35 + 7:1–27).

Too much violates Meinhold's design for it to be effective in guiding reading or even to be recoverable to most readers. For example, there is no good explanation for the intrusive 3:13–20 and 6:1–19 ("Zwischenstücke"), which, along with 4:1–9 (the fifth instruction), disrupt the design. Moreover, Meinhold's description of the themes of various passages is unnatural and tendentious, aimed at producing the desired correspondences. For example, the label given 2:5–8 (which Meinhold identifies, unnaturally, as the beginning of the *Hauptteil* of the chapter) is "right relation to God," although that is only part of what is said in that section. "Ways of justice" in 2:8 belongs with theme (b) as much as "righteousness, justice, and equity" in v 9 does. In fact, the theme of social relations is no more prominent in the sections assigned to (b) than in (a). Prov 4:12–19 recalls the theme of 2:12–15, but to draw that connection would confuse Meinhold's diagram on p. 46. Similar artificialities in unit segregation and thematic labeling weaken and blur the proposed schema, which, after all, could function only if it were clear and unambiguous. Pivotal to Meinhold's proposal is his idea of the structure of chapter 2, which I discuss in "The Design of Lecture II," after the commentary on that chapter.

The strongest assertion of unity comes from P. Skehan (1947a), who argues that the entirety of Prov 1–9 was precisely crafted. Chapters 2–7 comprise seven columns of uniform length, bracketed in the framework of chapters 1 and 8–9. These are the "seven columns" of Wisdom's house mentioned in 9:1. Skehan's argument, however, requires reorderings and excisions of verses as well as self-serving unit divisions, such as the break between the sixth column, ending at 7:6 (though, as he admits on p. 13, "Prov 7:6 might seem a strange way to end a column") and the seventh, starting at 7:7. See also the discussion of Skehan's analysis of chapter 2, in the discussion of the design of that chapter.

The present essay argues that there is considerable cohesiveness in Prov 1–9, but it is not the result of single authorship. The authorship was, in a sense, collective, the work, perhaps, of several generations. The process described here is not simply the assembling of earlier texts by a later redactor, but a process of growth, in which later authors read, learned from, and elaborated the themes of the earlier texts. The stages of development, as I reconstruct them, were as follows:

1. The base text, comprising a Prologue and a cycle of poems ("the Ten Lectures") by a single author, was written as an introduction to chapters 10–29.
2. Five poems (the interludes), probably by different authors, were added at different times to the Ten Lectures.
3. A few minor scribal insertions were introduced along the way.
4. In the Septuagintal tradition, the process of expansion continued, both in the Hebrew base text and in the Greek textual tradition. These are translated and discussed in the Textual Notes.

Ten Lectures	*Interludes*	*Minor Insertions*	*LXX Additions**
Prologue. 1:1–7			
I. 1:8–19			
	A. 1:20–33		
II. 2:1–22			
III. 3:1–12		3:3a	
	B. 3:13–20		3:16a
IV. 3:21–35			3:22a
V. 4:1–9			
VI. 4:10–19			

Ten Lectures	*Interludes*	*Minor Insertions*	*LXX Additions**
VII. 4:20–27			
VIII. 5:1–23		4:27a, 27b	
	C. 6:1–19	6:8a–8c, 11a	
IX. 6:20–35			
X. 7:1–27			
	D. 8:1–36	8:13a, 19	7:1a
	E. 9:1–6 + 11, 13–18	9:7–10, 12	8:21a
			9:10a, 12a–12c, 18a–d

* Including only substantive additions; excluding doublets and unparalleled LXX material that is a reworking of the MT, as well as hexaplaric expansions.

I. THE LECTURES AND PROLOGUE

A. The Ten Lectures

There is little logical progression from lecture to lecture, nor is there any evident organizational principle in their disposition. The message of the whole would not change significantly if the lectures were in a different order. But this is not to say that the organization of the Ten Lectures is chaotic and haphazard. In form, they constitute a *cycle*, in which ten poems develop a single central theme in different settings and perspectives. (The concept comes from song cycles, such as Mahler's *Das Lied von der Erde* or *Des Knaben Wunderhorn.*) The lectures are variations on a theme: how to withstand seduction (cf. Aletti 1977: 129–44). The programmatic Lecture II understands wisdom's main purpose to be the *guarding* of the young from temptation (2:11). All the lectures address the temptations confronting young men on the brink of adulthood.

There is considerable homogeneity in the structure and language of the lectures. They are all formulated as father-to-son instructions. Each develops a central topic in a tripartite structure, consisting of (1) an exordium (itself tripartite, comprising (a) address to the son, (b) exhortation, and (c) motivation); (2) a lesson; and (3) a conclusion.[205] They tend toward long chains of reasoning, unlike anything elsewhere in Proverbs (and unusual in the Bible as a whole). This homogeneity can be explained by two hypotheses:

Redaction: One possibility is that the lectures were written by different authors and collected by a redactor. This hypothesis is preferred by most commentators, for example Whybray (1994: 26–28) and McKane (p. 7). It entails the assumption that the lectures belonged to a rigid and uniform genre.

There is indeed a well-recognized genre of "instruction" in ancient Near Eastern Wisdom that uses the elements described here, but it shows far greater

[205] Conclusions are lacking, or at least not well demarcated, in Lectures III (but 3:12 may serve that purpose) and V (unless 4:9 has that function).

flexibility and variety than do the lectures in Prov 1–9, and the three structural constituents are distributed differently. This is true both of the other instructions in Proverbs and in foreign Wisdom; see pp. 46ff. Since the instruction genre was not highly uniform, if we ascribe their compilation in Prov 1–9 to the process of compilation, we must suppose that the redactor searched out and assembled poems that happened to express the same ideas in the same way. If so, the result is still a literary unity, though produced by redaction rather than authorship. This is Meinhold's view (pp. 43–46). He regards the first nine chapters as a redacted collection, but one shaped according to a careful and complex design (see pp. 126, 322). This hypothesis is, however, self-defeating, for an intricate design such as he proposes would (if persuasive) argue for single authorship rather than for compilation.

Authorship: Alternatively—and more simply—the Ten Lectures may be ascribed to a single author, who composed them as a unit. The unit may have originally been intended either as an independent book or as an introduction to the rest of the book of Proverbs. The fact that these chapters serve *so well* as an introduction to the rest of the book supports the second alternative. The author (or the literary tradition behind him) took the defining elements of the ancient genre of instruction and introduced them into each literary unit, making each lecture a complete instruction. This reformulation, by placing repeated emphasis on the importance of hearkening to wisdom and on wisdom's benefits, becomes the vehicle for a teaching on the nature of wisdom, which is described in Essay 3.

Further evidence for unity of authorship is the way one lecture alludes to or prepares the ground for others. Lecture II in particular is not an isolated unit. Instead, it lays down methodological and theoretical foundations for the other lectures; see the comment on 2:2. Another instance of a lecture pointing beyond itself is the sentence "I lead you in routes of rectitude" (4:11), in which the "leading" alludes to the speaker's teachings outside Lecture VI; see the discussion after 4:19.

Indeed, all the exordia look beyond the lessons of the units they are in. The "words" and "precepts" and "wisdom" that the listener is to absorb are not limited to the words of the particular lectures that follow but refer to the entirety of the teachings. For example, when the father exhorts his son in 7:1–4 to keep his precepts and become an intimate of wisdom, he does not mean only the warning against the Strange Woman in 7:5–27. He refers to his teaching its entirety, which is an instance of wisdom itself, and this, when learned and assimilated, will protect the son against dangers such as described in the lesson proper. The lessons, in other words, instantiate, but certainly do not exhaust, the wisdom that the exordia praise.

B. The Prologue (1:1–7)

The Prologue was probably added at the same time that the ten lectures were prefixed to the early collections (chapters 10–29) and prior to the insertion of the interludes. The Prologue is oriented more to the goals of the lectures than the rest of the book. The Prologue defines as the book's primary audience the callow youth, the *naʿar* or *peti* (1:4), who is also the implicit audience of the Ten Lectures. For the Prologue (1:5), the wise man is a secondary audience, who may *also* benefit from the book by studying it with a more sophisticated hermeneutic.

The Prologue suggests no awareness of the personification of wisdom, so important in the interludes, or even of its (nonpersonified) reification, which is to say, the conception of wisdom as an independently existing entity.

The Prologue uses terminology important throughout the book. It is noteworthy, however, that *m*ᵉ*zimmah*, one of the faculties the Prologue promises to impart (1:4), constitutes a virtue only in Part I (2:11; 3:21; 5:2; and 8:12). Elsewhere in Proverbs *m*ᵉ*zimmah* is an undesirable quality (12:2; 14:17; 24:8).

It is likely that the Prologue was written by the author of the Ten Lectures as an introduction to the entire book, for it puts the book in the same light as the lectures do: primarily as a means of educating the young in ethics and prudential skills. The Prologue reads the entire book in the light of the Ten Lectures, converting the earlier collections of proverbs (chapters 10–29) into a manual whose prime purpose is educating the young.

II. THE INTERLUDES

The interludes are a mixed group of passages inserted in the lecture cycle at different times to introduce new themes and ideas.

A. Interlude C (6:1–19)

Interlude C, comprising four epigrams on undesirable character traits, has only tangential relation to the lectures and none to the other interludes. It is itself composite; its internal growth is discussed in "The History and Composition of Interlude C," after 6:19. This unit was a latecomer to the book. It draws heavily on the other parts of Proverbs (see p. 227) and is embedded in a late stratum, the Ten Lectures. This interpolation is quite different from the Ten Lectures in form and theme, and it interrupts the contiguity of two thematically related lectures. It is not, however, incompatible with the lectures' ideology and message, and the overall disruptive effect is not severe. The second pair of epigrams (6:12–15, 16–19) even reinforces the depiction of the troublemaker in 2:12–15.

B. The Wisdom Interludes (A, B, D, E)

The interludes, in my view, are a later stratum—itself composite—inserted in the series of lectures. To identify historical strata in a literary work, we must first form a profile—conceptual, literary, and linguistic—of material that clearly belongs to one stratum. Then we ask whether the remaining material fits this profile. Although a work by a single author can hold much diversity and even disorganization, at some point the discrepancies and roughnesses become prominent enough to indicate diverse origins, and that is the case here. The interludes and the lectures differ in their conceptual and literary characteristics. Linguistic divergences, however, other than those dependent on theme, are not evident.

(1) Concepts

The most striking difference between the lectures and the interludes lies in their concepts of wisdom. The lectures understand wisdom as residing within people's words and thoughts. In the Wisdom interludes, it transcends the individual mind. The ideologies of wisdom (described below in Essays 3 and 4) consistently reinforce the separation of the two strata.

(2) Literary Features

Whereas the lectures present themselves as spoken by a father to his son, the Wisdom interludes either do not address a particular audience (B) or address types of people identified in the text (A, D, E).

The lectures are constructed according to a careful tripartite design, as described previously. Their author shows a concern for schematic organization. It would be unlike such an author to create and then disrupt a neat set of ten similar units by dispersing five passages of very different character in his composition. Their location of these passages has its own logic (see p. 328), but this is not an extension of the logic of the lectures.

(3) Diversity in the Interludes

Further confirmation of the hypothesis that the interludes were not written by the same author as the lectures is the evidence that the interludes themselves do not have a single author.

The singularity of Interlude C is evident. But even within the Wisdom interludes, various inconsistencies argue against common authorship. In Interlude A, Wisdom condemns fools for ignoring her call, but such a call is issued only in D and E. The logical sequence of the interludes, which a single author would likely have followed, is E-D-A. In E, Wisdom first builds her house (9:1), although this is already presupposed in D (8:34). Wisdom's characterization too differs from one interlude to another. In A and D, Wisdom goes about the city, while E has her sitting at home and sending out her maids. In E, Wisdom speaks only a couple of sentences, whereas in A and D her words occupy most of the passage. Interlude B, moreover, has a different concept of Wisdom from the other Wisdom interludes, for it personifies wisdom only incidentally. It seems unlikely that the author of A, D, and E, having created an elaborate and subtle personification, would reduce this figure to one image among several.

Overall, these inconsistencies cause little disturbance. However, recognition of a more discordant inconsistency is based on an aesthetic judgment, namely that Interlude E, in its current placement, is an anticlimax. The author of D would have been unlikely to have proceeded to write E. Interlude D comes to a grand climax in Wisdom's account of her eminent origins, which leads into her blessing of her followers ("Happy is the man who listens to me [8:34]) and her warning against those who spurn her ("all those who hate me love death" [v 36]). The proclamation in 8:34–36 would provide a grand finale to Part I and a regal prelude to the proverb collections. In the present text, however, Interlude E intrudes between the call to seek wisdom and the wisdom itself, that is to say, the proverbs in the following collection. Instead, the unit concludes with the invitation of the slattern Folly. This invitation, though memorable in itself, comes as an intrusion and a letdown after Wisdom's proclamation and invitation in chapter 8. Therefore (and this is my only concern at present), Interlude E is unlikely to have been written by the author of D. And if the interludes have different authors, they cannot all belong to the author of the lectures.

(4) Cohesion Among the Interludes
To be a proper "stratum," instead of a random bunch of interpolations, a set of literary units must also have a degree of internal cohesion. The Wisdom interludes have this above all in the figure of Wisdom as a woman, but also in some unusual motifs, such as the location of Wisdom's proclamation in the gates and busy streets (1:20–21; 8:2–3; 9:3b)[206] and the characterization of the audience (1:22; 8:4–5; 9:4). These features belong mainly to A, D, and E, but they are prefigured in the encomium to wisdom in B, with its inchoate personification in 3:16–18. Even if the Wisdom interludes were composed and inserted by different authors (as previously argued), they cohere as a group, probably because they all respond to ideas and motifs found in the lectures and in one another.

(5) Continuity with the Lectures
The interludes (other than C) do not appear to have originated as isolated poems. Rather, they are outgrowths of the Ten Lectures.

Several motifs from the lectures are echoed (or, when applied to the fool, reversed) in the interludes. Some notable cases (with the related interlude passages indicated in brackets) are the obligations to seek wisdom (2:4 [1:28]), to listen to it (2:2; 4:20, 5:1, etc. [1:24; 8:32]), and to call to it (2:3 [1:28; the complementary motif is wisdom's call: 1:21; 8:1]); finding wisdom (4:22 [1:28; 3:13; 8:17, 35]); the disastrous consequences of despising wisdom and reproof (5:12–14 [1:29–32]). In the lectures, the personification of wisdom is found in inchoate form, as one metaphor alongside others, in 2:3–4; 4:8–9; 6:22; and 7:4. Lady Folly is abstracted from the features of the Strange Woman of the lectures. Her house must be avoided (5:8; 7:25 [9:13–18]), for the path to it leads to death (2:18–19, 5:5, 7:27 [9:18]).

Given the diverse authorship of at least some of the interludes, along with the resonances of the lectures in the interludes, we can picture the process of growth as a series of insertions by scribes learning from and building on the lectures rather than as a compilation and reorganization of unrelated texts by a redactor. The connections among the Wisdom interludes can be explained

[206]These passages share some distinctive locutions; see esp. the comment on 8:3.

not from having a single author but from a process of organic growth, with each successive author reading the earlier text and elaborating on it. From the idea of wisdom in the lectures they extrapolated a different, more abstract concept of wisdom, then embodied that concept in a personification.

If the Wisdom interludes are later insertions in the series of the lectures, they are not incidental or thoughtless intrusions. The Wisdom interludes draw upon the lectures and rethink their postulates. The Wisdom interludes are, in a sense, midrashic commentaries on the lectures.[207] Their placement makes sense as responses to the substance of the lectures.

(a) Interlude A complements the preceding lecture. To the threats of Lecture I, Interlude A adds mockery, now directed both against the wicked tempters and the naif who gives in to them. And, as Ramaq observed, the lecture's warning against yielding to the summons of criminals is matched by the interlude's warning against rebuffing the call of Wisdom.

(b) Interlude B, with its spirited encouragement to pursue wisdom, nicely complements Lecture III, which extols piety alone and even intimates a certain misgiving about independent human intelligence (3:5). This suggests a later author backing away somewhat from the preceding lecture's pietistic emphasis.

(c) In Interlude D, the public, legitimate invitation of Lady Wisdom has its antithesis in the furtive, nocturnal, and illicit invitation of the Strange Woman (7:9–10).

(d) Interlude E echoes motifs and locutions from the earlier chapters, especially chapter 8: Wisdom's house, her invitation, the Strange Woman's house and her invitation, and the audience of fools, as well as various phrases (one of them borrowed mechanically in 9:11). All these are expanded into the conceit of the two invitations in chapter 9.

We thus see four authors developing the figure of wisdom sequentially, each one learning about the figure of Lady Wisdom from his predecessors and exploring its potentials by drawing upon the Ten Lectures and the other Wisdom interludes. Ben Sira continues the process in Sir 24:1–33, and the Wisdom of Solomon goes even further in the exaltation of wisdom, especially in chapters 6–19.

Like architects adding new wings to an old mansion while striving for harmony with the older styles, the authors of the interludes wrote in awareness of the earlier stages and shaped a new harmonious whole, leaving only minor inconsistencies. The result is a concordant panorama of Wisdom's history, status, personality, and powers.

III. MINOR INSERTIONS

Prov 3:3a; 4:7 (?); 8:13a; 8:19; 9:7–10; 9:12. These additions are unrelated to each other and could have been inserted at any time in the book's composition.

---

[207] Interlude C does the same for passages elsewhere in Proverbs; see "The History and Composition of Interlude C," after 6:19.

Their identification and particular functions are discussed in the Commentary. They show the evolving nature of a biblical text, which remained open to scribal expansion and revision for some time into its history.

IV. SEPTUAGINTAL PLUSES

LXX-Prov 3:16a, 22a; 4:27a, 27b; 6:8a–8c, 11a; 7:1a; 8:21a; 9:10a [= 10γ]; 9:12a–12c, 18a–18d. In its Hebrew base text, in the work of the original translator, and in the activity of subsequent revisors, the Septuagint carried forward the process of growth and reinterpretation. Some of the LXX pluses were probably in the translator's Hebrew text (3:16a; 7:1a; 9:12a–12b); others were composed in Greek and probably added after the OG translation (4:27a–27b; 6:8a–8c, 11a; 8:21a; 9:12c, 18a–18d). In addition, there are numerous expansions and hexaplaric doublets in the LXX; these are not considered here. See the Textual Notes for translation and discussion.

All these additions are amplifications and reinforcements of the Hebrew or the OG and in some way reinterpret their contexts. LXX 3:16a and 7:1a enhance the piety of the passages they are in. LXX 3:22a expands the promised advantages of wisdom. LXX 4:27a and 27b revise the imagery of v 27 to make it more familiar to the Greek reader and also to underscore the religious message. LXX 6:8a–8c praises the bee so as to reinforce (somewhat imprecisely) the exemplum of the ant as an industrious worker. LXX 6:11a too elaborates an analogy found in the preceding context, namely the runner. LXX 8:21a is meant to guide the reader in the transition to a new topic. The major additions in Interlude E, namely 9:12a–12c and 9:18a–18d, decipher, each in its own way, the "foolish woman" of 9:13–18 as the attractions of foreign culture. These all belong to an early stage of the book's history of interpretation.

In sum, Prov 1–9 is the outgrowth of a long effort of a long succession of sages and scribes. The strata did not disappear, nor did one bury the other. The contributions of the different authors were cumulative and continue to be heard.

ESSAY 2. THE ORIGINS OF PERSONIFIED WISDOM

How did the figure of Lady Wisdom come into being? This question will be approached from three angles: (A) the literary development of the figure; (B) the models or prototypes on which it was shaped; and (C) the social-historical setting that gave rise to the creation of this figure. The *idea* embodied in Lady Wisdom is considered in Essay 4.

I. LITERARY PRECEDENTS

The personification of wisdom has no exact parallel elsewhere in the Bible or ancient Wisdom literature. Nevertheless, we can trace its growth from earlier literary usages.

A. Personification as a Trope

The trope of personification is frequent and significant in the Hebrew Bible. Geographical and social units (Jerusalem, Israel, Babylon, etc.) are often treated as if they are persons. Closer to the type of figuration in the Wisdom interludes is the incarnation of abstractions; for example: "Kindness and truth meet; righteousness and peace kiss" (Ps 85:11 [Eng. 10]) and "Justice retreats, righteousness stands at a distance, for truth stumbles in the street, and honesty cannot enter" (Isa 59:14).

Egyptian literature has an example of an extended allegorical personification of an abstract virtue, the Late Egyptian tale "Truth and Falsehood" (Pap. Chester Beatty II; AEL 2.211–14), in which Truth and Falsehood are two brothers. Though the story is a deliberate allegorical transformation of the myth of Horus and Seth, the brothers in the tale are not gods. Their names are written with the sign used to designate humans, not the one for divinities, and Truth, though named Maʿat like the goddess, and having a feminine noun for its name, is a male in the story. Thus Truth and Falsehood are not hypostases of the sort common in Egyptian religion, in which an abstract quality becomes a deity, as when, for example, perception is hypostatized as the god Sia. This tale shows that personification does not in itself indicate hypostatization, even in a culture with numerous mythological hypostases.

B. Inchoate Personifications of Wisdom

The personification of wisdom evolves from a trope found elsewhere in Proverbs, namely inchoate personification, where person metaphors are used in passing but not developed as figures. Various metaphors speak about wisdom as if she were a woman without cohering into a consistent woman figure or governing the development of the passage as a whole.

Sometimes Wisdom is the object of verbs indicating actions normally done to humans. Prov 2:3 says, "if you call out (*qrʾ*) to understanding, cry aloud (*ntn qol*) to good sense"; similarly, Prov 7:4: "Say to wisdom, 'You are my sister,' and call understanding 'friend.'" The human quality lies in the way that people are to treat wisdom, not in what wisdom is or does. The "as if" relationship is clear, and the humanness is given no special importance.

Sometimes the actions or qualities predicated of wisdom are of the sort normally attributed to humans. In Prov 6:22, wisdom is said to "guide," "watch," and "converse" with her faithful. But even here, the trope is not prominent, for in the preceding verse, wisdom is compared to a necklace, in the next verse to a lamp. In 3:16, Wisdom has right and left hands like a human or humanoid goddess, but shortly after she is called a tree (v 18). Similarly, in 4:6–9, wisdom is said to "guard" and "keep" her followers and to grace them with garlands. These are cases of true personification, but the metaphor is still incidental and not developed further.

The personification interludes take up this incidental metaphor and elaborate it into a full-blown, self-standing image of Wisdom as a woman, who acts and reacts on her own. The existence of inchoate personification shows that the full-fledged personification of wisdom is an organic literary development in the book of Proverbs.

C. A Foreign Personification of Wisdom

Only once in foreign Wisdom literature is wisdom personified—in the Aramaic Ahiqar, ll. 94b–95. The text is fragmentary and its interpretation depends on the reconstruction:[208]

[mn] šmyn [ḥn]ynu ʿmmʾ	From heaven the peoples receive favor.
[ḥk]mt[h mn] ʾlhyʾ h[y]	Wisdom is from the gods.
ʾp lʾlhn yq[y]rh h[y]	Also, she is precious to the gods.
ʿ[d lʿ]l[mn lh] mlkwt	Rulership is hers f[or eve]r.
bš[my]n śymh hy	She/it has been placed in heaven,
ky bʿl qdšn nśʾ[h]	because the lord of the holy ones has exalted her.

The passage (as reconstructed) speaks of wisdom as an eternal entity given by the gods to humanity and thus distinct from both. The personification is inchoate, not developed. The next sentence says that wisdom has been "placed" or "laid away" (*śymh*). This verb, together with the statement of wisdom's preciousness, pictures wisdom as a treasure rather than as a person (cf. 3:15; 8:11).

There are significant similarities between the personification of wisdom in Ahiqar and Proverbs. In Prov 8, Wisdom is in effect "from God," though that

[208]The reconstruction is Lindenberger's (1983: 68–69), whose book also has alternative restorations and renderings. Most of these do not bear on the nature of the personification.

locution is not used. Though Lady Wisdom in Proverbs does not reign, she is the means of righteous rule (8:15–16). She is not exactly *in* heaven, but she was with God when he created it (v 27). And like wisdom in Ahiqar, Lady Wisdom is precious (v 11). Other parallels between various sayings in Ahiqar and Proverbs (see n. 32) strengthen the likelihood that the metaphor of woman-wisdom was known to the authors of the Wisdom interludes from Ahiqar, perhaps indirectly.

II. MODELS FOR WISDOM

Like all strange visions, the figure of Lady Wisdom took its features from realities and images familiar to the authors and readers. Determining the figure's models can help in re-creating something of the mind-set the authors and the original audience would have shared in picturing and understanding the Wisdom figure.

Some scholars argue for a single model for the figure, others for a combination. Some scholars argue for a common background picture for the personification passages, while others treat them separately. Most likely, features of several models are fused in this complex literary figure. The following survey touches on some highlights of the massive literature on this topic.

A. A Prophet?

In 1:20–33, Wisdom castigates fools in a manner reminiscent of the prophets, Jeremiah in particular. Lady Wisdom speaks *tokeḥah* "reproof" in the plazas, streets, and city gates. Amos, with himself in mind, says that people "hate the one who reproves [*mokiaḥ*] in the gate" (5:10). Ezekiel implies that as a prophet he would be an *ʾiš mokiaḥ*, a "man who reproves" (3:26), if he were not in a period of dumbness.

Wisdom similarly declares she will ignore the fools when disaster befalls them (1:26–31). This behavior is not prophetic but divine. This is how God behaves toward unworthy supplicants when they cry out in distress, according to Mic 3:4; Isa 1:15; Jer 11:11; Hos 5:6, and other passages. But, unlike God, Wisdom does not herself execute retribution.

In regard to the reverberations of prophecy, especially Jeremiah's, in Wisdom's words, see A. Robert 1934; B. Gemser 1963: 23; Kayatz 1966: 122–29; and S. Harris 1995: 87–109. See the excursus "Interlude A and Jeremiah," after chapter 1.

According to G. Baumann (1996: 289–91), the Wisdom figure is like a prophetess. Though Wisdom does not use the messenger formula, she serves as a messenger and mediator of Yahweh's word. Wisdom claims special knowledge of God, as does a mantic. She pronounces with prophetic authority on the divine sphere and demands trust. Like a prophet, she addresses a situation that calls for decision (*Entscheidungssituation*) (p. 290).

In my view, Lady Wisdom is not a prophet figure, though there are echoes of prophetic usages in her discourses. Parents and other teachers chastise, warn, and threaten, and they too insist on their authority. The similarities between Lady Wisdom and some of the prophets may be in part due to the fact that prophets sometimes take on a teacher's role (most clearly in Isaiah; see esp. 7:16; 28:9–13; and, more generally, Fichtner 1949 and Whedbee 1971). Unlike a prophet, Wisdom neither declares God's judgment nor claims to be mediating his word, which is the prophet's defining role. At most, prophetic usages provided a few pigments for Wisdom's portrait.

Some interpreters regard Lady Wisdom's role as mediation, though not primarily prophetic. Camp (1985: 272–81) argues that Wisdom is a mediator between the divine and human realms and that she takes on the symbolic role of the king. "As counselor, lover, and administrator of divine justice, female Wisdom assumes the functions and images once belonging to the king and his court" (p. 291).

It is true that Wisdom exists on an intermediate plane: below God as his creation and "child" and above humanity as their superior and patroness. But she does not *mediate*. God never speaks to her, and she does not quote him, even indirectly, or transmit his word to mankind. Nor does she exercise power in her own right. She does serve as counselor to human authorities (8:14–16), but in this capacity she does mediate God's will, for a counselor speaks his own wisdom, not another's. In Proverbs, moreover, Lady Wisdom is not an executor of his will, as an angel or (ideally) a king is.

Lady Wisdom attains the status of mediary in Ben Sira. God sends her forth with the charge to dwell in Zion (24:8), and since Wisdom is Torah (24:23), she conveys his word to the world by her very being.

B. A Herald?

Going about the city and making public proclamations (A, D) is the office of the herald. Zeraḥiah ben Shealtiel suggested this connection; see the comment on 8:4. This role could well belong to the background imagery of Interlude E.

C. An Angel?

Though not a member of the divine court or God's messenger, in status Lady Wisdom resembles an angel. She is a heavenly creature, residing in angelic proximity to God. She exists outside the mundane sphere, yet traverses it and speaks to people. Ben Sira ascribes angelic status to her when he says that "She opens her mouth in the assembly of the Most High" (24:2); cf. 1 Enoch 42:2.

D. A Canaanite Goddess?

W. F. Albright (1919–20) first suggested that Lady Wisdom combines features of Semitic goddesses, in particular Ishtar. B. Lang (1986: 57–70) goes further and maintains that the Wisdom figure actually is a wisdom goddess. She is the "goddess of the king," patroness and intimate of rulers. She may be the daughter of the Canaanite mother goddess Athirat and the high god El (whose name, Lang conjectures, was replaced with Yahweh's in chapter 8).[209] Or perhaps she was born of El by "male pregnancy." However, no Canaanite wisdom goddess is known. Lang is explaining the obscure by the unknown.

G. Boström (1935; see on 7:6–17) maintains that Lady Wisdom was devised as the antithesis of the Strange Woman, who is an Aphrodite-Astarte figure. (This premise is disputed in the Commentary, ad loc.) Lady Wisdom is thus a displacement and a "compensation for the lost Astarte" (1935: 173). Others too have seen her as derivative of one or more Canaanite goddesses.

The weak spot in all these theories is that Lady Wisdom bears scant resemblance to these goddesses. (Lang's theory has the advantage that no Canaanite wisdom goddess is known, so we cannot say that Lady Wisdom does *not* resemble her.) Lady Wisdom is not sexually aggressive, desirous, or desirable. She does not represent the realm of fertility and vegetation. To be sure, she is said to *serve as* a "tree of life" (3:18), but that is a different image from the personified-woman trope. Wisdom's gifts are not the fruit of the womb or the bounties of the fields but statecraft, wealth, honor, abundance in the storehouses, and life. Plenty in the storehouses (8:21) means grain, but that is just one item among many. Fertility is not in focus.

E. The Goddess Maᶜat?

The influential theory of C. Kayatz (1966: 93–119) holds that the prototype for Lady Wisdom in Prov 8 was Maᶜat, the Egyptian goddess of truth/justice (these are a single concept in Egyptian thought). Several features supposedly indicate an Egyptian background, with the goddess Maᶜat the specific model. These are: the mutual love formula ("I love him who loves me" and variations); the self-predication (or "self-revelation") formula ("I am X . . ."); Wisdom's existence before creation; Wisdom as child of God playing before him; Wisdom as lover and beloved; her service as dispenser of life and protection; and her status as the effective power in the royal regime (p. 119 and *passim*).

There is, however, no reason to single out Maᶜat as Wisdom's prototype. Nowhere does Maᶜat give a speech like Lady Wisdom's; in fact, she never seems to speak at all. Moreover, none of these features are exclusive to Maᶜat. All have parallels in various proclamations of kings and gods, especially Isis (see later)—and not only in Egypt.

---

[209] J. E. McKinlay (1996: 32–65, *passim*) proposes that behind the figures of Wisdom and Folly may lie the repressed memory of Ashera, the goddess who offers life. McKinlay advocates a "'resisting' gender reading, which allows the double-faceted power of women to recognize" (p. 64). Such a reading enables us to hear a distant echo of Ashera (p. 64). McKinlay does not point to any positive features of Ashera in these portrayals, so all that remains of this supposed background is its posited repression.

Maʿat (both as the concept of truth/justice and as its divine hypostasis) was the foundation principle of Egyptian society and was deeply embedded in Egyptian religion. Unlike some other Egyptian deities (notably Isis), Maʿat never developed an international persona. It is doubtful that ancient sages, Egyptian or Israelite, could have extracted the concept of Maʿat from scattered Egyptian cultic and mortuary texts and grafted it on to an Israelite figure of wisdom.

It is likely that some of the Egyptian clichés and images that Kayatz pointed out, such as the mutual love[210] and self-predication formulas, the preexistence of a personified abstraction, and perhaps the motif of a beloved child playing before her divine father, are softly echoed in Prov 8. The focus on the first moment of creation ("the start of his works of old," v 22b) calls to mind the Egyptian notion of the "first time"—the moment of creation, which is paradigmatic for renewal in all time. But these similarities do not constitute a special link between Wisdom and Maʿat.

F. The Goddess Isis?

If Wisdom resembles any Egyptian goddess, it is Isis—not so much in her native Egyptian form (which would not be accessible to a foreign audience) as in the universalistic, international persona she acquired in Hellenistic times, when she became the most popular goddess in the Near East and the Aegean. As giver of the first laws and principles, she was called Thesmophoros (Law Bearer) and Thesmothetis (Law Giver) (Diodorus 1.25, 27). As the consummately wise goddess, she had the epithets Phronesis (Intelligence) and Sophia (Wisdom) or Sophia Theou (Wisdom of God); see Reitzenstein 1904: 44.

Isis's virtues and powers were proclaimed in aretalogies, compositions in praise of gods, which had their origins in Egyptian texts and traditions but were mostly written and disseminated in Greek. It has been convincingly argued that the image of Isis influenced the depiction of wisdom in Ben Sira (Hengel 1974: 1.157–160 and n. 331) and the Wisdom of Solomon (Kloppenborg 1982: 57–84; Collins 1997: 203–4). W. J. Knox (1937) first observed that Wisdom in Prov 8 resembles Isis in several ways and suggested that this text too is an "orthodox" response to the attractions of Isis worship.

Isis speaks in her aretalogies much as Lady Wisdom does in hers. Compare the following lines of the great aretalogy from Cyme (Bergman 1968: 301) with Prov 8:

(3a) I, Isis, am the ruler of all lands,
(3b) and I was educated by Hermes. . . .
(4) I set down laws for men and legislated that which no one can alter.
(5) I am the eldest daughter of Kronos.

[210]This formula appears, however, in 2 Sam 19:7a, in a passage which shows no particular Egyptian or sapiential affiliations.

In ll. 12–15, she grandly recounts her work as creator, then continues:

(16) I have made justice powerful. . . .
(28) I have made justice more powerful than gold and silver.

In a Hellenistic magical stele, Isis bids all men:

Come to me, come to me.
See, my mouth possesses life.
I am a daughter known in her city,
at whose utterance reptiles are expelled,
because my father (Reᶜ) educated me to knowledge.
I am his daughter, the beloved one (born) of his body. . . .
I am Isis, the divine,
mistress of magic, who does magic,
effective in pronouncing spells.[211]

The portrayal of Lady Wisdom in Proverbs does not include many of the major attributes ascribed to Isis elsewhere, such as her beneficence to farmers and mariners (whose skills are her gift) and her expertise in magic.[212] Nevertheless, these forms of knowledge, like all technical skills, would have been considered *ḥokmah* in ancient Israel, though they do not fall in the purview of Proverbs.[213]

The main impediment to locating Lady Wisdom's background in Isis traditions is that the Hellenistic Isis religion began to spread abroad only in the late third century B.C.E., which seems too late for even the latest stratum of Proverbs. Only the aretalogies present a cluster of correspondences between Wisdom and Isis and not just isolated parallels, and texts of this sort are not attested before the first century B.C.E. The Isis-Wisdom connection requires positing that texts with at least the key features of the Isis aretalogies existed earlier. There is evidence that they are indeed a continuation of the ancient Isis hymnology and hold many ancient elements; see Žabkar 1988: 159–60 and *passim*.

Even if this background could be confirmed, it would not mean that Lady Wisdom is an Isis figure, but only that Hellenistic Isis texts were a source of the author's notions about how a wise goddess would speak and reveal herself. These were then transferred to Lady Wisdom so that she could *displace* Isis in Hellenistic Jewish sentiments.

The Isis identification does not exclude Maᶜat's relevance entirely, since in later times the two goddesses were sometimes identified syncretistically, so that Isis became a manifestation of Maᶜat or its provider (see the Cyme aretalogy, quoted previously). Yet the ancient goddess Maᶜat was not herself a significant

---

[211] Metternich Magical Stele, ll. 57–59; Sander-Hanson 1956: 35–42; cf. Kayatz 1966: 89.

[212] In Wis. Sol., Wisdom is the shipbuilder (14:2) and diviner (8:2).

[213] Ben Sira (38:24–34), who follows Proverbs' lead in defining *ḥokmah* in intellectual-ethical terms, explicitly excludes the craftsman and farmer from wisdom as such.

forerunner of Lady Wisdom. See further the assessment of the Egyptian parallels in my article "World Order and Maʿat" (Fox 1995).[214]

G. Human Women?

Wisdom is cast in the image of a woman. This was probably inevitable, given the feminine gender of the most important nouns for wisdom, *ḥokmah*, *tᵉbunah*, and *binah*. Nevertheless (contrary to Hermisson 1990, who believes that Wisdom is female only by virtue of grammatical gender), some specifically feminine characteristics are relevant to the portrait of Lady Wisdom and were drawn from the roles of actual women. This issue is of special interest for feminist theologians, who have welcomed (or repudiated) Lady Wisdom as a rare feminine element in the unremittingly patriarchal and masculine theology of Yahwism.[215]

Among the feminists who reject the values of Prov 1–9, including those spoken by Lady Wisdom, the most vehement is A. Brenner (1993: 125–26). Brenner believes that the "spokesperson" of the teachings in Prov 1–9 is the F(emale) voice, who has, however, betrayed itself by adopting the M[ale] ideology. "The price, here as in other passages in Proverbs, is the subscription of an identifiable F voice to misogyny and self-inflicted gender depreciation and gender disparagement" (p. 126).

According to Newsom (1989, esp. 155–57), Lady Wisdom speaks with the cultural voice of the "socialfathers" and grounds its values (p. 156; and see p. 257). The last statement seems true, and inevitably so. What may be doubted is the implication that these values were at variance with those of the socialmothers.

C. Camp's innovative and influential study, *Wisdom and the Feminine in the Book of Proverbs* (1985), proposed that several roles of human women were woven into the picture of Lady Wisdom: the wife as counselor; the wise wife who builds her house (cf. 14:1); the lover who seeks and is sought by her beloved (8:17, 34–35; cf. Cant 3:1–4; 5:2–6:2); the wife as provider (8:18–21; compare the Excellent Woman in 31:10–31). (See esp. Camp 1985: 90–109 and chapters 3, 7, and 9, *passim*.) Some of these roles have male counterparts, but the fact that they *could* be filled by women meant that it was not discordant to assign them to a feminine personage.

To these feminine features we can add the gracious hostess (9:1–6) and the less congenial image of a spurned woman nursing a grudge (1:24–31; cf. Cant 8:6b). Moreover, Wisdom is distinctly female by virtue of having her antithesis in Lady Folly and the Strange Woman, who use and abuse their feminine attractions.

---

[214]In a paper at a Society for Biblical Literature meeting (November 21, 1998), Hector Avalos observed similarities between the Isis aretalogies and Prov 8 on the one hand, and aretalogies of the Babylonian goddess Gula on the other. These similarities seem to me less precise, but it is fair to conclude that the features of Lady Wisdom's oration reflect an ancient Near Eastern tradition of divine self-praise. Compare also "To him who fears me I give life" (Gula Hymn 107) with Prov 10:7.

[215]See Camp 1985 (esp. chapter 9); Schroer 1996; McKinlay 1996; and Baumann 1996: 50–54, 316–25, with the literature cited there.

Wisdom, moreover, has features of a mother figure who, as noted before (see "Mothers as Teachers," after 1:8), is also a teacher. Wisdom stands in a parent-like relation to humans, as her divine guardian does to her (8:30–31). She calls them "sons" (v 32a), just as the teacher in the lectures calls his audience "son" or "sons" (the plural in 4:1; 5:7; and 7:24a). T. Frymer-Kensky says that Proverbs depicts wisdom as female because the mother is the primary source of wisdom to young children. Additionally, women were associated with important aspects of cultural knowledge, such as medicine and midwifery (1992: 179–83). Nevertheless, Lady Wisdom is not the mother of humanity, and her love is not an unconditional, all-forgiving maternal compassion (pp. 180–81).

It would be wrong to say that Lady Wisdom *is* a mother figure or *is* a lover figure. She has features of both, in different passages, according to their needs and messages. Instead, Lady Wisdom is an agglomeration of roles and activities, some of them found among human women.

The role of women in transmitting cultural knowledge does not account for the choice of a female model for the figuration. Even if much cultural knowledge is dispensed by women, the kind of wisdom that Lady Wisdom represents, such as statecraft, is not. We may say, however, that a female personification was *compatible* with wisdom. The fact that wisdom and women have a "certain affinity" in biblical thought (Baumann 1996: 321) contradicts the modern stereotype of ancient Israel as having justified male power on the assumption that women were intellectually or spiritually inferior. As Baumann says (p. 320–21), if most people had considered women characteristically "unwise," a female personification of wisdom would be inconceivable. Wise women were a recognized reality in ancient Israel, and Lady Wisdom is, figuratively, a wise woman. Still, is Lady Wisdom's gender essential to the message?

First of all, Wisdom *is* portrayed as a woman, and whatever the degree of the distinctively female in the portrayal, her femaleness is now a fact which the readers cannot escape. But we may still pose the question of what would be different if Wisdom had been personified as a man (called, perhaps, *śekel*, "Perceptiveness," "Intelligence"[216]), who was God's "firstborn," his *yeled šaʿăšuʿim* "delightful child" (as God calls Israel in Jer 31:20), and who now bids mankind to hearken to his counsel.

The first loss would be the tint of eros in the mutual attraction of Wisdom and humanity in chapters 8–9 (see pp. 294f.). The *śekel*-figure would lack an eros-like attraction to match the draw of Lady Folly, whose slattern call emulates the explicitly sexual pull of the Strange Woman.

A deeper difference would be that this personage would inevitably acquire a different kind of authority, one not quite suitable for describing the way wisdom works in the world. The praise of *śekel*'s antiquity, wealth, and power would make his authority *institutional*, a derivative of social and political relationships. A

[216]Egyptian mythology has this very figure in the god Sia ("perception"), who is Re's firstborn in some texts.

male with Lady Wisdom's qualities would be too much like a monarch. A first-born "son" of God would be his deputy, like the Davidic king in Zion (Pss 2:6–7; 89:28), who rules the kings and "the judges of the earth" through his God-given might (e.g., Pss 2; 110), and who not only teaches justice but actively executes it.

Lady Wisdom is not a king figure. She is powerful, and she is the principle of just dominion, but she does not herself exercise rulership. Instead, others rule *by* her. Her influence is verbal, working through persuasion and appeal to affection, not through exercise of office and power. Her power and appeal come from the just workings of the universe and the good sense of individual minds rather than from the constraints and compulsions of political institutions.[217]

H. A Teacher?

One model dominates the portrayal and provides the grid which holds together the component features, and that is the *teacher*, who in the Ten Lectures is the father.[218] The father-teacher's rhetoric and personality come to the fore in the Ten Lectures, in which the interludes are embedded.

The teacher model is most prominent in Interlude D, in which Wisdom speaks in forms similar to those the father has been using in the Ten Lectures. This model, after all, is fresh in the reader's mind. Interlude D is an extended exordium, comprising an address to the audience (8:4), an exhortation to listen (8:5–6, 8–10, 32–36), and an extended motivation extolling wisdom (8:12–31). The praise of wisdom's benefits, which is the way the exhortation is motivated in all the exordia,[219] is here elaborated into a long oration in the self-praise form; see "The Design of Interlude D" after chapter 8. Since mothers too are teachers, and their message is identified with the father's (1:8; 4:3; 6:20; cf. 31:1), this role is quite consonant with a female personification. Likewise, Wisdom's invocation in Interlude E (9:4–6 + 11) resembles the exordia of the lectures.

This model is recognizable also in Interlude A, where Wisdom's speech maintains some components of a lecture, namely an exordium (1:23) and a conclusion/capstone (1:32–33). Wisdom chastises and mocks the naive and the

---

[217]Though Wisdom's rule is indirect, that does not mean that she works mainly through "indirection." Camp (1985: 139–40) believes that indirection is a hallmark of women's behavior and also of the sage's, for which reason female imagery is "extraordinarily apt for the figurative presentation of Wisdom" (p. 140). But, as Camp herself notes, indirection is hardly confined to women. If Esther is indirect, she has learned the talent of male courtiers. And one need but mention Jacob, the father of Israel, and David, its greatest king, as exemplars of exceptional talents for indirection and manipulation. It is irrelevant that some women also have these skills. One person who does *not* work in this way, however, is Lady Wisdom in Proverbs. This figure, like the human faculty she embodies, is exceptionally direct, a quality epitomized in the prominent trope of Wisdom as the straight path.

[218]Lang (1986: 56–59) suggests this for 8:1–11 and 8:32–36, but unnecessarily identifies teachers with schoolmasters.

[219]Assuming that a motivating sentence was lost after 5:2, as argued in the Commentary.

foolish in A, and this too belongs to a wisdom teacher's role. The value of chastisement is affirmed by several proverbs (see the comment on 1:23), and within the ten lectures, the teacher pours scorn on fools and evildoers. A favorite topos in Egyptian school texts was the letter of rebuke to the lazy, prodigal pupil by his father or teacher. Some of these chastisements (for example, Menena's letter, quoted in the comment on 1:23) sound like Wisdom's rebukes in Interlude A. Though this parallel (and others in its genre) do not show literary dependence of Proverbs on such compositions, they do illustrate the ways a father-teacher could be expected to address a dissipated or recalcitrant son.

The use of the teacher as the primary model for Lady Wisdom ties this figure closely to the Ten Lectures, in which wisdom is praised and exemplified. In the Wisdom interludes, Wisdom is both the teacher and the wisdom taught.

I. A Variety of Models

While we can tease out some of the literary, mythological, and real-life background images that entered into the portrayal of Lady Wisdom, we should remember that they *are* background and are not to be equated with Lady Wisdom. After all, she cannot be imagined as both mother and lover of those she calls. Nor could a woman legitimately be the lover to all who seek her. And Lady Wisdom cannot be envisaged as subject to the subordination that Israelite women experienced. Components of her portrayal must come from known types of person (real or mythological), but these need not coalesce into a single human type to create a unity. Camp describes the unifying effect of personification by contrasting it to the rhetorical operation of individual proverbs:

> Personification . . . involves a reduction of the ambiguous, multi-faceted and/or unique to the typical. . . . Proverbs are able to bring the "multiplicity of experience" to terms in a performance context by virtue of their concreteness, their reference to some one particular thing or idea with which all participants are familiar. Personification, on the other hand, is unitary because of its generality, the level not of particularity but of abstractness that it brings to a given set of phenomena. (1985: 215–16)[220]

Though inevitably abstracting features from a variety of persons in the sketch of Lady Wisdom, the authors of the personification interludes are not *alluding* to them. A new and independent literary figure has been composed of fragments of reality.

---

[220]That a single author could personify wisdom by means of different and even incompatible models is shown by Ben Sira 15:2–3: "[Wisdom] will come before him like a mother, and like the wife of one's youth she will receive him. And she will feed him the bread of intellect, and give him the water of understanding to drink." This passage is clearly based on Prov 9:1–6 and thus shows that Ben Sira detected the roles of both wife and mother in Proverbs' figuration of wisdom.

III. SOCIAL AND HISTORICAL SETTING

A. The Socioeconomic Background (Mack's Theory)

Besides investigating the literary and external context in which the Wisdom figure took shape, one can inquire into the social-economic setting that gave rise to it and whose problems it sought to meet.

B. Mack (1985: 143–50) proposed that the wisdom figure arose as a response to social breakdown, a rupture between conventional categories of wisdom about society and the realities of the torn social fabric. The wisdom figure is "a first-level abstraction of the enduring value of the system of conventional wisdom" (p. 145). This abstract wisdom is first located outside society, in a transcendent reality, "the divine ordering of the natural world" (p. 145). Then, by making Wisdom reappear in the streets, the author reveals his "desire to affirm the presence of a wisdom no longer at home in society" (p. 146).

Mack does not say just when this breakdown occurred. Indeed, it is hard to think of a time in the biblical record when someone did not see social and moral disintegration about him. The question is whether the personification texts offer themselves as a response to social breakdown and the crumbling of traditional concepts—and they surely do not. On the contrary, Mack's theory is helpful for highlighting a very different setting for the entirety of Prov 1–9 from the one he suggests.

Nothing in the personification passages or elsewhere in Prov 1–9 suggests a backdrop of social disorder, not even an uneasiness that this is pending. There is no sense of looming social upheaval, threats to livelihood, subversion of community, or disintegration of family. Even the adulterer does not seem to have this effect. It is his *own* family and patrimony he wrecks (5:9–10, 16). The authors do not lament the prosperity of the wicked, do not even raise this possibility, except as a momentary state. The mechanisms of retribution are secure and undoubted.

Proverbs, here and elsewhere, is well aware that society includes fools and troublemakers, but it does not depict them as pervasive in society or as constituting socioeconomic groupings. They are aberrant individuals, just stupid folk who cause harm above all to themselves and whose punishment is inevitable (1:31–32; 8:36; 9:18).

According to Interlude E, Wisdom's influence extends throughout the world (8:15–16). She is the helper of kings and commoners. She loves mankind and accepts their love in return (8:17, 34–35). She takes up permanent residence in the city, meaning every city, and summons all to her. Her primeval origin and her proximity to God do not distance her from society but only emphasize her permanence within it.

The personification poems breathe an atmosphere of social and ideological security. They do not do this polemically, as an antidote to decay and uncertainty, but as something taken for granted. They presuppose and reaffirm a consensus that the principles of wisdom and justice are universal.

B. The Historical-Religious Role of the Wisdom Figure (Baumann's Theory)

G. Baumann, in *Die Weisheitsgestalt in Proverbien 1–9* (1996), argues that the Wisdom figure was created to meet the theological needs of the Persian period, which she calls a *Krisenzeit*, a time of crisis.

The Wisdom figure, Baumann says, is a synthesis of different aspects of wisdom, and it combines human and divine wisdom (pp. 267; 310–11). She is described in terms used elsewhere of Yahweh. She speaks with a plenitude of power, and the rewards for obeying her are the same as for obeying Yahweh.[221] Her exact status is deliberately left ambiguous: "She can be understood as a god-like [*gottänliche*] figure beside Yahweh or as 'only' a creature subordinated to him," depending on the stringency of the monotheistic sensibilities of each reader (p. 314).

Wisdom's primogeniture and presence at creation bestow upon her "the competence of a world-order expert" ("die Kompetenz einer 'Weltordnungsexpertin'") in a broad sense: having been present at creation, she can teach people in later times about the fundamental ordering of the world and right behavior (p. 274).

The post-exilic period was a *Krisenzeit*. The older wisdom had posited a world order with an effective "Deed-Consequence Nexus,"[222] but this was now called into question. The theological challenge to Yahweh's world order in a time of injustice was met by the creation of the Wisdom figure, who could serve as a credible "witness" to the existence of the world order and its goodness (p. 310).

> [The Wisdom figure] is meant to show people in the time of crisis a path that traverses received and familiar ways and makes it possible to again have confidence in the good order of the world, [a confidence] that had disappeared when the Deed-Consequence Nexus was brought into question by the events of everyday life. (p. 310)[223]

The world order was originally good, but it was undermined by human deeds in the course of history. A return to Wisdom's teaching can turn human fate to the good (p. 310). Apparently (though the reason is uncertain) Yahweh himself could no longer offer such mediation or assurance about the goodness of the world order (p. 313).

Because of her immediacy and intermediate status, people can love and follow Wisdom as a "personal goddess" (p. 313), similar (mutatis mutandis) to

---

[221] See the Commentary on 1:8.

[222] See "The 'Deed-Consequence Nexus,'" after 1:8–19.

[223] "[Die Weisheitsgestalt] soll den Menschen in der krisenhaften Zeit einen Weg weisen, der in überkommenen und bekannten Bahnen verläuft und ihnen wieder das Vertrauen in die gute Ordnung der Welt ermöglicht, das mit der Infragstellung des Tun-Ergehen-Zusammenhangs durch die Widerfahrnisse des alltäglichen Lebens geschwunden ist" (p. 310).

IDEAS OF WISDOM: INTRODUCTION TO ESSAYS 3 AND 4

The book of Proverbs, read as a whole, pursues a central theme throughout its numerous and divers maxims and observations. This theme, scarcely touched upon elsewhere in ancient Near Eastern Wisdom literature, is *wisdom*—not just wise behavior or wise teachings, but wisdom itself. The book of Proverbs is not only about doing, it is about *knowing*. This concern, even more than the specifics of the teachings, demands our attention if we wish to understand the special message and purpose of Israelite Wisdom.

Concern for wisdom in this sense is to be found throughout the book; it is so pervasive that it usually escapes notice. The most intensive reflection on wisdom comes in Part I, which is a hermeneutical preamble to the rest of the book. Within this unit, there are two ideas of wisdom, each conveyed in its own voice and each belonging to a different literary stratum—the lectures (discussed in Essay 3) and the interludes (Essay 4). These essays consider what these ideas are and how they are conveyed.

The *what* and the *how* can be discussed separately, but in reality they are almost inseparable, for the nature of wisdom is to a large degree determined by the personae who speak it, their rhetoric, and their relations to their audience. This is especially true in the personification interludes, where the persona *is* wisdom, but it pertains in the lectures as well, where the conduit of wisdom is the father. The authors of the Ten Lectures and the Wisdom interludes chose to speak to us by means of personae instead of the direct authorial voice. The creation of effective personae was instrumental in imbuing the readers not only with knowledge but also with attitudes and perspectives that will guide their behavior for the years to come.

Essay 3. Wisdom in the Lectures

I. What Is Wisdom?

As a way of discovering the meaning of wisdom in the Ten Lectures, we can ask why it is that the wisdom they teach is supposed to be so difficult to learn. The father regularly demands that the listener, his son, strive for wisdom with all his might. The effort required is described as arduous and prolonged. The exhortations encourage the son in this task. For example:

My son,
if you take in my words,
  store up my precepts within you,
making your ear attend to wisdom,
  directing your heart to good sense. . . . (2:1–2)

Even while absorbing the father's precepts, the son must pursue wisdom tenaciously. And even then, wisdom is reached only with God's help, "For the Lord grants wisdom, at his behest come knowledge and good sense" (2:6). So demanding is the learner's task that the author unfolds a theory of learning whose practical purpose is to encourage the neophyte to persevere. This is discussed in "The Idea of Education," after chapter 2.

Yet on the face of it, the teachings do not seem all that difficult. Their content does not seem to demand study and erudition to master intellectually, for even the young and callow can learn its truths. They are never esoteric and, though there may be some enigmas, as 1:6 suggests, there is nothing that *has* to be read that way. The message of the lectures is plain and unambiguous, and the precepts tell nothing that anyone would admit to being ignorant of: Don't rob; don't kill; don't commit adultery; be honest; trust God. As great as these principles are, having wisdom must mean something more than simply *knowing* them.

The reason that the wisdom the author is seeking to impart is at once difficult and obvious is that it is not reducible to the book's precepts. The author is aiming at a higher and harder goal: wisdom as a power. The knowledge of wisdom, once achieved, resides in the learner as a potential and must be activated by God in order to become the power of wisdom, an inner light that guides its possessor through life.

The function of this power is explicitly defined in sentences dependent on the exhortations: protection from sinful men and women—not from the harm they may cause directly, but from the temptations they pose:

Shrewdness will watch over you,
  good sense protect you,
to save you from the way of the evildoer,
from the man who speaks distortions; (2:11–12)

and also . . .

to save you (also) from a strange woman—
an alien who speaks smooth words. (2:16; cf. 7:5)

Seduction is the main (indeed, almost the only) peril warned against in the lectures. The wisdom that can withstand it is not erudition, sapience, or unusual intellect. Nor is it the aptitude for discovering new truths. It does require (according to 4:23–25) purity of heart, tongue, and eyes, meaning thought, speech, and desire. This wisdom is bound up with (though not identical to) the fear of God, which is both the starting point of the quest for wisdom (1:7; 9:10) and its culmination (2:5). Such wisdom is the ability to discern right from wrong and also the *desire* to pursue the right, because inert wisdom would not provide protection.

Wisdom has an attitudinal or emotional as well as an intellectual component. That is why the son is urged not only to learn wisdom but to love and desire it (4:6–8). Wisdom is a configuration of soul; it is *moral character.* And fostering moral character, it is no overstatement to say, is at all times the greatest goal of education. It is also the greatest challenge, for moral character comes down to desiring the right things, and how can we teach desire?

II. HOW WISDOM IS TAUGHT

The literary setting implied in the Ten Lectures, as in almost all instructional wisdom, is father-to-son teaching. The father's pedagogical rhetoric aims at guiding desire: fostering the right ones, suppressing the wrong ones. Imparting information is not enough, for static cognition may not engender moral character. With the goal of moral character clearly in view, the author minimizes advice on most of the virtues propounded elsewhere in Proverbs, such as interpersonal skills, diligence, and even social justice, touching upon these in only a few verses (3:9–10, 27–30; 4:23–24). He strips matters down to essentials and assigns to wisdom one primary function: to fortify its possessor against temptation.

Leo Perdue (1981) has identified the social-psychological setting of Wisdom instructions as *liminality,* a stage transitional to a new and elevated status. Though Perdue does not discuss Prov 1–9, this concept applies well to the situations pictured here. The youth addressed in Proverbs is about to come into independence and adult responsibilities, yet he lacks maturity and good sense. His moral cast is not yet hardened. He stands at the crossroads where the two paths diverge, and he must now, immediately, enter into the right path, the path to life.

The author knows that young men (represented by the "son" or "sons" within the text) are terribly vulnerable to peer pressure and their own raging libidos, and he is aware that the longings for camaraderie and sexual relief tug at them with a fearsome power that can easily overwhelm their still-precarious powers of reason and self-control. The lectures seek to help young men withstand these drives and channel them to proper uses, namely, concern for a good reputation and marital sex.

As we are painfully aware today, the surrender to the yearning for peer approval, fast money, and casual sex can be literally deadly. In the lectures, the father must convince his son (and the author his readers) of this. The teacher seeks to connect deed with consequence deep in the son's mind, so that he not only knows the principle of reward and punishment, he *feels* it. To do this, more is required than sententious warnings and somber maxims or even a logical demonstration of cause and effect, for by themselves these are abstract and lack rooting in the listener's short experience. The author must fashion a persona who can reach its audience, the readers. The persona, for his part, has his own rhetoric in addressing his son. The main qualities of his rhetoric are the following:

A. Authority

The father makes demands, not suggestions. He intones exhortations and injunctions with magisterial certitude, demanding attention and obedience. He is not holding out options; the only alternative to Wisdom's way, which is also *his* way, is the road to death. Though his teachings can be considered counsels (though not called *ʿeṣot* in these chapters[226]), obedience to them is not optional, for they are also *miṣwot*, which are commandments or authoritative precepts, not elective counsels (see the comment on 2:1). The authority behind these precepts is not that of law or divine command, and it has no sanctions to enforce it. It is the authority of *ethos*, the credibility of the speaker's character and his affinity to the audience. This authority derives from the speaker's paternal position and his role as the tradent of ancient teachings.

B. Promise and Warning

This is the most obvious tactic in the father's rhetorical arsenal. He heaps up promises of rewards for obedience: long life, health, prosperity, honor, favor, happiness, and protection, especially against temptation. And he warns of severe punishments for defiance: disaster, disgrace, and death. He rarely explains just how these consequences will come to pass, for retribution may ensue in many and unexpected ways. The outcome alone is certain.

C. Intimacy

In order to make a lasting impression, the father must not only command, he must *persuade*. To this end, he chooses an intimate, paternal intonation. When

[226] Lady Wisdom, however, speaks of her *ʿeṣah* in 1:25, 30; 8:14, so the term could presumably apply to the father's, too.

he tells how his own father gave him instruction (4:3–4), he is aligning himself with his son, letting the boy know that he went through the same experience himself. He speaks to the budding adult in a confidential, man-to-man tone, alerting him to the pull of greed, conformity, and, above all, lust, with a vividness that reveals his own nagging susceptibility to their attractions. The wise man is not devoid of such desires, and he does not demand that his son be. Wisdom does not mean purity of that sort, a childlike innocence that knows not good or evil. The fruit of the tree of knowledge has already been eaten, and wisdom now lies in *knowing*: in knowing what dangers will confront a man, how great their sway, and how horrendous their consequences. Wisdom also means knowing oneself. For the most insidious perils ultimately lie within, and only an internal power can withstand them. This is wisdom, a power of intellect and character, founded on fear of God.

D. Vividness

To bring the youngster to an awareness of what he will confront, the father conjures up memorable scenes that both tantalize and repulse. He paints the enticements in vivid, even lurid, colors, quoting the temptress in words bordering on the lewd, as in 7:18:

> Come, let's slake our thirst on love [*dodim*] till dawn,
> take our delight in lovemaking [*ʾŏhabim*].

The sexuality is explicit, for *dodim* refers to physical, sexual lovemaking, including coitus, and *ʾŏhabim* means sex, not necessarily with emotional involvement (Hos 8:9). Why does the father veil the vice in such allure?

The vividness is meant to make *appearances* clear and palpable, so that the son will be aware of their power. He shows the seductive woman's appeal to all the senses, her titillating offer of stolen pleasures, her ostensible attentiveness to her victim (7:15). In like manner, he recounts the gang's promise of wealth, power, and fellowship. The impact is all the greater, then, when he tears away the veil and bares the foul and fatal realities behind the façades. The would-be buddies, he informs his son, are fraudulent, and they are out to trap *you*. The sexy seductress, behind her sensuous looks and honeyed words, is shabby, exploitative, and treacherous. The sweetness of her mouth leaves a bitter aftertaste. Her perfumed abode is but a grave where her victims rot (2:18–19; 7:27).

E. Irony

The teacher revels in ironies. An ironic sensibility reminds us that we can control our actions but not their consequences. If a man digs a pit, *he* will fall into it (26:27). Worse, the irony of retribution shows the sinner to be ludicrous, a thought that may sting him worse than fear of bodily harm.

The ironic voice mocks the sinner. He may be wise in his own eyes, but others (even his comrades) see him as the fool he is. The greedy youth who succumbs to the invitation of the thugs is really their dupe, a silly bird taking the bait (this is one of the several points of the ambiguous 1:17). The oversexed young man who follows a loose woman to her bed squanders, ironically, his own powers of generation (5:9, 16). He sins in secret and is humiliated in public (5:14). He embraces a sylph in silky bedclothes only to be scorched by the glowing embers of her husband's ire (6:27, 34–35). The sinner indulges his cravings out of self-love, but down deep he hates himself, and he is his own destroyer (1:19; 5:22; 6:32b). Not only is he wicked; he is a *fool*.

The supple and multifaceted rhetoric of the wisdom teacher seeks to fortify the youngster's soul against its own fierce passions. Then the other skills and virtues, such as diligence, prudence, effective speech, social grace, justice, and compassion, will find sheltered ground on which to thrive, and to these much of the rest of Proverbs will be devoted.

ESSAY 4. WISDOM IN THE INTERLUDES

I. WHAT IS WISDOM?

In the Ten Lectures, the exordia, which call the son to attention and praise wisdom, are prefatory to the lessons, which hold the main messages. Some readers recognized the potential of these exordia to bear a message of their own and incorporated their essence in four poems, namely the Wisdom interludes.

Interlude B, the encomium of wisdom, is transitional to Interludes A, D, and E. Interlude B isolates wisdom as a topic in its own right and celebrates its powers in superlatives, using some incidental person-metaphors to do so.

The personification interludes express their concept of wisdom most dramatically by means of the figure of Wisdom, as she emerges in full personification in Interludes A, D, and E. Lady Wisdom is a strange being, a personification of a mental power who claims to have preceded creation and to exist in a daughterlike relationship to God. She transcends mundane reality and human minds, individually and collectively, yet is active in the busiest spheres of human existence. She is not simply a symbol of ordinary human wisdom, yet she is in some way identified with it.

The personification interludes expound their new concept of wisdom by means of the mythos of Lady Wisdom. I use the Greek form "mythos" to recall Plato's use of the word, a narratival trope that serves as an explanatory paradigm in areas where literal discourse must be supplemented by poetic imagination. This mysterious mythos requires decoding.[227] Indeed, it may be an enigma of the sort the Prologue says we will find in the book (1:6). What reality does it disclose?

B. Mack (1970) draws a distinction between myth proper and "myth-ology," the latter being the reappropriation of myth and mythic language for theological reflection. This is close to my use of "mythos," though I do not presume an antecedent myth.

Mack classifies the Wisdom figure as "myth-ology," for "the figure of wisdom becomes the language expression for a category of 'knowledge' which does not belong to man as man on the basis of observation and human experience but which may now be understood as God's wisdom, a wisdom which stands over against man and confronts him with itself" (p. 52).

While this distinction needs refinement, to reject it as anachronistic, as C. Camp does (1985: 52), is to make assumptions about the limits of Israelite mentality that do not do it justice. Certainly the concept would not be an anachronism if the poems were written in Hellenistic times, when philosophical refinements were more at home. In fact, Camp's own interpretation of Wisdom (see in Essay 2, §9) treats the figure as "myth-ology" rather than myth, though in a different way from Mack. Camp also says that Mack's interpretation is philosophical and unisemic and "lacks the fluidity inherent in poetry" (p. 53). In actuality, Mack's distinction recognizes the fluid and evolving

---

[227] Speaking of Platonic myths, I. Edman says, "These myths are not allegories; they are not symbolic paraphrases of demonstration. They are poetic creations which give in the immediacy of an imaginative picture a sense of the atmosphere, the beauty, the validity of some human aspiration, some human faith, some human vision which the senses cannot touch nor the methods of dialectic prove" (from the introduction to *The Works of Plato* (1928), p. xxxii. This may be applied to Proverbs' personification interludes as well.

uses of imagery, motifs, and language, rather than assuming that if a figure has mythlike traits it *is* mythological.

A. Some Decodings

1. One ancient interpretation equates Wisdom with Torah. This is the idea of Ben Sira 24 (see n. 231) and a commonplace of Midrash, which applies all that is said about wisdom to Torah. Much in Lady Wisdom's portrayal, however, does not accord with the concept of Torah, meaning God's verbal revelation to Israel. After all, "all the judges of the earth" (8:16) do not govern by Torah, even at their best, and the Torah cannot be reconciled with the scornful woman of Interlude A. (The identification I propose later allows Torah as one *application* of the mythos but not as its immediate referent.)

2. Another classic decoding explains Lady Wisdom as a hypostasis of God's own wisdom, not the wisdom he bestows but the wisdom in his own mind.

"Hypostasis," as the term is used in modern scholarship, refers to "mythic objectifications or personifications of divine qualities, gifts or attributes or of abstract concepts or aspects of human existence, whereby such entities assume an identity of their own" (*Encyclopedia of Religion*, 6.546). On the Wisdom figure as hypostasis, see Schencke 1913: 15–25; Ringgren 1947: 89ff.; Whybray 1965b: 78–94; Pfeifer 1967: 25–27; cf. R. Marcus 1950–51: 157–71.

Running counter to the hypostasis interpretation are a number of facts: Wisdom is a created being (8:22–23)[228] and therefore exists *outside of* God (v 30). God's own wisdom is mysterious and infinite, not accessible to all. Wisdom, as described in chapter 8, serves humanity, not God. If Lady Wisdom were a stable hypostasis, she would probably have a single name, *Wisdom* (this happens with *Sophia* in Wis Sol), whereas in Prov 1–9 she has three designations: *ḥokmah*, *binah*, and *t^{e}bunah* ("Wisdom," "Understanding," "Good Sense"). Though God is wise and uses wisdom, Lady Wisdom is not exactly divine wisdom.

3. The most influential modern reading of this mythos was proposed by Gerhard von Rad (1970: 189–228; ET 144–76). Von Rad identifies wisdom in Prov 8 and related texts as the primeval order itself, or as the order-mystery (*Ordnungsgeheimnis*), or as the order-producing force (*Ordnungsmacht*) with which God informs the world. This force speaks to man, influences him, and corrects him. It is a means of revelation alongside priesthood and prophecy (p. 213).

In my view, Lady Wisdom gives voice neither to the primeval order nor to God's words. All that she does is to summon humans, praise her own excellence, and react to people with emotions corresponding to the way they behave toward her. She says nothing about the world other than the fact that she saw it being formed, and she reveals no "mystery of order." Wisdom is not a channel of revelation of the divine will so much as a means of conforming to it. Nevertheless, von Rad has provided an important insight by describing Lady Wisdom as representing a real and independent power in the world and beyond it.

[228] The issue does not depend on the crux *qanani* in Prov 8:22; see the Commentary.

Some scholars believe that not only was Lady Wisdom modeled on a goddess, she was believed to really be one (see pp. 334ff.). Scholars are often unclear as to whether they think that Lady Wisdom was considered a goddess or was a demythologized literary outgrowth of an earlier divinity, but D. N. Freedman puts it bluntly: "Lady Wisdom emerges as superhuman, a heavenly person, and a companion of God from before Creation: that's a goddess in my book!" (DNF).

Freedman's criteria for divinity fail to allow for personification as a literary trope. There are numerous examples of personifications that do not presuppose the actual existence of the person described. A variety of principles and powers are personified in the midrash, such as Torah (= Wisdom) (*Gen. Rab.* 1.2), Truth and Kindness (*Gen. Rab.* 8.5), and the Principle of Mercy *middat haraḥămim* (*Ozar Hammidrašim* §407.5). The latter is a "female" by virtue of the feminine gender of *middah*. But none of these were really considered to be gods in the way that Isis, for example, was believed to be a goddess by her devotees. When the Torah is imagined as a person who assists God in creation (*Gen. Rab.* 1.2), this is only an incidental rhetorical trope, one of many, and was understood as such. Personified Torah's humanlike characteristics do not carry over into other contexts.

The personification poems in Prov 1–8 treat Wisdom in the same way that the midrash does Torah. In fact, the personification interludes are themselves a sort of midrash—homiletic exploration and exposition—on the earlier texts of Proverbs, especially the Ten Lectures. Lady Wisdom is indeed godlike, but that is a literary guise, and we should grant the author and readers the literary competency needed to use and read tropes in an appropriate manner.

B. Wisdom's Attributes

An adequate reading of Lady Wisdom must account for these facts within the mythos:

1. The figure of Lady Wisdom represents a wisdom that encompasses the actual teachings of human sages, such as the book of Proverbs holds. Lady Wisdom is designated by the same terms as they: *ḥokmah*, *binah*, and *t*^{e}*bunah*. If these words had a unique meaning in the mythos (such as "world order" or "mystery of order"), the personification passages would be disconnected from the rest of the book. The myth would be depicting an entirely different wisdom under the pretense of speaking of the same thing. But strong ties of phraseology, structure, and motif indicate an intention to bind the interludes to their context. Nevertheless, and paradoxically:

2. The wisdom of the mythos exists independently of the human mind, since Lady Wisdom preceded all creation.

3. This wisdom was not an active agent in creation. Lady Wisdom was not an assistant, an adviser, or a demiurge. Nor does the poem show her acting as an artisan or bearer of the arts to humanity. The notion that Wisdom was an *ʾomman*, an artisan (disputed in the Commentary to 8:30), is one of the most ancient and widespread interpretations. But this notion seems to be deliberately repudiated

in 8:30–31, which emphasizes that Wisdom played while God worked. God alone (as in Gen 1 and Job 38) imposes order on chaos.

4. The image of Wisdom playing *before* God implies that wisdom was an object of divine contemplation. Wisdom's role in relation to God is intellectual and aesthetic. In Prov 8, as von Rad observes, "this world-imminent wisdom is viewed less from the perspective of he rational aspect of the economic order than from the perspective of an aesthetic aspect" (1970: 205).[229]

5. In spite of her all-important role in human creativity, Wisdom does not seem to directly affect the course of human events. Though she is everywhere at once, she somehow remains aloof, preaching and advising rather than bringing about and shaping events. Her doings are largely confined to feelings and words. She loves and she hates. She does not herself execute punishment; fools do that to themselves (8:36; cf. 1:31–32; 9:12). She calls, and those who respond gain her love, whereupon they prosper (8:34–35). She offers bounteous benefits, but she does not bestow them directly, in the way that God bestows peace or a good rain. Rather, people who live by wisdom earn the promised rewards by their own merits, just as the carpenter, and not the carpenter's skill, is what makes the furniture. Wisdom does build herself a house, but that is just to set the stage for her discourse.

In the Wisdom interludes, Wisdom fills her role less by doing than by *being*. We may reflect that this is a commonsense view of the way wisdom works on the natural plane. Human wisdom (whether as knowledge or intelligence) does not accomplish things on its own, but must be activated and realized by the deeds of its possessors.

6. Wisdom in the mythos is extra-temporal, unbound by time and thus immutable. We cannot picture her growing or maturing as humans discover more truths or shrinking and withering if truths are forgotten or ignored. Her history is really ontology: she is at once a child to God and a patron to humans. The differences in status belong to hierarchy, not development.

7. Wisdom is unlocalized, unbounded by space. Being everywhere, she is, in a sense, nowhere. She says, "When he established the heavens, there was I" (8:27). Where? It cannot be the heavens, for God did not carry out the creation of the heavens in the heavens. "There" is nonspatial; it refers to an event—the work of creation. Yet Wisdom is not simply outside space. At creation, she was "near" God and "before" him, playing on the stage he had just erected, the "habitable world," the *tebel*. Now she indwells in all creative, rational human activity: in the marketplace, on the highways, and in every righteous decision in affairs of state.

C. Wisdom as a Universal

The concept that best accounts for Wisdom's features is that of a *universal*. To be sure, the author does not attach a philosophic or abstract label to the figure,

[229]". . . wird diese der Welt immanente Weisheit weniger unter dem rationalen Aspekt der ökonomischen Ordnung als unter einem ästhetischen Aspekt gesehen."

nor is there any indication that he would have recognized the concept of universal as such, by whatever term might have been current. Nevertheless, it is an appropriate way of designating the concept embodied in Lady Wisdom. A universal, in the "realistic" usage, is a "single substance or Form, existing timelessly and independently of any of its particular manifestations and apprehended not by sense but by intellect."[230]

Lady Wisdom symbolizes the perfect and transcendent universal, of which the infinite instances of human wisdom are imperfect images or realizations. Like a Platonic *idea*, the wisdom-universal exists objectively and not only as an abstraction or mental construct. It dwells in special proximity to God—"before him," present to his mind—while maintaining a distinct and separate existence. As a universal, it exists simultaneously in the supernal realm (universal, extra-temporal, extra-mundane) and the human world (time-bound, worldly, belonging to particular peoples, realized in specific words). This transcendent wisdom now and ever presents itself to humanity, meaning that the wisdom that people can learn, such as the wise teachings of Proverbs, are manifestations or precipitates of a universal, unitary wisdom. God's wisdom and man's wisdom, though incomparable in magnitude, are in essence the same.

The great principle of the Wisdom interludes is that all knowledge proceeds from a single source beyond time and locale, communicating itself to human sages and through them to others. The personification interludes embody this idea in the mythos of a woman: Wisdom speaking wisdom. To use an analogy from modern linguistics, we can say that the limitless teachings and wise ideas that humans can shape, learn, and transmit are *generated* from the transcendent wisdom in the same way as an infinity of possible utterances are "generated" from the deep structure of language.

Wisdom in the mythos is an objective reality alongside God and man. It is manifest in, but distinct from, the infinity of wise things that humans can know and say and do.

II. PERSONA AND PERSONALITY

The personality of Lady Wisdom is central to the rhetoric of the interludes, for in them persona and message coincide, and both are called wisdom.

Out of the lectures' exhortations and exaltations of wisdom, Lady Wisdom emerges in the interludes as a character in her own right and takes on female

[230]A. D. Wesley, in *Encyclopedia of Philosophy* 8.196, on whose discussion of universals (8.194–206) my use of the concept is based. In philosophical terms, the concept described here would be comparable to the "realist" theory of universals, which supposes them to exist independently of the human mind. This is similar to the Platonic concept of universals ("ideas"). I mention this by way of analogy, but a diffuse influence is not out of the question. The interludes may well be Hellenistic in origin.

In an earlier study (1997c) I used the term "archetype," which would fit well except that it now has indelible Jungian connotations.

form. What the father says about wisdom in the lectures, Wisdom says about herself in the interludes. Even the way the father derides sinners and fools is echoed in Wisdom's mockery of the arrogant in Interlude A. This is not just a datum of literary history. It belongs to the present experience of reading Prov 1–9 and the rhetorical strategy of personification, whereby incidental motifs in the father's words emerge as the leading themes in the interludes. The two voices, though heard distinctly, are now entwined, with the father's praise of wisdom in the lectures seconded and extended in Wisdom's praise of herself.

The demeanor of personified Wisdom differs from one interlude to another. In A, she displays a certain petulance alongside her solemn declarations of moral principles. There is even a whiff of Schadenfreude in her rather eager anticipation of the calamity awaiting those who spurned her. In D, she is majestic, lofty, and serene. She declaims in forms usually reserved for deities and monarchs, as she expresses pride in her sublime history and station. In E, she is an energetic and liberal hostess.

Common to all three pictures is a surprising facet of Wisdom's personality: She *wants* human attention. That is why she is furious when men ignore her (1:23–27) and why she excoriates fools not exactly for their folly or sins but rather for their mulish resistance to her call. In her eagerness to attract adherents, she both sends out her maidservants and goes herself to the busiest quarters of the city (9:3). There she invites all men, including some rather unsavory types, to her *symposium* (9:4). The real point of Wisdom's self-praise in D becomes clear in her renewed charge to mankind: "And now, my sons, listen to me" (8:32a).

Wisdom *needs* humanity. Or, we may say, before people came on the scene, she could only frolic before God, waiting for her real mission to begin. In the absence of humans, wisdom is, after all, inert. Lady Wisdom continues to "play," but she also roams about in search of man. Wisdom realizes her potential only through human activity. Her desire for love shows that human minds—from the callow juvenile's to the educated sage's—fill an essential role in the intellectual economy of the universe. Wisdom is not a static body of knowledge, a mass of facts and rules. It is certainly not an esoteric corpus of truths resistant to human penetration. Wisdom is like a living, sentient organism, requiring interaction with other minds for its own vitality and realization.

III. WHERE CAN WISDOM BE HEARD?

How, then, can we, the readers of Proverbs, hear Wisdom's voice in our own lives, and what does it sound like? When Lady Wisdom declares, "Happy is the man who listens to me" (8:34), *where* should we turn our attention? In abstract terms, how does the transcendent Wisdom manifest itself in the mundane sphere?

The scope of the audible, that is to say, perceptible, wisdom that the interludes describe cannot embrace the entirety of wisdom, which includes technical skills, magic, and esoteric knowledge, for these arts do not "call" to people in the sense of demanding attention or obedience. The phrase *šamaʿ l-* "listen to" (as in 1:33 and 8:34) always implies obedience or conformity to another's will, not simply hearing or absorbing information. Then again, Wisdom cannot be demanding attention only to the words quoted in the personification passages, for these are essentially self-praise and do not make demands other than that we listen to wisdom, which leaves us still wondering *what* wisdom.

Like the exordia in the Ten Lectures, Interlude D directs our attention not to itself but to *other* utterances. When Lady Wisdom urges us to listen to wisdom, she is not just telling us to read Prov 8, but to give thought to the proverbs in the following chapters. But wisdom is not confined to the book of Proverbs, for the world's princes, who can possess wisdom (8:16) cannot be expected to study the book of Proverbs, nor were the sayings of Solomon present at creation, as Lady Wisdom was.

The wisdom that the personification passages would have us hear and heed can be only teachings *of the kind* taught in the book of Proverbs. This does not mean only the literary genre we call Wisdom literature, which does not set itself apart from other genres. The wisdom that Wisdom speaks is *musar* (8:33), which refers to all admonitions bearing an ethical and religious message.

The book of Proverbs is one precipitate of the primeval, universal wisdom, as this is transmitted by and filtered through individual sages, such as Solomon and all fathers and mothers. Though not mentioned in Proverbs, the sacred books of Israel would belong to this wisdom, as would all intelligent thoughts and ideas that conform to wisdom's principles.

But Israel does not have a monopoly on wisdom. Since the transcendental wisdom pervades all of God's "habitable world," the learning of the nations, insofar as it conforms to the ethical standards of Proverbs, is genuine wisdom or, we may say, Wisdom's voice. This viewpoint is shared by 1 Kgs 5:10–11, for the comparison of Solomon's wisdom to the wisdom of renowned foreigners presupposes the validity of the latter.

Wisdom, in its essence rather than in its infinite particulars, is God's gift to humanity, and Israel partakes in this cosmopolitan wisdom. Israel's portion (as the ascription of Proverbs to Solomon implies) is greater than others', and Ben Sira correctly picks up Proverbs' implication when he says that Wisdom lodged in Israel.[231] But it is not confined there.

---

[231]There is thus no radical innovation in Ben Sira's claim that wisdom found its home in Israel (24:1–22), where it took the form of Torah (24:23–29). Though Ben Sira does say that "all wisdom is the fear of the Lord, and in all wisdom is the doing of Torah" (19:20), he does not deny that wisdom can exist elsewhere. The first man had *some* wisdom (24:28), and wisdom reigns over all the peoples (24:6). Ben Sira's point is that wisdom dwells in Israel permanently and securely, because the "covenant-book of the Most High" is the book of wisdom par excellence. It is "as full as the Pishon with wisdom" (24:25). Wisdom itself encompasses or somehow extends beyond Torah, for *topeś torah yadrikennahh* "He who holds Torah will come to it [wisdom]" (15:1). In spite of Ben Sira's "nationalizing" of wisdom (as it is often termed), he regards Torah as an instance—the premier one, of course—of a universal power.

The subtext of Proverbs' universalism is not the commendation of foreign wisdom but rather the assurance to Jews that they need not look elsewhere to find the sort of wisdom that is so admired by the peoples. Israel has its own *philosophia*.[232]

IV. THE VOICES TOGETHER

The voice of Wisdom and the voice of the teacher do not merge; they are heard in counterpoint. The teacher offers wise and life-saving teachings, and Lady Wisdom tells us that wisdom embraces such teachings but is greater than their sum total. The teacher is wise, but wisdom itself transcends any human's wisdom. It is a single principle that comprehends all sagacious teachings and astute thoughts. Personified as a woman, it is a heavenly creature, residing in angelic proximity to God. At the same time (again like an angel), it is ubiquitous in everyday life, traversing the streets and speaking to all men. We carry this image of Lady Wisdom with us as we enter the proverb collections that hold the wisdom of Solomon and other ancient sages. The image informs us that the sundry, often homely, proverbs of the father-teacher, of Israel's anonymous sages, even of Solomon himself, speak with a single voice, and this is Wisdom's own.

From this counterpoint, we learn that the intimate, down-to-earth teaching of the home, which strives to imbue the growing child with the hard but simple lesson of moral character based on fear of God, is an instance, perhaps the most important, of the grand and sublime power that pervades all creation. The fusion of these two voices in Prov 1–9 tells us that in the adages and observations of Israel's sages in the coming chapters we will hear at once the echo of transcendental wisdom and the reverberations of the wisdom taught in the home.

---

[232]Ben Sira undertakes an extension of this endeavor, namely "to convince Jews and even well-disposed Gentiles that true wisdom is to be found primarily in Jerusalem and not in Athens, more in the inspired books of Israel than in the clever writings of Hellenistic humanism" (Di Lella: 16).

TEXTUAL NOTES ON PROVERBS 1–9

◆

The Textual Notes have two interdependent goals: to identify ancient textual variants and to describe the underlying exegesis of the ancient translations, in particular the Greek.

After the discussion of each verse, I list textual variants. Differences in implicit vocalization belong to oral tradition or the translators' assumptions and are not textual variants. There are numerous differences for which a textual basis is possible but cannot be determined, such as variations in grammatical number and the use of the article, copulas, conjunctions, and words for "all." These can be freely varied by both translators and scribes, and it is not usually possible to determine the underlying Hebrew. It must be emphasized that to identify a variant, whether found in a Hebrew manuscript or retroverted from an ancient translation, is not to imply that it is *correct*. Adjudication among variants belongs to literary analysis and is relegated to the Commentary.

BIBLIOGRAPHY: For textual commentary see the still-valuable study of A. Baumgartner (1890) (= "Baum."). Some of the observations of Toy 1899 are still useful. For basic concepts and methodology, see Tov 1992.

THE TEXTUAL TRADITIONS

I. HEBREW

A. Masoretic Text

I use the BHS edition of Leningrad Codex B19^{A} (1008/9 C.E.). The variants in the Aleppo Codex (10th c.) are only orthographic: Plene-lene differences and a greater use of compound shewas with gutturals in the Aleppo.

B. Qumran

Only a few lines of Proverbs have turned up among the Dead Sea Scrolls: 4QProv^{a} (= 4Qum102), preserving parts of 1:27–2:1, and 4QProv^{b} (= 4Q103), with 13:6b–9b; 14:6–10; 14:31–15:8 and 15:19b–31. In 4QProv^{b}, the right column is written stichometrically, with one couplet per line, showing that the stichometric division of Hebrew verse, based on parallelism, was recognized in ancient times. The script of Prov[a] belongs to the mid-first century B.C.E., that of Prov[b] to the turn of the era. There is also a quotation (or paraphrase) of 15:8 in the Damascus Covenant XI 20–21.

II. SEPTUAGINT

A. Background

The Septuagint (LXX) is by far the most valuable of the versions for text criticism, for the history of interpretation, and for the transmission history of the book of Proverbs, and will therefore receive special attention. The LXX is the most important aid in identifying ancient variants. It also reveals an early interpretation of Proverbs and is a Wisdom text in its own right. The Textual Notes will address the LXX from these perspectives.

Though the Septuagint inevitably reflects exegesis and expresses the translators' own tendencies and beliefs, I differ from J. Cook's view that "the Septuagint should principally be seen as an *exegetical writing* (CSP 12)," "the earliest exegetical commentary on the Hebrew text" (p. 35). LXX-Prov is primarily a *translation*, one aiming at a faithful representation of the Hebrew, and it is best understood in terms of that goal. All translations are based on and reflect exegesis, though this tends to be noticeable only when one disagrees with the interpretation. The category "exegetical" is too vague to help us explain variations from the Hebrew or, more precisely, from a "zero-degree" or purely mimetic[233] rendering, which we hypothesize for the sake of describing "variations" in the actual translation.[234] "Exegetical" is more usefully reserved to describe words, phrases, or lines intended to explain another element in the translation.

LXX-Prov does introduce additional elements for exegetical purposes, but only a few are really tendentious. The moralizing additions, such as "and the downfall of lawbreakers is evil" (1:18$^{\beta}$) are not evidence that translation elsewhere is unusually "free." This is especially so because the LXX additions almost always serve to underscore, not contradict, the ethics expounded in the Hebrew, so there was no need for the translator to go against the grain elsewhere. When the exegetical and tendentious features are accounted for and the expansions are set aside, the LXX proves to be, on the whole, a fairly faithful rendering of a Hebrew original, and it can be used as evidence for textual variants. Hence the following notes are less inclined than CSP to account for differences by positing exegetical and ideological motives when none such are evident, but they nonetheless seek to identify the translator's attitudes and ideas.

[233] See n. 23 in the Introduction.

[234] This hypothetical, zero-degree translation would be a one-to-one mapping of source to target, with complete correspondence in rendering morphological elements and a unique correspondence between each lexeme in the source language and the lexeme that renders it in the target language.

The dating of the Greek translation can be determined only loosely. Mid- to late-second century B.C.E. is generally accepted. The Wisdom of Solomon shows dependency on LXX-Prov in a few verses, most clearly Wis 6:14 on 1:21, but Wis Sol's own dating is in considerable dispute. On the basis of the translation's minimal recourse to the belief in an afterlife, as well as its generally universalist outlook, M. Dick (1990: 21, 50) advocates an early-second-century dating. J. Cook (1993) supports a similar dating on the grounds of the translator's familiarity with Hellenistic literary style and (contrary to Dick's observation) his suspicion of foreign thought. These are weak criteria. There is no suspicion of foreign thought in the material that definitely belongs to the original translation ("Old Greek," OG), for the two major additions in chapter 9 were probably introduced later. The universalism comes from the parent text.

Edition

In the absence of a critical edition of LXX-Proverbs, I use Rahlfs's *Septuaginta*, with attention to inner-Greek variants only when relevant to text-critical decisions or when they are important to the meaning of the verse. It must be emphasized that there is no attempt to mention or account for all Gk variants. For this, CSP can be consulted for the chapters it examines.[235] I note significant variants in the uncials and occasionally call attention to interesting variants in the minuscules by referring to "MSS." In the absence of stemmata, listing of minuscule numbers would be of little value.

The lack of a critical edition is unfortunate, but the handicap is mitigated by the fact that changes later introduced in the LXX almost always harmonized it with the MT. The inability to identify some of these changes may camouflage true variants but would not create false ones.

Bibliography: J. A. Jäger's (1788) and P. de Lagarde's (1863) pathbreaking studies were important in subsequent research but are of limited value today. A. Baumgartner (1890) (= "Baum."); Bertram (1936); Gerleman (1956); Tov (1990).

The major study of LXX-Prov is J. Cook's *The Septuagint of Proverbs*, 1997 (= "CSP"). I have not attempted to incorporate the detailed data he brings, much of which is concerned with inner-Septuagintal issues and the nuances of Greek words, but mention his conclusions only insofar as they bear on my narrower purposes, which are more text-critically oriented.

B. Verse Numbering in the Septuagint

There is much confusion and variation in the way chapters and verses are numbered in the LXX, and all the systems are at variance with the MT numbering.

[235] Prov 1, 2, 6, 8, 9, and, in less detail, 30:32–33; 31:1–9; 25:1–8; 31:10–12.

So far as possible, I use the MT numeration even for LXX references, though I sometimes refer to the Greek numeration in brackets when the departure is considerable. I follow Rahlfs when referring to Greek verse numbering.

Additional verses: As in Rahlfs, additional verses in the LXX are indicated by letters; e.g., "15:18a" refers to the addition following 15:18. (In the MT, letters refer to verse segments.)

Transposed verses: The "additional" verses in Rahlfs are not always true additions, since he assigns transposed verses their own number, e.g., Rahlfs's "15:28a" is MT's 16:7. I use the MT number in such cases, but, where relevant to the discussion, add Rahlfs's number in parentheses, e.g., "16:7 [15:28a]."

Verse subdivisions: The lines (stichs) of verses in the LXX are designated by raised Greek letters, e.g., $1{:}7^{\beta}$ = second line of 1:7 (7^{β} is not the same as MT's 7b and does not exist in the MT).

C. *The Order and Number of the Septuagint-Proverbs*

A prominent feature of LXX-Proverbs is its numerous pluses. According to Mezzacasa (1913: 2), the LXX has about 130 stichs and thirty partial sentences not represented in the MT. Some of these existed in the Hebrew text used by the translator and thus represent a richer form of the textual tradition of Proverbs. Other pluses were added later, in the transmission of the Greek text. There are numerous missing lines and verses as well. In such cases, the MT may hold later additions.

The LXX's sequence differs from the MT's at a number of points. There are some minor variations, such as 8:32b appearing after v 34; 16:6, 7, 8 and 9 being interspersed in 15:27–29; and 20:20–22 being placed after 20:9. The major changes occur at the end of the book. Following 24:22a–22e, which is an extended warning about the king's dangerous powers, the LXX's order is 30:1–14; 24:23–34; 30:15–33; 31:1–9; 25:1–29:27; 31:10–31 (with vv. 25–26 in reverse order).

The variant order is often thought to show that these units circulated as independent collections and were assembled differently in the MT and the LXX traditions (thus Toy, p. xxxiii). Against this is the fact that the units within chapters 24–25 have the same sequence even when dispersed in the LXX, as do the units in chapters 30–31. It seems unlikely that this would have happened if the relocated materials were circulated separately, as is assumed by the theory.

Cook (CSP 312–15) argues that 31:1–9 was moved in order to make 31:10 be adjacent to 29:27, thereby creating a contrast between the "unrighteous man" (*anēr adikos*; 29:27) and the "virtuous woman" (*gynaika andreian*; 31:10). Cook also thinks that 25:1–7 was placed before 31:1–9 because the theme of both is the king. The join of 29:27 + 31:10, however, seems too minor a gain to explain the major movement, however, when the movement of a single verse would do the same. The association of two passages on kingship is more striking and may have played a role in the movement of 31:1–9, but it does explain why chapter 30 also was split in two. In any case, there is no reason to ascribe the relocations to the OG translator rather than to a Hebrew scribe or a later Greek copyist, Cook believes (CSP 313).

From the literary standpoint, MT's order is preferable. It appropriately has the short poems in 30–31 in appendices and keeps the uniform proverbial material of chaps 10–29 together.

There are only two differently located blocks in the end of LXX-Prov, 30:1–14 (35 stichs) and 30:15–33 (45 stichs), and the Septuagintal order may have resulted from their accidental displacement, in a way that recalls the dislocation of Sir 30:25–33:13a in the Greek. Major dislocation may arise from displacement of leaves. In the case of Ben Sira, that happened prior to all extant Greek MSS. Or a copyist may skip over a major block, which is then restored at the wrong place.

D. LXX-Proverbs as a Recension

Many LXX variants cannot be explained either as scribal errors or as by-products of the translator's belief, style, or whim. These irreducible variants include most of the transpositions of verses and larger blocks of verses, as well as the addition of new verses and proverbs. Some variants depend on a different Hebrew base text. Such differences show that LXX-Proverbs is, as Tov (1990) has argued, a translation of a parallel recension or edition of the book of Proverbs. While we may well agree that "the Hebrew parent text from which this Greek version was constructed did not differ extensively from the Massoretic text" (CSP 334), it *did* differ, and we can determine where and how it did so only by examining every verse.

Since we are dealing with two recensions, we need not always choose between alternative textual forms, nor need our explanations of variants be limited to the alternatives of "translation technique" *or* scribal error. Adages, in speech and in writing, undergo constant change, sometimes deliberate, sometimes accidental. If transmission gives rise to two proverbs, both are legitimate proverbs and can be interpreted.

Fluidity of transmission is characteristic of Wisdom literature and demonstrably at work, for example, in Ptahhotep, Anii, Shuruppak, and the Aḥiqar tradition. Almost every type of LXX variant has parallels within the transmission of Egyptian Wisdom literature (and other genres as well). The later scribes often substituted synonyms, made changes of person and tense, added words or lines to elaborate or "improve" a proverb, occasionally omitted material, and sometimes changed the order of sentences and even entire units. In a few cases, they were able to introduce a radically new sense into the text by a few subtle and clever modifications (see esp. Fecht 1958). Many LXX variants could have arisen as deliberate reshapings of the text in the Hebrew transmission; the same may be said of MT variants.

III. PESHIṬTA

The Syriac translation of Proverbs is a fairly literal translation of a Hebrew text very close to the MT. It is heavily influenced by the LXX, which the translator was clearly relying on for help in his work. Nevertheless, the Syriac maintains a certain distance from the LXX, sometimes negotiating a path between the two major versions, sometimes merging or rendering the text twice to reflect his two sources (Joosten 1995).

The Syriac is independent evidence for a textual variant when it diverges from both the MT and the Septuagint or when it can be retroverted to the same reading as the LXX but treats it differently from that version. Sometimes (e.g., 17:12; 21:10) the Syriac seems to be drawing on the LXX for the interpretation while still working from the Hebrew. For a good example of Syr's procedure, see the note on 6:3.

Syr does not usually maintain the major LXX pluses (two lines or longer). Exceptions are 9:12a–12c and 9:18a–18d; 13:13a; 25:20a; and 27:21a. It is unclear why these alone were translated. In none of these cases does the Syr testify to a Hebrew original. A Greek vorlage can sometimes be demonstrated; see the notes to 9:12a, 12b, 18a, 18b.

The edition used here is the Leiden Peshiṭta (Di Lella 1979). Variants from the Leiden apparatuses are mentioned only when they are arguably original rather than inner-Syriac and when they bear upon the meaning or the reconstruction of the vorlage. Syriac manuscript variants are referred to simply as "var." (pl. varr.) or "MSS"; Di Lella's apparatus should be consulted for details.

Bibliography: A. Baumgartner (1890); H. Pinkuss (1894) (= "Pink."); G. Kuhn (1931); A. Di Lella (1979); M. Weitzman (1994); J. Joosten (1995). Pinkuss's is still the only comprehensive study of this version.

IV. TARGUM

The Aramaic Targum (Tg) to Proverbs, unlike many other Targumim to the Hagiographa, shows very little midrashic paraphrase or expansion. Tg-Prov features are described by Melammed (1972: 18–20) and Healey (1991: ix–10).

Tg-Proverbs is directly dependent on the Syriac. This is the consensus view, first proposed by J. A. Dathe (1764). Maybaum (1871) argued for Syriac dependency on the Targum but had few followers. Dathe's hypothesis has been supported by Pinkuss (1894: 110–13), Melammed (1972), Díez Merino (1984: chapter 3 and p. 307), and R. J. Owens (1997). (The last surveys and evaluates the various theories.) Healey (1991: 9) cautiously (but needlessly) posits the existence of a common source for Tg and Syr.

Tg-Prov transcribes the Syr while making dialectical and orthographical adjustments and harmonizing the translation with a Heb text very close to the MT. Tg is nearly identical to Syr in about 300 of its 915 verses (Kaminka 1931–32: 171). D. Snell (1998) counted the words that the Targum and the Syr have in common (setting aside LXX pluses) and found a 72 percent correlation. Disagreements with the Syr are almost always due to Tg's attempt to adjust to the MT.

Kaminka (1931–32) maintained that the numerous Tg-LXX agreements are evidence that both versions rest on a pre-Tannaitic Hebrew vorlage, one perhaps going back to the third century B.C.E. (p. 173) and, moreover, that Tg is older than the LXX and influenced it. This theory is vitiated, however, by the fact that almost all the Tg-LXX agreements (Pinkuss [p. 110], counts more than 100; cf. Kaminka [pp. 178–91]) appear also in the Syriac (e.g., 1:21; 6:30; 7:22; 8:13), whereas there are many instances where Syr and LXX agree against Tg. The few cases where Tg seems closer to the LXX than to the Syr are mostly incidental to harmonization of Tg with the MT (e.g., 6:7a) or due to coincidental agreement in interpretation.

M. Weitzman (1994: 81–83) has gathered evidence for Jewish use of the Peshiṭta by medieval rabbis, allowing him to date the work to the last third of the first millennium C.E.

The arguments for the Tg's dependency on the Syr are strong, and for this reason the Tg is rarely of text-critical value. In a very few cases, Tg may support a minor variant independently, by using a synonym rather than a transliteration of the word used in the Syr (e.g., 9:1).

Edition

No critical edition is available. The major texts are Tg^L = Lagarde, *Hagiographa Chaldaica* (1873) and Tg^Z = Zamora text (= San Bernado 116-Z–40), dated 1517 C.E.; in Díez Merino 1984. Unless otherwise noted, I use Tg^Z. Other variants are available in Healey's textual notes. In the "Syr (Tg)" means that Tg treats the verse in the same way as Syr, apart from trivial adjustments.

Bibliography: Pinkuss (1894); A. Kaminka (1931–32); Minsker (1940); E. Z. Melammed (1972); L. Díez Merino (1984); Healey (1991); Weitzman (1994); Owens (1997).

V. VULGATE

Jerome translated Proverbs into Latin in 398 C.E., toward the end of his career (d. 405 C.E.). He worked from the Hebrew with the help of the Septuagint and with heavy reliance on the literal translations of Aquila, Theodotion, and Symmachus.

Jerome's Hebrew vorlage was almost identical with the consonantal MT. His interpretations seem to draw upon Christian and rabbinic exegesis (C. Gordon 1930). The Vulgate offers little evidence for textual variants in Proverbs, but it occasionally supports another version against the MT. Its main value, not exploited here, is for the history of interpretation.

Bibliography: Gordon (1930).

Comments

Prologue. 1:1–7

1:1. LXX: ". . . who ruled in Israel." Compare the rendering of *mlky yhwdh* by a relative clause in Isa 1:1 and 1 Kgs 4:1.

1:3. LXX creates three lines (stichoi): $^{\alpha}$ *dexasthai te strophas logōn*/$^{\beta}$ *noēsai te dikaiosynēn alēthē* /$^{\gamma}$ *kai krima kateuthynein*, "$^{\alpha}$ To receive twistings of words,/$^{\beta}$ to understand true righteousness, /$^{\gamma}$ and to guide justice aright."

Strophas logōn ("twistings of words" = convoluted sayings) is a puzzling translation of *mwsr*, which is otherwise rendered consistently by *paideia*, *sophia*, and synonyms. Mezz. suggests that it is a paraphrastic interpretation intended to avoid repeating the word of the preceding verse. But the translator is little concerned with avoidance of repetition (except, occasionally, in the case of the same word in parallel lines; e.g., 3:25)—certainly not to the point of changing a common term into an obscure one. In both Sir 39:2 (no Heb preserved) and Wis 8:8, *strophē* is associated with "enigmas." Wis 8:8 reads [*sophia*] *epistatai strophas logōn kai luseis ainigmatōn*, "[Wisdom] knows the intricacies of argument and the resolutions of riddles" (trans. Winston, AB). Sir 6:22 (Heb) reveals an "etymological" interpretation of *musar* in the sense of twisted and difficult, probably associating it with *s-w-r* "turn aside" (CSP 50): "For *musar* is like her name: not to many people is she straight" ("straight" = *nkwḥh*, translated *phanera* "evident"). (Being "not straight" is equivalent to *ʿqwbh* "uneven, rough land," which is the way wisdom is to the fool; v 20.) The LXX may also be playing on *hśkl* and the homonymous *śkl* "cross"; cf. Gen 48:14 (Kuhn 1931).

"Righteousness" (*ṣdq*) = *dikaiosynēn alēthē* "true righteousness." *Alēthē* is an adjectival elaboration of *dikaiosynēn*. CSP (64) notes that the translator often adds adjectives for explication, e.g., *neos* in v 4 and *chryseon* in v 9.

LXX takes *wmyšrym* as an inf., "to guide straight," which can hardly be explained as a graphic error (contrary to Lag., who retroverts to *lmyšr*, an Aramaizing inf.). The LXX shows considerable flexibility in the treatment of grammatical forms.

For unclear reasons, Syr renders *hśkl* as *wdḥltʾ* "and fear."

1:4. LXX translates *pty* as *akakos* "innocent." In contexts where the *peti* has not yet sinned, the LXX uses *akakos* "innocent" (1:22; 8:5; 14:15; 21:11). If he has sinned, he is an *aphrōn*, a fool (7:7; 9:4, 16; 14:18; 19:25; 22:3; 27:12). (*Akakos* is also used for forms of *t-m-m* "innocent" in 2:21 [some MSS] and 13:6.) In this way, the translator reinforces moral polarities by dividing an ambiguous class into two morally antithetical groups (see Giese 1990: §2.11–13). Also used for *peti* is *nēpios* "childlike" (1:32; also Ps 19[18]:8; 116[114]:6; 119[118]:130). For MT's *nʿr* LXX has *paidi de neǭ* "the young youth," adding an adjective to emphasize that the verse refers to the earliest stage of instruction and to more clearly distinguish the elementary stage of education in vv 2–4 from the advanced stage in vv 5–6.

1:5–6. LXX treats both sentences as indicatives, using the future. *Mlyṣh* = *skoteinon logon*, a "dark saying."

Syr 5a: "add *to his* wisdom," for clarity.

1:7. LXX prefixes a couplet($^{\alpha-\beta}$) taken from Ps 111 [110]:10: "$^{\alpha}$ The beginning [*archē*] [^{A} *aretē* "noblest"] of wisdom is the fear of God, $^{\beta}$ good intelligence for all who do it [namely, wisdom]." CSP judges all four lines to be OG, but with the translator responsible for the quotation from Psalms. Others regard $^{\gamma-\delta}$ as hexaplaric (Fritsch 1953: 170). Since *aretē* does not derive from the Greek of either Ps 111:10a or Prov 9:10, it seems that the couplet reflects a Hebrew vorlage already present in the OG translator's text. Within this couplet, *aretē* represents an alternative interpretation of *rʾšyt* (see Commentary).

In 7$^{\gamma}$, *yrʾt YHWH* is translated *eusebeia de eis theon* "reverence toward God."

Syr transposes *dʿt* and *ḥkmh* in 7a and b, as in Ps 111:10a and Prov 9:10, probably influenced by LXX's 7$^{\alpha-\beta}$.

Variant: prefixed couplet, $^{\alpha-\beta}$.

Lecture I. 1:8–19

1:8. "My son": The OG always omits the superfluous possessive of *b^{e}nî* "my son" with the vocative. This and similar differences in the treatment of the vocative will not be noted further. There are also a number of pluses and minuses in the LXX representation of "my son." The minuses are probably earlier, but it seems that scribes and especially translators could take liberties with this word, and it is difficult to determine what the parent texts had.

"Laws" and "rules": LXX contrasts the "laws [*nomous*] of your father" with "the rules [*thesmous*] of your mother." (*Paideian* in ^{B} looks like an adjustment to the expected rendering of *mwsr*, though CSP regards it as original.) Compare how the *nomos* (of the father) is coupled with the *thesmos* (of the mother) in 6:20. This coupling is deliberate, because *mṣwh* "precept" is rendered *nomos* in that verse only. The weightier word is *nomos*, being the standard designation of the divine as well as the paternal *torah* ("instruction"). *Thesmos* appears in the LXX only in 1:8 and in 6:20 (not noted in Hatch-Redpath). In Jewish Hellenistic literature, *thesmos* means "custom," "rule," "mode of practice," both pagan (*5 Sib.* 19) and Jewish (*Test. Neph.* 8:10). It refers to the Torah proper only in the mouth of a hostile gentile (4 Macc 8:7). (In Sir 28:19, read *desmois* with LXX^{BS}.) Hence the choice of *thesmos* in Prov 1:8 seems intended to ascribe greater authority to the father's words. Syr *nmwsʾ* for *mwsr* derives from the LXX^{ASC} rendering, since Syr elsewhere translates it as *mardutaʾ*.

1:9. LXX has "golden [*chruseon*] collar," for rhetorical heightening.

Syr resolves the metaphor "chaplet of grace" as "loveliness for your head."

1:10. LXX joins 10 to 11aα; MT numbers given in brackets: [10] "$^{\alpha}$ Son, let not wicked men mislead you, $^{\beta}$ nor should you consent [11aα] $^{\gamma}$ if they urge you, saying. . . . " The conditional in $^{\alpha}$ is turned into a hortative, perhaps because the apodosis is at a distance (v 15). *Mēde boulēthę̄s* agrees with MT's vocalization of *tbʾ* as *tōbēʾ* (derived from *ʾ-b-h*), as does Syr *ttpys* "be persuaded."

1:11. LXX [MT 11aβ] translates *n'rbh* as *koinōnēson* "share." Lag. (sim. Toy) explains *koinōnēson* as a rendering of *nʿrbh* ("let us go surety") or *nḥbrh* ("let us join") for MT's *n'rbh,* but neither reading makes good sense here, and *ʿrb* is never rendered *koinōnein*. LXX 18 (using *metechein*) shows the same puzzling understanding of *'rb*. The LXX missed the image of ambush entirely and consequently understood *nṣpnh* as a transitive and added *eis gēn* to make sense of the verb: ". . . let us hide the innocent man in the earth unjustly [*adikōs*]."

Syr *bʿt'* "deceitfully." *Bʿt'* = *ḥnm* only in Prov 1:11, 17; and 3:30 and is probably based on the LXX.

1:12. For unclear reasons, LXX 12$^{\beta}$ substitutes a sentence from Ps 34[33]:17b; 109[108]:15b: "and let us remove his memory from the earth." Since Gk of those verses differs from the existing LXX text in word order and the wording (*exoletheusai* rather than *airein*), the borrowing was from the Heb text and was presumably present in LXX-Prov's vorlage.

1:13. LXX correctly translates *nmṣ'* as *katalabōmetha* "seize," a sense *mṣ'* often has; see Iwry 1966.

Syr has *ʿwtrh w'yqrh* "his wealth and his honor." The understanding of *yqr* as a noun equivalent to Aramaic "honor" rather than as the adj. "precious" (cf. LXX-Prov 24:4) occasioned the pairing.

1:14. The third sentence in LXX, "$^{\gamma}$ and let there be to us one pouch," is a hexaplaric doublet, partly marked by an asterisk in SyH (Vul and OL omit).

1:15. OG lacks "(my) son." Both readings, with *bny* (Baum.) or without it (Lag., Toy) are possible and probably found in Hebrew MSS. "My son" does seem to overload the line, but compare the asymmetries in 1:10; 3:12, 28.

For MT's *ntybtm* "their path," LXX, Syr, Tg, and some Heb MSS have pl. "paths," perhaps because the verse is speaking about a plurality of people.

Variant: omit *bny.*

1:16. The verse is omitted in LXX$^{B,C,\ S^*}$ and MSS but present in $S^{c.a,\ A^*}$. In the MSS that have this verse, it is sometimes placed before, sometimes after, v 17, showing that it is a later addition to the LXX. Still, it might be original in the MT and lost by parablepsis by the OG translator (*ky* to *ky*; thus DNF).

Syr adds "innocent" (*zky'*) to "blood," taken from Isa 59:7 or influenced by Prov 1:11.

1:17. LXX: "For not unjustly [*ou gar adikōs*] are nets spread out for birds." *Adikōs* corresponds to Heb *ḥnm* only here and in Prov 1:11. The additional negative probably indicates that the translator understood the verse as a rhetorical question (as does Radaq, though with a different interpretation), which was then converted into a negative. (For examples of this technique in LXX-Job see Orlinsky 1958: 244–46). The translator apparently understood "birds" as metaphors for the wicked, mentioned in the preceding sentence, who get what they deserve. Possibly, however, "birds" are gullible youths.

Syr condenses: "And wrongfully [*bʿt'*, as in v 11b] do they spread nets on [*ʿl*] a bird." The presence of *ḥnm* in vv 17 and 11b led the translator to assume that both verses refer to the ensnaring of victims. BHS is mistaken in saying that *baʿal* is omitted in the versions. In fact, *bʿl knp* is translated as a unit.

1:18. LXX: "$^{\alpha}$ For the very ones who take part [*metechontes*] in murder store up evils for themselves, $^{\beta}$ and the downfall of lawbreakers is evil." LXX assumes that the "blood" (perhaps construing *ldmm* as *ldmym* [thus Tg]) is the victims' and adjusts accordingly. MT's *y'rbw* is translated *metechontes*, again understanding the root *'-r-b* to mean "participate in," as in v 11a, where the synonymous *koinōnēson* is used. The verb *ṣpn* (G) is again taken as transitive, requiring the addition of a complement, *kaka*. LXX 18$^{\beta}$ is a moralizing expansion. It is too unlike MT 19a to regard it as a paraphrase of the MT and thus as evidence for the reading *'ḥryt* (*pace* Mezz., BHS), which in any case is never translated *katastrophē*.

Syr: "and they lie in wait for blood and hide themselves [*wmṭšyn npšthwn*$^{pl.}$]." Like the LXX, Syr treats this verse as a continuation of the preceding and (in spite of LXX 1:19$^{\beta}$) neutralizes the adversative force of *whm*. Both versions understand the point of the verse to be that the bandits are harming their victims, not themselves. The differences from MT result from that assumption.

1:19. LXX adds *tę̄ gar asebeią̄* in $^{\beta}$, "for by impiety (they carry away their own soul)." This is a moralizing expansion and does not reflect *bʿwlh* (*beʿawlāh*) for MT *bʿlyw* (contrary to Lag., Mezz., Toy, following Jäger). Heb *bʿlyw* is implicit in "their own soul."

Syr, 19b: ". . . and take [*nsbyn*] the lives [*npšt'*$^{pl.}$] of their possessors"—probably a misunderstanding of MT, in accordance with Syr's assumption that the only casualties mentioned are the victims of the crime, not its perpetrators. LXX and Syr (≈ Tg) support MT's *'rḥwt* "way," against a conjectural *'ḥryt* "end" (BHS).

Interlude A. 1:20–33

1:20. LXX: "$^{\alpha}$ Wisdom praises herself [*hymneitai*]. . . ." The middle *hymneitei* is to be understood reflexively, since a passive would not accord with the context. Syr (*mštbḥ'* = Tg) (likewise in 8:3) also implies that Wisdom is praising herself.

1:21. Instead of MT's hapax *hmywt* ("bustling crossroads"), LXX (*teicheōn*) read *ḥmwt* or *ḥmywt*. The latter would be the pl. of *ḥmyt*, a form attested in Amarna (Tur-Sinai, p. 105) as well as in Ugaritic and Phoenician (Dahood 1963: 5). LXX 1:21$^{\beta}$ ≈ LXX 8:3$^{\alpha}$. *Dynastōn* "princes" = *śrym*, a distorted dittography of MT's *šʿrym* "gates." After 21$^{\alpha}$, LXX adds *paredreuei* ("sits constantly beside"). It may be parsing *tqr'* as if from *qārah* "happen upon," "meet"; cf. 9:18. Gk *paredreuei* (only here and in 8:3) shows Wisdom as a judge sitting in the city gate. $^{\gamma}$ is a hexaplaric corrective, $^{\beta}$ the original. Gk *epi de pulais poleōs* = *(b)šʿrym bʿyr* (Baum.).

Syr's *bryt'*$^{pl.}$, i.e., *beryātā'* "streets," "broad places" = MT. Tg takes the letters of Syr's reading and, by metathesis, reads *byrt'* "fortress," "palace" (cf. *b. Ber.* 53b: *br'š hbyrh* "at the top of fortress"). Syr (Tg) has "in the cities" for MT's sg., to make the universality of the scene explicit.

1:22. LXX: "$^{\alpha}$ As long as the innocent [*akakoi*] hold on to [*echōntai*] righteousness, they shall not be put to shame. $^{\beta}$ But the fools, being fond of arrogance, $^{\gamma}$ are impious and hate knowledge." We should probably emend *echōntai* to *erōntai* ("love") (Lag.). The Heb is treated very loosely and the second person ignored. The translator may have thought it made no sense for Wisdom to be calling fools, who are inherently deaf to her. (Compare how LXX uses softer terms for the fools that Wisdom addresses in 8:5. This does not, however, happen in 9:4.) Also, the assumption that the *peti* is morally innocent—*akakos* (see 1:4)—distorted the import of the verse and brought with it various disruptions, too many to ascribe just to an aesthetic preference for antithetical parallelism (Gerleman 1956: 18).

Syr harmonizes the third per. *ḥmdw* with the second per. of the rest of the sentence. Tg restores the third per.

1:23. LXX: "$^{\alpha}$ And they have become subject [*hypeuthynoi*] to reproaches. $^{\beta}$ Behold I will send forth to you the utterance [*rhēsin*] of my breath, $^{\gamma}$ and I will teach you my word." LXX maintains the third per. from v 22. For the much-discussed *tšwbw* "turn back" (see Commentary), LXX uses a hapax, *hypeuthynoi* "become subject to (reproaches)." This is probably paraphrastic, insofar as "turn back to" implies subjecting oneself to something. Still, an underlying *tḥwbw* (Mezz.) or *yḥwbw* (Lag., Toy) "become guilty" is possible. LXX elaborates *rwḥy* "my spirit" as "the utterance of my breath," for clarity.

Syr renders 23a as a conditional: "*If* you turn. . . ." This is meant to explain how Wisdom can demand that the fools "return" to her reproof when none has yet been quoted.

1:24. For Heb "stretched forth my hand," LXX substitutes "held forth words [*exeteinon logous*]," providing an action that seems more appropriate to Wisdom's behavior in this context.

Syr's *wʾrymt qly* "and I lifted up my voice" (rather than "stretched forth my hand") shows a rationalization like LXX's but independent of it. (Several Syr MSS have *ʾydy* "my hand"; Tg has "hands.") Syr (Tg) (a): "you did not believe" = Heb *wtʾmynw*, a metathesis, which consequently forced Syr to add the negative (cf. Baum.).

Variant: *wtʾmynw* (MT *wtmʾnw*).

1:25. For *wtprʿw* ("brushed aside," "ignored"), LXX has "set at naught [*akyrous epoieite*]," which is almost identical to 5:7b, where the verb is *swr* "turn aside." *Akyros* does not occur elsewhere where the Heb is available, but the verb *akyroun* is an Aquilan gloss for the synonymous *hēpēr* "annul" (Reider 1966: 11), and the translator may be relating *wtprʿw* to that verb.

1:26. In $^{\beta}$, LXX has "ruin" (*olethros*) for *pḥd* "fear"; similarly, in 3:25 *pḥd* it translates *ptoēsis* "fall," "disaster," in both cases showing that the reference is to *what* is feared and not to the emotion.

1:27. LXX: "$^{\alpha}$ and whenever your trouble arrives suddenly [*aphnō*], $^{\beta}$ and catastrophe appears like a whirlwind, $^{\gamma}$ and when there come to you affliction and siege [*poliorkia*], $^{\delta}$ or when ruin comes to you." LXX's *aphnō* ("suddenly" or "unawares") resolves the metaphor of stormwind (sim. Syr). Line $^{\delta}$ is probably OG and $^{\gamma}$ a later adjustment to MT. Baum. says that $^{\delta}$ was added to provide a parallel to the third line, but the LXX does not make major adjustments for literary reasons, and sometimes it even overrides parallelism, as in the next verse. *Poliorkia* interprets *ṣwqh* as "siege," a correspondence perhaps learned from Jer 19:9.

Syr joins 26 and 27a. The minority reading *ʿlykwn* "on you" (= MT, Tg) (see Leiden apparatus) is preferable to *ʿlyhwn* "on them."

Ketiv *kšʾwh*; qeré *kšwʾh* (*k*ᵉ*šôʾāh*) (the latter is correct).

1:28. LXX continues the second pl. of v 27 into 28$^{\alpha}$, but 28$^{\beta}$ switches to third pl. "Bad men" (*kakoi*) is added as the subject in $^{\beta}$, to make it clear that Wisdom's obduracy is only for the wicked. This word was in the OG, because LXX v 32 presupposes a prior mention of wicked men, who are distinguished from the imprudent innocents.

Syr *wnqdmwn lwty* ("they will come early to me"), an etymologizing translation of *yšḥrnny*; cf. Isa 26:9.

1:29. LXX has *sophian* "wisdom" for Heb *daʿat*. Elsewhere, *sophia* = *daʿat* only in 1:7$^{\alpha}$, where it is borrowed from Ps 111[110]:10. LXX^{A} and some MSS have *paidian* instead of *sophian*, but the former does not correspond to *daʿat* elsewhere in LXX-Prov and is later (thus CSP, contrary to Lag.).

1:31. LXX's *asebeias* "wickedness" for MT's *mwʿṣwt* "devices" enhances the moral clarity (Dick 1990: 25).

1:32. LXX's highly paraphrastic translation shows how it understands the entire unit: "$^{\alpha}$ Inasmuch as they harmed [*ēdikoun*] simple ones [*nēpious*], they shall be killed, $^{\beta}$ and interrogation [*exetasmos*] shall destroy sinners." In vv 22–32, LXX draws a distinction between wicked men (*kakoi, asebeis*) and callow youths (*akakoi, nēpioi*). As in LXX 1:17, the translator regards naive youths—such as the son being addressed—as the direct victims of the wicked. "Interrogation" associates *šlwt-* with *šʾlh* ("question," etc.) and pictures judicial interrogation. The *exetasmos* in Wis 4:6 probably belongs to the final judgment of the sinner.

Since the relation of v 32 to v 31 is problematic, Syr starts 32 with *mtwl hnʾ* ("because of this"), which must look back to vv 29–30 as the cause of the punishment. Syr's *ṭwʿyy* "errors of" = Heb *šlwt* ("complacency"), associating it with Aram *šālû* "neglect"; cf. Ezra 6:9.

With regard to chapter 1 as a whole, Cook (CSP 99–110) observes that the LXX translator, who demonstrates an excellent control of Greek, uses a greater variety of lexemes than the MT, including some unusual ones. (Seventy-four lexemes are in some way unique.) The translator brings out the unity of the chapter by adding particles and introducing syntactic connections. He also underscores MT's ethical dualism of good and evil.

Lecture II. 2:1–22

2:1. LXX makes the verse into a conditional: "Son, if, having received the utterance [*rhēsin*] of my injunction, you will hide (it) with yourself. . . ." For *ʾmry wmṣwty*, LXX reads *ʾmry mṣwty* (understood as *ʾimrê miṣwātî*), a *yod-waw* haplog. The sg. of *rhēsis* can represent the pl. *ʾămārîm* (4:5; 7:24 [LXX^{A}]).

Syr *blbk* "in your heart" for "in you" (based on 4:1) specifies *where* the teaching is hidden; sim. in 7:1.

2:2. LXX: "$^{\alpha}$ your ear will hearken to wisdom, $^{\beta}$ and you will direct your heart to understanding, $^{\gamma}$ and you will direct it to admonition [*nouthetēsin*] for your son." Line 2^{γ}, with an obelus in SyrH, is OG. In it, "for your son" = *lbnk* in the vorlage (though that must be wrong in context), in place of MT's *lbk*. This would be due to a near-dittog. of *bet* and *nun*, which are very similar in many scripts. The dir. obj. *autēn* in 2^{γ}, however, presupposes *kardian* and must be a later adjustment to the hexaplaric 2^{β}.

LXX v 2 is best read consequent upon v 1, since v 2 does not start with *kai*. This makes the understanding of wisdom into a *reward* for accepting the father's precepts. (For a similar notion in Egyptian Wisdom, see "Prologues to Wisdom Books, §4, after 1:7.) Especially interesting is the notion that attainment of wisdom will enable a man to teach his own son. Though arising from a scribal error, the idea would have made sense to a translator within the Wisdom tradition; see p. 81.

Syr (which treats *lhqšyb* as future) carefully postpones the apodosis until v 5.

Variant: *lbnk* (MT *libbᵉkā*).

2:3. In LXX 3^{α}, *sophia* = *bynh* (elsewhere only in 3:5), perhaps under the influence of the memorable 8:1a. (LXX-Prov usually uses *phronēsis* or *synesis* for *bynh*.) Though 3^{γ} ("and seek knowledge [*aisthēsin*] with a great voice") is lacking in [BS] and incorrectly given an asterisk in SyrH, it is OG. The more literal 3^{β} is hexaplaric and missing from important MSS (Fritsch 1953: 178; CSP).

Tg reads *ʾm* "if" as *ʾēm* "mother," hence: "For you will call understanding 'mother.' . . ." See the Commentary.

2:5. Tg cautiously phrases MT's "knowledge of God" as *wydʿtʾ mn qdm ʾlhʾ* "knowledge from before God."

2:6. In 6^{β}, LXX's "from his presence/face" (*apo prosopou autou*) instead of MT's "mouth" suggests to Toy that LXX is avoiding the notion of verbal inspiration of wisdom. But theological inhibitions about such an idea would not have been necessary. *Peh* and *panim* are synonym-variants that can interchange both within Hebrew and in translation.

Variant: *mpnyw* (MT *mippîyw*).

2:7. LXX: "$^{\alpha}$ And he stores up deliverance [*sōtērian*] for those who walk straight. $^{\beta}$ He shields their way [*tēn poreian autōn*]. . . ." LXX takes *mgn* as a verb and sees MT's *lhlky tm* as one word, *lhlyktm*. The majority LXX reading *sōtērian* associates *twšyh* "resourcefulness" with *tšwʿh* "salvation," as in Job 30:22 qeré.

Syr translates *twšyh* as *sabrāʾ* "hope" only here, perhaps under the influence of LXX's *sōtērian*. The usual renderings are *ywlpnʾ* ("instruction") and *ḥkmtʾ* ("wisdom").

Ketiv *wṣpn*; qeré *yṣpn* (*yiṣpōn*).

2:8. MT has sg. *ḥsydw* "his faithful one" in the ketiv and pl. *ḥăsîdāyw* in the qeré (= 1 Sam 2:9). The latter (= LXX) is correct, since the sg. *ḥāsîd* for some reason does not take first or third per. suffixes and has the second sg. suffix only in Ps 16:10 (qeré) and Deut 33:8.

Sg./pl. variants in qeré-ketiv are frequent. Sometimes, as here, they may represent different spellings of the plural, with the qeré intended to clarify the ambiguous defective spelling (see Barr 1981: 29).

For *ḥsydw*, LXX has *eulaboumenōn auton* "those who revere him" (sim. 30:5; cf. Mic 7:2), which is not the usual translation of *ḥsyd*. Syr similarly has *ḥsywhy*$^{pl.}$ "his pious ones."

Ketiv *ḥsydw*; qeré *ḥsydyw* (*ḥăsîdāw*).

2:9. For MT's *myšrym* "equity," LXX has *katorthōseis* "right actions." The latter word (accented differently) could be the pl. of the noun *katorthōsis* (thus Lag.). However, in 2 Chr 3:17 and Ps 97[96]:2, *katorthōsis* corresponds to forms of *k-w-n* and means "setting up." As a verb, *katorthōseis* means "you will make straight" (CSP). It parses *myšrym* as a ptcp. (*m^{e}yaššărîm*); cf. (*kateuthunein*) in 1:3, where *myšrym* is apparently considered an Aramaic inf. LXX-Prov translates *mʿgl* as *axonas*, lit. "wheels," "wagons"; cf. 2:18; 9:12b.

Syr (Tg) awkwardly construes *myšrym* as a construct ("and the rightness *of* all good paths").

2:10. LXX makes v 10 the protasis of a conditional: "For *if* wisdom comes to your [^{B} the] mind [*dianoian*], and knowledge appears beautiful [*kalē einai doxę̄*] to your soul. . . ." MT speaks of the *feeling* of pleasure (*ynʿm* = "be pleasant to"), for which LXX substitutes intellectual awareness of wisdom's excellence.

2:11. This is the apodosis of v 10: "(then) good counsel [*boulē kalē*] will guard you, and pious thought [*ennoia de hosia*] will keep you." "Good counsel" and "pious thought" are moralizing renderings of the neutral *m^{e}zimmah* and *t^{e}bunah* (Mezz.; Dick 1990: 24). Lag. suggests that the pluses are glosses to the OG, but they were present early enough to have influenced Syr. Moreover, they provide the antithesis to the "evil counsel" of LXX 2:17$^{\alpha}$.

Syr, drawing on the LXX, also moralizes, but differently: "Good thought [*trʿytʾ ṭbtʾ*] will protect you, and understanding of the just [*wswklʾ dkʾnʾ*$^{pl.}$] will preserve you."

2:12. LXX's prefixes *kai* "and" to 12$^{\beta}$, making a distinction between "the way of evil" and "the man who speaks nothing-faithful [*mēden piston*]." In MT, *raʿ* is probably a noun ("wicked man") and identical with the parallel *ʾiš* "man."

Syr: "that you may be saved. . . ." Diathesis for smoother syntax.

2:13. LXX: "$^{\alpha}$ Aha [*ō*]! (you) who abandon [nom. pl.] straight ways, $^{\beta}$ to go in ways of darkness. . . ." The vocative radically diverges from the syntax of MT's long conditional sentence. Perhaps *ō hoi egkataleipontes* = *hwy hʿzbym* (MT *hʿzbym*), but given the textual dissimilarity, the Gk is probably a deliberate smoothing of the abrupt switch in the Heb from sg. to pl.

2:15. In $^{\beta}$, LXX ("of whom the courses [*hai trochiai*] are bent") and Syr ("their paths are crooked"; = Tg) choose a more obvious image for MT's "devious *in* all their tracks"; see Commentary.

2:16. LXX now undertakes a revision of the Strange Woman warning: "so as to make you far from the straight way, and alienated [*allotrion*] from the righteous judgment [*tēs dikaias gnōmēs*]." This reflects a deliberate midrashic reworking of the verse, which in the MT speaks of the "strange woman" and "the alien." See later, "The Strange Woman in the Septuagint."

Syr adds a subject, which is not readily available from context: "*Wisdom* will save you from the foreign woman who changes [*mhpkʾ*, lit. "turns"] her words." In other words, she's a double-talker. (Syr-Prov has a different rendering for *heḥĕlîq*/*ḥālāq* every time it occurs.) Rather than repeating *nwkrytʾ* twice (as it does in 5:20 and 27:13), Syr, which lacks a separate equivalent for *zr(h)*, fuses *zrh* and *nkryh*, as in 7:5.

2:17. LXX: "$^{\alpha}$ Son, let not evil counsel overpower you, $^{\beta}$ which (counsel) has abandoned the teaching of youth, $^{\gamma}$ and forgotten the godly covenant" ($^{\alpha}$ *huie, mē se katalabę̄ kakē boulē* $^{\beta}$ *hē apoleipousa didaskalian neotetos,* $^{\gamma}$ *kai diathēkēn theian epilelēsmenē*). The LXX begins a new section by prefixing an entire line (17$^{\alpha}$), as in 8:21a. LXX derives Heb *ʾlwp* ("companion") from *ʾillep* "to teach." Gk "godly covenant" (MT *bryt ʾlhyh*) need not witness to *ʾlhym* "God," which would be *theou*. The translator may be thinking that (as Ehrlich suggests) the possessive is inappropriate when "evil counsel" is the possessor.

Syr independently uses the same etymology for *ʾlwp* but renders it *mrabbyānāʾ* "foster-father," "one who raises." Tg^{Z} has *mrbytʾ* "training." Tg^{L} has *mrbyynʾ* = Syr and is thus original.

2:18. LXX: "$^{\alpha}$ For she has placed [*etheto*] her house beside death, $^{\beta}$ her courses [*axonas*] beside Hades [*para tǭ hądę̄*] with the earthborn [*meta tōn gēgenōn*]." "Has placed" = *šth*, an error for MT's *šḥh*. *para tǭ ądę̄* is OG, *meta tōn gēgenōn* is from Theod. In 9:18 too, *gēgeneis* = *r^{e}paʾim*. In Jer 32[39]:20 *en tois gēgenesin* corresponds to *bʾdm* in MT. In Greek mythology, *gēgenetēs* sometimes refers to the Titans or Giants, born of Gaia (Liddell and Scott, 347b). This association is relevant to the Rephaim, who are identified as Anaqim and described as giants in Deut 2:10. Heb *rpʾym* is sometimes translated *gigantes* "giants" (e.g., Gen 14:5; Josh 12:4; 13:12), as is *ʿnqym* "Anaqim," in Deut 1:28.

A conjectural emendation for *byth* is *ntybtyh* "her paths" (Ehrlich) or *ntybth* "her path" (BHS, with ref. to 7:27—where it proposes *ntybwtyh* for *byth* and refers to 2:18!). See the Commentary.

Syr: "She has forgotten [*tʿt*] the thresholds [*ʾskptʾ$^{pl.}$*] of her house and the ways of her paths." "Forgotten" corresponds to *škḥh*; perhaps thus in Syr's vorlage but possibly taken accidentally from v 17 (Toy). *ʾl-mwt* is implicitly vocalized as *ʾullāmôt* (or *ʾēlammôt*) "porches").

Variant *šth* (MT *šāḥāh*).

2:19. LXX: "$^{\alpha}$ All who go in it shall not return $^{\beta}$ and will surely not take possession [*katalabōsin*] of the straight paths, $^{\gamma}$ for they are not possessed by years of life [*ou gar katalambonontai hypo eniautōn zoēs*]." In 19$^{\alpha}$, "in it" (*en autę̄*) must have *kakē boulē* as its antecedent. In $^{\beta}$, *eutheias* may be due to the influence of vv 13 and 15. Line $^{\gamma}$ has the obelus in SyrH and is probably OG, though CSP observes that both $^{\beta}$ and $^{\gamma}$ are partly based on the Hebrew and may be a double translation of 19b original to OG. The awkwardness of $^{\gamma}$ shows that it is struggling with a Heb text, not freely paraphrasing, but the text cannot be reconstructed.

Lag. suggests an original *yuśśᵉgû miššᵉnōt,* but that is poor Heb and can hardly be reconciled with MT's *yśygw ʾrḥwt ḥyym.* "Years of life" (*šnwt ḥyym*) is found in MT 4:10, where the OG (10^{γ}) has "ways of life." Somehow the locutions got switched around in Gk or Heb.

Syr: ". . . and are not mindful of [*mtdkryn*] the way of life." MT's *yśygw* is understood as grasping something *mentally.*

2:20. LXX: "$^{\alpha}$ For if they had gone in good paths, $^{\beta}$ they would have found the smooth paths of righteousness." This overrides the syntax of the Heb (final clause; second m. sg.) and makes the sentence a conditional in the third m. pl. The verse cannot be reconciled with the Heb. The translator is overriding the second pl. setting of the entire chapter.

Syr renders the verbs as imperatives.

The Strange Woman in the Septuagint

In 2:16–20, the LXX replaces MT's warning against the "strange woman" with one against "evil counsel," mentioned in LXX 2:17. This is not exactly an interpretation of the strange woman, since she is not mentioned in 2:17 but only in v 16.

M. Hengel (1974: 1.155) identifies this "evil counsel" with Hellenistic wisdom. If, however, the essential feature of the evil counsel were its foreignness, the translator would have enhanced rather than bypassed the alien character of the vice. This could easily have been extracted from *zārāh* and *nokriyyāh* in v 16. J. Cook (1987: 40; CSP 136–37) identifies "good counsel" and "evil counsel" with the rabbinic concepts of *yēṣer haṭṭôb* and *yēṣer hārāʿ,* "the good inclination" and "the evil inclination." But the "counsel" described in this chapter is not an internal, psychological drive, nor is *boulē* a good equivalent for the rabbinic concept of *yeṣer.*[236] Cook also believes that the warning is directed against foreign wisdom (CSP 138).

When Prov 2 in the LXX is read as a whole, it is evident that the "evil counsel" is neither foreign nor psychological, nor is it an abstract concept. It is the urgings and insinuations of the evil man, who "speaks nothing reliable" (v 12), whose influence would dislodge the naive from the right path (v 16). "Evil counsel" comprises everything that such people, male or female, encourage susceptible young men to do. An example is quoted in vv 11–14. *This* is the evil counsel that is incidentally personified in LXX v 18. Such blandishments can be withstood only with the support of the "good counsel" (v 11), which is the wisdom that comes from one's teachers and God. The "good counsel" is wisdom, the "bad counsel" is folly, but in a concrete sense. A further level of abstraction is not drawn here.

---

[236] *Yṣr* is rendered *diaboulion* "counsel," "deliberation," in Sira 15:14, and Heb *yṣr* certainly underlies *diaboulion* in Sir 17:6. In both cases, however, *yṣr* is neither the evil nor the good inclination but rather (as in BH), man's ability to plan and make choices.

2:21. LXX lines $^{\alpha-\beta}$, though absent in $^{B,130,\ 106}$, are OG (CSP); $^{\gamma-\delta}$ are hexaplaric. In $^{\alpha}$, the verb *yšknw* is treated as a noun: *oikētores*, "inhabitants."

In Syr 21b, read *mštyryn* "remain" (confirmed by Tg) for *mštḥryn*.

2:22. LXX adds *hodoi* "ways (of the wicked)," probably based on Ps 1:6b. CSP explains the word as an attempt to enhance the dualism by matching the "good ways" (*tribous agathas*) in v 20. If that were the motive, however, we would expect the same words to be used.

A CG manuscript vocalizes *ysḥw* as *yusḥû*, which may be right, even though it arose later in the Hebrew MS tradition.

Lecture III. 3:1–12

3:1. LXX has pl. *nomimōn* for MT's sg. *tôrātî*. MT's *mṣwty* (pl.) is rendered *ta rhēmata mou*, corresponding to *ʾmry* or *dbry*. The Heb words are synonym-variants; see 7:2b. Since there is no reason for the LXX to depart from its usual rendering of *mṣwh* (*entolē*), one of these variants was probably in the vorlage.

Variant: *ʾmry* (= *ʾămāray*) or *dbry* (= *d^{e}bāray*) (MT *miṣwôtay*).

3:2. Syr's *nttwspn*$^{pl.}$ *lk* "will be added to you, may reflect *ywspw*, which could read as passive (for MT *ywsypw*), but Syr may simply be compensating for the lack of an explicit subject. In the editions of the Peshitta, *wšlmʾ* "peace" is attached to the next verse. This may represent a text that read *wywspw lk šlwm*. Perhaps the translator forgot *wšlmʾ*, then restored it as an afterthought, but intending it as a second subject of *nttwspn*$^{pl.}$.

3:3. LXX "$^{\alpha}$ Let not mercies [*eleēmosynai*] and loyalties [*pisteis*] desert you; $^{\beta}$ bind them upon your neck, $^{\gamma}$ and you will find favor." The LXX (with most commentators) understands *ḥesed* and *ʾĕmet* as virtues required of the listener. OG lacked 3c ("and inscribe them on the tablet of your heart"). It was supplied (from Theod, according to SyrH) in various forms and positions in $^{S,\ A,\ MSS.}$ Since 3c is entirely germane and needed for the parallelism, the omission was almost certainly accidental, a homeoteleuton from the *kaph* at the end of the second line to the *kaph* at the end of the third. OG (in ^{B}) joins 4a to v 3$^{\gamma}$.

Syr starts v 3 with *wšlmʾ*, from MT v 2. "Tablets" are in the pl. (*lwḥʾ*$^{pl.}$).

3:4. LXX: "$^{\alpha}$ And perceive [*pronoou*] good [*kala*] $^{\beta}$ before the Lord and men!" Having attached *wmṣʾ* to the previous sentence, LXX needs an impv. and mistakes *wśkl* for one.

Syr: (a) "and you will find love and blessing and understanding" (*wtškḥ rḥmʾ*$^{pl.}$ *wṭybwtʾ wswklʾ*). Syr (= Tg) read *wṭwb* (for MT's *twb*) and translated it by the cognate *wṭybwtʾ* "and blessing." Syr metathesized *śkl* and *ṭwb* in translation.

Variant: *wṭwb* (MT *ṭôb*).

3:5. LXX: "$^{\beta}$ and do not exalt yourself [*epairou*] for your wisdom [*en sę̄ sophią*]." *Epairesthai* (only here for *niš*ʿ*an*) allows the translator to avoid the implication that one should *not* rely on one's wisdom. After all, relying on one's wisdom is what the book is all about. Instead, the translation's message is, as Jeremiah put it: "Let not the wise man boast of his wisdom" (9:22a).

Syr adds *dnpšk* ("yourself," i.e., "your *own* wisdom") for emphasis; sim. Tg *dlbk* "your heart's wisdom." Both may have the same concern the LXX seems to evince.

3:6. LXX: "$^{\alpha}$ In all your ways, declare [*gnōrize*] it [*autēn*], $^{\beta}$ that you may make your ways straight." The vorlage may have had *hdʿhw* (*hōdîʿēhû*) for *dāʿēhû*, because LXX uses *gnōrizein* only for the H/A-stem of *y-d-ʿ* (or a synonym), never for the G, and there would be no reason for *dʿhw* to throw the translator off track. Having understood the verb in v 6a as "make known" rather than "know," LXX took the dir. obj. to be *wisdom* (hence the fem. *autēn*). This goes against the Heb grammar but accords with LXX's assumption that the wisdom mentioned in v 5 is of the virtuous sort. Some MSS borrow from 3:23b the thematically related line $^{\gamma}$ "and let not your foot stumble" (asterisked in SyrH).

3:8. LXX's *tǭ sōmati sou* represents either *lšʾrk* or *lbśrk* (both meaning "your flesh")" for MT's *lšrk* "your navel." The metaphor of "moistening" the bones is paraphrased as *epimeleia* "treatment," "caring for"; sim. 13:4; 28:25. Kuhn and others emend the Gk to the more literal *pimelē* "fat," but this would have to be done in all three verses. SyrH confirms *epimeleia*.

Syr *bsrk* ("your flesh") supports Heb *lšʾrk* or *lbśrk* = LXX. Syr *duhnāʾ* ("fat") adjusts "moistening" of bones to the common metaphor of *fatness* signifying health, whether in the bones (as in 15:30 and Ps 109:18), or in the body as a whole (13:4; 28:25), though a different Gk word is used elsewhere.

Variant: *lšʾrk* (MT *l*^{e}*šorrekā*).

3:9. LXX: "Honor the Lord from your honest [*dikaiōn*] labors, and offer first-fruits to him [*aparchou autǭ*] from your fruits of righteousness [*dikaiosynēs*]." "Honest" and "righteous" are added and the syntax of 9b is altered. The translation is paraphrastic and moralistic, teaching that you may honor God only from *honest* earnings.

3:10. LXX has *plēsmonēs sitou* ("a surfeit of grain") for *śbʿ* "grain." Lag. regards *plēsmonēs sitou* as a conflation of *šbr* and *śbʿ*. But since a note in SyrH says that *sitou* is found in neither the LXX nor the Heb, it is probably a scribal gloss within the Greek transmission (although we would expect the more literal *plēsmonē* to be the later variant), rather than a later Greek recourse to an original (and unattested) Heb. Also, as Ehrlich keenly notes, *šeber* is not the proper designation for grain as one's own possession, but only for grain viewed as a marketable commodity.

3:11. LXX: "$^{\beta}$ and be not faint [*ekluou*] when rebuked by him." Only here is *tqwṣ* "despise" rendered by *ekluesthai* or a synonym for faintness, perhaps because faintheartedness rather than disgust seemed the expected reaction to suffering. MT's *btwkḥtw* "his chastisement" is made into a circumstantial clause.

Syr interprets the verb similarly: ". . . do not be wearied (*tmʾn*)." Elsewhere Syr uses *ʿwq* for Heb *q-w-ṣ*.

3:12. LXX: "$^{\alpha}$ Because him whom the Lord loves he instructs [*paideuei*] $^{\beta}$ and he afflicts every son whom he accepts [$^{\beta}$ *mastigoi de panta huion hon paradechetai*]." LXX's *paideuei* for *hokiaḥ* recalls *paideias* in v 11 (*elegchei* [$^{B\dagger,\ SyrH}$], preferred by Lag. and Baum., is an adjustment to MT). In $^{\beta}$, *mastigoi* construes *wk'b* as a verb in the D or G-stem, though the D does not exist in BH and the G lacks the required causative sense (an H-form would be required).

The second line is especially interesting. An *'al tiqre'* interpretation in *Mid. Ps.* 94:2 shows that the MT can be construed as in the LXX even without consonantal alteration: *'al tiqre' wk'b 'ela' wk'b*, "Do not read *ûk^{e}'āb* but rather *w^{e}kē'ēb*. LXX is thus not good for *wyk'b* = *w^{e}yak'îb* in the vorlage. "Every" is added, as often, for emphasis. The verse is quoted in this form in Hebrews 12:6. DNF suggests that the original consonantal text was *wyk'b k'b* ("and afflicts as a father does . . .") and that the first word was lost in the MT, the second in the LXX vorlage. The smoothest reading would repeat the dir. obj., thus: *w^{e}yak'îbô k^{e}'āb 'et bēn yirṣeh*, "and afflict him as a father (does) to a son he favors."

In 3:12b, Syr has "like a father who punishes [*drd'*] his son," apparently reading *yrdh* (an Aramaism) for MT's *yrṣh* (Pink.).

Interlude B. 3:13–20

3:13. LXX: "$^{\alpha}$ Happy [*makarios*] the man who has found wisdom, $^{\beta}$ and the mortal who knows understanding!" The synonyms for the repeated *'adam* are varied in both LXX (*anthrōpos, thnētos*) and (independently) Syr (*brnš', br bsr'*). The second term in each pair is rare, and it is hard to see what Heb word could generate both.

3:14. LXX: "$^{\alpha}$ For it is better to traffic in her [*autēn emporeuesthai*] $^{\beta}$ than in treasures of gold and silver." LXX construes *sḥrh* as an inf., "to traffic in her." Apparently *msḥr* was lost by near haplography with *sḥrh*, though it may have been eliminated as superfluous. The rest of the verse is rendered loosely.

Syr fills out the comparison in 14b: "(more) excellent [*mytrn$^{pl.}$*] (than)."

3:15. LXX: "$^{\alpha}$ She is more precious than costly stones; $^{\beta}$ no evil [*ponēron*] can oppose [*antitaxetai*] her. $^{\gamma}$ She is familiar to all who approach her [$^{\gamma}$ *eugnōstos estin pasin tois eggizousin autę*]. $^{\delta}$ No valuable equals her worth." (*Eugnōstos* here means "easy to get to know.") Throughout this section, the fem. pron. in reference to wisdom can be translated either "she" etc. or "it" etc.

3^{α} and $^{\delta}$ are hexaplaric and witness to *ḥpṣym*, without the suffix (as in MT 8:11). Lines $^{\beta}$ and $^{\gamma}$ have the obelus in SyH and are OG. (The same sentence was translated in the expected fashion in 8:11b and would have presented no problem here.) But these lines cannot be reconciled to MT and render a different vorlage. There is no evident motive for the translator to have composed them.

3^{β} is distant from MT. Lag. emends *ponēron* to *pothēton* ("longed for"), but the latter never corresponds to *ḥepeṣ*. Moreover, *antitaxetai* connotes hostility (cf. v 34), making *ponēron* a suitable dir. obj. in Gk, though not necessarily in the Heb. The text is opaque to the underlying Hebrew.

3^{γ} can be retroverted (supplying the vocalization) to *nôda'at hî' l^{e}kōl q^{e}rōbeyhā*. (Cf. *ouk eugnōstoi* = *lō' tēda'* in 5:6.) LXX's "to (all) who approach her" would represent *qrbh* in the vorlage, which would be vocalized as *q^{e}rōbeyha*, "who are close to her." For the sentiment of the retroverted saying, see Sir 6:18–22 (a passage influenced by Prov 3:13–18), which advises the reader to draw close (*qrb*) to wisdom, for she yields her bounty to those who accept her discipline, while she is troublesome to the fool. The conjectured Hebrew of Prov 3:15$^{\gamma}$ is possibly echoed in Sir 4:24, *ky b'mr nwd't ḥkmh.*

Syr's *mdm l'* "nothing" = *kl ḥpṣym l'*, confirming *ḥpṣym* for *ḥpṣyk* independently of the LXX.

Variants: *ḥpṣym* (MT *ḥăpāṣeykā*).

Ketiv *mpnyym* (an error); qeré *mipp^enînîm.*

3:16. To "length of life," LXX adds "and years of living [*etē zōēs*]," a phrase imported from 3:2. According to Gerleman (1956: 25) this was intended to make the line "materially conformable to" (i.e., quantitatively balanced with) its parallel (comparing 3:16; 17:15; 23:21). But since many additions produce imbalance (e.g., 3:23$^{\alpha}$; 5:22$^{\beta}$; 10:22$^{\beta}$; 12:4$^{\beta}$), the occasional creation of balance is probably fortuitous.

3:16a. LXX: "$^{\alpha}$ From her mouth proceeds righteousness, $^{\beta}$ and she bears law and mercy on (her) tongue." 16$^{\alpha}$ resembles Isa 45:23a, and $^{\beta}$ is based on Prov 31:26[25]b. In both cases the affinity is to the Hebrew, not the LXX of those verses. Hence the couplet was probably present in the vorlage (Tov 1990: 49). Tov retroverts the couplet to *mpyh tṣ' ṣdqh wtwrt ḥsd 'l lšwnh.* The additional verse adds religious virtues to the practical benefits noted in 16.

3:18. LXX: "$^{\beta}$ and for those who lean on her, (she is) as firm as (leaning) upon the Lord" ($^{\beta}$ *kai tois epereidomenois ep' autēn, hōs epi kurion asphalēs*). LXX enhances the religious message by an explicit assertion: To embrace wisdom is to embrace the Lord. The only meaning of *tmk* that the translator knows is "lean on" (see at 4:4). Lag. believes that "as upon the Lord" reflects a dittography *(*twm*)*kyh kyh*, but the unique rendering of *m'šr* as "firm" (as in MH *m^e'uššar* "strong") indicates that the translator is deliberately importing a religious theme.

Syr 18 "$^{\alpha}$ She is a tree of life for those who strengthen themselves [*mḥmsnyn*$^{pl.}$] by her, $^{\beta}$ and those who support her [read *msmkyn lh*] are blessed [*twbyhwn*]." Syr mistranslates Heb *mḥzykym* "grasp" as *mḥmsnyn*$^{pl.}$ "those who strengthen themselves." Syr's *mskyn* ("hope for") should be corrected to *msmkyn* "support," as in 5:5 (Pink.). The pl. of *twbyhwn* in Syr (= Tg) belongs to the Syriac idiom (and is taken into Tg), and it is no evidence for Heb *m'šrym*, as BHS implies. But even without this support, *m^e'uššārîm* is a reasonable emendation. The error could have been occasioned by parablepsis with the *yod* of *yhwh* in v. 19 (DNF).

3:19. Syr: "his wisdom," "his understanding"—adjusting to the next verse.

3:20. For *yr'pw*, several MSS have *y'rpw*; cf. Sir 43:22, *m'rp 'nn ṭl.* But both metatheses are probably erroneous.

Lecture IV. 3:21–35

3:21. The LXX translates the difficult *ylzw* (*yālûzû*) as *mē pararruēs* "do not slip aside." Hebrews 2:1 rephrases this as *pararuōmen*, lit. "flow." LXX probably read a metathesized *yzlw* (= Kenn. 95 p.m.), parsed as if from *n-z-l* "flow" (cf. Baum.). The LXX rendering is unlikely to be interpretive, because in the nearly identical 4:21, *ylyzw* is translated *ekleipein* "abandon." Since the LXX was not induced to introduce the notion of flowing in 4:21, in spite of the presence of "springs" in the Gk of that verse, it must have read *yzlw* here. Similarly Vul *ne effluant haec*. In 3:21b, LXX adds "my," as often, for specificity.

Syr: "may it not be trivial [*nzl*] in your eyes to keep my teaching and my thoughts" (= Tg^{L}; Tg^{Z} corrects toward MT). Heb *ylyzw* is translated "trivial" in Syr 4:2. Syr is relating the rare *yz(y)lw* to *z-l-l* and like LXX probably reading *yzlw*. Syr's *bʿynyk*$^{pl.}$ need not represent *bʿynyk* in the vorlage (Pink., Baum.; 2 MSS), since the choice of preposition would have been constrained by the translator's understanding of the verb.

Variant: *yzlw* (MT *yāluzû*).

3:22a. LXX: "$^{\alpha}$ And it will be healing for your flesh, $^{\beta}$ and treatment [*epimeleia*] for your bones. . . ." This translates 3:8 but in a wording different from the Greek of that verse. Hence the expansion (which embellishes wisdom's benefits) was in the LXX's vorlage (Tov 1990: 50).

Variant: additional verse, cf. 3:8.

3:23. LXX: "$^{\alpha}$ so that you may confidently [*pepoithōs*] tread all your paths in peace [*en eirēnę̄*], $^{\beta}$ and your foot not stumble [lit. "stumble by your foot"]." "Confidently" and "in peace" are a doublet, the former the closer to MT and presumably the later.

3:24. In 24$^{\alpha}$, LXX (= SyrH) has *tšb* "sit down" for MT *tškb* "lie down."

Syr turns the conditional into an indicative, "you will sleep and not fear, etc." Syr reflects the repeated *tškb* but creates variation by rendering it *tdmk . . . wtškb*. Tg = Syr, but some MSS have *tškwb wtdmwk* in 24a.

Variant, 24a: *tšb* (MT *tiškab*).

3:25. LXX: "$^{\alpha}$ And you will not fear an approaching alarm [*ptoēsin epelthousan*] $^{\beta}$ or the approaching [*eperchomenas*] attacks [*hormas*] of sinners." The wicked are the source rather than the casualties of the danger. The tenses of *eperchesthai* seem to be a rhetorical variation.

Syr uses *ḥiʾpaʾ* ("attack," "eruption") for MT's *šoʾat-*. Syr agrees with LXX in regarding the violence as coming *from* the sinners.

3:26. For MT's *bᵉkislekā* ("your hope"), LXX has *epi pasōn hodōn sou* "upon all your paths." This reflects *bmsltk* "in your road" (or "highway") in the vorlage (Toy). Gk *hodos* = Heb *mᵉsillah* (pl.) in Judg 20:31, 32, 45. The hypothetical *bmsltk* could easily arise from the lexical variant *bksltk* (*kislāh* [Job 4:6] = *kesel*).

For *ereisei*, "make firm" (that is, your feet), Lag. prefers *tērēsei* ([23, 297]), which, however, looks like a harmonization. For *lkd*, LXX has *saleuein* (only here), but the proposed corrections to *agreuthę̄s* or *sullēphę̄s* (see Lag., Baum.) are distant. $^{\beta}$ is paraphrastic.

Syr: "be with you," relating *ksl* "hope" to the homographic "loin." Similarly, Vul *in latere tuo*. Tg: *bsʿdk* "at your aid."

Variant: *bmsltk* (MT *bᵉkislekā*).

3:27. LXX understands the verse as enjoining charitable deeds: "$^{\alpha}$ Do not abstain from doing good *to the poor* [*endeē*], $^{\beta}$ whenever your hand has (the ability) to *help* [*boēthein*]."

Ketiv *ydyk*; qeré *yād^{e}kā*.

3:28. MT's *rʿyk* is not represented in LXX and does seem to overload the line. After 28a, LXX adds, $^{\beta}$ "when you are able to do good," reinforcing its interpretation of the verse as enjoining acts of charity.

LXX has an additional line, $^{\gamma}$ *ou gar oidas ti texetai hē epiousa*, "for you do not know what the morrow will produce." This is the equivalent of 27:1. Since the Greek of 27:1 is different (*ginōskeis* for *oidas*), 3:28$^{\gamma}$ was probably present in the LXX's vorlage of this verse rather than transferred in the Gk. The three lines of the LXX may represent an ancient variant of MT 3:28. The logical association between doing good to other people (28$^{\alpha\beta}$) and ignorance of the morrow is not self-evident. (Toy calls it "a not very appropriate gloss, taken from 27:1.") Yet the topos is used often in Egyptian Wisdom, especially to bolster advice to treat others well, on the grounds that one does not know his own future. See Anii (21.4–10; AEL 2.142); Ptahhotep (339–50, esp. 343, 345; AEL 1.69); Amenemope (§18 = 19.11–15; AEL 2.157); O. Petrie 11 (vso. 5); and Pap. Ramesseum I (A 18).

Syr connects this verse to the preceding by putting the last clause (*wkd ʾyt lk* "and when you have [it]") first. Syr joins "tomorrow" to the preceding: *wtʾ twb mḥr* "come back tomorrow." Tg adjusts to MT in both regards.

Ketiv *lrʿyk* (pl.); qeré *l^{e}rēʿăkā* (sg.)

3:29. LXX: "$^{\alpha}$ Do not devise evil against your friend [*philon*], $^{\beta}$ who dwells nearby [*paraoikounta*] and trusts in you." By reading *lbṭḥ* as an independent finite verb, LXX nicely avoids the implication that one is permitted to devise evil against someone who does *not* dwell with him trustingly. Compare its treatment of v 30.

Syr = MT.

3:30. LXX: "$^{\alpha}$ Do not be quarrelsome with a man for no reason, $^{\beta}$ lest he do some harm to you [*mē ti eis se ergasētai kakon*]." LXX's rephrasing of 30b as a warning ("lest" for "if not"), while more utilitarian than MT (Baum.), is probably due to discomfort with MT's implication that it *would* be acceptable to quarrel for purposes of revenge.

Syr: (a) "Do not litigate [*tdwn*] with a man deceitfully [*bʿtʾ*]." Syr regards the quarreling—perhaps correctly—as litigation. Syr omits 30b, probably to avoid the appearance of tolerating revenge. Tg is close to Heb.

Ketiv *trwb*; qeré *tārîb*.

3:31. LXX: "$^{\alpha}$ Do not incur [*ktēsę̄*] the reproaches of bad men [*kakōn andrōn*], $^{\beta}$ nor envy [*zēlōsę̄s*] their ways." Or: "nor emulate," for *mēde zēlōsę̄s*. LXX renders Heb *tqnʾ* (*t^{e}qannēʾ*) as if it were *tqnh* = *tiqneh* "acquire." (Compare how LXX equates *ksh* with *ksʾ* and translates *thronos* in 12:23.) LXX adds "evil" to "men" (or, possibly, double-translates *ḥms*). Heb *ḥms* is rendered *oneidos* as in 26:6 and Job 19:7. Instead of MT's *tbḥr* "choose" (*bḥr* = *zēloun* only here), LXX seems to have had *ttḥr*, which in Ps 37:1, 7, 8 is rendered *parazēlou*. (In Prov 24:19a, however, *ttḥr* = Gk *chaire*.)

3:32. LXX: "$^{\alpha}$ For impure before the Lord is every transgressor, $^{\beta}$ and he does not sit in counsel [*ou sunedriazei*] among the righteous." Lag. deletes *ou* (thus in MS 106) as a dittography of the following *su-*. It is more likely that having misidentified the antecedent of the suffix of "his counsel" as the transgressor, the translator added the negative to make sense of the sentence (cf. 1:7). *Akathartos* ("impure") for *tw'bh* is a peculiarity of LXX-Prov. In translating *tw'bt YHWH*, LXX-Prov often but inconsistently prefers the Aramaic-sounding circumlocution with "before" the Lord, using *enanti* [3:32], *enōpion* [11:1; 20:10], or *para* [16:5; 17:15]; cf. 8:7.

3:33. LXX and Syr treat the nouns of the second line as pl., and LXX's *eulogountai* construes *ybrk* (MT *y^{e}bārēk*) as a passive "are blessed" (= Vul).

3:34. For *yālîṣ* (God) "scorns," "mocks," LXX uses the more dignified *antitassetai* "opposes" (used in 3:15b). LXX, Syr, Tg, and Vul ignore the difficult particle *'im*, on which see the Commentary.

Syr: "And he will overthrow [*wnsḥwp*] mockers, but he will care for [*nraḥep*; lit. "hover over"] the wise [*ḥkym'$^{pl.}$*]." Syr too apparently thought that it was unseemly to say that God treated the mockers in kind. Syr's *nrḥp* is probably a corruption of *nrḥm* "will have mercy," a plausible rendering of the MT *ytn ḥn* (*ḥen* is regularly translated *raḥme'$^{pl.}$*, including in 13:15). *ḥkym'$^{pl.}$* "the wise" may be an inner-Syr corruption of *mkyk'$^{pl.}$* "the oppressed."

The kere has *wl'nyym* "and to the poor"; the qeré reads *w^{e}la'ănāwîm* "and to the humble." Heb *'ny* and *'nw* are often confused graphically and are not always distinguishable semantically. We should not assign them different meanings in the frequent qeré-ketiv pair.

Ketiv *wl'nyym*; qeré *w^{e}la'ănāwîm*.

3:35. LXX: "$^{\beta}$ but the wicked exalt disgrace [*hypsōsan atimian*]." This apparently means that the wicked glorify the things that in reality disgrace them. LXX's *hypsōsan* for Heb *mrym* is a natural attempt to deal with the difficult word. Vul treats *mrym* as a noun, *exaltatio*. Syr (Tg) leaves the sense vague: *nqblwn ṣ'r'* "receive trouble."

In 3:21–35, the LXX places greater emphasis on moral and charitable obligations than does the MT. LXX regards 3:27 as requiring charity to the poor, one of the interpretations discussed in the Commentary. In 3:29, 30a, the LXX precludes the inference that sometimes devising evil and quarreling without cause *are* permitted. In v 30b, it similarly excludes the inference that revenge is permissible.

Lecture V. 4:1–9

4:1. Syr: "(b) and hear knowledge and understanding [*yd't' wswkl'*]," parsing *ld't* (inf. in MT) as *l^{e}da'at*.

4:2. LXX "$^{\beta}$ Do not abandon my law [*nomon*][^{MSS}: *logon*]." LXX interprets Heb *leqaḥ* etymologically, as "that which is taken," then rephrases this as *dōron* "gift" (= Vul *donum*) (Baum.). But this happens only here.

4:3. For MT's *rk wyḥyd*, LXX has *hypēkoos kai agapōmenos* ("obedient and beloved"). *Hypēkoos* may reflect the graphically similar *dk* "humble," interpreted to mean "obedient" (Heidenheim). Toy believes that LXX may have derived the notion of submissiveness from MT's *rk* "soft." Lag. retroverts *kai agapōmenos* to *wydyd*. But *yḥyd* is rendered *agapētos* in Gen 22:2, 12, 16; Amos 8:10; Zech 12:10; Jer 6:26, and that sense is appropriate here.

For MT's *lpny* "before" (namely, "my mother"), several MSS and a *sebirin* reading have *lbny* "to the sons of," a visual error, as in Ps 80:3a.

4:4. LXX: "$^{\alpha}$ who said [pl.] and taught [pl.] me: $^{\beta}$ Let our word [*ho hēmeteros logos*] rest firmly [*ereidetō*] upon [*eis*] your heart." The LXX—and this must be deliberate—makes both parents the teachers by translating *dbry* as "*our* word" and the verbs in 4a as plural. It reverses the order of the verbs, putting them in their "logical" sequence, "saying" before "teaching." As for 4b, LXX-Prov does not seem to know the verb *tāmak* in the sense of "grasp," but only "support" (as in MH), the sense required in Prov 3:18; 11:16; 31:19. This led to some infelicities. The end of MT 4b is attached to v 5.

Syr: 4b "Let my word become strong in your heart" (*ttḥyl mlty blbk*). Syr too takes *tmk* to mean "support," "rest [something] upon," hence "be strengthened." We should not retrovert the Heb to *ysmk* (N-stem), contrary to Pink., Delitzsch.

After 4b, Syr adds *wnmwsy ʾyk bbtʾ dʿynʾ* ("and [keep] my law as the pupil of the eye"), taken from 7:2b (4:4b = 7:2a). After *wʾmr ly* "said to me," Tg (but corrected in Tg^{Z}) adds YY "the Lord," a double dittography (Pink.).

4:5. LXX: "[MT 4c] $^{\alpha}$ Keep (the) commandments [*phylasse entolas*], [MT 5b] $^{\beta}$ do not forget and do not overlook the speech of my mouth" (*mēde paridęs rhēsin emou stomatos*). In the OG (= LXX^{B}), the sentence begins with *šmwr mṣwty* (4c), then omits the end of 4c and all of 5a. Missing, then, are *-y wḥyh qnh ḥkmh qnh bynh*. The words *ktēsai sophian ktēsai synesin* ("get wisdom get understanding") were evidently added early in a margin, whence they were copied in LXX^{Sca} after "do not forget" and in LXX^{A} after "the speech of my mouth." LXX^{A} adds two lines translating MT v 5 literally. V 5a is supplied in SyrH with an asterisk. These variants belong to the attempt to harmonize the LXX with the MT and, contrary to McKane, show nothing about the Hebrew vorlage. LXX^{B}, however, probably reflects a Heb variant: the accidental parablepsis of the end of 4b and all of 5a. The fem. sg. verbs in 6, as Baum. notes, presuppose the existence of the nouns in 5a, which argues for the originality of that line.

Syr lacks *ʾl tškḥ*. It was restored in Tg. Syr treats *mʾmry* as sg. (pl. in Tg).

4:6. Syr 6b: *tšwzbk* "deliver," an intensification of MT's *tṣrk* "guard." Tg: *tyśwgbk* "elevate."

4:7. Absent in LXX. SyrH supplies a literal translation, assigning it to "all," i.e., Theod, Aq, and Sym. The absence might be original; see the Commentary.

4:8. Gk *pericharakoun* ("surround with a stockade," "fortify") associates *slslh* with *solelah* "siege wall" (Lag., Baum.). *Pericharakoun* usually has hostile connotations ("encamp against"); it occurs in the LXX only here and in Jer 52:4. Vul: *arripe illam* "seize her," loosely for *slslh*. For unclear reasons, in 8b LXX switches the subj. and obj.

Syr (Tg) renders *slslh* as *ḥbbyh* ("love her"); a similar understanding is found in *Tos. Sota* 5, 7; see the Commentary. In 8b, Syr arranges the verbs in their logical sequence: *wʿpqyh dtyqrk* "and embrace her, that she may honor you." Tg[Z]: *wḥbqh wyyty yqrk* "and embrace her that your honor may come"—perhaps thinking it unseemly for wisdom to show honor to mortals.

4:9. LXX starts with *hina* "so that," to provide a logical connector between the verses.

Syr: "And she will put on your head the beauty of grace [*y'ywt' drwḥp'*], and with a chaplet of glory [*wbklyl' dšwbḥ'*] she will satisfy you [*tsbʿk*]." Cf. 1:9, where *lwyt ḥn* is similarly literalized as *y'ywt'* "beauty." Pink. emends *tsbʿk* to *tsyʿk* ("she will aid you"), which is the rendering of *mgn* in 2:7 (reading the word as *māgēn* "shield").

Lecture VI. 4:10–19

4:10 Line $^{\beta}$ is more literal than its doublet $^{\gamma}$, which is probably the OG: *hina soi genōntai pollai hodoi biou* ("so that there may be for you many *ways* of life"). "Years of life" corresponds to MT "ways of life" in one doublet of LXX 2:19; see the note.

Syr: (b) "your life."

4:11. For "(taught you) *in* (the) way of wisdom," LXX and Syr have "*ways* of wisdom," as a dir. obj.

4:12. Syr uses "(steps will not) *shake*" [*nzwʿn*$^{pl.}$], apparently substituting a more transparent image for *yṣr* "be straitened."

4:13. LXX has "hold to *my* instruction," representing *bmwsry*. The end of the verse, *ky hy' ḥyyk*, is rephrased as *eis zōēn sou* ("for your life"), perhaps because it was not clear how the instruction can *be* one's life. See the note on 8:30bc.

Syr: *bmrdwty* "*my* discipline" [= LXX].

Variant: *bmwsry* (MT *bammûsār*).

4:14. For MT's *t'šr* (*tᵉ'aššēr*) "go in," "follow" (a path), LXX's has *zēlōsęs* "envy" or (as it is to be understood here) "emulate." In English too, "following someone's ways" means to *emulate* his behavior. Aq, Theod: *mēde makarisęs* "nor declare fortunate," construing *t'šr* as "declare fortunate." Vul *nec tibi placeat* "let . . . not please you," relating *t'šr* to *'ošer* "joy."

Syr has *ṭṭn/tyṭn* "envy" (as in 3:31; 23:17; Pss 37:1; 73:3); = Tg. This construes *t'šr* as "declare/consider fortunate" and was perhaps influenced by LXX's *zēlōsęs*.

4:15. LXX 15$^{\alpha}$, *en hǫ an topǫ stratopedeusōsin* ("In whatever place they encamp"), is puzzling, since the LXX correctly understood *prʿ* to mean "ignore" or "reject" in 1:25; 13:18; and 15:32, though it translated differently at each occurrence. Suggested retroversions, all of them farfetched, are *rbʿhw*, parsed as (Aram) *r-b-ʿ* "lie, crouch down" (Kuhn); *mirʿēmô* (Lag.); and *mirʿēhu* (Jäger). LXX varies the repeated word *ʿbr* "pass" by translating *epelthęs* and *parallaxon*.

Syr: (aα) *wb'tr' dšryn* "And in the place they encamp." Syr looks to LXX to explain *prʿhw* but stays closer to the Heb for the rest of the verse. Syr adds *mnh* "from it" at the end of the verse, for clarity. For *prʿhw* Tg has *'ryš*, which should be emended to *'dyš* "pass by," "ignore."

Radaq mentions a qeré-variant, qeré *śᵉṭê*, no longer preserved.

4:16. LXX: "α For they do not sleep, if they do not do evil. β Their sleep is removed, and they do not sleep" (α *ou gar mē hypnōsōsin, ean mē kakopoiēsōsin.* β *aphęrētai ho hypnos autōn, kai ou koimōntai*). LXX's *koimōntai* reflects *yškbw*, for MT's *ykšwlw* (Lag.). Since LXX reads *yškbw*, MT's conditional *ʾim loʾ* ("if not") had to be ignored. The reading *yškbw* was probably occasioned by a mistaken expectation of a parallel to *yšnw* "sleep."

Syr 16a has *ʿdmʾ* "until," for "if not" (twice). 16bβ *ʿdmʾ dʿbdyn ṣbynhwn* ("until they do their will"). Syr was apparently trying to make sense of the awkward intransitive *ykšwlw* (MT's ketiv) and understood "if they do not stumble" (ketiv) as implying that the wicked do their will and stumble into *sin*. Pink. retroverts Syr to *ymšwlw* "rule," but that would not provide the required meaning.

The qeré *yakšîlû* and the ketiv *ykšwlw* are different expansions of consonantal *ykšlw*. The latter spelling would best explain the *k-š* metathesis reflected in LXX's *yškbw*.

yškbw (MT *ykšwlw*).

Ketiv *ykšwlw*; qeré *ykšylw* (*yakšîlû*).

4:17. LXX renders 17b as *oinǭ de paranomǭ methyskontai* ("and get drunk on sinful wine"), correctly parsing *ḥmsym* as an abstract pl. The unique choice of *methyskesthai* for *šth* "to drink" emphasizes the sinner's dissolute character.

Syr uses *mʾkwlthwn* "their food" for *lḥmw* (*lāḥᵉmû*) "they eat," probably reading the rare verb *lḥmw* as *laḥmô*, then adjusting the number of the suffix. Tg: "bread of the evildoer [*duršyʿʾ*]," misreading Syr's *ʿwlʾ* = *ʿawlāʾ* as *ʿawālā*.

4:18. LXX: "α The ways of the just (pl.) shine like light; β they go forward and give light until the day sets in" (α *hai de hodoi tōn dikaiōn homoiōs phōti lampousin,* β *proporeuontai kai phōtizousin heōs katorthōssę hē hēmera*). "Shine" (*phōtizousin*) vocalizes *wngh* as *nōgēah* (ptcp.), and "they give light" may imply that the righteous give spiritual illumination by teaching; see, e.g., Ps 19[18]:9; 119[118]:130; Sir 24:32. MT's difficult *nkwn* is rendered mechanically: *katorthōsę*, lit. "becomes straight."

In Syr, 18a is made into an independent sentence: "and its light goes [*wʾzl nwhrh*] until the day has set in [*tqn*]."

4:19. LXX's *skoteinai* ("dark") and Syr's *ḥšwkʾ-hy* ("is dark") ignore the comparative *k* of *kʾplh*, perhaps because the comparison between a way and darkness seems unbalanced. In a similar vein, several MSS have the more obvious (and prosaic) *bʾplh* ("*in* the dark") for *kʾplh*.

Lecture VII. 4:20–27

4:21. LXX (consequent upon v 20): "α so that your springs [*pēgai*] not abandon you. β Guard them [*autas*] in your heart." In α, some minuscules add (springs) "of your life" (*tēs zōēs sou*), which is not OG (*contra* Lag., Baum.) but a gloss (based on 4:23) identifying the springs. The translator read *mʿynyk* (*mēʿêneykā*) as *maʿyāneykā* "your springs" and made the dir. obj. "them" (*autas*, fem.) refer to these rather than to the father's words. LXX correctly translated *mʿynyk* in the nearly identical 3:21a, and it may be that an exegetical tradition compelled the translator to treat the word as "springs" in 4:21 in spite of the resulting complications, namely the implication that the springs should be preserved in the heart.

The gloss in 21$^{\alpha}$ rightly identifies the "springs" as the source of life. More precisely, the springs are wisdom itself, which is held in the heart and, according to 4:23, is the source of life. According to LXX 8:35, life proceeds from wisdom.

Syr: *l' nzln*$^{pl.}$ *b'ynyk*$^{pl.}$ "let them not be trivial in your eyes," associating *ylyzy* with *z-l-l*; cf. 3:21.

4:22. LXX: "$^{\alpha}$ For they are life to those who find them [*autas*], $^{\beta}$ and healing to all flesh [*pasę̄ sarki*]." Again, the dir. obj. *autas* (fem. pl.) must refer to the springs. The variants *autōn* in SyrH and some MSS and *autēn* in ^{B} (the latter referring to *rhēsis*) are inner-Gk adjustments. In 22b, "all flesh," meaning all mortals, may represent *lkl bśr* (without the third m. sg. sfx.).

In Syr, 22b is *wbsrh klh m's'* "and it heals all his flesh." Heb *marpē'* is parsed as an act. ptcp. (D or H-stem), as in 12:18; sim. Tg's *m'sy*. The choice is deliberate, because *marpē'* is recognized as a noun and translated *'sywt'* in Prov 6:15; 15:4; 16:24; and 29:1.

4:23. In 23$^{\beta}$, "for from these [*toutōn*] are the outlets [*exodoi*] of life," "these" are the springs. The image seems to be of rivulets or channels bringing life (or life-giving actions) from the springs, meaning wisdom, which are in the heart.

Syr: (a) *bkl zwhr*, "with every caution." Tg: "*More than* every caution [*zhwr'*; var *zyhwr'*] keep your heart, for from it is the outlet of life."

4:24. Syr (b): "and keep thoughts of deceit [*rny' d't'*] far from your lips." Where Syr has *rny'* "thoughts," Tg has *knt'* "winding." This probably represents an error in Tg's Syr text, in which *knt'* and *rny'* would look alike.

4:25. LXX has $^{\beta}$ *ta de blephara sou neuetō dikaia* "let your eyelids assent to righteousness," which has the gist of the MT but a different image. In Prov 21:1, *neuein* ("to nod," "gesture," hence "affirm") = *ḥpṣ* "wish." (*Neuein* is not used elsewhere in the LXX.) LXX is being logical: The eyelids don't *go straight*, but they *can* gesture affirmation. For a hostile use of eye gestures, see 6:13 and the comment there. Sir 27:22–23 (Gk) uses *dianeuein* of winking the eye.

Syr = MT. Tg: (a) "Let your eyes be bright [*n'wrn* ^{L}]. Pink. emends *n'wrn* to *nḥwrn* "look," but *n'wrn* is original, arising from a confusion of Syr's *nḥōrān*$^{pl.}$ "let them look" with the homonym *ḥwr* "be clear, shine."

4:26. In 26$^{\beta}$, LXX's *kateuthyne* ("make straight") represents *ykynw* (*yakînû*) or understands MT's *yknw* that way (sim. Aq, Sym, Theod). In ^{a}, LXX lacks "all," a word that is more often a LXX plus vis-à-vis the MT. Verse 26a is quoted in Hebrews 12:13, where the word order differs but the Hebrew syntax is construed in the same way.

Syr: (a) "Remove your foot from evil paths." The paraphrase is influenced by v 27 in the LXX, which alone mentions "paths" (Pink.).

4:27. LXX = MT, except that in the second line, LXX adds "way" ("the evil way"), to maintain the metaphor of path.

4:27a. LXX: "$^{\alpha}$ For God knows the ways that are on the right; $^{\beta}$ but those on the left are perverted [*diestrammenai*]." In contrast to v 27, LXX 27a equates the right and left with good and evil, respectively, which is a Greek, not a biblical, cliché. This identification disturbs the original metaphor of a single true path, from which all divergences lead astray. The warning in 4:27 against inclining to the right apparently puzzled a Greek scribe, who "corrected" it in 27a.

4:27b. LXX: "$^{\alpha}$ And he will make your paths straight, $^{\beta}$ and your journeys he will guide in peace." This verse rephrases MT v 27 in a way that introduces God's activity (Dick 1990: 27) and construes the straightness as well-being rather than rectitude. LXX's 27a and 27b are two distinct restatements of v 27 and probably represent later scribes' interpretations of that verse, which the OG translator did not have trouble with. Both additions are represented in Vul but not in Syr.

Lecture VIII. 5:1–23

5:1. LXX has *emois de logois* ("to my words") = *ldbry* (*lidbāray*) in 1b, for MT's *ltbwnty* ("to my understanding"). This is due to leveling with 4:20b, probably in the Heb, since the wording in the Gk is somewhat different. SyrH (= MSS 23, 252) has a doublet adjusting to MT.

Syr's *wlmʾmry* ("and to my word") represents the same consonantal text as LXX (*wldbry*) but treats it as sg. A Syr variant, *wlswkly* ("and to my understanding"), adjusts to the MT, as does Tg's *lbywny*.

Variant: *wldbry* (MT *litbûnātî*).

5:2. LXX (continuing v 1): $^{\alpha}$ "so that you may guard good insight [*ennoian agathēn*]. $^{\beta}$ And the knowledge [*aisthēsin*] of my lips is commanded you." "Good" is a moralizing enhancement, though *ennoia* itself introduces the moral connotation that Heb *m^{e}zimmah* lacks. LXX reads "my lips" (*śpty*) for MT's "your lips" (*śptyk*) and "is commanded you" for "keep" (MT *ynṣrw*; third pl.). *Entellesthai* almost always renders Heb *ṣiwwāh* "command," which is not used as a verb in Proverbs. The motive for these differences is unclear. LXX creates a neater parallelism by treating *lšmr* in v 2a as a finite verb. No variant is indicated.

Syr uses *wtzdhr* "and be careful" for MT's inf.

After 5:2, we should supply a verse along the lines of 7:5; see the Commentary.

5:3. LXX: "$^{\alpha}$ Do not hearken to the base woman, $^{\beta}$ for honey drips from the lips of the harlotrous woman, $^{\gamma}$ who for a season anoints your throat." ($^{\alpha}$ *mē prosechе phaulę̄ gynaiki.* $^{\beta}$ *meli gar apostazi apo cheileōn gynaikos pornēs,* $^{\gamma}$ *hē pros kairon lipainei son pharygga.*) Line $^{\alpha}$ is added to provide a logical bridge to the motive clause in v 3. Vul adds a similar phrase to the end of v 2. "Harlotrous woman" = *znh* (*zōnāh*), for MT *zrh* (*nun-reš* interchange; see Prov 6:7; 7:4; and probably 21:6; cf. Kaminka 1931–32: 178). In $^{\gamma}$, *pros kairon* ≠ MT's *wḥlq*, but no graphically similar variant is evident in either Gk or Heb. Lag. emends to *pro elaiou* = *miššemen*. The latter is, however, already represented in the LXX by *lipainei*, which vocalizes *mšmn* as *m^{e}šammēn* "lubricates" (D masc. ptcp.). The Gk had *ḥkkh* (*ḥikk^{e}kāh*) "your palate," a dittography of *kaph* (MT *ḥkh* "her palate"). Note that *ḥēk* "palate" is usually translated by Gk *pharynx* (the throat, incl. the pharynx), as here or *larynx* (the upper windpipe).

Syr: "(b) and her words [*mlyh*$^{pl.}$] are smoother [*rkykn*$^{pl.}$] than oil," resolving the metaphor "palate" as "words," as in 2:16. Tg = MT, but Tg^{Z} lacks "of the alien." The adj. *ḥālāq* is understood to mean "smooth" in Syr only here; elsewhere Syr usually construes the word etymologically, from the notion of "divide," and translates *ḥlq* with a form of *p-l-g* "to divide."

Variants: *znh* (*zōnāh*) (MT *zārāh*); *ḥkkh* (MT *ḥikkāhh*).

5:4. LXX translates 4a paraphrastically by adding *hysteron mentoi . . . heurēseis* ("Later, however, you will find her . . ."). A closer rendering, "her end is bitter," might be misunderstood to mean that she herself dies a hard death. This is an example of how LXX-Prov guides and limits interpretation without necessarily distorting the meaning. The comparative degree of the adjectives *pikroteron* "more bitter" and *ēkonēmenon mallon* "sharper than" is used for literary intensification (cf. 6:6). However, *kaph* and *mem* are very similar in many square scripts, and the variants *mlʿnh* and *mḥrb* are possible.

Syr: *wḥrthyn* "and their [f. pl.] end," referring to the aftereffects of "her words," which are sweet at first (v 3). In 4b, Syr returns to fem. sg.: "she is sharper" [*ḥryp' hy*], referring to the Strange Woman. Tg has "her end" = MT. Syr uses the comparative: *mn gdd'*: . . . *mn syp'* (= LXX).

5:5. LXX: "$^{\alpha}$ For the feet of folly will lead $^{\beta}$ those who are intimate with her with death down to Hades. $^{\gamma}$ Her steps are not firm." ($^{\alpha}$ *tēs gar aphrosynēs hoi podes katagousin* $^{\beta}$ *tous chrōmenous autę meta thanatou eis ton hądēn.* $^{\gamma}$ *ta de ichnē autēs ouk ereidetai.*) Because no antecedent is available in the immediate context for "her" in 5$^{\alpha}$, "folly" is substituted for the sfx. pron. Lag. and Jäger explain *aphrosynē* as a synecdoche for "the foolish woman." The abstraction, however, points to a cautious allegorical interpretation, which is reinforced by v 19; see the discussion later.

Though both LXX and Syr translate *yrdwt* ("go down") as a causal, "bring down," we need not assume a Heb variant. Both versions are paraphrastic, explaining that not only does the wicked woman die, she *kills*. In Jer 9:17, both LXX and Syr treat the G of *y-r-d* as causative, as does LXX in 5:5. (Even Naḥmias explains *yōrdôt* in 5:5 as causative and compares 1 Sam 23:6 and Jer 9:17.)

The translator's assumption that *tmk* means "lean on" or the like, rather than "grasp," as is here the case (see Textual Note on 4:4), causes a number of tangles. He is obliged to supply a negative to avoid an intolerable statement. He joins *š'wl* to the first clause rather than taking it as the dir. obj. of *tamak*. To make sense of *mwt š'wl*, he makes it into an adverb of means (*meta* + gen.) rather than location.

Such contortions show that it is inadequate to characterize the translation as "free" just because it varies from (our interpretation of) the MT. The translator is trying to render his Hebrew text as precisely as possible. When his linguistic assumptions differ from the ones current today, his translation may appear to be "free," but it is actually bound to the Hebrew text *as he understood it*.

Syr: (a) "Her feet lead down [*mḥtn*$^{pl.}$] to death; (b) Sheol supports her steps [*šywl hlkth' msmk'*]" (*šywl* is f. sg.). Syr parses *yrdwt* as a transitive, as in LXX. Tg (*nḥtn* "go down") adjusts to MT. On the treatment of *tmk*, see at 4:4. Tg^{L}

msmkn (f. pl.) follows Syr but makes "her steps" the subject; the meaning is uncertain.

5:6. LXX: "For she goes not upon the ways of life. $^{\beta}$ Her courses are slippery and not well-known" [$^{\beta}$ *sphalerai de hai trochiai autēs kai ouk eugnōstoi*]. *Sphalerai* means "likely to make one stumble"; the paths may be rough or slippery. This produces a more obvious metaphor than MT's "her courses wander." MT's *lʾ tdʿ* was parsed as second sg. ("you do not know") and converted into an adjectival construction, "not well known." In other words, they are foreign or alien, and one who goes on them $^{\alpha}$ trips and $^{\beta}$ gets lost. Compare the image in 9:12b.

Syr: "(b) for her paths are a trackless wasteland and not known" (*twšʾ ʾnwn gyr šbylyh*$^{pl.}$ *wlʾ ydyʿyn*). Syr uses the same metaphor, but with a different word (*ḥwrbʾ*) in 9:12c: The wicked travel in a pathless wasteland. For "ways of life," Syr has the sg. "way of life," in accordance with the usual metaphor of the two paths. Syr learned "not well-known" from LXX but independently dealt with the metaphor of paths "wandering."

5:7. LXX: "$^{\alpha}$ Now, then, son, hear me, $^{\beta}$ and do not treat my words as invalid" [*akyrous poiēsęs*]. As in 7:24 and 8:32, the LXX changes "sons" to sg. for the sake of consistency. "Treat as invalid" probably reflects *tsyrw* (H-stem) (lit. "put aside") for MT's *tswrw* (G-stem).

5:8. LXX: $^{\beta}$ "do not approach the front doors [*prothyrais*; ^{A}] of her house [*oikōn*]." (The variant in Rahlfs, *pros thyrais* [^{BS} etc.], is ungrammatical and corrupt [Zuntz 1956: 129].) *Prothyrais* (often for *petaḥ*) is emphatic: Don't approach *even* her outer doors. The pl. of *oikōn* (lit. "houses") is not "scribal inadvertence" (Toy) but used in reference to a residential complex; cf. 7:8.

Syr = MT.

5:9. LXX has *zōēn sou* "your life" = *ḥyk* or *ḥyyk* (*ḥayyekā*), a graphic error for MT's *hwdk* (*hōdᵉkā*) "your glory." The error was perhaps encouraged by the parallel "your years," which was understood to mean "life" and rendered accordingly (*bion*). The pl. of "cruel men" is influenced by the parallel plural. The Gk often smooths out sudden shifts in number.

Syr (= Tg) *ḥylk*, for MT *hwdk*. Pink. believes that Syr represents Heb *hwnk* ("your wealth," which *ḥylʾ* sometimes means), but *ḥylk* in the sense of "your strength" is probably a clarification of the somewhat puzzling *hwdk* "your glory." For MT's *lʾkzry*, Syr uses the pl., *lʾylyn dlʾ mrḥmnyn* "to those who show no mercy," as in LXX. Tg^{Z} has *lbr ʿmmyn* "to a foreigner" and Tg^{L} has *lnwkrʾyn* "to aliens." These may reflect a midrashic association of *ʾakzār* with *zār* "foreign" (as in Rashi to Job 19:13), under the influence of v 10.

Variant: *ḥyk* (= *ḥayyekā*) (MT *hwdk*).

5:10. "Enter" is added in LXX 10$^{\beta}$ to provide a verb for the second line; sim. Syr *tʿl* "enter."

5:11. LXX: "$^{\alpha}$ And you repent in the end, $^{\beta}$ when the flesh [pl.] of your body is worn out" ($^{\alpha}$ *kai metamelēthēsę* [^{A} *metamelēthęs*] *ep' eschatōn*, $^{\beta}$ *hēnika an katatribōsin sarkes sōmatos sou*). LXX represents several variants: (1) *wnḥmt* for MT *wnhmt*; (2) *bʾḥryt* for MT *bʾḥrytk*; (3) *bblwt* for MT *bklwt*; (4) *bśr šʾrk* for

MT *bśrk wšʾrk*. Variants 1–3 are due to confusion or haplography of similar letters. Variant 4 is a construct of synonyms. (= Syr). The pl. of *sarx* is often used for sg. *bāśār*. These synonyms appear in construct, but in the opposite order, in Lev 18:6 and 25:49. The LXX's and the MT's forms of the line seem equally possible.

Syr: *wbsybwtk*, "And in your old age," an interpretation of MT's "and in your end" (cf. Clemens Alexandrinus 122.24 *epi gērōs*). Syr *ttwyk npšk* ("your soul repents") assumes Heb *wnḥmt* (*w^{e}niḥamtā*) = LXX. Syr's *bsrʾ dgwšmk* "the flesh of your body" = LXX, but using the sg. of "flesh" and thus probably reflecting the Heb variant independently.

Variant: *wnḥmt bʾḥryt bblwt bśr šʾrk* ("And you will be regretful in the end, when the flesh of your flesh wears away").

5:13. LXX: "$^{\alpha}$ I did not listen to the voice of him who educated me and who taught me [*paideuontos me kai didaskontos me*], $^{\beta}$ nor did I set my ear." The verse is divided after *lmlmdy*, disturbing the parallelism (thus too in v 5). MT's *mwry* and *lmlmdy* are taken as singular, in other words, as referring to the father. Syr = MT.

5:15. LXX: "$^{\alpha}$ Drink waters from your vessels $^{\beta}$ and from the wells of your spring" ($^{\alpha}$ *pine hydata apo sōn aggeiōn* $^{\beta}$ *kai apo sōn phreatōn pēgēs*). The LXX joins *nzlym* ("liquids") to "your well" rather than reading it as an additional object of "drink" (cf. the similar error in 5:13). Consequently, LXX must restructure the syntax. MT's *bwrk* and *bʾrk*, both meaning "well," are treated as plurals, "vessels" and "wells" (Gk *phrear* = *bʾr*, as almost always in the LXX, not *nzlym*). It is unclear what these "vessels" (or "reservoirs") and "wells" are meant to signify. Baum. notes that a wife is referred to as a vessel in 1 Thess 4:4 (*to heautou skeuos*) and a cup (*kws*) in *b. Ned*. 20b, but the plural of "vessels" *aggeiōn* does not accord with this interpretation.

Syr = MT. Tg = MT, but worded differently from Syr.

5:16. LXX: "$^{\alpha}$ Let not the waters be spilt by you from your spring, $^{\beta}$ but let your waters go through your (own) plazas" ($^{\alpha}$ *mē hyperekcheisthō soi ta hydata ek tēs sēs pēgēs,* $^{\beta}$ *eis de sas plateias diaporeuesthō ta sa hydata*). The translator construes *mʿyntyk* as *mēʿênōteykā* "from your springs." He must then supply a subject ("the waters") from v 15. The negative particle is supplied in 16a to make sense of the verse, an expediency taken in 1:17, 3:32; 5:5; etc. (It is removed in LXX^{ASc}.)

Gerleman (1956: 18) offers this verse as an example of a Greek predilection for antithetical parallelism. The antithesis arose, however, for the sake of sense, not rhetoric. Since the translator understood "waters" to signify sexual powers, the verse could not mean that your waters *should* be spilt outside.

Syr: "(a) And your waters will overflow in your streets (b) and in your streets they will flow" (*wnštpʿwn myk$^{pl.}$ bšwqyk$^{pl.}$ wbšwqyk$^{pl.}$ nrdwn*). Syr combines the "springs" and "waters" of MT into "waters," which are probably to be understood as the male generative powers or as the semen itself (Isa 48:1; RH). Syr, unlike LXX (see previously), understands the spilling of waters as a blessing, namely fecundity, not as something to avoid. Syr *nrdwn* ("will flow") = Heb *plgw*, for MT *palgêy-*. Tg = MT.

5:17. LXX: "$^{\beta}$ and let no stranger [*allotrios*] partake [*metaschetō*] with you." As in 16$^{\beta}$, a jussive is added to a nominal clause. MT's *zrym* is treated as sg.

Syr (Tg) supplies a verb meaning "partake" (*nštwtpwn*) in 17b, as in LXX, but maintains the pl. of *zrym*.

5:18. LXX: "$^{\alpha}$ Let your spring of water be for you alone, $^{\beta}$ and enjoy yourself together with the wife of your youth" ($^{\alpha}$ *hē pēgē sou tou hydatos estō soi idia*, $^{\beta}$ *kai syneuphrainou meta gynaikos tēs ek neotētos sou*). "Your spring" (*mqwrk*) is glossed "of water." "For you alone" (*soi idia*) = *lk lbdk*, or loosely for *lbdk* alone; the translator would not have ignored a clear and appropriate adjective like *brwk* "blessed." For MT's "get pleasure from" (*śmḥ m-*), LXX speaks of the (shared) pleasure of the *couple* (*syneuphrainou meta* + gen.). The vorlage was probably *śmḥ b-*, perhaps attested by Syr (*wḥdy ʿm*), Vul (*laetare cum*), *Mid. Shoḥer Tov*, ad loc., and some Heb MSS. See Commentary.

Syr: "Your source" (*mqwrk*) is translated *brk*, "your well," i.e., your wife. Syr *wḥdy ʿm* probably represents *wśmḥ b-*. Tg = MT.

Variants: *lbdk* (MT *bārûk*); *bʾšt* (MT *mēʾēšet*).

5:19. LXX: "$^{\alpha}$ A doe of affection and a filly of your grace, let her be together with you. $^{\beta}$ And may your own one guide you and associate with you at all times, $^{\gamma}$ because, consorting in her affection, you will become very great" ($^{\alpha}$ *elaphos philias kai pōlos sōn charitōn homileitō soi.* $^{\beta}$ *hē de idia* [*philia* $^{\text{Sc, V, O, SyrH}}$] *hēgeisthō sou* [var. *soi*] *kai synestō soi en panti kairǭ* $^{\gamma}$ *en gar tę̄ tautēs philią symperipheromenos pollostos esę̄*).

In 19$^{\alpha}$, LXX reads *ḥnk* for MT's *ḥn*; the *kaph* is a corruption of the similar-looking *dalet* of *ddyh* ("her breasts").

Baum. suggests that *hē de idia* in 19$^{\beta}$ represents *lbdh* (= *l^{e}baddāhh*) for MT *ddyh* (Baum.), but that is graphically distant. "Your own one" means "your wife" and is the opposite of *tēs mē idias* "one not your own" = *nkryh* in v 20. "Your own (woman)" interprets *ddyh* (*dōdeyhā*) as "her love," meaning *her*—the woman wife herself. The hexaplaric reading in $^{\beta}$ is *philia*, implicitly vocalizing *ddyh* as *dōdeyha* "her love" (*philia* = *dōdîm* in Prov 7:18) or reading *dwdyh*. Though not OG, this is the correct vocalization; see the Commentary.

LXX represents *yrwk* twice, as *hēgeisthō sou* (vocalizing *yōrûkā*) and as *synestō soi* ("associate with you"). The former has the obelus in SyrH and is OG. The second too may be original, because *synestō* does not look like an adjustment to the MT's *y^{e}rawwukā*. The OG clearly wishes to emphasize the notion of *being with* this female, as is shown by *homileitō soi* in 19$^{\alpha}$. Skehan (1946: 291) proposes that *homileitō . . . synestō soi* translates *tśyḥk* and *tnḥh ʾtk* of 6:22, which, he believes, originally belonged after 5:19 (in the order 6:22bca). But the verbal resemblance is slight, and the theory is convoluted. It is, however, likely that the translator was influenced by the *idea* of wisdom guiding a man and being with him, expressed in 6:22 and often implicit; e.g., 3:3; 4:5; 7:3–4; 8:35.

LXX's "let her lead you" in 19$^{\beta}$ shows that the translator is thinking of the woman in this verse as other than a human, because the translator would not have considered it desirable to let a man's wife "lead" him. Gk *hēgeisthai*, esp. with the genitive, implies rule and control as well as guidance. In the LXX, it commonly translates words for various types of rulers and chiefs, particularly *mōšel* "ruler." Without rejecting the literal sense of the verse, the translator implies an allegorization of the woman as Lady Wisdom, an idea perhaps inspired by the implicit vocalization of *yrwk* as *yōrûkā* "teach/lead you" (thus too in Syriac). Wis 7:12 says that Wisdom *hegeitai—controls* or *disposes* of—good things. The LXX of this verse, then, hints at an allegorization of the two women, Wisdom and Folly.

In 19^{γ}, *pollostos esę* = *tśgh* (*tiśgeh*) "become great," a different vocalization of MT's *tišgeh*. The LXX prefers spiritual to sexual association. Vul, Aq = MT.

Vocalizing the text to reflect LXX's understanding, 5:18 reads: (a) *ʾayyelet ʾăhābîm w^{e}ya‘ălat ḥēn*, (b) *dōdeyhā yōrukā b^{e}kol ‘ēt*, (c) *b^{e}ʾahăbātāhh tiśgeh tāmîd*.

Syr's *ʾwrḥth$^{pl.}$ ylp* ("learn her ways") paraphrases MT's *ddyh yrwk*. Syr clearly vocalizes the second word as *yōrûkā* "teach you." "Her ways" for MT's *ddyh* could represent *drkyh* (see Pink., p. 110), but that is graphically distant. Syr's "her ways" is probably a reflex of the underlying allegorical identification of the woman with wisdom, with the metaphor of "love" explained as "ways," calling to mind *Wisdom's* ways (3:17; 4:11; 8:32; 9:6). Syr sums up the difficult phrase at the end of the verse as *wbrḥmth r‘y* "and feed upon her love," taking the image, though not the exact phrase, from Cant 6:2. The idiom *r‘y b-* implies consorting sexually (29:3; contrast 13:20; 22:24).

Tg: (a) *ʾyltʾ drḥmwtʾ wdyṣtʾ dḥṣdʾ* (b) *hwwnʾ ʾylyp bkl zmn* (c) *wbrḥmwtʾ tgrm* (var. *tgrs* $^{C, R}$) "A gazelle of love and a roe of kindness, learn good behavior at all times and in her love grow strong [var. study] always." Tg too interprets Heb *ddyh* (*dadeyhā* in the Tg's pointed text) as a metaphor, but interprets it more specifically as good behavior. If Tg had seen *drkyh*, it would have translated it *ʾrḥthʾ* (cf. 3:17; 7:25; etc.). Tg (^{Z}, ^{L}) reads *tgrm* "grow strong" (?), which can be explained as an understanding of *tšgh* as *tśgh*. Other MSS have *tgrs* "read," "study," which is probably an inner-Targumic variant further allegorizing the figure of the legitimate wife as Torah, as in the midrash (e.g., *Mid. Prov.*; *j. Ber* 80b). Tg derives the notion of *learning* from *yrwk*, although it would have used a vocalized MT with *y^{e}rawwukā*. Since Tg treats this notion differently than Syr, it is likely that an exegetical tradition lies behind the rendering. The midrashic interpretation allegorizes the breast as Torah (*Mid. Prov.*; *Sifré* Deut 321; *b.* ‘*Erub* 54b) but maintains *yrwwk* as "slake your (spiritual) thirst."

There is considerable confusion in the versions in the treatment of *ddym* in its various occurrences. While the hexaplaric reading in Prov 5:19 construes *ddym* as *dōdeyhā* "her love," which also seems to underlie OG's *hē de idia*, the reverse happens in the Song of Songs, where the LXX awkwardly translates *ddym* (written both plene and lene in MT) as "breasts" in Cant 4:10 (MT *dōdayik*) and 7:13 (*dōday*), and even in 1:2, 4, where the *dōdîm* (actually, "love") belong to the male; thus too Vul. Syr translates *d(w)dym* as "breasts" when the possessor is the woman in Cant 4:10 and 7:13, but "love" in reference to the man in 1:2, 4. Vul has *ubera eius* "her breasts" in Prov 5:19 as well as 7:18 (MT *dōdîm* "lovemaking").

Variants: *ḥnk* (MT *ḥēn*). For vocalic variants, see previously.

5:20. LXX: "ᵅ Be not great with another woman, ᵝ nor embrace the arms of one not your own" (ᵅ *mē polys isthi pros allotrian* ᵝ *mēde synechou agkalais tēs mē idias*). Heb *wlmh* (lit. "and why") is correctly understood as "so that not," i.e., "lest." MT's *tišgeh* is again read as *tiśgeh* "become great/many"; cf. v 19. "Being great" here means having many progeny. A man's sons must come from his legitimate wife if they are to be his heirs and successors. LXX's *tēs mē idias* correctly construes Heb *nkryh* as a woman other than one's own wife. LXX lacks "(my) son."

Syr paraphrases MT's *lāmāh* as a prohibition and underlines the admonition by introducing 20b with *ʾp lʾ*.

Tg *ʾḥrynʾ* "other" for *nkryh* shows that Tg does not regard the Strange Woman as necessarily a foreigner.

5:21. Heb *mpls* is translated *skopeuei* "watches" in LXX. Syr rephrases this as *glyn qdmwhy* "are revealed before him." (Syr uses a different word for each of the six occurrences of the verb and is obviously guessing at its meaning.)

5:22. LXX: "ᵅ Transgressions will hunt down a man [*andra*], ᵝ and each one [*hekastos*] is bound in the cords of his own sins." MT's *ʾt hršʿ* is not represented, but "a man" and "each one" are supplied for explicitness. The explication of the pronoun in ᵝ as *hekastos* "each one" shows that *ʾt hršʿ* was not available as an antecedent.

Syr: "(a) in his sins an evildoer [*ʿwlʾ*] is caught." Syr turns the difficult syntax of 22a into the passive to match 22b. It represents *ʾt hršʿ*. Tg: *ḥwbwy дršyʿʾ* *qmṭyn lyh* . . . "The sins of the wicked man seize him," adjusting to MT. "Sins" pl. = LXX (MT sg.).

Variant: omit *ʾet-hārāšāʿ*.

5:23. LXX: "ᵅ He dies by lack of instruction ᵝ and is cast out from the greatness of his own sustenance; ᵞ and he perishes through folly" (ᵅ *houtos teleutą meta apaideutōn,* ᵝ *ek de plēthous tēs heautou biotētos exerriphē* ᵞ *kai apōleto di' aphrosynēn*). "Cast out" interprets *šagah* as "go astray," hence (since a punishment is required here, not a sin) "be cast out." The hapax *biotētos* "sustenance" seems to derive from a different vorlage, because the translator would have no problem with *ʾwltw*, "his folly," but no likely variant in Heb or Gk is evident. Gk *ek plēthous* = *m rb* "from (the greatness of)" for MT's *bᵉrōb*. The doublet in ᵞ is an addition, assimilating v 23b to MT. Setting "folly" in the absolute, for MT's "his folly," recalls the added *aphrosynēs* in v 5 and reminds us that the failing underlying the sexual transgression is folly itself.

Variants: *wmrb* (MT *ûbᵉrōb*).

Interlude C. 6:1–19

6:1. LXX: "ᵅ Son, if you go surety for your friend, ᵝ you will deliver [*paradōseis*] your hand to an enemy [*echthrǭ*]." LXX makes v 1b an apodosis. *Echthros* = *zar* only here. It may have been used because of an assumption that 1b is the consequence of 1a. The translator reads the verse to mean that going surety for a friend will turn him into your enemy. CSP observes that Sir 6:5–17 uses the same words in speaking of a "friend" (*philos*) who turns into an "enemy" (*echthros*). "Hand" sg. (= Vul) for MT's pl.

Syr too starts the apodosis at v 1b: ". . . you have surrendered [*'šlmt 'ydk*] to an alien [*nwkry'*]." "Surrendered" [lit. "delivered your hand]" is influenced by LXX. Syr has "hand" (sg.) for MT's pl. Tg = MT. The sg. is correct.

Variant: *kpk* (MT *kpyk*).

6:2. LXX: "$^{\alpha}$ For a strong trap for a man are (his) own lips [*cheilesin*, $^{\beta}$ and he is caught by the lips of his own mouth." LXX is too distant from the Heb to witness to textual variants, but *śptyk* "your lips" in 2b is supported by Syr (the hexaplaric variant is *rhēmasin*).

Syr, 2b: *bmmll' dspwtk*$^{pl.}$ "by the word of your lips." Syr's "your lips" is independent of LXX here but partly resembles it. Syr probably reflects a synonym variant, *śptyk*. (It is self-serving to transfer Syr's variant from 2b to 2a, then use it to emend 2a, as BHS does.) Syr's "your lips" may reflect a stage on the way to the different repetitions in MT ("your mouth" twice) and LXX ("lips" twice).

Variant: *śptyk* (MT *pîkā*).

6:3. LXX: $^{\alpha}$ "Do, son, what I command you, and be saved, $^{\beta}$ for you have come into the hands of bad men [*kakōn*] through your friend. $^{\gamma}$ Go, without being lax, $^{\delta}$ and also importune your friend, for whom you have gone surety" ($^{\gamma}$ *ithi mē ekluomenos*, $^{\delta}$ *paroxyne de kai ton philon sou, hon eneguēsō*]. LXX elucidates MT's *z't 'pw'* ("this therefore") as "what I command you." In $^{\beta}$, *kakōn* ("of evil men") is a different vocalization of MT's *rē'ekā*. This rendering was probably motivated by the assumption that the source of the trouble is evil men (namely, the moneylenders), rather than the borrower. LXX thus introduces a moralistic concern. The gloss in $^{\delta}$ "for whom you have gone surety" shows that the translator is carefully sorting out the various parties in the transaction.

In 3$^{\gamma}$, MT's undignified "go and grovel" is supplanted by a vague warning to avoid being lax (or despondent *ekluesthai*). Rather than reading *l' ttrph* (CSP), the translator is probably guessing the meaning of a rare verb from context, deriving the notion of persistence from the next verse.

In 3$^{\delta}$, LXX's sg. for MT's *r'yk* is clearly correct. The latter is actually a plene orthography for the sg.; cf. 2 Sam 12:11. For the phenomenon, see Sperber 1966: 261.

Syr: "(a) Do thus, my son, and save yourself, because for the sake of [*'l 'py*$^{pl.}$] your friend you have fallen into the hands of your enemy [*b'ldbbk*]: (b) Therefore coax [*grg*] your friend, for whom you have gone surety." This is an attempt to deal with the problem of why it should be a misfortune to fall into a *friend's* power. A hostile party is introduced into the scene as in the LXX, but using a different word ("your enemy" rather than "bad men").

This verse gives insight into Syr's flexible reliance on the LXX. Following LXX, Syr (1) understands the misfortune in 3a as falling into hostile hands and adds "in the hands of your enemy"; (2) combines the rare verbs in 3b; and (3) adds the same relative clause modifying "your friend" (sg., as in LXX) in 3b. At the same time, Syr is basically working from MT. Unlike LXX, Syr (1) agrees with

MT in 3a (LXX 3$^{\alpha}$); (2) retains "your friend" in 3b; and (3) uses "your enemy" where LXX has "evil men," thus avoiding the LXX's moralistic categories. Syr (4) also gives the verbs in 3b a different sense and (5) omits *lk* "go" in 3b. Thus we see a translator who calls upon the LXX for exegetical help but has independent control of the Hebrew. Tg = MT.

6:4. LXX repeats the negative and makes *tnwmh* a verb—*epinustazęs* "drowse off." Syr repeats the negative in 4b; Tg omits it.

6:5. LXX: "$^{\alpha}$ so that [*hina*] you may be saved as a gazelle from a trap [*brochōn*] $^{\beta}$ and as a bird from a snare [*ek pagidos*]." In the first line, for MT's *myd* ("from a hand"), LXX has *ek brochōn* ("from a trap"). This probably reflects *mmṣ(w)d* (= *mimmāṣōd*) or *myd mṣwd*. The original presence of a word for "trap" is evidenced by Sir Gk 27:20, which draws on the phraseology of Prov 6:5 but independently of the LXX: *exephygen hōs dorkas ek pagidos*. *Yod-ṣade* confusion is most likely to arise in the old script. In 6$^{\beta}$, LXX *ek pagidos* = *mpḥ*, a synonym variant.

Syr (Tg): (a) "from a trap [*mn nšb'*]" = LXX. (b) *mn bpḥ'* "from a snare" = Heb *mpḥ* (= LXX). *Yqwš* elsewhere is translated *twqlt'*. Several Heb MSS have *mpḥ* here as well.

Variants: *mmṣd* (MT *myd*); *mpḥ* (MT *miyyad yāqûš*).

6:6. LXX: "$^{\alpha}$ Go [*ithi* $^{A^{*}Bc}$] to the ant, O sluggard, $^{\beta}$ and seeing its ways, emulate (him) [*kai zēlōson idōn tas hodous autou*] $^{\gamma}$ and become wiser than that one." LXX turns the couplet into a tristich, adding "emulate" to make the practical lesson clear. LXX uses the comparative degree, "wiser than that one," because to the literal-minded translator, it is hardly adequate to be merely *as wise* as the ant. The comparison assumes that the ant *is* wise, a notion that could have been learned from 30:24. *Deut. Rab.* (5.2) also extracts an a fortiori lesson from this verse: "You, for whom I did appoint officers and officials—how much the more so should you hearken to them (Prijs 1948: 31). An epigram on the ant in Pseudo-Phocylides (164–70) is based on LXX-Prov but emphasizes the ant's diligence (as in MT) rather than its wisdom.

Syr *'tdm' lšwšmn' wḥzy 'wrḥth*$^{pl.}$ "Emulate the ant and see its ways" is influenced by the LXX's *zēlōson*. Syr lacks "O sluggard" and joins *wḥkm* to the next sentence, which it begins, "And learn that. . . ." Tg restores the words (*'ṭl'* and *w'tḥkym*) but otherwise follows Syr.

6:7. LXX: "$^{\alpha}$ For (though) he has no field, and has no enforcer, and is not under a master. . . ." For MT's *qṣyn* "leader," LXX has *geōrgiou* "field" (gen.). This must represent *qṣyr* "harvest" in the vorlage (= Syr), which the translator could understand only as a metonymy for field. V 7 is formulated as a genitive absolute, which is to say, a circumstantial or concessive clause, with the next verse as main clause. On *n-r* interchanges, see 5:3. Cook (CSP) thinks that *geōgorion* was derived from "immediate context," but it is hardly required by context.

Syr (with different verse division): "and learn that it has no harvest [*ḥṣd'*] and has no ruler [*šlyṭ'*] over it, nor is there anyone who presses it [*w'p l' mn d'kp lh*]." Syr independently witnesses to *qṣyr*. Tg: *ḥṣd'* "harvest" = Syr. Syr repeats the negative.

Variant: *qṣyr* (MT *qṣyn*).

6:8. For *ʾgr* "stores up," LXX has "and he makes (provisions) [*parathesin*] great." The meaning of *ʾagar* seems deduced from context; it is rendered differently in 10:5.

Syr = MT.

6:8a–c. "(8a) Or go to the bee, and learn how diligent [*ergatis*] she is and how seriously she performs [*poieitai*] work—(8b) (she) whose products kings and commoners use for health, and who is desired and well-known to all. (8c) Though weak in strength, having honored wisdom she excels [*tēn sophian timēsasa proēchthē*]." Instead of *poieitai* in 8a, the variant in LXX^{V}, *emporeuetai* ("traffics in"), may be OG (Zuntz 1956: 136).

The epigram in LXX 6:8a–c is an original Greek composition inserted here because of association with the ant. Admiration for the bee is Greek. Aristotle praises the industriousness (*ergatis*) of the bee, which he describes immediately after the ant (*Historia animalium*, 622B; noted by Gerleman 1956: 31). (Cook [CSP 166] holds that the hapax *ergatis* shows that the translator had access to Aristotle. Influence [perhaps indirect] from Aristotle is likely, but we cannot assume that the OG translator wrote this composition.)

Ben Sira (11:3) says the same of the bee: "The bee is weak among flying animals, but her fruit is the best of products" (*rʾš tnwbwt*; Gk has "of sweet things") Pseudo-Phocylides too uses this topos (171–74), emphasizing the bee's industriousness. (This immediately follows an epigram on the ant, 164–70, indicating dependency on LXX-Prov.) The late Egyptian Phibis (25:3), to demonstrate the disproportionate effects little things can have, says, "The little bee brings the honey." Interestingly, Saʿadia, without reference to the LXX passage, adds: "The ants as well as the bees, by nature lacking the faculty of intelligence, gather their food at the appropriate season."

The epigram does not fit its present context and probably was not composed for it. Whereas Prov 6:6–8 describes the ant as an example of independent enterprise whose efforts benefit itself, the LXX addition lauds the bee for her value to *others*.

The point of the praise is that the bee's wisdom compensates for its physical weakness (Giese 1992b: 411). Whereas MT teaches the work ethic of the value of present labor, LXX asserts that the combination of work and wisdom can overcome a lack of power. Accordingly, the poor wise man can supplant the ungodly rich one (Giese 1992b: 411). Cook (CSP 168) believes that the translator composed the addition, whose purpose is to interpret a "dualism" in the contrast between rich and poor in a "religious way." But this contrast is well in the background and cannot be the *purpose* of the addition), nor is there a significantly religious message here.

6:9. Syr = MT, but transposing the last two words. LXX, Tg = MT.

6:10. LXX: "$^{\alpha}$ For a little while you sleep [*oligon de hypnois*], β and for a little while you lie down [*kathēsai*], $^{\gamma}$ and you will slumber a bit [*mikron de nustazeis*], $^{\delta}$ and for a little while you may embrace [*enagkalizę̄*] your bosom with your hands." 6:10$^{\alpha}$, which has nothing corresponding in MT (or Syr), reflects *mʿṭ šbt* (*šebet*) (Lag., Baum.), a dittography of *mʿṭ šnt* (MT *meʿat šēnôt*). LXX treats the verbal nouns in 10$^{\beta\gamma\delta}$ as finite verbs in the second m. sg. The identical Heb verse is treated differently in the LXX of 24:33.

Syr also renders the nouns as verbs (second masc. sg. imperf.) and omits *lškb*. Tg = MT.

6:11. LXX: "$^{\alpha}$ Then [*eit'*] your penury shall come upon you like an evil wayfarer [*kakos hodoiporos*], $^{\beta}$ and your neediness like a good runner [*agathos dromeus*]." LXX creates a moral antithesis between an "evil wayfarer" and a "good runner." (This does not happen in LXX 24:34, though it too has *agathos dromeus*.) Cook sees this antithesis as further evidence of the translator's (undeniable) penchant for a "dualism of good versus bad" (CSP 171). This may be the motive, but we should note that "good" must here mean *effective*, that is, speedy. Thus the antithesis created by the addition of *kakos* and *agathos* is superficial and semantically asymmetrical.

"Runner" for *mgn* is a guess from context, but Rashi reasons similarly: "like a man who goes *fast*, like an *ʾiš magen* who comes quickly to defend his master."

Syr (sim. Tg) has *wtdrkk* "and come upon you," reading *mhlk* or *wmhlk*, without the *kaph*. The duplicate in MT 24:34 has *wbʾ mthlk*. The *kaph* of comparison is appropriate semantically in both places but was lacking in Syr 6:11 as well as in some Heb MSS and probably lost by near haplography with the *mem*. The versions treat 24:34 quite differently from 6:11. Syr interprets *ʾyš mgn* as "a vigorous man" (*gbrʾ kšyrʾ*).

Variant: *mhlk* (MT *kimhallēk*).

6:11a. LXX: "$^{\alpha}$ But if you are tireless, your harvest will come like a fountain, $^{\beta}$ and your neediness [*endeia*] will depart like a bad runner [*kakos dromeus*]." The second part of the first line has the obelus in SyrH. Fritsch (1953: 179) believes that all of LXX 11a is OG, while 11 is hexaplaric. But "bad runner" in 11a$^{\beta}$ shows an awareness of the Gk of 11$^{\beta}$, which diverges from the Heb. LXX 6:11a is an extension of 6:11 by the translator or a later scribe.

LXX 6:11a is a new proverb extending the image of good and bad runners (cf. Tov 1990: 46). Vul retains 11a, but without "bad runner." Syr omits.

6:12. LXX's "a man foolish and lawless" (*aphrōn kai paranomos*) combines the two phrases in MT 12a. For MT's "goes (in) crookedness of mouth" (*hôlēk ʿiqšût peh*), the literal-minded translator substitutes a more predictable metaphor, "goes on paths that are not good."

Syr's *bʿqšywtʾ* ("in twistedness") eliminates the incongruity by leaving out "mouth." Tg = MT.

6:13. In 13$^{\gamma}$, LXX's "He teaches with hints of his fingers [*didaskei de enneumasin*]" assumes that Heb *mrh* (*mōreh*) "points" means "teaches" and so must add a seemingly appropriate modifier, "with hints." The translation implies that the scoundrel teaches others his wicked ways.

Syr has "eyes" (= qeré), "foot" (= ketiv).

Ketiv *bʿynw*, qeré *beʿênāyw*; ketiv *brglw*, qeré *beraglāyw*.

6:14. In 14^{γ}, LXX renders *mdynym yšlḥ* ("sends strife") as "such a one causes troubles [*tarachas*] to a city [*polei*]." "Troubles" and "to a city" are doublets. The first renders the ketiv *mdnym* "strifes," the second, the consonantal qeré *mdynym*, which it associates with *m^edînāh* in its Aramaic sense, "city." This association is made transparent in SyrH *lmdy(n)tʾ*.

Syr (Tg) treats Heb *tḥpkwt* as a verb, "And he turns about [*wmthpk*] in his heart," thereby connoting scheming or unreliability rather than perversity. Syr 2:16 says the same of the Strange Woman. To "foments strife" (Syr *šgš* ≈ MT), Syr adds *byt tryn*$^{pl.}$ ("between two people") for clarity. (Tg omits.)

Ketiv *mdnym*; qeré *midyānîm*.

6:15. LXX's *diakopē* for Heb *petaʿ* is puzzling. Elsewhere *diakopē* = *pereṣ* or *mipraṣ*. Perhaps it does serve "to emphasize the downfall of the foolish transgressor" (CSP), but a word for "suddenly" would have done the same. Gk *kai syntribē* = *wšbr*.

Syr (Tg) = MT.

Variants: *wšbr* (MT *yiššābēr*).

6:16. In LXX, vv 16–19 continue the description of the villain begun in v 12. LXX 16 reads "$^{\alpha}$ For he rejoices [*chairei*] in all things that the Lord hates, $^{\beta}$ and he is shattered [*syntribetai*] through impurity [*akatharsian*] of soul." LXX missed the numerical sequence and understood *šš* (*šēš*) as *śāś* ("he rejoices"). He clearly read *wšbr* (which he parsed as *w^ešubbār*) instead of *šbʿ* ("seven"). For possible examples of *ʿ-r* interchange, see LSF §131. *ʿayin* and *reš* were similar in some varieties of the archaic script.

Consequent upon the reading of *wšbr* for *wšbʿ*, the translator assumed that MT's *twʿbt npšw* ("the loathing of his [namely, God's] soul") must be an attribute of the evildoer, *his* impurity. This was all occasioned by a slight scribal error. The translator will often override syntactical constraints in favor of representing the individual word-meanings as he understands them; see the note on 5:5.

Syr: *ʾslyt* "abhors," parsing MT's *twʿbt* (qeré) as a fem. ptcp. (*tōʿebet*). Tg uses a noun, *ʾslywt* "abhorrence" (apparently a hapax), adjusting to MT while maintaining Syr's writing. Tg-Prov regularly (except in 26:25) uses *mrḥq(t)ʾ* ("repulsive") for *toʿebah*.

The pl. of the ketiv is correct; cf. 26:25.

Ketiv *twʿbwt* (pl.); qeré *tôʿăbat* (sg.).

Variant: *yšbr* (MT *w^ešebaʿ*).

6:17. Whereas MT's pointing *dām nāqî* construes *dm nqy* as "innocent blood," LXX's *haima dikaiou* takes it as a bound form, *dam-nāqî* "blood of the innocent," which is probably correct. See the comment on 1:11.

Syr = MT.

6:18. In 18^{β}, LXX's *epispeudontes kakopoein* "hurrying to do evil," merges the two synonyms *mmhrwt lrwṣ* and treats *lrʿh* as an infinitive.

Syr = MT, but treating *rglym* as sg. This shows that Syr will override grammatical number even when it is consonantally unambiguous.

6:19. LXX construes *ypyḥ* as *yāpîaḥ* "to blow," hence *ekkaiei* "kindles." Heb *mdnym* is associated with *dyn* "judgment" and translated *kriseis* "judgments."

Lecture IX. 6:20–35

6:20. LXX: "α Son, keep the laws [*nomous*] of your father, β and reject not the customs [*thesmous*] of your mother." On the paralleling of the *nomos* of the father with the *thesmos* of the mother, see the Textual Note to 1:8.

6:21. LXX uses *psychę̄* for *lb* "heart," as in Prov 6:21; 15:32 [16:3]; and 26:25. This rendering shows that the "binding" was understood as a metaphor for attention and devotion.

6:22. LXX: "α Whenever you go about, lead it and let it be with you. β Whenever you lie down, let it guard you, γ so that when you are awake, it may converse with you" (α *hēnika an peripatę̄s, epagou autēn, kai meta sou estō* β *hōs d'an katheudę̄s phylassetō se,* γ *hina egeiromenǭ syllalę̄ soi*). LXX implicitly vocalizes *tnḥh* as *tanḥehā* and adds *wthyh*, a doublet of *tnḥh*. The conflation may be OG or later. It is unlikely (*contra* CSP) that *ʾtk* "with you" by itself would have been expanded into an independent clause; cf. Syr. DNF suggests that words might have been lost by homeoteleuton, since six of seven cola in vv 20–22 end with *kaph*.

In the LXX, the imperatives make the verse into a continuation of the exhortation rather than a promise of reward. The addition of *hina* in γ means that the *purpose* of wisdom's protection is her "conversation," which alludes to the study of wisdom. Wisdom is a reward in and of itself; see the Textual Note to 2:2.

Syr diverges considerably from MT: "(a) And when you go about, join them to you and let them be with you [*ʾqp ʾnwn lk wʿmk nhwwn*]. (b) Keep them that they may keep you [*ṭr ʾnwn dnnṭrwnk*]. (c) And when you wake up, they will be to you (as) a meditation [*rnyʾ*]." Syr resembles LXX in 22a but treats the sentence differently. Syr carries forward the plural of v 21. Syr reflects *wetanḥehā ʾittekā wetihyeh ʾittāk*, as in LXX, but repeating *ʾtk*. For MT's *bškbk*, Syr has *šmrh*, perhaps a dittography of *tšmr*. Syr's *rnyʾ* "object of meditation" relates Heb *tśyḥk* to *śîaḥ* "conversation," "meditation." The variants in (a) and (b) cannot be explained as stylistic or "interpretive," but show a different text. Context and parallelism support MT against all of these variants.

Variants: *tanḥehā wetihyeh ʿittāk* (MT *tanḥeh ʾōtāk*); *šmrh*. (MT *bešokbekā*).

6:23. LXX: "α For a commandment of law (is) a lamp and a light, β and reproof and instruction (are) (the) way of life" (α *hoti lychnos entolē nomou kai phōs* β *kai hodos zōēs elegchos kai paideia*). LXX combines the nouns differently. If retroverted precisely, 23α would be equivalent to *ky nr mṣwt twrh wʾwr wdrk ḥyym tkḥt wmwsr*. CSP suggests that the restructuring, esp. in *entolē nomou*, is the translator's attempt to make a clearer reference to the Mosaic law. There does seem to be an allusion to Torah in LXX's use of *nomos*, but an interpreter could elicit that from the MT as well, as did subsequent Jewish interpreters. The LXX seems to represent a somewhat different vorlage, as reconstructed here. There is nothing to commend the *correctness* of these variants.

Syr (b): *mksnwtʾ wmrdwtʾ* = *twkḥt wmwsr* = LXX; = Tg^L^.

Variants: *mṣwt twrh wʾwr* (MT *miṣwāh w^e^tôrāh ʾôr*); *tkḥt* (sg.) (MT *tôk^e^ôt*, pl. cstr.); *wmwsr* (MT *mûsār*).

6:24. LXX: "^α^ to preserve you from a married woman [*apo gynaikos hypandrou*] ^β^ and from the slander [*diabolēs*] of the tongue of a stranger (fem.) [*glōssēs allotrias*]." (The last phrase may mean "from a strange tongue.") Heb *ʾšt rʿ* is vocalized as *ʾēset rēaʿ*, lit. "(the) wife of a neighbor" (cf. v 29) for MT's *ʾēšet rāʿ* "a woman of evil." LXX's implicit vocalization fits the context better, though we would expect *ʾēšet rēʿekā* "the wife of your neighbor," and we should probably emend thus (*kaph-mem* haplography); see the Commentary. The MT vocalization *rāʿ* would have been occasioned by the loss of the *kaph*.

The LXX understands "smoothness" (*ḥlqt*) as slander rather than as flattery or seduction, perhaps influenced by the homonym *ḥlq* "division." Various idioms using *ḥ-l-q* in regard to speech are associated with dishonesty (Ps 5:10; 12 [LXX 11]:3, 4). In Prov 28:23, however, LXX uses *glōssocharitountos* "flattering."

Syr: *ʾnttʾ byštʾ* ("evil woman") = MT. Like the LXX, Syr understands "smoothness" as slander (*mʾkl qrṣʾ*). Tg = Syr but substituting *šʿwʾ* "smoothness" for "slander."

6:25. LXX: "^α^ Let not the desire of beauty overcome you, ^β^ nor let yourself be caught by your eyes, ^γ^ nor let yourself be seized by her eyelids" (^α^ *mē se nikēsę̄ kallous epithymia* ^β^ *mēde agreuthę̄s sois ophthalmois* ^γ^ *mēde synarpasthę̄s apo tōn autēs blepharōn*). LXX in 25^α^ is paraphrastic. It implies that though you cannot prevent feeling desire, you *can* refuse to let it control your actions. Similarly, the *Mekilkta* to Exod 20:17 interprets the tenth commandment as prohibiting the *carrying out* of forbidden desires.

Line ^β^ is OG and ^γ^ a later adjustment to MT 25b (Lag.). CSP believes that either the original translator or a later hand added ^γ^ as an explication of the second line, but it does not explicate. In ^γ^, "nor let yourself be seized" is diathesis. LXX implies that the real danger comes from within, from man's unruly lusts.

Syr: "(a) Do not desire her beauty in your heart, (b) and do not be caught by her eyes [*wlʾ ttṣyd bʿynyh^pl.^*], (c) and do not let her capture you by her eyelids [*wlʾ tšbyk btmryh^pl.^*]." Syr reproduces the doublet under the LXX's influence but changes "your eyes" to "her eyes" in b, approximating MT. Tg omits Syr's 25b.

6:26. The LXX uses *timē* ("value") to translate *bʿd*, probably for the wordplay on *timias* "precious" (namely, *psychas* "souls").

Syr's *dwmyh* "the likeness (of a harlot)" should be emended to *dmyh* "the price of" (Pink.). Tg apparently saw the former and translated, strangely, *mṭwl ddmyʾ* . . . "because a harlotrous woman resembles a loaf of bread." A variant in ^L^ and other MSS tries to force sense out of this by adding *mltʾ d-* "the word of (a harlot resembles)," picking up the theme of 6:24b.

6:27. LXX and Syr treat *tśrpnh* "be burnt" as active, "burn up."

6:28. LXX expands *gḥlym* into *anthrakōn pyros* "coals of fire"; sim. Syr, *gwmrʾ^pl.^ dnwrʾ*. The verb *tkwynh* is active in LXX.

6:29. LXX: "^α^ Thus the one who approaches [*eiselthōn pros*] a married woman [*gynaika hypandron*] will not go unpunished, ^β^ nor (will) anyone who touches her." LXX divides the verse after *l' ynqh* and thus finds two offenses: approaching a married woman and touching her.

Syr (b): *wqrb lh* "and approaches her," for MT's "touch her"—a cautionary heightening of the warning; cf. LXX. Tg(L) is more explicit: "Thus it is with everyone who goes in to commit adultery with her [*lmygwr ʿmh* L]."

6:30. LXX: "α It is not surprising if one who steals is caught, β for he steals in order to fill his soul, which hungers" (α *ou thaumaston ean halǭ tis kleptōn*, β *kleptei gar hina emplēsę̄ tēn psychēn peinōsan*). (Syr supports *peinōsan* [fem. sg. pres. ptcp.] against the BSV variant, *peinōn* "when he is hungry" [masc. sg. ptcp.].) The verb "is caught" is imported from the next verse to improve the logic, since a thief must be caught before people take note of him. Baum. postulates that LXX had *ky ylkd*, a corruption of *ky ygnwb*, but the translator is paraphrastic here. He adds the notion of the thief's being caught and changes the public's lack of contempt into surprise. He did not want to allow for the possibility that a thief could ever avoid capture and disgrace.

Syr: "(a) One who stole who gets caught is not to be wondered at [*l' lmtdmrw b'yn' dmttḥd dgnb*], (b) for he stole that he may sate his soul [*npšh*], which hungered." Syr follows LXX's interpretation, and Tg follows Syr. (TgL, *l' mlmtdmrw*, is correct; Z has *l' mtrš* "is not crushed.")

6:31. LXX's *halǭ* correctly renders *wnmṣ'* as "caught" rather than "found." To 31b, LXX adds "he will save himself" to explain that the nature of the payment is ransom from vengeance rather than punitive fines or recompense (Baum.).

Syr repeats the subject *dgnb*. Tg ≈ MT.

6:32. LXX: "α But the adulterer, through lack of mind [*phrenōn*], β brings about the destruction of his soul." The LXX restructures the syntax to bring out the causal relationship between mindlessness and destruction.

Syr 32b: *wmḥbl npšh* "and he destroys himself," making MT's *mšḥyt npšw* into a verbal sentence (≈ LXX). Syr joins *hw' yʿśnh* to v 33.

6:33. LXX adds an emphatic *eis ton aiōna* "forever."

Syr repeats *hw' yʿśnh* from 32b by dittography, which it translates *whwyw ʿbd*; thus: "It is he who causes grief to approach him."

6:34. LXX's *kriseōs* for MT's *nqm* suggests that the translator has judicial proceedings in mind (cf. 5:14). He may also wish to avoid the implication that private vengeance is acceptable.

6:35. LXX: "α He will not exchange (his) enmity for any ransom, β and he will not be reconciled by many gifts." The divergences are an attempt to understand MT's difficult *l' yś' pny kl kpr*, lit. "will not lift the face of [i.e., accept] any ransom." Vul adds *pro redemptione* "for redemption."

Syr renders Heb *koper* as *qwrbn'* "oblation" or "sacrificial offering" (only here). It seems that Syr is suddenly changing the subject to God, who will reject atonement offerings in the case of adultery. Tg: "He will not favor anyone who gives him a gift," parsing *kpr* as a ptcp.

Lecture X. 7:1–27

7:1 As in 2:1, Syr translates "with you" as "in your heart" (*blbk*), specifying the place of hiding; likewise in 2:1.

7:1a. LXX: "$^{\alpha}$ Son, honor the Lord and you will be strong, $^{\beta}$ and besides him fear no other" ($^{\alpha}$ *huie tima ton kyrion kai ischyseis,*$^{\beta}$ *plēn de autou mē phobou allon*). This addition interrupts the exhortation with an irrelevant thought and is secondary. The expansion may have been present in the vorlage as *bny kbd ʾt yhwh wḥzq, wmlbdw ʾl tyrʾ ʿwd*; cf. Deut 4:35. Syr omits.

7:2. In 2$^{\beta}$, LXX has *tous de emous logous* ("my words"), as in 4:10 = *dbry* or *ʾmry*, a synonym variant that could occur in either the Heb or the Gk; cf. 3:1b.

Syr *ʿynʾ* "eye" for MT's *ʿynyk* "your eyes."

Variant: *ʾmry* or *dbry* (MT *miṣwôtay*).

7:3. LXX's *platos* ("width" or "flat surface") usually translates *rōḥab* or *merḥāb*. Here it may imply "the entire width" = the entirety (thus too in 3:3 ^{A}, where it is hexaplaric, and in an added phrase in 22:20).

Syr: (a) *bṣwrk*, "on your neck," as in 3:3 (Tg = MT); (b) *lwḥʾ*$^{pl.}$ "tablets," as in 3:3 (for MT sg.).

7:4. LXX restructures the syntax: "$^{\alpha}$ Say that wisdom is your sister, $^{\beta}$ and make prudence an acquaintance for yourself" ($^{\beta}$ *tēn de phronēsin gnōrimon peripoiēsai seautǭ*). Lag. retroverts the last two words to *tqnh* (thus Baum., Toy), but *peripoiein* is not used for *qnh*.

Syr translates, "and call understanding knowledge" (*mdʿʾ* (*maddaʿāʾ*) for MT *mōdāʿ* ("friend")—a mechanical use of the consonantal text which doesn't make much sense. Tg *mwdʿʾ* = MT.

7:5. LXX: "$^{\alpha}$ so that it (she) may keep you from a strange and wicked woman [*gynaikos allotrias kai ponēras*], $^{\beta}$ if she should assail you with words for favor [*ean se logois tois pros charin embalētai*]." In 6:24, the "smoothness" of the woman's words is understood as slander, here as ingratiation. Lag. emends *ponēras* to *pornēs* ("harlot"), but that would not render *nkryh*. Since LXX does not have a distinct gloss for *nokriyyāh*, it substitutes a modifier for it. For unclear reasons, LXX is very peraphrasic in 5$^{\beta}$. The same sentence is handled very differently in 2:16.

Syr combines *zrh* and *nkryh* into *nwkrytʾ* as in 2:16. *mylh*$^{pl.}$, "whose words are seductive." Tg uses *ḥylwnytʾ* "profane" for *zrh*.

The Strange Woman in Proverbs 7

This chapter, esp. in vv 6–17, is replete with paraphrastic liberties (even when the Hebrew is clear), as well as rare words, neologisms, and unique renderings that show the translator to be deliberately reshaping the scene. Many differences stem from the notion that it is the Strange Woman, not the speaker, who is looking out the window.

The loose correspondences throughout this chapter make it an unstable basis for textual retroversion, except when the differences have a clearly mechanical explanation. Few of the LXX's divergences here can be ascribed to textual processes. The fact that such reinterpretation does not require a textual justification is shown by the way that Syr agrees with LXX on the outlines of the narrative while reflecting a vorlage much closer to MT.

Whether or not she is a prostitute, the woman looking out the window in the LXX's rewriting is not Aphrodite Parakyptousa—the Aphrodite who leans out the window. She is not even modeled after this goddess (contrary to Boström 1935: 120–23), for the woman in LXX-Prov 7 is hidden behind a lattice, not on view to passersby.

Contrary to G. Boström [1935: 106], it is certainly not the case that the LXX preserves elements of an older text while the *MT* underwent deliberate changes for the sake of discretion, to avoid revealing the Strange Woman as the Aphrodite figure she supposedly is. (Boström makes several emendations to achieve this effect.) If the original author were worried about the Aphrodite cult, there would be no reason for later scribes to *obscure* the danger.

The syntax of LXX 7:6–10, which must be simplified in English translation, is a long series of relative (participial) clauses dependent on the main clause in 10^{α}.

Throughout this section, Syr shows strong LXX influence but differs in many particulars. In spite of having recourse to the MT, Syr formulates the section as a past tense narrative and has the *woman* looking through the window in vv 6–8. It must be granted, however, that in the consonantal text of the Syr, all the verbs translated as third fem. sg. in that section could as well be first c. sg., as in MT, were it not for the third fem. sfx. of *byth* "her house" in 6a, and that may be an early mistake due to the mention of the woman in v 5.

Tg, as usual, uses Syr as the basis and adjusts toward MT, in this case restoring the first-person narrator. Vul does the same. The details of this adaptation will not be mentioned.

7:6. LXX: "$^{\alpha}$ For from the window, out of her house, $^{\beta}$ she peers onto the plazas [*eis tas plateias parakyptousa*]."

Syr: "For from the window of her house and from the balcony she looked out." (Syr *kssṭrwn* can mean "upper room" as well as "balcony.") Syr follows LXX in making the woman the observer.

7:7. LXX: "for whichever mindless lad she may espy from among (the) foolish youths."

Syr: "And she saw youths, and she observed among the simple and among those who lack a mind" [*wḥzt šbrʾ*$^{pl.}$ *wḥrt bṭllyʾ*$^{pl.}$ *wbḥsyr*$^{pl.}$ *rʿynʾ*]. While following LXX's concept of the scene, Syr attempts to imitate MT's wording, but condenses *bbnym nʿr* to *bṭlyʾ*$^{pl.}$.

Tg, for unclear reasons, has *wtmhyt* "and I was surprised," where MT has *naʿar*.

7:8. LXX, continuing v 7, with reference to the lad: "passing [sg.] by the corner on (the) thoroughfares of her houses [*oikōn autēs*]." The parallelism is collapsed, probably because *yṣʿd* "strides" was missing (cf. Syr). The formal pl. "her houses" is used of the woman's dwelling in 5:8 and of the Excellent Woman's house in 31:27, probably in reference to a stately residential complex.

Syr ". . . who were passing [pl.] in the street next to the corners of the paths of her house." Syr too lacks *yṣʿd*. Syr assumes that this verse continues to describe the plurality of youths mentioned in v 7. Tg uses sg. *ʿbyr* "passing" and restores *yṣʿd* as *mhlk*.

7:9. LXX: "$^{\alpha}$ And speaking [*kai lalounta*] in the evening darkness [*en skotei hesperinǭ*], $^{\beta}$ when (there is) nocturnal silence and darkness [*hēsychia nykterinē ę kai gnophōdēs*]." It is hard to see how the awkward *kai lalounta* arose. It takes the place of but does not translate the missing *yṣʿd* at the end of 7:8. The inner-Gk emendations proposed are farfetched. LXX makes it appear as if the woman is speaking from her window, which is a plausible picture, except that she meets the boy in v 11 and embraces him in v 13. Syr, which also lacked *yṣʿd*, has nothing corresponding to *lalounta*. *hēsychia* might be deriving Heb *ʾyšwn* from *y-š-n* "sleep" (Baum.), but this happens only here.

Syr: "in the evening, at the setting of the sun, in the darkness [*bḥšwkʾ*] of the night and in the gloom [*bʿmṭnʾ*]." Syr's *bḥšwkʾ* = MT, against LXX's "silence." "Setting of the sun" is idiomatic. Tg "in the setting of the day [*ywmʾ*]."

7:10. LXX: "$^{\alpha}$ And the woman meets him, having a harlotrous appearance [*eidos*], $^{\beta}$ which makes the hearts of youths flutter [$^{\beta}$ *hē poiei neōn exiptasthai kardias*]." LXX 10$^{\beta}$ is a guess for MT's *nṣwrt lb* ("hidden of heart"), a notion the translator may have found confusing because, according to 4:23, hiddenness of heart is a virtue. In vv 10–12, the woman has moved into the street without transition.

Syr: "And the woman went out to meet him in the attire [*ʾskymʾ*] of a harlot, which makes the hearts of youths flee [*mprdʾ lbhwn dʿlymʾ$^{pl.}$*]." Syr again combines LXX and MT. Syr's *mprdʾ* "makes flee" is an interpretation of LXX's "makes flutter." Tg ≈ Syr.

7:11. In 11$^{\alpha}$, LXX has *anepterōmenē de estin kai asōtos* ("She is agitated and profligate")—unique renderings of *hmyh hyʾ wsrrt* and probably based on the description of the woman in v 12.

Syr = MT, but using the *ʾswṭyʾ* = *asōtos*, as in LXX, for *srrt*.

7:12. LXX: "$^{\alpha}$ For sometimes [*chronon gar tina*] she roams [*rhembetai*] outside, $^{\beta}$ and sometimes [*chronon*] in the plazas, next to every corner she lies in wait." *rhembetai* is an explanatory addition. LXX makes a single sentence of the words from the second *pʿm* to the end of the verse; perhaps it lacked the *waw* of *ʾeṣel*.

Syr follows LXX in structuring the verse as two independent clauses and in supplying "roams" (*phyʾ*) in the first. MT's *kl* "all" is omitted. Tg has *pnytʾ dʾyʾ* "suitable corner." Perhaps "*every* corner" seemed exaggerated.

7:14. LXX's present tense, "today I pay [*apodidōmi*] my vows," indicates that she is about to bring the offerings.

Syr lacks *ʿālay*. Tg = MT.

7:15. LXX: "$^{\alpha}$ For this reason I went forth to an encounter with you. $^{\beta}$ Longing for [*pothousa*] your face, I found you." LXX has a bipartite structure lacking in MT.

Syr, 15a = MT. 15b: "for I was expecting [*mskyʾ hwyt*] to see you, and I found you." Syr too creates a bipartite verse. Tg, 15b: "for I was waiting to perceive [*lrgšʾ*; see Pink.], and [^{L} + I said] I will guide you [*ʾydbrynk*]." The reason for this divergence is unclear. Pink. suggests that Tg read *w^{e}ʾōṣîʾekkā*.

7:16. In 16$^{\beta}$, LXX's *estrōka* ("I have spread") is often thought to represent *hṭty* (*hiṭṭîtî*) "I have stretched out" for MT's hapax *ḥṭbwt* (BHS et al.). But the correspondence is unparalleled, and the retroversion distant graphically from the MT. Probably LXX is dealing with an unknown Heb word by creating a parallel for *tetaka* ("I have spread").

Syr (b) *qrmth* "I have spread it" for *ḥtbwt* = LXX.

7:17. In LXX$^{\beta}$, *ton de oikon mou* ("my house") is a misreading of *ʾhlym* (actually "aloes") as *ʾohŏlî* "my tent," understood to mean house, as in Gen 9:21, 27; 31:33, etc.

7:18. LXX: "$^{\alpha}$ Come and let us enjoy affections [*philias*] till dawn. $^{\beta}$ Come on [*deuro*], and let us roll ourselves [*egkylisthōmen*] in love [*erōti*]!" *Egkyliesthai,* lit. "roll in" or "roll up in," has the abstract sense of "be involved in," but the connotation of physically rolling is vividly germane here and not lost. The verb is used in translating *mtgll bʿwntyw* ("roll in his sins") in the Gk of Sir 12:14.

Syr 18b: "and we will embrace each other in desire" [*wnʿpq ḥd lḥd brgtʾ*]—understanding MT's *ntʿlsh* similarly to LXX; + *waw.* Tg^{Z} *nʿsyq ḥd lḥd* "busy ourselves with each other in desire," supplying a vaguer verb out of delicacy.

Vul translates *ddym* (MT *dōdîm*) *uberibus* "breasts"; cf. 5:19.

7:19. In LXX, "my man" replaces the blunt "the man"; sim. Syr.

7:20. LXX: $^{\beta}$ . . . *d i' hēmerōn pollōn* "after many days," a loose rephrasing of the rare *keseʾ*. Aq, correctly: *eis hēmeran panselēnou* "at the day of the full moon." Thus Vul.

Syr (b) *wlywmtʾ*$^{pl.}$ *hw sgyʾʾ*$^{pl.}$ ("and after many days") LXX. The Peshiṭta elsewhere uses Syr *kesaʾ* ("full moon") for Heb *keseʾ*, but here it is following the LXX closely. Tg has *lywmʾ dʿydnʾ* "on the appointed day," apparently also uncertain about the meaning of *keseʾ*.

7:21. LXX: "$^{\alpha}$ She led him astray by much conversation [*pollę̄ homilią*], $^{\beta}$ and by traps [*brochois*] from her lips she drove him aground [*exōkeilen auton*]." (*Homilia* can also mean "instruction.") LXX replaces the benign-sounding "smoothness" (*ḥlq*) with the scarier image of traps, perhaps influenced by the imagery (but not the wording) of 6:2. The translator had already eliminated smoothness of speech from the woman's features in 7:5. This motif is lacking in LXX 2:16 and 5:3 as well (in the latter, for textual reasons). It seems that the translator thought that verbal smoothness was not an unambiguous indicator of danger and deceit, because mellifluous rhetoric can be a worthy talent.

Syr: "(a) *bswgʾʾ dmlyh*$^{pl.}$ "by her many words." The translator may have been puzzled by the ironic mention of the woman's *leqaḥ* "doctrine."

7:22. LXX: "$^{\alpha}$ And he followed her, bird-brained, $^{\beta}$ as an ox is led to slaughter, $^{\gamma}$ and as a dog to bonds . . ." ($^{\alpha}$ *ho de epēkolouthēsen autę̄ kepphōtheis,* $^{\beta}$ *hōsper de bous epi sphagēn agetai,* $^{\delta}$ *kai hōsper kuōn epi desmous*). According to Liddell-Scott, the rare *kepphōthoushthai* means something like "be ensnared like a stormy petrel (?)," hence "be easily cajoled," or "become feather-brained." LXX is reading *ptʾm* "suddenly" as *p^{e}tāʾîm* "silliness" and translating it by an elegant word. Lacking a clue as to the meaning of *ʿks*, the translator introduced a

Gk cliché, "a dog to bonds" (Gerleman 1956: 33). MT's *mwsr* (*mûsar*) is implicitly vocalized *môsēr* "bond" (from *ʾ-s-r*). LXX read *ʾyl* ("stag") for MT's *ʾwyl* and spliced it, in spite of the syntax, to v 23. In $^{\beta-\gamma}$, LXX's vorlage had *kšwr ʾl ṭbḥ ywbʾ* (*yûbāʾ*) *wkʿks ʾl mwsr.*

Vul $^{\gamma}$ *et quasi agnu lasciviens* "like a lamb sporting." Vul obtains the meaning of *ʿks* from Isa 3:16 (correctly treating the word in the present verse as an inf.) and construes *ʾl* (MT *ʾel*) as *ʾêl* "lamb," properly "ram" (Pink.).

Syr "(a) And he went [*ʾzl hwʾ*] after her like a simpleton [*šbrʾ*], (b) and like an ox that goes to a butcher [*dʾzl lwt ṭbḥʾ*]. (c) And like a dog to bondage [*ʾswrʾ*]." Line (c) = LXX. At the end of the verse, *ʾwyl* is joined to v 23. Tg^{L} ≈ Syr, while Tg^{Z} adds *dsyklʾ* "fool" to the end of (c), awkwardly adjusting to MT.

Variants: *ywbʾ* (MT *yābôʾ*); *ʾyl* (= *ʾayyāl*) (MT *ʾĕwîl*; see next verse).

7:23. LXX: "$^{\alpha}$ or as a stag struck by an arrow in the liver. $^{\beta}$ And he hurries as a bird to a snare, $^{\gamma}$ not knowing that he runs for [= at the cost of] life" [$^{\alpha}$ *ē hōs elaphos toxeumati peplēgōs eis to hēpar,* $^{\beta}$ *speudei de hōsper orneon eis pagida,* $^{\gamma}$ *ouk eidōs hoti peri psychēs trechei*]. In $^{\alpha}$, LXX attaches *ʾyl* (*ʾayyāl*) (MT *ʾĕwîl*) from the end of 22. To make sense of the impossible syntax that resulted in 23b, the translator turned 23^{β} into a main clause. In $^{\gamma}$, *trechei* ("runs") is added to provide a verb for the indefinite "he" (MT *hwʾ*) that ends the verse.

Syr: "(a) and like a stag into whose liver an arrow flies [*wʾyk ʾylʾ dmprḥ gʾrʾ bkbdh*]. (b) And he hurries like a winged creature to the snare. (c) And he does not know that it is to the death of his soul that he is going [*dlmwtʾ hw dnpšh ʾzl*]." Though similar to LXX in the beginning of the verse, Syr differs in 23a, where *mparaḥ* might be an attempt to imitate the sound of Heb *y^{e}pallaḥ*, and in 23c, which supplies a verb for "he." Syr is thus independent support for *ʾyl*.

Tg = Syr, but using *ṣyprʾ* for Heb *ṣpwr* where Syr has *ḥywt knpʾ* "winged creature." Since Tg takes the trouble to adapt to the MT in this detail while staying with Syr in the treatment of the last word in MT's v 22, it too probably had *ʾyl* rather than *ʾwyl* at the end of 22c.

7:24. LXX adjusts MT's "sons" to "son" for the sake of consistency, as in 5:7 and 8:32.

Syr (≈ Tg) = MT.

7:25. OG omits v 25b by parablepsis from *ʾl* to *ʾl*; it is restored in hexaplaric MSS (according to SyrH, from Theod). The verse is present in Syr and Tg.

7:26. LXX: "$^{\alpha}$ For, wounding many, she has cast (them) down [*trōsasa katabeblēken*], $^{\beta}$ and innumerable are those whom she has murdered." LXX treats *ḥllym* as a third fem. sg. verb, perhaps because of the unusual syntax, with the elided relative pron.

Syr treats *rbym* as an adjective, "many slain" [*swgʾʾ dqṭylʾ$^{pl.}$*] = Tg. The versions did not recognize *rbym* as the predicate.

7:27. LXX again reads *yrdwt* (G) as a causative, "lead down"; see 5:5.

Syr: "The ways of her house are the ways of Hades, which go down to the chambers [*twnʾ$^{pl.}$*] of death." The first "ways" (*ʾwrḥtʾ$^{pl.}$*) smooths out the awkward predication (lit. "her house is the ways . . .") and does not necessarily witness to *ntybwt byth*. The latter is a possible emendation, but not required syntactically here as it is in 2:18. Tg adjusts the syntax to MT and explains the meaning of "death" as *qytwnʾ qbrʾ* "chamber of the grave."

Interlude D. 8:1–36

8:1. LXX: "$^{\alpha}$ You [sg.] shall call wisdom, $^{\beta}$ so that prudence may respond to you" ($^{\alpha}$ *sy tēn sophian kēryxeis* $^{\beta}$ *hina phronēsis soi hypakousę̄*). The second person in 1a is a misreading of the ambiguous *tqrʾ*. The effect is to make the audience the youth addressed in 7:1–5. LXX's "respond to you," for MT's more indefinite "gives her voice," is influenced by the mutuality formula of 8:17.

Syr: "For this reason [*mṭl hnʾ*] call wisdom [*ḥkmtʾ ʾkrz*], and understanding will answer you." The imperatives resemble LXX's parsing of the verbs as second person sg. Syr too connects the verse to the preceding chapter (cf. the Gk variant *dio su . . . kēryxon* ^{MSS}). The causal conjunction interprets the call to Lady Wisdom as a rejection of the Strange Woman's appeal. Tg makes wisdom the subject of the verb as in MT but keeps the causal connection to the preceding by starting with *mṭwl hyknʾ*.

8:2. LXX: "$^{\alpha}$ For [*gar*] she is upon the lofty heights; $^{\beta}$ and she stands between [*ana meson*] the roads." The causal *gar* is not quite suitable. MT's *ʿly drk* is omitted, perhaps by condensation with *ntybwt*. The versions agree in construing *byt* as if it were Aram (Syr) *beyt* "between."

Syr adds "wisdom" at the end of 2a for clarity and transposes *ʿly drk* with *byt ntybwt*.

8:3. LXX: "$^{\alpha}$ For by the gates of the princes she sits; $^{\beta}$ in the entrances she praises herself" [$^{\alpha}$ *para gar pylais dynastōn paredreuei*, $^{\beta}$ *en de eisodois hymneitai*]. LXX 8:3$^{\alpha}$ = 1:21$^{\beta}$. 3$^{\beta}$ ≈ 1:20α. The puzzling *dynastōn* is transferred from 1:21, where it represents *śrym*, a distorted dittography of *šʿrym*. *Paredreuei* too is based on 1:21a, q.v. Vul: *iuxta portas civitatis* "next to the city gate"—free but correct.

Syr: "(a) At the gates, by her mouth she cries [*bpwmh qryʾ*]. (b) And at the entrances of the gates of the cities [*dkrkʾ*$^{pl.}$; ^{MSS} om.] she praises herself [*mštbḥʾ*]." "Of the cities" is explanatory. "Praises herself" for *trnh* follows LXX. *Bpwmh qryʾ* is a misunderstanding of *lpy* as if meaning "by [her] mouth." MT's *qrt* is equated with Syr *qᵉrāt*, from *qrʾ*; cf. LXX 9:3. Heb *qeret* is translated by *mdyntʾ* "city" in Prov 11:11, by *qrāʾ* again in 9:14 (Syr 15) and Job 29:7, and perhaps by *ʾemar* "said" in 9:3. Tg (with ^{L}): *bpwmh dqryyʾ* "at the entry of the city." Syr's Dt *mštbḥʾ* could be passive (as in v 31), but the reflexive is more appropriate here, since Wisdom is the speaker.

8:4. Before 4b, *proiemai emēn phōnēn* ("and I send forth my voice") is added for syntactic parallelism.

Syr (Tg) prefixes *wʾmrʾ* "and she says" to introduce the quotation, because it does not understand *trnh* as a *verbum dicendi*.

8:5. For Heb *hbynw lb*, LXX has *enthesthe kardian* "take in heart" (i.e., intelligence). This is commonly assumed to represent *hkynw lb* (Jäger Lag., BHS, etc.), but *hēbîn* is closer than *hēkîn* to Gk *entithenai*, which means "place in," "incorporate," "instill." Cf. *Test. Naph.* 2:2 and 3 Macc 5:28, where *entithenai* means implant something in the mind. "Heart" is here the intelligence or understanding itself (see Commentary) rather than the organ of understanding.

Syr reformulates the difficult *hbynw lb* as *nstklwn blbhwn*, "will understand [or "may they understand"] in their hearts," again using a future for an impv. and making this a purpose clause dependent on the preceding. The result of this reformulation is that Wisdom does not speak to the foolish (who, by definition, would ignore her call), but addresses only people in general. Tg 5a = MT; 5b = Syr.

8:6. In 6^{α}, LXX adds *mou* "(hear) *me*." For the difficult *ngydym*, LXX has *semna* "august things," relating it to *nāgîd* "prince." Similarly Theod: *hēgemonika* "authoritative things"; Vul: *de rebus magnis*, "about great things." In 6^{β} LXX has: "and I will bring forth [*anoisō* ^{BS}] straight things from (my) lips," (^{A} has *anoigō* "I open up," closer to MT). "Bring forth" is an accommodation to the seemingly awkward predication in MT, lit. "and the opening of my lips is straight things" (compare the adjustment in LXX 6:34).

Syr *šwmʿwny* "hear me" = LXX. *Ngydym* is translated *šryrtʾ* "truth," probably by association with Heb *neged* "straight ahead"; see the Commentary.

8:7. In 7^{β}, LXX's *ebdelygmena de enantion emou cheilē pseudē* ("and abominated before me are deceitful lips") represents a variant consonantal vorlage: *wtʿbty śpty ršʿ*; cf. 11:20. But rather than speaking of wickedness in general (*rešaʿ*), LXX focuses on verbal deceit, thereby creating a neater antithesis (influenced by 12:22). The circumlocution "abominated *before me*," which reduces anthropopathism (see on 3:32), is here applied to Wisdom, as if she were a divinity.

For "my palate," Syr has *pwmy* "my mouth," the usual term for the organ of speech. Syr (Tg) = LXX in 7b.

Variant: *tʿbty* (MT *tōʿăbat-*).

8:9. LXX's *enōpia* "in front of" parses *nkḥym* (*n*^{e}*kōḥîm*) as an adj. from the adverb *nōkaḥ* "before."

Syr renders this word as *glyn*$^{pl.}$ "are revealed," again working directly from the Heb text but taking exegetical direction from the LXX. Syr 9b is *lʾynʾ dṣbʾ lmdʿ ʾnyn*$^{pl.}$ "to the one who wishes [var. pl.] to know them." This means that wisdom's words are accessible to anyone desirous of wisdom and not only to the educated. Tg = Syr.

8:10. LXX's *paideian* = *mwsr* "instruction," for MT's *mûsārî*. 10^{γ} *anthaireisthe de aisthēsin chrysiou katharou* ("Prefer knowledge to pure gold") is OG (Lag., Fritsche). Though absent in LXX^{BS*}, it is further from the MT and shows a Heb variant: *bḥr* (parsed as impv.) for *nbḥr*. Syr, moreover, was influenced by 10^{γ}. LXX 10^{β} is an adjustment to MT.

Syr (Tg^{L}) 10a: *mrdwtʾ* = *mwsr* = LXX. Syr 10b: "and choose for yourselves [*wgbw lkwn*] knowledge more than refined gold." This conflates the variants *bḥr* (LXX) and *nbḥr* (MT), though possibly the former was just borrowed from LXX.

Variants: *mwsr* (MT *mûsārî*); *bḥr* (MT *nibḥār*).

8:11. Syr begins with a doublet of 10b and entangles it with 11a: "Because wisdom is better than refined gold and better than precious stones." As it stands, it gives a reason, albeit tautologous, for 10b. Tg = MT.

8:12. LXX's *kai ennoian* = *wmzmwt,* as in 1:4.

For Heb *šknty,* Syr has *bryt* "I created" (var. *qnyt* "acquired"). Syr's *bryt* is probably an error for *dryt* "I dwell" (*dolath* resembles *beth* in estrangelo). Syr's *bryt* is witnessed by Tg^{L} but adjusted to MT in Tg^{Z}, *dryt*." (Tg^{L}'s *bryt* can be explained only by mechanical dependence on the Syr as we have it and thus original. Tg^{Z}'s reading is therefore secondary within the Targumic transmission, even though *dryt* was probably the original Syr.) In 12b, Syr's *wydʿtʾ wtrʿytʾ* reflects a copula, like LXX. Tg^{Z} = MT.

Variant: *wmzmwt* (MT *m^{e}zimmôt*).

8:13. LXX: "$^{\alpha}$ The fear of the Lord hates [*misei*] injustice, $^{\beta}$ insolence, and arrogance and the ways of wicked people [*hodous ponērōn*]. $^{\gamma}$ I hate [*memisēka,* perf.] twisted ways of evildoers [*diestrammenas hodous kakōn*]." In $^{\alpha}$, *misei* construes Heb *śnʾt* as *śānēʾt,* a fem. ptcp. (sim. Vul). "Way" (*drk*) is pluralized. The translator accidentally transferred *hodous* from $^{\beta}$ to $^{\gamma}$. CSP thinks this was done for the sake of rhyme, but *logous* would have served just as well. (In fact, Lag. emends to *diestrammenous logous*.) The transfer happened in the reverse direction in 11:20.

Syr (Tg): (a) *snyʾ byšwtʾ* "hates evil" = LXX. The awkwardness of 13a witnesses to Syr's direct exegetical dependence on the LXX.

8:14. LXX's *asphaleia* for *twšyh* is unparalleled. For *ʾny bynh* "I am understanding," LXX's *emē phronēsis* and Syr's *dyly hw swklʾ* appear to witness to *ly bynh,* which actually occurs in 2 MSS K-R. In all cases, however, the use of the possessive may arise through imitation of the parallel clauses.

Tg condenses the verse into a single sentence: "Mine are counsel and forethought and understanding and power" (Tg^{L}).

8:15. LXX translates *yḥqqw* etymologically as *graphousin* "inscribe."

Syr's *mṭlty* ("because of me") for Heb *by* ("through me") in 15a makes wisdom an agent as well as a means of justice. Syr renders *yḥqqw* as *bdqyn* "examine" or "declare," as often. Emendation to *yḥqrw* (Baum.) is not necessary. Tg 15a = Syr. In 15b, Tg^{Z} moralizes: *wšlṭwny mšyḥyn bṣdqwtʾ* "are anointed in righteousness."

8:16. In $^{\beta}$ LXX has *tyrannoi di' emou kratousi gēs* ("and through me potentates control the earth"), perhaps reading *wndybym by yšpṭw ʾrṣ* (possibly without *by* "through me"), though these are not the usual lexical correspondences. Vul's *decernunt* "they discern" also has a verb for MT's *špṭy. kl* "all" is not represented.

There is an inner-Masoretic variant for the last word in 16: *ʾāreṣ* in Hillel Codex and some editions (witnessed by LXX, Vul, and several medieval commentators) and *ṣedeq* in Leningradensis, Aleppo, and many editions. Both variants (*dzdyqwtʾ* and *dʾrʿʾ*) appear in seventh-century Syr MSS. Tg's *tryṣwtʾ* = *ṣedeq*.

Variants: *yšpṭw* (MT *šōp^{e}ṭê*); *ʾāreṣ* and *ṣedeq*, both Masoretic.

8:17. LXX and Syr support the qeré.

Ketiv *ʾhbyh* (= *ʾōhăbeyhā* "those who love her"); qeré *ʾōhăbay* ("those who love me").

8:18. The versions interpret *hwn ʿtyq* "enduring riches (?)" variously: LXX: *ktēsis pollōn* ("the acquisition of many things"); Sym: *bios palaios* ("ancient life," apparently reading *ḥym* [or Aram *ḥyn* = *ḥayyîn*] for *hwn*); Theod: *hyparxis palaia* ("ancient wealth"); Vul: *opes superbae* ("splendid works"); Syr *qnynʾ ʿtyqʾ* ("ancient property"); Tg^{L}, unusually: *wmmwnʾ wmzlʾ* "and wealth and fortune."

8:19. LXX adds *karpizesthai* ("enjoy my fruit") in 19^{α} and *kreissō* ("better than") in 19^{β} to reduce ellipsis. "Precious stone" (*lithon timion*) is a guess for *paz*, as in Pss 19[18]:11 and 21[20]:4. Vul *lapide pretioso*.

Syr's *dhbʾ snynʾ* ("refined gold") combines *ḥrwṣ* and *paz*. Tg has *wmdhbʾ dʾwbrwzyn* "unalloyed gold," a doublet for emphasis.

8:20. LXX adds a verb, *anastrephomai* ("I walk about"), at the end of 20^{β} to avoid ellipsis.

8:21. To "I will fill" at the end of the verse, LXX adds *agathōn* ("with goods") for specificity.

For MT's *yeš* "possessions, Syr has *sbrʾ* ("hope") and Tg *šnyʾ sgyʾtʾ* ("many years"), both tending to mute the materialism of Wisdom's promises.

8:21a. LXX: "$^{\alpha}$ If I tell you things that happen daily, $^{\beta}$ I shall (also) remember to recount things of old." The prosaic addition provides a transition to the new topic. Because of the historical importance of this passage and the divergences of the LXX from the apparent original meaning, 8:21a–31 will be translated in full.

8:22. LXX: "The Lord created me the first of his ways for his works" (*kyrios ektisen* ^{ASB} [var. *ektēsato* "acquired"] *me archēn hodōn autou eis erga autou*). Like modern scholars, the versions are divided on whether the meaning of *qnny* is "created" (OG, Syr, Tg) or "acquired" (LXX ^{MSS}, Aq, Sym, Theod; Philo; Vul *possedit*). Baum. discusses the role these variants played in Christological debates about whether Sophia/Christ was created (as the Arians held) or preexistent (thus the Athanasians). Heb *qānāh* is translated by *ktizein* only here and in Gen 14:19, 22. (The standard rendering [61×] is *ktasthai*.) CSP is probably right that the purpose of the choice of *ektisen* was to underscore God's solitary role in creation.

LXX (= Sym and Vul) takes *drkw* (MT *darkô*) as plural. LXX's *eis* construes *qdm* as a preposition, like Aram *qᵉdām* (which, however, is not rendered *eis*), but *eis* is difficult here. The phrase *eis erga autou* (when read without reference to the Heb) seems to imply that wisdom was created *for*—that is, to serve—God's works. LXX omits *mʾz* ("of old"), which became awkward after *qdm* was translated *eis*. The motive for the omission of *mʾz* cannot be to show that wisdom was not around "from all eternity" (CSP) because that is not implied by *mʾz*. The LXX consequently condenses the couplet into a sentence.

In his Epistle CXL, *ad Cyprian*, Jerome transliterated 22a as *adonai canani bresith dercho*. *Bresith* agrees with the likely adverbial function of *rʾšyt* (cf. Vul *initium*) and is some evidence for a variant *brʾšyt*.

Syr: "The Lord created me [*brny*] at the beginning [*bryš*] of his creations [*bryth*$^{pl.}$], and prior to [*wmn qdm*] all his deeds [*ʿbdwhy*$^{pl.}$]." Syr understands *rʾšyt* adverbially; it does not necessarily read *brʾšyt* (BHS). "His creations" is an (accurate) paraphrase of *drkw* "his way(s)." Syr + *klhwn* "all" (his works); om. *mʾz* (= LXX). Tg adjusts to MT.

8:23. LXX: "$^{\alpha}$ Before the ages he founded me, $^{\beta}$ in the beginning ($^{\alpha}$ *pro tou aiōnos ethemeliōsen me,* $^{\beta}$ *en archē* . . ." (LXX joins 23b syntactically to 24). The major change is the diathesis from passive to active in vv. 23–25, which focuses attention entirely on God as sole creator (CSP). *Ethemeliōsen me* = *nsdty* (*nōsadtî*) for MT's difficult *nissakti*. Though *kaph-dalet* interchanges are not well attested, they are possible in the square script. A good example is the qeré-ketiv variant *yd/yk* in 1 Sam 4:13 (assuming that the change took place prior to the use of final letters). Sym *prokecheirismai* for *prokechrismai* "anointed before."

In vv 23–25, LXX levels out MT's various ways of saying "before" by repeating *pro* + genitive.

Syr: "(a) And before the ages [*wmn qdm ʿlmʾ*$^{pl.}$] he established me [*ʾtqnny*], and from the beginning, and before he would establish [*ntqn*; var. *nʿbd* "make"] the earth." Syr ≈ LXX. Syr separates *mrʾš* and *mqdmy*. Syr adds a verb (*ntqn*) in 23b to fill the ellipsis. Note that Syr uses *tqn* of other acts of creation in vv 23, 25, and 27 and probably finds this a reasonable way to deal with the obscure *nskty* too. Tg uses *ʾyttqnyt* "I was established" for *nskty*, influenced by Syr's *ntqn* but conforming to MT's passive.

Variant: *nsdty* (*nōsadtî*) (MT *nissaktî*).

8:24. LXX: "$^{\alpha}$ before making the earth, $^{\beta}$ and before making the abysses, $^{\gamma}$ before the springs of the waters came forth" [$^{\alpha}$ *pro tou tēn gēn poiēsai,* $^{\beta}$ *kai pro tou tas abyssous poiēsai,* $^{\gamma}$ *pro tou proelthein tas pēgas tōn hydatōn*] (joined with 25). The first part of LXX 24$^{\alpha}$ (Rahlfs) = MT 23b. LXX supplies verbs in $^{\alpha}$ and $^{\gamma}$. In $^{\beta}$, the verb *poiēsai* is made to apply to the abyss. That this change was not intended to skirt the suggestion that wisdom was "begat" or "born" (*ḥôlāltî*) is shown by the use of *gennạ* in the next verse. MT's *nkbdy* is not represented. It seems unlikely that LXX would have ignored the word, whose basic meaning ("honorable") was known and not inappropriate. It seems that LXX read *nbky* (see Commentary) and combined *nbky* and *mʿynwt* (both meaning "fountains") in *tas pēgas*. The change from *nbky* to MT's *nkbdy* could result from *b/k* metathesis plus *d/b* (or *d/k*) near-dittography. (On *d/b* confusion, see LSF §131.)

Syr *ʾtyldt* ("I was born") retains the anthropomorphism of *ḥwllty*. Tg = Syr, but Tg^{Z} substitutes a more cautious *ʾytqnyt* "I was acquired." Syr 24b: *myʾ*$^{pl.}$ *bmbwʿ*$^{pl.}$ "waters in fountains," perhaps reading *nbky mʿynwt*; cf. LXX. Tg etymologizes *nkbdy* nicely: *mʿyny ʿšwny dmyʾ* "fountains, strongholds of water" = MT.

Variant: *nbky* (MT *nikbaddê*).

8:25. LXX: "$^{\alpha}$ before the mountains were sunk [*hedrasthēnai*], $^{\beta}$ before all hills, he begot [*gennạ*] me." (After $^{\alpha}$, LXX^{S} inserts *kai plasthēnai tēn gēn* "and the earth was formed" from Ps 90[89]:2). The use of *gennạ* for *ḥwllty* hardly reduces possible mythic overtones (contrary to Küchler 1992: 137). On the contrary, treating *ḥwllty* as an active verb sharpens them. *Gennạ* serves as the main verb of vv 24 and 25. The present tense of *gennā* in a series of aorists is puzzling (the aorist is used elsewhere in this narrative). The translator may have seen *ḥwll ʾty*, which he understood as *ḥōlēl ʾōtî*. Vul uses *iam concepta eram* "I was now conceived," in spite of the incongruity.

Syr = MT, using *ʾtbṭnt* "I was conceived/born" for *ḥwllty*.

8:26. LXX: "$^{\alpha}$ The Lord made lands and uninhabited places $^{\beta}$ and the populated heights of that which is under the heaven" ($^{\alpha}$ *kyrios epoiēsen chōras kai aoikētous* $^{\beta}$ *kai akra oikoumena tēs hyp' ouranon*). LXX supplies an explicit subject, "Lord," and omits *ʿd lʾ* "before," possibly because of homeoarcton with the *ʿayin* of *ʿśh*. The omission makes the description of creation start here in this verse. The phrase *oikoumena tēs hyp' ouranon* ("the populated [heights] of that which is under the heavens") is a double translation of *tbl* "inhabited land," while *ʿprwt* is ignored. "Uninhabited places" seems to understand *ḥwṣwt* as "fields" (see the Commentary). (In Job 5:10, *ḥwṣwt* is rendered *tēn hyp' ouranon*.)

Syr (= Tg^{L}) has *nḥlʾ*$^{pl.}$ "wadis" for *ḥwṣwt*; sim. Vul *flumina*. This is a puzzling interpretation not learned from LXX. Tg^{Z} has *ʾšqqy* "streets," adjusting to MT.

For Leningradensis's *ʿoprôt-* (with *qameṣ qaṭan*, from an unattested **ʿoper* or **ʿoprāh*), Aleppo and many MSS correctly read *ʿaprôt-* (from *ʿāpār*), as in Job 28:6.

8:27. LXX: "$^{\alpha}$ When he prepared the heaven, I was present with him , $^{\beta}$ and when he marked out his throne upon the winds" ($^{\alpha}$ *hēnika hētoimazen ton ouranon symparēmēn autō̢* $^{\beta}$ *kai hote aphōrizen ton heautou thronon ep' anemōn*). *Symparēmēn* ("was-with-and-near") emphasizes Wisdom's proximity to God. MT's "there" (*šām*) is paraphrased as "with/near him," since no place has been mentioned for "there" to point to. "His throne" for *ḥwg* ("circle") is based on the idea that the heavens are God's throne (Isa 66:1) and that he is located on the "circle of the heavens" (*ḥûg šāmāyim*; Job 22:14). LXX's "winds" for *thwm* "abyss" seems to be a reflex of the same picture. The deeps are not the "logical" place for God's throne (CSP). Note that different words for "when" are used in this and the next verse. Since no interpretive motive is relevant in cases like this, we see the translator's inclination to variety for its own sake, one which CSP (*passim*) documents extensively.

Syr *ʿmh* "with him" (for *šm*) LXX.

8:28. LXX: "$^{\alpha}$ When he made sturdy that which is above the sky, $^{\beta}$ and when he made firm the springs of that which is beneath the sky" (*hēnika ischyra epoiei ta anō nephē, kai hōs asphaleis etithei pēgas tēs hyp' ouranon*). . . ." In 28$^{\alpha}$, *asphaleis etithei* does not necessarily reflect *bʿzwzw* (with the third masc. sg. suffix) for MT's *bʿzwz* (BHS), because the translator would be obliged to supply a subject in some form. The circumlocution "that which is beneath the sky" is used for *thwm* "abyss" (only here) for the sake of a neater antithesis to "that which is above the sky" (itself a mistranslation).

8:29. LXX: [$^{\alpha}$, $^{\beta}$ lacking]. "$^{\gamma}$ And [+ *hōs* when ^{B}] he made sturdy [*ischyra epoiei*] the foundations of the earth." LXX 29$^{\gamma}$ corresponds to MT v 29c. "Made sturdy" represents *bḥzqw* (*b^{e}ḥazz^{e}qô*) in the vorlage, for *bḥwqw* "when he engraved." (The former is correct; see the Commentary.)

MT 29ab is missing in OG. The reason for the loss is not evident. The mythological background of the line is already submerged in the Hebrew and would not call for suppression. The omission was probably accidental, homeoarcton from *bśwmw* to *bbḥwqw*. DNF observes that if the lines were written stichometrically, the words could be vertically aligned, which would facilitate parablepsis. The lines are supplied in ^{ASs} etc. from Theod (asterisked in SyrH): "$^{\alpha}$ When he set his commandment [*akribasmon*] on the sea, $^{\beta}$ and waters should not transgress his mouth." CSP (245) does not identify these lines as hexaplaric.

Vul has a double interpretation of 29a: *quando circumdabat mari terminum suum* "when he compassed the sea with its limit" (cf. Tg), followed by *et legem ponebat aquis* "and set a law to the waters" (cf. Syr).

Syr and Tg = MT, but interpreting *ḥwq* differently. Syr: *kd sm nmws' lym'* "When he set a law for the sea." Tg: "When he set [*šwy*] for the sea its borders [*tḥwmyh*]." By prefixing a *waw* to the last clause, *wkd ʿbd* "and when he made," Syr makes it—and perhaps all the "when"-clauses starting with 27b—circumstantial to v 30. Tg *lyh* "him" for *pyw* "his mouth."

Variant: *bḥzqw* (MT *b^{e}ḥuqqô*).

8:30a. LXX: "$^{\alpha}$ I was with him, arranging [$^{\alpha}$ *ēmēn par' autǭ harmozousa*]." Gk *harmozousa* may mean "suiting myself (to him)," or "arranging (namely, all things)," or "fitting together" (CSP), or (literally) "harmonizing," "being in tune" (Gerleman 1950: 26). In Nah 3:8, the place name "Amon" (in No-Amon, i.e., Thebes) is rendered *harmosai* (corrected to *Amōn* in a doublet). In Ezek 23:42, *qwl hmwn* is translated *phōnēn harmonias*, as if reading *qwl 'mwn*. *Harmozein* for Heb *'mwn* thus belongs to the LXX lexicon. Nevertheless, the choice of this verb in the present passage seems to echo the Pythagorean notion of the "music of the spheres," which is called *harmonia*. Gerleman (1956: 57) finds in this verse the Stoic conception that wisdom brings all things into harmony. This is possible, but need not come directly from Stoic philosophy.

Hexaplaric glosses of *'mwn* are *estērigmenē* ("set firm," "steady") (Sym, Theod) and *tithēnoumenē* "nursed" (Aq). Both treat *'mwn* as a pass. ptcp.

Vul: (a) *cum eo eram cuncta conponens* "I was with him arranging everything." This is based on the LXX but does not necessarily capture the intended meaning of *harmozousa*.

Syr: (a) "I was creating with him" (*ʿmh mtqn' hwyt*). Syr makes 30a the main clause for the clauses starting in v 27b or 28.

> (27a) When he created the heavens I was with him. (27b) And when he made the circuit on the surface of the abyss, (28) and when he strengthened the clouds above, and when he strengthened the fountains of the abyss, (29) (and) when he placed a law to the sea, and the waters do not transgress his mouth, and when he made the foundations of the earth, (30) I was creating with him.

(Since 29 does not begin with a *waw*, it may begin a new sentence.) This construction makes Wisdom an active participant in creation, as God's assistant, and not only as present during the work. *Mtqn*ʾ "create" is the verb used consistently in this chapter for God's creative acts.

Tg 30a: *whwyt ṣydwy mhymnt*ʾ [^{L}, correctly; var. *mhymnwt*ʾ ^{Z}].I was with him (as) a trusted one. Tg parses *ʾāmōn* as a passive from *ʾ-m-n* "be firm."

8:30bc. LXX: "$^{\beta}$ I was the one in whom he rejoiced. $^{\gamma}$ Daily I rejoiced in his presence at all times . . ." ($^{\beta}$ *egō ēmēn hę̄ prosechairen* $^{\gamma}$ *kath' hēmeran de euphrainomēn en prosōpǭ autou en panti kairǭ*). LXX paraphrases (correctly) the meaning of the somewhat opaque *wʾhyh šʿšwʿym*, lit. "I was delights," making it a clearer verbal sentence. (Compare how LXX treats the nominal predicates in 7:27 and 8:6.) LXX awkwardly attaches the adverbial *ywm ywm* to the following clause. LXX's verbs in $^{\beta}$ and $^{\gamma}$ suggest a more decorous, celebratory type of rejoicing, as in Job 38:7.

Syr (= Tg^{Z}): (b) "In me he was rejoicing [*ḥdʾ-hwʾ*] every day, (c) and at all times I was rejoicing before him" ≈ LXX.

8:31. LXX: "$^{\alpha}$ while he rejoiced, having completed the inhabited world," $^{\beta}$ and he took pleasure in the sons of men" ($^{\alpha}$ *hote euphraineto tēn oikoumenēn syntelesas*, $^{\beta}$ *kai eneuphraineto en huiois anthrōpōn*). (The verbs *eupraineto* and *eneuphraineto* are transposed in ^{BS}.) LXX makes v 31 a temporal clause dependent on v 30, thereby associating v 31 with God's rejoicing at creation, in accordance with Gen 1:31. The creation passage is also the source of *syntelasas*, used in Gen 2:1–2 for *klh* (Dp, D). LXX's *tēn oikoumenēn* fuses the synonyms of *tbl ʾrṣw*. For MT's *wšʿšʿy* "my delighting" in $^{\beta}$, LXX read *wšʿšwʿyw* (or *wšʿšwʿw*, parsed as pl.), lit. "his delights" (BHS), but rephrased it as a verbal clause. The assumption that God was the one who rejoiced led the translator to override the fem. gender of *mśḥqt*.

Syr (b) "and I was praised [*wmštbḥʾ hwyt*] by the sons of man"—harking back to v 3. Tg too understands *šʿšʿy* as "praise" but renders it with a noun, *šbwḥyy* "my praises," to conform to MT.

Variant: *wšʿšwʿyw* or *wšʿšwʿw* (= *w*^{e}*šaʿăšuʿāyw*) (MT *w*^{e}*šaʿăšuʿay*).

8:32–34. At this point, LXX^{B} proceeds in the order MT 32a, 34a, 32b, 34b–36, omitting 33. LXX's order makes sense but is inferior in literary balance. Verses 32b and 33 are missing from OG (^{BS}) due to parablepsis from *wʾšry* to *ʾšry*. They are supplied in the Hexapla (^{A}, SyrH with an asterisk). The OG thus read 32a, 34a, 34b, 35, 36. The following notes proceed in the MT order.

8:32. LXX (MT 32a): "Now therefore, son, hear me," using sg. for MT's pl. "sons," as in 5:7; 7:24. Syr (Tg) = MT. For MT 32b, see LXX 34$^{\beta}$.

8:33. Missing in OG. Syr = MT, with *tṭʿwn* "err" for MT *tprʿw*.

8:34. LXX: "α Fortunate is the man [*anēr*] who shall hearken [*eisakousetai*] to me, $^{\beta}$ and the man [*anthrōpos*] who shall keep [*phylaxei*] my ways, $^{\gamma}$ being watchful [*agrypnōn*] at my doors daily, $^{\delta}$ guarding [*tērōn*] the posts of my entryways." LXX 34$^{\beta}$ = MT 32b. Syr (Tg) = MT, but using finite verbs for *lšqd* and *lšmr*. Tg returns to an inf. for the latter.

8:35. LXX: "$^{\alpha}$ For my exits are the exits of life, $^{\beta}$ and favor is readied with the Lord [$^{\alpha}$ *hai gar exodoi mou exodoi zōēs*, $^{\beta}$ *kai hetoimazetai thelēsis para kyriou*]." LXX$^{\alpha}$ corresponds to the ketiv *mṣʾy mṣʾy*, which it implicitly vocalizes *moṣāʾay* *mōṣāʾê*- "my exits are the exits of (life)" (= Syr *mpqny*$^{pl.}$ *mpqnʾ*$^{pl.}$). Using these consonants but vocalizing *mōṣ*^{eʾ}*ay mōṣ*^{eʿ}*ê* gives better sense: "for those who find me are finders of life." *Exodoi* may refer either to exits or to the ways of escape from difficulty. GELS proposes the latter, but 1:20 supports the former. MT's *ypq* is parsed as a passive (*hetoimazetai*, only here), and its sense is surmised from context. (The word is inconsistently translated in the LXX.)

Qeré: *mōṣ*^{eʾ}*î māṣāʾ* "my finder has found (life)." Ketiv: *mṣʾy mṣʾy*, to be vocalized *mōṣ*^{eʾ}*ay mōṣ*^{eʿ}*ê* "my finders are finders of (life)." The pl. in the ketiv is awkward before the sg. of the verb in 35b, and 18:22 supports the qeré.

Ketiv *mṣʾy mṣʾy*; qeré *mōṣ*^{e}*îʾ māṣāʾ*.

Variant: *mṣʾy* (MT qeré *māṣāʾ*).

8:36. LXX has pl. in 36a and omits "all" in 36b. Syr follows LXX, while Tg has sg. in 36a.

Interlude E. 9:1–18

9:1. LXX's *hypēreisen* ("set down") reflects *hṣbh*, i.e., *hiṣṣîbāh*, for MT's *ḥṣbh* (*ḥāṣ*^{e}*bāh*) "hewed." LXX om. "her" in "her pillars." Syr's *wʾqymt* ("set up") supports LXX's Heb *hṣbh*, as does, independently, Tg's *ʿtydt* ("prepared"). This is one of the very few places where Tg attests independently to a non-Masoretic reading.

Variant: *hṣbh* (= *hiṣṣîbāh*) (MT *ḥāṣ*^{e}*bāh*).

9:2. LXX: "$^{\alpha}$ She has slaughtered her sacrifices; $^{\beta}$ she has mixed her wine into a krater [*eis kratēra*], and she has prepared her table." "Into a krater" was added to elaborate the picture of a *symposium* for the Hellenistic reader. (CSP rightly observes that *kratēra* is too generally used to be a specific relation to Hellenistic mystery cults, *contra* Sandelin 1986: 70.) Gk's "krater" does not represent a lost *bks* (*b*^{e}*kōs*) (Lag.), because *kôs* "cup" (always plene in the absolute) is almost always translated *poterion* (as in Prov 23:31), never *kratēr*, which was the bowl from which cups were filled.

Syr (b): *ptwryh*$^{pl.}$ ("her tables"), which suggests a larger banquet.

9:3. LXX: "$^{\alpha}$ She sent forth her manservants, $^{\beta}$ summoning [f. sg.] with a high proclamation to the krater, saying [f. sg.]" ($^{\alpha}$ *apesteilen tous heautēs doulous* $^{\beta}$ *sygkalousa meta hypsēlou kērygmatos epi kratēra, legousa*). The masc. *doulous* for the fem. pl. *nʿrwt* may reflect the translator's notion of propriety or his assumptions about which servants would be sent out; cf. Matt 22:3. *Meta hypsēlou* draws the notion of "high" from *mrwmy*, while *kērygmatos* parses *qrt* (MT *qāret*) as a form of *qrʾ* "call." Cf. 8:3. *Kratēra* was copied from v 2. *Legousa* is probably a transitional addition (cf. 9:15) rather than a second rendering of *qrt*.

Syr: "(a) And she has sent forth her manservants [*ʿbdyh*$^{pl.}$] (b) that they might cry out upon the heights and say." Syr follows LXX in changing "maids" into manservants, but then smooths out an apparent unevenness by having *them* doing the calling. The difficult phrase *ʿl gpy mrwmy qrt* is simplified as "on the heights." A *verbum dicendi* is added for transition, as in 8:4.

Tg has "(sends) her girls/maidservants" (*tlythʾ*) = MT, but makes them the subject of the verb *dtqryyn* "that they might call," as in Syr. The final phrase is rendered *rmtʾ ʿšyntʾ dnṣyrn* (^{L}), "fortified heights which are guarded," picturing an acropolis.

9:4. LXX omits *lw* "to him" (homeoarcton).

Syr: *lwty* ("to me") for *hēnnāh* "hither." Syr's *wēʾmar leh* parses MT's *ʾmrh* as first person, which accords better with the first line. Tg = MT.

9:5. LXX adds *hymin* "(mixed) for you."

9:6. LXX: "$^{\alpha}$ Abandon folly and live, $^{\beta}$ and seek prudence that you may live, $^{\gamma}$ and keep understanding straight through knowledge" ($^{\alpha}$ *apoleipete aphrosynēn kai zēsesthe,* $^{\beta}$ *kai zētēsate phronēsin hina biōsēte* [$^{BS^*}$ om. *hina biōsēte*] $^{\gamma}$ *kai katorthōsate en gnōsei synesin*). Heb *ptʾym* is (correctly) translated an abstraction ("folly") by LXX and the Three. LXX 6^{β} is a doublet of $^{\alpha}$ and corresponds to MT 6a as its obverse ("seek prudence" is equivalent to "abandon folly"). On this technique, see the note on 1:17. If anything is secondary, it is line $^{\alpha}$. Line 6^{β} is a "free rendering" of MT 6b (CSP). CATTS says that *gnōsei* = *bdʿt* for MT's *bdrk,* but this is distant graphically. Rather, *b^e^derek* is understood as "by means of" and rendered by Gk *en*. MT's *ʾšrw* is equated with *yšr* "go straight."

In $^{\alpha}$, in place of *kai zēsesthe,* MSS $^{BS^*A}$ have *hina eis ton aiōna basileusēte* "that you may rule forever," an expansion based on Wis 6:21 (Lag.) and reflecting the notion that Wisdom's words are (as in Wis Sol) addressed to the world's rulers.

Syr: (b) *wʾwrḥʾ tryṣtʾ ʾtrʿw* "and think in the right way." Syr does not recognize the lexeme *ʾiššer* "go (in a path)," but translates it differently the three times it has that meaning: "think" (9:6b); "envy (4:14b); and "rejoice" (23:19b). These are all based on the notion of "consider/declare fortunate," which is its basic sense in 3:18 and 31:28. The LXX has influenced the rendering here: *tryṣtʾ* ≈ *katorthōsate*. Tg = MT.

9:7. LXX $^{\alpha}$ = MT. $^{\beta}$ [in Rahlfs] "He who rebukes the wicked harms himself" (*elegchōn de ton asebē mōmēsetai heauton*). A doublet in several minuscules (23, 68, 109, 147, 157, 151, 252, 295, 297) suggests a different interpretation, namely that the rebukes hurt him who is chastised, not the rebuker: $^{\gamma}$ *hoi de elegchoi tǭ asebei mōlōpes autǭ* "and the rebukes to the wicked are bruises to him." The same interpretation is reflected in Syr, perhaps independently. SyrH has both, giving the second the obelus.

Syr: "(a) The punishment of the wicked gives him dishonor, (b) and the evildoer's (own) blemish rebukes him" [(a) *mrdwtʾ lbyšʾ yhbʾ lh ṣʿrʾ* (b) *wmks lʿwlʾ mwmh*]. Syr assumes that the one hurt by chastisement is the one who receives it and therefore thinks that "to him" refers to the evildoer. Tg ≈ MT.

9:8. LXX translates *lēṣ* broadly as *kakous* "bad men"; sim. Syr *byšʾ* "bad man. LXX uses a variety of terms to translate *lēṣ*, all of them implying arrogance or wickedness, but not specifically mockery. Tg = MT.

9:9. LXX: $^{\alpha}$ "Give the wise man an opportunity [*aphormēn*]," supplying a dir. obj. for "give"; sim. Syr *ʾptʾ* "opportunity," Vul *occasionem*. LXX parses *lqḥ* (MT *leqaḥ* "teaching") as if it were an inf. and translates *prosthēsei tou dechesthai* ("and he will receive even more"). The same phrase in 1:5a is handled differently. Syr's *ywlpnh* ("his learning") moves closer to MT. Tg has *ʾlyp* "teach" for "give" in 9a.

9:10. LXX: "α The beginning of wisdom is the fear of the Lord, β and counsel [*boulē*] of holy ones [*hagiōn*] is understanding. γ ["10a" in Rahlfs] For to know the law is (the part of) a good intellect [*to gar gnōnai nomon dianoias estin agathēs*]." There is considerable inner-LXX variation in this verse. The use of *boulē* "counsel" for "knowledge" (MT *daʿat*) may show that the translator has in mind the counsel that saints provide; cf. Syr. The word *hagioi* may mean either (human) saints (e.g., Ps 16[15]:3; 34[33]:10) or angels (e.g., Ps 89[88]:6, 8; Job 5:1). The former is probably intended here, since it is the saints who give counsel; and see Wis 6:10, quoted later. Line γ is a doublet. It has the obelus in SyrH, and Lag. considers it the older translation of MT 10b. Toy, however, calls it a gloss by a "legalistic scribe," whereas Seeligmann (1953: 179) considers it a midrashic expansion based on Prov 13:15 that identifies wisdom with study of Torah. It certainly has that function, but wisdom was identified with Torah before LXX-Prov, and the expansion could be the work of the original translator (thus CSP) no less than a later scribe. In γ, MT's *qdwšym* is understood as "holy matters," hence "the Law." Wis 6:10 says that "those who observe holy things in a holy way shall become holy" (playing on cognate forms of *hosia*). γ is reused in LXX-Prov 13:15β (or possibly comes from there).

Syr (b): "knowledge of saints [*zdyqʾ*$^{pl.}$]." In other words, fear of God is defined as the knowledge that the saints possess; = MT. Tg = MT, but with "God" for "Lord."

9:10a = LXX 10$^{\gamma}$.

9:11. LXX *toutǭ gar tǭ tropǭ* "for in this way" = *ky bh* for MT *ky by*. The change (probably occurring in the Hebrew) was consequent upon the insertion of vv 7–10, which interrupt Wisdom's speech. The fut. pass. *prostethēsetai* ("will be added") for MT's *wywsypw* (H-stem) remedies the lack of a subject.

Syr (= Tg^{L}) *bh* (= LXX) for MT's *by*. Tg^{Z} has *by*, adjusting to MT.

Variant: *bh* (= *bahh*) (MT *bî*).

9:12. LXX is expansive: "α Son, if you become wise, you will be wise for yourself and for your neighbors, β but if you prove [*apobęs*] evil [*kakos*], you alone will draw up [*anantlēseis* = *an antlēseis*] evils [*kaka*]." LXX adds "son." The phrase "and for the neighbors" is a cautionary addition, lest one think that the wise man benefits *only* himself. MT's *tiśśāʾ* "you will bear" is understood (inaccurately) as *drawing up*—metaphorically drawing up evils as one draws water. *Kakos* and *kaka* are added in order to place the contrast between α and β on an ethical axis. Syr is very close to the LXX.

Addition 1. 9:12a–12c

9:12a. LXX: "α He who relies on deceits—he shepherds the winds. β This one will pursue a flying bird" (α *hos ereidetai epi pseudesin houtos poimanei* [*poimainei* ^{BSc}] *anemous*. β *ho d'autos diōxetai ornea petomena*). (^{S} lacks β.) Addition 1 is based on a Heb vorlage, as the following notes argue. The Heb vorlage of this verse had, approximately, *twmk šqr yrʿh rwḥ, whwʾ yrdp ṣpwr mʿwpptt* (or *ʿph*).

Syr: "He who prates [*srb*] deceitfully shepherds the winds and pursues the fowl of the sky." *Srb* ("brag," "prate," "contradict") corresponds to Gk *thrasus* "overconfident" and Heb *gbhn* "haughty" in Sir 4:29. Here, *srb* must represent a form of *erizein* "to quarrel," perhaps *erizetai* or an itacistic *ereizetai*, an error for *ereidetai*. (Compare the inner-LXX variants *erisai/ereisai* in Gen 49:6 and the *ereidei/erizei* variants in Prov 29:23, discussed by Barr 1974.)

Variant: additional verse, perhaps *twmk šqr yrʿh rwḥ, whwʾ yrdp ṣpwr mʿwpptt* (or *ʿph*).

9:12b. LXX: "$^{\alpha}$ For he has abandoned the roads of his own vineyard, $^{\beta}$ and has strayed (from) the paths of his own field" ($^{\alpha}$ *apelipen gar hodous tou heautou ampelōnos* $^{\beta}$ *tous de axonas tou idiou geōrgiou peplanētai*).

Axonas is an etymologizing translation of *mʿgly* (or *mʿglwt*), understood as "axles," hence "wagon"; cf. 2:9, 18. The appearance of this word here supports the hypothesis of a Hebrew vorlage, for an original Gk composition would have used a more usual word for "paths." The Strange Woman's paths according to 5:6 are *ouk eugnōstoi* "not well known."

Further evidence for a Hebrew vorlage is the awkward middle *peplanētai* + accus. (This verb in mid./pass. can govern the accus. of place and mean "wander *about in*" [Liddell & Scott 1940: 1411a], but that would not make sense here, since the man in question has *left* his proper territory.) The Gk looks like a mimetic rendering of *tʿh mʿgly* (or *mʿglwt*). Hebrew, however, requires a *m(in)* in this construction. So while the awkwardness in the Gk allows us to reconstruct its vorlage as *tʿh mʿgly-*, we have to suppose that the latter resulted from a haplography for *tʿh mmʿgly*.

Syr "(a) For he has abandoned the way of his vineyard, (b) and has neglected the paths of his husbandry [*wṭʿʾ šbyly*$^{pl.}$ *pwlḥnh*]. . . ." "Husbandry" (*pwlḥnʾ*) is the usual meaning of Gk *geōrgion*, namely "cultivation," "husbandry." But *geōrgion* can also mean "field" (cf. 24:30; 31:16), which is the sense required here by parallelism and context. The Syr saw an ambiguous word and chose the wrong sense. This misunderstanding shows that Syr is entirely dependent on the Gk in this passage, since the Syr translation of Heb *śdhw* would have been *ḥaqleh*, not *pwlḥnʾ*.

Variant: additional verse, perhaps *ky ʿzb drky krmw, u(m)mʿgly śdhw tʿh*.

9:12c. LXX: "$^{\alpha}$ He traverses a waterless desert $^{\beta}$ and a land assigned to droughts; $^{\gamma}$ and he gathers barrenness with (his) hands" ($^{\alpha}$ *diaporeuetai de di' anydrǭ erēmou* $^{\beta}$ *kai gēn diatetagmenēn en dipsōdesin* $^{\gamma}$ *synagei de chersin akarpian*). It is difficult to reconstruct a Heb vorlage for 12c, esp. for $^{\gamma}$. The description of the desert is influenced by LXX Jer 2:6b; note esp. *en tę̄ erēmǭ* and *gę̄ anydrǭ kai akarpǭ* in that verse. Prov 9:12c is probably an inner-Gk extension of 12b, to teach us that the deceitful man has chosen a barren, fruitless land in place of his own field and vineyard.

Syr "(a) to travel in a wasteland [var. path] without water. (b) And away from that which is trodden he travels in a parched land. (c) He too acquires nothing" ([a] *lmrdʾ bḥwrbʾ* [var. *bʾwrḥʾ*] *dlʾ myn*$^{pl.}$. [b] *wmn ʾydʾ ddryšʾ rdʾ bṣhyʾ*. [c] *ʾp hw nknš lʾ mdm*). (The variant *bʾwrḥʾ* is supported by the fem. *ʾydʾ*.) Syr is a free treatment of Gk. Syr 5:6 says that the Strange Woman's paths are "a trackless wasteland and unknown."

Addition 1 as an Interpretation of the Strange Woman

There are two major interpolations in the LXX of chapter 9, 9:12a–12c (Addition 1) and 9:18a–18d (Addition 2). These introduce different allegorical interpretations of the chapter.

The notes previously mentioned several reasons to suppose that a Hebrew scribe introduced 9:12a–12b in LXX's vorlage as a hermeneutic guide to the chapter. Verse 12c was probably added in the Greek.

Addition 1 is a somewhat disjointed remonstrance against trusting in deceits. The "deceits" warned against are not mundane frauds, such as chicanery in business dealings, for to rely on them does not mean leaving one's own territory. The author does not specify the deceits, thereby allowing the warning to be applied to all temptations of foreign origin. The most relevant referent is foreign doctrines and beliefs,[237] since these are something that one might choose to rely on, the antitheses of what one *should* rely on, namely the true wisdom (3:18), which has been granted Israel.

Addition 1 serves as a pivot between the two invitations, Wisdom's and Folly's. Though vv 1–12 contains later insertions (vv 7–10 + 12), in the composite text as represented in the MT, the entirety of the passage belongs to Wisdom's invitation. The hypothesized Hebrew author of 12ab and the Greek supplementer of 12c would have had the composite text. Addition 1 points back to vv 1–12 and identifies wisdom as the man's own vineyard and field, which he has abandoned. It points forward to the folly described in vv 13–18 by allusion to the foreign wasteland the foolish man chooses. Addition 1 thus introduces and guides the interpretation of the following passage. Additions meant to introduce a subsequent passage are not common, but see Prov 1:17[a] and 8:21a.

Addition 1 speaks of a man who places his faith in deceits, abandoning the paths of his own fertile land to wander in bleak alien territories. The text (in vv 13–18) proceeds to describe the guiles of the shameless woman Folly, who invites men to her house, where death awaits them.

This figure can hardly be dissociated from the fraudulent attractions described in the wasteland metaphor in Addition 1. The connection is strengthened by the images of vineyard and field.[238] "Vineyard" and "field" are elsewhere metaphors for a man's own wife, the source of legitimate delight and fruitfulness, as opposed to the barren and forbidden "terrain" of another woman. These connotations of sexuality associate the motifs of Addition 1 with the two women, the legitimate and the illegitimate, of this chapter, but their purpose is only to help

[237]Cook refers to "foreign cultural perspectives during the inter-testamental period, which endangered [the Jews'] way of life." One challenge was the "explicit emphasis placed on the individual in Greek culture" (CSP 271). LXX 9:12 addresses this.

[238]Vineyards are allusions to women in Cant 1:6; 8:11; and Isa 5:1. In all these verses, there is a complex interplay of literal and metaphorical senses. The garden is a figure for the maiden, particularly with respect to her sexuality, in Cant 4:12; 5:1; and 6:2.

organize the chapter's metaphorical system. The erotic associations are quickly transferred to the relevant realm: the terrain of the spirit.

9:13. LXX: "α A foolish and brazen woman comes to lack (even) a morsel; β she knows no shame" (α *gynē aphrōn kai thraseia* β *endeēs psōmou ginetai,* γ *hē ouk epistatai aischynēn*). LXX understands *ʾšt ksylwt* as "foolish woman" rather than as an abstraction. For *ptywt*, LXX had *pt* or (pl.) *ptwt*, which it understood as "bread," hence "morsel," then added *endeēs* to make sense of the sentence. *Aischynēn* reflects *klmh* (k^e*limmāh*) for MT *māh* (Jäger). The image of a brazen woman refusing to be ashamed (*hikkālēm*) is found in Jer 3:3.

Syr: "A woman lacking sense is seductive [*mšdlnyʾ*] and does not know shame." Syr lacks *hmyh*, unless *ḥsyrt rʿynʾ* combines *ksylwt* and *hmyh*. *Mšdlnyʾ* ("seductive," "flattering") is an etymological rendering of *ptywt*. Syr *bhttʾ* ("shame") = LXX = Heb *klmh* (k^e*limmāh*). Tg is based on MT, but clarifies *māh* (unusual in the sense of "anything") as *ṭbtʾ* "good."

The versions, including Vul, construe *ʾšt ksylwt* as "foolish woman" rather than as an abstraction. The subsequent verses are ambiguous as to whether the speaker is an actual or a figurative woman.

Variant: *klmh* (MT *māh*).

9:14. LXX gives the gist of Heb *ʿl ksʾ mrwmy qrt* as β *epi diphrou emphanōs en plateiais* "on a chair, publicly, in the plazas."

Syr has (b) *ʿl kwrsyʾ rmʾ* "on a high chair," taking the image from LXX but diverging from its wording. MT's *qrt* ("city"), understood as "call" in Syr 8:3, is elided here as in 9:3. Tg ". . . *ʿl qrsyʾ rmʾ wʿšynʾ* "a high and strong chair"; cf. v 3.

9:15. In LXX *drk* "way" is not represented in OG (it is supplied in A as *hodon*), but it is probably implicit in *pariontas* "passing by" (CSP).

In 15b, Syr has *dtryṣyn*$^{pl.}$ *ʾrḥthwn*$^{pl.}$ ("whose paths are straight"), a more usual idiom; sim. Tg. At the end of the verse, Syr adds *wʾmrʾ* ("and says") as a connective.

9:16. For *pty* "innocent," "callow," LXX has a much harsher *aphronestatos* "most foolish." In β, *parakeleuomai legousa* ("I exhort, saying") is an expansive rendering of *wʾmrh* that maintains the first sg. (w^{e}*ʾōm*^{e}*rāh*), as in LXX 4a.

Syr *wʾmr* "and I will say" = w^{e}*ʾōm*^{e}*rāh* = LXX (as in 9:4b). Tg puts the entire sentence in the third person and restructures the syntax: "Whoever is foolish comes (*nʾtʾ* L) to her [*lwth*], and (likewise) the senseless one. And she says to him."

9:17. LXX: "α Take hidden breads with pleasure, β and the very sweet water of theft" (α *artōn kryphiōn hēdeōs hapsasthe* β *kai hydatos klopēs glykerou*). LXX transposes the clauses and treats *ynʿm* as an adv. and *ymtqw* as an adj. (Vul renders both as comparative adjectives.) The imperative "take" is prefixed and the syntax restructured to avoid the notion that "hidden breads" and "stolen waters" really *are* pleasant and sweet.

Syr (Tg) = MT.

9:18. LXX: "α But he does not know that the earthborn perish with her, β and he meets with the springboard (?) of Hades" (α *ho de ouk oiden hoti gēgeneis par' autę̄ ollyntai,* β *kai epi peteuron hą̄dou synantą̄*). On *gēgeneis* "earthborn," "mortal," see the note on 2:18. Since the ghosts are not actually "there" (*šām*), namely in the foolish woman's house, the literal-minded translator modifies this to say that mortals *perish* there (cf. 2:18–19; 7:26–27). *Synantą* parses *qrw'yh* as an active verb from *q-r-h* "meet." The LXX hapax *peteuron* [var. *petauron*] for MT's *bʿmqy* "in the depths of" is puzzling. It means "springboard" or "tightrope" (GELS). CSP translates "snare" without explanation. Are we to picture a springboard such as was used in Greek athletics? Emending to the dissimilar *stegastron* "covering" (Lag.) is no help.

Syr translates *dgnbr'*$^{pl.}$ *lwth 'bdyn* ("But he does not know that mighty men perish with her"). This follows LXX's interpretation but uses *gnbr'*$^{pl.}$ for *rp'ym*, as usual in Syr (based on Deut 2:1). Tg (a): "But he does not know that she has brought down [*'pylt*] mighty men [^{L} *gnbry*] there." Tg equates the Rephaim with the Nephilim and adds *'pylt* to play upon the root *n-p-l* (Healey, p. 27).

Addition 2. 9:18a–18d

9:18a. LXX: "$^{\alpha}$ But get away [*apopēdēson*]; tarry not in the place, $^{\beta}$ nor direct your eye toward her."

The command not to gaze at the foolish woman (as LXX understands *'št ksylwt*) shows that the author of Addition 2 thinks of her attraction in sexual terms, though that is not necessarily implied in the description of Lady Folly and is not the come-on she uses here.

Syr = LXX. Syr's *šwr* "leap" imitates one of the senses of *apopēdan* and shows Syr's dependence on LXX.

9:18b. LXX: "$^{\alpha}$ For thus you may pass through strange water $^{\beta}$ and cross over a strange river" (*houtōs gar diabēsę hydōr allotrion,* $^{\beta}$ *kai hyperbēsę potamon allotrion*). ^{BS*} lack β. The omission is accidental, since the other verses of the addition are couplets.

Syr = Gk (confirming *diabēsę* as opposed to LXX^{S*} *diabēsetai* and the existence of $^{\beta}$).

9:18c. LXX: "$^{\alpha}$ From strange water keep away, $^{\beta}$ and from a strange spring drink not." This expands on the theme of foreign dangers by replacing the foolish woman by another metaphor. The "strange water/river" must represent foreign cultures, not foreign woman (in spite of the woman/water metaphor in 5:15–18), for the author would not wish the reader to "pass through" or "cross over" the woman in question.

J. Cook (CSP 284) identifies the waters with the River Styx, but the Styx is fatal in the crossing, not in drinking or touching it, nor would the reader be advised to pass through the River Styx. Cook believes that the Strange Woman throughout is Greek philosophy.

Although v 18b has informed us that we may safely "pass through" strange water, 18c insists that we *keep away* from it and avoid imbibing it. This apparent contradiction makes sense if strange water is a cipher for alien cultures generally rather than foreign doctrines or philosophies, for one could avoid the latter without "passing through" them.

Jews of the Diaspora must dwell within alien societies. They must traverse them in their life course. The goal is to survive the passage untouched, as the Israelites passed through the Red Sea (Exod 14:29) and as they pass through waters in the new Exodus (Isa 43:2). While negotiating foreign "seas" and "rivers," one must keep a distance from the water and avoid the temptation to imbibe their cultures.

Syr = Gk.

9:18d. LXX: "$^{\alpha}$ so that you may live a long time [*hina polyn zēsęs chronon*], $^{\beta}$ and years of life be added to you" (based on LXX 9:11$^{\beta}$).

Syr: "So that many days and years of life may be added [*nttwspn*$^{pl.}$] to you." Syr reformulates the line under the influence of v 11.

Addition 2 as an Interpretation of the Strange Woman

A Greek origin is likely for Addition 2, since it is aimed at a Diaspora audience (see later). Since its interpretation of the foolish woman is not in evidence elsewhere in Prov-LXX, Addition 2 was probably introduced after the original translation.

This addition to chapter 9 interprets the foolish woman of 9:13–18 as a symbol for another, more abstract evil—some aspect of foreign life—which it redefines by means of a further symbol, strange waters.

Foreignness is the principal issue in both additions, but with a significant difference. According to the images in Addition 1, it is possible simply to stay home and avoid the foreign realm, whereas in Addition 2, traversing an alien area seems to be an inescapable, or at least accepted, fate, and the goal is to do so unharmed. This difference makes sense if we explain the "desert" of Addition 1 as foreign belief and the "water" of Addition 2 as foreign culture or, more generally, as the experience of life in foreign lands.

For Addition 1, native and foreign are regions of the intellect, whether in philosophy or in religion. (Compare "bad waters" = heretical ideas, in *ʾAbot* 1:11.) For Addition 2, the symbolic geography maps life in the Diaspora generally. The addition offers a modus vivendi for the Diaspora: Pass through the culture but don't assimilate it.

Both additions assume, independently, that 9:13–18 refers to foreignness. The source of this assumption is twofold: The foolish woman is equated with the Strange Woman described in chapters 2, 5, and 7, and her "strangeness" is understood to be ethnic foreignness. The latter idea was not derived from the OG. In the OG, *allotria* has the same sense as in Hebrew: a woman not your own, or *hē mē idia*, as *nokriyyah* is accurately translated in 5:20.

BIBLIOGRAPHY

* Works marked by an asterisk are referenced by name of author only, ad loc. unless otherwise indicated.

Diacritics are used in names for precision in the following listing but not in the body of the Commentary.

I. EGYPTIAN SOURCES

◆

The major sources of Egyptian Wisdom literature and their places of publication are listed below. Parentheses indicate texts that are related to, but not within, the genre of Wisdom Instructions.

Eclectic texts are usually referenced by the section numbering (in capital roman numerals) in the KÄT editions.

For an extensive translation of Egyptian literature, see M. Lichtheim, *Ancient Egyptian Literature* (3 vols.) 1973–80.

For dating and contents, see the Introduction, X.

Amenemḥet I: Pap. Millingen; Pap. Sallier I, II etc. Volten 1945, Helck 1969. AEL 1.135–39, AW 169–77. (This is a political apologia in the guise of a Wisdom Instruction.)

Amenemḥet Priest of Amon (tomb autobiography): Helck, *Urk. 18. Dyn.*, nos. 1408–1411. AW 389–91.

Amenemope: Pap. BM 10474 et al. Lange 1925. AEL 2.146–63, AW 234–56.

Amennakhte: Various ostraca (only the introduction and two maxims remain). Posener 1955 and COHL III, no. 1596; Beckenrath *SAK* 1983 (numbering according to Posener's edition). See also Bickel and Mathieu 1993: 33–35. AW 231–33.

Anchsheshonq: Pap. BM 10508. Glanville 1955; LEWL 70–92; quote taken from AEL 3.159–84; also AW 257–91.

Anii: Quack 1994. Five papyri, one writing tablet, and some nine ostraca. Unless otherwise noted, references are to Pap. Boulaq IV ("B") in Quack's edition.[239] Commentary in Volten 1937. Text, transl., commentary: Quack 1994. AEL 2.135–46, AW 196–217.

Brooklyn Wisdom Papyrus: Pap. Brooklyn 47.218.135. Jasnow 1992.

Pap. Chester Beatty IV: HPBM, pls. 37–44. A miscellany of Wisdom texts. AW 218–30.

Djedefḥar (or Ḥardjedef): NK ostraca and wooden tablet of Late Period. Brunner-Traut 1940; Posener 1951, 1966; Helck 1984. AEL 1.58–59, AW 101–3.

Duachety (or Chety; first part called the "Satire of the Trades"): Pap. Amherst (Eighteenth Dynasty); Pap. Sallier II, Pap. Anastasi VII, and Pap. Chester Beatty XIX (Nineteenth Dynasty); plus wooden tablets and scores of ostraca. Brunner 1944; Helck 1970a. AEL 1.184–92, AW 155–68.

[239] Note that Suys's cols. 1–10 (the numeration commonly used in translations) = Quack's cols. 14–23. Suys transcription is faulty and outdated, and translations based on it must be regarded with caution.

"Eloquent Peasant": (MK) Four incomplete papyri. AEL 1.169–84, AW 358–67.
Ḥori (O. Gardiner 2, rco.): Fischer-Elfert 1986: 1–4. Bickel and Mathieu 1993: 49–50.
Kagemeni: Pap. Prisse 1–2. Text: Gardiner 1946; AEL 1.59–61, AW 133–36.
Kemit ("The Compilation"): Writing board and many ostraca. Posener 1951, pls. 1–21; Barta 1978. LAE 15–16; AW 368–69.
Louvre Demotic Papyrus 2414: LEWL 94–95. AW 292–94.
"Loyalist Teaching": Collated from the stele of Seḥetibre (which incorporates a partial version of the instruction) and numerous fragmentary copies by G. Posener, *L'Enseignement loyaliste* (1976). (Original version from the time of Sesostris I.) References according to Posener's edition. AEL 1.125–29 (partial), AW 178–84.
"A Man to His Son": Text: Helck 1984. AW 185–93.
Menena (or Menna), a letter including proverbs and instructions: Oriental Inst. Ost. 12074. Gugliemi 1983; J. L. Foster 1984. AW 399–402.
Merikare: Pap. Leningrad 116A, Pap. Moscow 4658, Pap. Carlsberg 6; ostraca. Volten 1945; Helck 1977; COHL 18: pls. 2–21. AEL 1.97–109, AW 137–54.
O. Petrie 11 ("Instruction According to Old Writings"): HO LXXXVIII vso. (title) + I rto. LEWL 7, AW 215–17.
Phibis ("Demotic Wisdom Book"): Pap. Insinger; Pap. Carlesberg: Lexa 1926; Volten 1941 (partial). LEWL 197–234; AW 295–349. Quoted from AEL 3.184–217.
Ptaḥḥotep: Pap. Prisse. Žába 1956. AEL 1.61–80, AW 104–32.
Ramesseum Papyri I and II: J. W. B. Barns 1956, I: pll. 1–6, pp. 1–10; II: pll. 7–9, pp. 11–14. AW 178–84 (partial).
"Satirical Letter": Pap. Anastasi I. Gardiner 1911. Selections in AW 396–402.

II. MESOPOTAMIAN SOURCES

◆

(For a comprehensive translation of Mesopotamian literature, see BTM.)

Aḥiqar: Aramaic; 6th–5th c. in origin; widely translated and revised. Aramaic: Lindenberger 1983. Syriac and other versions in Coneybeare et al. 1913.
Shube'awilum: Three (from Ugarit, Emar, and Boghazhkeui, but of Mesopotamian origin). Latter part of second millennium. Text Dietrich 1991; text and translation in Nougayrol et al. 1968. Translation BTM 1.332–35.
Shuruppak (Suruppak): Three Sumerian versions, dating from ca. 2500 B.C.E. to ca. 1800 B.C.E. (texts and translation in Alster 1974) and a fragment of an Akkadian translation, ca. 1100 B.C.E. Text and translation in Alster 1974: 33–51.

III. TRADITIONAL JEWISH EXEGESIS

◆

Midrashim, Medieval Commentaries, and Some Later Commentaries in the Traditional Mode. Printed texts are listed, with reference to the most accessible edition or editions. For a list of commentaries regularly employed in this commentary, see the Introduction, VII.

Alsheikh

Moshe ben Ḥayyim Alsheikh (1508–1601, Safed). *Rav Peninim*. Vilna: The Widow and Brothers Rom. (Abridged trans.: E. Munk, Jerusalem, 1991).

Baḥyeh

Baḥyeh ben Asher (13th c., Saragosa). (Through chap. 15). Collated by Y. Heine. Jerusalem, 1950.

Benjamin ben Judah

Benjamin ben Judah (1285–1330, Rome). Ed. by H. Berger. Pressburg: Alkalay, 1901.

Elijah, Gaon of Vilna

Tana' debey Eliyahu. Prague: J. Scholl, 1814.

"Frankfort"

Anonymous Frankfort Manuscript (MS dated 1340, commentary 11th–13th c.; France or Provence). Ed. by Georg Kantorowsky, *Ein anonymer hebräischer Commentar zu den Proverbien*. Breslau: H. Fleischmann, 1907.

Gavishon

Abraham ben Jacob Gavishon (1520–78, Algeria). *ʿOmer Hašik^{e}ḥah*. Jerusalem: Kedem, n.d.

Gerundi, Sheshet

Sheshet ben Isaac Gerundi (13th–14th c., Gerona and Palestine). Ed. by Karl Koch. Erlangen: Vollrath, 1893 (repr. Jerusalem: Hasekhel, 1992).

Gerundi, Yonah

Yonah ben Abraham Gerundi (1200–1263, Spain). Commentary to Proverbs, etc. Ed. by Y. Gloskinus. Spring Valley, N.Y.: Feldheim, 1993.

Hame'iri

R. Menachem ben Shelomo Hame'iri (1249–1316? Provence, Toledo). Ed. by Menachem Mendel Meshi-Zahav. Otzar Haposqim. Jerusalem, 1969.

Ibn Janaḥ

Yonah Abu al-Walid Marwan ibn Janaḥ (first half of 11th c., Spain). *Peruš Lekitvey Haqodeš*. Tel Aviv, 1926, 1936. See also Ibn Janaḥ's *Sefer Hariqmah* in the modern scholarship section.

Ibn Yaḥyah

Yosef ben David ibn Yaḥyah (1494–1534, Italy). Bologna, 1539; also in the *Q^{e}hilat Yaʿaqov* Bible (Amsterdam, 1724–27).

Immanuel of Rome

Immanuel ben Solomon (1260–ca. 1330, Rome). Naples, 1487. Repr. with intro. by David Goldstein, Jerusalem: Magnes, 1981.

Isaac ben Arama

Isaac Arama (1420–94, Spain). *Yad Avshalom.* Ed. by I. Freimann. Leipzig, 1858–59.

Isaiah di Trani

Isaiah ben Mali di Trani (13th c., Italy). Commentary. Ed. by A. J. Würtheimer. Jerusalem: Ketav Yad vaSefer, 1978.

Jephet ben Ali

Jephet ben Ali Halevi (Karaite) (Second half of 10th c., Basra and Jerusalem). *Der Commentar des Karäers Jephet ben 'Ali Halevi zu den Proverbien.* Ed. by Israel Günzig. Krakau: J. Fischer, 1898. Cf. G. Tamani, "La Tradizione delle opere di Yefet ben Ali." *Bull. d'Etudes Karaites* 1983: 67–68.

Kaspi

Yosef ibn Kaspi (1279–1340, Spain). *Ḥaṣoṣarot Kesef* ("Trumpets of Silver"), in *ʿAsarah Kley Kesef* ("Ten Instruments of Silver"). Ed. by Isaac Last. Pressburg: Alkalay, 1903 (repr. Jerusalem: Makor, 1969–70). Unless otherwise noted, references are to MS A.

Malbim

Meir Loeb ben Yechiel Michael (1809–79, Poland). *Musar Haḥokmah* (Commentary on Proverbs) in *ʾOtzar Haperushim,* vol. X. [Vilna: The Widow and Brothers Rom, 1923]. ET C. Wengrov, see Malbim, below.

Mezudat David

David Altschuler (18th c., Galicia). Rabbinic Bible.

Midrash Proverbs (ca. 9th c.)

Ed. by B. Visotzky. New York: Jewish Theological Seminary, 1990.

Midrash Shoḥer Tov

Jerusalem: Midrash Pub., n.d.

Naḥmias

Yosef ben Yosef ibn Naḥmias (first half of 14th c., Toledo). Ed. by A. L. Bamberger. Berlin: Itschkowsky, 1911 (repr. Israel, 1969[?]).

Pinto

Josia ben Joseph Pinto Commentary on Proverbs. Amsterdam: Isaac Timpelo, 1729.

Pseudo-Ibn Ezra

A Commentary on the Book of Proverbs Attributed to Abraham Ibn Ezra. Ed. by S. R. Driver. Oxford: Clarendon, 1880.

Radaq

R. David Qimḥi (1160–1235?, Spain). Ed. by Talmage 1990. See also Qimḥi's *Sefer Hashorashim* in the modern scholarship section.

Ralbag

R. Levi ben Gershon (Gersonides) (1288–1344, France). Rabbinic Bible.

Ramaq

R. Moses Qimḥi (d. 1190, Spain). See Talmage 1990. (A flawed edition appears in the Rabbinic Bible, where it is incorrectly ascribed to Abraham Ibn Ezra.)

Rashi

Solomon ben Isaac (1040–1105, Troyes). Rabbinic Bible.

Riyqam

R. Yoseph Qimḥi (ca. 1105–1170, Spain). See Talmage 1990.

Saʿadia
Saʿadia Gaon (882–942, Egypt, Palestine, Babylonia). Commentary translated into Hebrew from Judeo-Arabic and edited by Yosef Qafiḥ. Jerusalem, 1975–76 (?).
Shadal
Samuel David Luzzatto (1800–65, Italy). See Luzzatto 1876.
Yalqut Machiri
Machir bar Abba Mari, Hamachiri (14th c., southern France). *Yalqut Hamachiri*. Ed. by Yehuda Shapira. Berlin: Itzkowsky (repr. Jerusalem, 1964); ed. by Eliezer Grünhut. Jerusalem, 1902 (1964).
Zeraḥiah ben Shealtiel
Zeraḥiah ben Isaac ben Shealtiel Ḥen (13th c., Barcelona). *Imrey Daʿat*. Ed. by I. Schwartz. Vienna: Hafferburg & Mann, 1871.

IV. Modern Scholarship

◆

Abrahams, Israel
1948 *Hebrew Ethical Wills*. 2 vols. Philadelphia: Jewish Publication Society.
Ahlström, Gösta W.
1979 "The House of Wisdom [Prv 9,1]." *Svensk Exegetisk Årsbok* 44: 74–76.
Albright, William Foxwell
1919–20 "The Goddess of Life and Wisdom." *AJSL* 36: 258–94.
1945 "A New Hebrew Word for 'Glaze' in Proverbs 26:23." *BASOR* 98: 24–25.
1955 "Some Canaanite-Phoenician Sources of Hebrew Wisdom." *VTSup* 3: 1–15.
1982a "The Hapax *ḥarak* in Proverbs 12,27." *Bib* 63: 60–62.
1982b "Philological Observations on Five Biblical Texts (Prv 14,35)." *Bib* 63: 370–89.
Aletti, J. N.
1976 "Proverbes 8,22–31. Etude de structure." *Bib* 57: 25–37.
1977 "Séduction et parole en Proverbes I–IX." *VT* 27: 129–44.
Allegro, John M.
1964 "The Wiles of the Wicked Woman." *PEQ* 96: 53–55.
Alster, Bendt
1974 *The Instructions of Suruppak*. Copenhagen Studies in Assyriology 2. Copenhagen: Akademisk.
1975a "Paradoxical Proverbs and Satire in Sumerian literature." *Journal of Cuneiform Studies* 27: 201–27.
1975b *Studies in Sumerian Proverbs*. Copenhagen Studies in Assyriology 3. Copenhagen: Akademisk.
Alt, Albrecht
1951 "Die Weisheit Salomos." *TZ* 76: 139–44 (ET in SAIW 102–12).
Altenmüller, Hartwig
1983 "Bemerkungen zu Kapitel 13 der Lehre des Amenemope." Pp. 1–17 in *Fontes atque pontes*. Ed. by H. Brunner. Bamberg: Manfred Görg.

Alter, Robert
1985 *The Art of Biblical Poetry.* New York: Basic Books.
Anat, M. A.
1969 "Von der Form zur Bedeutung im Buch Mischle." *Beth Mikra* 39/4: 77–86.
Anbar (Bernstein), M.
1972 "Proverbes 11,21; 16,5: *yd lyd* 'sur le champ.'" *Bib* 53: 537–38.
Anderson, Bruce W.
1967 "Human and Divine Wisdom in Proverbs: Readings in Biblical Morality." Pp. 55–60 in *Understanding the Old Testament.* Englewood Cliffs, N.J.: Prentice Hall.
Anderson, Gary A.
1991 A *Time to Mourn, A Time to Dance.* University Park: Pennsylvania State University Press.
Andrew, M. E.
1978 "Variety of Expression in Proverbs XXIII 29–35." *VT* 28: 120–30.
Anthes, Rudolf
1977 "Zur Echtheit der Lehre des Amenemhet." *FAL* 42–54.
Arambarrí, Jesus
1990 *Der Wortstamm 'Hören' im Alten Testament.* Stuttgarter Biblische Beiträge 20. Stuttgart: Katholisches Bibelwerk.
Arzt, Paul Josef
1993 "Braucht es den erhobenen Zeigefinger?" *Protokolle zur Bibel* 2: 77–87.
Assmann, Jan
1975 *Ägyptische Hymnen und Gebete.* Zurich: Artemis (= ÄHG).
1979 "Weisheit, Loyalismus und Frömmigkeit." SAL 12–70.
1989 "State and Religion in the New Kingdom." Pp. 56–88 in *Religion and Philosophy in Ancient Egypt.* Ed. by W. K. Simpson. YES 3. New Haven, Conn.: Yale University Press.
1990 *Maʿat: Gerechtigkeit und Unsterblichkeit im alten Ägypten.* Munich: C. H. Beck.
Assmann, Jan, Erika Feucht, and Reinhard Grieshammer, eds.
1977 *Fragen an die altägyptische Literatur.* Wiesbaden: Reichert (= FAL).
Audet, Jean-Paul
1962 "Origines comparées de la double tradition de la loi et de la sagesse dans le Proche-Orient ancien." *Int. Congress of Orientalists* (Moscow) 1: 352–57.
Auffret, Pierre
1980 "Note sur la structure littéraire de Proverbes 22,8–9 selon la restitution proposée par J. Carmignac." *Folia Orientalia* 21: 43–46.
Augustin, Matthias
1983 *Der schöne Mensch im Alten Testament und im hellenistischen Judentum.* Frankfurt am Main: Peter Lang.
Avishur, Yitzhaq
1975 "Phoenician Topoi in Proverbs 3" [Hebrew]. *Shnaton* 1: 13–25.
Backhaus, F. J.
1993 "Qoheleth und Sirach." *BN* 69: 32–55.
Badawy, Alexander
1961 "Two Passages from Ancient Egyptian Literary Texts Reinterpreted." ZAW 86: 144–45.

Barbiero, G.
1982 "Il testo massoretico di Prov 3,34." *Bib* 63: 370–89.
Barker, Kenneth L.
1989 "Proverbs 23: 7—'To Think' or 'To Serve Food'?" *JANES* 19: 3–8.
Barley, Nigel
1972 "A Structural Approach to the Proverb and the Maxim." *Proverbium* 20: 737–50.
1974 "The Proverb and Related Problems of Genre Definition." *Proverbium* 23: 880–84.
Barns, John W. B.
1956 *Five Ramesseum Papyri*. Oxford: Griffith Inst., Oxford University.
Barns, John W. B., and H. Zilliacus
1967 *The Antinoopolis Papyri*. Part III. London: Egypt Exploration Society.
Barr, James
1974 "*Erizō* and *ereidō* in the Septuagint: A Note Principally on Gen. XLIX.6." *JSS* 19: 198–215.
1975 "Baʾareṣ—*Molis*: Prov. XI.31, I Pet. IV.18." *JSS* 20: 149–64.
1981 "A New Look at Kethibh-Qere." *OTS* 21: 19–37.
Barré, Michael L.
1981 "'Fear of God' and the World View of Wisdom." *BTB* 11: 41–43.
Barta, Winfried
1978 "Das Schulbuch Kemit." *ZÄS* 105: 6–14.
Barucq, André
1976 "Dieu chez les sages d'Israel." *BETL* 41: 169–89.
Bauckmann, E. G.
1960 "Die Proverbien und die Sprüche des Jesus Sirach." *ZAW* 72: 33–63.
Bauer, Hans, and Pontus Leander
1922 *Historische Grammatik der Hebräischen Sprache des ATs*. Bd. I. (repr. 1962. Hildesheim: Georg Olms) (= B-L).
Bauer, Jean Baptiste
1958 "Encore une fois Proverbes VIII 22." *VT* 8: 91–92.
Baumann, Gerlinde
1996 *Die Weisheitsgestalt in Proverbien 1–9*. Forschungen zum Alten Testament 16. Tübingen: Mohr-Siebeck.
Baumgartner, Antoine J.
1890 *Etude critique sur l'état du texte du Livre des Proverbes d'après les principales traductions anciennes*. Leipzig: W. Drugulin.
Baumgartner, Walter
1933 *Israelitische und altorientalische Weisheit*. Tübingen: J. C. B. Mohr.
Baumgartner, Walter, and Johann Jakob Stamm
1967–90 *Hebräisches und Aramäisches Lexikon*. 4 vols. Leiden: Brill (HALAT).
Beardslee, William A.
1980 "Plutarch's Use of Proverbial Forms of Speech." *Semeia* 17: 101–11.
Beaucamp, Evode
1982 "Sagesse et salut dans l'Ancien Testament." *LTP* 18: 239–44.
Bechtel, Lyn M.
1991 "Shame as a Sanction of Social Control in Biblical Israel." *JSOT* 49: 47–76.
Beckenrath, Jürgen von
1983 "Ostrakon München ÄS 396." *SAK* 10: 63–69.

Becker, Joachim
1965 *Gottesfurcht im Alten Testament.* Rome: Pontifical Biblical Inst.
Beckman, Gary
1986 "Proverbs and Proverbial Allusions in Hittite." *JNES* 45: 19–30.
Ben Sira
1973 *Sefer Ben Sira* [Heb]: Text, Concordance, and an Analysis of Vocabulary. A publication of The Historical Dictionary of the Hebrew Language. Jerusalem: Academy of the Hebrew Language.
Bentzen, Aage
1957 *Introduction to the Old Testament.* Copenhagen: G. E. C. Gad.
Berger, Klaus
1989 *Die Weisheitsschrift aus der Kairoer Geniza.* Tübingen: Francke.
1991 "Die Bedeutung der wiederentdeckten Weisheitsschrift aus der Kairoer Geniza für das Alte Testament." ZAW 103: 113–21.
Berger, P. R.
1987 "Zum Huren bereit bis hin zu einem Rundlaib Brot: Prov 6,26." ZAW 99: 98–106.
Bergman, Jan
1968 *Ich bin Isis.* Uppsala: Universitet.
1979 "Gedanken zum Thema 'Lehre–Testament–Grab–Name." SAL 74–103.
Bergmeier, Roland
1981 "Weisheit-Dike-Lichtjungfrau." *JSJ* 12: 75–86.
Berndt, Rainer
1994 "Skizze zur Auslegungsgeschichte der Bücher *Prouerbia und Ecclesiastes* in der abendländlischen Kirche." *Sacris Erudiri* 34: 5–32.
Bertram, Georg
1936 "Die religiöse Umdeutung altorientalischer Lebensweisheit in der griechischen Übersetzung des ATs." ZAW 12: 153–67.
1953 "Die religiöse Umdeutung altorientalischer Lebensweisheit in der griechischen Übersetzung des ATs." ZAW 12: 153–67.
1969 "Weisheit und Lehre in der Septuaginta." ZDMG Sup. I: 302–19.
Bickel, Susanne, and Bernard Mathieu
1993 "L'écrivain Amennakht et son enseignement." *BIFAO* 93: 31–51.
Bickell, Georg
1891 "Kritische Bearbeitung der Proverbien." *Wiener Zeitschrift für die Kunde des Morgenlandes* 5: 79–102.
Bien, Günther
1988 "Ueber den Begriff der Weisheit in der antiken Philosophie." *Studia Philosophica* 47: 33–51.
Bjørndalen, Anders Jørgen
1970 "'Form' und 'Inhalt' des Motivierenden Mahnspruches." ZAW 82: 347–61.
Blanshard, Brand
1967 "Wisdom." *Encyclopedia of Philosophy* 8.322–24. New York: Macmillan.
Blenkinsopp, Joseph
1983 *Wisdom and Law in the Old Testament.* Oxford: Oxford University Press.
1991 "The Social Context of the Outsider Woman." *Bib* 72: 457–72.
Blocher, Henri
1977 "The Fear of the Lord as the 'Principle' of Wisdom." *TynBul* 28: 3–28.

Bloomfield, Morton

1984 "The Tradition and Style of Wisdom Literature." Pp. 19–30 in *Biblical Patterns in Modern Literature*. Ed. by D. H. Hirsch and N. Aschkenasy. Chico, Calif.: Scholars Press.

Blumenthal, Elke

1980 "Die Lehre für König Merikare." *ZÄS* 107: 5–41.

Bonnard, P. E.

1979 "De la Sagesse personnifiée dans l'Ancien Testament à la Sagesse en personne dans le Nouveau." Pp. 117–49 in *La Sagesse de l'Ancien Testament*. Ed. by M. Gilbert. Leuven: Leuven University.

Bonora, Antonio

1987 "La via dell'amore in Pr 30,18–20." *RivB* 35: 51–55.

Boström, Gustav

1935 *Proverbiastudien: Die Weisheit und das fremde Weib in Sprüche 1–9*. Lund: C. W. K. Gleerup.

Boström, Lennart

1990 *The God of the Sages*. Stockholm: Almqvist & Wiksell.

Botterweck, G. Johannes, and Helmer Ringgren, eds.

1970ff. *Theologisches Wörterbuch zum Alten Testament*. Stuttgart: W. Kohlhammer (= TWAT).

1974ff. *Theological Dictionary of the Old Testament*. Grand Rapids, Mich.: Eerdmans (= TDOT).

Bratcher, Robert G.

1983 "A Translator's Note on Proverbs 11,30." *BT* 34: 337–38.

Brenner, Athalya

1993 "Proverbs 1–9: An F Voice?" Pp. 113–30 in *On Gendering Texts*. Ed. by A. Brenner and F. van Dijk-Hemmes. Leiden: Brill.

Brenner, Athalya, and F. van Dijk-Hemmes

1993 *On Gendering Texts*. Leiden: Brill.

Brongers, H. A.

1965 "Bemerkungen zum Gebrauch des adverbielen *Weʿattāh* im Alten Testament." *VT* 15: 289–99.

1977 "Miscellanea Exegetica" [part III: *tušiyya*]. Pp. 30–49 in *Übersetzung und Deutung* (FS Alexander R. Hulst). Ed. by A. R. Hulst. Nijkerk: F. Callenbach.

Brown, John P.

1981 "Proverbs-Book, Gold-Economy, Alphabet." *JBL* 100: 169–91.

Brown, William P.

1996 *Character in Crisis*. Grand Rapids, Mich: Eerdmans.

Brueggemann, Walter

1972 *In Man We Trust*. Richmond: John Knox.

1977 "A Neglected Sapiential Word Pair." *ZAW* 89: 234–58.

1990 "The Social Significance of Solomon as a Patron of Wisdom." SIANE 117–32.

Brunner, Hellmut

1944 *Die Lehre des Cheti, Sohnes des Duauf*. Ägyptologische Forschungen, XIII. Glückstadt: J. J. Augustin.

1954 "Das hörende Herz." *ThLZ* 79: 697–700 (= 1988b: 3–5).

1955 "Die Lehre vom Königserbe im frühen Mittleren Reich." AS 4–11.

1956 "Das Herz als Sitz des Lebensgeheimnisses." *AfO* 17: 140–41 (= 1988b: 6–7).

1957 *Altägyptische Erziehung*. Wiesbaden: Harrassowitz.

1958 "Gerechtigkeit als Fundament des Thrones." *VT* 8: 426–28.

1961 "Ptahhotep bei den koptischen Mönchen." ZAW 86: 145–47.

1963 "Der freie Wille Gottes in der ägyptischen Weisheit." SPOA. Pp. 103–20 (= 1988b: 85–102).

1966 "Die 'Weisen', ihre 'Lehren' und 'Prophezeiungen' in altägyptsicher Sicht." *ZÄS* 93: 29–35 (= 1988b: 59–65).

1978 "Zur Datierung der 'Lehre eines Mannes an seinen Sohn." *JEA* 64: 142–43.

1979 "Zitate aus Lebenslehren." SAL 105–71.

1981 "L'éducation en ancienne Egypte." Pp. 65–86 in *Histoire Mondiale de l'éducation*. Ed. by G. Mialaret and J. Vial. Paris: Presses Universitaires.

1984 "Zentralbegriffe ägyptischer und israelitischer Weisheitslehren." *Saeculum* 35: 185–99.

1988a *Altägyptische Weisheit*. Zurich: Artemis (= AW).

1988b *Das hörende Herz*. (Kleine Schriften zur Religions- und Geistesgeschichte Ägyptens). Ed. by W. Röllig. OBO 80. Göttingen: Vandenhoeck & Ruprecht.

1991 "Die menschliche Willensfreiheit und ihre Grenzen in ägyptischen Lebenslehren." Pp. 32–46 in *Biblische und ausserbiblische Spruchweisheit*. Ed. by H.-J. Klimkeit. Wiesbaden: Harrassowitz.

Brunner-traut, Emma

1940 "Die Weisheitslehre des Djedef-Hor." *ZÄS* 76: 3–9.

1979 "Weiterleben der ägyptischen Lebenslehren in den koptischen Apophthegmata am Beispiel des Schweigens." SAL 173–216.

Bryce, Glendon E.

1972 "Another Wisdom-'Book' in Proverbs." *JBL* 91: 145–57.

1975 "Omen-Wisdom in Ancient Israel." *JBL* 94: 19–37.

1978 "The Structural Analysis of Didactic Texts." Pp. 107–21 in *Biblical and Near Eastern Studies*. Ed. by Gary A. Tuttle. Grand Rapids, Mich.: Eerdmans.

1979 *A Legacy of Wisdom*. Lewisburg, Pa.: Bucknell.

Buccellati, Giorgio

1981 "Wisdom and Not: The Case of Mesopotamia." *JAOS* 101: 35–47.

Buchanan, George Wesley

1965 "Midrashim pré-Tannaites." *RB* 72: 227–39.

Buchberger, Hannes

1989–90 "Zum Ausländer in der altägyptischen Literature—eine Kritik." WO 20–21: 5–34.

Buhl, Frants

1914 "Die Bedeutung des Stammes *lûṣ* oder *lîṣ*." Pp. 81–86 in *Studien zur semitischen Philologie und Religionsgeschichte* (FS Julius Wellhausen). BZAW 29. Giessen: Töpelmann.

Burden, J. J.

1990 "The Wisdom of Many." *OT Essays* 3: 341–59.

Burkard, Günter

1977 *Textkritische Untersuchungen zu ägyptischen Weisheitslehren des alten und mittleren Reiches*. ÄA 34. Wiesbaden: Otto Harrassowitz.

Caminos, Ricardo

1954 *Late-Egyptian Miscellanies*. London: Oxford University (= CLEM).

Camp, Claudia
1985 *Wisdom and the Feminine in the Book of Proverbs*. Sheffield: Almond.
1987 "Woman Wisdom as Root Metaphor: A Theological Consideration." Pp. 45–76 in *The Listening Heart* (FS Roland E. Murphy). JSOTSup 58. Ed. by K. Hoglund et al. Sheffield: Sheffield Academic Press.
1988 "Wise and Strange: An Interpretation of the Female Imagery in Proverbs in Light of the Trickster Mythology." *Sem* 42: 14–36.
1991 "What's So Strange about the Strange Woman." Pp. 17–31 in *The Bible and the Politics of Exegesis* (FS N. Gottwald). Ed. by D. Jobling et al. Cleveland: Pilgrim.
Camp, Claudia, and Carole Fontaine
1990 "The Words of the Wise and Their Riddles." Pp. 127–59 in *Text and Tradition*. Ed. by Susan Niditch. Atlanta: Scholars Press.
Canney, Maurice A.
1923–24 "The Hebrew *Meliṣ*." *AJSL* 40: 135–37.
Caquot, André
1978 "Israelite Perceptions of Wisdom and Strength in the Light of the Ras Shamra Texts." IW 25–33.
1979 "Deux proverbes Salomoniens." *Revue d'Histoire et de Philosophie Religieuses* 59: 577–81.
Carasik, Michael
1994 "Who Were the 'Men of Hezekiah' (Proverbs XXV 1)?" *VT* 44: 289–300.
Carmignac, Jean
1980 "Critique textuelle de Proverbes 22,8–9." *Folia Orientalia* 21: 33–41.
Caspari, W.
1928 "Über den biblischen Begriff der Torheit." *Neue Kirchliche Zeitschrift* 39: 668–95.
Cassuto, M. D. (Umberto)
1974 *The Book of Exodus* [Hebrew]. Jerusalem: Magnes.
Cathcart, Kevin J.
1970 "Proverbs 30,4 and Ugaritic *ḤPN*, 'Garment.'" *CBQ* 32: 418–20.
Causse, A.
1938 "La Sagesse et la propaganda juive à l'époque perse et hellénistique." Pp. 148–54 in *Werden und Wesen des Alten Testament*. BZAW 60. Berlin: Töpelmann.
Cazelles, Henri
1959 "L'Enfantement de la Sagesse en Prov., VIII." *BETL* 12: 511–15.
1963 "Les débuts de la sagesse en Israel." *SPOA* Pp. 27–40.
1979 "Les nouvelles études sur Sumer (Alster) et Mari (Marzal) nous aident-elles à situer les origines de la sagesse israélite?" *BETL* 51: 17–27.
1995 "Aḥiqar, *Ummân* and *Amun*, and Biblical Wisdom Texts." Pp. 45–55 in *Solving Riddles and Untying Knots, Essays in Honor of Jonas Greenfield*. Ed. by Z. Zevit, S. Gitin, and M. Sokoloff. Winona Lake, Ind.: Eisenbrauns.
Černý, Jaroslav
1939 *Late Ramesside Letters*. Bibliotheca Aegyptiaca IX. Brussels: Fondation égyptologique Reine Elisabeth.
1978 *Papyrus hiératiques de Deir el-Médineh*. FIFAO 8,22.
Černý, Jaroslav, and Alan H. Gardiner
1957 *Hieratic Ostraca*. Oxford: Griffith Inst., Oxford University Press (= HO).

Chajes, Hirsch Perez

1899 *Proverbia-Studien zu der sog. Salomonischen Sammlung, C. X–XXII, 16.* Berlin: C. A. Schwetschke.

Claasen, W. T.

1983 "Speaker-oriented Functions of *kî* in Biblical Hebrew." *JNSL* 11: 29–46.

Clements, Ronald E.

1988 "Solomon and the Origins of Wisdom in Israel." Pp. 32–35 in *Perspectives on the Hebrew Bible* (FS W. J. Harrelson). Ed. by J. L. Crenshaw. Macon, Ga.: Mercer University.

1993 "The Good Neighbor in the Book of Proverbs." Pp. 209–28 in *Of Prophets' Visions and the Wisdom of Sages*. Essays in Honor of R. N. Whybray. JSOTSup 162. Sheffield: Sheffield Academic Press.

1996 "The Concept of Abomination in the Book of Proverbs." Pp. 211–25 in *Texts, Temples, and Traditions: A Tribute to Menahem Haran*. Ed. by M. V. Fox et al. Winona Lake, Ind.: Eisenbrauns.

Clifford, Richard J.

1975 "Proverbs IX: A Suggested Ugaritic Parallel." *VT* 25: 298–306.

1993 "Woman Wisdom in the Book of Proverbs." Pp. 61–72 in *Biblische Theologie und gesellschaftlicher Wandel* (FS N. Lohfink). Ed. by G. Baraulik, W. Gross, and S. McEvenue. Freiburg: Herder.

1999 *Proverbs* (OTL). Louisville, Ky.: Westminster/John Knox.

Clines, David J. A.

1993 *The Dictionary of Classical Hebrew*. Sheffield: Sheffield Academic Press (= DCH).

Cody, Aelred

1980 "Notes on Proverbs 22,21 and 22,23b." *Bib* 61: 418–26.

Cohen, Amoz

1979 "Wer einen Feigenbaum pflegt, wird seine Frucht essen (Spr 27,18)." *Beth Mikra* 80: 81–82.

Cohen, Chaim

1996 "The Meaning of *ṣalmawet* ["darkness]." Pp. 287–309 in *Texts, Temples, and Traditions: A Tribute to Menahem Haran*. Ed. by M. V. Fox et al. Winona Lake, Ind.: Eisenbrauns.

1997 "Two Misunderstood Verses in the Book of Proverbs." *Shnaton* 11: 139–52.

Cohen, Jeffrey M.

1982 "An Unrecognized Connotation of *nšq peh*." *Bib* 32: 416–24.

Collins, John J.

1977 "Cosmos and Salvation: Jewish Wisdom and Apocalyptic in the Hellenistic Age." *HR* 17: 121–42.

1980 "Proverbial Wisdom and the Yahwist Vision." *Semeia* 17: 1–17.

1997 *Jewish Wisdom in the Hellenistic Age*. Louisville, Ky.: Westminster/John Knox.

Coneybeare, Frederick C., J. R. Harris, and A. S. Lewis

1913 *The Story of Aḥikar*. Cambridge: Cambridge University Press.

Conrad, Joachim

1967 "Die Innere Gliederung der Proverbien: zur Frage nach der Systematisierung des Spruchgutes in den älteren Teilsammlungen." ZAW 79: 67–76.

Conzelmann, Hans
1964 "Die Mutter der Weisheit." Pp. 225–34 in *Zeit und Geschichte* (FS Rudolf Bultmann). Ed. by Erich Dinkler. Tübingen: J. C. B. Mohr.

Cook, Johann
1987 "Hellenistic Influence on the Book of Proverbs (Septuagint)?" *BIOSCS* 20: 30–42.
1991a "Hellenistic Influence in the Septuagint Book of Proverbs." Pp. 341–53 in *VII Cong. of the IOSCS (1989)*. Ed. by C. E. Cox. SCS 31. Atlanta: Scholars Press.
1991b "Reflections on the Role of Wisdom in Creation with Special Reference to the Intertestamental Period." *Acta Academica* 23: 47–66.
1993 "The Dating of Septuagint Proverbs." *ETL* 69: 383–99.
1994a "Are the Syriac and Greek Versions of the *ʾiššah zarah* (Prov 1 to 9) Identical?" *Textus* 14: 117–32.
1994b "A Comparison of Proverbs and Jeremiah in the Septuagint." *JNSL* 20: 49–58.
1994c "*ʾIššah Zara* (Proverbs 1–9 Septuagint): A Metaphor for Foreign Wisdom?" ZAW 106: 458–75.
1996 "Exodus 38 and Proverbs 31." BETL 126: 537–49.
*1997 *The Septuagint of Proverbs: Jewish or Hellenistic Proverbs?* VTSup 69. Leiden: Brill.

Cooper, Alan
1987 "On Reading the Bible Critically or Otherwise." Pp. 61–79 in *The Future of Biblical Studies: The Hebrew Scriptures*. Ed. by R. E. Friedman and H. G. M. Williamson. Atlanta: Scholars Press.

Cornelius, Izak
1994 "The Visual Representation of the World in the Ancient Near East and the Hebrew Bible." *JNSL* 20: 193–218.

Cosser, William
1953–54 "The Meaning of 'Life' (*Hayyim*) in Proverbs, Job, and Ecclesiastes." *Glasgow University Oriental Society Transactions* 15: 48–53.

Couroyer, Bernard
1949 "Le Chemin de vie en Egypte et en Israël." *RB* 56: 412–32.
1961 "Amenemopé, I, 9; III, 13: Egypte ou Israël." *RB* 68: 394–400.
1963 "L'origine égyptienne de la sagesse d'Amenemopé." *RB* 70: 214–21.
1983 "La Tablette du coeur." *RB* 90: 416–34.
1987 "Le 'Dieu des Sages' en Egypte, I." *RB* 94: 574–603.

Couturier, Guy
1962 "Sagesse Babylonienne et sagesse Israélite." *Sciences ecclésiastiques* 14: 293–309.
1980 "La Vie familiale comme source de la sagesse et de la loi." *Science et Esprit* 32: 177–92.

Cowley, A. E.
1923 *Aramaic Papyri of the Fifth Century* B.C. (repr. 1923). Osnabrück: O. Zeller.
1929 "Two Aramaic Ostraca." *JRAS* 61: 107–11.

Cox, Dermot
1977 "Ṣedaqa and Mišpaṭ." *Studium Biblicum* 27: 33–50.
1982a "Fear or Conscience?: *Yir'at YHWH* in Proverbs 1–9." *Studia Hierosolymitana* 3: 83–90.

1982b *Proverbs*. Wilmington: Michael Glazier.

Crenshaw, James L.

1969 "Method in Determining Wisdom Influence upon 'Historical' Literature." *JBL* 88: 129–42 (repr. SAIW 481–94).

1970 "Popular Questioning of the Justice of God in Ancient Israel." *ZAW* 82: 380–95. (repr. SAIW 289–304.)

1974 "Wisdom." Pp. 225–64 in *Old Testament Form Criticism*. Ed. by John H. Hayes. San Antonio, Tex.: Trinity University Press.

1976 *Studies in Ancient Israelite Wisdom* (selected, with a prolegomenon, by James L. Crenshaw). New York: Ktav (= SAIW).

1977 "In Search of Divine Presence." *Review and Expositor* 74: 353–69.

1980 "Impossible Questions, Sayings, and Tasks." *Semeia* 17: 19–34.

1981a "Wisdom and Authority: Sapiential Rhetoric and Its Warrants." *VTSup* 32: 10–29.

1981b *Old Testament Wisdom*. Atlanta: John Knox.

1983 *Theodicy in the Old Testament*. Philadelphia: Fortress.

1984 "A Mother's Instruction to Her Son (Proverbs 31:1–9)." Pp. 9–22 in *Perspectives on the Hebrew Bible* (FS Walter J. Harrelson). Ed. by J. L. Crenshaw. Macon, Ga.: Mercer University.

1985 "Education in Ancient Israel." *JBL* 104: 601–15.

1987 "The Acquisition of Knowledge in Israelite Wisdom Literature." *Word and World* 7: 245–52.

1989a "Clanging Symbols." Pp. 51–64 in *Justice and the Holy* (FS Walter Harrelson). Ed. by D. A. Knight and P. J. Paris. Atlanta: Scholars Press.

1989b "Poverty and Punishment in the Book of Proverbs." *Quarterly Review* 9: 30–43.

1992 "Prohibitions in Proverbs and Qoheleth." Pp. 115–24 in *Priests, Proverbs and Scribes*. Ed. by E. Ulrich et al. (FS J. Blenkinsopp). JSOTSup 149. Sheffield: Sheffield Press.

1993 "The Concept of God in Old Testament Wisdom." Pp. 1–18 in *In Search of Wisdom*. Ed. by L. Perdue et al. (Essays in Memory of John G. Gammie). Louisville, Ky.: Westminster/John Knox.

1998 *Education in Ancient Israel*. New York: Doubleday.

Crepaldi, Maria Grazia

1982 "Il tempo nei libri sapienziali." *Studia Patavina* 29: 25–47.

Crook, M. B.

1954 "The Marriageable Maiden of Prov 31,10–31." *JNES* 13: 137–40.

Cross, Frank M., and David Noel Freedman

1953 "A Royal Psalm of Thanksgiving." *JBL* 72: 15–34.

Crossan, J. D., ed.

1980 "Gnomic Wisdom." *Semeia* 17. Chico, Calif.: Scholars Press.

Dahood, Mitchell

1960 "Immortality in Proverbs 12,28." *Bib* 41: 176–81.

1963 *Proverbs and Northwest Semitic Philology*. Rome: Pontifical Biblical Institute.

1965 "Hebrew-Ugaritic Lexicography III." *Bib* 46: 311–32.

1968 "The Phoenician Contribution to Biblical Wisdom Literature." Pp. 123–48 in *The Role of the Phoenicians in the Interaction of Mediterranean Civilizations*. Ed. by W. A. Ward. Beirut: American University.

1973 "Honey That Drips: Notes on Proverbs 5,2–3." *Bib* 54: 65–66.
1982a "The Hapax *ḥarak* in Proverbs 12,27." *Bib* 63: 60–62.
1982b "Philological Observations on Five Biblical Texts." *Bib* 63: 370–89.

Dalley, Stephanie
1989 *Myths from Mesopotamia*. Oxford: Oxford University Press.

Dathe, J. A.
1764 *De ratione consensus versionis Chaldaicae et Syriacae Proverbiorum Salomonis*. Leipzig.

Daube, David
1964 *The Sudden in Scripture*. Leiden: Brill.
1985 "A Quartet of Beasties in the Book of Proverbs [30,24]." *JThS* 36: 380–86.

Davies, E. W.
1980 "The Meaning of *Qesem* in Prv 16,10." *Bib* 61: 555–56.

Davies, Graham
1995 "Were There Schools in Ancient Israel?" Pp. 199–211 in J. Day et al. *Wisdom in Ancient Israel: Essays in Honour of J. A. Emerton*. Cambridge: Cambridge University Press.

Day, John, Robert Gordon, and H. G. M. Williamson
1995 *Wisdom in Ancient Israel: Essays in Honour of J. A. Emerton*. Cambridge: Cambridge University.

Deist, Ferdinand
1978 "Prov 31: 1. A Case of Constant Mistranslation." *JNSL* 6: 1–3.

Delitzsch, Franz
*[1873] *Biblical Commentary on the Proverbs of Solomon*. ET James Martin. Repr. 1983. Grand Rapids, Mich.: Eerdmans.

Delitzsch, Friedrich
1920 *Die Lese- und Schreibfehler im AT*. Berlin/Leipzig (= LSF).

Derousseaux, Louis
1970 *La Crainte de Dieu dans l'Ancien Testament*. Paris: Cerf.

Deutsch, Hermann
1885 *Die Sprüche Salomo's nach der Auffassung im Talmud und Midrasch*. Berlin: A. Mampe.

De Vries, Simon J.
1978 "Observations on Quantitative and Qualitative Time in Wisdom and Apocalyptic." IW 263–76.

Dhorme, Edouard
[1967] *A Commentary on the Book of Job*. ET: Harold Knight. Nashville: Thomas Nelson.

Dick, Michael B.
1990 "The Ethics of the Old Greek Book of Proverbs." *Studia Philonica Annual* 2: 20–50.

Dietfried, Gewalt
1985 "'Offne deinen Mund für den Stummen'—zu Proverbia 31,8." *Dielheimer Blätter zum Alten Testament* 21: 133–38.

Dietrich, M.
1991 "Der Dialog zwischen šupe'ameli und seinem 'Vater.'" *UF* 23: 33–74.

Dietrich, M., O. Loretz, and J. Sanmartin
1976 *Die keilalphabetischen Texte aus Ugarit*. Teil 1, Transkription. AOAT 24. Neukirchen-Vluyn: Neukirchener Vlg. (= KTU).

Díez Merino, Luis

1984 *Targum de Proverbios*. Madrid: Consejo Superior de Investigaciones Cientifícas.

Di Lella, Alexander A.

1979 *Proverbs: The Old Testament in Syriac according to the Peshiṭta Version*. 2.5. Leiden: Brill.

1993 "The Meaning of Wisdom in Ben Sira." Pp. 133–48 in *In Search of Wisdom*. Ed. by L. Perdue et al. (Essays in Memory of John G. Gammie). Louisville: Ky.: Westminster/John Knox.

Di Lella, Alexander A., and Patrick Skehan

*1987 *The Wisdom of Ben Sira*. AB 39. New York: Doubleday.

Doll, Peter

1985 *Menschenschöpfung und Weltschöpfung in der alttestamentlichen Weisheit*. Stuttgarter Bibel-Studien 117. Stuttgart: Katholisches Bibelwerk.

Domeris, W. R.

1996 "Shame and Honour in Proverbs: Wise Women and Foolish Men." *OTE* 8: 86–102.

Donald, Trevor

1963 "The Semantic Field of 'Folly' in Proverbs, Job, Psalms, and Ecclesiastes." *VT* 13: 285–92.

1964 "The Semantic Field of Rich and Poor in the Wisdom Literature of Hebrew and Accadian." *Oriens Antiquus* 3: 27–41.

Donner, H., and W. Röllig

1962 *Kanaanäische und Aramäische Inschriften*. Vols. I–III. Wiesbaden: Harrassowitz (= KAI).

Dorsey, David A.

1991 *The Roads and Highways of Ancient Israel*. Baltimore: Johns Hopkins University Press.

Drioton, Emil

1959 "Le Livre des Proverbes et la sagesse d'Aménémope." In *Sacra Pagina: Miscellenea Biblica Congressus internationalis Catholici de Re Biblica*, Vol. I. Ed. by J. Coppens, A. Descamps, and E. Massaux (Bibliotheca ephemeridum theologicum Lovaniensium 12 and 13). Gembloux: J. Duculot.

Driver, G. R.

1932a "Problems in 'Proverbs.'" ZAW 50: 141–48.

1932b "Studies in the Vocabulary of the Old Testament." *JThS* 33: 38–47; 34: 375–85.

1934 "Hebrew Notes." ZAW 52: 51–56.

1940 "Hebrew Notes on Prophets and Proverbs." *JThS* 41: 162–75.

1947 "Hebrew Roots and Words." WO 1: 406–15.

1950 "Hebrew Notes." *VT* 1: 241–50.

1951 "Problems in the Hebrew Text of Proverbs." *Bib* 32: 173–97.

1954 "Problems and Solutions." *VT* 4: 223–45.

1967 "Playing on Words." Pp. 1.121–29 in *Papers of the Fourth World Congress of Jewish Studies*. Jerusalem.

Driver, S. R.

1880 *A Commentary on the Book of Proverbs Attributed to Abraham Ibn Ezra*. Oxford: Clarendon (= "Pseudo-Ibn Ezra").

Drubbel, Adrien
1936a "Le Conflit entre la sagesse profane et la sagesse religieuse." *Bib* 17: 45–70.
1936b *Les livres sapientiaux d'Isräel dans leurs sources pré-exiliques*. Rome: Pie X.
Duesberg, Hilaire
1938 *Les Scribes inspirés*. Paris: de Brouwer.
Duhaime, Jean-L.
1980 "Perception de Dieu et comportement moral chez les sages d'Israël." *Science et Esprit* 32: 193–97.
Dunsmore, Marion Hiller
1925 "An Egyptian Contribution to the Book of Proverbs." *JR* 5: 300–308.
Dürr, Lorenz
1932 *Das Erziehungswesen im Alten Testament und im antiken Orient*. MVAG 36,2. Leipzig: J. C. Hinrichs.
Eaton, John
1989 *The Contemplative Face of Old Testament Wisdom*. Philadelphia: Trinity Press.
Ebeling, Erich, and Bruno Meissner, eds.
1932 *Reallexikon der Assyriologie*. Berlin: W. de Gruyter.
Ehrlich, Arnold B.
*1908–14 *Randglossen zur hebräischen Bibel*. Hildesheim: Georg Olms. (Repr. 1968; unless otherwise specified, references are to the notes on Proverbs, vol. 6, 1913, ad loc.]
Eissfeldt, Otto
1913 *Der Maschal im Alten Testament*. BZAW 24. Giessen: Töpelmann.
Elioni, M.
1977 *Meḥqarim BeQohelet UveMishley*. Jerusalem: Society for Biblical Study.
Emerton, John A.
1964 "A Note on Proverbs xii.26." ZAW 76: 191–93.
1965 "'Spring and Torrent' in Psalm LXXIV 15." *VTSup* 15: 122–33.
1968 "A Note on the Hebrew Text of Proverbs i. 22–3." *JTS* 19: 609–14.
1969 "Notes on Some Passages in the Book of Proverbs" (Prv. 14,31; 19,16; 24,21; 26,9; 28,12). *JTS* 20: 202–20.
1979 "A Note on Proverbs 2,18." *JTS* 30: 153–58.
1984 "The Meaning of Proverbs 13,2." *JTS* 35: 91–95.
1988 "The Interpretation of Proverbs 21,28." ZAW 100: 161–70.
1991 "A Further Consideration of D. W. Thomas's Theories about *Yādaʿ*." *VT* 46: 144–63.
Encyclopedia Miqra'it
1965–88 *Encyclopedia Miqra'it* [Hebrew]. Jerusalem: Bialik (= EM).
Englund, Gertie
1987 "The Treatment of Opposites in Temple Thinking and Wisdom Literature." Pp. 77–88 in *The Religion of the Ancient Egyptians. Cognitive Structures and Popular Expressions*. Ed. by G. Englund. Uppsala: Acta Universitatis Upsaliensis.
Erman, Adolf
1924 "Eine ägyptische Quelle der 'Spruch Salomos.'" *SPAW* (phil-hist. Kl. 15): 86–93.

Eshel, Hanan, and Esti Eshel
1987 *L^{e}mishneh Hahora'ah šel Hamilah Delet BeMishley* ["The Ambiguity of the Word *delet* in Proverbs" (Hebrew)]. *Megadim* 3: 52–54.
Estes, Daniel J.
1997 *Hear, My Son: Teaching and Learning in Proverbs 1–9*. Grand Rapids, Mich.: Eerdmans.
Faulkner, Raymond O.
1955 "Ptaḥḥotpe and the Disputants." AS 81–84.
Fecht, Gerhard
1958 *Der Habgierge und die Maat in der Lehre des Ptahhotep (5.und 19. Maxime)*. ADAIK I. Glückstadt-Hamburg-N.V.: Augustin.
Fensham, F. C.
1971 "The Change of Situation of a Person in Ancient Near Eastern and Biblical Literature." *Annali dell'Instituto Orientale di Napoli* 21: 155–64.
Fichtner, Johannes
1933 *Die altorientalische Weisheit in ihrer israelitisch-jüdischen Ausprägung*. BZAW 62. Giessen: Töpelmann.
1949 "Jesaja unter den Weisen," *TLZ* 74: 75–80.
1955 "Der Begriff des 'Nächsten' im Alten Testament." *Wort und Dienst* 4: 23–52.
1965 *Gottes Weisheit*. Arbeiten zur Theologie 2. Reihe, 3. Stuttgart: Calwer.
Firchow, Otto
1955 *Ägyptologische Studien*. Ed. by Otto Firchow. Deutsche Akad. d. Wiss. Institut für Orientforschung. Berlin: Akademie Verlag (= AS).
Fischer-Elfert, Hans-Werner
1983 *Die satirische Streitschrift des Papyrus Anastasi I.* (KÄT). Wiesbaden: Harrassowitz.
1984 "'Ich bin das Schiff—du bist das Ruder.'" HO I.3, 3; COHL 1254–56.
1986 *Literarische Ostraka der Ramessidenzeit in Übersetzung*. KÄT. Wiesbaden: Harrassowitz.
1997 *Lesefunde im literarischen Steinbruch von Deir el-Medineh*. KÄT 12. Wiesbaden: Harrassowitz.
Fishbane, Michael
1974 "Accusations of Adultery." *HUCA* 45: 25–45.
Fontaine, Carole R.
1982 *Traditional Sayings in the Old Testament*. Sheffield: Almond.
1985 "Proverb Performance in the Hebrew Bible." *JSOT* 32: 87–103.
1990 "The Sage in Family and Tribe." SIANE 155–64.
1993 "Wisdom in Proverbs." Pp. 99–114 in *In Search of Wisdom*. Ed. by L. Perdue et al. (Essays in Memory of John G. Gammie). Louisville, Ky.: Westminster/John Knox.
Forti, Tova
1996 "Animal Images in the Didactic Rhetoric of the Book of Proverbs." *Bib* 77: 48–63.
Foster, Benjamin R.
1993 *Before the Muses*. Bethesda, Md.: CDL (= BTM).
1994 "Wisdom and the Gods in Ancient Mesopotamia" (*Or* [ser. 2] 43: 344–65.
Foster, John L.
1977 *Thought Couplets and Clause Sequences in a Literary Text: The Maxims of Ptah-Hotep*. Toronto: The Society of the Study of Egyptian Antiquities.

1984 "Oriental Institute Ostracon 12074: 'Menna's Lament' or 'Letter to a Wayward Son.'" *Journal of the Society for the Study of Egyptian Antiquities* 14: 88–99.

1986 "Texts of the Egyptian Composition 'The Instruction of a Man for His Son' in the Oriental Institute Museum." *JNES* 45: 197–211.

Fox, Michael V.

1968 "Aspects of the Religion of the Book of Proverbs." *HUCA* 39: 55–69.

1973 "Jeremiah 2: 2 and the 'Desert Ideal.'" *CBQ* 35: 441–50.

1980 "Two Decades of Research in Egyptian Wisdom Literature." ZAW 107: 120–35.

1983 "Ancient Egyptian Rhetoric." *Rhetorica* 1: 9–22.

1985a "LXX Proverbs 3: 28 and Ancient Egyptian Wisdom." *HAR* 8: 63–69.

1985b *The Song of Songs and the Ancient Egyptian Love Songs*. Madison: University of Wisconsin Press.

1986 "Egyptian Onomastica and Biblical Wisdom." *VT* 36: 302–10.

1989 *Qohelet and His Contradictions*. JSOTSup 71. Sheffield: Almond Press.

1992 "Review of *Die Weisheit Israels—ein Fremdkörper im Alten Testament?* by F.-J. Steiert." *JBL* 111: 134–37.

1993a "Review of *Wurzeln der Weisheit* by C. Westermann." *JBL* 111: 529–32.

1993b "The Social Location of the Book of Proverbs." Pp. 227–39 in *Texts, Temples, and Traditions: A Tribute to Menahem Haran*, ed. M. V. Fox et al. Winona Lake, Ind.: Eisenbrauns, 1996.

1993c "Wisdom in Qohelet." Pp. 115–32 in *In Search of Wisdom*. Ed. by L. Perdue et al. (Essays in Memory of John G. Gammie). Louisville, Ky.: Westminster/John Knox.

1993d "Words for Wisdom." ZAH 6: 149–69.

1994 "The Pedagogy of Proverbs 2." *JBL* 113: 233–43.

1995 "World Order and Maʿat: A Crooked Parallel." *JANES* 23: 37–48.

1996a "*ʾAmon* Again." *JBL* 115: 699–702.

1996b "The Social Location of the Book of Proverbs." Pp. 227–39 in *Texts, Temples, and Traditions: A Tribute to Menahem Haran*. Ed. by M. V. Fox et al. Winona Lake, Ind.: Eisenbrauns.

1996c "The Strange Woman in Septuagint Proverbs." *JNSL* 22: 31–34.

1997a "Ideas of Wisdom in Proverbs 1–9." *JBL* 116: 613–33.

1997b "Who Can Learn? A Dispute in Ancient Pedagogy." Pp. 62–77 in *Wisdom, You Are My Sister* (FS R. E. Murphy). Ed. by M. L. Barré (CBQMS 29). Washington: Catholic Biblical Association.

1997c "What the Book of Proverbs Is About." *Congress Volume, VTSup*: 48: 153–67.

1997d "Words for Folly." ZAH 10: 1–12.

Fraine, J. de

1967 "*Margemah* (Prov 26,8)." Pp. 1.131–35 in *Papers of the Fourth World Congress of Jewish Studies*. Jerusalem: World Union of Jewish Studies.

Frankenberg, W.

1895 "Über Abfassungs-Ort und -Zeit, sowie Art und Inhalt von prov. I–IX." ZAW 15: 104–32.

Franklyn, Paul

1983 "The Sayings of Agur in Proverbs 30: Piety or Scepticism?" ZAW 95: 238–51.

Franzmann, Majella

1991 "The Wheel in Proverbs XX 26 and the Ode of Solomon XXIII 11–16." *VT* 41: 121–22.

Freedman, David Noel

1997 "Proverbs 2 and 31: A Study in Structural Complementarity." Pp. 47–55 in *Tehilla le-Moshe* (FS Moshe Greenberg). Ed. by M. Cogan et al. Winona Lake, Ind.: Eisenbrauns.

Friedländer, Moriz

1904 *Griechische Philosophie im Alten Testament*. Berlin: Reimer.

Fritsch, Charles T.

1953 "The Treatment of the Hexaplaric Signs in the Syro-Hexaplar of Proverbs." *JBL* 72: 169–81.

Frymer-Kensky, Tikva

1992 *In the Wake of the Goddesses*. New York: Free Press.

Gaboriau, F.

1968 "Enquête sur la signification biblique de connaître." *Angelicum* 45: 3–43.

Gammie, John G.

1974 "Spatial and Ethical Dualism in Jewish Wisdom and Apocalyptic Literature." *JBL* 93: 356–85.

1987 "The Septuagint of Job: Its Poetic Style and the Relationship to the Septuagint of Proverbs." *CBQ* 49: 14–31.

1990 "Paranetic Literature: Toward the Morphology of a Secondary Genre." *Semeia* 50: 41–75.

Gammie, John G., W. A. Brueggemann, W. L. Humphreys, and J. M. Ward, eds.

1978 *Israelite Wisdom: Theological and Literary Essays in Honor of Samuel Terrien*. New York: Union Theological Seminary (= IW).

Gammie, John G., and Leo G. Perdue, eds.

1990 *The Sage in Israel and the Ancient Near East*. Winona Lake, Ind.: Eisenbrauns (= SIANE).

Garbini, Giovanni

1984 "Proverbi per un anno. Il libro dei *Proverbi* e il calendario." *Henoch* 6: 139–46.

García Martínez, Florentino

1994 *The Dead Sea Scrolls Translated*. Leiden: Brill (= DSST).

Gardiner, Alan H.

1911 *Egyptian Hieratic Texts*. Series I: Literary Texts of the New Kingdom. Leipzig: Hinrichs.

1937 *Late-Egyptian Miscellanies*. BibAeg VII. Brussels: La Fondation Egyptologique (= LEM).

1946 "The Instruction Addressed to Kagemni and His Brethren." *JEA* 32: 71–74.

1947 *Ancient Egyptian Onomastica*. London: Oxford.

Garrett, Duane A.

1990 "Votive Prostitution Again: A Comparison of Proverbs 7:13–14 and 21:28–29." *JBL* 109: 681–82.

Gaspar, Joseph W.

1947 *Social Ideas in the Wisdom Literature of the Old Testament*. Washington, D.C.: Catholic University of America.

Gasser, Johann Conrad

1904 *Die Bedeutung der Sprüche Jesu ben Sira für die Datierung des althebräischen Spruchbuches*. Gütersloh: C. Bertelsmann.

Gaster, Theodor H.

1954 "Proverbs [viii 30]." *VT* 4: 77–78.

Gemser, Berend

1953 "The Importance of Motive Clauses in Old Testament Law." *VTSup* 1: 50–66.

1960 "The Instructions of 'Onchsheshonqy and Biblical Wisdom Literature." *VTSup* 7: 102–28 (repr. SAIW 134–60).

*1963 *Sprüche Salomos*. HAT I.16, 2nd ed. Tübingen: J. C. B. Mohr.

1968 "The Spiritual Structure of Biblical Aphoristic Wisdom." Pp. 138–49 in *Adhuc Loquitor*. Ed. by A. Van Selms and A. S. Van der Woude. Leiden: Brill (repr. SAIW 208–19).

Genug, John Franklin

1911 "Meaning and Usage of the Term *tušiyyah*." *JBL* 30: 114–22.

Geradon, Bernard de

1974 *Le Coeur, la langue, les mains*. Paris: Desclée De Brouwer.

Gerleman, Gillis

1950 "The Septuagint Proverbs as a Hellenistic Document." *OTS* 8: 15–27.

*1956 *Studies in the Septuagint. III: Proverbs*. Lund: Gleerup.

Gerstenberger, Erhard

1965 *Wesen und Herkunft des "apodiktischen Rechts."* WMANT 20. Neukirchen-Vluyn: Neukirchener Vlg.

1969 "Zur alttestamentlichen Weisheit." *Verkundigung und Forschung* 14: 28–44.

Gese, Hartmut

1958 *Lehre und Wirklichkeit in der alten Weisheit*. Tübingen: J. C. B. Mohr.

1984 "Wisdom Literature in the Persian Period." Pp. 189–218 in *The Cambridge History of Judaism*, vol. 1. Ed. by W. D. Davies and L. Finkelstein. Cambridge: Cambridge University Press.

Gesenius, Wilhelm, and Frants Buhl

1915 *Hebräisches und aramäisches Handwörterbuch über das Alte Testament*. Leipzig: Vogel.

Gewalt, Dietfried

1985 "'Öffne deinen Mund für den Stummen'—zu Proverbia 31,8." *Dielheimer Blätter zum Alten Testament* 21: 133–38.

Gibson, J. C. L.

1978 *Canaanite Myths and Legends*. Edinburgh: T. & T. Clark.

Giese, Ronald L., Jr.

1990 "Wisdom and Wealth in the Septuagint of Proverbs." Ph.D. diss., University of Wisconsin–Madison.

1992a "Quantifying Wealth in the Septuagint of Proverbs." *JBL* 111: 409–25.

1992b "Strength through Wisdom and the Bee in LXX Prov 6,8^{a-c}." *Bib* 73: 404–11.

1993a "Compassion for the Lowly in Septuagint Proverbs." *JSP* 11: 109–17.

1993b "Dualism in the LXX of Prov 2:17." *JETS* 36: 289–95.

Gilbert, Maurice

1979a "Avant-propos." *BETL* 51: 7–13.

1979b "Le discours de la Sagesse en Proverbs, 8. Structure et cohérence." *BETL* 51: 202–18.

1979c *La Sagesse de l'Ancien Testament.* Ed. by M. Gilbert. Leuven: Leuven University.

1980 "La Sagesse personnifiée dans les textes de l'Ancien Testament." *Cahiers Evangile* 32: 5–36.

1991 "Le Discours menaçant de Sagesse en Proverbes 1,20–33." Pp. 90–119 in *Storia e tradizioni di Israele*. Brescia: Paideia.

1995 "Qu'en est-il de la Sagesse?" Pp. 19–60 in *La Sagesse Biblique*. Lectio Divina 160. Paris: Cerf.

Glanville, Stephen R. K.

1955 *The Instructions of ʿOnchsheshongy.* Catalogue of Demotic Papyri in the British Museum, Vol. II. London: British Museum.

Glazier-McDonald, Beth

1987 *Malachi*. SBLDS 98. Atlanta: Scholars Press.

Glück, J. J.

1964 "Proverbs XXX 15a." *VT* 14: 367–70.

1977 "The Figure of 'Inversion' in the Book of Proverbs." *Semitics* 5: 24–31.

Glueck, Nelson

1927 *Das Wort ḥesed im alttestamentlichen Sprachgebrauche*. Giessen: Töpelmann. (ET: A. Gottschalk; Cincinnati: Hebrew Union College, 1967.)

Godbey, Allen H.

1922–23 "The Hebrew *Mašal*." *AJSL* 39: 89–108.

Godlovitch, S.

1981 "On Wisdom." *Canadian Journal of Philosophy* 11: 137–55.

Goedicke, H.

1967 "Die Lehre eines Mannes für seinen Sohn." *ZÄS* 94: 62–71.

Goldingay, J. E.

1977 "Proverbs V and IX." *RB* 84: 80–93.

1994 "The Arrangement of Sayings in Proverbs 10–15." *JSOT* 61: 75–83.

Golka, Friedemann W.

1983 "Die israelitische Weisheitsschule oder 'der Kaisers neue Kleider.'" *VT* 33: 257–70.

1986 "Die Königs- und hofsprüche und der Ursprung der israelitischen Weisheit." *VT* 36: 13–36.

1989 "Die Flecken des Leoparden." Pp. 149–65 in *Schöpfung und Befreiung* (FS C. Westermann). Ed. by R. Alberz et al. Stuttgart: Calwer.

1993 *The Leopard's Spots: Biblical and African Wisdom in Proverbs*. Edinburgh: T & T Clark.

Gordis, Robert

1943 "The Social Background of Wisdom Literature." *HUCA* 18: 77–118.

Gordon, Cyrus H.

1930 "Rabbinic Exegesis in the Vulgate of Proverbs." *JBL* 49: 384–416.

Goshen-Gottstein, I. M.

1957 "The History of the Bible-Text and Comparative Semitics." *VT* 7: 195–201.

1963 "Theory and Practice of Text Criticism." *Textus* 3: 130–58.

Gottlieb, Isaac B.

1990 "Pirqe Abot and Biblical Wisdom." *VT* 40: 152–64.

Graetz, Heinrich
1884 "Exegetische Studien zu den Salomonischen Sprüchen." *Monatschrift für die Wissenschaft des Judentums* 33: 145–447 (*passim*).
Greenberg, Moshe
1977 "The Use of the Ancient Versions for Interpreting the Hebrew Text." *VTSup* 29: 131–47.
1995 *Studies in the Bible and Jewish Thought*. Philadelphia: Jewish Publication Society.
Greenfield, Jonas C.
1985 "The Seven Pillars of Wisdom (Prov 9:1). A Mistranslation." *JQR* 76: 13–20.
Greenspahn, Frederick E.
1994 "A Mesopotamian Proverb and Its Biblical Reverberations." *JAOS* 114: 33–38.
Gressman, Hugo
1927 *Israels Spruchweisheit im Zusammenhang der Weltliteratur*. Berlin: Karl Curtius.
Grimm, Karl J.
1901 "The Meaning and Etymology of the Word *tušiyyah* in the OT." *JAOS* 22: 35–44.
Grollenberg, Luc
1952 "A Propos de Prov., VII, 6 et XVII, 27." *RB* 59: 40–43.
Grossberg, Daniel
1994 "Two Kinds of Sexual Relationships in the Hebrew Bible." *HS* 35: 7–25.
Gruber, Mayer I.
1980 *Aspects of Nonverbal Communication in the Ancient Near East*. 2 vols. Rome: Biblical Institute Press.
1986 "Hebrew *q*[e]*dešah* and Her Canaanite and Akkadian Cognates." *UF* 18: 133–48.
Grumach, Irene: see Shirun-Grumach
Gugliemi, Waltraud
1983 "Eine 'Lehre' für einen reiselustigen Sohn (Ostrakon Oriental Institute 12074)." *WO* 14: 149–66.
Gunn, Battiscombe
1926 "Some Middle-Egyptian Proverbs." *JEA* 12: 282–84.
Gunneweg, Antonius H. J.
1992 "Weisheit, Prophetie und Kanonformel. Erwägungen zu Proverbia 30,1–9." Pp. 253–60 in *Alttestamentliche Glaube und Biblische Theologie* (FS H. D. Preuss). Stuttgart: Kohlhammer.
Habel, Norman C.
1972 "The Symbolism of Wisdom in Proverbs 1–9." *Int* 26: 131–57.
Halbe, Jörn
1979 "'Altorientalisches Weltordnungsdenken' und alttestamentliche Theologie." *ZTK* 76: 381–418.
Halperin, David J.
1981 "*The Book of Remedies* [cited in bBer 10b, Pes 56a], the Canonization of the Solomonic Writings, and the Riddle of Pseudo-Eusebius." *JQR* 72: 269–92.

Haran, Menachem

1972 "The Graded Numerical Sequence and the Phenomenon of 'Automatism' in Biblical Poetry." *VTSup* 22: 238–67.

1988 "On the Diffusion of Literacy and Schools in Ancient Israel." *Congress Volume*. Ed. by J. A. Emerton; Jerusalem, 1988. *VTSup* 40: 81–95.

1996 *Haʿăsuphah Hamiqra'it* ["The Biblical Collection"]. Jerusalem: Mosad Bialik.

Harrington, Daniel J.

1996 *Wisdom Texts from Qumran*. London & New York: Routledge.

Harris, Scott L.

1995 *Proverbs 1–9: A Study of Inner-Biblical Interpretation*. SBLDS. Atlanta: Scholars Press.

Hartman, Louis F., and Alexander A. Di Lella

1978 *The Book of Daniel*. AB 23. Garden City, N.Y.: Doubleday.

Hasan-Rokem, Galit

1990 "And God Created the Proverb. . . ." Pp. 107–20 in *Text and Tradition*. SBL Semeia Studies. Ed. by Susan Niditch. Atlanta: Scholars Press.

Hatch, Edwin

1889 *Essays in Biblical Greek*. Oxford: Clarendon.

Haupt, Paul

1926 "Mistranslated Lines in Proverbs." *JBL* 45: 350–57.

Hausmann, Jutta

1991? "Studien zum Menschenbild der älteren Weisheit." Habilitationschrift Augustana-Hochschule (unpub.). Neuendettelsau. n.d.

1992 "Beobachtungen zu Spr 31,10–31." Pp. 261–66 in *Alttestamentliche Glaube und Biblische Theologie* (FS H. D. Preuss). Stuttgart: Kohlhammer.

Hausmann, Jutta, and Hans-Jürgen Zotta, eds.

1992 *Alttestamentlicher Glaube und biblische Theologie* (FS H. D. Preuss). Stuttgart: Kohlhammer.

Hayes, W.

1948 "A Much Copied Letter of the Early Middle Kingdom." *JNES* 7: 1–10.

*Healey, John F.

1991 *The Targum of Proverbs*. The Aramaic Bible, XV. Collegeville, Minn.: Michael Glazier.

Heidenheim, M.

*1865ff. "Zur Textkritik der Proverbien." *Deutsche Vierteljarschrift* 2 (1865) 395–414 (Prov 1–3); 3 (1867) 51–60 (Prov 4–7); 327–46 (Prov 8–9); 445–60 (Prov 10–14); 468–87 (Prov 15–31).

Heijerman, Mieke

1994 "Who Would Blame Her? The 'Strange' Woman of Proverbs 7." Pp. 21–31 in *Reflections on Theology and Gender*. Ed. by F. van Dijk-Hemmes and A. Brenner. Kampen: Kok Pharos.

Heinisch, Paul

1933 *Die persönliche Weisheit des Alten Testaments in religionsgeschichtlicher Beleuchtung*. Münster-in-Weisf.: Aschendorff.

Helck, Wolfgang

1956 *Urkunden der 18. Dynastie*. Berlin: Akademie. Leipzig (= Urk.).

1969 *Der Text der "Lehre Amenemhets I. für seinen Sohn."* KÄT. Wiesbaden: Harrassowitz.

1970a *Die Lehre des Dw3-Htjj*. 2 vols. KÄT. Wiesbaden: Harrassowitz.
1970b *Die Prophezeiung des Nfr.tj*. KÄT. Wiesbaden: Harrassowitz.
1977 *Die Lehre für König Merikare*. KÄT. Wiesbaden: Harrassowitz.
1984 *Die Lehre des Djedefhor und Die Lehre eines Vaters an Seinen Sohn*. KÄT. Wiesbaden: Harrassowitz.

Helck, Wolfgang, and Otto Eberhard, eds.
1972ff. *Lexikon der Ägyptologie*. Wiesbaden: Harrassowitz (= LÄ).

Hempel, Johannes
1929 [Remarks on Cowley, "Two Aramaic Ostraca" (1929)], ZAW 47: 150–51.
1936 *Gott und Mensch im Alten Testament*. Chap. 1: "Die Furcht vor Jahve," pp. 4–33. BWANT 38. Stuttgart.

Hengel, Martin
1974 *Judaism and Hellenism* (ET J. Bowden). Philadelphia: Fortress.

Herbert, A. S.
1954 "The Parable (*Māšāl*) in the Old Testament." *Scottish Journal of Theology* 7: 180–96.

Herdner, Andrée
1963 *Corpus des tablettes en cunéiformes alphabétiques découvertes à Ras Shamra-Ugarit de 1929 à 1939*. Paris: Geuthner.

Hermisson, Hans-Jürgen
1968 *Studien zur israelitischen Spruchweisheit*. WMANT 28. Neukirchen: Neukirchener Vlg.
1971 "Weisheit und Geschichte." Pp. 136–54 in *Probleme biblischer Theologie* (FS Gerhard von Rad). Ed. by H. W. Wolff. Munich: Chr. Kaiser.
1978 "Observations on the Creation Theology in Wisdom." IW 43–57.
1990 "Zur 'feministischen' Exegese des ATs." *EpD/Evangelische Information* 52a/90: 3–7.

Hesselgrave, Charles Everett
1910 *The Hebrew Personification of Wisdom; Its Origin, Development and Influence*. New York: G. E. Stechert.

Hildebrandt, Ted
1988a "Proverbs 22: 6a: Train Up a Child?" *Grace Theological Journal* 9: 3–19.
1988b "Proverbial Pairs: Compositional Units in Proverbs 10–29." *JBL* 107: 207–24.
1990 "Proverbial Strings: Cohesion in Proverbs 10." *Grace Theological Journal* 11: 171–85.
1992 "Motivation and Antithetic Parallelism in Proverbs 10–15." *JETS* 35: 433–44.

Hitzig, F.
1858 *Die Sprüche Salomons*. Leipzig: Weidmann.

Ho, Ahuva
1991 *Ṣedeq and Ṣedaqah in the Hebrew Bible*. New York: Peter Lang.

Höffken, Peter
1985 "Das Ego des Weisen." *TZ* 41: 121–34.

Hoglund, Kenneth G., E. F. Huwiler, J. T. Glass, and R. W. Lee
1987a *The Listening Heart* (FS Roland E. Murphy). JSOTSup 58. Sheffield: Sheffield Academic Press.
1987b "The Fool and the Wise in Dialogue." Pp. 161–80 in *The Listening Heart* (Hoglund et al., 1987a).

1987c "Murphy's Axiom: Every Gnomic Saying Needs a Balancing Corrective." Pp. 1–13 in *The Listening Heart* (Hoglund et al. 1987a).

Holladay, William

1958 *The Root šubh in the Old Testament*. Leiden: Brill.

Holmes, James S.

1988 *Translated!* Amsterdam: Rodopi.

Hornung, Erik

1979 "Lehren über das Jenseits?" SAL 217–24.

1982 *Conceptions of God in Ancient Egypt*. Ithaca, N.Y.: Cornell.

Hornung, Erik, and Othmar Keel, eds.

1979 *Studien zu altägyptischen Lebenslehren*. OBO 28. Freiburg (= SAL).

Horst, P. W. van der

1978 *The Sentences of Pseudo-Phocylides*. Leiden: Brill.

Hubbard, David A.

1966 "The Wisdom Movement and Israel's Covenant Faith." *TynBul* 17: 18.

Hudal, Alois

1914 *Die religiösen und sittlichen Ideen des Spruchbuches*. Rome: Pontifical Biblical Institute.

Hugenberger, Gordon P.

1993 *Marriage as a Covenant*. VTSup 52. Leiden: Brill.

Humbert, Paul

1929 *Recherches sur les sources égyptiennes de la littérature sapientiale d'Israel*. Neuchâtel.

1937 "La 'Femme étrangère' du Livre des Proverbes." *Revue des études sémitiques* 4: 49–64.

1939 "Les adjectifs 'Zâr' et 'Nokrî' et la 'Femme Etrangère' des proverbes bibliques." *Mélanges Syriens* 1.259–66.

1950 "'Qânâ' en Hêbreu biblique." Pp. in 259–67 in *FS Alfred Bertholet*. Tübingen: J. C. B. Mohr.

1960 "Le substantif *tôʿēbā* et le verbe *tʿb* dans l'AT." ZAW 72: 217–37.

Hurvitz, Avi

1968 "The Chronological Significance of 'Aramaisms' in Biblical Hebrew." *IEJ* 18: 234–40.

1986 *ʿIyyunim Bilšono šel Sefer Mišley: L^{e}šimmušo šel Mivneh Hasmikhut baʿal X*" ["Studies in the Language of the Book of Proverbs: Concerning the use of the Construct Pattern *baʿal* X" (Hebrew)]. *Tarbiz* 55: 1–17.

1988 "Wisdom Vocabulary in the Hebrew Psalter: A Contribution to the Study of the 'Wisdom Psalms.'" *VT* 38: 41–51.

1990 "*Ṣaddiq* = 'wise' in Biblical Hebrew and the Wisdom Connections of Ps 37." Pp. 109–13 in *Goldene Äpfel in silbernen Schalen*. Frankfurt a.M.: Lang.

1991 *Š^{e}qiʿey Ḥokmah Besefer T^{e}hillim* [*Wisdom Language in Biblical Psalmody* (Hebrew)]. Jerusalem: Magnes.

Ibn-Janaḥ, Jonah

[1965] *Sefer Hariqmah*. 2 vols. Ed. by M. Wilensky (first ed. 1929). Jerusalem: Academy for the Hebrew Language.

Imschoot, Paul van

1938 "Sagesse et Esprit dans l'A.T." *RB* 47: 23–49.

Irwin, William A.

1961 "Where Shall Wisdom Be Found?" *JBL* 80: 133–42.

1984 "The Metaphor in Prov 11,30." *Bib* 65: 97–100.

Israeli, Shlomit

1990 "Chapter Four of the Wisdom Book of *Amenemope*." Pp. 464–83 in *Studies in Egyptology Presented to Miriam Lichtheim*. Ed. by Sarah Israelit-Groll. Jerusalem: Magnes.

Iwry, Samuel

1966 "whnmṣᶜ—a striking variant reading in 1QIsa[a]." *Textus* 5: 34–43.

Jacob, Edmond

1971 "Sagesse et alphabet. A propos de Proverbes 31: 10–31." *Homages à André Dupont-Sommer*. Paris.

1978 "Wisdom and Religion in Sirach." IW 247–60.

Jacobson, Arland D.

1990 "Proverbs and Social Control." Pp. 75–88 in *Gnosticism & the Early Christian World*. Ed. by James E. Goehring et al. Sonoma, Calif.: Polebridge.

Jäger, Johannes G.

1788 *Observationes in Proverbium Salomonis versionem alexandrinam*. Meldorf (= Jäg.).

Jakobson, Roman

1979 "Notes on the Makeup of a Proverb." *Linguistic and Literary Studies* 4: 83–85.

Jamieson-Drake, David

1991 *Scribes and Schools in Monarchic Judah*. JSOTSup 109. Sheffield: Almond.

Jasnow, Richard

1982 "An Unrecognized Parallel in Two Demotic Wisdom Texts." *Enchoria* 11: 59–61.

1992 *A Late Period Hieratic Wisdom Text (p. Brooklyn 47.218.135)*. SAOC 52. Chicago: Oriental Institute.

Jenkins, R. Geoffrey

1987 "The Text of P. Antinoopolis 8/210." Pp. 65–77 in *VI Congress of the International Organization for Septuagint and Cognate Studies*. Ed. by Claude Cox. SBLSCS 23. Atlanta: Scholars Press.

Jenks, Alan W.

1985 "Theological Presuppositions of Israel's Wisdom Literature." *Horizons in Biblical Theology* 7: 43–75.

Jepsen, Alfred

1965 "*Ṣedeq* und *Ṣᵉdaqah* im Alten Testament." Pp. 78–89 in *Gottes Wort und Gottes Land* (FS H.-W. Hertzberg). Göttingen: Vandenhoeck & Ruprecht.

Jequier, G.

1911 *Les Papyrus Prisse et ses Variants*. Paris: P. Geuthner.

Johnson, A. R.

1955 *Mašal*. VTSup 3: 162–69.

Joosten, Jan

1995 "Doublet Translations in Peshitta Proverbs." Pp. 63–72 in *The Peshitta as a Translation*. Ed. by P. B. Dirksen and A. van der Kooij. Leiden: Brill.

Joüon, Paul, and Takamitsu Muraoka

1991 *A Grammar of Biblical Hebrew*. Rome: Pontifical Biblical Inst. (= GBH).

Kaiser, Walter C.

1978 "Wisdom Theology and the Centre of Old Testament Theology." *EvQ* 50: 132–46.

Kalugila, Leonidas
1980 *The Wise King*. Lund: Gleerup.
Kaminka, A.
1931–32 "Septuaginta und Targum zu Proverbia." *HUCA* 8–9: 169–91.
Kaspi, Yosef ibn
*1903 *Ḥaṣoṣ^{e}rot Kesef* in *'Aśarah K^{e}ley Kesef*. Ed. by Isaac Last. Pressburg: Alkalay & Son.
Kaufmann, Yehezkel
1960 *The Religion of Israel*. Trans. and ed. by M. Greenberg. Chicago: University of Chicago.
Kayatz, Christa
1966 *Studien zu Proverbien 1–9*. WMANT 22. Neukirchen-Vluyn: Neukirchener Vlg.
Keel, Othmar
1971 "Eine Diskussion um die Bedeutung polarer Begriffspaare in den Lebenslehren." SAL 225–34.
1974 "Die Weisheit 'spielt' vor Gott." *Freiburger Zeitschrift für Philosophie und Theologie* 21: 1–66.
Kellenberger, Edgar
1982 *ḥäsäd wä'ämät als Ausdruck einer Glaubenserfahrung*. ATANT 69. Zürich: Theologischer Vlg.
Keller, Carl A.
1977 "Zum sogenannten Vergeltungsglauben im Proverbienbuch." Pp. 223–38 in *Beiträge zur atl. Theologie* (FS W. Zimmerli). Göttingen: Vandenhoeck & Ruprecht.
Kitchen, Kenneth A.
1969 "Studies in Egyptian Wisdom Literature—I: The Instruction of a Man for His Son." *OrAnt* 8: 189–208.
1977–78 "Proverbs and Wisdom Books of the Ancient Near East." *TynBul* 28: 69–114.
1979 "The Basic Literary Forms and Formulations of Ancient Instructional Writings in Egypt and Western Asia." SAL 235–82.
1988 "Egypt and Israel During the First Millennium." *Congress Volume: Jerusalem, 1986*. Ed by J. A. Emerton. VTSup 40: 106–25.
Kleinig, John W.
1983 "The Banquet of Wisdom—An Exegetical Study of Proverbs 9: 1–12." *Lutheran Theological Journal* 17: 24–28.
Kloppenborg, John S.
1982 "Isis and Sophia in the Book of Wisdom." *HTR* 75: 57–84.
Knox, Wilfred L.
1937 "The Divine Wisdom." *JThS* 38: 230–37.
Koch, Klaus
1972 "Gibt es ein Vergeltungsdogma im Alten Testament?" Pp. 130–80 in *Um das Prinzip der Vergeltung in Religion und Recht des Alten Testaments*. Ed. by K. Koch. Darmstadt (first published in *ZTK* 52 [1955] 1–42; ET in Crenshaw 1983, 57–87).
König, Eduard
1897 *Lehrgebäude der hebräischen Sprache*. II.2 (Syntax). Leipzig: J. C. Hinrichs.
Körbert, R.
1982 "Zu Prov 23,1–2." *Bib* 63: 264–65.

Kovacs, Brian W.
1974 "Is There a Class-Ethic in Proverbs?" Pp. 171–89 in *Essays in OT Ethics*. Ed. by J. L. Crenshaw and James Willis. New York: KTAV.
Krantz, Eva S.
1996 "'A Man Not Supported by God': On Some Crucial Words in Proverbs XXX 1." *VT* 46: 548–53.
Kraus, Hans-Joachim
1951 *Die Verkündigung der Weisheit*. Neukirchen: Kreis Mohrs.
Krispenz, Jutta
1989 *Spruchkompositionen im Buch Proverbia*. Frankfurt a.M.: Peter Lang.
Kruger, Paul A.
1987 "Promiscuity or Marriage Fidelity? A Note on Prov. 5:15–18." *JNSL* 13: 61–68.
Küchler, Max
1966 *Frühjüdische Weisheitstraditionen*. OBO 26. Fribourg: Universitätsverlag.
1992 "Gott und seine Weisheit in der Septuaginta. (Ijob 28; Spr 8)." Pp. 118–43 in *Monotheismus und Christologie*. Ed. by H.-J. Klauck. Freiburg: Herder.
Kugel, James L.
1981 *The Idea of Biblical Poetry*. New Haven: Yale University Press.
Kuhn, Gottfried
1931 *Beiträge zur Erklärung des Salomonischen Spruchbuches*. BWANT 57. Stuttgart: W. Kohlhammer.
Lackoff, George, and Mark Johnson
1980 *Metaphors We Live By*. Chicago: University of Chicago Press.
Lagarde, Paul de
*1863 *Anmerkungen zur griechischen Übersetzung der Proverbien*. Leipzig: Brockhaus (= Lag.).
1873 *Hagiographa Chaldaica*. Leipzig: Repr. Osnabrück: Zeller, 1967.
Lambert, W. G.
1960 *Babylonian Wisdom Literature*. Oxford: Clarendon (= BWL).
Lanczkowski, Günter
1955 "Reden und Schweigen im ägyptischen Verständnis." AS 186–96.
Landes, George M.
1956 "The Fountain at Jazer." *BASOR* 144: 30–37.
1978 "Jonah: A *Māšāl*?" IW 137–58.
Lang, Bernhard
1972 *Die weisheitliche Lehrrede*. SBT 54. Stuttgart: KBW.
1979 "Schule und Unterricht im alten Israel." *BETL* 51: 186–201.
1981 "Vorläufer von Speiseeis in Bibel und Orient. Eine Untersuchung von Spr 25,13." *AOAT* 212: 219–32.
1983 "Die sieben Säulen der Weisheit (Sprüche IX 1) im Licht israelitischer Architektur." *VT* 33: 488–91.
1986 *Wisdom and the Book of Proverbs*. New York: Pilgrim.
1995 "Figure ancienne, figure nouvelle de la sagesse en Pr 1 à 9." Pp. 61–97 in *La Sagesse Biblique*. Lectio Divina 160. Paris: Cerf.
Lange, Hans O.
1925 *Das Weisheitsbuch des Amenemope*. Copenhagen: A. F. Host.

LaPointe, Roger
1970 "Foi et vérifiabilité dans le langage sapiential de rétribution." *Bib* 51: 349–67.
Lebram, J. C.
1965 "Nachbiblische Weisheitstraditionen." *VT* 15: 167–237.
Leclant, Jean
1963 "Documents nouveaux et points de vue récents sur les sagesses de l'Egypte ancienne." SPOA 4–26.
Leiden Peshitta, Proverbs: See Di Lella
Lemaire, André
1981 *Les écoles et la formation de la Bible dans l'ancien Israel*. Fribourg: Editions Universitaires.
1984 "Sagesse et écoles." *VT* 34: 270–81.
1990 "The Sage in School and Temple." SIANE 165–81.
Lévêque, Jean
1974 "Le Contrepoint théologique apporté par la réflexion sapientielle." *BETL* 33: 183–202.
1985 *Les motivations de l'acte moral dans le livre des "Proverbes."* Pp. 105–21 in *Ethique, Religion et Foi*. Ed. by J. Doré et al. Paris: Beaucheshe.
Lewis, Theodore J.
1996 "Toward a Literary Translation of the Rapi'uma Texts." Pp. 115–49 in *Ugarit, Religion and Culture*. FS John Gibson. Ugaritisch-Biblische Literature 12. Ed. by N. Wyatt, W. G. E. Watson, and J. B. Lloyd. Münster: Ugarit-Verlag.
Lexa, Frantisek
1926 *Papyrus Insinger*. Paris: Geuthner.
Lichtenstein, Murray H.
1973 "The Poetry of Poetic Justice." *JANES* 5: 255–65.
1982 "Chiasm and Symmetry in Proverbs 31." *CBQ* 44: 202–11.
Lichtheim, Miriam
1973–80 *Ancient Egyptian Literature*. Vols. 1–3 (= AEL). Berkeley: University of California.
1979 "Observations on Papyrus Insinger." SAL 283–305.
1983 *Late Egyptian Wisdom Literature in the International Context*. OBO 52. Freiburg: Universitätslag (= LEWL).
1992 *Maat in Egyptian Autobiographies and Related Studies*. OBO 120. Göttingen: Vandenhoeck & Ruprecht.
1997 *Moral Values in Ancient Egypt*. OBO 155. Göttingen: Vandenhoeck & Ruprecht.
Liddell, H. G., and Robert Scott
1940 A *Greek-English Lexicon*. Oxford: Clarendon (repr. 1968).
Lindenberger, James M.
1983 *The Aramaic Proverbs of Ahiqar* (Johns Hopkins Near Eastern Studies). Baltimore: Johns Hopkins University Press.
Lipiński, E.
1967 "Peninna, Iti'el et l'Athlète." *VT* 17: 68–75.
1968 "Macarismes et Psaumes de congratulation." *RB* 75: 321–67.
1973 "Les 'voyantes des rois' en Prov. XXXI 3." *VT* 23: 246.

Lipscomb, W. Lowndes, with James Sanders
1978 "Wisdom at Qumran." IW 277–85.
Loewenstamm, Samuel E.
1987 "Remarks on Proverbs XVII 12 and XX 27." *VT* 37: 221–24.
Loprieno, Antonio
1980 "Amenemope ed i Proverbii: Un Problema di Comparazione Lessicale." *Vicino Oriente* 3: 47–76.
Loretz, Oswald
1974 "ʾjš Mgn in Proverbia 6,11 und 24,34." *UF* 6: 476–77.
1985 "Ein kanaanäisches Fragment in Proverbia 9, 1–3a.5." *Studi Epigrafici e Linguistici* 2: 127–31.
Lowe, A. D.
1980 "Some Correct Renderings in Ancient Biblical Versions." Pp. 24–38 in *Oriental Studies Presented to B. J. Isserlin*. Ed. by R. Y. Ebied and M. J. L. Young. Leiden: Brill.
Lust, J., E. Eynikel, and K. Hauspie
1996 *A Greek-English Lexicon of the Septuagint*. Stuttgart: Deutsche Bibelgesellschaft.
Luzzatto, Samuel David (Shadal)
*1876 *Comments of Shadal on Prophets and Writings* [Hebrew]. Lemberg: C. Budweiser.
Lyons, Ellen L.
1987 "A Note on Proverbs 31.10–31." Pp. 237–45 in *The Listening Heart*. Ed. by K. Hoglund et al. Sheffield: Sheffield Academic Press.
Maag, V.
1965 "*B^e^lijaʿal* im AT." *TZ* 21: 287–99.
Mack, Burton L.
1970 "Wisdom Myth and Myth-ology." *Int* 24: 46–60.
1973 *Logos und Sophia*. SUNT 10. Göttingen: Vandenhoeck & Ruprecht.
1985 *Wisdom and the Hebrew Epic*. Chicago: University of Chicago.
Magass, Walter
1985 "Die Rezeptionsgeschichte der Proverbien." *Linguistica Biblica* 57: 61–80.
Maier, Christl
1995 *Die "Fremde Frau" in Proverbien 1–9*. OBO 144. Göttingen: Vandenhoeck & Ruprecht.
Maimonides, Moses
1904 *The Guide for the Perplexed*. ET M. Friedländer. London: Routledge (repr. 1956).
Maire, Thierry
1995 "Proverbes XXII 17ss.: Enseignement à Shalishom?" *VT* 45: 227–38.
Malbim (Meir Loeb b. Yechiel Michael)
*1923 *Musar Haḥokmah* (Comm. on Proverbs). Vilna: Rom.
1982 *Malbim on Mishley*. Abridged trans. by Charles Wengrov. Jerusalem: Feldheim.
Malchow, Bruce V.
1985 "A Manual for Future Monarchs." *CBQ* 47: 238–45.
Mandry, Stephen A.
1972 *There Is No God!: A Study of the Fool in the Old Testament*. Rome: Catholic Book Agency.

Marcus, Ralph
1943 "The Tree of Life in Proverbs." *JBL* 62: 117–20.
1950–51 "On Biblical Hypostases of Wisdom." *HUCA* 25: 157–71.
Margalith, Othniel
1976 *ʾArbaʿ Pesuqim B^esefer Mišley* ["Four Verses in Proverbs." (Hebrew)]. *Beth Mikra* 67: 517–23.
Martin, Tony Michael
1981 "Sages and Scribes." SBT 11: 93–94.
Maybaum, S.
1871 "Über die Sprache des Targum zu den Sprüchen und dessen Verhältnis zum Syrer." *Archiv für wiss. Erforschung des AT* 2: 66–93.
McAlpine, Thomas H.
1987 *Sleep, Divine and Human, in the OT.* JSOTSup 38. Sheffield: JSOT Press.
McCreesh, Thomas P.
1985 "Wisdom as Wife: Proverbs 31:10–31." *RB* 92: 25–46.
McKane, William
1965 *Prophets and Wise Men.* Naperville, Ill.: Allenson.
*1970 *Proverbs.* OTL. London: SCM.
1979 "Functions of Language and Objectives of Discourse according to Proverbs 10–30." *BETL* 51:166–85.
McKinlay, Judith E.
1996 *Gendering Wisdom the Host.* JSOTSup 216. Sheffield: JSOT Press.
Meinhold, Arndt
1987 "Gott und Mensch in Proverbien III." *VT* 37: 468–77.
*1991 *Die Sprüche.* Zürcher Bibelkommentare 16 (2 vols). Zürich: Theologischer Vlg.
1992 "Der Umgang mit dem Feind nach Spr 25,21f. als Masstab für das Menschsein." Pp. 244–52 in *Alttestamentliche Glaube und Biblische Theologie* (FS H. D. Preuss). Stuttgart: Kohlhammer.
Melammed, Ezra Z.
1972 *Targum Mishley. Bar Ilan* 9: 18–91.
Metzger, Bruce M.
1972 "Literary Forgeries and Canonical Pseudepigrapha." *JBL* 91: 3–24.
Meyers, Carol L.
1974 *The Tabernacle Menorah: A Synthetic Study of a Symbol from the Biblical Cult.* ASORDS 2. Missoula, Mont.: Scholars Press.
Mezzacasa, Giacomo
*1913 *Il Libro dei Proverbi di Salomone: Studie Critico sulle Aggiunte Greco-Alessandrine.* Rome: Pontifical Biblical Institute (= Mezz.).
Michel, Dieter
1992 "Proverbia 2—ein Dokument der Geschichte der Weisheit." Pp. 233–43 in *Alttestamentlicher Glaube und Biblische Theologie* (FS H. D. Preuss). Ed. by J. Hausmann and H.-J. Zobel. Stuttgart: Kohlhammer.
Milgrom, Jacob
*1991 *Leviticus 1–16.* AB 3. New York: Doubleday Anchor.
Miller, Patrick D.
1970 "Apotropaic Imagery in Proverbs 6,20–22." *JNES* 29: 129–30.
1982 *Sin and Judgment in the Prophets.* SBLMS 27. Chico, Calif.: Scholars Press.

Minsker, Frank
1940 "Syriacisms in the Targum to the Book of Proverbs." Rabbinic Thesis. Hebrew Union College, Cincinnati.
Mitchell, Christopher
1987 *The Meaning of BRK "To Bless" in the OT.* SBLDS 95. Atlanta: Scholars Press.
Moffatt, James
*1954 *A New Translation of the Bible.* New York: Harper & Row (orig. 1922).
Montet, Pierre
1963 "Les fruits défendus et la confession des péchés." SPOA 53–62.
Moore, Rick D.
1994 "A Home for the Alien: Worldly Wisdom and Covenantal Confession in Proverbs 30,1–9." ZAW 106: 96–107.
Moran, William L.
1963 "The Ancient Near Eastern Background of the Love of God in Deuteronomy." *CBQ* 25: 77–87.
Morenz, Siegfried
1959 "Ein weitere Spur der Weisheit Amenopes in der Bibel." ZAW 84: 79–80.
1963 "Aegyptologische Beiträge zur Erforschung der Weisheitsliteratur Israels." SPOA 63–72.
Morgan, Donn F.
1981 *Wisdom in the Old Testament Traditions.* Oxford: Blackwell.
Moss, Alan J.
1993 "Wisdom, The Wife, as Beloved, Home-Builder, and Teaching Mother." Ph.D. Diss., University of Queensland.
Mowinckel, Sigmund
1955 "Psalms and Wisdom." *VTSup* 3: 205–24.
Mühll, Peter von der
1976 "Das griechische Symposion." Pp. 483–505 in *Ausgewählte kleine Schriften.* Ed. by B. Wyss. Basel: Fr. Reinhardt (orig. 1957).
Müller, August, and Emil Kautzsch
*1901 *The Book of Proverbs: A Critical Edition of the Hebrew Text.* Leipzig: Hinrichs.
Müller, Hans-Peter
1970 "Der Begriff 'Rätsel' im Alten Testament." *VT* 20: 465–89.
1977 "Die weisheitliche Lehrerzählung im Alten Testament und seiner Umwelt." *WO* 9: 77–98.
Murphy, Roland E.
1962 "The Concept of Wisdom Literature." Pp. 46–54 in *The Bible in Current Catholic Thought.* Ed. by John L. McKenzie. New York: Herder & Herder.
1969 "Form Criticism and Wisdom Literature." *CBQ* 31: 475–83.
1977 "What and Where Is Wisdom?" *Currents in Theology and Mission* 4: 283–87.
1978 "Wisdom—Theses and Hypotheses." IW 35–41.
1981a "The Faces of Wisdom in the Book of Proverbs." *Mélanges . . . Cazelles.* AOAT 212: 337–45.
1981b "Hebrew Wisdom." *JAOS* 101: 21–34.
1981c *Wisdom Literature* (Forms of the Old Testament Literature, XIII). Grand Rapids, Mich.: Eerdmans.

1984 "The Theological Contributions of Israel's Wisdom Literature." *Listening* 19: 30–40.
1985 "Wisdom and Creation." *JBL* 104: 3–11.
1986 "Wisdom's Song: Proverbs 1: 20–33." *CBQ* 48: 456–60.
1987 "Proverbs 22:1–9." *Int* 41: 398–402.
1988 "Wisdom and Eros in Proverbs 1–9." *CBQ* 50: 600–603.
1990 *The Tree of Life*. New York: Doubleday.
1993 "Recent Research on Proverbs and Qoheleth." *Currents in Research: Biblical Studies* 1: 119–40.
1998 *Proverbs* (WBC). Dallas, Tex.: Word Books.

Murray, Oswyn
1983 "The Greek Symposion in History." Pp. 257–72 in *Tria Corda* (FS A. Momigliano). Ed. by E. Gabba. Como: New Press.

Naḥmias, Joseph ben Joseph
*1912 *Commentary on Proverbs* [Hebrew]. Ed. by Moshe Bamberger. Berlin: Itskowski.

Navarro Peiro, Angeles
1976 *Biblia babilónica: Proverbios*. Madrid: Consejo Superior de Investigaciones Cientificas.

Nebe, Gerhard Wilhelm
1972 "Lexikalische Bemerkungen zu *ʾwšwn* 'Fundament, Tiefe' in 4 Q 184, Prov 7,9 und 20,20." *RevQ* 8: 97–103.

Nel, Philip Johannes
1977 "The Concept 'Father' in the Wisdom Literature of the Ancient Near East." *JNSL* 5: 53–66.
1978 "A Proposed Method for Determining the Context of Wisdom Admonitions." *JNSL* 6: 33–39.
1981a "Authority in the Wisdom Admonitions." ZAW 93: 418–27.
1981b "The Genres of Wisdom Literature." *JNSL* 9: 129–42.
1982 *The Structure and Ethos of the Wisdom Admonitions in Proverbs*. BZAW 158. Berlin: Töpelmann.

Newsom, Carol A.
1989 "Woman and the Discourse of Patriarchal Wisdom: A Study of Proverbs 1–9." Pp. 142–60 in *Gender and Difference*. Ed. by Peggy L. Day. Minneapolis: Fortress.
1992 "Proverbs." Pp. 145–52 in *The Women's Bible Commentary*. Ed. by C. A. Newsom and S. H. Ringe. Louisville, Ky.: Westminster/John Knox.

Niccacci, Alviero
1979 "Proverbi 22,17–23,11." *Studium Biblicum Franciscanum* 29: 42–72.
1983 "Aspetti della religiositá egizia e biblica." *Terra Santa* 59: 188–92.
1984 "La teologia sapienziale nel quadro dell' Antico Testamento a proposito di alcuni studi recenti." *Studium Biblicum Franciscanum* 34: 7–14.
1990 *The Syntax of the Verb in Classical Hebrew Prose*. JSOTSup 86. Sheffield: Sheffield Academic Press.

Niditch, Susan
1976 "A Test Case for Formal Variants in Proverbs." *JThS* 27:192–94.

Nilsson, Martin P.
1955 *Die hellenistische Schule*. Munich: Beck.

Nir, Rafael
1995 *Hapitgam K^e^text Zaʿir* ["The Proverb as a Mini-Text" (Hebrew)]. *Hadassah Kantor Jubilee Book*. Ed. by O. Schwarzwald and Y. Schlesinger. Ramat Gan: Bar Ilan.

Nöldeke, Theodor
1871 "Das Targum zu den Spruchen von der Peschita abhängig." *Archiv für wiss. Erforschung des ATs*, 2.1: 246–49.

Nordheim, Eckhard von
1985 *Die Lehre der Alten*, vol. 2. Leiden: Brill.

Norrick, Neal R.
1985 "How Proverbs Mean: Semantic Studies in English Proverbs." *Trends in Linguistics* 27: 1–213.

North, F. S.
1965 "The Four Insatiables." *VT* 15: 281–82.

Noth, Martin, and D. Winton Thomas, eds.
1955 *Wisdom in Israel and in the Ancient Near East*. VTSup 3. Leiden: Brill.

Nougayrol, Jean
1963 "Les Sagesses babyloniennes: Etudes récentes et textes inédits." SPOA 41–51.

Nougayrol, Jean, Charles Virolleaud, and Emmanuel Laroche
1968 [Wisdom of Shube'awelum]. R.S. 22.439. *Ugaritica* 5: 273–97.

Ockinga, Boyo
1984 *Die Gottebenbildlichkeit im alten Ägypten und im Alten Testament*. ÄAT 7. Wiesbaden: Harrassowitz.

Oesterley, W. O. E.
*1929 *The Book of Proverbs*. Westminster Commentaries. London: Methuen.

Olivier, J. P. J.
1975 "Schools and Wisdom Literature." *JNSL* 4: 49–60.

Orlinsky, Harry
1958 "Studies in the Septuagint of the Book of Job: Chapter II." *HUCA* 29: 229–71.

Otzen, Benedict
1975 "Old Testament Wisdom Literature and Dualistic Thinking in Late Judaism." *VTSup* 28: 146–57.

Owens, Robert J., Jr.
1998 "The Relationship between the Targum and Peshitta Texts of the Book of Proverbs." *Targum Studies* 2: 195–207.

Oxford Book of Aphorisms
1983 *The Oxford Book of Aphorisms*. Ed. by John Gross. Oxford: Oxford University Press.

Oyen, Hendrik van
1967 *Ethik des Alten Testaments*. Gütersloh: Gerd Mohn.

Paran, Meir
1978 *Ḥudo šel Hadegem Qal-Vaḥomer B^e^sefer Mišley*. ["The Point of the A Fortiori Pattern in Proverbs" (Hebrew)]. *Beth Miqra* 73: 221–23.

Pardee, Dennis
1982 *Handbook of Ancient Hebrew Letters*. Chico, Calif.: Scholars Press (= HAHL).

1988 *Ugaritic and Hebrew Poetic Parallelism, A Trial Cut (ʿnt I and Proverbs 2)*. VTSup 39. Leiden: Brill.

Parkinson, R. B.
1997 *The Tale of Sinuhe and Other Ancient Egyptian Poems*. Oxford and New York: Clarendon.

Passoni dell'Acqua, Anna
1982 "L'elemento intermedio nella versione greca di alcuni testi sapienziali e del libro Salmi." *RivB* 30: 79–90.
1984 "La Sapienza e in genere l'elemento intermediario tra Dio e il creato nelle versioni greche dell'Antico Testamento." *Ephemenides Litugicae* 98: 97–147.

Paul, Shalom
1979 "Unrecognized Biblical Legal Idioms." *RB* 86: 231–39.

Pedersen, Johannes
1955 "Wisdom and Immorality." Pp. 238–46 in *Wisdom in Israel and in the Ancient Near East Presented to Professor Harold Henry Rowley*. Ed. by Martin Noth and D. Winton Thomas. *VTSup* 3. Leiden: Brill.

Peels, Hendrick
1994 "Passion or Justice? The Interpretation of *b*^{e}*yôm nāqām* in Proverbs vi 34." *VT* 44: 270–74.

Peet, T. Eric
1923 *The Rhind Mathematical Papyrus*. Liverpool: Liverpool University Press.

Peles, M.
1981 "Proverbia, nach ihren Themen geordnet." ZAW 93: 324.

Perdue, Leo G.
1977 *Wisdom and Cult*. SBLDS 30. Missoula, Mont.: Scholars Press.
1981 "Limnality as a Social Setting for Wisdom Instructions." ZAW 93: 114–26.
1994 *Wisdom and Creation*. Nashville: Abingdon.

Perdue, Leo G., Bernard B. Scott, and William J. Wiseman, eds.
1993 *In Search of Wisdom*. Essays in Memory of John G. Gammie. Louisville, Ky.: Westminster/John Knox.

Perles, Felix
1895 *Analekten zur Textkritik des Alten Testaments*. Munich: Theodor Ackermann.
1922 *Analekten zur Textkritik des Alten Testaments*. Leipzig: Gustav Engel.

Perlitt, Lothar
1976 "Der Vater im Alten Testament." Pp. 50–101 in *Das Vaterbild in Mythos und Geschichte*. Ed by H. Tellenbach. Stuttgart: Kohlhammer.

Perry, Theodore A.
1993 *Dialogues with Kohelet*. University Park: Pennsylvania State University Press.

Peshitta: See Di Lella 1979

Peterson, Bengt Julius
1966 "A New Fragment of *The Wisdom of Amenemope*." *JEA* 52: 120–28.

Pfeifer, Gerhard
1967 *Ursprung und Wesen der Hypostasenvorstellungen im Judentum*. Arbeiten zur Theologie, I. Reihe, Heft 31. Stuttgart: Calwer.

Pfeiffer, Robert H.
1926 "Edomitic Wisdom." ZAW 44: 13–25.

1933 "Wisdom and Vision in the Old Testament." ZAW 58: 93–101.

Piankoff, Alexandre

1930 *Le "Coeur" dans les textes égyptiens*. Paris: Paul Geuthner.

Pinkuss, Hermann

*1894 "Die syrische Übersetzung der Proverbien." ZAW 14: 65–141, 161–222.

Pirot, Jean

1950 "Le 'Mâšâl' dans l'Ancien Testament." *Recherches des Sciences Religieuses* 37: 565–80.

Plath, Siegfried

1963 *Furcht Gottes*. Arbeiten zur Theologie, II. Reihe, Bd. 2. Stuttgart: Calwer.

Pleins, J. David

1987 "Poverty in the Social World of the Wise." *JSOT* 37: 61–78.

Plöger, Otto

1964 "Besprechung von U. Skladny, *Die Ältesten Spruchsammlungen in Israel*." *Gnomon* 36: 297–300.

1965 "Wahre die richtige Mitte; solch Mass ist in allem das Beste!" Pp. 159–73 in *Gottes Wort und Gottes Land*. Ed. by H. G. Reventlow. Göttingen: Vandenhoeck & Ruprecht.

1971 "Zur Auslegung der Sentenzensammlung des Proverbienbuches." Pp. 402–16 in *Probleme Biblischer Theologie* (FS G. von Rad). Ed. by Hans Walter Wolff. Munich: Chr. Kaiser.

*1984 *Sprüche Salomos* (*Proverbia*). *BKAT* 17. Neukirchen-Vluyn: Neukirchner Verlage.

Polaček, Adalbert

1969 "Gesellshaftliche und juristiche Aspekte in altägyptischen Weisheitslehren." *Aegyptus* 49: 14–34.

Polk, Timothy

1983 "Paradigms, Parables, and *Měšālîm*: On Reading the *Māšāl* in Scripture." *CBQ* 45: 564–83.

Posener, Georges

1938ff. *Catalogue des ostraca hiératiques littéraires de Deir el Médineh*. Cairo. Vols. 1 (1938; FIFAO I), 2 (1951; FIFAO XVIII = OHDM), 3.3 (1977–80) (FIFAO XX) (= COHL). [Reference by ostracon number.]

1951 *Ostraca hiératiques littéraires de Deir el Médineh* (FIFAO XVIII). Cairo, 1951 (= OHDM).

1955 "L'Exorde de l'instruction éducative d'Amennakhte." *RdÉ* 10: 61–72.

1963a "Aménémopé 21,13 et bj3j.t au sens d'"oracle.'" ZAW 90: 98–102.

1963b "Sur une Sagesse égyptienne de basse époque (Papyrus Brooklyn no. 47.218.135)." SPOA 153–56.

1966 "Quatre tablettes scolaires de basse époque (Aménémopé et Hardjédef)." *RE* 18: 45–65.

1973a "Le chapitre IV d'Aménémopé." ZÄS 99: 129–35.

1973b "Une nouvelle tablette d'Aménémopé." *RE* 25: 251–52.

1976 *L'Enseignement Loyaliste: Sagesse égyptienne du Moyen Empire*. Geneva: Librairie Droz.

1979 "L'Enseignement d'un homme á son fils." SAL 308–16.

1981 "Sur le monothéisme dans l'ancienne Egypte." *Mélanges . . . Cazelles*. AOAT 212: 347–51.

Postel, Henry J.
1976b "The Form and Function of the Motive Clause in Proverbs 10–29." Ph.D. diss., University of Iowa.

Preuss, Horst Dietrich
1972 "Das Gottesbild der älteren Weisheit Israels." *VTSup* 23: 117–45.
1977 "Erwägungen zum theologischen Ort alttestamentlicher Weisheitsliteratur." *EvTh* 30: 417.

Prijs, Leo
1948 *Jüdische Tradition in der Septuaginta*. Leiden: Brill.

Puech, Emile
1988 "Les Ecoles dans L'Israël préexilique: données epigraphiques." *VTSup* 40: 189–203.
1991 "4Q525 et les Péricopes des Béatitudes en Ben Sira et Matthieu." *RB* 98: 80–106.

Qimḥi, David
[1847] *Sefer Hashorashim*. Ed. by J. H. R. Biesenthal and F. Lebrecht. Berlin: G. Berthge (repr. Jerusalem 1967).

Quack, Joachim Friedrich
1994 *Die Lehren des Ani*. OBO 141. Göttingen: Vandenhoeck & Ruprecht.

Rabin, Chaim
1948 "*Meʿʿaṭ ḥibbuq yadayim lišqab*. (Proverbs vi, 10; xxv, 33)." *JJS* 1: 197–98.

Rad, Gerhard von
1970 *Weisheit in Israel*. Neukirchen-Vluyn: Neukirchener Vlg. (ET *Wisdom in Israel*; James D. Martin. London: SCM, 1972.)

Ramaroson, Léonard
1970 "'Charbons ardents': 'sur la tête' ou 'pour le feu'? (Pr 25,22a—Rm 12,20 b)." *Bib* 51: 230–34.

Rankin, Oliver Shaw
1936 *Israel's Wisdom Literature*. New York: Schocken.

Ranston, Harry
1930 *The Old Testament Wisdom Books and Their Teaching*. London: Epworth.

Redford, Donald B.
1992 *Egypt, Canaan and Israel in Ancient Times*. Princeton: Princeton University Press.

Reider, Joseph
1957 *The Book of Wisdom*. New York: Harper.
1966 *An Index to Aquila*. Ed. by Nigel Turner. VTSup 12. Leiden: Brill.

Reitzenstein, Richard
1904 *Poimandres*. Darmstadt: Wissenschaftliche Buchgesellschaft (repr. 1966).

Rendtorff, Rolf
1977 "Geschichtliches und weisheitliches Denken im Alten Testament." Pp. 344–53 in *Beiträge zur at. Theologie* (FS W. Zimmerli). Göttingen: Vandenhoeck & Ruprecht.

Renfroe, F.
1989 "The Effect of Redaction on the Structure of Prov 1,1–6." ZAW 101: 291–93.

Rice, Eugene, Jr.
1958 *The Renaissance Idea of Wisdom*. Cambridge, Mass.: Harvard University Press.

Richardson, H. N.
1955 "Some Notes on *lyṣ* and Its Derivatives." *VT* 5: 163–79.
Richter, Wolfgang
1966 *Recht und Ethos*. SANT XV. München: Kösel.
Rinaldi, G.
1982 "Nota: *Maktêš* (Prov 27,22)." *Bibbia e Oriente* 24/133: 174.
Ringgren, Helmer
1947 *Word and Wisdom: Studies in the Hypostatization of Divine Qualities and Functions in the Ancient Near East*. Lund: H. Ohlsson.
*1962 *Sprüche*. ATD 16. Göttingen: Vandenhoeck & Ruprecht.
Robert, André
1934 "Les Attaches Littéraires Bibliques de Prov. I–IX." *RB* 43: 42–68, 172–204, 374–84.
1940 "Le Yahwisme de Prov 10,1–22,16; 25–29." Pp. 163–82 in *Mémorial Lagrange*. Paris: Gabalda.
Roberts, Colin H.
1950 *The Antinoopolis Papyri*. Part I. London: Egypt Exploration Society.
Römheld, Diethard
1989 *Wege der Weisheit*. BZAW 184. Berlin: De Gruyter.
Roth, Martha T.
1987 "Age at Marriage and the Household: A Study of Neo-Babylonian and Neo-Assyrian Forms." *Comparative Studies in Society and History* 29: 715–39.
Roth, W. M. W.
1965 *Numerical Sayings in the OT*. VTSup 13. Leiden: Brill.
Rottenberg, Meir
1980 "Recent Exegesis of the Proverbs of Solomon." *Beth Mikra* 82: 263–71.
1983 *Hapitgamim šebesefer Mišley*. Tel Aviv: Reshafim.
Ruffle, John
1977 "The Teaching of Amenemope and Its Connection to the Book of Proverbs." *TynBul* 28: 29–68.
Rüger, Hans Peter
1959 "Vier Aquila-Glossen in einem hebräischen Proverbien-Fragment aus der Kairo-Geniza." ZNW 50: 275–77.
1977 "Amon—Pflegekind. Zur Auslegungsgeschichte von Prv. 8:30a." Pp. 154–63 in *Übersetzung und Deutung* (FS A. R. Hulst). Nijkerk: F. Callenbach.
1981 "Die gestaffelten Zahlensprüche des ATs und aram. Achikar 92." *VT* 31: 229–34.
1991 *Die Weisheitsschrift aus der Kairoer Geniza*. WUNT 53. Tübingen: J. C. B. Mohr.
Ruhl, Charles
1989 *On Monosemy*. Albany: State University of New York Press.
Rylaarsdam, J. Coert
1946 *Revelation in Jewish Wisdom Literature*. Chicago: University of Chicago Press.
Saʿadia Gaon
n.d. *Commentary on Proverbs*. Hebrew transl. by David Kafiḥ. Jerusalem: n.p.
Saebø, Magne
1986 "From Collection to Book." Proceedings of the Ninth World Congress of Jewish Studies, Division A, Jerusalem: World Union of Jewish Studies.

Sagesses du Proche-orient ancien
1963 Paris: Presses Universitaires (= SPOA).
Sakenfeld, Katherine Doob
1978 *The Meaning of Ḥesed in the Hebrew Bible.* HSS 17. Missoula, Mont.: Scholars Press.
Salisbury, Murray
1994 "Hebrew Proverbs and How to Translate Them." Pp. 434–61 in *Biblical Hebrew and Discourse Linguistics.* Ed. by Robert D. Bergen. Dallas, Tex.: Summer Institute of Linguistics (Eisenbrauns).
Sandelin, K.-G.
1986 *Wisdom as Nourisher.* Abo: Academiae Aboensis.
Sander-Hansen, C. E.
1956 *Die Texte der Metternichstele.* Analecta Aegyptiaca 7. Copenhägen: Munksgaard.
Sanders, James A.
1967 *The Dead Sea Psalms Scroll.* Ithaca, N.Y.: Cornell.
Sauer, Georg
1963 *Die Sprüche Agurs.* BWANT 4. Stuttgart: Kohlhammer.
Savignac, Jean de
1954 "Note sur le sens du verset VIII 22 des Proverbes." *VT* 4: 429–32.
Scharff, Alexander
1941–42 "Die Lehre für Kagemni." ZÄS 77: 13–21.
Schencke, Wilhelm
1913 *Die Chokma (Sophia) in der jüdischen Hypostasenspekulation.* Kristiania: Jacob Dybwad.
Schmid, Hans Heinrich
1966 *Wesen und Geschichte der Weisheit.* BZAW 101. Berlin: Töpelmann.
1968 *Gerechtigkeit als Weltordnung.* BHT 40. Tübingen.
1988 "Alttestamentliche Weisheit und ihre Rationalität." *Studia Philosophica* 47: 11–31.
Schmidt, Johann
1936 *Studien zur Stilistik der alttestamentlichen Spruchliteratur.* ATAbh 13,3. Münster: Aschendorff.
Schmidt, Werner H.
1992 "Wie kann der Mensch seinin Weg verstehen." Pp. 287–97 in *Alttestamentliche Glaube und Biblische Theologie* (FS H. D. Preuss). Ed. by J. Hausmann et al. Stuttgart: Kohlhammer.
Schnabel, Eckhard J.
1985 *Law and Wisdom from Ben Sira to Paul.* WUNT 2. Reihe. Tübingen: J. C. B. Mohr.
Schneider, Heinrich
1961 "Die 'Töchter des Blutegels in Spr 30,15." Pp. 257–64 in *Lex Tua Veritas* (FS Hubert Junker). Ed. by Heinrich Gross and Franz Mussner. Trier: Paulinus.
1962 *Die Sprüche Salomos.* Herder Bibelkommentar. Freiburg: Herder.
Schroer, Silvia
1996 *Die Weisheit hat ihr Haus gebaut.* Mainz: Grünwald.

Scoralick, Ruth
1995 *Einzelspruch und Sammlung: Komposition im Buch der Sprichwörter Kapitel 10–15*. BZAW 232. Berlin: W. de Gruyter.
Scott, Charles T.
1976 "On Defining the Riddle: The Problem of a Structural Unit." Pp. 77–90 in *Folklore Genres*. Ed. by Dan Ben-Amos. Austin: University of Texas.
Scott, Melville
*1927 *Textual Discoveries in Proverbs, Psalms, and Isaiah*. New York: Macmillan.
Scott, R. B. Y.
1955 "Solomon and the Beginnings of Wisdom in Israel." *VTSup* 3: 262–79.
1960 "Wisdom in Creation: The *'Amon* of Proverbs VIII 30." *VT* 10: 213–23.
*1965 *Proverbs, Ecclesiastes*. AB 18. New York.
1970 "The Study of Wisdom Literature." *Int* 24: 21–45.
1972 "Wise and Foolish, Righteous and Wicked" [Prv 10–29]. *VTSup* 23: 146–65.
Seeligmann, I. L.
1953 "Voraussetzungen der Midraschexegese." *VTSup* 1: 150–81.
Segal, Moshe Zvi
1958 *Sefer Ben Sira Hašalem* [*The Complete Book of Ben Sira*]. Jerusalem: Bialik.
Segert, Stanislav
1987 "'Live Coals Heaped on the Head.'" Pp. 159–64 in *Love and Death in the Ancient Near East: Essays in Honor of M. H. Pope*. Ed. by J. H. Marks and R. M. Good. Guilford, Conn.: Four Quarters.
Seitel, Peter
1976 "Proverbs: A Social Use of Metaphor." Pp. 125–43 in *Folklore Genres*. Ed. by Dan Ben-Amos. Austin: University of Texas.
Shachter, Jacob
1963 *Sefer Mišley Basifrut Hatalmudit* [*The Book of Proverbs in Talmudic Literature*] (includes his commentary, "Words of Jacob.") Jerusalem, pub. by author.
Shapiro, David
1987 "Proverbs." Pp. 313–30 in *Congregation*. Ed. by David Rosenberg. New York: Harcourt Brace Jovanovich.
Sheppard, Gerald T.
1980 *Wisdom as a Hermeneutical Construct*. BZAW 151. Berlin: De Gruyter.
Shirun-Grumach, Irene
1972 *Untersuchungen zur Lebenslehre des Amenope*. Münchner Ägyptologische Studien 23. Munich: Deutscher Kunstverlag.
1979 "Bemerkungen zu Rhythmus, Form und Inhalt in der Weisheit." SAL 317–51.
Shupak, Nili
1987 "The 'Sitz im Leben' of the Book of Proverbs in the Light of a Comparison of Biblical and Egyptian Wisdom Literature." *RB* 94: 98–119.
1993 *Where Can Wisdom Be Found?* OBO 130. Göttingen: Vandenhoeck & Ruprecht.
1999 "The Father's Instruction to the Son in Ancient Egypt" [Hebrew]. Pp. 13–21 in *Hinukh Vehistoria*. Ed. by R. Feldhay. Jerusalem: Merkaz Zalman Shazar.

Simpson, D. C.
1926 "The Hebrew Book of Proverbs and the Teaching of Amenophis." *JEA* 12. 232–39.

Sjöberg, Ake W.
1976 "The Old Babylonian Eduba." Pp. 159–79 in *Sumerological Studies in Honor of T. Jacobsen*. Ed. by St. J. Lieberman. Chicago: University of Chicago.

Skehan, Patrick W.
1946 "Proverbs 6:15–19 and 6:20–24." *CBQ* 8: 290–97 (= Skehan 1971: 1–8).
1947a "The Seven Columns of Wisdom's House in Proverbs 1–9." *CBQ* 9: 190–98.
1947b "A Single Editor for the Whole Book of Proverbs." *CBQ* 10: 115–30.
1967 "Wisdom's house." *CBQ* 29: 468–86.
1971 *Studies in Israelite Poetry and Wisdom*. CBQMS 1. Washington, D.C.: Catholic Biblical Association.
1979 "Structures in Poems on Wisdom: Proverbs 8 and Sirach 24." *CBQ* 41: 365–79.

Skehan, Patrick W., and Alexander A. Di Lella
1987 *The Wisdom of Ben Sira*. AB 39. New York: Doubleday (= Di Lella).

Skladny, Udo
1962 *Die ältesten Spruchsammlungen in Israel*. Göttingen: Vandenhoeck & Ruprecht.

Slater, William J.
1991 *Dining in a Classical Context*. Ed. by W. J. Slater. Ann Arbor: University of Michigan.

Smalley, Beryl
1986 *Medieval Exegesis of Wisdom Literature*. Ed. by Roland E. Murphy. Atlanta: Scholars Press.

Snaith, Norman
1967 "Biblical Quotations in the Hebrew of Ecclesiasticus." *JThS* 18: 1–12.

Sneed, Mark
1995 "Wisdom and Class: A Review and Critique." *JAAR* 62: 651–71.
1996 "The Class Culture of Proverbs: Eliminating Stereotypes." *JSOT* 10: 296–308.

Snell, Daniel C.
1983 "'Taking Souls' in Proverbs XI 30." *VT* 33: 362–65.
1987 "Notes on Love and Death in Proverbs." Pp. 165–68 in *Love and Death in the Ancient Near East: Essays in Honor of M. H. Pope*. Ed. by J. H. Marks and R. M. Good. Guilford, Conn.: Four Quarters.
1989 "The Wheel in Proverbs XX 26." *VT* 39: 503–7.
1991 "The Most Obscure Verse in Proverbs: Proverbs XXVI 10." *VT* 41: 353–55.
1998 "The Relation between the Targum and the Peshiṭta of Proverbs." ZAW 110: 72–74.

Snijders, L. A.
1954 "The Meaning of *zar* in the OT." *OTS* 10: 1–154.

Soden, Wolfram von
1990 "Kränkung, nicht Schläge in Sprüche 20,30." ZAW 102: 120–21.

Sommers, C. F.
1989 *Vice and Virtue in Everyday Life*. San Diego: Harcourt, Brace, and Jovanovich.

Sperber, Alexander
1966 *A Historical Grammar of Biblical Hebrew*. Leiden: Brill.
Spiegel, Joachim
1935 *Die Präambel des Amenemope und die Zielsetzung der ägyptischen Weisheitsliteratur*. Glückstadt: J. J. Augustin.
Stadelmann, Luis I. J.
1970 *The Hebrew Conception of the World*. Rome: Pontifical Biblical Inst.
Steiert, Franz-Josef
1990 *Die Weisheit Israels—ein Fremdkörper im Alten Testament?* Freiburg: Herder.
Storøy, Solfrid
1993 "On Proverbs and Riddles." *SJOT* 7: 270–84.
Story, Cullen I. K.
1945 "The Book of Proverbs and Northwest Semitic Literature." *JBL* 64: 319–37.
Suter, David Winston
1981 "*Māšāl* in the Similitudes of Enoch." *JBL* 100: 193–212.
Suys, Emil
1934 "La théologie d'Aménémopé." *Miscellania Biblica* 2: 1–36.
1935 *La Sagesse d'Ani*. Rome: Pontifical Biblical Inst.
Talmage, Frank (Ephraim)
1990 *Perušim L^{e}sefer Mišley L^{e}veyt Qimḥi* [*Commentaries on the Book of Proverbs by Joseph Kimḥi, Moses Kimḥi, and David Kimḥi* (Hebrew)]. Jerusalem: Magnes.
Tate, Marvin E.
1990 *Psalms 51–100*. WBC 20. Dallas, Tex.: Word Books.
Taylor, Archer
1987 "The Study of Proverbs." *Proverbium* 1: 1–10
Thackery, H. St. J.
1912 "The Poetry of the Greek Book of Proverbs." *JThS* 13: 46–66.
Thomas, D. Winton
1935 "The Root *šnh* = [Arab.] *sny* in Hebrew." ZAW 2–3: 207–8.
1937a "Notes on Some Passages in the Book of Proverbs." *JThS* 38: 400–403.
1937b "The Root *šnh* = [Arab.] *sny* in Hebrew, II." ZAW 55: 174–76.
1941 "A Note on *lyqht* in Proverbs xxx. 17." *JThS* 42: 154–55.
1953 "A Note on *bl ydʿh* in Prov 9:13." *JThS* 4: 23–24.
1955 "Textual and Philological Notes on Some Passages in the Book of Proverbs." *VTSup* 3: 280–92.
1962 "*ʾw* in Proverbs XXXI 4." *VT* 12: 499–500.
1963a "*Blyʿl* in the Old Testament." Pp. 11–19 in *Biblical and Patristic Studies in Memory of R. P. Casey*. Ed. by J. N. Birdsall and R. W. Thomson. Freiburg: Herder.
1963b "A Note on *daʿat* in Proverbs XXII. 12." *JThS* 14: 93–94.
1964a "Additional Notes on the Root *ydʿ* in Hebrew." *JThS* 15: 54–57.
1964b "The Meaning of *ḥataʾt* in Proverbs X. 16." *JThS* 15: 295–96.
1965 "Notes on Some Passages in the Book of Proverbs." *VT* 15: 271–79.
Thompson, John Mark
1974 *The Form and Function of Proverbs in Ancient Israel*. The Hague: Mouton.

Toeg, Aryeh
1974 "*Bammidbar 15: 22–31—Midraš Halakah*" ["A Halakhic Midrash in Num 15:22–31" (Hebrew]). *Tarbiz* 43: 1–20.
Toorn, Karel van der
1989 "Female Prostitution in Payment of Vows in Ancient Israel." *JBL* 108: 193–205.
Torrey, Charles C.
1954 "Proverbs, Chapter 30." *JBL* 73: 93–96.
Tov, Emanuel
1990 "Recensional Differences between the Masoretic Text and the Septuagint of Proverbs." Pp. 43–56 in *Of Scribes and Schools*. Ed. by H. W. Attridge, J. J. Collins, and T. H. Tobin. Lanham, Md.: University Press of America.
1992 *Textual Criticism of the Hebrew Bible*. Minneapolis: Fortress.
Towner, W. Sibley
1995 "Proverbs and Its Successors." Pp. 157–75 in *Old Testament Interpretation*. Ed. by J. L. Mays, D. L. Petersen, and K. H. Richards. Nashville: Abingdon.
Toy, Crawford H.
*1899 *The Book of Proverbs*. ICC. Edinburgh: T. &. T. Clark (repr. 1959).
Trible, Phyllis
1975 "Wisdom Builds a Poem: the Architecture of Proverbs 1:20–33." *JBL* 94: 509–18.
Tsumura, David
1978 "The Vetitive Particle *ʾy* and the Poetic Structure of Proverbs 31:4." *Annual of the Japanese Biblical Institute* 4: 23–31.
Tur-Sinai, Naphtali Herz (= Harry Torczyner)
1924 "The Riddle in the Bible." *HUCA* 1: 125–49.
*1947 *Mišley Š^{e}lomoh*. Tel Aviv: Yavneh.
1967 *P^{e}šuṭo šel Miqraʾ* [*The Plain Meaning of the Bible* (Hebrew)] 4.1. Jerusalem: Kiryat Sefer.
Ulrich, Eugene, et al., ed.
1992 *Priests, Prophets, and Scribes* (FS J. Blenkinsopp). JSOTSup 149. Sheffield: Sheffield Academic Press.
Van Leeuwen, Raymond C.
1986a "Proverbs XXV 27 Once Again." *VT* 36: 105–14.
1986b "Proverbs 30:21–23 and the Biblical World Upside Down." *JBL* 105: 599–610.
1986c "A Technical Metallurgical Use of *yṣʾ*." *ZAW* 98: 112–13.
1988 *Context and Meaning in Proverbs 25–27*. SBLDS 96. Atlanta: Scholars Press.
1990a "Limnality and Worldview in Proverbs 1–9." *Semeia* 50: 111–44.
1990b "The Sage in the Prophetic Literature." SIANE 295–306.
1992 "Wealth and Poverty: System and Contradiction in Proverbs." *HS* 33: 25–36.
1997 *Proverbs*. New Interpreter's Bible, V. Nashville: Abingdon.
Vattioni, F.
1967a "La casa della saggezza (Prov. 9,1; 14,1)." *Augustinianum* 7: 349–51.
1967b "La "straniera" nel libro dei Proverbi." *Augustinianum* 7: 352–57.
1969a "Note sul libro dei Proverbi." *Augustinianum* 9: 124–33.
1969b "Note sul libro dei Proverbi II." *Augustinianum* 9: 531–36.
1972 "Studi sul Libro de Proverbi." *Augustinianum* 12: 121–68.

Vawter, Bruce
1980 "Prov 8:22: Wisdom and Creation." *JBL* 99: 205–16.
1986 "Yahweh: Lord of the Heavens and the Earth." *CBQ* 48: 461–67.

Vergote, Jozef
1963 "La notion de Dieu dans les livres de sagesse égyptiens." SPOA 159–90.

Vischer, Wilhelm
1975 "L'Hymne de la sagesse dans les Proverbs de Salomon 8,22–31." *Etudes Théologiques et Religieuses* 50: 175–94.

Visotzky, Baruch (Barton)
1990 *Midrash Mishle*. New York: Jewish Theological Seminary.
1991 *Reading the Book*. New York: Doubleday.
1992 *The Midrash on Proverbs*. New Haven, Conn.: Yale University Press.

Volten, Aksel
1937 *Studien zum Weisheitsbuch des Anii*. Copenhagen: Levin & Munksgaard.
1941 *Das Demotische Weisheitsbuch*. Analecta Ägytiaca, II. Copenhagen: Munksgaard.
1945 *Zwei altägyptische politische Schriften*. Analecta Ägyptiaca IV. Copenhagen: Munksgaard.
1963 "Der Begriff der Maat in den Ägyptischen Weisheitstexten." SPOA 73–102.

Volz, Paul
1921 *Hiob und Weisheit*. SAT 3,2. Göttingen: Vandenhoeck & Ruprecht.

Vries, Simon J. de
1978 "Observations on Quantitative and Qualitative Time in Wisdom and Apocalyptic." IW 263–76.

Waard, Jan de
1993 "Metathesis as a Translation Technique?" Pp. 249–60 in *Traducere Navem* (FS K. Reiss). *Studia Translatologica* A, 3. Tampere: Tampereen.

Waegeman, Maryse
1990 "The Perfect Wife of Proverbs 31:10–31." Pp. 101–7 in *Goldene Äpfel in silbernen Schalen*. Frankfurt a.M.: Lang.

Waldman, Nahum M.
1976 "A Note on Excessive Speech and Falsehood." *JQR* 67 (1976–77): 142–45.

Walle, Baudouin van de
1963 "Problèmes relatifs aux méthodes d'enseignement dans l'Egypte ancienne." SPOA 191–207.

Wallis, G.
1960 "Zu den Spruchsammlungen Prov 10:1–22,16 und 25–29." *TLZ* 85: 147/8.

Waltke, Bruce K.
1979a "The Book of Proverbs and Ancient Wisdom Literature." *BS* 136: 221–38.
1979b "The Book of Proverbs and Old Testament Theology." *BSac* 136: 302–17.

Waltke, Bruce K., and Michael P. O'Connor
1990 *An Introduction to Biblical Hebrew Syntax*. Winona Lake, Ind.: Eisenbrauns.

Washington, Harold C.
1994a "The Strange Woman . . . of Proverbs 1–9 and Post-Exilic Judean Society." Pp. 217–42 in *Second Temple Studies* 2. Ed. by T. C. Eskenazi and K. H. Richards. Sheffield: JSOT Press.
1994b *Wealth and Poverty in the Instruction of Amenemope and the Hebrew Proverbs*. SBLDS 142. Atlanta: Scholars Press.

Watson, Wilfred G. E.
1984 *Classical Hebrew Poetry*. JSOTSup 26. Sheffield: Sheffield Academic Press.

Wehmeier, Gerhard
1970 *Der Segen im AT*. Basel: F. Reinhardt.

Wehrle, Josef
1993 *Sprichwort und Weisheit: Studien zur Syntax und Semantik der Tob . . . min-Sprüche im Buch der Sprichwörter*. St. Ottilien: EOS.

Weiden, W. A. van der
1970a *Le Livre des Proverbes*. BibOr 23. Rome: Pontifical Biblical Institute.
1970b "Prov. XIV 32b, 'Mais le juste a confiance quand il meurt.'" *VT* 20: 339–50.

Weinfeld, Moshe
1972 *Deuteronomy and the Deuteronomic School*. Oxford: Clarendon.
1982 *L^{e}gilguleyha šel Miš'alah B^{e}Yisra'el Uve'ammim*" ["Concerning the Transformations of a Wish in Israel and the Nations (Proverbs 3:4)" (Hebrew)]. *EI* 16: 93–99.
1995 *Social Justice in Ancient Israel and in the Ancient Near East*. Jerusalem: Magnes.

Weingreen, Jacob
1973 "Rabbinic-type commentary in the LXX version of Proverbs." Pp. 407–15 in *Proceedings of the Sixth World Congress of Jewish Studies*. Jerusalem: World Organization for Jewish Studies.

Weitzman, M. P.
1994 "Peshitta, Septuagint, and Targum." Pp. 51–84 in *VI Symposium Syriacum*. Ed. by René Lavenant. *Orientalia Christiana Analecta* 247. Rome: Pontifical Biblical Inst.

Wente, E. F.
1967 *Late Ramesside Letters*. SAOC 33. Chicago: Oriental Inst. (= LRL).
1990 *Letters from Ancient Egypt*. SBLWAW 1. Ed. by E. S. Meltzer. Atlanta: Scholars Press (= LAE).

Westbrook, Raymond
1988 *Studies in Biblical and Cuneiform Law*. Cahiers de la RB 26. Paris: Gabalda.

Westermann, Claus
1956 *Sprüche, Prediger, Hohelied*. Stuttgart: Quell.
1984 *Vergleiche und Gleichnisse im Alten und Neuen Testament*. Calwer Theologische Monographien 14. Stuttgart: Calwer.
1990 *Wurzeln der Weisheit*. Göttingen: Vandenhoeck & Ruprecht. (ET: J. D. Charles, *The Roots of Wisdom*. Louisville, Ky.: Westminster/John Knox, 1995.)
1991 *Forschungsgeschichte zur Weisheitsliteratur 1950–1990*. Stuttgart: Calwer.

Whedbee, J. William
1971 *Isaiah and Wisdom*. Nashville: Abingdon.

Whybray, R. N.
1965a "Proverbs VIII 22–31 and Its Supposed Prototypes." *VT* 15: 47–56 (repr. SAIW 390–400).
1965b *Wisdom in Proverbs*. SBT 41. London: SCM Press.
1966 "Some Literary Problems in Proverbs I–IX." *VT* 16: 482–96.
1972 *The Book of Proverbs*. CBC. Cambridge: Cambridge University Press.
1974 *The Intellectual Tradition in the OT*. BZAW 135. Berlin: W. de Gruyter.
1978 "Slippery Words. IV. Wisdom." *ExpTim* 89: 359–62.

1979 "Yahweh-sayings and Their Context in Proverbs 10:1–22, 16." *BETL* 51: 153–65.
1982 "Prophecy and Wisdom." Pp. 181–96 in *Israel's Prophetic Tradition*. Ed. by Peter Ackroyd. Cambridge: Cambridge University Press.
1989 "The Social World of the Wisdom Writers." Pp. 227–50 in *The World of Ancient Israel*. Ed. by R. E. Clements. Cambridge: Cambridge University Press.
1990 *Wealth and Poverty in the Book of Proverbs*. JSOTSup 99. Sheffield: Sheffield Academic Press.
1992 "Thoughts on the Composition of Proverbs 10–29." Pp. 102–14 in *Priests, Proverbs and Scribes*. Ed. by N. E. Ulrich et al. Sheffield: Sheffield Academic Press.
1994 *The Composition of the Book of Proverbs*. JSOTSup 168. Sheffield: Sheffield Academic Press.
1995 *The Book of Proverbs: A Survey of Modern Study*. History of Biblical Interpretation 1. Leiden: Brill.
1996 "City Life in Proverbs 1–9." Pp. 243–50 in *"Jedes Ding hat seine Zeit . . ."*: (FS D. Michel). Ed. by A. A. Diesel et al. BZAW 241. Berlin: de Gruyter.

Wildeboer, D. G.
*1897 *Die Sprüche*. KHAT XV. Freiburg: J. C. B. Mohr.

Williams, James G.
1980 "The Power of Form: A Study of Biblical Proverbs." *Semeia* 17: 35–58.
1981 *Those Who Ponder Proverbs*. Sheffield: Almond.

Williams, Ronald J.
1961 "The Alleged Semitic Original of the 'Wisdom of Amenemope.'" *JEA* 47: 102f.
1972 "Scribal Training in Ancient Egypt." *JAOS* 72: 214–21.
1981 "The Sages of Ancient Egypt in the Light of Recent Scholarship." *JAOS* 101: 1–20.

Wilson, Frederick M.
1987 "Sacred and Profane? The Yahwistic Redaction of Proverbs Reconsidered." Pp. 313–34 in *The Listening Heart*. Ed. by K. Hoglund et al. Sheffield: Sheffield Academic Press.

Winston, David
*1979 *The Wisdom of Solomon*. AB 43. Garden City, N.Y.: Doubleday.

Wittenberg, G. H.
1987 "The Situational Context of Statements Concerning Poverty and Wealth in the Book of Proverbs." *Scriptura* 21: 1–23.

Wolf, Philip
1897 "The Septuagintal Rendering of Hebrew Synonyms in the Book of Proverbs." Rabbinic thesis, Hebrew Union College, Cincinnati.

Wolff, Hans Walter
1937 *Das Zitat im Prophetenspruch*. EvTh Beiheft 4. München: Kaiser.
1955 "Erkenntnis Gottes im Alten Testament." *EvTh* 15: 426–31.

Wolters, Al
1985 "*Ṣôpiyyâ* (Prov 31:27) as Hymnic Participle and Play on *Sophia*." *JBL* 104: 577–87.
1988 "Proverbs XXXI 10–31 as Heroic Hymn: A Form-critical Analysis." *VT* 38: 446–57.

1995 "The Meaning of *Kîšôr* (Proverbs 31:19)." *HUCA* 65: 91–104.

Woude, A. S. van der

1995 "Wisdom at Qumran." Pp. 244–56 in *Wisdom in Ancient Israel: Essays in Honour of J. A. Emerton*. Ed. by J. Day et al. Cambridge: Cambridge University Press.

Würthwein, Ernst

1960 *Die Weisheit Ägyptens und das Alte Testament*. Marburg: Elwert.

Yee, Gale A.

1982 "An Analysis of Prov 8,22–31 according to Style and Structure." ZAW 94: 58–66.

1989 "'I Have Perfumed My Bed with Myrrh': The Foreign Woman (*'iššâ zārâ*) in Proverbs 1–9." *JSOT* 43: 53–68.

1992 "The Theology of Creation in Proverbs 8:22–31." Pp. 85–96 in *Creation on the Biblical Traditions*. Ed. by Richard J. Clifford and John J. Collins. CBQMS 24. Washington, D.C.: Catholic Biblical Association.

Žába, Zbynek

1956 *Les Maximes de Ptahhotep*. Prague: Editions de l'Académie Tchécoslovaque des Sciences.

Žabkar, Louis V.

1988 *Hymns to Isis in Her Temple at Philae*. Hanover, N.H. and London: Brandeis University Press.

Zer-Kavod, Mordecai

1975 *Ḥidot Besefer Mišley* [*Riddles in the Book of Proverbs* (Hebrew)]. *Beth Mikra* 64: 7–11.

Zer-Kavod, Mordecai, and Yehudah Keel

1983 *Sefer Mišley* [*The Book of Proverbs* (Hebrew)]. Jerusalem: Mosad HaRav Kook.

Zimmerli, Walther

1933 "Zur Struktur der alttestamentlichen Weisheit." ZAW 51: 177–204 (ET in SAIW 175–207).

*1962 *Sprüche*. ATD 16. Göttingen: Vandenhoeck & Ruprecht.

1963 "Ort und Grenze der Weisheit im Rahmen der alttestamentlichen Theologie." SPOA 121–38 (ET in SAIW 314–26).

Zohary, Menahem

1987 *M^{e}qorot Rashi* [*Rashi's Sources* (Hebrew)]. Jerusalem: Kanah.

Zuntz, G.

1956 "Der Antinoe Papyrus der Proverbia und das Prophetologion." ZAW 68: 124–84.